The Ottoman-Iranian Borderlands

Using a plethora of hitherto unused and underutilized sources from the Ottoman, British, and Iranian archives, *The Ottoman-Iranian Borderlands* traces seven decades of intermittent work by Russian, British, Ottoman, and Iranian technical and diplomatic teams to turn an ill-defined and highly porous area into an internationally recognized boundary. By examining the process of boundary negotiation by the international commissioners and their interactions with the borderland peoples they encountered, the book tells the story of how the Muslim world's oldest borderland was transformed into a bordered land. It details how the borderland peoples, whose habitat straddled the frontier, responded to those processes as well as to the ideas and institutions that accompanied their implementation. It shows that the making of the boundary played a significant role in shaping Ottoman-Iranian relations and in the identity and citizenship choices of the borderland peoples.

Sabri Ateş is an assistant professor of history at Southern Methodist University in Dallas, Texas. He has published a book in Turkish entitled *Tunalı Hilmi Bey: An Intellectual from the Ottoman Empire to Modern Turkey* (2009), as well as several articles in *Comparative Studies of Asia, Africa and the Middle East* and *Iranian Studies*.

The Ottoman-Iranian Borderlands

Making a Boundary, 1843–1914

SABRİ ATEŞ

Southern Methodist University

CAMBRIDGE
UNIVERSITY PRESS

32 Avenue of the Americas, New York NY 10013-2473, USA

Cambridge University Press is part of the University of Cambridge.

It furthers the University's mission by disseminating knowledge in the pursuit of education, learning and research at the highest international levels of excellence.

www.cambridge.org
Information on this title: www.cambridge.org/9781107545779

© Sabri Ateş 2013

First published 2013
First paperback edition 2015

A catalogue record for this publication is available from the British Library

Library of Congress Cataloguing in Publication data
Ates, Sabri.
The Ottoman-Iranian borderlands : making a boundary, 1843–1914 / Sabri Ates.
    p.   cm.
ISBN 978-1-107-03365-8
1. Turkey – Boundaries – Iran.   2. Iran – Boundaries – Turkey.
3. Turkey – Foreign relations – Iran.   4. Iran – Foreign relations – Turkey.   I. Title.
DR479.I7A84   2013
956'.015–dc23   2013004058

ISBN 978-1-107-03365-8 Hardback
ISBN 978-1-107-54577-9 Paperback

For Elizabeth

Contents

List of Illustrations

Acknowledgments

From its birth as an idea at a small café in Greenwich Village to today, this project has been through many incarnations and, with the help of generous individuals and institutions, has dwelled in many climes. I am concerned that I will not be able to mention them all, and the list of those who rightfully deserve credit will be only partial.

During my years at New York University, I had the privilege to study with many supportive professors and friends, including Peter Chelkowski, Khaled Fahmy, Michael Gilsenan, Mohammad Mehdi Khorrami, Zachary Lockman, Robert McChesney, Molly Nolan, and Ariel Salzmann. I am deeply indebted to them, for their criticisms and suggestions at different stages have significantly improved my work. Thanks are also due to all my friends in the dissertation-writing group that over a long period benefited from the gracious hospitality and guidance of ever-supportive Michael Gilsenan. It has also been a great pleasure to work in the Clements Department of History at Southern Methodist University, where I have found great support from my colleagues; the administrative staff; and the previous and present chairs, Jim Hopkins and Kathleen Wellman. I could not imagine a better working environment.

To my friends, I owe a special debt of gratitude. In Istanbul, Seda Altuğ, İlke Şanlıer, Yüksel Taşkın, Murat Yüksel, and Nuri Akgül opened their homes and provided me with more support than I could have hoped for. In Iran, Farshad Fazlollahi showed the best of Iranian hospitality and made my stays pleasant and most comfortable. I also thank Chista Crouther and Noushin Faghihi-Nejad for their friendship and for introducing me to Farshad and his cohort. Dr. Shervin Ziabaksh-Tabari, Bahar Bazgerd, their son Parham, and the Bazgerd family's warm hospitality will be long remembered. A summer at Felor Alemohammad's was most pleasant. In Iran, I also had the good fortune of meeting Kaveh Bayat, who provided me with friendship, support, and various materials I have yet to use. Dr. Nasrollah Salehi has also gone beyond the call of duty in his continuing support and friendship and contributions to this project.

In England, Kate Fleet was most helpful during my short stay at Cambridge. In London, Faruk Hacıhafızoğlu and Zafer Yörük provided me with warm friendship and lodging. I would also like to acknowledge my deepest gratitude to Ayşe Aslan.

Tasha Darbes deserves heartfelt appreciation for the time she spent on this project in its dissertation stage, as do Edward Countryman and Rudi Matthee for their comments and suggestions on more recent iterations of the manuscript. Over the years, I have incurred many debts of gratitude to librarians and archivists, including those of the Başbakanlık Arşivi in Istanbul; the Majlis Library in Iran; the Public Records Office (Kew) and British Library–India Office in London; the libraries at NYU; and, last but not least, the libraries of SMU, specifically Billie Stowal and the ILL staff. For maps, I thank Norman Belza of SMU and Boundary Cartography. I also thank Saqi Books and John Tchalenko for letting me reproduce two maps from *Images from the Endgame*, and the Finnish Museum of Photography for its permission to reproduce some images I first saw in John Tchalenko's book. Thanks are also due Chris Seaton for allowing me to use a photograph from the Albert Wratislaw Collection.

This long adventure would have not been possible without financial support from New York University's Department of Middle Eastern and Islamic Studies, the Kevorkian Center for Near Eastern Studies, and the Graduate School of Arts and Science. My work in Turkey during the dissertation- and book-writing stages was made possible by two generous grants from the American Research Institute in Turkey. Koç University's RCAC and its staff made our stay in Istanbul an unforgettable time filled with good friends and a great work environment. I also thank SMU's Department of History and University Research Council for providing summer research support and Cambridge University's Skilleter Center for making my time in Cambridge and London possible. I also thank the reviewers of my manuscript, my editor at Cambridge Marigold Acland, and assistant editor Sarika Narula, together with Cherline Daniel of Integra-PYD, who through a very long process have been most accommodating and helpful.

My academic life would not have been possible without my mentor Ariel Salzmann, who took me under her wing and has continued to be a great source of support and inspiration. Similarly Zachary Lockman, a most insightful and generous scholar, has for many years provided immense support and mentorship. It is from him and Ariel Salzmann that I learned what a daunting task it is to be an *ustad*. I only hope that I will be able to follow their examples.

Finally, my family – my parents, Suveyla and Ibrahim; my in-laws, Kathy and Dan; and the brothers, sisters, brothers- and sisters-in-law, nephews, and nieces whose care I was away from but whose warm support has always been with me. Their unconditional love, acceptance, confidence, pride, and support have given me strength to go through the daunting task of writing this book.

This book is dedicated to my love and wife, Elizabeth, who selflessly spent countless hours editing, "cut-editing," and learning about the geographies, peoples, and histories of the Zagros and Mesopotamia while nurturing me and our daughter, Suheyla.

Note on Transliteration and Usage

For reasons of simplicity and consistency, except for *ayn* and *hamza*, I have eliminated diacritical marks except when quoting from a published or secondary work or providing the title of a published book. For example, I render *dâr al-Islâm* and *thughūr* as *dar al-Islam* and *thughur*. Names and places that are rendered differently in Ottoman, Persian, and English sources present special difficulties. The goal has been to make them accessible to English speakers while following the most common international usage. In these cases, such as for the word *pasha* or Dervish, I have used the standard English spelling or Anglicized form. When this is not possible, I have followed the *New Redhouse Turkish-English Dictionary* or *Encyclopædia Iranica* sans diacritical marks. For place names, I have tried to use the most modern version, which a reader could find on contemporary maps. However, in some instances, my usage does not follow a convention but rather reflects an arbitrary selection. The present-day town of Mahabad is a good example. It is referred to as Sawj Bulaq/Savojboulagh/Savejboulagh/Saujbulagh/Soujbulakh/Sablax/Savucbulak/Savuçbulak/Savojbulagh, from which list I adapted the last one. Dates are given in the Common Era calendar, but I have also included the catalog dates of documents from the Ottoman archives. Place names on maps follow the map makers's original spellings.

Abbreviations

ABBREVIATIONS FOR THE OTTOMAN ARCHIVES (BOA)

A.	Sadaret
A.AMD	Amedi Kalemi
A.DVN	Divan-ı Hümayun Kalemi Kataloğu
A.DVN.MHM	Divan-ı Hümayun Muhimme Kalemi
A.DVN.NMH	Nâme-i Hümayun Kataloğu
A.DVNS.MHM	Sadaret Mektubi Muhimme Kalemi
A.MKT	Mektubi Kalemi
A.MKT.MHM	Mektubi Muhimme Kalemi
A.MKT.UM	Umum Vilâyat
BEO	Bâb-ı Âli Evrak Odası
BOA	Başbakanlık (Prime Ministry) Archives
CEVDET HR	Cevdet Hariciye
HAT or HH	Hatt-ı Hümayun
HR.SYS	Hariciye Siyasi
I.DH	İrade Dahiliye
IMM	İrade Meclis-i Mahsus
I.MSM	İrade Mesaili Muhimme
I.MVL	İrade Meclis-i Vala
MVL	Meclis-i Vâla Evrakı Hülasa Kayıt Defterleri
Y.	Yıldız
Y.A.HUS	Sadaret Hususi Maruzat Evrakı
Y.PRK	Perakende Evrakı
Y.PRK.EŞA	Elçilik Şehbenderlik Maruzatı
Y.PRK.KOM	Perakende Komisyonlar

| Y.PRK.SRN | Serkurenalık Evrakı |
| Y.PRK.UM | Umum Vilayetler Tahriratı |

OTHER ABBREVIATIONS

AHR	*American Historical Review*
BL-IOR	British Library, Oriental and India Office Records
IJMES	*International Journal of Middle East Studies*
IMFA	Iranian Ministry of Foreign Affairs
IMoFA	Iranian Minister of Foreign Affairs
JRGS	*Journal of Royal Geographical Society of London*
KE	Kânun-u Evvel
KS	Kânun-u Sani
L/P&S	India/Political/Secret (BL-IOR)
MES	*Middle East Studies*
OMD	Ottoman Ministry of Defense
OMFA	Ottoman Ministry of Foreign Affairs
OMoFA	Ottoman Minister of Foreign Affairs
OMW	Ottoman Ministry of War
PRO FO	Public Records Office, Foreign Office, Kew Gardens

MAP 1. Ottoman-Iranian Borderland
Made by Boundary Cartography.

Introduction

THE NATURE OF THE OTTOMAN-IRANIAN FRONTIER

From their first confrontation in 1514 through the Ottoman occupation of northwestern Iran between 1905 and 1912, the Ottomans and the dynasties ruling Iran fought over the borderlands extending from the Persian Gulf to Mount Ararat. However, domination of these regions, inhabited by various autonomous ethnocultural groups, remained an elusive dream, as the borderland peoples defied the authority of both powers, who in turn refused to recognize each other's sovereignty. A host of historical, military, social, religious, political, geographic, and environmental factors prolonged the process of the transformation of the Ottoman-Iranian frontier into a boundary for almost four centuries. In the meantime, control of this ill-defined and highly porous expanse and the peoples inhabiting it shifted frequently, as it continued to be a place of perpetual motion, of separation as well as crossing and mixing.

In the words of a pioneering historian of the borderlands, this frontier functioned as an "ancient interacting frontier" rather than a "sudden" one.[1] Swinging like a pendulum between Iranian and Ottoman rule, and organized by patterns of interaction developed over centuries, it was a classic frontier zone. Failing to extend their authority on a permanent basis, the competing imperial powers engaged in a continuous process of conciliation and coercion with local elites, which provided ample opportunities for "localized political autonomy and relative freedom of socio-economic

---

[1] Owen Lattimore, *Studies in Frontier History: Collected Papers, 1928–1958* (New York: Oxford University Press, 1962), 25.

1

borderland movement."[2] Such autonomy, an outcome of the bargaining process between the state and local semi autonomous structures and communities, gradually came to an end with the delimitation and demarcation of the frontiers, which began in earnest only in the mid-nineteenth century, as agendas of reform and modernization gained pace.[3] A British and Russian intervention in 1840, triggered by the threat of renewed military conflict in the frontier, also speeded the process by which this borderland was to be permanently fixed and its political order transformed from "a suzerain to a sovereign reality."[4] This intervention, in conjunction with *tanzimat* reforms on the Ottoman side and a less ambitious modernization project on the Iranian side, dramatically altered the nature of the frontier and the lives of the borderland peoples. Beginning in 1843, the intermittent work of diplomats, soldiers, engineers, translators, cartographers, archeologists, and botanists from Istanbul, Tehran, St. Petersburg, British India, and London slowly carved a thin dividing line. The finalized boundary was formally recognized after more than seven decades of such labors, days after the beginning of the First World War. Still, partial changes were made to that line as late as the 1930s and again in the 1970s.

Boundary studies are gradually becoming part of Ottoman and Iranian historiography.[5] However, despite its significance in shaping Ottoman-Iranian relations, the notion of *frontier* has only recently emerged as an organizing theme of this historiography. Yet a cursory look at Ottoman-Iranian wars and the treaties they produced over the centuries reveals that frontiers are at the heart of their entangled histories. Neglect of this fact is due, in part, to a well-established tradition in Middle Eastern

---

[2] Richard Schofield, "Narrowing the Frontier: Mid-Nineteenth Century Efforts to Delimit and Map the Perso-Ottoman Boundary," in Roxane Farmanfarmaian ed., *War and Peace in Qajar Persia* (New York: Routledge, 2008), 150.

[3] For the notion of bargaining as a tool of state building, see Dina Rizk Khoury, "Administrative Practice between Religious Law (*Shari'a*) and State Law (Kanun) on the Eastern Frontiers of the Ottoman Empire," *Journal of Early Modern History* 5.4 (2001): 305–30; and Rudi Matthee, *The Politics of Trade in Safavid Iran* (Cambridge, UK: Cambridge University Press, 1992), 62.

[4] B. D. Hopkins, "The Bounds of Identity: The Goldsmid Mission and the Delineation of the Perso-Afghan Border in the Nineteenth Century," *Journal of Global History* 2.2 (2007): 2.

[5] For Iran, see Schofield, Matthee, O'Shea, and especially Kashani-Sabet's works in the bibliography. The Iran-Iraq war prompted an expansive and partially partisan literature on their mutual frontiers; see Schofield and Keith McLachlan, *A Bibliography of the Iran-Iraq Borderland* (London: Menas Press Ltd, 1987). For the Ottoman side, see Kemal H. Karpat and Robert W. Zens, eds., *Ottoman Borderlands: Issues, Personalities and Political Changes* (Madison: University of Wisconsin Press, 2003); and A. C. S. Peacock, ed., *The Frontiers of the Ottoman World* (Oxford, UK: Oxford University Press, 2009).

historiography, one that proposes that the Iranian-Ottoman boundary – at present shared by Iran, Turkey, and Iraq – is one of the oldest in the world, already established in 1639. Yet this frontier, which first began to take shape in the early sixteenth century, was not a formal border. As was the case with most premodern borderlands, there was no exact line of demarcation and the entire region was characterized by multiple social, linguistic, and political identities. Even by the nineteenth century, it was not a pacified and settled borderland. Indeed, until the mid-nineteenth century, the territorial limits of both the Ottoman Empire and Iran were to a large extent defined by the pledged allegiance of local groups; as the primary loyalty of these groups was to their own territories, such allegiances shifted as the incessant struggle for hegemony continued.

This book tells three intertwined stories of this frontier. First, it recounts the transformation of the Ottoman-Iranian frontier into a boundary. Second, it analyzes how their mutual borderland shaped Ottoman-Iranian relations during the life of the Qajar dynasty in Iran (1796–1925). Third, it highlights the role played by borderland communities in the process of boundary making. It also answers the question of how the making of this "ancient" boundary became an international problem requiring the intervention of great powers in the 1840s. While thus taking into account regional and global economic, political, and military ambitions, this book nevertheless privileges the local context, illuminating what happened when state actors created the foundation for the emergence of new identities through the introduction of new administrative structures and the imposition of state subjecthood on the borderlanders.

The multifaceted processes that transformed a permeable borderland into a legally defined boundary drastically altered the human and political geography of the region. Affecting patterns of exchange, notions of belonging, and migratory movements of itinerant populations, these processes also necessitated a complicated separation of myriad ethno-religious and tribal groups – including Lurs, Arabs, Kurds, Turks, Jews, Armenians, Persians, and Nestorians – into citizens of Iran or the Ottoman Empire. Some groups complied, whereas others resisted by fashioning alternative ideas of sovereignty, identity, and spatial organization. Nonetheless, backed by military might and modern technologies of mapping and surveying, as well as by Ottoman, Iranian, and European geographical discourses of sovereignty, territoriality, and citizenship, the frontier commissioners opened the way for the eventual displacement of local practices that, antagonistic to such discourses, favored a porous border. As Benedict Anderson has noted in another context, "Triangulation by triangulation, war by war, treaty by treaty, the alignment of map and power proceeded."[6]

The demarcating of the boundary was also facilitated by shifting ideas of territorial sovereignty that "gradually heightened the importance of the boundaries of kingdoms at the expense of other divisions; local, pacific boundaries eventually merged with militarized state frontier defenses into a single concept of sovereign divisions between states."[7] Charles Maier has described such shifts as the "transformation of territoriality," in which a bounded territory and the control of populations within it increasingly became "the premise of state sovereignty."[8] In the Ottoman-Iranian borderland, as in Europe, this "evolving premise of social organization" emerged around the mid-seventeenth century; experienced decisive modifications in the eighteenth century; and culminated in the nineteenth century, when states successfully intensified efforts to territorialize, integrate, and reclaim space with the help of new technologies. As Robert Sack has argued, the geographic/spatial strategies of territoriality developed during this period aimed "to affect, influence, and control people, phenomena, and relationships by delimiting and asserting control over a geographical area."[9] This book argues that the resulting contest between states for control over a finite space and its inhabitants was inextricable from the process of transformation of borderlands into boundaries. Following the lead of Paolo Novak, I also attempt to show how this spatial strategy "unfolds in its actuality."[10]

The borderlands – that is, the spatiotemporal areas most profoundly impacted by this actuality – were home to demanding geographies, climates, and ecosystems that helped produce and shape the histories of a variety of human cultures and modes of life. Yet, despite the significant differences that distinguished the Ma'dan or Marsh Arabs in the south, for example, from the Jalali or Haydaran Kurds in the north, the borderlanders were connected by social, religious, and kinship networks, as well as a frontier ethos, that transcended geography or environment.

---

[6] Benedict Anderson, *Imagined Communities* (London: Verso, 1991), 173.
[7] Daniel Power, "Introduction," in Daniel Power and Naomi Standen, eds., *Frontiers in Question: Eurasian Borderlands, 700–1700* (New York: St. Martin's Press, 1999), 5.
[8] Charles S. Maier, "Transformations of Territoriality 1600–2000," in Oliver Janz, Sebastian Conrad, and Gunilla Budde, eds., *Transnationale Geschichte: Themen, Tendenzen Und Theorien* (Gottingen: Vandenhoeck & Ruprecht, 2006), 34.
[9] Robert Sack, *Human Territoriality: Its Theory and History* (New York: Cambridge University Press, 1986), 19.
[10] Paolo Novak, "The Flexible Territoriality of Borders," *Geopolitics* 16.4 (2011): 742.

This is not to say that they lived without conflict. To the contrary, their world of narrow mountain passes and gorges, deserts and marshes, large rivers and thousands of small creeks was also home to vendettas, tribal allegiances, and multigenerational conflicts. Highway robbery, theft of flocks, and other raids were also part of daily life. Consequently, without the intervention of states, borderlanders developed intricate ways of negotiating and resolving conflict to manage the scarce resources they shared. The same challenging geographical and environmental conditions that necessitated such strategies also allowed them to evade or limit state control of their lives, thus permitting their semi-independent social structures to thrive. At the same time, those conditions blocked the emergence of alternative forms of power and ultimately created conditions that would make subjugation to central states possible and even desirable.

It should be noted that central states were never altogether absent from the borderlands; rather, they ruled indirectly. The process of replacing indirect with direct rule ran parallel to the process of territorializing sovereignty. Both were part of the larger project of increasing state capacity, which in turn marks the transition from premodern to modern forms of borders and hegemony. Negotiation and indirect rule thus needed to give way to more direct forms of governance in which appointed representatives replaced the hereditary aristocrats who had long brokered between state and society.[11] The end result – that is, the destruction of local autonomies, the inscription of interstate boundaries, and the imposition of uniform state identities – had far-reaching consequences that even today ripple through the borderland: traditional ways of life were shattered, migratory patterns were altered, and long-held mechanisms of conflict resolution were abandoned without being replaced.

Delimitation and demarcation also meant the end of the notion of frontier as an outer limit open to state expansion. Now, limits of legitimate state authority had to be defined by boundary conferences and the surveys that followed.[12] To borrow from Howard Lamar and Leonard Thomson, the making of the boundary signified the "closing" of the frontier that occurs when "a single political authority" establishes its hegemony over the border zone, making it less porous and mutable.[13] In this book, however, such a

---

[11] Khoury, "Administrative Practice," 305.

[12] Michael Kodarkowsky, *Russia's Steppe Frontier: The Making of a Colonial Empire 1500–1800* (Bloomington: Indiana University Press, 2002), 49.

[13] Howard Lamar and Leonard Thompson, "Comparative Frontier History," in Lamar and Thompson, eds., *The Frontier in History: North America and Southern Africa Compared* (New Haven, CT: Yale University Press, 1981), 3–14.

closing is not imagined as total or totalizing. Not the erection of an impregnable wall, it is rather the tightening of a frontier filter.[14]

Similarly, taking my inspiration from Peter Sahlin's work on the borderlands of France and Spain, I do not see the act of "b/ordering" as a unidirectional imposition from above or "a mere expression of imperial fiat" that limits itself to global or regional imperial actors or centers.[15] To the contrary, it is a process that also foregrounds the voices of the borderlanders and their territorial strategies and rationalities.[16] Although concerned with charting Ottoman-Iranian relations, my project thus aims as well to bring borderland peoples back into history, giving voice to an indigenous agency whose role in the making of local as well as imperial histories has been consciously silenced.[17] As Thongchai Winichakul maintains in a different context, although the dispute was about territories, too little attention has been paid to the people residing in those territories or even to the territories themselves. Existing studies mislead us by considering only the perspective of those who became the ruling powers of the emerging nation-states. The fates of tiny tributaries and the people, especially the nomadic people, of the disputed regions remain virtually unknown, as if they occupied a void with no view, no voice, and no history of their own.[18]

This is not because of a lack of written records, but, to the contrary, because of the ideological construction of Turkish and Iranian national historiographies, and an accompanying hostility aimed at scholars situated outside the confines of the nationalist linear time frame. As Mark Bassin argues in another context, however, an additional factor is perhaps even more important than an a priori political bias, which should be taken into consideration.[19] When a teleology is created, the course of events it describes – in this case, the formation of the modern nation states of Iran and Turkey (and Iraq) – leads inexorably to a preordained conclusion, which inevitably leaves a significant gap in our knowledge. To begin to fill

---

[14] Pekka Hämäläinen and Samuel Truett, "On Borderlands," *The Journal of American History* 98.2 (2011): 358. For the state of borderland studies, see this inspiring article.

[15] Ibid.; Peter Sahlins, *Boundaries: The Making of France and Spain in the Pyrenees* (Berkeley: University of California Press, 1989).

[16] Novak, "Flexible Territoriality," 748. I borrowed the notion of "b/ordering" from Novak.

[17] For the role of mobile groups in Ottoman history, see Reşat Kasaba, *A Moveable Empire: Ottoman Nomads, Migrants, and Refugees* (Seattle: Washington University Press, 2009).

[18] Thongchai Winichakul, *Siam Mapped: A History of the Geo-Body of a Nation* (Honolulu: University of Hawaii Press, 1994), 96.

[19] Mark Bassin, *Imperial Visions: Nationalist Imagination and Geographical Expansion in the Russian Far East, 1840–1865* (Cambridge, UK: Cambridge University Press, 1999).

this gap, while also highlighting the interdependent nature of historical processes, this book investigates how imperialist interventions, the rivalry between the Ottoman and Qajar states, the local peoples' reactions to the new limits placed on their social and economic habitats, and the habitat itself all worked in concert to shape the boundaries of the Ottoman Empire and Iran. Above all, however, this study privileges the peoples at the margins of the empires. In this sense, it is a project of spatial and temporal de-marginalization that attempts to reclaim the roles and recover the voices of the occupants of this land in-between.

The length of the frontier defines the geographical scope of the book, but I make no claim to give an exhaustive account of the themes, sources, actors, or geographies of the borderland. No doubt it is impossible to explain such a long and contentious trajectory in all its complexity or to do justice to all groups involved. I aim, rather, to show that the borderland peoples were not merely swallowed up by the imperial cultures that encroached on them. Instead, they actively participated in, or fought against, the creation of the imperial frontiers and the modern state. As such, this study challenges teleological and ethnocentric conceptions of the past that mislead us into considering only the point of view of history's winners. By denying the agency of the people at the margins, such ethnocentric or, as David Weber has called them, "myopic histories" not only propagate incomplete versions of the past, but also facilitate the continuing denial of rights and responsibilities to the region's marginalized peoples.[20] By treating the borderlanders as subjects rather than objects in global power plays, I hope to provide a more inclusive, egalitarian version of Middle Eastern history and shed new light on the past as well as some of the most contentious issues of our day, such as the origins of the Kurdish question and the frontier issues that led to the eight-year-long war between Iran and Iraq. Nevertheless, it should be stated at the outset that a lack of local archival material inevitably hampers any attempt to tell a different kind of history. Ironically, perhaps, it is through official documents that the borderlanders establish a presence in this narrative.[21]

Situating itself within the larger field of border/borderland studies that aims at what Hämäläinen and Truett called "unsettling centrist paradigms" and nation-state–centered teleologies, this study claims to be

---

[20] David Weber, *Spanish Borderlands in North America* (New Haven, CT: Yale University Press, 1992), 5.
[21] See Michiel Baud and Willem van Schendel, "Toward a Comparative History of Borderlands," *Journal of World History* 8.2 (1997): 211–42.

neither an Ottoman history nor an Iranian one.[22] Readers looking for such histories should refer to the extensive and well-established literature that already exists. It is, more simply, a history of the making of the Ottoman-Iranian boundary in the long nineteenth century. Even within this limited scope, it is hardly exhaustive. It does not analyze, among many other themes, the myriad forms of boundary crossing, such as trade and pilgrimage, that deserve their own books; neither does it give extensive consideration to the Ottoman and Iranian geographical literature, which is vast.

A NOTE ON TERMINOLOGY

Throughout the book, I use the words *borderland*, *border*, and *frontier* interchangeably. However, I privilege the term *borderland* because, as recent scholarship has stressed, it does not imply only encounters between states straddling a line but more broadly describes an interdependent cross-boundary region that "encompasses areas immediately beside a state's external border, or straddling it, and also administrative regions abutting a border whose centers are physically and socially distant from that border."[23] This notion of the borderland thus facilitates a recognition that the state is not the only agent of history, allowing historians to break the shackles of the nation and, consequently, of nationalist historiography. As I argue in later chapters, both notions of and lived realities in the frontier began to change with the rise of the idea of a fixed political boundary or territoriality, which many identify with the Westphalian system, during the Russo-British interventions of the second half of the nineteenth century. *Boundary* thus refers to this notion of a cartographically identifiable line marking the territorial limits of states. The process of making a boundary involves both *delimitation*, the marking on maps of the range of territory that will contain the final boundary, and *demarcation*, the actual construction of the boundary on the ground by members of survey commissions.[24]

Delimitation and demarcation were parts of a process, not a rupture in time and space. As Weber argues, frontiers represent place and process, linked inextricably. Cross-border interactions of state and non-state actors,

---

[22] Hämäläinen and Truett, "On Borderlands," 339.

[23] James Anderson and Liam O'Dowd, "Borders, Border Regions and Territoriality: Contradictory Meanings, Changing Significance," *Regional Studies* 33.7 (1999): 595.

[24] For the definition of these terms, see Winichakul, *Siam Mapped*, chap.3; Baud and van Schendel, "Toward a Comparative History"; Anderson and O'Dowd, "Borders"; John Robert Victor Prescott, *The Geography of Frontiers and Boundaries* (Chicago: Aldine Publishing Company, 1965), 64; and Power, "Introduction," 3.

or the process of expansion and contraction, gave shape to the contested place we refer to as the frontier.[25] Political geographers understood this process as the successful evolution from frontier to boundary.[26] As Sahlins argues regarding France, however, such thinking relied on binary notions of progress and linear development unsupported by historical evidence. The most historical part of the frontier, the concept of the *linear boundary*, long preceded modern delimitation efforts.[27] In his famous article on the notion of *frontière*, Lucien Febvre warns against defining the frontier as premodern and the boundary as modern, an impulse that privileges the evolutionary perspective described earlier, which traces a progressive movement "from the broad, sterile and empty separating zone to the simple non-substantial line of demarcation; from the lack of the precision of a line which often wandered to the rigorous determination of a mathematically defined contour."[28] Instead of studying the frontier as an isolated phenomenon, he maintains, we should analyze it in relation to the state; concepts of sovereignty; the transition from subjects, vassals, and members of restricted communities into the body of citizens and the militarization of the nation or universal conscription. Accordingly, this book defines boundary making as part of a state-building process that relies, in part, on increasing the capacity of states at the margins, but it does not treat borders solely as lines or as zones. Instead, it suggests that they are filters.[29] As the rise in the capacity of states and their powers of surveillance led to the institutionalization and standardization of state practices and the penetration of the peripheries, the porosity of these filters decreased over time.[30] Treating boundary formation and the rise of state capacity as concomitant processes allows us to describe different stages or degrees of frontier formation or territoriality in terms of different

---

[25] Weber, *Spanish Borderlands*, 12.

[26] See Sahlins, "State Formation and National Identity in the Catalan Borderlands during the Eighteenth and Nineteenth Centuries," in T. M. Wilson and Hastings Donnan, eds., *Border Identities: Nation and State at International Frontiers* (Cambridge, UK: Cambridge University Press, 1998), 37.

[27] Sahlins, *Boundaries*, 4.

[28] Lucien Febvre, *A New Kind of History and Other Essays* (New York: Harper Torchbooks, 1973), 212. Also Wilson and Donnan, "Introduction" in *Border Identities*; and Malcolm Anderson, *Frontiers: Territory and State Formation in the Modern World* (Cambridge, UK: Polity Press, 1996), 9.

[29] See also Anderson and O'Dowd, "Borders."

[30] The literature on state building or the establishment of the modern states and the drawing of the borderlands is too extensive to list here. The concept of *state capacity* is adapted from Doug McAdam, Sidney Tarrow, and Charles Tilly, *Dynamics of Contention* (New York: Cambridge University Press, 2001).

stages or layers of a filter, tightening not only in time but also in space as the borderland is transformed into bordered lands.[31]

DIVIDING THE *UMMA*, DEFINING ITS FRONTIERS

As a European power, the Ottomans were hardly ignorant of European notions of frontiers and boundaries. Indeed the historical trajectory of the Ottoman-Iranian borderland traces the same path to territoriality that has so far been identified as post-Westphalian. At the same time, non-European notions of territorial limits had long shaped political thought and action in Ottoman and Iranian lands. Specifically, concepts of frontier and of separation between the lands of Islam, or *dar al-Islam*, and the lands of disbelief, or *dar al-harb*, were integral to the development and spread of Islam from its beginning.[32] The need for such distinctions arose from the fact that except for during the formative period of Islam, the ideal of an Islamic community, or *umma*, united under the authority of a single caliph, was never a reality. From the eighth century onward, the *umma* was divided under often competing sovereigns only nominally under the caliph's authority. When the Mongols extinguished the remnants of the Abbasid caliphate in the mid-thirteenth century, the Islamic community had already been divided into fifteen separate Muslim-ruled states. In time, Muslims overwhelmingly accepted the reality of territorial pluralism, and "authoritative Muslim writers have come to elaborate a new 'consensus of speech' (ijma'al-qawl), which argues that the territorial state is a natural, and even worthy institution."[33] Consequently, in addition to distinguishing between Islamic and non-Islamic lands, there arose the need to define the internal boundaries of the *umma*.

The former division – that is, between *dar al-Islam* and *dar al-harb* – has been the subject of numerous studies. Indeed, it has been a dominating concept, if not an organizational theme, in Ottoman historiography for the past century, especially as it related to concepts of *jihad* and *ghaza*.[34]

---

[31] I borrow this last concept from Jeremy Adelman and Stephen Aron, "From Borderlands to Borders: Empires, Nation-States and the Peoples in Between in North American History," *The American Historical Review* 104.3 (1999).

[32] Ralph W. Brauer, *Boundaries and Frontiers in Medieval Muslim Geography* (Philadelphia: American Philosophical Society, 1995), 9–11.

[33] James P. Piscatori, *Islam in a World of Nation-States* (New York: Cambridge University Press, 1986), 45.

[34] Colin Heywood, "The Frontier in Ottoman History: Old Ideas and New Myths," in Power and Standen, *Frontiers in Question*, 228.

Although equally prone to political and military conflict, however, interstate relations within the *dar al-Islam*, along with their theoretical implications and practical consequences, have not received the same level of scrutiny.

As the major power defending and expanding the frontiers of *dar al-Islam* in Europe, Ottoman claims to supremacy in the world of Islam were strengthened when the symbols of the caliphate, the carefully preserved holy relics kept in Cairo, were taken to Istanbul in 1517, after the Ottomans defeated the Mamluks and conquered Egypt and Syria. Because the holy cities of Mecca and Medina had been under Mamluk control, the victory also allowed the Ottomans to take the title of *khadim al-haramayn*, or "Servitors of the two Holy Sanctuaries," which further boosted their legitimacy. Lacking lineal descent from the prophet's family, the Ottoman sultans justified using the title of caliph of all Muslims by highlighting their role as guardians of the frontiers of *dar al-Islam* and protectors of pilgrimage routes: "In this fashion a new concept of Caliphate came to be based on actual power and influence with God's support, and eventually served as a policy aimed at establishing Ottoman mastery over the world of Islam."[35]

Three years before their victories in Egypt and Syria, the Ottomans had dealt the nascent Safavid state a crushing blow at Chaldiran. The Safavids, and the Shi'ism they championed, nevertheless continued to pose a serious challenge to Ottoman claims of supremacy and reshaped Ottoman self-image and religious policies. Ottoman religiosity, true to its frontier origins, had previously been syncretistic, and the body politic uninterested in rigorously defining and enforcing an orthodoxy.[36] As Cemal Kafadar argues, it was the rise of the Safavids that stimulated a "heightened concern of governments with imposing orthodoxy."[37] Halil Inalcık shares this view: "It was, indeed, the dangerous struggle against the *Kızılbash* sect on the one hand and the Ottomans' Caliphate policies on the other that made the Ottoman Sultans, from Suleyman the Lawgiver onwards, increasingly concerned with the more stringent application of the religious law."[38]

Embracing the idea that all of humanity had the potential to become Muslim and so be bounded by one law and governed by one ruler, the Ottoman Empire continued expanding its western frontiers with the goal of reducing the *dar al-harb* to submission. However, as the first caliph

[35] Halil İnalcık, "Islam in the Ottoman Empire," in Halil İnalcık, *Essays in Ottoman History* (Istanbul: Eren Kitabevi, 1998): 232–34.

[36] Cemal Kafadar, *Between Two Worlds: The Construction of the Ottoman State* (Berkeley: University of California Press, 1995), 76.

[37] Ibid., 73.

[38] İnalcık, "Islam in the Ottoman Empire," 235.

demonstrated, the empire also recognized a duty to fight against the dissenters or rebellious Muslims of Arabia and to defend the *umma* against all types of subversion.[39] As Shi'ism was seen as an aberration, from 1512 onward, Ottoman sultans ordered fatwas to be issued for the elimination of the Safavid shahs and declared war on Iran to suppress unwelcome theological innovations, punish heretical leaders, and suppress rebellion. Indeed, in his letters to Shah Ismail from this period, the Ottoman sultan addresses the Safavid leader as a rebel (*bağī*) and heretic in the lands of Islam and defines himself as *khilafat Allah*, the caliph of God, and the guardian of the frontiers of Islam.[40]

The Shi'i law of jihad, in contrast to the Ottoman one, linked the special duty of waging holy war with the doctrine of *wilaya*, or allegiance to the imam. According to Shi'i legal theory, "not only would the failure of a non-Muslim to believe in Allah justify waging a jihad, but also the failure of a Muslim to obey the imam would make him liable for punishment by a jihad."[41] Sunni Islam, of course, rejected the Shi'i imam as supreme authority; these contrasting religious ideologies pitted the Ottomans and the dynasties ruling over Iran against each other, imbuing their mutual frontiers with military and ideological significance not altogether different from that ascribed to Ottoman frontiers with Christian Europe. Consequently, despite lack of known anti-Sunni or anti-Ottoman fatwas coming from Iran, at times of crisis or at the urging of the palace or military, Ottoman religious authorities readily issued anti-Shi'i fatwas declaring Iran to be *dar al-harb* and permitting the enslavement or killing of its people and the pillaging of their property. Subsequently, clashes between the Safavids and Ottomans were represented in ideological and religious or confessional terms, and their frontiers became the grounds of military-ideological clashes that continued into the Afshar and Zand eras. It was only with the 1823 Erzurum Treaty that the Ottomans agreed to drop sectarian issues from the terms of a treaty. Despite the ongoing Ottoman-Qajar sectarian competition in Iraq, the Erzurum Congress of 1843–47 and its concluding treaty, signed with the mediation of Russia and Britain, similarly excluded religious issues. As Russia and Britain increasingly took the lead as mediators and then arbitrators in the

---

[39] D. Sourdel, A. K. S. Lambton, F. de Jong, and P. M. Holt, "Khalīfa," *Encyclopaedia of Islam*, 2nd ed., P. Bearman et al., eds. (Brill, 2011), http://referenceworks.brillonline.com.

[40] Feridun Bey et al., eds., *Mecmua-yi Münşeat-i Feridun Bey or Münşe'at-i Selātīn* (Istanbul: Darüttıbattil'âmire, 1265–1274 [1848–1857]), vol. I, 382.

[41] Majid Khadduri, *War and Peace in the Law of Islam* (New York: AMS Press, 1979), 66.

processes of delimitation and demarcation, the role played by sectarian differences continued to diminish. The long nineteenth century, which roughly corresponds to the Qajar era, thus witnessed the secularization of Ottoman-Iranian relations, including how they defined their mutual border.

ISLAMIC CONCEPTS OF FRONTIER

The most common Arabo-Islamic concept used to define boundaries between the lands of Islam and unbelief is *thaghr*. The plural form, *thughur*, designates a frontier zone or march, the lines of fortifications protecting gaps along frontiers between *dar al-Islam* and *dar al-Harb* and the coastlands of the *dar al-Islam* vulnerable to maritime attack.[42] In medieval Muslim literature, *thughur* is thus essentially a military term used to describe situations in which non-Islamized peoples dominated the adjoining territory.[43] The frontier zone between the Seljuks of Rum and Byzantium and between the Ottomans and Byzantium, which evolved over a long time, showed characteristics of *thughur*, or marches or marchland, and is referred to as *uc* in Turkish. Persian sources used the concept for the same purposes.[44] Still, it should be noted, as Michael Bonner observes in the example of the Arab-Byzantine frontier, that such nomenclature "do[es] not derive from administrative history so much as from a series of superimpositions made by medieval writers on geography and related subjects."[45]

As happened elsewhere, in this march environment, unorthodox, syncretistic dervishes Islamized a mixed border population and directed it to *ghaza*, or raids with a religio-economic purpose. The men, not always Muslims, who perpetuated *ghaza* in the Byzantine lands or the marchland, where suzerainty was debatable or negligible, were called *ghazi* or *uc* Turks. They were organized under a *bey* or *emir* [qaid], a leader with an established following and a recognized realm. The "competitive,

---

[42] For a detailed account, see J. D. Latham and C. E. Bosworth, "al-Thughūr (a.)," *Encyclopaedia of Islam*, 2nd ed. Also Brauer, *Boundaries and Frontiers*; and Michael Bonner, "The Naming of the Frontier: 'Awāṣim, Thughūr, and the Arab Geographers," *Bulletin of SOAS* 57.1 (1994): 17–24.

[43] Brauer, *Boundaries*, 14, 18; and Heywood, "Frontier," 244. The oldest Persian geographical account, *Ḥudūd al-'Ālam*, describes towns such as Malāzgird, Qālīqala (Erzurum), Jazira in this manner; see Vladimir Minorsky, trans. and ed., *Ḥudud al-'Ālam: The Regions of the World* (London: Luzac, 1937), 143, 148–49.

[44] See Loghatname-e Dekhoda, *thughur*.

[45] Bonner, "The Naming of the Frontier," 18.

expansion oriented enterprise" of such *Uc emiri* or *Uc beyi* "was called a *beglik* or emirate."[46] The Ottoman *beglik* was one among many Turco-Muslim entities that emerged in the *thughur* or *uc* (pl. *ucat*) of western Anatolia. Historians have long debated the question of how the Ottoman state rose from a *beglik* at the Muslim Seljuk and Christian Byzantine *thughur/uc* to a world empire. Among various explanations, the so-called *ghaza* thesis attracts the most attention.[47] Discussion regarding this thesis centers on the nature of the *ghaza* (holy war or not) and the identity of *ghazis* (Turks or a mixed frontier people). Notwithstanding such debates, it is obvious that the geographic location of the nascent state and the institutions it developed in the borderland played a crucial role in its development.[48]

Ottoman expansion into Europe and its transition to a centralized empire, especially following the conquest of Constantinople, did not completely erase its characteristics as a frontier state. The *ghazis, akıncıs* (raiders), *uc eris*, or *ehl-i hudud* (frontiersmen) were drawn to the empire's western frontiers for various purposes. They continued to operate through the seventeenth century, during which time a controlled level of violence was maintained at the *ucat*.[49] The Ottoman state and its *ghazi* vanguards thrived on an open frontier. Reminiscent of Frederic J. Turner's thesis regarding the frontier's central role in American history is Halil Inalcık's claim that the initial *ghazi* character of the Ottoman sultanate "influenced the state's historical existence for six centuries."[50] As Riffat Abou-el-Haj asserts, the ability to maintain continuous warfare with the infidel was the legitimating justification of its dynasty's claim to leadership of the Islamic community. The western frontier remained open and the *ghazi mentalité* survived until the 1699 Treaty of Karlowitz, which marked the formal closure of the Ottoman frontier in Europe and forced the Ottomans to accept international border commissions to delimit and demarcate the

---

[46] Kafadar, *Between Two Worlds*, 14.
[47] Literature on the *ghazâ* thesis abounds. Among others, see Kafadar, *Between Two Worlds*; Heath W. Lowry, *The Nature of Early Ottoman State* (Binghamton: SUNY Press, 2003); and Linda T. Darling, "Contested Territory: Ottoman Holy War in Comparative Context," *Studia Islamica* 91 (2000): 133–63.
[48] A. C. S. Peacock, "Introduction," *The Frontiers of the Ottoman World* (Oxford: Oxford University Press, 2009), 12.
[49] Mark L. Stein, *Guarding the Frontier: Ottoman Border Forts and Garrisons in Europe* (London: Tauris Academic Studies, 2007), 27.
[50] Itnalcık and Donald Quataert, *An Economic and Social History of the Ottoman Empire, 1300–1914* (Cambridge, UK: Cambridge University Press, 1994), 11.

frontier with the Habsburgs. From then onward, the Ottoman story in Europe was mainly one of contraction.[51]

Certainly, the empire's frontiers to the west were crucial in shaping the Ottoman polity in various ways. Equally important, however, were its frontiers to the east, which have not benefited from the same degree of historical inquiry. There is no doubt that the "transfrontier contention for hegemony" between Iranians and Ottomans had transformative effects on both states.[52] Their frontiers, however, were not shaped by the *uc* mentality or the ideology of *ghazi* warriors; neither did they witness the military culture that developed at the fortresses of the *thughur*. Moreover, unlike the west – where, for example, Muslims of various persuasions, including Turks, Kurds, and Arabs, colonized the Balkans[53] – the Ottoman-Iranian frontier did not function as a pioneer frontier or a frontier of settlement. The Ottoman administrative system also differed greatly here. For instance, it did not employ its usual fiscal and administrative methods of incorporation, such as the *defter*, or official registers, and the *timar* system of nonhereditary prebends. Moreover, unlike in the west, large Kurdish or Arab tribal confederations and local hereditary dynasties guarded their own frontiers as well as those of the sultan or the shah whose suzerainty they recognized. Thus, Ottomans and Iranians ruled not by fiat but by negotiation/conciliation with local magnates, chiefs, and dynasts that, through various mechanisms, were integrated into the imperial administration. Walter Posch's analysis of the political-military nature of the Ottoman-Iranian frontier in Kurdistan describes one case that sheds light on this reality:

[A] Safavid town and its environs under *qızılbash* rule (like Ūrmīya for instance) had a glacis inhabited by – in most cases one – pro-Safavid Kurdish tribe, the Bradōst in this case, which, in one or the other way, might be tied or might be loosely connected to this town. This pro-Safavid tribe bordered the pro-Ottoman Kurds (the Shanbō) in the approaches of the next Ottoman town (Bitlis, later Van). The two tribes were, on the other hand, departed by natural barriers like mountain ranges.[54]

---

[51] Rifaat A. Abou-el-Haj, "The Formal Closure of the Ottoman Frontier in Europe: 1699–1703," *Journal of the American Oriental Society* 89.3 (1969): 469. For the making of the Ottoman-Habsburg frontier after the 1699 Treaty of Karlowitz, see John Stoye, *Marsigli's Europe* (New Haven, CT: Yale University Press, 1994), chap. 7.

[52] Weber, *Spanish Borderlands*, 13.

[53] Inalcık, "Ottoman Methods of Conquest," *Studia Islamica* 3 (1954): 122–28; and Heywood, "Frontier," 240–41.

[54] Walter Posch, "What Is a Frontier? Mapping Kurdistan between Ottomans and Safavids," in Éva M. Jeremiás, ed., *Irano-Turkic Cultural Contacts in the 11th–17th Centuries* (Philiscsaba: Avicenna Institute of Middle Eastern Studies, [2002] 2003), 208.

As a result of such social and geographical realities and the negotiations they necessitated, these frontier areas remained semiautonomous buffer zones between Iran and the Ottoman Empire. Hence, when a Kurdish or Arab tribe defended its territory, it simultaneously defended the border of the sultan's or shah's power.[55] Such tribes also played primary and secondary roles in complex diplomatic maneuvers aimed at establishing links with prospective anti-Safavid or anti-Ottoman allies and clients, including securing the frontier, scouting, intelligence gathering, and providing transportation. Even though some historians, following the lead of the official chroniclers, describe the shifting alliances of borderlanders as indicative of their fickle nature, such moves were in fact as calculated as those of any agent seeking alliances and security. Thus, as Rhoads Murphey maintains, "they retained sufficient fluidity and dynamism to defend their own interests and in exceptional circumstances, especially during wartime, even to extend their sphere of influence within those states."[56] Because tribal confederations – for example, the Marsh Arabs of southern Iraq – were the guardians of the marches, periods of war put them on equal terms with provincial governors and "extended their territorial jurisdiction for the most influential and strategically located tribal confederations who took enhanced responsibilities far beyond their traditional peacetime role as guardians of the border."[57] Consequently, in contrast to what happened in Anatolia or the Balkans, the slaves (*kul* or *ghulam*) of the sultan did not replace the native aristocracy in the Ottoman-Iranian frontier region.

From the beginning, frontiers played a significant role in the Safavid-Ottoman confrontations that eventually led to their transformation into a boundary. The eponymous founders of the Ottoman state, Osman Ghazi (d. 1324), and the Sunni-Sufi order of Safaviyah, Sheikh Safi (d. 1334), were contemporaries, and both of their dynasties developed in syncretistic frontier environments. The transformation of the Safavi religious brotherhood into a temporal power and its consequent military success were closely related with its activities in Anatolia and the Caucasian borderland. Like the rise of the

---

[55] Posch, *What Is a Frontier?*, 208; and Inalcık, "Ottoman Methods of Conquest."

[56] Rhoads Murphey, "The Resumption of Ottoman-Safavid Border Conflict, 1603–1638: Effects of Border Destabilization on the Evolution of State-Tribe Relations," *Orientwissenschaftliche Hefte*, Mitteilungen des SFB "Differenz und Integration" 5: Militär und Integration, Halle (2003): 151–55. For Iran, see Matthee, "The Safavid-Ottoman Frontier: Iraq-i 'Arab as Seen by the Safavids," *International Journal of Turkish Studies* 9.1–2 (2003): 167–69.

[57] Murphey, "Resumption," 151, 154.

Ottomans in the west, here too the ethos of *ghaza* and jihad, especially in Shirvan and Georgia, played a substantial role in the formation of the polity. As the spiritual masters or *murshid-i kamil* of the Sufis, the Safavid leaders, in their bid for temporal power, encouraged their followers to *ghaza* and jihad against non-Muslim Daghestanis, Circassians, and Georgians.[58] More importantly, troops of *qezelbash ghazis* or *shahi sevan* (those loyal to the shah) fiercely fought Sunni Uzbeks and Ottomans, and their wars resembled contemporaneous religious wars in Europe.[59]

Perhaps because of the nature of these wars, the Ottoman chronicles do not shy away from using the word *thughur* or its Turkish version *suğur* when referring to their frontiers with Iran. Similarly, Iranian sources use the same terminology to describe the frontier in Iraq-i 'Arab.[60] However, *hadd* and especially its plural *hudud* is the term most commonly used by Ottoman and Iranian historians when referring to their mutual frontiers. Apart from its meaning of boundary and limit, *hudud* is also a technical term denoting "the punishment of certain acts which have been forbidden or sanctioned by punishment in the Ḳur'ān."[61] In a theological context, *hadd* indicates finiteness, a necessary attribute of all things created, and strongly connotes prevention, restraint, and prohibition. Its geopolitical meaning, which describes a place whose transgression without proper documentation is punishable, reveals its theological roots. Muslim geographers used the singular form, *hadd*, to emphasize the point at which a geographical entity, such as a city, mountain range, sea, desert, or country, came to an end.[62] Denoting a zone of transition from one sovereignty to another, the plural *hudud* applied to both the internal and external frontiers of a Muslim entity. Still, depending on the context in which it is used, *hudud* could correspond to European concepts of frontier or boundary as well. Indeed, most documentation produced by the Ottoman frontier commissioners

---

[58] See Eskandar Beg Monshi, *Tārīkh-e 'Ālāmāra-ye 'Abbāsī*, trans. Roger M. Savory (Boulder, CO: Westview Press, 1978); Monshi I, 35; and Savory I, 30–33, 56. From here onward, *'Ālāmāra* Monshi refers to the Persian version edited by Iraj Afshar and *'Ālāmāra* Savory to the English translation.

[59] Among many examples, see *'Ālāmāra* Savory I, 60, 71, 85, 105; Monshi I, 36–38; and *Tarih-i Osman Paşa*, transliterated by Yunus Zeyrek (Ankara: T. C. Kültür Bakanlığı, 2001).

[60] Matthee, "The Safavid-Ottoman Frontier," 167–68.

[61] "Hudud," *Encyclopaedia of Islam*, 2nd ed.

[62] Loghatname-e *Dekhoda*, "hadd"; Bauer, *Boundaries*, 12; and "Hudūd," *Encyclopedia of Islam*, 2nd ed. In *Hudud al-'Ālam*, both *ḥadd* and *hudūd* are used. Minorsky translated the first as "frontier" and the second as "limit."

of the nineteenth century uses the concept of *tahdid-i hudud* (limiting, demarcating the boundaries). Even the earliest commissioner used the almost identical *kat-ı hudud* to define his mission.

While the Ottoman survey commission of 1848–52 published its diary under the title *Seyâhatnâme-i Hudûd*, or *Itinerary of the Frontier*, the Iranian commissioner published his report under the title *Risalah-i Tahqiqat-i Sarhaddiyah*, or *Explorations at the Borderland*. No doubt both commissioners referred to the same region. By *hudud* or *serhadd*, (or *sarhadd*) they both meant the frontier or borderland as a social and economic region adjacent to both sides of the boundary. In Ottoman parlance, frontier provinces such as Erzurum were *serhadd*, which Şemseddin Sami, in his renowned dictionary *Kamus-u Türki* defines as the beginning or the line of *hudud*. Redhouse, in his lexicon, defines *serhadd* as "a frontier, a frontier place, a march."[63] *Loghatname-e Dehkhoda*, the preeminent dictionary of the Persian language, in addition to providing the words *marz* and *thugur* as equivalents, defines *serhadd* as *sar + hadd* (beginning, extremity of the *hadd*), a definition imparting a meaning much closer to the European notion of boundary. The wardens of the marches were therefore called *serhaddar* or *marzdar* (or *marzuban*).[64] For the Safavids, Arabistan, Luristan-i Fayli, Georgia, and Kurdistan – regions ruled by high-ranking *wali*s and bordering the Ottoman Empire – were *sarhadd*.[65] For the Ottomans, all provinces bordering other sovereignties were *serhadd* or *serhadd-i mansure* (*sarhadd al-mansura*, the victorious frontier), *serhaddat-ı İslamiye* (frontiers of Islam), or *serhadd-i Hakani* (the royal frontier). The governors of such provinces were also called *muhafız*, *serhaddat muhafızları*, or occasionally *serhad sipehdarları*.[66] To further complicate matters, *sarhadd* is interchangeably used with *marz u boum* or *marz*, which the *Dekhoda* defines as *thughur*. In addition to connoting the *sarhadd* of a country, *marz u boum* has the meaning of one's native country or homeland. Yet, from the various meanings the *Dekhoda* provides, it is

---

[63] Şemseddin Sami, *Kamus-i Türk-i* (Istanbul: Ikdam Matbaası, 1897, reprint).

[64] *Loghatnameh-e Dehkhoda*, http://www.loghatnameh.org.

[65] Minorsky, *Tadhkirat Al-Mulūk, A Manual of Safavid Administration* (London: Luzac & Co, 1943), 43.

[66] For examples, see *Şâni-zâde Târîhi*, 745; Naşûhü's-Silāḥī Maṭrākçī, *Beyān-ı Menāzil-i Sefer-i ʿIraḳeyn*, ed. H. G. Yurdaydın (Ankara: TTK Yayınevi, 1976), 340–41; *Şem'dânî-zâde Fındıklılı Süleyman Efendi târihi, Müri't-tevârih*, prepared by M. Münir Aktepe (Istanbul: İstanbul Üniversitesi Edebiyat Fakültesi, 1976–1981), 157; *Tarih-i Selâniki* 13, 32, 182, 189, 222, 285, 328, 703; Ahmed Cevdet Paşa, *Târih-i Cevdet* (Istanbul: Matbaa-i Osmaniye, 1309 [1893]) v. 6, 205; and *Tarih-i Osman Paşa*, 17.

possible to conclude that *marz* and *hadd* are used almost synonymously and are closest to the European idea of boundary. Indeed, the *Dekhoda* notes that *marz* is the *hadd* of everything and *boum* is cultivated land, whereas *marz* is the edges of that land, which is why they call the *sarhadds* of a vilayat (province) a *marz*.

More familiar with the Ottoman usage, Redhouse defines *marz* as a frontier district, any district, a country, or a region, and *merzbum* as a country or a region. *Merzban* or *merzwan* thus describes the warden (*hakem, mir*) of a frontier (*sarhadd*), whereas a *merzuban* is "a lord of a frontier district, a marquis" and *merzebe* "being or becoming a lord of the marches," which *marzanishan* inhabit. Instead of the Persian *merzban*, Ottoman chronicles and documents refer to the lords of the marches as *serhad muhafızı* or *hafez al-hadd*, protectors of frontier provinces. The *Dekhoda* defines *merzban* as keeper or protector (*hafez*) of the *marz*, *thughur*, and *hudud*, among other things.[67]

Among all these terms, the word closest to the European notion of boundary, used by both Ottoman and Iranian sources, is *sınur* or *sinur/ sinor* (from the Greek *sínoron*). This meaning is most obvious when *Tarih-i Selânikî* defines one of the tasks of Shah Abbas's envoy to Istanbul as defining the *sinur* of the *serhadd-i memalik*, or the boundaries of the borderland or outer lands.[68] Similarly, the *Tārih-i Na'imā* and *Şanizāde Tārihi* from different centuries use the word *sınur* to denote the place one transgresses (*sınırı tecavüz*).[69] In the same manner, describing Ottoman troops campaigning in the Caucasus, *'Ālamāra-ye 'Abbāsī* notes that they crossed the *sınur* into the province of Akıska (*dakhile sinur-e in taraf bud*), thus making *sınur* an unmistakable equivalent of boundary.[70] In the following chapters, I resign myself to the use of the European terms *frontier* and *boundary*, suggesting that they correspond roughly to *sarhadd/hudud* and *sinur*; hence the transformation of the *sarhadd/hudud/ frontier* into the *sınur/boundary*.

---

[67] *Darande-e keshvar o molk* (owner, holder of a country, land, province), *negahban, negah darande* (guardian, keeper), *hakem, shahrban* (ruler of part of the country), *sardar, amir, saheb manseb* (commander, holder of a rank), *zamindar* (landlord).

[68] "Tekrâr *serhaddi* memâlik *sınıru* ta'yin olunmak içun ve name-i hümâyûn cevâb-ı bâ-sevâbı içün" in Mustafa Selaniki *Tarih-i Selânikî*, ed. Mehmet İpşirli (Ankara: TTK Yayınevi, 1999), vol. I, 252.

[69] Naîmâ Mustafa Efendi, *Tarih-i Na'îmâ: Ravzat ül-Hüseyn fî hulâsat-i ahbâr'l-hafikayn*, prepared by Mehme İpşirli (Ankara: TTK, 2007) v. I, 60–1; and Şânî-zâde Mehmed 'Atâ'ullah Efendi, *Şânî-zâde Târîhi*, prepared by Ziya Yılmazer (İstanbul: Çamlıca, 2008), 49.

[70] *'Ālamāra* I, Monshi, 232.

OTTOMAN-IRANIAN TREATIES AND FRONTIERS

After years of military and ideological confrontations, the Ottomans and Safavids signed the first treaty defining the frontiers in the town of Amasya on May 21, 1555. This marked the first time the Ottomans recognized Safavid Iran as a legitimate entity.[71] Not withstanding its vagueness on the frontier, referred to as *hudud* or *serhadd* throughout, the treaty allowed each party to acknowledge the other's respective domains.[72] Notably, this was also the year that the Peace of Augsburg officially established the legal basis for the existence of Protestant and Catholic sovereigns in the Holy Roman Empire. Neither the treaty of Amasya nor that of Augsburg, however, put an end to the religio-political confrontations they sought to ameliorate. Amasya granted the Ottomans Iraq, most of Kurdistan, and Western Armenia; ceded Tabriz, Revan, and Nakhjavan to Iran; and divided Georgia between them. At this time, Erzurum, Diyarbakr, Zulkadriyye, Baghdad, and Shahrizor were also securely in Ottoman hands, with the local Kurdish principalities in Erzurum, Van, and Shahrizor provinces serving as buffers between the parties. Ottoman sources of the period, like those produced by Matrakçı Nasuh, use cities rather than lines to mark the limits of the Ottoman Empire, creating ambiguous transitional zones in which frontiers were not be crossed by stepping over an invisible boundary but rather by arriving at the first town on the other side.[73] As state frontiers were fluid, state limits in Matrakçı's works were visualized through a "constellation of points" – that is, of cities and towns – rather than by unbroken lines.[74]

   The peace engendered by the 1555 treaty lasted about two decades. Twelve years of brutal warfare on the Caucasian frontiers resulted in the signing of a second Ottoman-Safavid treaty in 1590. In his letter to the shah, Sultan Murad III made it clear that the purpose of this treaty was to define the frontiers by establishing the *hudud* and *sınur* based on the

---

[71] For a history of early Iranian-Ottoman treaties, see Remzi Kılıç, *XVI-XVII Yüzyıllarda Osmanlı-İran Siyasi Antlaşmaları* (Istanbul: Tez Yayınları, 2001). The most detailed source on early Iranian-Ottoman relations is still Kütükoğlu, *Osmanlı-İran*. For the beginning of the eighteenth century, see Münir Aktepe, *Osmanlı-İran Münasabetleri ve Silahşör Kemani Mustafa Ağanın Revan Fetihnamesi 1720–1724* (Istanbul: Istanbul Universitesi Ed. Fak. Yayınları, 1970).
[72] See Sadrazam's letter to Shah Tahmasp's envoys, *Münşe'at-i Selātīn* I, 619–20.
[73] Kathryn A. Ebel, "Representations of the Frontier in Ottoman Town Views of the Sixteenth Century," *Imago Mundi* 60.1 (2008): 6.
[74] Ibid., 7.

Amasya Treaty, also known as Suleiman's *sınur*.[75] Invoking the ancient principle of *uti possidetis*, which argued that a territory should remain with its possessor at the end of the conflict, the sultan reiterated Ottoman claims to Bagdad, Shahrizor, Van, and Erzurum. He also argued that lands occupied by the Kars castle and Ahıska *beglerbeglik*, along with their dependencies, should remain under the control of the Ottoman *hakims* of *serhadd*. More noteworthy was his request that plenipotentiaries (*vekil*) from both sides work with local elders to delimit the boundaries of Hemin, Darna, and Dartang (sanjaks in the Zohab region), again according to Suleiman's *sınur*. In return, he guaranteed that Ottoman authorities would respect the frontiers as long as Iranian authorities sent 100 bales of silk annually and did not transgress their limits or intervene in the affairs of Baghdad and Daghestan.[76] This was the first time an Ottoman-Iranian treaty mentioned the appointment of plenipotentiaries to delimit boundaries of disputed districts. Nevertheless, the parties soon found themselves mired in conflict once more. Almost ten years of intermittent confrontation, which devastated the borderlands and their inhabitants, led to yet another round of talks, initiated in 1611, about peace and how to delimit and demarcate the frontiers (*kat'ı sınır* and *ta'yin-i suğur*). In possession of Azerbaijan, Georgia, and Shirvan, the shah asked that boundaries be drawn according to the Amasya Treaty, whereas the Ottomans requested the return of Sunni-inhabited lands.[77] The war officially ended with what Ottoman sources call the Nasuh Pasha, or Istanbul Treaty of 1612.

This treaty required the delimitation of the frontiers (*kat'ı hudud*) and the prevention of interference (*men'i sudud*) in internal affairs; therefore, Istanbul authorized the muhafız of Baghdad and the beylerbeg of Van to appoint a plenipotentiary. The shah likewise authorized the hakim of Revan to demarcate the frontiers in accordance with the 1555 treaty. In 1614, the appointees drafted a *sınırname*, or frontier document, but disagreed on the ownership of Ahıska, then in Ottoman hands. The Ottoman delegate did not accept the Iranian claim that elders of Ahıska alive in the time of Suleiman agreed that the province belonged to Iran.[78] Thus, with the treaty's ink barely dry, the parties prepared for yet another

[75] *Münşe'at-i Selātīn* II, 170.
[76] Ibid., 172–73.
[77] *Tārih-i Na'īmā* II, 382–83.
[78] Kütükoğlu, *Osmanlı-Iran*, 277–79; Feridun Bey, *Münşeat*, II, 255; *Tārih-i Na'īmā* II, 391, 404–5, 421; Kılıç, *XVI-XVI Yüzyıllarda*, 168.

confrontation; following the unsuccessful 1616 siege of Revan and a devastating loss at Jang-i Sahra-yı Serav (Serab), Ottoman commanders appealed for peace. The Treaty of Serav, signed on September 26, 1618, reiterated many clauses of the previous treaty regarding frontiers and sectarian conflicts. The only difference was that the Iranians agreed to leave the castles of Kars and Ahıska to the Ottomans and their tribute was reduced from 200 to 100 bales of silk.[79]

This was followed by another long period of wars, devastating to the greater borderland. The Ottoman conquest of Baghdad, which brought to a close sixteen years of campaigning, resulted in another treaty – referred to as the Sultan Murad-Shah Safi Treaty or the Zehav/Zohab or Qasr-i Shirin Treaty – which was signed at Zohab near Qasr-i Shirin on 14 Muharram 1049/May 17, 1639, and, following the shah's approval, ratified by Murad IV in January 1640.[80] Two centuries later, the Ottoman plenipotentiary to the 1843–47 Erzurum Congress on the Ottoman-Iranian frontier quoted this important document thusly:

Of the frontier places towards Baghdad and Azerbaijan, Jessau and Bauderani, should belong to our Imperial self; the town of Mendeljin and the intervening plains as far as Dairtenk (the place called Sair-mil being fixed as the boundary of Dairtenk) also should belong to our Imperial self, and the mountain on the other side thereof to the other party; that the Mil Bashi being designed as a boundary to Dairna and Dairtenk they should belong to our imperial side, and the divisions called Zeyau-ed-din and Hauruni, of the tribes of Jauf, should belong to us, and Bera and Zairduli remain to the other party; that the fortress of Zenjir, which is situated on a hill, being demolished and made waste, the villages to the west of the said demolished fortress remaining with our Imperial side, those to the east thereof should remain with the other party; and those parts of the mountain above the fortress of Zaulim near the town of Shehr-e Zor, which look towards the said fortress, should be taken possession for our Imperial self, and the fortress of Avraman, with its dependent villages, should remain to the other party; that the pass of Chagan be a boundary on our Imperial side, and Mihriban, with its dependencies, should remain to the other party; and that the fortresses of Kotur and Maukew on the frontier of Van, with that of Maghauzberd towards Kars, should be pulled down on/by both sides.... And besides the above-mentioned articles, Akhiskha, and Kars, and Van, and Shehr-e Zur, and Baghdad and Bussorah, and all the forts and habitations, districts and lands, plains and deserts, hills and mountains within their limits, be not disturbed by the other party.[81]

---

[79] *Tārih-i Naʿīmā* II, 421, 425–28; Kılıç, *Osmanlı-İran*, 172–73.

[80] Kılıç, *Osmanlı-İran*, 195.

[81] *Schofield I*, 160–62. For a slightly different version of the 1639 treaty, see J. C. Hurewitz, *Diplomacy in the Near and Middle East* (New York: Octagon Books, 1972), vol. I, 21–23.

One copy of this treaty, purported to be a letter sent to the shah by the Ottoman grand vizier Kara Mustafa Pasha, was dubbed *sınırname*, or frontier document. It emphasizes that the treaty's purpose was to delimitate frontiers and boundaries, "ta'yin-i ahval-i sınur ve hudud."[82] Like its predecessors, and unlike the treaties that would result from the Erzurum Congress and other nineteenth- and twentieth-century negotiations, the 1639 agreement did not lay down a precise line but rather designated entire regions lying between the two states as frontiers. Still, it did define parts of the frontier less ambiguously than earlier treaties by making reference to mutually recognizable landmarks (including military installations) and inhabitants.[83] As Stanford Shaw has argued, the 1639

FIGURE 1. An Ottoman frontier fort.
Reproduced from Ms. Bishop (Isabela L. Bird), *Journeys in Persia and Kurdistan* (London: John Murray, 1891), vol. 1, 78.

---

[82] BOA.IE.HR 1/18 14 Muharram 1049/17 May 1639. Another document, BOA.IE.HR 4/407, 29 Z 1085–26 March 1675, billed as the letter Mustafa Pasha sent to confirm the agreement, repeats the general terms of the treaty.

[83] Maurice Harari, "The Ottoman-Iranian Boundary Question: A Case Study in the Politics of Boundary Making in the Near and Middle East" (Ph.D. diss., Columbia University, 1953), 7. Maria T. O'Shea argues that due to shifting loyalties, the frontier zone defined by the treaty was more than 160 kilometers wide from the Zagros to the Tigris. See O'Shea, "The Demarcation of the Ottoman/Iranian Border," in Keith McLachlan ed., *The Boundaries of Modern Iran* (New York: St. Martins Press, 1994), 52.

treaty was honored in the following years, "but less out of genuine friendship rather than as a consequence of internal weakness, preoccupation with the reform, and foreign aggression."[84] Although small-scale skirmishes continued to occur, this document helped establish the longest period of stability in Ottoman-Iranian relations, eighty years without major confrontations. In a similar fashion, after thirty years of war (1618–48) in which religion played a primary role, the European states established what has been called the Westphalian state system of 1648. It will not be an exaggeration to suggest that these processes were part of an intercontinental phenomenon that encompassed Western Europe and Eurasia. Thence forward, territorial sovereignty would gradually replace hegemony defined by suzerainty, and the gradual secularization of frontiers and relations, especially in the case of Ottoman-Iranian frontiers, would gain ground.

The quiet on the eastern frontier, which lasted from 1639 to 1724, freed the Ottomans to settle many scores in the west. However, the Afghan occupation of Iran and the end of Safavid rule overturned the West Asian order suddenly and radically, as Ariel Salzmann has argued.[85] The 1639 frontiers were abruptly obliterated, resulting in years of renewed upheaval. In September 1746, at the village of Kurdan near Tehran, Nadir Shah met an Ottoman envoy and signed a new treaty that essentially restated the 1639 treaty, restoring the earlier borders.[86] Like previous treaties, it also reiterated an Iranian promise to discontinue the ritual cursing by Shi's of the companions of the prophet, including his wife Aisha and the first three caliphs, as well as an Ottoman pledge to protect Iranian pilgrims traveling to *'atabat-i 'aliyat.*[87] As he sued for peace, Nadir Shah reportedly lamented the defining role sectarian differences had played in Ottoman-Iranian relations: "How much time has the family of 'Uthman since the reign of Selim spent mobilizing troops, expending wealth, and destroying lives in order to halt the cursing of the first three caliphs?"[88] Although he failed to achieve religious reconciliation, as Ernest Tucker argues: "The 1746 Kurdan treaty formally

[84] Stanford Shaw, "Iranian Relations with the Ottoman Empire in the Eighteenth and Nineteenth Centuries," in Peter Avery et al., eds., *Cambridge History of Iran*, vol. 7 (Cambridge, UK: Cambridge University Press, 1991), 297.

[85] Ariel Salzmann, *Tocqueville in Ottoman Empire* (Leiden: E. J. Brill, 2004), 39.

[86] Ernest Tucker, *Nadir Shah's Quest for Legitimacy in Post-Safavid Iran* (Gainesville: University Press of Florida, 2006), 98. BOA.HAT 804/37147-B, written in 1840, maintains that the treaty signed with Nadir Shah reiterated articles in the Sultan Murad treaty regarding *hudud* and *sınur*.

[87] Tucker, *Nader Shah*, 98.

[88] Ibid., 91.

defined a new basis for relations between Iran and the Ottomans and remained the basis of future relations, even during the chaos that arose in Iran during the last few months of Nadir's reign and continued after his death."[89] Despite continuing instability in Iran, the modus vivendi established by the 1746 treaty lasted until the mid-1770s. It was only toward the end of Karim Khan Zand's rule (1750–79) that new and serious complications emerged.

In the early 1770s, the governor of Baghdad, Ömer Pasha, violated the conditions of the Treaty of Kurdan by overtaxing and oppressing Iranian pilgrims. At the same time, he exerted his authority over Shahrizor, the province of the Kurdish Baban dynasty.[90] Responding to the violations of the treaty's terms, Karim Khan made a series of demands that the Porte ignored. In response, he began carrying out raids into eastern Anatolia and Iraq. His forces laid siege to and later occupied Basra; ravaged the regions of Darna, Mahrud, Mendelchin, and Badra *muqataas*; and occupied Shahrizor and lands five hours from "the city of Kerkuk, which is a sancak of Kurdistan," as Cevdet Pasha notes.[91] In addition, he (like Omar Pasha) intervened in Baban affairs and also seized Zohab from its Baghdad-appointed governor, Abdullah Pasha of Bajalan [Bajlan]. On one hand, these clashes demonstrate the ongoing importance of sectarian tensions. For example, in response to Karim Khan's aggression, Sultan Abdulhamid I (r. 1774–89) demanded a fatwa be declared against him.[92] Such fatwas were common, but as an indication of the further secularization of Ottoman-Iranian relations, this one differed from its predecessors by defining the enemy not as a Shi'i apostate, but rather as a rebel (*baghi*) against the sultan. On the other hand, the territorial dimensions of the dispute would be especially germane to the future of the frontier conflict. Indeed, the fates of Zohab and the lands of the Baban would emerge as two of the most contentious issues in the competition between the two states. The resolution of the latter dispute, in particular, would signal the transition from contested suzerainty to bounded sovereignty.

[89] Ibid., 99. For the Persian text of the treaty, see BOA.A.DVNS.NMH, III, pp. 60–61. For a Turkish translation, see BOA.HAT 7/220, 29.Z.1159/January 12, 1747.

[90] Tucker, *Nader Shah*, 111. For the details of the Zand-Ottoman competition over Iraq and the Baban, see John Perry, *Karim Khan Zand: A History of Iran, 1747–1779* (Chicago: University of Chicago Press, 1979).

[91] *Tārih-i Cevdet* II, 52–56 and 114–15. For a detailed treatment of this topic, see Perry, *Karim Khan Zand*, chap. 11.

[92] For this fatwa, see *Tārih-i Cevdet* II, 305, Appendix 3.

A NOTE ON SOURCES AND METHODOLOGY

This book situates itself within borderland literature and Ottoman historiography. With regard to the latter, it relies heavily on the British National Archives (then PRO), the India Office Records of the British Library, and the Başbakanlık Osmanlı Arşivi. It was my good fortune that the Başbakanlık opened the files of Osmanlı-Iran Hududu for the first time when I started work on this project. These extensive files, which would no doubt take a lifetime to thoroughly digest, include intergovernmental and intra-governmental correspondence and the reports and records of various commissions. Among the Başbakanlık's many collections, the files of Hariciye Siyasi have been especially valuable. The Ottoman chronicles *Târih-i Cevdet*, *Es'ad Efendi Tarihi*, and *Şânî-zâde Târîhi* have been vital sources of information for the early period of Ottoman-Qajar relations. Equally invaluable have been the works of the frontier commissioners, including the Iranians Mirza Ja'far Khan and Mirza Mohib Ali Khan, and the Ottomans Dervish Pasha, Hurşid Pasha, and Tahir Pasha. Richard Schofield's voluminous *The Iran-Iraq Border: 1840–1958* brings together an impressive number of documents and saved me from months, if not years, of research in British archives and libraries. Despite its focus on Ottoman historiography, Iranian perspectives are not absent from this project. In addition to consulting English and Turkish translations of the most important Persian documentation regarding boundary negotiations, I have made frequent use of pertinent Persian sources, including books written by the Iranian frontier commissioners mentioned earlier and occasionally used volumes of documents on Ottoman-Iranian relations published by the Iranian Ministry of Foreign Affairs.

Still, because of its chronological and geographical breadth, not to mention the innumerable actors involved, one book simply cannot provide an exhaustive account of the story of the making of the Ottoman-Iranian boundary. This book therefore focuses on those parts of the boundary whose delimitation most occupied the commissioners and the peoples who resided therein. These contentious areas include Zohab-Qasr-i Shirin, Shatt al-Arab, Lahijan-Vezne, and Posht-e Kuh. Consequently, the reader will find many groups and places absent from the following pages. One notable absence is the Armenian issue, which I have largely omitted for two reasons. First, a considerable literature about this important subject already exists. Second, even though the process impacted them significantly, Armenians did not directly participate in the making of the frontier and are rarely mentioned in frontier negotiations.[93] Other absences include the topics of trade, the administrative structure of the frontier, and fortifications and the military establishments along the border. It is my hope that other scholars will take up these topics or use this study as a springboard to produce more detailed provincial or ethno-tribal histories that have yet to be written.

As Hämäläinen and Truett note, traditional histories of "borderlands bent toward the telos of the nation and its territorialized incorporation of space."[94] This book, however, is not primarily concerned with the linear story of the relation between nation and border formation. To the contrary, even though many of the histories that inspired my project focus on examples of successful nation-state formation, mine is partially the history of a failure or an unmaking of a nation, precisely because the making of this border effectively precluded the formation of a possible Kurdish nation-state, making Kurds the globe's largest non–nation-state ethnic group. Moreover, even if we could trace many proto–nation-state policies to this period, the making of the boundary in and of itself was not an attempt to make the nation and its boundaries congruous.

If we unlink the border from the nation, how do we define the limits of a border region? How do we decide where it starts and ends? Or, to borrow again from Hämäläinen and Truett, what are the borders of this borderland history, and what is the relation between the narrative and spatial horizons of this story? Chronologically, the book starts with the Qajar dynasty's rise and ends with the First World War. Spatially, in Ottoman parlance, the provincial capitals of Erzurum and Van were accepted as *serhadd* – that is, as frontier cities – and in the southern part, the governors of Baghdad and Basra were responsible for policies regarding the frontier. On the Iranian side, the governors of Tabriz, Urumieh, Kermanshah, and Luristan – some of whom were the grand chiefs of large tribal confederations (such as the Lur and the Kalhor) – were responsible for the protection of the frontiers and the appointment of frontier wardens. Hence, the borderland would be the lands in between the authorities of these governors, and the people in between the borderland peoples or borderlanders. Therefore, in the north, the lands between Lake Van and Lake Urumieh constitute the borderland; in

[93] For the most recent treatment of the issue, see Janet Klein, *The Margins of Empire: Kurdish Militias in the Ottoman Tribal Zone* (Stanford, CA: Stanford University Press, 2011); and Michael A. Reynolds, *Shattering Empires: The Clash and Collapse of the Ottoman and Russian Empires 1908–1918* (Cambridge, UK: Cambridge University Press, 2011).

[94] Hämäläinen and Truett, "On Boundaries," 356.

the middle, the lands between Kermanshah and Baghdad; and in the south, the lands between Basra and the eastern part of the Island of Khizr (Abadan). More strictly, borderlanders were those individuals and groups (towns, villages, cities, tribes) whose lives were directly affected by the delimitation and demarcation of the boundaries. As such, people in Van or Urumieh were borderlanders, as were the people residing between these towns. Meanwhile, nomads such the Mangur tribe, whose lives were profoundly shaped by the transformations of the boundary, could be placed at what Baud and van Schendel's define as the *border heartland*, whereas the cities of Baghdad, Erzurum, Kermanshah, Van, and Tabriz would be the *outer borderland*, and the lands and peoples in between the *intermediate borderland/ers*.[95]

STRUCTURE OF THE BOOK

Chapter 1 covers the first half of the nineteenth century and explores how the concurrent processes of boundary making and state making happened at the margins of both states, and how the borderland peoples responded to them. Writing locals and localities back into history, it focuses on a Kurdish periphery dominated by dynasties and powerful tribal confederations. After providing a broader context of Ottoman-Qajar relations in which to understand the events that led to the making of the boundary, the first chapter details various Kurdish rebellions waged either to protect the relative autonomy of local dynasties or to carve out an alternative state-space in contravention to the imperial boundary. The suppression of these rebellions facilitated the integration of the borderland's settled and itinerant communities into the geo-body of centralizing states increasingly defined by imperial boundaries. This chapter thus examines the initial phase of the tumultuous process of turning tribespeople into Ottomans and Iranians, and itinerants into settled tax-paying citizens.

Completing this process required defining the limits of Iranian and Ottoman sovereignty. To this end, the first border conferences were held in the frontier town of Erzurum between May 1843 and May 1847. Chapter 2 provides an account of these lengthy negotiations by focusing on how the frontier was redefined in accordance with the needs of the centralizing states as well as a post-1815 international order intent on mapping the world according to its interests. By analyzing complex

---

[95] Baud and van Schendel, "Toward a Comparative History," 221–22.

negotiations surrounding questions of territory and landownership, commerce, religio-legal issues, and cross-border migrations by itinerant populations, it shows how delegates from four imperial capitals (Ottoman, Iranian, British, and Russian), in consultation with local actors, laid the groundwork for making the boundary.

While Chapter 2 details conceptual, legal, and diplomatic aspects of boundary making, Chapter 3 scrutinizes the work of the first survey commission (1848–52) to show how the boundary line, theoretically defined in Erzurum, was demarcated on the ground. Describing the commission's efforts to locate this line in the variegated geography of the borderland, it emphasizes the interactions between boundary commissioners and borderland communities and highlights the effects of delimitation on the latter, including Arab, Turcoman, and Kurdish tribes whose habitats straddled both sides of the newly mapped line.

The transformation of the frontier into a boundary was interrupted by a major military conflict between three of the principal boundary makers: the Crimean War of 1853–56, in which Russia fought against the Ottoman Empire and England. This war intensified turmoil in the borderland and also exacerbated the rise of sectarianism – specifically, of Shiʻi-Sunni and Christian-Muslim animosities – which thereafter played a detrimental role in the life of the borderlanders, reaching its climax with the Russo-Ottoman War of 1877–78, a watershed event that reshaped the religio-political geography of the region and set the stage for many of the tragedies the borderlanders would witness in coming decades. By providing a history of the northern borderland region during and between these wars, Chapter 4 considers the crucial question of how boundary making and imperialist intervention led to the rise of sectarianism and shaped the future of the frontier and its peoples.

One result of this seismic change was that from 1905 to 1912, Ottoman forces occupied the Sunni parts of the Shiʻi shah's land, claiming them in the name of the Sunni caliph sultan. Iran, Russia, and England came together to reject this occupation. The borderland communities, squeezed between global and regional actors and forced to make identity and citizenship choices, variously resisted or cooperated with it. Analyzing this final, unstudied episode of Ottoman expansionism, Chapter 5 reveals the dynamics informing Ottoman-Iranian relations and the citizenship choices of the borderlanders during the tumultuous period of constitutional revolutions on both sides.

It was only because of the distractions of Italy's occupation of Libya and the Balkan Wars, as well as pressure from the great powers, that

Istanbul ended its endeavor to turn northwestern Iran into the northeastern Ottoman Empire. Their land and power greatly diminished, the Ottomans withdrew from Iran and accepted the final demarcation of the frontiers. In the company of their Iranian and Ottoman colleagues, the Russo-British members of the last international frontier commission, which surveyed the region in 1913 and 1914, arbitrated the boundary line that many assume has been there since 1639. The concluding chapter details this commission's interactions with various borderland communities and shows the role these negotiations played in definitively demarcating the limits of the Ottoman Empire and Iran.

I

The Kurdish Frontier and Ottoman-Qajar Relations

Struggles for hegemony over the Mesopotamian plain and the Zagros mountain range date back to the times of the Persian and Greek Empires. After serving as a passageway for conquering Mongols, Arabs, and Turks, in the sixteenth century these areas became the stage for Ottoman-Safavid encounters. Focused on the Caucasus, Azerbaijan, Kurdistan, Baghdad, and Basra regions, these encounters resulted in Iranian supremacy in Azerbaijan, eastern Kurdistan, and parts of the Caucasus, and Ottoman control in the rest. Later, the same regions would be the physical loci of wars fought between the Ottomans and the Afshar, Zand, and Qajar dynasties ruling over Iran. At the end of the eighteenth century, as the Qajars established hegemony over most Safavid-controlled lands and attempted to solidify their hold over surrounding areas, a new era of Ottoman-Iranian antagonism began, in which the hitherto ill-defined, porous borderland emerged as the most contentious matter.[1]

The Porte refused to recognize the founding Qajar ruler, Agha Muhammad Khan (r.1789–97), and his successor, Fath'Ali Shah (r.1797–1834). It was thus not surprising that Istanbul declined to support Tehran when the latter waged war with Russia. Regarding the Qajars as ignorant, tribal, and potentially conflictive, Istanbul refused to demonstrate Muslim unity by declaring *ghaza* and jihad against "Moskof."[2]

---

[1] For the contours of Qajar history, this book relies on Abbas Amanat's *Pivot of the Universe: Nasir Al-Din Shah Qajar and the Iranian Monarchy, 1831–1896* (Berkeley: University of California Press, 1997).

[2] Ahmed Cevdet Paşa, *Târih-i Cevdet* (Istanbul: Matbaa-i Osmaniye, 1893), vol. VI, 203–5, 207–8, 250–1; for Sadrazam's answer to Agha Muhammad, 391–92. Hereafter *Târih-i Cevdet*.

Attempts to create unity against a common enemy, and the inability to achieve it, would remain a constant until the 1830s.

Whereas Russia thus influenced Ottoman-Qajar relations from the beginning, Britain's involvement emerged later, in the wake of the Wahhabi desecration of holy Shiʻi sites in Baghdad province in early 1802. FathʻAli Shah responded decisively by promising to punish the offenders and attack Baghdad. The British ambassador, meanwhile, tried to convince Istanbul to combine forces with Iran against the Wahhabis. Guided by sectarian animosity and their historical rivalry over Iraq, Istanbul again refused to cooperate and refused to allow Shiʻi Iranian forces to enter the domains of the Sunni caliph.[3]

Even as Russian and British influence increased, local people and populations also helped shape Qajar-Ottoman relations. For example, the governors of Baghdad, Erzurum, and Van on the Ottoman side and of Azerbaijan and Kermanshah on the Iranian one emerged as key state actors. The occupants of the borderland, including hereditary dynasts such as the *wali*s of Ardalan and Posht-e Kuh, together with large tribal confederations such as the Kurdish Shekak, Haydaran, Jalali, Jaf, Kalhor, Sinjabi, and Arab Banu Lam, Muntafik, and Kaʻb also played significant parts by providing a buffer zone or first protective layer around each state's domain. None of these, however, played as important a role in the first fifty years of Ottoman-Qajar relations as the Babans of Suleimanieh. Theirs was a quintessential case of a frontier principality squeezed between major powers and struggling to remain autonomous. Shaped by the vague or disputed sovereignty of the central states, their own divided loyalties, and a multiplicity of state and non-state actors, the Babans' story exemplifies the role of the borderlanders as well as the complexities of the transition from suzerainty to sovereignty in an undefined frontier.

Through the example of the Babans and other Kurdish principalities, this chapter argues that the elimination of indirect rule was an important phase in the process of centralization or imperial reassertion, which put an end to borderland accommodation and, crucially, evolved in parallel with the creation of the boundary lines. For the imperial centers, then, the elimination of the lords of the marches, who hitherto held power at the borderland, facilitated the making of the boundary even as the making of the boundary facilitated their elimination. To demonstrate the parallel

---

[3] *Târih-i Cevdet* VI, 171–72; Yahya Kalantari, "Feth Ali Şah Zamanında Osmanlı-İran İlişkileri" (Ph.D. diss., Istanbul Universitesi, 1976), 33.

processes of centralization and boundary making, the following pages detail how the borderland and its peoples, along with emerging Russian and British interference, initiated the transformation of Ottoman-Qajar relations from interstate struggle to international coexistence.[4] The chapter privileges the Kurdish principalities because they embody strikingly resilient forms of local rule in both Iranian and Ottoman domains, and their vigorous, ultimately failed, defense of their dwindling autonomy represents a turning point in the borderland's history.[5]

Following the formulation developed by Jeremy Adelman and Stephen Aron, I analyze a critical stage in the transformation of the borderlands into bordered lands and show how the borderland peoples lost their ability to manipulate or negotiate with state power, play rival states against each other, and "live autonomously in interstitial spaces" as a result of the territorialization of the state-space.[6] The result was what Charles Maier has defined as "a new quality of territoriality" that privileges "what happens *within* the borders. The area within will no longer be construed as a passive enclosure to be awarded to great families or captains of the realm," and, as a result, the process of mastering the interior is inaugurated.[7] This process might be defined in Foucauldian terms as *governmentality*, which begins with the surveying and mapping of the borderland that allows the center to achieve territorial integrity and control. Ending indirect local control through strategies that constituted and consolidated state power, Istanbul attempted to unify its domains by creating a newly demarcated "national" space.[8] As Maier argues, the decline of the landed order, or *ancien régime*, during this period was a global phenomenon instigated as central states abandoned their "confederal organization" during

---

[4] Jeremy Adelman and Stephen Aron, "From Borderlands to Borders: Empires, Nation-States and the Peoples in Between in North American History," *The American Historical Review* 104.3 (1999): 816. The authors suggest that the "shift from inter-imperial struggle to international coexistence turned borderlands into *bordered* lands."

[5] For Ottoman mechanisms of authority at the margins of empire see Eugene Rogan, *State in the Late Ottoman Empire: Transjordan, 1850–1921* (Cambridge, UK: Cambridge University Press, 1999), and Janet Klein, *The Margins of Empire: Kurdish Militias in the Ottoman Tribal Zone* (Stanford, CA: Stanford University Press, 2011).

[6] Pekka Hämäläinen and Samuel Truett, "On Borderlands," *The Journal of American History* 98.2 (2011): 344; Adelman and Aron, "From Borderlands," 816.

[7] Charles S. Maier, "Transformations of Territoriality 1600–2000," in Oliver Janz, Sebastian Conrad, and Gunilla Budde, eds., *Transnationale Geschichte: Themen, Tendenzen Und Theorien* (Gottingen: Vandenhoeck & Ruprecht, 2006), 41–42.

[8] Jonathan Murdoch and Neil Ward, "Governmentality and Territoriality," *Political Geography* 16.4 (1997), 308.

widespread civil wars and replaced decentralized structures of politics with administratively and territorially cohesive regimes.[9]

THE END OF THE *ANCIEN RÉGIME* AND THE RISING CAPACITY OF STATES AT THE BORDERLAND

As McAdam, Tarrow, and Tilly argue, increasing state capacity or extending state power in the borderland was composed of four complementary processes: (1) the replacement of indirect rule by direct rule; (2) the penetration of the geographic peripheries; (3) the standardization of state practices and identities; and (4) instrumentation, that is, growth in the means (and capacity) of carrying out intended policies.[10] Certainly, Istanbul's empire-wide citizenship project – its effort to turn borderlanders into Ottomans – was more ambitious than Iran's. Both projects, however, required the extension of the state's infrastructural power into the peripheries, which they accomplished at various levels and with varying degrees of success through, among other activities, the making of the boundaries, the forceful replacement of local notables and interest groups with salaried appointees, the reorganization of regional administrative divisions, the reform of landholding patterns, the forced settlement of itinerant populations, the introduction of new taxes, and the conscription of hitherto unconscripted locals. In addition, standardization at the margins meant the introduction of travel documents, including passports, and an increase in the number of customhouses and border patrols, all of which required a fixed boundary. These kinds of measures, which shifted structural power-holding mechanisms, were fiercely challenged by the local hereditary dynasties that jealously guarded their diminished ancestral domains, as well as by the nomadic and seminomadic tribes that employed transborder pastures now claimed by rival sovereigns. As the states aggressively pushed for the territorialization of their sovereign space, such groups vehemently defended their precarious autonomy.

Hereditary dynasties were a feature of Kurdistan from the first days of the Ottoman-Safavid encounter, in which the Kurds played significant

---

[9] Maier, "Transformation," 43. For socio-organizational changes of the Ottoman *ancien régime* in the premodern period with a particular attention to Iran, cartography, and the borderlands, see Ariel Salzmann, *Tocqueville in Ottoman Empire* (Leiden: E. J. Brill, 2004).

[10] Doug McAdam, Sydney Tarrow, and Charles Tilly, *Dynamics of Contention* (Cambridge, UK: Cambridge University Press, 2001), 78 (emphasis added).

roles.[11] Even though the Ottomans had successfully eliminated or incorporated much larger political entities in the Balkans and Anatolia, they recognized that the situation on the eastern frontier was distinct. Not only was the region geographically remote from Istanbul and close to the Safavid centers, but the local dynasties also wielded considerable power. As such, Istanbul was forced to cooperate with local rulers, whose alliances with the sultan proved invaluable to the region's military defense and sociopolitical organization. In turn, such alliances helped local rulers preserve relative autonomy.[12] In Kurdistan proper, the Safavids followed a similar policy by allowing the House of Ardalan, centered in Sinne, to dominate the periphery and control many of the lesser dynasts. Inevitably, the central governments needed to sustain the local power elite that protected the guarded domains and controlled their populations. Those elites, most of which predated and outlived not only the Safavids but also most of the life of the Ottoman Empire, likewise needed the support of the center to shield them from local adversaries and the rival empire. The result was a flexible and symbiotic relationship that was mutually beneficial but not without tensions. Ottoman and Iranian relations with borderland populations, grounded in local relationships, could thus be described as a "history of entanglements – of shifting accommodations," rather than of imperial domination.[13] The logic of empire and the precarious geopolitical conditions of the borderland required such interdependence or interpenetration, which survived as long as the Ottoman-Iranian competition for hegemony over the borderland; as a result, many districts retained their special status into the first half of the nineteenth century. Indeed, thanks to their proximity to the ambiguous border, some powerful emirs were able to balance the two empires against each other and maintain a de facto independence, as van Bruinessen has argued.[14] Only the rise of the intertwined processes of centralization and boundary making put an end to the centers' beneficial but risky relationships with the lords of the marches.

[11] For Kurdistan between Iran and the Ottoman Empire and the notion of tribe in Kurdistan, see Martin van Bruinessen's magisterial *Agha Shaikh and State: The Social and Political Structures of Kurdistan* (London: Zed Books, 1992), chap. 3, and his "Kurds, States and Tribes," in Faleḥ A. Jabar and Hosham Dawod, eds., *Tribes and Power: Nationalism and Ethnicity in the Middle East* (London: Saqi, 2003): 165–83.

[12] For the impact of the Safavids on the Eastern policy of Suleiman, see Jean-Lois Bacqué-Grammont, "The Eastern Policy of Suleymân the Magnificent, 1520–1533," and Rhoads Murphey, "Suleymân's Eastern Policy," both in Halil Inalcik and Cemal Kafadar, eds., *Suleiman the Second and His Time* (Istanbul: The Isis Press, 1993).

[13] Hämäläinen and Truett, "On Borderlands," 347, 352.

[14] van Bruinessen, *Agha*, 174.

In the Ottoman-controlled provinces of Baghdad, Van, and Erzurum, the ruling families – or dynasts, as Janet Klein has defined them[15] – that survived into the nineteenth century included the Babans, Cizra Botan (Jazirah ibn-Omar), Hakkari, Egil, Bitlis, Mush, Palu, Bradost, Bahdinan, Imadiye, Soran, and Mahmudi. The Iranian side, meanwhile, was dominated by the Ardalan family (which governed Iranian Kurdistan for centuries) and their subbranches in Saqqez and Baneh (Bana), as well as the rulers of Mukri and Maku, the *wali*s of Posht-e Kuh and Hawiza. A variety of administrative arrangements existed between the centers and these peripheral rulers, most of whom were also the official wardens of the marches.

For example, the Ardalan established themselves in Sinne (Senna-Sanandaj), and their "state" – supported by the Jaf, Kalhor, Mandami, and Shaikh Esma'ili tribes – was incorporated into the Safavid state as an autonomous frontier province, whose ruler was designated as a *wali*.[16] This status remained unchanged during the first half century of Qajar rule.[17] Chronicling the frontier Kurds at the beginning of the nineteenth century, J. M. Kinneir affirmed that they lived under "the rule of a number of independent princes, who govern their subjects as absolutely as either the King of Persia, or the Grand Seignor." He went on to describe the court of the *wali* of Ardalan as follows:

The most powerful of these chiefs are the *Wallees* of *Ardelan* and *Solimanea*. The former, although he condescends, for the preservation of peace, to pay an annual tribute to the King of *Persia*, is, in every other sense of the word, independent. He has the power of life and death over his vassals; but governs them more as a patriarch than a tyrant. He is said to be the lineal descendant and representative of the Great Salah a deen, and holds his court at *Senna*.[18]

Although they suffered from occasional inter-imperial or, more frequently, inter-familial competition, such "nobiliary counties" in time became adept at exploiting their situation in the periphery.[19] Their power, however, did

---

[15] Janet Klein, "Power in the Periphery: The Hamidiye Light Cavalry and the Struggle over Ottoman Kurdistan, 1890–1914" (Ph.D. diss., Princeton University, 2002).

[16] For a history of Ardalan, see Sheerin Ardalan, *Les Kurdes Ardalan: Entre Le Perse et L'Empire Ottoman* (Paris: Geuthner, 2004). For the intertwined history of the Baban and Ardalan, see Muhammad Mardukh Kordestani, *Tarikh-i Mardukh: Tarikh-i Kurd va Kurdistan* (Tehran: Kharang, 1379–2000).

[17] For the sociopolitical organization of Kurdistan throughout modern history, see van Bruinessen, *Agha*.

[18] John MacDonald Kinneir, *A Geographical Memoir of Persian Empire* (London: John Murray, 1813), 142–43, 146 (emphasis in original).

[19] Maria T. O'Shea, "The Question of Kurdistan and Iran's International Borders," in Keith McLachlan, ed., *The Boundaries of Modern Iran* (New York: St. Martin's Press, 1994), 51.

not survive the Qajar drive to replace them with provincial governors appointed from the countless members of the royal family. Aman-Allah Khan Bozorg (r.1799[80?]–1824[25?]) was the last powerful *wali* of Ardalan and the dynasty gradually declined after him. In 1851, as the first Ottoman-Iranian frontier survey commission passed through Ardalan, the Russian survey commissioner Tchirikof evoked a very different political landscape from that described by Kinneir:

> No more than forty years ago these valis were very powerful; they had at their disposal considerable military forces, and their relation to Tehran was that of vassal princes. At the end of the forties dissensions had weakened them, and the delimitation commissioners during their stay at Senne, were able to see in the country the full weight of Government control. Two battalions of regular troops took the place of the original army, with its picturesque uniform and steel chain-armour. These battalions were formed and trained as a contingent of the Shah's army, and the vali himself was only their commander (sertip=general).[20]

In 1867, following the death of its last hereditary *wali*, Nasir-al-Din Shah (r. 1848–96) terminated "Ardalan's special status as a semi-autonomous frontier province (which it shared with Arabistan [Kuzestan] and the Post-e Kuh) and named his own uncle, Farhad Mirza Mo'tamad-al-Dawla, as *hakem* (governor) of what had become simply the province of Kurdistan, thus putting an end to the Ardalan dynasty"[21] and, concomitantly, Kurdish autonomy. Instituting the appointment of family members to provincial governmental positions, the Qajars gradually transitioned from suzerain to a sovereign reality, eroded the rule of local power holders, established the relative domination of the center, and by eliminating a relatively centralized authority atomized the frontier society.

THE ADMINISTRATIVE ORGANIZATION OF OTTOMAN KURDISTAN

With partial exceptions, no nobiliary counties on the Ottoman side achieved the power and continuity of the Ardalan. Still, they enjoyed significant autonomy and many lasted almost as long as their counterparts in Iran. As we turn our attention to the example of Ottoman Kurdistan, which is this chapter's primary focus, it is important to recognize that our

---

[20] Y. I. Tchirikof, *Traveling Diary of Yegor Ivanovich Tchirikof*, 17, in British Library, IOR, L/P/S 11/29 and also PRO.FO 881/10116. Hereafter Tchirikof, *Diary*.

[21] P. Oberling, Banī Ardalān, in EIr and V. Minorsky, Kurdistan, EI and Kordestani, 'Ali Akbar Vaqaya' Nigar, and Muhammad Ra'uf Tavakkoli. *Hadiqah-'i Nasiriyah dar jughrafiya va tarikh-i Kurdistan* (Tehran: Tavakkoli, 1985), 139.

information about the history and sociopolitical and economic organization of this region is limited.[22] Acknowledging this lack, a rudimentary
account of relations between the Kurdish dynasts and Istanbul is provided
to better understand the transformation of the periphery that accompanied
the boundary-making process.

The pact between the Ottomans and the Kurdish rulers, or *hukkam*,
was sealed during the first days of the Ottoman-Safavid wars, when Sultan
Selim I (r. 1512–20) asked the Sunni Kurdish grandees to recognize his
overlordship and fight against the *qezelbash* (Shi'i Iranians). In response,
"the Kurdish *begs* in the region from Urumiya to Malatya, Diyarbakır to
Damascus" readily offered their religiously sanctioned allegiance (*bey'at*)
to the sultan.[23] In return, they received grants of autonomy that can be
compared to the Roman *extra provinciam*, which guaranteed independence from the governor's control or interference. Such independence, in
this context, was defined in terms of *Maktu'al-kadem ve mefruz'al-kalem*,
roughly translated as "separated from the treasury account" or free from
qalam (bureaucratic processing) and "off limits to all trespass" or *qadam*
(interference by government agents).[24] As a reward for their services and in
recognition of their power, Sultan Selim, as described by the sixteenth-
century reformist Aziz Efendi, granted that

From that time on, apart from the requirement of doing battle and combat with the
heresy-embracing "redheads" they were freed from all obligation to pay the extraordinary impositions (*tekalif*), and autonomy was granted to them over their ancestral lands (*odjak*) and homes (*yurt*) on the traditional basis as "cut off from the feet
[of intruders] and set aside from the pen [of surveyors] and so on" confirmed in
perpetuity generation after generation in order to console and gratify their minds.[25]

Suleiman the Magnificent (r. 1520–66), too, issued the Kurdish commanders
"grants of proprietorship (*mülkname*) containing clear terms of conferral
and extended to them the shade of imperial protection."[26] The contribution

---

[22] The best is still van Bruinessen, *Agha*. For a list of relevant works, see Lokman Meho and
Kelly L. Maglaughlin, *Kurdish Culture and Society: An Annotated Bibliography*
(Westport, CT: Greenwood Press, 2001).

[23] Halil İnalcık, "Autonomous Enclaves in Islamic States," in *History and Historiography of
Post-Mongol Central Asia and the Middle East: Studies in Honor of John E. Woods* Eds. Judith
Pfeiffer, Sholeh A. Quinn, and Ernest Tucker (Weisbaden: Harrasowitz, 2006), 125, 127.

[24] 'Azîz Efendi and Rhoads Murphey, *Kanûn-nâme-i Sultânî Li 'Azîz Efendi: Aziz Efendi's
Book of Sultanic Laws and Regulations* (Cambridge, MA: Harvard University Office of
the University Publisher, 1985) 13, 58.

[25] Ibid., 13.

[26] Ibid., 14. Orhan Kılıç, "Yurtluk-Ocaklık ve Hükümet Sancakları Üzerine Bazı Tespitler,"
in *OTAM*, vol. 10 (1999), 127.

of the Kurdish *begs* pleased this sultan so much that he proclaimed the following:

> Just as God, be He praised and exalted, vouchsafed to Alexander, "the two horned" to build the wall of Gog, so God made Kurdistan act in the protection of my imperial kingdom like a strong barrier and an iron fortress against the sedition of the demon Gog of Persia … It is hoped that, through neglect and carelessness, our descendants will never let slip the rope of obedience [binding] the Kurdish commanders [to the Ottoman state] and never be lacking in their attentions to this group.[27]

As the sultan's words suggest, the ties that bound the Kurds to the Ottoman Empire created a crucial buffer zone against the pro-Safavid central Anatolian masses and messianic Safavid expansionism, guaranteeing an Ottoman border that began at Zagros rather than in the central Anatolian steppe. Following Suleiman's rule, the number of privileged sanjaks continued to increase, at times providing forces of fifty thousand to sixty thousand soldiers to fight the "redheads." As Aziz Efendi notes, however, their rulers gradually lost much of their power to tyrannical provincial governors. Nonetheless, they managed to maintain a certain degree of authority.[28] As the state-space became increasingly territorialized, however, local desires for autonomy collided with the goals of Istanbul's centralization campaign and the boundary-making process. To better understand local responses to this situation, it is worth providing details about the land tenure system that developed as a result of the grants of autonomy given from the sixteenth century onward.

In Ottoman Kurdistan, this system was based on regular Ottoman sanjaks with *timar*, the prevalent system in the empire's core areas, as well as two types of less commonly found privileged administrative units. The first was called *yurtluk* (family property or family estates), *ocaklık* (hereditary autonomous appanage, ancestral lands, family estate, or province), or, more commonly, *yurtluk-ocaklık*. The second and more privileged was *hükümet*, also known as *ocaklık*.[29] Although we lack exact information on how much of Kurdistan was administrated by *yurtluk-ocaklık*s and *hükümet*s – or *Kürd hükümeti/ Ekrad begligi*, as they were also called – "a common feature of the frontier territories was the condominium, that is the joint rule of the

---

[27] 'Aziz Efendi and Murphey, *Kanûn-nâme*, 14.

[28] For relations between the Ottoman center and provinces, see essays in Suraiya Faroqhi, *The Cambridge History of Turkey. Vol. 3, Later Ottoman Empire, 1603–1839* (Cambridge, UK: Cambridge University Press, 2008), Part 3.

[29] In a 1706 petition from Bedirkhan, the bey of Cizre indicates to the sultan that the district, denominated as a *hükümet*, was bequeathed to him as an *ocaklık*. See BOA Cevdet DAH, 13221, 9.M.1178/23 April 1706. *Hukuma* denotes political as well as judicial authority.

former power elite and the Ottoman authorities."[30] Those nobiliary counties dominated Ottoman Kurdistan.[31]

The resulting system, according to Halil İnlacık, was based on an idea, present in numerous Islamic states, of "a special kind of sultanic land grant (*tamlîk, temlîk*), bestowing absolute and hereditary immunities vis-à-vis the administration, making it a virtually autonomous enclave within the territory of the state."[32] As *tamlik*, the autonomous lands created by this system assumed the full qualities of a *mulk*, that is, the proprietor could sell, donate, pawn, or make a *waqf* out of them. Moreover, they were granted perpetually and bestowed with a *berat* (a sultanic diploma bearing his seal) or *ahidname* (a written sultanic pledge granting privilege, authority, or immunity) that regulated their relations with the central government and included privileges and obligations.[33] As we will see in Chapter 3, in the Ottoman-Iranian borderland, the freedom that *berat* holders enjoyed would create problems when the proprietorship of contested territories came under negotiation. When claiming lands under their rival's authority, the Ottomans, for example, often argued that members of Kurdish dynasties sold them to Iranians without Istanbul's knowledge, which could only mean that until the early nineteenth century, they had enjoyed *mulk* status.

The authority of these privileged units extended to such tasks as raising troops for campaigns, taxation, public administration, and justice. Those closer to the borderland (such as the *mir*s of Rawanduz, Mahmudi, Hakkari, and Baban) were also the guardians of the frontier. As long as they remained loyal to the house of Osman, all *yurtluk-ocaklık sancak*s

---

[30] Gabor Agoston, "A Flexible Empire: Authority and Its Limits on the Ottoman Frontiers," in Kemal H. Karpat and Robert W. Zens, eds., *Ottoman Borderlands: Issues, Personalities and Political Changes* (Madison: University of Wisconsin Press, 2003), 20–23. Baki Tezcan maintains that in Diyarbekir province in 1521–22, administrative units called *cemâ'at-i Kürdan* (Kurdish communities) covered a larger area than those of regular districts. Tezcan, "The Development of the Use of 'Kurdistan' as a Geographical Description and the Incorporation of This Region into the Ottoman Empire in the 16th Century," *The Great Ottoman-Turkish Civilization* 3 (Ankara: 2000), 546.

[31] As it is difficult to come up with English equivalents of *yurtluk-ocaklık* and *hükümet*, I have adopted Agoston's "nobiliary counties," which he used to describe Hungarian condominiums where the former power elite ruled jointly with Ottoman authorities. Agoston, "A Flexible Empire," 25. With regard to the nature of *hükümet*s such as Bitlis, Cizre, and Baban, Tom Sinclair's concept of "tribal principalities" does not fit my understanding of these institutions. Sinclair, "The Ottoman Arrangements for the Tribal Principalities of the Lake Van Region in the Sixteenth Century," 119–43, and Mehmet Öz, "Ottoman Provincial Administration in Eastern and Southeastern Anatolia: The Case of Bidlis in Sixteenth Century," both in Karpat and Zens, *Ottoman Borderlands*.

[32] Halil İnalcık, "Autonomous Enclaves in Islamic States," 112–13.

[33] Ibid.

and *hükümet*s "passed from father to son or to other relatives; if there were no legitimate heirs, the province could not be given to 'outsiders' or 'foreigners' but only to somebody from the region in agreement with the emirs of Kurdistan."[34] Over time, however, the number of *yurtluk-ocaklık*s and *hükümet*s changed, as did the balance of power between Kurdish lords and central and local authorities.[35]

The hereditary rulers of *yurtluk-ocaklık*s possessed the traditional symbols of power, *tabl u alem*, or a drum and a flag.[36] Nonetheless, tax registers were drawn up in their *sancak*s and the *timar* system was introduced to parts of their lands. Their most important obligation to the central government, however, was to participate in imperial campaigns under the authority of the governor-general (*beylerbeyi*) of the province.[37] Likewise, rulers of the more privileged *hükümet*s in places such as Bitlis, Hakkari, Cizre, and Baban were also expected to participate with their troops in such campaigns.[38] However, their lands were exempt from the land survey, and all their tax income belonged to the *amir*.[39] Hence, in contradistinction to *yurtluk-ocaklık*s, no revenue accrued from *hükümet*s to the central state. Moreover, the *timar* or *zeamet* systems were not introduced, no census or registers were drawn up, and no Ottoman troops or officials were stationed in their lands.[40]

Hükümet holders also had power over local judicial affairs because, unlike Ottoman Turks, most Kurds belonged to the Shafi'i rather than the Hanafi branch of Sunni Islam. Hence, the, *hükümet*s were authorized by the central government to appoint *qadi*s (judges) from among *ulama*

---

[34] Agoston, "A Flexible Empire," 20–1, and van Bruinessen, *Agha*, chap. 3.

[35] David McDowall, *A Modern History of the Kurds* (New York: I. B. Tauris, 1977), 28.

[36] In the sixteenth century, the administrative units of Kurdistan province were called *eyalet*, as opposed to *livâ* or *sancak*, the usual Ottoman term for county. See Tezcan, "Development of the Use of 'Kurdistan' as a Geographical Description," 546–47.

[37] Orhan Kılıç, "Van Eyalet'ine Bağlı Sancaklar ve Idari Statüleri (1558–1740)," *Osmanlı Araştırmaları* 21 (2001): 189–210.

[38] For the extent and nature of Bitlis Hükümet and its relations with Istanbul in earlier centuries, see Robert Dankoff, ed., *Evliya Çelebi in Bitlis: The Relevant Sections of the Seyahatname* (Leiden: E. J. Brill, 1990).

[39] Kumiko Saito, personal communication.

[40] According to Kumiko Saito (personal communication), there were exceptions to that rule and in some seventeenth-century *hükümet*s, *tahrir*s (census) were carried out for *jizya* (non-Muslim poll tax). One only hopes that Saito's meticulously researched dissertation (University of Tokyo) on Ottoman land tenure in Kurdistan will be published in Turkish or English soon. Sinclair notes that *tahrir* was carried out in Bitlis. Tom Sinclair, "Administration and Fortification in the Van Region Under Ottoman Rule in the Sixteenth Century," in A. C. S. Peacock, *The Frontiers of the Ottoman World* (Oxford, UK: Oxford University Press, 2009), 221.

educated in well-established regional Shafi'i *madrasas*.[41] Magisterial affairs, the maintenance of law and order, crime prevention, and most importantly the maintenance of order among mostly antagonistic tribes (including the arbitration of blood feuds) were the prerogatives of *hükümets*. The regional elites were thus not only brokers between state and society, but also between different segments of society.[42]

The number of *hükümets* rose from eight to eleven between the sixteenth and eighteenth centuries.[43] However, by the first quarter of the nineteenth century, no *hükümets* were left, although *yurtluk-ocaklıks* could be found in the provinces of Trebizond, Lazistan, Erzurum, Çıldır, Hakkari, Van, and Kurdistan. Although the central state gradually diminished hereditary domains and their privileges, it did not successfully eliminate the ruling families, who continued to rule their ancestral domains with the bureaucratic titles of *mutesellim, mutasarrıf,* or *müdür*. Their days, however, were numbered. With the ascension of Mahmud II (r. 1808–39), the Ottoman government cast the net of centralization over ever-larger areas. Its push to replace indirect with direct rule, change landholding patterns, force itinerant populations to settle, introduce new taxes, and enforce conscription affected numerous segments of society and brought elites and commoners together in resistance. Their resistance, in turn, shaped the borderland's unfolding history, as the case of the Babans of Suleimanieh illustrates.

BABANS BETWEEN THE OTTOMANS AND QAJARS

According to Vladimir Minorsky, the celebrated scholar of the frontier region and Russian frontier commissioner of 1913–14, under the rule of the Baban, the city of "Sulaymāniyya had a more or less autonomous existence from the end of the 11th/17th century to 1267/1850. The representatives of this local dynasty cleverly maintained their position between the two rival powers, Turkey and Persia, but they were really under the [Ottoman] pashas of Baghdad."[44] Describing lower Kurdistan as extending

---

[41] I thank Kumiko Saito for drawing my attention to this point and providing information.

[42] For the Kurdish emirates' internal organization, van Bruinessen, *Agha*, 161–70.

[43] 'Aynî 'Alî Efendi, Kavânin-i Âli '*Osmān* der Hulāsa-i Mezāmīn-i Defter-i Divān, ed. Tayyib Gökbilgin (Istanbul: Enderun Kitabevi, 1979), 30; and Kılıç, "Yurtluk-Ocaklık."

[44] Minorsky, *Bābān* in EI. In English, the most detailed information about the Babans is found in S. H. Longrigg, *Four Centuries of Modern Iraq* (Oxford, UK: Oxford University Press, 1925). For the Babans at the beginning of nineteenth century, see Claude Rich, *Narrative of a Residence in Koordistan and on the Site of Ancient Nineveh* (London: James Duncan, 1836), vol. 1. Cevdet Pasha also provides valuable information in his celebrated *Târîh-i Cevdet*. Metin

"from Armenia and the territories of the chief of *Julamerick* to the district of *Mendeli*, which is its frontier toward *Kuzistan*," Kinneir wrote the following around 1810:

> The province is divided into the districts of *Solymania, Kerkook, Erbille, Amadea, Shahre-van, Zohaub, Bidri*, and *Mendeli*, each of which has a separate *Hakem*, or governor. But he who resides at *Solymania* rules over the greatest portion of territory; and as he must, by birth, be a Kurd, usually assumes the title of *Pasha of Kurdistan*.[45]

In addition to the previously mentioned places, Halabja and the highly cultivated plain of Shahrizor were also under the authority of the Baban pashas, as were Koi and Harir sanjaks. Together with Rawanduz, these sanjaks formed Shahrizor (also Shahrizol or Šahrazūr) *eyalet* or province.[46]

Whereas the Babans used their in-between position to advance their autonomy, Tehran and Istanbul used the same status to extend their authority. Meanwhile, the governors of Baghdad, on the one hand, and Kermanshah and Azerbaijan, on the other, siphoned money and resources from the Baban. Interfamily rivalries, exacerbated by interventions from the center, rendered such schemes possible, as relatives vying for the Baban crown turned to Iranians or Ottomans as potential allies, thus deepening their precarious status, endangering their autonomy, and increasing the ambiguity of the limits of both states. Keeping a mansion in Baghdad, the Babans also sent family members as hostages to the Qajar court, as well as annual gifts to Tehran and, if need be, Tabriz. Such diplomacy or shows of recognition of dual suzerainty were necessary. Many of the itinerant tribes under Baban authority, including the Jaf and Pishder, spent their summers in lands considered Iranian.[47]

They similarly sent annual gifts to Baghdad's *mamluk* governors, who, with Iran's consent, appointed the Baban pashas and thus posed the greatest threat to their power. Cevdet Pasha describes this threat, bluntly, as a war between the *mamluk*s and the aristocrats (*asilzadeler*) that benefited only the *mamluk*s.[48] Indeed, the first Baban crisis in the Ottoman-Qajar period started in 1805 when the new governor of Baghdad, 'Ali Pasha

Atmaca's dissertation "Politics of Alliance and Rivalry on the Ottoman-Iranian Frontier: The Babans (1500-1851)" (Freiburg University, 2012) is the first comprehensive study of the Babans. For nineteenth-century Iraq, see Gökhan Çetinsaya, "Challenges of a Frontier Region: The Case of Ottoman Iraq in the Nineteenth Century," in Peacock, *The Frontier*, 271–87.

[45] Kinneir, *A Geographical Memoir*, 295–96.

[46] See Hurşîd Paşa, *Seyâhatnâme-i Hudud*, transcribed by Alaatin Eser (Istanbul: Simurg, 1997), 168.

[47] *Târih-i Cevdet* I, 339, 344.

[48] *Târih-i Cevdet* IV, 102.

(r.1802–7), dismissed 'Abd-al-Rahman Pasha, the hereditary ruler of the Baban provinces. Defiant, 'Abd-al-Rahman Pasha routed forces from Mosul sent to unseat him, before being defeated by forces from Baghdad, at which point he took refuge in Sinne, the capital of the *wali* of Ardalan, or Iranian Kurdistan.[49] The ensuing events provide a clear picture of the complex role played by the Kurdish frontier in Ottoman-Iranian relations. Fath 'Ali Shah asked the Baghdad governor for the reinstatement of the Baban pasha. The governor, in turn, sent a representative to Tehran to request that 'Abd-al-Rahman be returned or resettled in the interior of Iran. 'Abd-al-Rahman himself also met with the shah, who presented him with a dagger and appointed him governor of Baban sanjak. The shah also asked 'Ali Pasha to acknowledge his decision or face a campaign. When this request was ignored, 'Abd-al-Rahman, in the company of Aman-Allah Khan, the *wali* of Ardalan, advanced to his old seat of power, Suleimanieh. Unable to resist, the region's new Baban *mutasarrif*, Khalid Pasha Baban, withdrew to Baghdad.[50] Claiming that Iran's involvement in the matter was a breach of treaties, 'Ali Pasha gathered twelve thousand soldiers and began to march toward Iran. He was swiftly stopped by Istanbul, however, which wanted to maintain good relations with its neighbor, because both parties were then at war with Russia.

Obeying orders, 'Ali Pasha redirected his forces to Suleimanieh, where he obliged 'Abd-al-Rahman to return to Sinne, but only for a short time. Following further large-scale clashes between Ottoman and Iranian frontier forces at Merivan, where the Iranians bested the Ottomans in late 1806, 'Ali Pasha dispatched a celebrated Shi'ite jurist to negotiate with prince-governor Mohammad-'Ali Mirza Dawlatshah (1789–1821) in Kermanshah.[51] As a result of these negotiations, and as a sign of ambiguous dual suzerainty over the Babans, 'Abd-al-Rahman was reinstated.[52] The Sublime Porte supported this outcome and ordered 'Ali Pasha to refrain from further anti-Iranian activities. Following the exchange of envoys, it was also agreed that the governors of Shahrizor would be appointed with Iranian consent and Iranian pilgrims and travelers would

[49] Longrigg, *Four Centuries*, 231.

[50] Kordestani, *Tarikh-i Mardukh*, 379–81; Kalantari, "Feth Ali Şah," 41–42. Shukrullah Sanandaji, and Hishmatallah Tabibi, *Tuhfa-i Nasiri dar tarikh wa jugrafiya-i Kurdistan* (Tehran: Mu'assasa-i Intisharat-i Amir Kabir, 1987), 177–78.

[51] Kalantari, "Feth Ali Şah," 43–45 and Hasan-e Fasā'ī, *Fārsnāma-ye Nāṣeri*, trans. *Heribert Busse* (New York: Columbia University Press, 1972), 119.

[52] Abbas Amanat, "Dawlatšāh, Moḥammad-'Alī Mīr-za," in *EIr*; Kalantari, "Feth Ali Şah," 42; *Târih-i Cevdet* VIII, 51–52.

not be harassed. In January 1807, the Ottoman governor of Erzurum and the Qajar crown prince and governor of Azerbaijan, 'Abbas Mirza, also exchanged envoys for the release of Ottoman prisoners taken during the clashes and to negotiate an alliance against Russia.[53] It is no coincidence that the Ottoman authorities carried out negotiations with the two princes. 'Abbas Mirza and his brother and rival Dawlatshah ruled their provinces with monarchial authority and dominated Ottoman-Iranian relations in the first quarter of the nineteenth century, often carrying out policies independent of Tehran. Dawlatshah's authority increased when, in 1224/ 1809, the shah appointed him *wali* of the frontier region from Kermansah to Khuzestan, where he served unchallenged for the rest of his life, creating serious problems for the Ottoman frontier administration.[54] Because the *mirzas* tended to act independently of Tehran, the pro-centralization Ottoman statesman Cevdet Pasha opined that Iran was a "Republic of United Tribes" rather than a centralized state.[55]

Partly as a result of the Russo-Iranian wars of 1804–13 and the Russo-Ottoman wars of 1806–12, and partly to Napoleon Bonaparte's push for an Ottoman-Iranian alliance against Russia, a short period of rapprochement followed what we might call the first 'Abd-al-Rahman crisis, or the wars of Baban succession. By 1807, Ottoman-Iranian representatives were busy negotiating possible cooperation between the Muslim states. In a clear shift from the sectarian discourse that dominated previous Ottoman-Iranian exchanges, they now spoke in terms of the community of believers (*camia-i Islamiye*) and the need to protect the *serhadat* or frontiers of Islam by cooperating against Russia. 'Abbas Mirza's strong push for an alliance, in particular, seems to have worked for a time. Hence, when, in 1808, Baghdad's governor and his Baban allies forced 'Abd-al-Rahman to take refuge again in Sinne, Tehran quickly sent a special envoy to Baghdad to arrange his reinstatement.[56]

While dealing with the *mamluks*' whims and the prince of Kermanshah, 'Abd-al-Rahman increased his power and mended relations with Istanbul, which did not bode well for Iran. In 1810, he even helped Istanbul's abrasive representative Halet Efendi depose yet another of Baghdad's *mamluk* governors, Küçük Süleyman Pasha, who, among other offenses,

---

[53] Kalantari, "Feth Ali Şah," 46. Faridun Adamiyat, *Amir Kabir va Iran* (Tehran: Intisharati Kharezmi, 2006), 64.

[54] Amanat, "Dawlatšāh, Moḥammad-ʿAlī Mīr-za."

[55] "Iran devleti aşair-i müctemia cumhuriyetine benzerdi," *Târih-i Cevdet* X, 231.

[56] *Târih-i Cevdet* IX, 206–7. For 'Abd-al-Rahman's career in this period, see Longrigg, *Four Centuries*, 232–38.

"ravaged the territories of *Mosul* and *Diarbekr* and at the same time quarreled with his own vassal the Pasha of Kurdistan."[57] Despite the power he wielded thereafter, the coveted governorship was not transferred to 'Abd-al-Rahman because Halet realized that such an appointment would deliver the whole province to the Baban dynasty, parts of which had been pro-Iranian. Thus Baghdad was, for the time being, left in *mamluk* hands, and the Babans in a precarious situation.[58]

As both parties were still fighting Russia, Istanbul ordered the military and civil authorities of the eastern frontier to cooperate with Iran.[59] When this cooperation did not materialize, 'Abbas Mirza sent Hac Huseyn Agha [as *maslahatguzar*] to Istanbul, in October 1810, to press again for an alliance. Responding positively, Istanbul sent a *büyükelçi*, Yasinizade Abdulvahab Efendi, to Tehran. The *qadi* of Selanik and a highly respected scholar who later rose to the rank of *sheikh al-Islam*, Yasinizade, after meeting Fath 'Ali Shah, returned to Tabriz on January 21, 1811, and remained there until the end of 1813. In the royal letter that accompanied him, written to 'Abbas Mirza, the sultan urged for cooperation against "the enemy of our religion, Moskof," while advising collaboration with England, a friend of both parties and enemy of Russia.[60] Indeed, the British representative was present at the Tabriz meetings.

The negotiations between Yasinizade and the crown prince resulted in a treaty promising cooperation against Russia. In addition, Yasinizade convinced 'Abbas Mirza to release Armenians that Iranian troops had enslaved in a skirmish with the *muhafiz* of Van and return pillaged property from the same area. Iranians also agreed to refuse fugitives and respect mutual frontiers. Istanbul, in turn, promised fair treatment of Iranian pilgrims, to tax Iranian merchants the same as Ottoman merchants, and to likewise refuse fugitives.[61] Iran promised to stop protecting 'Abd-al-Rahman and interfering in Baban affairs but once again reiterated its demand that Baban or Shahrizor *umara* be designated with their consent and that Baghdad's governors be friendly.[62] It seemed, momentarily, that the agreement would stick.

[57] Kinneir, *A Geographical Memoir*, 308–9.
[58] *Târih-i Cevdet* IX, 206–17.
[59] Ibid., 147.
[60] Ibid., 219–21. For the text of the letter, see 312–14 and Kalantari, "Feth Ali Şah," 80.
[61] Kalantari, "Feth Ali Şah," 89–91; *Şâni-zâde Târîhi*, 787, 814–15, 831–35; *Târih-i Cevdet* X, 231–32.
[62] Fasā'ī, *Fārsnāma-ye Nāşeri*, 135–36; *Târih-i Cevdet* IX, 221, and X, 32. Also Faik Reşit Unat, *Osmanlı Sefir ve Sefaretnâmeleri* (Ankara: TTK, 1968), 206–7.

Then, in 1811, uneasy with 'Abd-al-Raḥman's independence, Dawlatshah and 'Abdullah Pasha (r.1810–13), the governor of Baghdad, began to pressure 'Abd-al-Rahman to appoint sub-Baban administrators to Zohab, Darna, and Baclan. When he resisted, Dawlatshah gathered an army of sixty thousand and besieged him at Koi sanjak. As Cevdet Pasha notes, however, 'Abdullah quickly withdrew his support from Dawlatshah when he realized that a victory by the prince would result in penetration of the region by *rafidhis* (Shi'is) and increased Sunni suffering. His ally lost, the prince withdrew. Eager to appease him, 'Abd-al-Rahman sent Dawlatshah one of his sons as a hostage together with a considerable *pishkesh* or gifts.[63] Unhappy with 'Abd-al-Rahman's pace with the Iranians, in early summer 1812, it was 'Abdullah's turn to march on the frontier principality, and 'Abd-al-Rahman once again put up a fight; lacking the firepower to prevail, he took refuge with Dawlatshah whose subsequent interventions came to nothing.[64]

While tension increased between Baghdad and Kermanshah, Istanbul independently signed a treaty in Bucharest on September 28, 1812, which concluded the six-year-long Russo-Ottoman wars. This signing, however, was in contravention to the cooperation promised by Yasinizade's embassy. Tehran took umbrage, even as Russia evacuated Ottoman territories while continuing to wage war against Iran on the eastern front.[65] Struggling to defend itself, Tehran, informed of the Baban debacle, sent Dawlatshah with a large force to attack Ottoman territory. In August 1812, they moved toward Baghdad, laying waste to the countryside. Afraid of losing his position, Baghdad's governor reached a deal with Dawlatshah to put an end to Persian looting in exchange for 'Abd-al-Rahman's reinstatement. As Cevdet Pasha points out, such events worsened relations between the two states and eventually brought about the end of the Baban dynasty while increasing the need for a defined frontier.[66]

On June 18, 1813, while Yasinizade was still in Tabriz, Istanbul sent a second envoy, Celaleddin Efendi, to Tehran. His negotiations, however, were unproductive, and he was ordered to join Yasinizade. Together, they made little headway. Iran agreed not to collect on 'Abd-al-Rahman Pasha's annual promise of ten thousand tumans but refused to pay compensation

---

[63] *Târih-i Cevdet* IX, 223; Kordestani, *Tarikh-i Mardukh*, 381–82.

[64] *Târih-i Cevdet* X, 90–91; Kordestani, *Tarikh-i Mardukh*, 382; Sanandaji, *Tuhfa-i Nasiri*, 189–90.

[65] *Târih-i Cevdet* X, 31.

[66] Amanat, "Dawlatšāh"; *Târih -i Cevdet*, X, 90–92, 101–2; Kordestani, *Tarikh-i Mardukh*, 382; Kalantari, "Feth Ali Şah," 95.

for Dawlatshah's pillaging, arguing that Iraqi Arabs constantly robbed their pilgrims to Atabat. Unable to make progress, on September 17, 1813, Celaleddin left Tabriz without Yasinizade and without informing his hosts. In the same year, London mediated the disastrous Golestan Treaty with Russia, by which Iran lost considerable territory in the Caucasus. The alliance they had hoped to build with the Ottomans could have lessened the damage. No doubt the Qajars would hold a grudge against Istanbul.

Soon thereafter, 'Abd-al-Rahman died. Honoring the preferences of Kurdistan's *begzade*, *agha*, *sadat*, and *mashaikh*, and with Iranian consent, his elder son, Mahmud Beg, was made a pasha and the *mutasarrif* of all Baban sanjaks.[67] These developments resulted in a temporary lull in tensions but kept the status of the Baban lands in an ambiguous dual suzerain realm. However, in a few years, 'Abbas Mirza and Dawlatshah restarted their aggressive policies. Wary, Istanbul ordered its frontier governors and the Kurdish *bey*s to cooperate in prohibiting Iranian forces from crossing the *sınır*.[68]

Nevertheless, in 1815, the new governor of Baghdad Sa'id Pasha (r.1813–16) tried to replace Mahmud Pasha with his uncle 'Abdullah. Because Mahmud was appointed with Iranian consent, and Iran saw itself as quasi-suzerain in Shahrizor, Tehran intervened. Ten thousand Iranian soldiers joined Mahmud's troops in Suleimanieh and forced the governor's troops to withdraw. In the meantime, a revolt against Sa'id took place in Baghdad. With support from Mahmud and other Kurdistan *bey*s, Davud Efendi, the revolt's leader, was appointed governor in November 1816 and received assurance that if he proved to be a wise and thoughtful vali, Mahmud would cut all ties with Iran and become a loyal Ottoman subject.[69] Istanbul, too, supported the rebel leader, because it viewed Sa'id as incompetent and unable to work with the Kurdish *bey*s, which disrupted the peace and tranquility of the borderland populations. This new, more forceful administrator, it hoped, would protect its frontiers (*hudud* and *sugur*) and frontier populations.[70]

However, Iran remained unwilling to allow the Ottomans to establish exclusive sovereignty over the frontier principality. Mahmud Baban was left between a rock and a hard place, as Dawlatshah prevented him from fulfilling his promise to cut ties with Iran. For these reasons, relations

---

[67] *Târih-i Cevdet* X, 102–3, 212; Kalantari, "Feth Ali Şah," 96–97.
[68] *Şâni-zâde Târîhi* II, 738–39; and X, 197.
[69] *Târih-i Cevdet* X, 224–26.
[70] *Şâni-zâde Târîhi*, II, 754–55.

between Davud and Mahmud deteriorated, as the former, ironically, accused the latter of plotting with Dawlatshah. Rather than confronting Dawlatshah directly, however, Davud sent his seal bearer to Mahmud to force him to end his relationship with Iran. At the same time, Mahmud responded to Dawlatshah's threats by sending his brother Hasan, the *bey* of Karadagh, as a hostage to Kermanshah in 1818. Hasan, however, advanced to Baghdad instead to ally himself with Davud, who, after occupying Harir and Koi, appointed the traitorous brother *mutasarrıf* of those sanjaks. Such machinations left Mahmud no choice but to cooperate with the Iranians, and Dawlatshah sent a force of ten thousand to aid him. This force advanced up to Kirkuk, while other Iranian detachments occupied Mandali, Jassan, and Badra *muqataa*s. Davud sent forces in response, but before a confrontation could take place, the Baban factions reconciled among themselves and Mahmud was restored to his post, calming the frontier for some time.[71] The complex developments surrounding the Baban succession display the tensions that arose over the status of a semi-autonomous borderland principality and the indeterminate geographic limits of Ottoman and Iranian sovereignties. The case of the Haydaran and Sipki tribes of the northernmost borderland, in turn, allows us to examine how the indeterminate subjecthood of the borderland tribes complicated Ottoman-Iranian relations.

TRIBES AND EMPIRES: THE CASE OF HAYDARAN AND SIPKI

The case of Haydaran and Sipki came to the fore during the revolt of Dervish Pasha, the *muhafız* of Van, which occupied the Porte and Tabriz from 1816 to 1819 and ravaged the Hakkari-Van-Urumieh region. Iran became involved when Dervish invited its Sipki Kurdish tribe to take refuge in Van, settling its members in Ercish. When he refused to return them, 'Abbas Mirza sent several thousand men to lay siege to Ercish's castle. He then asked Istanbul to move the Sipkis to the environs of Revan (Yerevan). In the meantime, succumbing to Iranian pressure, the *mir* of Hakkari, named Mustafa, moved with four thousand families to the Iranian side. Cevdet Pasha attributes such moves to two causes: the local rulers' fear of Istanbul's centralist, anti-*ayan* (local grandees) policies and the appeasement policies of the Qajar princes. As the subjecthood of many tribes in the Iranian *hudud* was debatable (*meşkuk*), their chiefs should be

---

[71] *Târih-i Cevdet* X, 227–29; Longrigg, *Four Centuries*, 243.

approached with kindness (*istimalet*), he noted, adding that "in that matter the Porte was not as successful as the Iranian *mirzas*."[72]

The *mirzas* had more in mind than kindness, however. When Istanbul was unable to persuade Dervish to return the Sipkis, 'Abbas Mirza sent Hussein Khan, the *sardar* of Revan, to attack Khoshab castle, the center of the Mahmudi dynasts. The governor of Erzurum and general commander of the east, Celaleddin Pasha, rushed to help the rebel pasha. With ammunition provided by his new ally, Dervish and the Mahmudi Kurds repelled the Iranians. This effort did not endear him to Istanbul, which, with the help of Kurdish grandees, was able to suppress his revolt in August 1819. With Dervish gone, Selim Pasha, the *mütesellim* of Mush, was able to convince the *mir* of Hakkari to return to Ottoman sovereignty. The Sipkis, meanwhile, also remained in Ottoman lands.[73]

By 1820, however, the Iranians were again complaining about the mistreatment of pilgrims, including members of the royal family. When 'Abbas Mirza attempted to circumvent the regional governors by communicating directly with Istanbul, Celaleddin imprisoned his envoy before he could proceed. The crown prince then appealed to the British representatives in Iran and Istanbul for his envoy's release.[74] This was followed by Iranian complaints about the Sipki's continuing migration to the Ottoman side, as well as the large Haydaran tribe's movement in the same direction.[75] Celaleddin and Selim, they argued, had incited both migrations. The Haydaran migration became a particular bone of contention, as evidenced by a large paper trail in the archives. A second envoy was sent, who successfully reached Istanbul to complain about the protection given to this group. While the envoy engaged in diplomacy, 'Abbas Mirza's troops plundered Ottoman lands and continued to threaten the Haydaran chief, Kasim Agha, with forceful return.[76]

At this time, Istanbul was embroiled in two revolts on its western frontiers, led by 'Ali Pasha of Janina and the Greeks. Still, it readied its forces on the eastern frontier for another possible confrontation with

---

[72] *Târih-i Cevdet* XI, 7.
[73] Sinan Hakan, *Osmanlı Arşiv Belgelerinde Kürtler ve Kürt Direnişleri* (Istanbul: Doz Yayınları, 2011), 27–39; Kalantari, "Feth Ali Şah," 109–13.
[74] *Şânî-zâde Târihi*, 1001–2; Adamiyat, *Amir Kabir*, 64–65.
[75] Ottoman chroniclers claim the Haydaran was a branch of the Shikaki living in Mayafârqin. From that region, they moved to Malazgird, Mush, and Ercish *sancaks* where they wintered, at times temporarily (*alâ tarîkı'l müsâfere*) retreating to Iran. Accordingly, in 1820, they returned from Iran to settle in their own lands. *Şânî-zâde Târihi*, 999–1001 and *Târih-i Cevdet* XI, 4–5.
[76] *Târih-i Cevdet* XI, 5–6.

Iran,[77] which was using aggressive tactics with the governor of Baghdad, warning him to show his respect during the shah's visit to Soltaniyah or face the consequences. Suspicious that they were trying to take advantage of the Greek War of Independence, Istanbul urged Davud Pasha to protect *hudud* and *sınur*.[78] Still, hoping to avoid confrontation, in late October 1820, Istanbul sent an envoy to ask once more for noninvolvement in Baban affairs, release of Baban prisoners, and refusal of fugitives. Despite Fath 'Ali Shah's amicable response, tensions increased. The *sardar* of Revan sent his brother Hasan Khan with a large force to bring the Haydaran back. Faced with strong resistance by Selim Pasha, Hasan withdrew from the Mush area at the interior after ravaging many Armenian villages and churches.[79] Increasingly concerned, Istanbul ordered its eastern governors to ready their forces. The *mutasarrıf* of the Baban *sancak* and other begs of Kurdistan, together with the *yurtluk-ocaklık* holders of the Diyarbekir *vilayat*, were instructed to do the same. Directives were also sent to Selim and the governor of Erzurum to send forces to aid the *muhafız* of Kars in case of Iranian transgressions. If one is to believe the official Ottoman chronicler of the time, on receiving news of these preparations, Mohammad 'Ali Mirza sent Davud conciliatory messages and gifts and withdrew his troops from the Baghdad frontier.[80] Cevdet Pasha has a different explanation. He suggests Davud was afraid he would lose his post as a result of so many non- *mamluk* governors gathering in Baghdad and so gave the Iranians what they wanted while informing the Porte they had left the frontier region after negotiations. Whatever the truth, Ottoman troops did not go to Baghdad. Nevertheless, in January 1821, Istanbul sent additional cannon and other equipment to Erzurum.[81]

Regardless of what Davud might have conceded to his brother, it seems that 'Abbas Mirza was not satisfied, and he presently withdrew his representative to Erzurum. Before leaving, 'Ali Khan informed Erzurum's governor that because of the maltreatment of its pilgrims, Iran would prohibit both the trade of provisions with the province of Van, which was suffering from famine, and pilgrims from going to hajj that year. In May 1821, Istanbul again warned the governors of the eastern provinces that taking advantage of the Greek revolt, Iran might cooperate with the Russians against the empire.[82]

---

[77] Ibid., 5–7; *Şânî-zâde Târihi*, 1015–16.
[78] Kalantari, "Feth Ali Şah," 103; *Şânî-zâde Târihi*, 945–47.
[79] Hakan, *Osmanlı*, 44; Kalantari, "Feth Ali Şah," 114–18.
[80] *Şânî-zâde Târihi*, 945–47.
[81] *Târih-i Cevdet* X, 230, and XI, 8.
[82] *Şânî-zâde Târihi*, 1141–42; *Târih-i Cevdet* XI, 10.

THE LAST OTTOMAN-IRANIAN WAR, 1821–1822

Soon afterward, the forces of the two *mirzas* entered Ottoman territories. It has been suggested that the Russian military commander in the Caucasus and the tsar's representative in Tehran provided much-needed funds for 'Abbas Mirza's campaign; in any case, British efforts to dissuade the crown prince proved ineffective.[83] In the north, 'Abbas Mirza commanded a force of around thirty-five thousand, trained in the European style, along with Hussein Khan (the *sardar* of the Khanate of Yerevan) and his brother, Hasan Khan. They were weakly opposed by *Serasker* (commander in chief) Hüsrev Pasha, whose thirty thousand men included provincial Ottoman troops, Kurdish light cavalry, and mounted infantry. In the south, Davud, with a similar force, faced Dawlatshah, whose forty thousand men were mainly drawn from the heavy mailed squadrons of the southern (Shi'i) Kurdish tribes, as well as the Bakhtiaris and Lars.[84]

Following his advance guard, which moved from Tabriz on September 10, 1821 (Zilhicce 12, 1236), 'Abbas Mirza quickly brought strategic points under control, but he was stunned by the ease with which his forces took the frontier stronghold of Bayazid. Soldiers posted at Toprak Kaleh, an Ottoman stronghold between Erzurum and Tabriz, quickly dispersed. Under the pretense of returning the Haydarans to Iran, the prince's troops continued through Ottoman territory, pillaging and taking prisoners along the way. Although they failed to take Van, they captured Eleshkird, Malazgird, Bulanık, parts of Mahmudi, Hakkari, and Bitlis and forced Selim Pasha of Mush to submit, despite his fierce resistance. He was, however, subsequently reinstated by 'Abbas Mirza and his brother was given the title of khan to signify Iranian suzerainty. As the winter intensified, the prince withdrew to Tabriz, leaving in charge local notables alienated by Istanbul's drive for centralization.[85]

To reverse the Iranian advance, Istanbul appointed an ex-sadrazam, Mehmed Emin Rauf Pasha, as the new *serasker* of the east and governor of Erzurum. Increasing his forces to forty thousand, in the age-old fashion, the Porte also obtained a fatwa from the *sheikh al-Islam* declaring the country of the *refavız-ı 'Ajam*, who attacked the frontiers of Islam, or *hudud-u Islamiye*, to be the abode of war, or *dar al-harb*, and its people

---

[83] Graham Williamson, "The Turco-Persian War 1821–1823: Winning the War but Losing the Peace," in, Roxane Farmanfarmaian, ed., *War and Peace in Qajar Persia* (London: Routledge, 2008), 89.

[84] Ibid., 93–95.

[85] *Tārih-i Cevdet* X, 10–11, and XI, 82; Kalantari, "Feth Ali Şah," 135–40.

ahl-al harb. Orders were then sent to the provinces to arrest or extradite Iranian merchants and visitors, as well as notables on their way to pilgrimage.[86] Rauf Pasha's movement into Azerbaijan, however, was delayed when Iranian forces left at Toprak Kale advanced to that town's fort. Ottoman forces, including those of Selim, quickly followed. In mid-May 1822, 'Abbas Mirza marched from Tabriz and emerged victorious from the Battle of Toprak Kale. He then set his eyes on Erzurum, where he hoped to force an apology from the governor and reclaim the Haydaran. His plans, however, were derailed by the emergence of cholera and the resulting loss of soldiers.[87]

If the prince justified his campaign by pointing to the misdeeds of the Erzurum's governor and the Haydaran and Sipki tribes, his brother referred to those of Baghdad's governor, especially as they pertained to the Baban issue and the indeterminate frontier. Before the war, unable to win over Mahmud Pasha Baban, Dawlatshah had pressured Davud to appoint Abdullah Bey Baban, who had taken refuge in Kermanshah, as the Baban *mutasarrif*. Informed of the prince's plan, Istanbul urged the governor to support Mahmud. In early October 1821, Dawlatshah moved from Kermanshah, while Davud sent Mahmud reinforcements. However, in the ensuing confrontation, Davud's *kethuda* (chief of staff), Mehmed Aga, defected and Mahmud's forces were defeated. Victorious, Dawlatshah appointed Abdullah Bey and advanced to Baghdad. According to Abbas Amanat, only the formidable city walls and the pleas of Shaikh Musa Najafi stopped him from taking the city.[88] Cevdet Pasha and Longrigg argue that Davud's strong defense and reconciliation with Mahmud allowed the Ottomans to emerge victorious. Yet it is obvious that with no help from Istanbul, Davud simply sued for peace. Some have suggested that he also agreed to pay ten thousand tuman compensation plus a yearly sum.[89] Disregarding Mahmud's services during the war, he accepted the appointment of 'Abdullah, as well as that of Khalid Pasha to Harir and Koi sanjaks; in return, Dawlatshah withdrew to Kermanshah. Davud's decisions, as Cevdet Pasha notes, threw the affairs of Kurdistan into disarray, which was hastened by Dawlatshah's death from cholera during his withdrawal, on November 22, 1822. In response, the *wali* of Diyarbakir, 'Ali Pasha, marched with Mahmud on Suleimanieh

---

[86] For the fatwa's text, see Kalantari, "Feth Ali Şah," 148.

[87] Williamson, "The Turco-Persian War," 95–97; *Tārih-i Cevdet* XI, 12.

[88] Amanat, "Dawlatšāh, and Kalantari, "Feth Ali Şah," 141–43.

[89] Williamson, "The Turco-Persian War," 95; Adamiyat, *Amir Kabir*, 65.

and routed the Iranian troops. At great human cost, they displaced Mahmud's uncle ʿAbdullah. Fath ʿAli Shah then ordered Dawlatshah's ambitious son Mohammad ʿAli Mirza to carry out a new campaign, which succeeded in occupying Mendeli. However, the resistance of Ottoman as well as tribal forces such as those of Shammar, accompanied by the ongoing cholera epidemic, compelled him to retreat.[90] In the end, with the consent of both parties, Mahmud was reinstated in Suleimanieh and ʿAbdullah in Koi, further blurring the status of the Baban lands.

THE ERZURUM TREATY OF 1823

The culmination of frontier raids carried out by ʿAbbas Mirza and Dawlatshah, the war of 1821–22 was inconclusive, despite Iran's many victories. The emergence of cholera, mutual concerns about Russia's advance, the war in Greece, and pressure from Iranian merchants trading with the Ottoman Empire all helped bring hostilities to an end.[91] ʿAbbas Mirza claimed he had waged the campaign not for land or against the sultan, but in defense of his family's honor; however, Sultan Mahmud II remained upset with Tehran and considered a countercampaign. ʿAbbas Mirza's pleas to Stratford Canning, the powerful British ambassador in Istanbul, might have changed his mind. Following negotiations between Rauf Pasha and the Iranian envoy, Mirza Mohammad ʿAli Ashtiyani, on July 28, 1823, the first Treaty of Erzurum was signed.[92] With its preamble emphasizing Islamic brotherhood, it was worded as if it were a renewal of previous treaties and existing *hudud*.[93] The terms it employed to describe geographical boundaries, the treatment of pilgrims, the rejection of fugitives, the freedom of prisoners of war, and the residence of ministers at their respective courts, relied heavily on language used in the 1746 Treaty of Kurdan. It additionally required that all occupied Ottoman territories – although which territories, exactly, remained unspecified – be returned within sixty days. True to the increasing importance of territoriality and control of populations, it also demonstrated a novel concern with the

---

[90] *Târih-i Cevdet* XI, 12–13; Kalantari, "Feth Ali Şah," 154–55; Longrigg, *Four Centuries*, 245.

[91] *Târih-i Cevdet* XI, 13.

[92] Mehmed Esʿad Efendi, *Vakʿa-nüvîs Esʿad Efendi Tarihi*, prepared by Ziya Yılmazer (Istanbul: OSAV, 2000), 229. Also *Târih-i Cevdet* XI, 77–78; Adamiyat, *Amir Kabir*, 64–65; Kalantari, "Feth Ali Şah," 155–65.

[93] For the Ottoman text of the treaty, see *Esʿad Efendi*, 236–46; and *Târih-i Cevdet* XI, 228–35; for the Iranian version, see *Guzidah-ʾi asnad* I, 294–99.

movements of tribes across frontiers. In addition, it emphasized the economics of cross-border relations by fixing a one-time custom due of 4 percent *ad valorem* and providing for the protection of merchants as well as estates of deceased Iranians.[94]

'Abbas Mirza's insistence on Iran's right to interfere in Baban affairs and its sovereignty over Zohab, now under Iranian authority, delayed the treaty's final signing. Happy with the postponement, the Ottomans hoped the Greek revolt would soon be suppressed so they would be in a stronger position to negotiate; to bolster their position, they sent additional troops to the frontier, almost provoking renewed military confrontation. To make matters worse, they noticed for the first time the exclusion of the *tarziyye*, or apology for the cursing of the first three caliphs and the companions of the prophet – a staple of previous treaties. According to Es'ad Efendi, Iran responded by claiming that the erroneous beliefs of the Safaviyah had been corrected by Nadir Shah's efforts to reconcile Shi'i and Sunni beliefs, and it was now firmly within the *ahl al-Sunna* tradition. Not wanting to engage in yet another discussion of Nadirid Ja'farism, Istanbul consented, making this the first Ottoman-Iranian treaty not to emphasize sectarian divisions.[95] 'Abbas Mirza asked that it be approved by the shah and his heir apparent, that is to say, 'Abbas Mirza himself. Istanbul agreed, in essence recognizing the prince as the next shah.[96]

Abandoning the language of sectarianism, the 1823 treaty marked the changing nature of the conflict and discourse between the two states. For example, its second article explicitly stated that Iranian pilgrims would be protected and treated like Muslims of other countries, that non-Islamic taxes would not be asked from them, and that Atabat visitors without merchandise should not pay *bâc* (market dues) and those with it should only pay legal taxes. Equally noteworthy is its seventh article, which established that every three years, each country would send a diplomatic representative to the other, thus initiating the era of permanent resident diplomats.[97] Likewise significant is the fact that the first Ottoman records listing Iranian subjects in the *Düvel-i Ecnebiye Defterleri*, or Registers of

---

[94] Previously Iranians, like other Muslims, paid 2½ percent of the value of goods imported, whereas non-Muslims paid 5 percent. Bruce Masters, "The Treaties of Erzurum (1823 and 1848) and the Changing Status of Iranians in the Ottoman Empire," *Iranian Studies* 24.1/4 (1991), 5.

[95] For Nadir's attempts to reconcile Shi'ism with Sunnism, see Ernest Tucker, *Nadir Shah's Quest for Legitimacy in Post-Safavid Iran* (Gainsville: University of Florida, 2006).

[96] *Es'ad Efendi Târihi*, 233–34.

[97] Ibid., 244–45.

Foreign States, date to 1822, just one year before the treaty was signed.[98] This was in contradistinction to Europeans, who were legally subjects of the "abode of war" granted permission to dwell in the "abode of Islam," and who had been listed in such defters since the sixteenth century.[99] As Bruce Masters notes, "[l]ike the Europeans before them, [Iranians] were to be given special consideration in their dealings with the central government and were entitled to state intervention should they encounter violations of the treaty by Ottomans, whether government officials or otherwise."[100] The 1823 treaty, therefore, signifies the gradual transformation of Iranians from ambiguous members of *umma* to citizens of Iran. The process of redividing the *umma* and defining the citizen had begun. This was also a step in the process of secularizing Iranian-Ottoman relations and moving toward a modern notion of international relations, which in turn furthered the transformation of the frontier into the boundary.

Laying the groundwork for such a transformation, both parties focused on keeping the borderlanders within their newly acknowledged territorial limits, which they now aimed to make coincide more precisely with the limits of their sovereignty. To this end, the first article of the Ottoman version of the treaty prohibited Iran from meddling in the affairs of Baghdad and Kurdistan, whereas both parties agreed that those tribes or parts of tribes that had recently crossed over from Iran could stay or return, as they wished. At the same time, both sides pledged to prevent further crossings and to cooperate to secure the borderland. The treaty did not prohibit seasonal migration between pastures on both sides of the border, but it did require borderland tribes (*ashair-e marzneshin*) to continue paying customary pasturage dues.[101]

Because the *casus belli* for Iran was the Haydaran and Sipki migrations to the Ottoman side, the treaty's third article – the so-called *Ekrâd maddesi* or "Kurdish article" – was especially contentious. During negotiations, Rauf Pasha rejected the claim that these tribes belonged to Iran and suggested that a commission resolve the disagreement after the treaty was signed. The Iranian envoy refused, arguing that 'Abbas Mirza had commanded him to resolve the issue without delay. It was finally concluded that the populations in question could remain where they were but should be prevented from raiding Iranian territory and allowed to return

[98] Ibid., 11.
[99] Başbakanlik Osmanlı Arşivi Rehberi (Ankara: 1992), 145. The first Iranian defter was a *Nişan Defteri*, followed by an *Ahkam Defteri* in 1823.
[100] Masters, "The Treaties," 9.
[101] *Es'ad Efendi*, 231–33.

permanently to Iran. If they chose the latter option, Ottoman authorities would refuse them if they tried to return, whereas Iranian authorities would prohibit them from raiding or crossing back over. The fourth article stipulated that in line with previous treaties, neither party would protect fugitives or tribes that crossed the frontier.[102]

The language of the 1823 treaty confirms the difficulty of controlling the cross-border movements of tribes straddling the frontier region, even as it affirms the weakening of religious sectarianism as the driving force behind interstate relations.[103] In this sense, it symbolizes an important shift in Qajar-Ottoman relations and predicts the transformation of the border-land into bordered lands. Its discursive maneuverings, however, did not put a decisive end to the problems of Iranian pilgrims or merchants or sectarian animosity.[104] Nor did they magically empower the states to enforce the limits of their sovereignty. As a consequence – or perhaps a symptom – of such shortcomings, the duties and responsibilities of the respective governments were weakly expressed in the document.[105] Exacerbating this failing was Iran's refusal to return some of the territories it had occupied, namely, places in Baghdad *vilayet* and Zohab. This refusal, as we will see, sowed the seeds of a conflict that would result in seemingly endless negotiations. Meanwhile, as Longrigg notes, "every scope and pretext for border restlessness remained."[106]

DEVELOPMENTS LEADING TO THE MAKING OF THE FRONTIER

Such border restlessness included challenges posed by local dynasties, cross-border tribal activities, border skirmishes, and occasional ransack-ing of frontier cities by forces on both sides. In late 1824, as 'Abbas Mirza and Davud Pasha took snipes at each other's frontier policies, Istanbul sent Pazarcıbaşızade Es'ad Efendi to ask Iran for the return of the still-occupied zones and to repeat its request for nonintervention in Baban affairs. He met with Iran's representative, Hussein Quli Khan, and Tehran's Baban can-didate, Abdullah Pasha Baban, in Baghdad, but to no avail. From

---

[102] Ibid., 243.
[103] Maurice Harari, "The Ottoman-Iranian Boundary Question: A Case Study in the Politics of Boundary Making in the Near and Middle East" (Ph.D. diss., Columbia University, 1953), 13.
[104] For a similar view see Adamiyat, *Amir Kabir*, 67.
[105] Harari, *Ottoman-Iranian*, 13. Also, Adamiyat, *Amir Kabir*, 65.
[106] Longrigg, *Four Centuries*, 247; Kalantari, "Feth Ali Şah," 172–76.

Bahgdad, Es'ad Efendi traveled to Tabriz, where he was once again stymied. The Iranians denied interfering in Baban affairs;insisted they collected pasturage dues only from those who crossed into their territory; and
demanded the dismissal of Davud, who, they now argued, was the root of
all problems.[107]

In 1825, acknowledging the failure of Es'ad Efendi's nearly yearlong
mission, Istanbul named Mehmet Said Galib Pasha, Erzurum's new governor as chief negotiator of frontier issues. Under him, the parties disputed
the ownership of various castles and towns in the eyelet of Van and the
districts of Hakkari and Khoshab, as well as the castles of Kotur, Chahrik,
and Derik. Of these, the district of Kotur was the main source of dispute:
the Ottomans claimed it belonged to Khosab, whereas the Iranians argued
it was part of Khoi. Galip Pasha finally accepted that the district had
changed hands in the past and, after additional meetings, agreed that
Kotur as well as Chahrik would remain in Iran, whereas the other disputed
districts, along with the castles of the Van eyelet, would be returned to
Istanbul. However, 'Abbas Mirza rejected the agreement, insisting that
Iran maintain control of Derik Castle in Hakkari and Abagha (locally
known as Abex in present-day Çaldıran) Castle in Khoshab.[108] Any conclusive resolution would thus require the delimitation and demarcation of
the boundary, and the parties agreed to appoint engineers to determine
ownership of the disputed lands and castles.

Before concrete action could be taken, the disastrous Russo-Iranian
War of 1826–28 erupted. Once more rebuffing Iran's call for an alliance
against Russia, Istanbul declared its neutrality and warned provincial
borderland authorities to prevent Kurdish tribes from fighting alongside
Iranians.[109] Defeated, Iran signed the catastrophic Turkmanchay Treaty,
leaving Russia large swaths of the Caucasus. While Tehran was busy with
the war, Galib Pasha, Nurullah Bey of Hakkari, and İshak Pasha, the
kaimmakam of Van, worked to secure territories and properties for the
sultan, including the castles at Derik, Bashkılan (modern Başkale), Pizan,
Erci, Divane, Eshkidan, and Lorikan, as well as the districts of Kilisa-i
Albak in Hakkari, Satmanis, Abagha (Ibex), and Mela Hasan in
Khosab.[110]

---

[107] Kalantari, "Feth Ali Şah," 179–81.
[108] Hakan, *Osmanlı* 49. Hakan maintains that it was agreed that Kotur belonged to Musa
      Bey of the Mahmudi family, who recognized Iranian sovereignty.
[109] Kalantari, "Feth Ali Şah," 188.
[110] See Hakan, *Osmanlı*, 49–50; Kalantari, "Feth Ali Şah," 183–86; Aykun, "Osmanlı-Iran
      Diplomatik İlişkilerinden Bir Kesit," *Osmanlı*, 691.

Soon, the Russo-Ottoman War of 1828–29 would begin. When Istanbul turned to Iran for help, the shah recalled its recent neutrality but left open the possibility of cooperation, if it were based on an official treaty rather than empty promises. As a result of negotiations carried out by Tehran's representative, Muhammad Sharif Shirvani, the parties signed their first treaty of alliance against Russia in March 1829; unfortunately, it produced no results. Because of the war, the Ottoman representative charged with exchanging the document could not reach Tabriz. Moreover, owing to Russia's pressure and policy of appeasement, Iran balked at its declared commitment to send troops. In any case, swift Russian advances on the eastern and western fronts forced the Ottomans to sue for peace, which was signed in Edirne on September 14, 1829.[111]

When the dust of war settled, the flow of envoys and correspondence surrounding the Van and Hakkari frontiers restarted, with Kotur and Chahrik again the main points of dispute. Unable to reach any agreement, the parties reiterated the need to send engineers to define the frontier. Although mostly fruitless, the negotiations between the two states did have one positive effect: the Porte determined to put an end to the reign of the *mamluk* viceroys of Iraq, who had caused serious problems for Iran and the Babans. When the Porte asked 'Abbas Mirza to refuse entry to Davud Pasha if he tried to cross the border, the Iranian prince happily complied. Without further Iranian assistance, Ottoman forces entered Baghdad and, in September 1831, routed the *mamluks*. The victory made Baghdad again a regular Ottoman province and opened the way for the complete integration of the borderland. The unexpected death of 'Abbas Mirza in 1833, and of Fath 'Ali Shah in 1834, however, left other matters in the borderlands unresolved – matters that, as we shall see, would haunt Ottoman-Iranian relations for decades to come.[112] Such unresolved issues were exacerbated by almost continuous skirmishes. For example, in 1835, Mahmud Khan of Mahmudi (Khosab), perhaps to assert his ancestral claims, attacked Kotur, which had previously been under his family's authority. Another attack by the similarly virtually independent *mir* of Rawanduz on Mergever and Urumieh further increased tensions.[113] However, it was the 1837 attack on Muhammarah by 'Ali Rıza Pasha, Davud's successor, that brought disputes over the borderland into the realm of international diplomacy.

[111] Kalantari, "Feth Ali Şah," 191–200.
[112] Ibid., 207–20.
[113] Alwyn Parker's Memorandum, 8 December 1906, *Schofield IV*, 91; Aykun, *Osmanlı-Iran*, 693.

Thought to rival the city of Basrah, Muhammarah (present-day Khorramshahr) was under the rule of the Arab Shiʻi Banu Kaʻb, a tribe that tentatively acknowledged Iranian sovereignty. Questions about Muhammarah thus revolved around the Kaʻb and ownership of the lands they inhabited on the left, or Iranian, bank of the Shatt al-Arab River. Over the years, Iran had claimed this bank at approximately sixty miles from its junction with the Persian Gulf and had stationed troops along it. Because the Porte claimed the same territory, it threatened war if the shah continued to refuse to withdraw his forces. ʻAli Rıza thus justified his pillage by claiming that the Kaʻb had revolted by refusing to pay taxes to their true master, the sultan. Adding insult to injury, at the time of the attack, Tehran was distracted by the siege of Herat, which brought it into a losing conflict with Britain.[114] After the incident, the ownership of Muhammarah, the southernmost part of the frontier, and the waters of the Shatt al-Arab as well as the access to the Persian Gulf these provided emerged as perhaps the most contentious of all disputes in the process of boundary making.

Tehran's first opportunity to retaliate came in 1839, when the army of the rebellious Egyptian governor Mehmed Ali defeated the sultan's troops and seriously threatened Istanbul at Nizip. Mirza Jaʻfar Khan, the Iranian ambassador to Istanbul, rushed to inform his government of the situation. With dreams of capturing Baghdad and its holy Shiʻi sites as well as settling scores in Muhammarah, Mirza Aqasi, the Iranian premier, planned for the shah to march to Isfahan, from which point the army could move into Iraq and Kurdistan. Alarmed, the Porte dispatched a high-level ambassador, Sarim Efendi, to Tehran.[115] A precursor to the frontier conferences, the ensuing discussion centered on indemnities of one million pounds sterling demanded by the Iranians for the sack of Muhammarah, the Bey of Revanduz's attacks on Iranian land, and Ottoman Jaf tribes' incursions into Zohab province. The proprietorship of Zohab, whose

---

[114] A. Henry Layard, *Early Adventures in Persia, Susnia and Babylonia* (London: Longmans, Green & Co., 1887), vol. 2, 432. The Iranian surveyor from 1848 to 1852, Mirza Jaʻfar Khan, agrees, adding that Muhammarah's rise threatened Ali Rıza Pasha's personal fortunes. Mirza Jaʻfar Khan, *Risalah-i Tahqiqat-i Sarhadiyyah*, ed. Muhammad Mushiri (Tehran: Bunyad-i Farhang-i Iran, 1348/1969) 34. Hereafter, Mirza Jaʻfar, *Tahqiqat*.

[115] Mirza Jaʻfar, *Tahqiqat*, 36–37. Ibrahim Aykun, "Erzurum Konferansı (1843–1847) ve Osmanlı-Iran Hudut Antlaşması" (Ph.D. diss., Erzurum Atatürk Üniversitesi, 1995), 23–26. Istanbul ordered Ali Rıza Pasha to restore Muhammarah to Iran, if it so belonged. *Schofield I*, 177–78. See also Mirza Taqi to Mirza Aqasi in Nasrollah Salehi, *Asnadi az Inʻikad-e ʻAhdnâmeh-e Dovvome Erzetelroum* (Tehran: Daftar-e Motalaat-e Siyasi va Bayn al-Milali, 1377/1999), 33–34. (Hereafer, Salehi, *Erzetelroum*.)

name had graced the first treaty dealing with frontiers, was hotly debated. According to Iran, it had historically been the *yurt* and winter pasture (*qeshlak*) of the Kermanshah tribes. The Ottomans, however, claimed that Iran had only retained Zohab in 1822, had refused to return it as the 1823 treaty stipulated, and was thus illegally appropriating its revenues.[116] Indeed, as mentioned previously, as late as 1811, the Babans were appointing the *hakim* of Zohab, and Kinneir described Zohab as part of Baban province in 1810.[117]

Tehran threatened war if its demands, which included the return of the refugee Qajar princes and a new treaty on trade, were not met. In response, Sarim Efendi prolonged negotiations as much as possible to avoid armed conflict, while urging Istanbul to strengthen its *sarhadd* troops as a precaution.[118] Diplomatic relations between the states continued to deteriorate, reaching a particularly low point in March 1841, when the Ottoman Council of Ministers denounced Iranian claims of indemnity for Muhammarah as exaggerated, because it was an Ottoman town and even if it was not, the damages recently inflicted by Iran on Suleimanieh had been comparatively much heavier.[119]

The Suleimanieh debacle was also related to the Baban succession. Immediately after resolving the Egyptian crisis by naming Mehmed Ali as hereditary governor of Egypt, Istanbul turned its gaze eastward and dismissed Mahmud Pasha Baban, who had been in and out of office several times. As Iran had helped him gain the post, he took refuge there while his cousin Ahmed Pasha replaced him in 1840. Later, Ahmed, too, was removed by the Ottomans and imprisoned in Baghdad. Tehran's attempt to restore Mahmud to power was prevented by Ahmed's brother Abdullah, the interim governor. When Necib Pasha replaced 'Ali Riza Pasha in Baghdad, Ahmed was released. But to sow dissension between the brothers, Baghdad's new governor gave Abdullah the significant rank

---

[116] Some British officials supported the Ottoman view, arguing that Dawlatshah occupied it in 1821. See J. Felix Jones, *Memoirs of Baghdad, Kurdistan and Turkish Arabia, 1857* (Buckinghamshire, UK: Archive Editions, 1998), 199–200; and Henry C. Rawlinson, "Notes on a March from Zohab, at the foot of Zagros, along the Mountains to Khuzistan (Susnia), and from Thence Through the Province of Luristan to Kirmanshah, in the Year 1836," *JRGS* 9 (1839).

[117] Kinneir, *A Geographical Memoir*, 295–96.

[118] Général Duhamel to Nesselrode, Julfa, May l7, 1840; Général Duhamel to Titoff, Isfahan August 16, 1840; "Tercüme-i Tahrir-i Sarım Efendi"; "Extrait d'une dépêche du Ministre Roussie en Perse, Ispahan, le 4/16 Juin 1840," all in BOA.HR.SYS. 719–1.

[119] Aykun, "Erzurum," 35–36.

of *kaimmakam* and governor.[120] Not to be outdone, Tehran insisted on the reinstallation of Mahmud and when its demand was not met sent Mahmud and two thousand soldiers to Suleimanieh. Other Iranian forces, under the command of Reza Qoli Khan, the governor of Ardalan, occupied parts of Shahrizor. However, Abdullah sacked their camp and forced their withdrawal to Sinne.[121] It was this attack that the Ottomans equated with 'Ali Riza's sack of Muhammarah, suggesting that claims resulting from the two assaults should annul each other. Meanwhile, Iran complained to Ottoman, British, and Russian representatives that Ottoman frontier authorities were corresponding with chiefs from the Sunni Kurdish tribes "with a view of exciting rebellion."[122]

As various documents from the period show, however, the Ottomans were not alone in inciting the tribes. Both parties continued to engage in conflicts over, and in strategic alliances with, various borderland groups, whose political and military machinations as well as migratory patterns continued to cause problems for their centralization projects. For example, in the northernmost part of the frontier, Iranian tribes such as the Jalali and Zilan increased their violent raids on communities living on the Ottoman side. These resulted in the migration of several thousand families to Iranian and Russian territories and so drew Russia into Ottoman-Iranian frontier problems. Believing that Tehran had purposefully unleashed these tribes and that, moreover, its troops had aided them, the Ottoman Council of Ministers argued that Tehran should pay compensation and ordered local authorities to resist the intruders.[123] Then, in 1842, the Jalali tribe pushed the two states to the brink of war once again. While continuing to blame each other for encouraging the tribe's cross-border depredations, both sides began amassing troops at Khoi and Bayezid. The shah ordered Iranian merchants in the Ottoman Empire to settle their business and return home, and the British consul in Erzurum noted the arrival of guns, money, and troops.[124]

Tribal cross-border attacks like those of the Jalali were, as we have seen, one steady cause of tension. As the Haydaran and Sipki cases of two decades earlier illustrate, migrations of tribes under the authority of one state to the lands of the other were another source of concern. One such

---

[120] Lorimer, *Four Centuries*, 287.
[121] Aykun, "Erzurum," 40.
[122] Iranian Prime Minister to Ottoman Grand Vizier, July 20, 1841, *Schofield II*, 149.
[123] Aykun, "Erzurum," 26–29. Général Duhamel to Titoff, Isfahan August 16, 1840, in BOA.HR.SYS. 719-1.
[124] Brant to Canning, Erzurum, September 2 and 21, 1842, *Schofield I*, 41–48.

case, which brought Ottoman, Iranian, and British authorities together, was that of the Zilan tribe, which crossed from Iran to the Ottoman Empire to escape the oppression of Shahzada Bahman Mirza, the governor of Azerbaijan. The situation generated a flurry of correspondence between the two states as well as the British consul of Erzurum, but the Zilan stayed put.[125] As we will see in the next chapter, their predicament occupied the frontier conferences for some time.

Despite the continuing futility of most negotiations, one important step was taken at this time. After being recommended for the third time – this time by Mirza Ja'far Khan, Russian Charge d'Affaires Titof, and Rifat Pasha – a joint engineering commission to demarcate the frontier was finally appointed. Its membership included the Russian Colonel Dainese and the Ottoman Es'ad Efendi. Although its work was inconclusive, its mere formation and the new patterns it generated – including the involvement of British as well as Russian representatives – opened the way for what would follow: Russo-British intervention, the Erzurum Frontier Conferences, and eventually the making of the boundary.[126] Still, tensions on the frontier continued to rise and an outbreak of serious hostilities seemed imminent. Perhaps concerned by the possible spillover effects of a war on its volatile Caucasian frontiers, Titow urged Sarim Efendi, now the OMoFA, toward a diplomatic solution.[127] Meanwhile, Iran prohibited caravans from entering Ottoman lands, bringing economic activities to a standstill. Calculating that Iran would attack from Baghdad and Bayezid, Istanbul amassed troops and large tribal contingents in Erzurum and Baghdad provinces. Tehran took countermeasures in Urumieh, Khoi, and Kermanshah. Looking for reinforcements, Ottoman governors reconciled with estranged Kurdish grandees such as Ismail Pasha of Imadiyah and Bedirkhan Bey of Cizre, while the Bey of Revanduz informed Baghdad's governor of his readiness to serve the sultan. Notwithstanding these preparations, both parties were fundamentally unprepared or unequipped to fight and so were open to Russo-British attempts at mediation.[128]

---

[125] Brant to Canning, Erzurum, December 9, 1842, *Schofield I*, 81–84; Aykun, "Erzurum," 42–44.

[126] Aykun, *Osmanlı*, 692. Mirza Ja'far claims that Russia and England were both protectors of the Ottoman Empire and forced Tehran to agree to the negotiations. See *Tahqiqat-i Sarhaddiya*, 37.

[127] Aykun, "Erzurum,"34–38. Also Titow to Sarım Efendi, Büyükdere July 3/15, 1842, in BOA.HR.SYS 719–1.

[128] Aykun, "Erzurum,"49–56.

GREAT POWER INTERVENTION AND THE MAKING
OF THE BOUNDARY

Up until this time "Russia was the acknowledged mediator in Ottoman-Iranian affairs";[129] however, in 1842, Tehran sought British intervention as well. Motivated by their own ongoing rivalry in Iran and the region's strategic position vis-à-vis their respective frontiers in the Caucasus and South Asia, Russia and Britain agreed to intervene jointly to prevent the outbreak of war. Even before this, as we have seen, their consuls had been increasingly involved in the border region. Consular intervention, however, was not enough. Hence, both ambassadors appealed to the sultan, who agreed to withdraw his troops provided the shah took similar measures.[130] In an attempt to preserve the status quo, the ambassadors pressured the two states to resolve their conflicts, especially the disputes over their frontier, by means of an international conference. Soon thereafter, Canning, the influential British ambassador, and Titow, his Russian counterpart, convinced OMoFA Sarim Efendi to agree to this plan.[131] Their colleagues in Tehran soon seconded their effort. In fact, neither the Ottomans nor the Qajars were in a position to reject the proposal.[132]

In October 1842, the Russian and British ambassadors informed the OMoFA that if Ottoman forces withdrew from Bayezid, Iranian forces would withdraw from Khoi, and they promised that their representatives would observe the withdrawal. The Ottoman Council of Ministers concluded that a peaceful solution was advisable. Additionally, Iran admitted the fault of its frontier authorities in the Suleimanieh affair and accepted the appointment of a plenipotentiary and the initiation of frontier conferences. Both sides withdrew on November 29.[133] Six months later, on May 15, 1843, the Erzurum frontier conferences began.

Learning from cases such as that of the Zilan, the mediating powers recognized that negotiations would not be limited to the disputed lands and that the social structures of borderland societies would create

---

[129] Canning's Report to Earl of Aberdeen, April 27, 1844, *Schofield I*, 306.
[130] Russian and British consuls to HH Behmen Meerza, November 7, 1842, *Schofield I*, 76.
[131] For Titow and Canning's meeting with Sarım Efendi at the *sahilhane* of OMFA, see BOA.I.MSM 38/1060.
[132] Harari, *Ottoman-Iranian*, 34. Even though Russia had significant influence in Istanbul, British sources claim that their ambassador, Canning, was the principal architect of the mediation scheme. See, for example, Layard, *Early Adventures*, vol. 2, 377, 407. Canning credited himself and the Russian envoy, together with their colleagues in Tehran, for preventing a confrontation, BOA.HR.SYS 719/1, 31. Also Aykun, "Erzurum," 64.
[133] BOA.IMM, 38/1071, December 3, 1842.

complications. Canning observed that the differences between Tehran and Istanbul had much to do with national rivalries (particularly the Shi'i-Sunni factor) and traditional grievances:

Yet: the chief bone of contention was the boundary . . . occupied in great measure by nomadic tribes, who often shifted their residence, and were constantly claimed as the subjects by both the contending Governments. A frontier line clearly laid down by mutual agreement, and maintained by series of forts, presented the only chance of affecting a durable settlement and removing a constant provocative to war between the two countries on whose pacific relations the general tranquility of the East so much depended.[134]

We have seen that such disputes, jealousies, and provocations were not limited to the northern part of the borderland. As the delegates convened in Erzurum, the situation in the middle part of the frontier was no better. Thus, shortly before the start of the conferences, Major Rawlinson, the British consul of Baghdad, along with Captain Felix Jones of the Indian navy, was sent to Zohab to collect information, procure an interview with the governor of Kermanshah, and prevent a cross-border collision that might endanger the success of the commission.[135] Even though the feared collisions were averted, the large Kalhor tribal confederation was in open rebellion against the governor of Kermanshah, Mohib 'Ali Khan, during the British representatives' visit. The poor cultivators revolted, Jones noted, "not to seek imaginary grievances, but to obtain the justice which has hitherto been denied to them," because ever-heavier tax burdens had become impossible for them to shoulder: "the rapacious agents" of the governor "resorted to a system which in a very short time left the brave but oppressed Ryot nothing but his sword to subsist by."[136]

While similarly limited confrontations were taking place on the Iranian side of the frontier, the Ottomans prepared to launch a larger and more ambitious campaign to subdue the lords of the borderland. Having eliminated Baghdad's *mamluk* governors, they now calculated various factors that would allow them to extend their anti-*ayan* (notables) and centralization policies to the Kurdish frontier. These included securing Russo-British support to solve the Egyptian question, finding solace in the British commitment to preserve the integrity of both Persia and the Ottoman

---

[134] Stanley Lane-Poole, *The Life of the Right Honourable Stratford Canning*, vol. II (London: Longmans, Green, and Co., 1888), 121.

[135] James Felix Jones, *Memoirs of Baghdad, Kurdistan and Turkish Arabia, 1857* (Reprint, Buckinghamshire, UK: Archive Editions, 1998), 137, 159.

[136] Ibid., 190.

Empire, and agreeing to the internationalization of the boundary-making process. Hence, at the very time that the four powers were negotiating the demarcation of the oldest frontier of the Islamic world – a process that will be detailed in the following pages – the *tanzimat* (reformation) state was embarking on a project of turning autonomous borderlanders into citizens.

Making and securing the boundaries allowed the central states to increase their surveillance capacity, abetting the state-making process in the peripheries. It was not only an act of defining the limits of the legitimate coercive capacity of the state, but also of imposing the same institutional and administrative arrangements and laws across its territory in ways characteristic of a modern state.[137] By introducing modern state institutions such as the boundary, and using the technologies of mapping, cartography, and surveys, along with the geographical discourses of sovereignty and territoriality, the states sought to replace indigenous discourses of spatiality and identity with their own categories and terms.[138] Hence, simultaneous with defining their outer limits, Iran and, to an even greater degree, the Ottoman Empire, with the help of the two great powers, set out to redefine the geographical, political, and cultural contours of the borderland.

PACIFICATION OF THE BORDERLAND: THE FIRST PHASE

In his initial drive to modernize the military and the bureaucratic administration of the empire, Sultan Mahmud II eradicated the Janissaries in 1826 and suppressed the *derebeys* (lords of the valleys) and *ayans* of Anatolia and the Balkans between 1820 and 1830. In 1831, a cadastral survey was launched to determine the economic and human potential of the empire. In the eastern borderlands in the same year, the *mamluk* rulers of Baghdad and Basra were deposed, and the hold of the Jalili family of Mosul was loosened. Having established Ottoman authority in the central and southern zones of the borderland, Istanbul was ready to launch its campaign against the Kurdish lords. Yet, this action was forestalled in 1831–32 by the Egyptian campaign into Syria led by Ibrahim Pasha, the son of Egypt's ruler, Mehmed Ali. As we have seen, Ibrahim's campaign reverberated throughout the empire and the borderland. The subsequent weakness of the Ottoman

---

[137] Eric Hobsbawm, *Nations and Nationalism since 1870: Program, Myth and Reality* (Cambridge, UK: Cambridge University Press, 1990), 80.

[138] Tongchai Winichakul, *Siam Mapped: A History of the Geobody of a Nation* (Honolulu: University of Hawaii Press, 1994) chap. 5.

army gave the diminished Kurdish principalities an opportunity to reclaim most of what they had lost to the centralizing state. Hence, while at loggerheads with Tehran and anxiously guarding against the Egyptians, Istanbul's armies first marched toward the Soran emirate of Muhammad Pasha of Rawanduz, known locally as Miré Kor.[139]

Miré Kor took leadership of the impoverished Soran emirate in 1814 and violently subdued area tribes, including the Shirwan, Bradost, Surchi, Khushnaw, and Mamash. He also seized the nearby town of Harir, the old Soran capital, from Baban hands. In 1831, he took over the Bahdinan emirate of Imadiyah (Amadiyah), which had been ruled by the same family since the time of Abbasids,[140] massacring many Yezidis before occupying the town of Aqra and expelling its ruler in 1833. By 1834, he controlled Arbil, Altun Kupru, Raniya, Zakho, and Duhok, and in 1835, he led an incursion across the frontier into Iran. The Ottoman advance coincided with his attempt to consolidate his ministate in defiance of Istanbul's authority.[141]

Pressured by Ibrahim Pasha and the Iranian forces, the pasha of Baghdad initially accepted Miré Kor's push for power as a *fait accompli* and granted him the title of pasha. This precarious peace broke down when Miré Kor sent his troops against Nisibin and Mardin farther north, seized Cizre, and was said to be in contact with Ibrahim (then in Syria). His expansionism also gained him many enemies among the local population. The notables of Imadiyah, for example, issued a formal complaint regarding his *zulm*, or oppression, to Mehmed Reşid Pasha, the former grand vizier and governor of Sivas, and the region's supreme authority. The Beg of Bradost and Bervari, the chiefs of Zibari and Mızuri, and the mufti and sheikhs of Zakho and Akre also signed the letter.[142]

In 1834, Istanbul had ordered the valis of Baghdad and Mosul to join Reşid Pasha's punitive campaign against the Kurdish emirates. Because of the conflict with Egypt, this campaign was delayed until 1836. Not surprisingly, when it restarted, its first stop was Miré Kor's nearly inaccessible capital, Rawanduz. In advance of the main army, Reşid carried out punitive expeditions against smaller local rulers, targeting the Yezidi Kurds of

---

[139] Miré Kor or Mir Muhammedé Kore (meaning the blind *mir/ amir* because he was blind in one eye) is the Kurdish version of Mir-i Kur.

[140] Kinneir, *A Geographical Memoir*, 301.

[141] Longrigg adds that he wrested Koi and Raniyah from the Babans and gave his brother Rasul governance over Imadiyah and Bahdinan. *Four Centuries*, 285.

[142] See Hakan, *Osmanlı* 68–74.

the Diyarbakır region. Because Mir Seyfeddin of Cizre, the *mütesellim*, was now under the authority of Miré Kor, the pasha also occupied that town. Seyfeddin took refuge in Baghdad and Reşid appointed his cousin Bedirhan to replace him.[143] Despite the movement of large numbers of troops, no confrontation took place between the forces of the pasha and the *mir*. If one is to believe the reports of the British agent Richard Wood, even as Istanbul's armies were closing in on Rawanduz, the Qajars were offering Miré Kor help and possible sanctuary while offering Istanbul cooperation against him. The Qajar force that crossed the frontier to support the *mir* included a Russian infantry battalion of eight hundred men. Realizing that Ottoman forces could not defeat Miré Kor with his support from Iran and Russia, and that a failed operation could cost them the province, Wood convinced the governor of Baghdad to offer a compromise: if Miré Kor submitted to Istanbul, he would be reinstated to protect the frontier against Iran:[144]

[He surrendered] on conditions very favorable to him: he was to remain the Governor of Rawanduz, but had to assert his submission to the sultan. His brother Resul Beg, who had taken refuge at Imadiye castle, surrendered after resisting a siege of twenty days. Miré Kor was sent to Istanbul, where the sultan bestowed many honors upon him; on the return voyage, however, he mysteriously disappeared.[145]

Miré Kor's disappearance, however, was not the effective end of the emirate of Rawanduz. His family was incorporated into the Ottoman system and remained influential in the frontier region for some time. One side effect of the suppression of Rawanduz was that sensing the threat, the Baban *mutasarrıf*, Suleiman Pasha, provided six hundred soldiers to the sultan and severed his relations with Iran. To further seal his new status with the state, one of his sons was decorated and the other appointed a *Binbaşı* in the regular army.[146]

KHAN ABDAL AND THE CITY OF VAN

Following the disappearance of Miré Kor, Reşid Pasha – and, after his 1837 death, his replacement as *müşir* of Sivas, Hafız Pasha – directed his attention to other parts of Kurdistan in a nearly four-year-long campaign. The first target was the Yezidi Kurds of Sincar and Telafar, whose en masse

---

[143] Ibid., 80.
[144] McDowal, *A Modern History of the Kurds*, 43–44.
[145] van Bruinessen, *Agha*, 176–77.
[146] Hakan, *Osmanlı*, 81.

resistance to taxation and conscription he bloodily suppressed, forcing them to pay taxes, submit to governmental authority, and send three thousand youth to serve in the army.[147] The second targets were Khan Mahmud and Abdal Khan, of Khoshab/Hoşab castle fame. The hereditary rulers of the town and district of Müküs (Mahmudi), by 1834, these brothers had brought the entire frontier province of Van under their patronage. As recently as 1825, their father had pled with Istanbul for help against 'Ajam aggressions, but, according to Consul Brant, they had gradually defied the sultan's authority and, toward the end of the 1830s, declared independence and stopped paying taxes.[148] After establishing his authority, Khan Mahmud, the eldest son, appointed his six brothers to different districts on the borders of Iran and around Lake Van.[149]

Some Ottoman pashas were of the opinion that a campaign against the Khan brothers should be postponed because the Iranians and the *mir* of Hakkari might come to their aid. As it turned out, however, the opposite happened. Nurullah Bey and the previous *mütesellim* of Cizre, Seyfeddin Beg, who harbored enmity toward the brothers, complied with orders from Hafız to attack Khan Mahmud. They prevailed and forced him to go to Erzurum to submit to the pasha on November 4, 1838, where he was imprisoned along with two of his brothers. Mahmud's remaining brothers fortified themselves in their castles but after negotiations submitted with little resistance. Khan Mahmud and two of his brothers were exiled to Istanbul, where they arrived in March 1839.[150]

The Ottoman pashas soon turned their sights on Nurullah Bey, despite his help with the suppression of Khan Mahmud, because his predecessors had occasionally defected to Iran.[151] Bedirkhan, possibly the strongest Kurdish notable at the time, was also not immune to their master plan. Hafız laid a forty-day siege on Cizre, which led to Bedirkhan's surrender. Joining the Ottoman forces to subdue one of his former allies, Said Beg of Finiq, he was given the rank of *miralay* (colonel) and incorporated into the Ottoman military system.[152] After the submission of Miré Kor in

---

[147] Ibid., 86–87.
[148] PRO.FO 78/2707, Consul Brant's detailed "General Report on Border Provinces," [possibly finished in 1852].
[149] Ibid.
[150] It appears they were allowed to return, because they commanded an important castle and kept a standing force to defend the frontier. See Hakan, *Osmanlı*, 88–114.
[151] BOA.HH 448/22316/, 1254–1838.
[152] Çadırcı, Musa, *Tanzimat Döneminde Anadolu Kentlerinin Sosyal ve Ekonomik Yapıları* (Ankara: Türk Tarih Kurumu Basımevi, 1991), 194–96; van Bruinessen, *Agha*, 177–82.

Rawanduz, the Khan brothers in Van, Bedirkhan in Cizre, and some lesser notables of the same districts, it seemed that Kurdistan's pacification was nearly complete. The *yurtluk-ocaklık* holders were incorporated into the hierarchy of the empire, the northern zone of the borderland was under control, and the path toward the finalization of the boundary was clear.

However, just as the first Egyptian campaign into Syria had allowed the Kurdish nobility to reclaim lost power, so again Ibrahim Pasha and his Egyptian armies reversed the balance of power. As is well known, at the 1839 Battle of Nizib, the Egyptian armies bested the Ottoman forces, and it was only Great Power intervention that saved the Grand Seignior. The reduced nobilary counties took advantage of the resulting instability and swiftly filled the power vacuum created in the region.[153] Ironically, their recent reincorporation by Istanbul actually aided them in the process. As an Ottoman *miralay*, for example, Bedirkhan was asked, in the style of the old *hükümet*s, to mobilize his troops for imminent battle with Ibrahim's forces.[154] Using this opportunity wisely, he added the power delegated by Istanbul to his existing authority and extended his control beyond his ancestral domains.

This new heyday for the Kurdish dynasts, however, was short lived. British and Russian support of Istanbul would once again change the course of events, and the Porte would "demand as before taxes and the *corvée*, money, and recruits."[155] The ensuing reassertion of central power, as Von Moltke observes, was an open invitation to revolt, but Istanbul quickly sent the superiorly armed fifty-thousand-strong army it had mobilized against Ibrahim to the Kurdish periphery.[156] Hence, after evading the enormous internal threat posed by the Egyptian challenge, with costly help from Russia and Britain, the Ottoman throne re-embarked on its restructuring of the borderland.

Meanwhile, on the other side of the border, the Iranian army had begun its own centralization campaign. In the early 1830s, 'Abbas Mirza subdued Khurasan, massacring Türkmens at Sarakhs. Tehran also suppressed the Ismaili rebellion in Yazd and Kirman in 1838 and throughout the 1840s dealt with the Babi challenge. In the border region itself, Tehran

---

[153] van Bruinessen, *Agha*, 176.

[154] McDowall, *A Modern History*, 45.

[155] Field-Marshal Helmuth von Moltke, *Essays, Speeches, and Memoirs*, vol. 1 (New York: Harper & Brothers, 1893), 278. Moltke was an early commenter on developments during and after the Battle of Nizib. At the time, he was advising the Ottoman army against the Egyptians.

[156] Ibid., 285.

gradually incorporated the Ardalan family through imperial marriages, while also, in the early 1840s, directing its attention southward. There, the first target was the Bakhtiari chief, Muhammad Taqi Khan, who was forced to escape his stronghold and take refuge with the Sheikh of Muhammarah, where he was captured.[157] However, according to H. A. Layard, Qajar plans for Muhammarah itself were imperiled because of the fear that Sheykh Thamir, who at the time rejected both Ottoman and Iranian authority, might ally himself with Baghdad's Ottoman governor.[158] The governor, however, had little time to ponder this dilemma; he was busy with his campaign against the Baban.

THE BABANS, FOR THE LAST TIME

After the conclusion of the turbulent career of Mahmud Pasha Baban, relations between the Babans and Istanbul improved. However, in the early 1840s, Ahmed Pasha, possibly following the example of the pashas of Baghdad and Sultan Mahmud himself, equipped his troops in the garb of the state's regular troops. Within a year, according to Felix Jones, he raised a disciplined (according to European tactics) force of eight hundred men, which troubled the governor general of the region, Necib Pasha, who responded by substantially increasing the taxes Suleimanieh had to send to Baghdad.[159] This put an enormous burden on the shoulders of Ahmed, forcing him, in turn, to increase taxes on his already burdened subjects. What is more, as he strove to keep the Iranians at bay, Ahmed was bribing various Baghdad authorities to ignore the tempting offers of his brother Abdullah Bey, who wanted to replace him.[160]

The making of the frontier temporarily halted Necib's *tanizmat*-inspired plan to eliminate the Babans, which coincided with discussions by the Erzurum conferees regarding the ownership of the Baban-ruled territory of Suleimanieh. In this context, Necib's uninhibited aggression irritated British representatives. His "interfering with internal government of Suleimanieh before the ratification of the future treaty," wrote Rawlinson, showed that "Suleimanieh may perhaps at no distant period be subject to some

---

[157] For this phase of Qajar penetration of its peripheries, see Arash Khazeni, *Tribes and Empire* (Seattle: University of Washington Press, 2010), 41–52.

[158] Henry A. Layard, *Discoveries in the Ruins of Nineveh and Babylon; with Travels in Armenia, Kurdistan and the Desert: Being the Result of a Second Expedition Undertaken for the Trustees of the British Library* (London: John Murray, 1853), 80–100.

[159] Jones, *Memoirs*, 208.

[160] Ibid., 209.

disturbance, as I think an attempt will be made to break in on the almost independent government of the Kurdish Pasha."[161] Aware of the relation between boundary making and the consolidation of state authority, Williams, the British commissioner for frontier negotiations, urged the British consul of Baghdad to induce Necib "to allow affairs to remain in *status quo*, in that province especially, until the new treaty shall have been ratified, and the frontier-line practically defined."[162] Necib desisted, but not for long.

In spring 1845, with the conferences still in session, he gathered troops to march against the Baban, Bohtan, and Soran principalities – the three most powerful semiautonomous dynasts of Ottoman Kurdistan. The pasha began with the *mir* of Soran – that is, the family of Rawanduz, which had regained its power – whom he declared a rebel against the sultan. He secretly invited Ahmed Pasha Baban, now in power, to join him, but the pasha declined because of fear of treachery as well as embarrassment over secretly commissioning two thousand muskets from a British dealer.[163] Angered, Necib redirected his forces toward the Baban. Rawlinson, who was on good terms with Ahmed Pasha, unsuccessfully attempted to convince him to be conciliatory. Necib advanced toward the province of Köy/Koi Sanjak with the declared goal of observing and adopting measures for agricultural improvement, but his real intention was to incite a crisis so as to assert Istanbul's power while curbing that of the Baban prince, Rawlinson noted.[164]

His move was received with suspicion by "the Kurds who were aware of the critical position of their own chief" and regarded the pasha's move as a hostile invasion.[165] When Baghdad officers entered the town to collect provisions, Kurdish locals resisted and imprisoned them for a day. The Baban governor of the district, with a "sufficiently respectful, but distinctly intimating" letter, informed Necib that "pending instructions from Ahmed Pasha the Ottoman troops could not be permitted to occupy the place."[166]

Ahmed's efforts at rapprochement came too late. Necib ordered him to "withdraw his troops from Koie and admit a free occupation of the country by the troops within five days, and appear in camp and render

[161] Williams to Canning, Erzurum, February 12, 1844, *Schofield I*, 213.
[162] Ibid.
[163] PRO.FO 78 / 2713, Rawlinson to Canning, British Consulate, Baghdad, May 13, 1845.
[164] Ibid.
[165] PRO.FO 78 / 2713, Rawlinson to Canning, Suleimanieh and Baghdad, July 9, 1845.
[166] Ibid.

personal homage to his superior that he would restore [Koie to] him."[167] Not getting a response, Necib deposed Ahmed, appointing his brother and rival, the previous governor Abdullah, in his stead. As had been prearranged, Necib requested that all possible troops from Mosul and Baghdad immediately march on the region. His force of about twelve thousand was numerically inferior but better trained and equipped than the Baban forces. Abdullah Bey Baban, now a pasha, accompanied Necib to win over malcontents from his brother's party through the influence of his name. Ahmed's efforts at reconciliation again proved fruitless.[168] The borderland was to be stripped of local dynasts, and he was no exception.

In response, he decided to resist and a general confederacy formed under his leadership, consisting of the chief of the Khusnaw tribe of Koi Sanjak (which had also been deposed by Necib) and the *mir* of Rawanduz. The tribal families and property were moved to secure places or sent across the frontier. The passes were secured and two separate Kurdish forces assembled at Koi and Bazian, the only places from which the Ottoman troops could penetrate the mountain chain. That the Ottoman maneuvers were part of the extension of the *tanzimat* state, and understood as such by the borderlanders, is clearly illustrated by the reaction of the plain's Arab tribes to the campaign against the Baban. It was reported that they, "who have been always in friendly communication with the Kurds,"[169] realized they would be made to submit next. Thus, they prepared to harass the Ottoman troops on their march from Baghdad. Given its size, Ahmed's force could have overwhelmed Necib; in the end, however, he promised to act only defensively and did not attack.[170]

For the *mir*s, the campaign was a matter of life or death; for the Ottoman pashas, it was the final move against autonomous entities whose end was long overdue. Rawlinson, our main source for this campaign, wrote that Necib had substantial grounds for believing the substitution of "Turkish for Kurdish power in that *pashalik* to be agreeable to the Porte." He also noted that the Baghdad governor's actions were premeditated and designed to

aim at the subversion of the native power in the mountain range, which divides Assyria from Media, and the establishment of Turkish governors and Turkish garrisons in all the towns of Kurdistan. If the expedition against Sulaimanieh is attended with success ... Kurt Mahomad Pasha will be left with a strong force of

[167] Ibid.
[168] Ibid.
[169] Ibid.
[170] Ibid.

Turkish infantry and artillery in Southern Kurdistan, and Abdollah Pasha will be made use of as a mere puppet to soothe the irritation of the Kurds at their subjection to a foreign race. Similar measures will then be conducted in succession against Rawanduz, Khosnau, the Hakkiari Chief, and Bedir Khan Bey, the chief of Jazireh; and ultimately it is hoped, the spirit of independence which has long reigned among the Kurds will be thoroughly broken, and the tribes will became subjects, rather than the tributaries of the Turkish Empire.[171]

All parties were aware of the intimate relationship among the making of the frontiers, the suppression of Kurdish autonomy, and the end of tributary status. Fearing that the operation would alarm Iran and threaten the precarious situation on the borders, Rawlinson obtained a written declaration from Ahmed Pasha that the detachment of the present force was unconnected to any hostile designs against Iran, which he forwarded to British minister of Tehran, Colonel Justin Sheil, for the information of the Iranian government. In the case of his defeat, Ahmed had no alternative but to seek asylum in Iran, in which case the question of his extradition would become a point of contention between the courts of Tehran and Istanbul. Informing his worried ambassador about the extensive preparations the Kurds were making, Rawlinson assured Canning that Ahmed's rebellion was "against Necib Pasha not against the Porte."[172]

It was, however, not the clash with Necib that brought about Ahmed's fall. As the former advanced to Koi sanjak, the latter was preparing to surround his camp. Finding his position critical, Necib dispatched two Tatars to Baghdad for aid, but both were intercepted and killed. He then enlisted to his service a sheikh much venerated by the Kurds and sent him to Ahmed, who, during the ensuing negotiations, killed the sheikh with a pistol. This enraged Ahmed's followers, many of whom switched allegiance to his brother, Abdullah. After skirmishes erupted, Ahmed fled to the powerful Jaf tribe, whose members were among his subjects, his army dispersed, and his guns fell into Necib's hands.[173]

Ahmed ended up in Sinne, at which point Count Modem and Colonel Sheil, the Russian and British ministers in Tehran, respectively, applied to Hajji Mirza Aqasi, the Iranian prime minister, for his removal from the frontier. They were promised that Ahmed would be given a place of residence remote from Suleimanieh.[174] This promise, it appears, was not kept, and Ahmed continued to be active in the frontier region. Nearly a

[171] Ibid.
[172] Ibid.
[173] PRO.FO 78/2713, Rawlinson to Canning, Moosul, July 12, 1845.
[174] PRO.FO 78/2713, Sheil to Aberdeen, Camp near Tehran, August 29, 1845.

year later, he carried out an unsuccessful attempt against his brother, which prompted an expedition from Baghdad.[175] After this expedition, Ottoman authorities were ordered to watch the frontier more closely, and Istanbul once again asked Tehran to send Ahmed into its interior.[176] This episode marked the effective end of Baban rule, but not of its influence in the region or, later, in Istanbul.

Simultaneous with the general campaign of the Ottomans, the Iranian governor of Urumieh started a limited campaign against various refractory chiefs residing in his frontier district. But once again it became obvious that suppression of such chiefs could not be completed without a clearly delimited boundary. Among the targets of the Iranian campaign was Hasan Agha, a chief whom Iranian authorities considered to be their subject. However, Nurullah Bey of Hakkari also claimed him as a dependent. Hence, Nurullah threatened to assist Hasan Agha should Iranian forces attack him. Concerned that such a clash would jeopardize the Erzurum conferences, the Russian and British ministers in Tehran interfered, and the Iranian prime minister ordered the suspension of coercive measures.[177] The *tanzimat* pashas, however, were less forgiving as they again turned their attention to the last vestiges of Kurdish autonomy: Bedirkhan of Cizre, Nurullah, and the Khan brothers of Van.

THE CASE OF THE CITY OF VAN AND THE *MIR* OF BOHTAN

Istanbul's attempts to penetrate the margins of the empire affected many segments of society, uniting them in resistance. What happened in Van is a case in point. In the years following their release from Istanbul, Khan Mahmud and his brothers, with local backing, regained the province and city of Van. After wresting control of Khoshab castle from Ottoman troops, with the goal of extending their territories, they carried out a campaign against Bitlis. This aroused the suspicion of the Ottoman pashas, who worried that Khan Mahmud was making alliances with Hakkari and Cizre, as well as Yahya Khan of Salmas, a member of the Hakkari family on the Iranian side. In fact, he was receiving aid from the Shekak tribe on

---

[175] Canning to Abderdeen, Constantinople, July 20, 1846, *Schofield I*, 576–77.
[176] PRO.FO 78/2714, Canning to Sheil, Constantinople, February 12, 1846. Ahmed Pasha later went to Istanbul, where he lived in exile. Afterward, his brother Abdullah was also deposed and sent to Istanbul. Abdullah was later appointed governor of Divaniye. See BOA.A.DVN 97/39, 18.L.1270/July 14, 1854.
[177] PRO.FO 78/2713, Sheil to Aberdeen, Camp near Tehran, August 29, 1845.

the Iranian side, and the Duderi and Koçer tribes of the Cizre region, who spent their summers in Mahmudi pastures.[178] When, in 1845, the regional governor general, Esad Pasha of Erzurum, pressed the city's people to explain their rebellion, they and Khan Mahmud sent a deputation to inform him that although they were faithful subjects of the sultan and ready to pay just dues, they refused to furnish recruits, receive a garrison, accept *tanzimat*, or submit to quarantine.[179] Esad Pasha gave the deputation forty days, expiring on December 22, 1845, to submit unconditionally. In their answer, made in March 1846 and bearing the seals of thirty-eight Muslims and sixteen Christians, the people reiterated that they were not resisting out of rebellion or unwillingness to pay taxes, but because for them *tanzimat* meant more taxes, government pressure, and conscription. They additionally urged the pasha not to deploy regular troops to their city, as local troops were protecting their castle (against Iran).[180]

Like the Ottoman pashas, James Brant advocated the end of the Kurdish dynasts and wrote that "until the Beys in all Koordistan [sic] be reduced to obedience, there will be no tranquility in this part of the empire, the frontier will always be in a disturbed state, and misunderstanding with Iran will never be terminated."[181] Both Brant and the pashas furthermore believed Bedirkhan to be the prime force behind the revolt. Made *mütesellim* in 1836 and subdued in 1838, Bedirkhan had reestablished himself following the Battle of Nizib and extended his authority from east of Rawanduz in the southeast, to west of Urumiya in the east, and to the gates of Mosul in the south. Establishing security and the rule of law in the lands under his control, he promoted crop cultivation and rebuilt destroyed villages, which resulted in a general prosperity. Exceeding even the powers of the traditional *hükümet* system, he had his own coins minted and Friday prayers recited in his name, both of which could only be done by rulers of an independent entity:[182] "He worked to modernize his army (somewhat) and centralize command, creating elite units recruited from all the tribes, who were now directly under his authority instead of under the traditional command of their respective chiefs. This move, like the one by the Babans and Mahmudis, contributed to the decrease in influence

---

[178] Hakan, *Osmanlı*, 126–29.
[179] PRO.FO 78/653, 8 January 1846, Brant to Aberdeen. Most of the information in the following pages is based on Brant's letters.
[180] Hakan, *Osmanlı*, 183.
[181] PRO.FO 78/653, Brant to Aberdeen, January 8, 1846.
[182] For the rise and fall of Bedir Khan see van Bruinessen, *Agha*, 177–82; and Klein, "Power in the Periphery," 109–10.

previously held by the tribal *agha*s."[183] This process, which I call the de-clanization or de-tribalization of Kurdistan, extended solidarity beyond tribal membership. The rise of a figure around whom various tribes could unite led to the erosion of the power of petty chiefs. This, one could claim, was the beginning of a new form of identity and allegiance formation and so posed a challenge to the Ottoman project of creating citizenship based on rights provided by *tanzimat* reforms. As such, it could not be tolerated. As Brant notes, not only did figures such as Bedirkhan, in the eyes of the center, destabilize the frontier and prevent its further penetration of the peripheries, but they also impeded rapprochement with Iran.[184]

There was, however, a more pressing reason to eliminate Bedirkhan. The Nestorians, possibly encouraged by the support they thought they would receive from Christian missionaries and the European countries they represented, were refusing to pay an annual tribute to Nurullah Bey of Hakkari. In response, Bedirkhan sent a large force to Hakkari in 1843, which slaughtered many Nestorians and forced many others to leave the region.[185] The attack, seen as one more event in a long chain of anti-Christian violence, was well publicized in Europe, and the British and French governments pressured the Ottomans to punish the rebel chief, whereas regional administrators defended Bedirkhan and characterized the Nestorians as insubordinates.[186] For example, the governor of Erzurum, Kamili Pasha, argued that British and American influence, along with Iranian interference, had encouraged them to pillage villages and turn mosques into churches.[187] Such local support, combined with Bedirkhan's ability to control swaths of Kurdistan and more general fears of British and French intervention, motivated Istanbul to allow him to remain in power, and he continued his anti-Nestorian policies. The French and British consuls, kept informed by missionaries, continued to pressure Istanbul and their foreign services to put a stop to this persecution. After he carried out yet another attack, Istanbul decided to deal with him definitively and ordered the *müşir* of the Anatolian army and the governors of Sivas, Diyarbakır, and Mosul to coordinate a campaign against him and against Van, whose

---

[183] Klein, "Power in the Periphery," 111, after van Bruinessen.
[184] PRO.FO, 78/653, Brant to Aberdeen, January 8, 1846.
[185] Klein, "Power in the Periphery," 114; and van Bruinessen, *Agha*, 180.
[186] Klein, "Power in the Periphery," 114. This part of Bedirkhan's career is well known. See van Bruinessen, *Agha*, 177–81; Hakan, *Osmanlı*, 157–93; Klein, "Power in the Periphery," 108–15. Literature on the Nestorians and missionary activities in this region is too extensive to quote here.
[187] Hakan, *Osmanlı*, 162.

inhabitants continued to defiantly proclaim "their ability to maintain their independence"[188] In response, Bedirkhan attempted to placate Istanbul: he pledged to leave Cizre, allow the return of those who had fled the region, pay what he owed, cease interfering in Nestorian affairs, and submit to the exclusive authority of the governor of Mosul. His promises, however, were in vain. Indeed, his requirement that the Friday Khutba be read in his name alone warranted his dismissal. Bent on establishing its territorial sovereignty, Istanbul would tolerate the Kurdish lords no more.

In spring 1847, Ottoman troops from the Anatolian and Arabistan armies began preparing their simultaneous attack on Van and Bedirkhan. The Porte ordered its pashas to break the "league of notables." This was accomplished when Sherif Bey of Mush, Nurullah of Hakkari, and Han Mahmud's brother Han Abdal defected.[189] To guarantee his services, Sherif Bey was made a *miralay* and Mush the center of preparations. Because Han Abdal controlled the Satmanis and Khoshab castles on the border, his defection distressed the Han Mahmud-Bedirkhan league, which had planned to take refuge in Khosab in case of defeat[190] and forced Bedirkhan into inconclusive negotiations with Iran. In the meantime, the *kaimmakam* of Harir, Resul Pasha of Rawanduz, who had been appointed after his brother's 1836 submission, escaped to Iran. Istanbul asked the Iranian and British consuls in Baghdad for his return. He voluntarily complied, and Tehran decided to refuse to aid or give refuge to Bedirkhan.[191]

Faced with twenty-five thousand soldiers under high-ranking generals, Bedirkhan and Han Mahmud determined to use force of arms.[192] Yet they were dealt another blow with the defection of Bedirkhan's cousin Ézdin Şêr – the son of Mir Seyfeddin, whom Bedirkhan had replaced – especially after he guided Ottoman troops to Bedirkhan's Dergul residence.[193] Clashes ensued between Khan Mahmud's forces and Ottoman troops in

---

[188] PRO.FO 78/654, Brant to Palmerston, November 11, 1846; and Hakan, *Osmanlı*, 192.

[189] For details, see Hakan, *Osmanlı*, 193–203.

[190] PRO.FO 78/702, Dispatches of Brant, April 10, and May 6, 1847; and Hakan, *Osmanlı*, 208–11.

[191] Hakan, *Osmanlı*, 217–19.

[192] Brant added, "entertaining little hope of successful resistance Bedir Khan prepared a retreat for his family and treasures in the country of Nurullah Bey near Julamerg, where he had built a strong fort with the intention of retiring thither if forced to abandon his province." PRO.FO 78/702, Dispatches of Brant, April 10 and May 6, 1847, and Brant to Palmerston, June 4 and 8, 1847.

[193] PRO.FO 78/702, Brant to Lord Covley, June 26 and July 3, 1847. As a reward for his cooperation, Ézdin Sher was named *kaimmakam* of Cizre, a rank lower than that of *mütesellim*, which Bedirkhan held.

the Ahlat, Bitlis, and Mush regions.[194] On June 14, 1847, Bedirkhan and a force of four thousand to five thousand men executed a night attack on the camp of Ferik Ömer Pasha of the Syrian army. Khan Mahmud launched an ambush on the Serasker's division the same night, but his was discovered and "his troops were prevented from passing the Bohtan River, which they were about to attempt on rafts, the bridge having been destroyed."[195]

According to Brant, after their failure, Bedirkhan released his followers from the oath of loyalty they had sworn. Because his Dergul stronghold had been occupied, he retreated with five hundred adherents to Erwex (Orak) castle, where his family awaited. Meanwhile, some of his followers, including his nephews Ibrahim Bey and Mossor capitulated, and their forts were garrisoned by regular (Albanian) troops. The disintegration of their nascent league dispirited the resistance in Van. When the Erzurum division arrived there, two of Khan Mahmud's brothers, who had been left to defend the city, surrendered to Ömer Pasha.[196] A contemporary reported that the sultan's troops, assisted by Yezidi Kurds, finally defeated Khan Mahmud near Tilleh, as he marched with the tribes of Van and Hakkari to aid Bedirkhan. After his surrender, Ottoman troops destroyed most of the region's castles, depriving it of its historical monuments, memory, and legacy.[197]

It appears that the Van revolt helped incite disturbances elsewhere. Some Kurds, for example, plundered villages in the district of Kighi, whereas the Dojik Kurds of Dersim plundered Terjan and Erzincan. Istanbul suspected extensive Kurdish coalitions. It is difficult, however, to prove whether the initiators of these and other disturbances were organized by the league of Bedirkhan, were responding to *tanzimat* measures, or were simply taking advantage of the chaos. It was speculated that Bedirkhan's success could have resulted in a general Kurdish uprising.[198] He failed, however, and surrendered toward the end of July 1847, near the

---

[194] Hakan, *Osmanlı*, 212–13.
[195] PRO.FO 78/702, Brant to Covley, June 26, 1847. In Ottoman documents, the commander of Bedirkhan's forces is Telli Bey. See Hakan, *Osmanlı*, 224.
[196] PRO.FO 78/702, Brant to Covley, July 3, 1847.
[197] Layard, *Discoveries in the Ruins of Nineveh and Babylon*, 50–54.
[198] PRO.FO 78/702, Brant to Covley, July 3, 1847. The [Alawi] Kurds of Dersim's Dojik Mountains took up arms right after Bedirkhan's defeat. Their rebellion, although relatively unknown, was the more vigorous of the two and provides a fascinating account of the ruthless extension of Ottoman state capacity and resistance to it. I do not include it, however, because it did not directly affect the borderland. For details, see Brant's letters to Canning and Palmerston in PRO.FO 78/870.

kaza of Eruh. In the same month, as the second Erzurum Treaty was being ratified, Erzurum received intelligence that Nurullah was ready to renounce his alliance with Bedirkhan.[199] By August, nearly every important Kurdish chief had surrendered and was awaiting exile to the empire's western regions.[200]

Soon afterward, however, rumors reached the *mushir* of the Anatolian army that Nurullah was attempting to unite the districts around Hakkari with Iran.[201] This case well illustrates the complexities of allegiance and belonging in the borderland. The Ottomans were suspicious of Nurullah because one of his wives was the sister of Yahya Khan of Salmas, whose other sister was the wife of the shah of Iran, Mohammad Shah. Hence, Istanbul urged Tehran to refuse Nurullah entrance if he crossed the frontier. Ottoman troops entered Julamerg (Colemerg) on December 9, 1848. Overwhelmed by their superior military might, Nurullah escaped to the frontier castle of Berderesh, and the tribes of Hakkari gradually submitted. While the Ottoman commanders were still determining what to do about the escaped Kurdish lord, the *hakim* of Berdesor on the Iranian side, 'Ali Ashraf Khan, accompanied by several hundred horsemen, came to Nurullah's rescue. Istanbul demanded his return from Iranian authorities, including 'Ali Ashraf Khan and Najaf Quli Khan, the *hakim* of Urumieh, as well as from the British and Russian consuls in Tabriz. The consuls likewise petitioned Iran to hand him over, promising that the Ottomans would guarantee his life, honor, and property. Iran responded that 'Ali Ashraf Khan was in revolt and had twice defeated the troops sent to subdue him. Additionally, because Yahya Khan was originally from Hakkari, there was danger of a general movement in support of Nurullah. Once again, such fears did not materialize. As result of joint pressure from Istanbul and the Russo-British representatives, Nurullah was forced to return. As if to signify the rise of a new class of actors in the peripheries – namely, the *ulama* – he took refuge with a respected Naqshbandi sheikh, Taha of Hakkari.[202] Soon, however, he was sent to Istanbul, and then to exile. Like Nurullah, the leaders of some other tribes, including the Zilan (who might have participated in the revolt), escaped to Iran while their remaining members petitioned to be settled on the Ottoman side.[203]

---

[199] PRO.FO 78/702, Brant to Palmerston, July 8, 1847.
[200] PRO.FO 78/702, Brant to Palmerston, August 9, 1847.
[201] BOA.A.MKT 112/50, 1264.5.17/ 29 July 1848.
[202] Hakan, *Osmanlı*, 266–71.
[203] They were settled in Kars. See BOA.A.MKT 168/63, 1265.2.16/May 28, 1849 and 222/20, 1265.10.16/November 28, 1849.

TAXES, CONSCRIPTION, RETRIBALIZATION:
THE STATE IS HERE TO STAY

With the suppression of all Kurdish chiefs of consequence and the replacement of indirect with direct rule, the stage was set for the extension of the *tanzimat* state and the demarcation of the boundaries. These processes, in turn, facilitated the penetration of the peripheries and the standardization of state practices, which were followed by growth in the capacity to carry out intended polices. The most visible measures were the exile and, as we shall see later, the co-optation of defeated notables, along with the introduction of new administrative units, taxes, and methods of conscription.[204] Resistance to state penetration, however, by no means ceased and accounts of small-scale rebellions continued to reach Istanbul. As Longrigg notes, the emerging regime "was precarious, nominal, barely operative in the tribes and remoter mountains, but at least, most of the rallying points of the Kurdish nation had been destroyed."[205]

Soon, however, a new rallying point emerged thanks to the already influential *ulama*. In 1850, the governor of the newly created Hakkari province informed Istanbul that it could curry local favor by granting Sheikh Taha of Nehri's request to build a mosque.[206] A year later, however, the governor's judgment was very different. In addition to the exiled Nurullah, he reported, a second danger loomed in the region: Sheikh Taha was uniting the people. He thus urged Istanbul to grant a previous petition by the sheikh for financial support to move to Mecca. His immediate removal was advisable, the governor wrote, because those escaping conscription were taking refuge with him, and he was using his influence to hinder conscription. Hakkari's proximity to Iran made this situation all the more precarious.[207] As we will see, the governor's concern may have been premature, but it was not misplaced: Taha's son Ubeidullah would emerge as a leader capable of uniting the Kurds.

Although it did not heed the governor's advice, Istanbul did implement a plan to empower lesser actors, whether sheikh or *agha*, to atomize the

---

[204] van Bruinessen suggests that Bedirkhan's revolt was provoked by administrative plans to divide Bohtan between Diyarbekir and Mosul *eyalet*s, which threatened his power. See *Agha*, n.107, 202–3.

[205] Longrigg, *Four Centuries*, 286.

[206] BOA.MVL 233/84, Vali of Hakkari to Istanbul, 24.L.1266/September 2, 1850.

[207] BOA.MVL 227/21, Commander of Hakkari to Ministry of Interior, 07.Ş.1267/June 8, 1851.

frontier society, a process I call the re-clanization of Kurdistan.[208] In places such as Rawanduz, the *ulama* were given salaries.[209] Similarly, many of the *Ekrad ve aşair beyleri* (*beys* of tribes and the Kurds), eager to fill the power vacuum, were sent robes of honor designating official recognition as chiefs of a certain tribe or locality.[210] Their lands were made into *nahiyes* (local districts, smaller than a *kaza*) and their chieftains appointed as salaried *müdürs*, or lesser administrators. This strategic co-optation, however, had its limits. For example, some chieftains, such as those of Van, were granted temporary salaries only "until the border was finalized and division of tribes [with Iran] was complete."[211]

Following the elimination of the chiefs of consequence, hundreds of other notables whom the government judged to have leadership skills were exiled to other parts of the empire. This policy intended to transform the encounter between the empire and its borderland subjects from a mediated or brokered one into an imposed one. But the central states still lacked the means to fully consolidate and expand their jurisdictional, administrative, and military authority over the borderland. The substitution of government appointees for local chiefs thus resulted in a dearth of recognized authorities capable of brokering between rival tribes. This, in turn, resulted in the further atomization and clanization of large tribal confederations, which van Bruinessen has described as "a rapid devolution from complex, state like to much simpler forms of social and political organization – as if [tribal organization had] taken a few steps back on the evolutionary ladder."[212] Unresolved feuds and other conflicts proliferated, often resulting in the creation of new subtribes and increasing instability.[213] Breaking the power of the Kurdish lords of the marches allowed the Ottoman state to increase its coercive force, and the resulting lack of administrative mechanisms of brokerage between state and society left a fractured social structure. This process, which forced Kurdish political institutions to devolve from proto-state to chiefdom to tribe, increased instability on the border in the short term, but further empowered the state in the long run.[214]

---

[208] For one such case, that of Sharafuddin Bey of Hizan, see BOA.A.MKT.UM 2/35, 1266.1.8/March 20, 1850.

[209] For Shaikh Abdulgafur, the *postnishin* of Naqshbandi *dargah*, see BOA.A.MKT.UM 242/1, 29.L.1272/July 3, 1856 and BOA.I.MVL 368/16126. For others see BOA.A.MKT. UM 280/54, 05.N.1273/July 10, 1856.

[210] BOA.I.DH 256/15827, 07.Za.1268/August 18, 1852.

[211] BOA.A.AMD 29/53, 28.3.1267/June 8, 1851.

[212] van Bruinessen, *Agha*, 181–82.

[213] Ibid. 193–95.

[214] Ibid.

It is important to recognize, however, that exile did not necessarily preclude co-optation. Bedirkhan, for example, was sent with his extended family to Candia, on the island of Crete. But there, he was given a salary; elevated to the rank of *mir-i miran*; and, in 1858, decorated with the Fourth Degree Majidi Decoration.[215] He was also allowed to collect revenue from his private lands, and many of his progeny rose to high office whereas others emerged as standard bearers of Kurdish nationalism. Similarly, Nurullah was given the rank of *dergah-ı âli kapıcıbaşılığı*, pardoned, and granted a salary increase, with the condition that he, too, live in Crete and not communicate with his native land.[216] Sherif Bey of Mush, in spite of his defection, was exiled to Damascus and allowed to retain revenue from his *yurtluk-ocaklık* lands.[217] Like the Bedirkhanis, some members of the Baban family also rose to high ranks in the empire.[218] Certainly, these exiles marked the end of the privileged status of *yurtluk-ocaklıks*. As a memo from the Ottoman prime minister's office argues, changing times (*inkılab-ı zaman cihetiyle*) demanded that noble families no longer be able to claim such lands as inheritance. Yet, like Sherif Bey of Mush, some families were allowed to continue collecting a fraction of revenues accrued.[219] Furthermore, as co-opted members of the bureaucratic-military elite, many clans continued to wield considerable authority in the borderland and elsewhere.

Ottoman documents, not surprisingly, portray the rebel dynasts as bandits (*eskiya*) who committed crimes and oppressed the poor (*fukara*).[220] Their defeat, however, did not result in peace or prosperity. The Ottoman survey commission, when passing through Suleimanieh in 1851, observed that many of its frontier districts were no longer cultivated and water distribution was in shambles. Additionally, large tribes such as the Jaf and Ilgavâre, which had previously paid *harc-ı hane* taxes to Baban-appointed

---

[215] Like Bedirkhan, the Ottoman pashas who helped suppress revolts were given decorations "peculiar to the conquests of Kurdistan." BOA.A.DVN.MHM 7/16 1265.C.3/April 27, 1849.

[216] BOA.A.MKT.UM 343/82, 09.B.1275/1859.

[217] BOA.A.MKT 225/82, Kurdistan Valisi M. Esad Muhlis'in yazısı, 1265.11.13/January 25, 1850.

[218] BOA.A.DVN 61/39, 1266.9.15/27 November 1849S and BOA.A.MKT.UM 10/35, 1266.4.24/July 6, 1850.

[219] For example, out of fifty thousand *ghurush* yearly revenue collected from villages registered to them, the seven sons and daughters of Evliya Pasha of Mahmudi received a total of twenty-four hundred. BOA.A.AMD 89/98, 1274/1858.

[220] For example, see telegram regarding Bedirkhan's surrender. BOA.A.MKT.UM 18/49, 1263.Ş.29/August 12, 1847.

officers on their seasonal migrations, had ceased paying those taxes even as they increasingly disrupted the lives of the province's inhabitants.[221] Certainly, in some places, the end of the dynasts brought a measure of relief to the peasantry. Around Bitlis, the production of oak, formerly monopolized by Bedirkhan and other grandees, was now open to the participation of villagers.[222] Still, for the most part, such respite, if it existed at all, was short lived. In Jelu district, where Nurullah's troops had massacred Nestorians, villagers continued to complain about oppression and overtaxation, this time by the Ottoman forces now patrolling the region.[223]

Indeed, new taxes proliferated throughout the borderland. The Zibar country between the Rawanduz and Nestorian valleys was made to pay taxes on tobacco, cotton, and fruit for the first time. In addition, their *saliyane*, a kind of yearly property tax, was raised. As Henry Austen Layard reports, the Zibaris and other tribes that had been placed under their authority in the districts of Shirwan, Gherdi, Bradost, and Shamdinan complied "rather than run the risk of an invasion, and still more dreaded evil conscription."[224] What is interesting in the Zibari case is that shortly before the introduction of these taxes, their chief had traveled to Mosul to receive his cloak of investiture. Thus, as the new representative of Istanbul, he had little choice but to make those under his control pay the taxes introduced by the *tanzimat* state. Not all chiefs faced similar dilemmas. To the contrary, those located closer to Iranian lands were sometimes offered economic incentives. For example, in Van province, Istanbul granted some chieftains, including those of the large Hesenan confederation, temporary salaries until the demarcation was completed.[225]

Such co-optation also allowed the central government to conscript hitherto unconscripted borderlanders. As forced conscription was so reviled that some even fled to Iran to avoid it,[226] a lottery system (*kur'a*) was introduced, in which lots were drawn in the presence of a *Kur'a*

---

[221] Mehmed Hurşid Paşa, *Seyâhatnâme-i Hudud*, transcription Alaatin Eser (Istanbul: Simurg, 1997), 181–84.

[222] Layard, *Discoveries in the Ruins of Nineveh and Babylon*, 37.

[223] Ibid., 35.

[224] At the time of Layard's visit, the *mir* of Rawanduz, Feyzullah Bey, while boasting of complete independence, was under the control of the Zibari chiefs. Layard, *Discoveries in the Ruins of Nineveh, and Babylon*, 371.

[225] See BOA.A.AMD, 29/53, 1267.3.28/July 9, 1851. It seems these salaries were given at the request of Ottoman pashas in the region. The agha of Hesenan was given 500 ghurus and others 1,950 ghurus, in addition to taxes they collected from the tribe.

[226] Layard, *Discoveries in the Ruins of Nineveh and Babylon*, 385–86.

Meclisi (Lottery Council) to determine conscripts.[227] As an official memo put it, many borderlanders, however, continued to resist what it called the beneficial system of conscription, such as the people of Palu and Şiro *kaza*s, which had until then enjoyed *yurtluk-ocaklık* status.[228] Similarly, the *nahiya*s of Mardin resisted until troops were sent to impose the new policies.[229] Villages in Cizre were likewise forced to surrender conscripts and pay taxes.[230]

Despite such resistance, the *tanzimat* state forged ahead with the planned shift from a suzerain to a sovereign political realm. It created new administrative units and posts for salaried appointees that facilitated the borderland's integration into the newly territorialized structure of the empire. One such unit was the short-lived *eyelet* of Kurdistan, composed of Diyarbakır *eyelet*;Van, Mush, and Hakkari *sancak*s;and Cizre, Bohtan, and Mardin *kaza*s. Created on December 5, 1847, it was abolished in 1867.[231] More illustrative of the process's impact on the region is the case of Hakkari, which was denominated as a *vilayet*, or larger administrative unit, and provided with troops from Albania. Its new governor, Ahmed İzzet Pasha, began residing in Nurullah Bey's stronghold, and his rule prompted one observer to declare, "the whole of this country, for the first time, has been brought under the direct control of the Porte."[232] Despite – or, better put, because of – this historic transformation, the frontier region remained unsettled and many tribes continued to refuse allegiance to any government. From the perspective of the central states and Great Powers, however, such resistance was not worrisome. The work of the frontier conferences and commissions, as Layard observed, would remove "the uncertainty which had so long existed as to the nationality of the various tribes ... and some of the principal causes of the unsettled state of Kurdistan, and of the frequent disputes between the two powers."[233]

[227] Musa Çadırcı, "Osmanlı İmpartorluğunda Askere Almada Kura Usulüne Geçilmesi– 1846 Tarihli Akerlik Kanunu," *Askeri Tarih Bülteni*, Sayı 18, Şubat 1985.

[228] [*kur'a-i şer'iyye usul-ü hasenesi*] See BOA.A.MKT.MHM 22/35, 1266.8.8 /October 20, 1850.

[229] BOA.MVL [Catalog no, 1086, p.8], From the Governor of Kurdistan and the 4th Army Commander to Istanbul, 12.L.1267/August 10, 1851.

[230] BOA.A.AMD 22/61 (1266–1849).

[231] Hakan, *Osmanlı*, 255–57.

[232] Layard, *Discoveries in the Ruins of Nineveh and Babylon*, 383.

[233] Ibid., 385–86.

2

Laying the Ground: The Concert of Zagros

The Turco-Persian Boundary Commissions, as they were called, began their arduous task at the beginning of 1842, during the final stages of the Ottoman *tanzimat* state's campaign to replace the indirect rule of the Kurdish lords with direct rule and extend its capacity in the borderland. Toward the end of the same year, the British and Russian commissioners met in Trebizond, the main port linking northwestern Iran with the northeastern Ottoman Empire, and proceeded to Erzurum, which would be their home for more than three years. Famous for its harsh winters, Erzurum was a sizeable frontier town with a cosmopolitan flair thanks to the presences of French, British, and Russian consulates and a few American missionaries.[1] The commissioners' host, Erzurum's governor, held the rank of vizier. Ruler of the borderland's northern section, his authority extended over the Ottoman provinces facing Russia and northwestern Iran as well as all the Kurdish notables in the region.

The Russian and British commissioners arrived in early January 1843, around the same time as the Ottoman representative, Nuri Efendi. The latter, however, unexpectedly died on March 1, and Enveri Efendi replaced him. Meanwhile, the first appointed Iranian representative fell ill, and his replacement did not arrive until April 18. Hence, it took some time for the various parties to organize themselves, even as they adjusted to the culture of this distant city, which comprised "the main land-route for trade between Europe and the Orient."[2] Still, hopes were high that their labors

---

[1] Robert Curzon, *Armenia: A Year at Erzeroom, and on the Frontiers of Russia, Turkey, and Persia* (London: J. Murray, 1854), 32–36, 44.

[2] Alexander Pushkin, *A Journey to Arzrum*, trans. Brigitta Ingemanson (Ann Arbor, MI: Ardis, 1974), 79. Pushkin was disappointed with the Asian poverty he witnessed when he traveled to Erzurum with the Russian army that occupied it in 1829.

would bring about the long-awaited delimitation and the lessening of the trans-border tensions that so frequently erupted into war.

Living in Erzurum proved to be difficult. As the months wore on, various members of the commission fell sick and others endured attacks or were even killed.[3] Despite these hardships, on May 15, the delegates from London, St. Petersburg, Tehran, and Istanbul began negotiations. They held weekly meetings for four years, until May 31, 1847, when they signed the Erzurum Treaty, which established the limits of territorial sovereignty and guaranteed noninterference in the domestic affairs of each state. Leaving aside the colorful details of the daily lives of the commissioners and making minimal reference to the non-frontier-related issues that occupied their time, the present chapter focuses on two cases: Zohab and Muhammarah to examine how the parties negotiated disputed lands and the Zilan tribe to analyze their dealings with cross-border migrations.

Introducing the two "Mohammedan powers" to the mediation of the Great Powers, the new international order represented by the commission required the limits of Ottoman and Iranian control to be demarcated.[4] Embroiled in their own "great game," Russia and Britain "wanted a more precise definition of the Ottoman-Iranian boundary to ease the expansion of their imperial interests in the region."[5] Moreover, England wanted to develop steamship navigation on the Tigris, Euphrates, and Shatt al-Arab, whereas Russia wanted to certify its role as the broker of Ottoman-Iranian relations and "protector" of Iran. In the post-Vienna world of 1815, the Erzurum Conferences laid the groundwork for the inclusion of Iran and the Ottoman Empire in a system of diplomacy that would establish what one might call a "Concert of Zagros." Similar to the "Concert of Europe," which finalized European boundaries in a way mutually tolerable to important powers and guaranteed the resulting territorial arrangements through a series of interlocking treaties, the Concert of Zagros laid the groundwork for the transformation of Ottoman-Iranian relations from an interstate struggle to an international coexistence regimented by bordered lands.[6]

---

[3] For the colorful details of commissioners' life in Erzurum see Curzon, *Armenia*.

[4] The terms "Mohammedan powers" and "Great Powers" were commonly used. See, for example, "Russian charge d'affaires to IMFA," in Nasrollah Salehi. *Asnadi az In'ikad-e 'Ahdnameh-e Dovvome Erzetelroum* (Tehran: Daftar-i Mutala'at-i Siyasi va Bayn al-Milali, 1377 [1999]), 101–2.

[5] Will D. Swearingen, "Geopolitical Origins of Iran-Iraq War," *Geographical Review* 78 (October 1988): 409.

[6] On the post-1815 order, see Paul W. Schroeder, "The 19th Century International System: Changes in the Structure," *World Politics* 39.1 (Oct. 1986), 1–26.

From 1843 to 1914, the technical and diplomatic corps that staffed this and subsequent frontier commissions were agents of territorializing sovereignty who worked to prevent a full-scale collision between the subjects of the shah and those of the sultan and, finally, marked down in black and white a frontier that conventional historiography assumes existed since 1639.

These conferences also served to warn the borderland peoples that the limits of their sovereigns' authorities were to be permanently set. As the previous chapter argued, the boundary-making process would transform relations between local elements and the center from a suzerain to a sovereign reality. Thenceforward, it would not be enough that the border-landers and the lords of the marches simply recognize the suzerainty of the ruler while remaining internally autonomous. They would have to be incorporated into sovereign domains. The commissioners explicitly articulated this goal, as when one of them wrote that the "congress at Erzeroom [met] to discuss the position of the boundary and to check the border incursions of the Kurdish tribes, both by argument and by force of arms."[7] Indeed, as we saw in the previous chapter, less than two months after the Erzurum Treaty was signed, Bedirkhan,the strongest of the Kurdish nota-bles, surrendered to the Ottoman pashas.

The negotiations proceeded in three stages. During the first, which lasted from the beginning of 1843 to the middle of 1844, the Ottoman and Iranian negotiators made claims and declared grievances on behalf of their respective governments. The second phase, which closed with the signing of the treaty in 1847, included the consideration of possible concessions by both parties and the presentation of the Anglo-Russian compromise plan. The third phase, which extended beyond the timeline of the conferences them-selves, ended with the treaty's final ratification.[8] Along the way, the commissioners confronted various crises while discussing territorial disputes, tariffs and customs, monetary compensation claims, religio-legal issues, legal jurisdiction, and problems regarding seasonally migrating tribes.

THE COMMISSIONERS AND THEIR WORK

The commission's plenipotentiaries included prominent diplomats and soldiers from every party. The Iranian negotiator Mirza Taqi Khan, later known as Amir Kabir, became a celebrated statesman. As Abbas Amanat

---

[7] Curzon, *Armenia*, vii.
[8] Maurice Harari, "The Ottoman-Iranian Boundary Question: A Case Study in the Politics of Boundary Making in the Near and Middle East" (Ph.D. diss., Columbia University, 1953), 43.

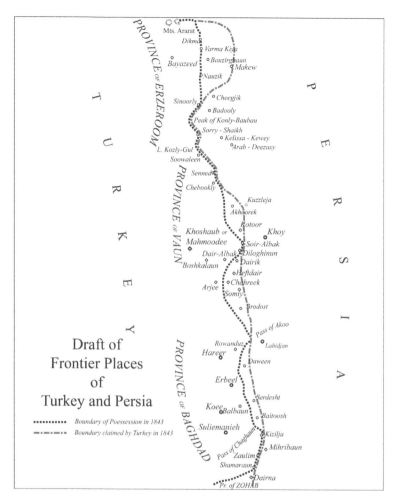

MAP 2. Frontier Places of Turkey and Persia
Adapted from PRO.MFQ 1/63/005, Map communicated to the Erzurum Commission by the Ottoman Commission in 1843.

observes, the Erzurum conferences put him on the political map.[9] According to Robert Curzon, a British commissioner, he was "beyond all comparison the most interesting of those assembled at the congress of Erzeroom," and his delegation's belated arrival was celebrated with formal greetings

---

[9] Abbas Amanat, *The Pivot of the Universe* (Berkeley: University of California Press, 1997), 92–93; and Faridun Adamiyat, *Amir Kabir va Iran* (Tehran: Intisharati Khawarizmi, 1385/ 2007).

and cannon and gunfire.[10] Istanbul's *murahhas*, or plenipotentiary, was Enverizade Esseyid Mehmet Enveri Saadullah Efendi, a member of the Supreme Council of Justice (Meclis-i Ahkam-ı Adliye). Because he replaced the deceased Mehmed Nuri Efendi, the former ambassador to London, Vienna, and Paris, his appointment delayed the conferences considerably. Moreover, his arrogance and occasionally undiplomatic language created so many problems that Istanbul considered replacing him.[11] The British commissioner, Colonel Fenwick Williams (1800–83) of the Royal Artillery, went on to serve as the British survey commissioner. Because of an unexpected illness, however, Curzon briefly replaced him and cosigned documents for him before departing toward the end of 1843.[12] The Russian commissioner, Colonel Dainese, later rose to the rank of general.[13] Three or four junior officers representing a pool of technical, military, and linguistic knowledge as well as a body of "native servants" accompanied each plenipotentiary.[14]

[10] Curzon, *Armenia*, 54–55; and Ibrahim Aykun, "Erzurum Konferansı (1843–1847) ve Osmanlı-Iran Hudut Antlaşması" (Ph.D. diss., Erzurum Atatürk Üniversitesi, 1995), 75. The main officers accompanying Mirza Taqi were Mirza Ahmad Khan Veqayi'negar Shirazi, the chargé d'affaires at Istanbul and author of *Tarikh-e Qajariyeh;* Mirza Mohammad Hussein Farahani, Mirza Taqi's private secretary, who later earned the title of Dabir al-Molk and appointment as minister of interior; Cheraghli Khan Zanganah, Mirza Taqi's close aide when he was prime minister; and Jan Davud Mesihi, the translator. Adamiyat, *Amir Kabir*, 71–72.

[11] Enveri Efendi's chief staff was composed of Bekir Pasha, Sabri Pasha (commander of Ottoman troops), Kâmil Efendi (*serkâtib* or first secretary), Rüştü Pasha (translator), and Zaim Agha (*kethüda* or chamberlain). Aykun, "Erzurum", 204–8. For complaints against Enveri, see BOA.HR.SYS, 719/1, 76, 79, 84, and Aykun, "Erzurum", chap. 7.

[12] At the time, Curzon (later Lord Zouche) was Canning's private secretary. In addition to his memoirs, *Armenia: A Year in Erzurum*, Curzon wrote *Visits to Monasteries in the Levant* (London: J. Murray, 1865). Joseph Dickson, the doctor of Tehran's British legation, and Zohrab Efendi, a translator for the British Embassy in Istanbul, also accompanied the British commission. Adamiyat, *Amir Kabir*, 73.

[13] Harari, *Turco-Persian*, 41–42. Also William Fenwick Williams, *The Siege of Kars, 1855: Defense and Capitulation* (London: Stationery Office, 2000). Colonel Dainese's secretary was Proseuriakof and his translator was Mr. Moukine.

[14] The verbatim record (*procès-verbaux*) of the formal conferences, concluding treaty, proposals, and other correspondence is in French. The British commission did forward the report of the first three conferences in English; however, French was used starting with the fourth to make Russian and British documents identical. Written and oral testimony in Turkish, Persian, and Arabic was also used. All commissions included a translator, the most prominent being James Redhouse (1811–92), author of the famous Turkish-English Lexicon. See Carter V. Findley, "Sir James W. Redhouse (1811–1892): The Making of a Perfect Orientalist?" *Journal of the American Oriental Society* 99.4 (Oct.–Dec. 1979): 573–600. Redhouse translated from Arabic, Turkish, and Persian into English or French, but Taylor Thomson translated some Persian documents into English, and Jean David, the Persian court's official translator, translated Mirza Taqi's letters to the mediating commissioners. The Russian Commission communicated with other commissioners in French. The Ottoman translator was Rüşdü

As would become the norm, the British and Russian commissioners were known as the mediating commissioners and Britain and Russia as the mediating powers. Accordingly, the Ottoman and Iranian commissioners were the negotiating, principal, or contracting commissioners.

The royal letter (*ferman*) of authorization (*ruhsatame*) appointing Enveri Efendi as *murahhas* "with complete permission and the most ample full-powers" provides clues about Ottoman expectations regarding the negotiations. In it, Sultan Abdülmecid I (r. 1839–61) declares his readiness to repulse Iranian aggressions, defend his territory, and protect the tranquility of his subjects. However, as Iran had requested the restoration of friendship and the appointment of a plenipotentiary to bring peace to the frontier, he adds, "It is evident that in order to avoid the shedding of human blood, I would not refuse restoration of peace and good-will, for which a desire had been expressed."[15] Nevertheless, he notes that Iran, in contravention to the 1823 treaty, "recently, and without just cause, broke faith, declared war against my imperial Government, invaded my royal guarded dominions, committed various depredations, and made a display of enmity." Hence, reconciliation would be contingent on the investigation of Iran's many unfounded demands. The new treaty, therefore, should guarantee the present and future safety of Ottoman domains and require that Iran make amends for past depredations. Finally, the sultan summarizes the central issues to be addressed by the commission as follows:

The disputes relating to my imperial frontiers towards Erzeroum and Baghdad, and also to the tribes and Koords, must be properly terminated; also the customs-dues, which according to a former treaty, are taken from the merchants and subjects of the said Power who come into or go out of my imperial guarded dominions, must be henceforward demanded and taken in conformity with the treaty of commerce lately concluded between my exalted empire and England, France and various other friendly powers; in short, every subject and every thing which branches off from the said basis, and has a relation to the guarantees for the present and the future, must be arranged and set in order according as is desired.[16]

The sultan, then, names the frontier as one of several problems with Iran and expresses his desire that the rival power be included in the new international system of treaties.

Pasha, who later gained fame as *mütercim*, the translator. Iranian and Ottoman reports were written in their own languages for their respective courts. Mirza Taqi understood Turkish and Enveri Efendi understood Persian. Afshar, *Amir Kabir*, 77. For the Persian version of *procès-verbaux*, see *Guzidah-i Asnad* I, 613–816.
[15] PRO.FO 78/2711, May 15, 1843.
[16] Ibid.

In a much shorter letter of authorization (*ekhtiyarnameh*), Mohammad Shah of Iran praises his plenipotentiary even while reminding him of the existing problems between the "exalted" states of Iran and Rum [the Ottoman Empire]. Unlike the sultan, who does not mention the mediating powers in his letter, the shah describes Russia and England as wanting to bring tranquility to Ottoman-Iranian relations out of good will. Appointing Mirza Taqi as deputy (*wakil*), the shah orders him to join "the representatives of the glorious states of Rome, Russia, and England" to negotiate all existing problems.[17] In a second official Iranian missive, the IMoFA (Iranian Minister of Foreign Affairs) gave high priority to a variety of issues, including territorial claims, control over and citizenship status of borderland tribes, the removal of the Qajar princes from Baghdad, the continuation of the 4 percent tariffs and concomitant exemption from the Balta Liman Treaty, and the resolution of various issues involving indemnities. In addition, in his secret code of conduct or *dastur al-aʿmal*, Mohammad Shah advised his *wakil* that if it were to be decided that Suleimanieh belonged to the Ottoman Empire, he should ensure that its governors be appointed by both sides and that the Baban governors pay Iran thirty thousand *tumans* annually. The shah also insisted that Muhammarah and the left (western) bank of the Shatt al-Arab remain with Iran.[18]

Although the negotiating commissioners were constrained by their sovereigns' demands and burdened by centuries of territorial disputes, "instructions enjoined the mediators essentially to hear and elicit evidence, note all claims and counterclaims, chair/co-chair meetings, take over-all responsibility for the organization and procedures of the meetings, report continuously on the progress of the conferences and related developments, and generally endeavor to restrain the principals from leading each other into an inevitable rupture of the negotiations."[19] With the mediating commissioners powerless to direct the conversation, the parties spent their first months together fruitlessly arguing about the limits of the full powers granted to the negotiating commissioners, especially Mirza Taqi.[20] Mirza Taqi's refusal to produce a full list of Iranian claims further exacerbated the situation. It was only when the mediating representatives guaranteed that his decisions would be binding for the shah that Enveri Efendi agreed to proceed.[21] Soon afterward,

---

[17] Ibid.
[18] Salehi, *Erzetelrum*, IMoFA's letter to Mirza Taqi, 28–29; Shah's secret instructions, 36–37.
[19] Harari, *Turco-Persian*, 43–44.
[20] Aykun, "Erzurum," 93–94; Afshar, *Amir Kabir*, 71, 80–81.
[21] PRO.FO 78/2711, Erzurum, May 28, 1843. Enclosure No. 2 "The letter of British commission to Colonel Sheil."

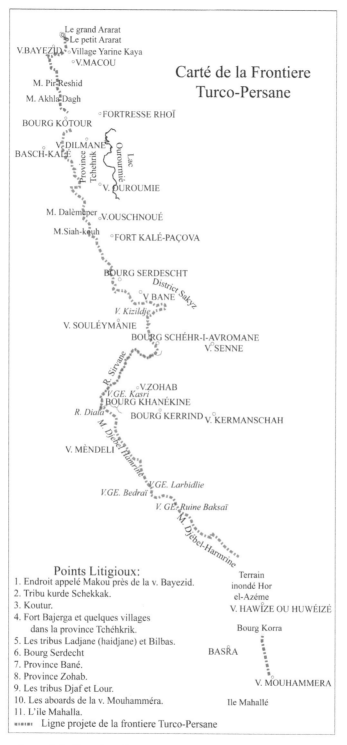

Le grand Ararat
Le petit Ararat
V.BAYEZID. Village Yarine Kaya
V.MACOU

Carté de la Frontiere
Turco-Persane

M. Pir-Reshid

M. Akhla-Dagh

FORTRESSE RHOÏ

BOURG KÔTOUR

V. DILMANE
BASCH-KALÉ

Province Tchehrik

Lac Ourourmié

V. OUROUMIE

M. Dalèmeper   V.OUSCHNOUÉ

M.Siah-kouh   FORT KALÉ-PAÇOVA

BOURG SERDESCHT

District Sakyz
V BANE

V. Kizildje

V. SOULÉYMÄNIE

BOURG SCHÉHR-I-AVROMANE
V. SENNE

R. Sirvane

V.ZOHAB
V.GE. Kasri
BOURG KHANÉKINE

R. Diala   BOURG KERRIND   V. KERMANSCHAH

M. Djébel Hamrine

V. MÈNDELI

V.GE. Larbidlie
V.GE. Bedraï
V. GE. Ruine Baksaï

M. Djébel-Harmrine

Points Litigioux:
1. Endroit appelé Makou près de la v. Bayezid.
2. Tribu kurde Schekkak.
3. Koutur.
4. Fort Bajerga et quelques villages
   dans la province Tchéhkrik.
5. Les tribus Ladjane (haidjane) et Bilbas.
6. Bourg Serdecht
7. Province Bané.
8. Province Zohab.
9. Les tribus Djaf et Lour.
10. Les aboards de la v. Mouhamméra.
11. L'ile Mahalla.
◼▪◼▪◼ Ligne projete de la frontiere Turco-Persane

Terrain
inondé Hor
el-Azéme

V. HAWÏZE OU HUWÉIZÉ

Bourg Korra

BASRA

V. MOUHAMMERA

Ile Mahallé

MAP 3. Carte de la Frontière Turco-Persane
Adapted from PRO.MFQ 1/523 Carte de la Frontière Turco-Persane.

the shah sent a new letter giving full authorization to Mirza Taqi to negotiate the issues laid out by each party and, most importantly, to find a solution to the Karbala problem, which will be discussed later and without which no treaty could succeed.[22] Frustrated by endless discussions and evasive answers, Curzon complained that the negotiating plenipotentiaries "pay but little respect to our meditation; we are constantly trotting about in the sun, smoking pipes, and listening to all this garbage, without any good coming of it."[23]

The plenipotentiaries, however, had their excuses. Mirza Taqi, for example, was reminded that although he had full authority (*vakalat al-mutlaqa*) to sign a treaty, it should not stray even a hair's breadth from the shah's instructions.[24] This warning was conveyed by the shah and reiterated by his prime minister, Hajji Mirza Aqasi, and the IMFA (Iranian Ministry of Foreign Affairs), both of whom chastised the plenipotentiary for failing to defend Iran's right to its tribes and lands.[25] Despite their own frustration, the mediating commissioners understood that Mirza Taqi's extravagant territorial claims and stubbornness were motivated by the inflexible instructions from Tehran.[26] Given the confines placed on the field negotiators' "full authority," it is not surprising that any time British and Russian compromises were offered, the center of mediation tended to move to the British and Russian ambassadors at Constantinople and the respective government(s). This, in turn, prolonged the conferences considerably.

The conferees' work was also delayed by various political and military crises. For example, news of the Ottoman massacre of a reported twenty-two thousand Shi'i Iranian pilgrims at Karbala resulted in a three-month suspension of negotiations as tensions in the borderland again reached a boiling point. Even more severe than the 1802 Wahhabi assault on the city,[27] the Karbala revolt was led by organized gangs and their clerical and

---

[22] "Mohammad Shah's firman to Mirza Taqi Khan," Salehi, *Erzetelrum*, 119.

[23] Curzon to Canning, Erzurum July 30, 1843, as cited in Stanley Lane-Poole, *The Life of the Right Honourable Stratford Canning*, vol. II (London: Longmans, Green, and Co., 1888), 24.

[24] Salehi, *Erzetelrum*, 122. Mirza Taqi noted that "he had been sent here with his hands tied behind his back." "British Commissioner to Sir Stratford Canning," January 21, 1844, *Schofield I*, 199.

[25] For examples, see "IMoFA to Mirza Taqi" Salehi, *Erzetelrum*, 47–48, 61–62.

[26] PRO.FO 78/2711, Williams to Canning, Erzurum, December 30, 1843, and March 11, 1844. They understood because most of the communication between Tehran and its plenipotentiary was copied or first submitted to them. This was not the case with the Ottoman representative, as Mirza Taqi complained. See "Mirza Taqi to Mirza Aqasi" in Salehi, *Erzetelrum*, 104–6. Also Adamiyat, *Amir Kabir*, 120–21.

[27] Adamiyat, *Amir Kabir*, 71.

notable allies, who were bloodily suppressed. As Cole and Moomen argue, this revolt was not only a by-product of Shi'i-Sunni rivalries but also the culmination of resistance to attempts by successive post-*mamluk* Baghdad governors to include Karbala within the *tanzimat* state.[28] Following fruit-less negotiations and a twenty-five days siege, on January 14, 1843, Baghdad troops entered the town. Many were slain and Karbala was pillaged in the ensuing battle, which no doubt included the participation of Iranians. Ottoman sources claim that the number of the dead was between three thousand and thirty-five hundred. Tehran's efforts to hide the news were unsuccessful, and the public reacted with outrage to the killing of Shi'is and the desecration of the city of Hussein's shrine during the pilgrimage season. Iran proclaimed itself in favor of declaring war against the Ottomans and the *mujtahids* called for jihad. The ineffective Muhammad Shah ordered troops and cannon readied to march to the frontier, and the Ottomans took countermeasures. The mediating parties expressed their displeasure.[29]

In a letter to his Ottoman counterpart, Hajji Mirza Aqasi invoked the discourse of Islamic brotherhood to charge that the governor's campaign was against religion and state and, most importantly, disrespectful of the *ahl al-Bayt*, the household of the Prophet. Aqasi asked for punishment of the culprits and execution of the murderers. Stressing the religious motive behind the massacres, he wrote that Iranians, like foreigners, should not be bound by Hanafi law and should freely perform their Ja'fari rites, just as Sunnis followed their own rites in Iran. He further emphasized the age-old Iranian demand for respect for and protection of Iranian merchants and pilgrims and expressed his regret that such matters required the interven-tion of the Great Powers.[30]

The Karbala incident so stressed Ottoman-Iranian relations that one commissioner thought "the moment has arrived when the prompt inter-ference of the mediating powers can alone prevent a war."[31] Only the

---

[28] Curzon, *Armenia*, 32–33. Moojan Momen and Juan Cole suggest that about five thousand people were killed in Karbala's brutal reconquest. "Mafia, Mob and Shiism in Iraq: The Rebellion of Ottoman Karbala 1824–1843," *Past and Present* 112 (August, 1986): 112–43. For the rise of Shi'i power in southern Iraq and the Ottoman-Iranian rivalry, see Yitzak Nakash, *The Shi'is of Iraq* (Princeton, NJ: Princeton University Press, 1994).

[29] Aykun, "Erzurum," 77–86; Adamiyat, *Amir Kabir*, 76.

[30] Salehi, *Erzetelrum*, 15–17.

[31] Williams to Canning, Erzurum, March 11, 1844, *Schofield I*, 245. In February 1844, Mohammad Shah warned his brother Bahman Mirza, the governor of Azerbaijan, to prepare for possible confrontation. "Mohammad Shah to Bahman Mirza," in Salehi, *Erzetelrum*, 72.

intense mediation of the British and Russians, who suggested that the problem be discussed outside of the Erzurum Conferences, saved the meetings and prevented war. As a result of their pressure, Istanbul sent Hajji Mirza Aqasi a letter maintaining that Tehran had received exaggerated reports and assuring him that Namık Pasha had been sent, with Russian and British representatives, to Karbala to investigate. Insisting that the campaign was not directed against Iranians, and promising to compensate losses, repair damaged holy places, and protect Iranian pilgrims and subjects, Istanbul emphasized its sadness and informed Tehran that it desired friendship.[32] Encouraged by the mediating powers, the Porte also suggested that a treaty should be concluded whose articles would appoint a commission to settle disputed sections of the frontier, provide for the mutual restoration and future regulation of the frontier tribes of Kurdistan, and address ongoing issues regarding commerce, tariffs, and the location of the Qajar princes. Tehran accepted these articles, while again insisting that it not be included within the framework of the Balta Liman Treaty.[33]

THERE WAS A TREATY OF 1639, BUT WHERE IS IT?

These steps brought the parties back to the negotiating table, and the negotiating parties set about supporting their territorial claims with documentary or *viva voce* evidence. To prove their rightful ownership of a certain district, both parties resorted to arguments based on historical precedent. These were difficult to prove, especially in light of the problem posed by the original treaty. Referred to as the Sultan Murad IV–Shah Safi Treaty, the Qasr-i Shirin/Kasrı Şirin Treaty, the Zohab/Zehav Treaty, or the 1639 Treaty, it supposedly defined the limits of the lands of the shah and the sultan, but neither party was able to produce the original document.

Blaming internal problems for the loss of its original copy, Ottoman negotiators provided two secondary versions, recorded in the *Târih-i Naîmâ* by Mustafa Naîmâ (1655–1716) and *Gülşen-i Maarif* by Mehmed Said Fera'i-zizâde (d. 1835).[34] This evidence provoked a critique

---

[32] Aykun, "Erzurum," 89–90.

[33] "Detailed Statement by Sir S. Canning on all points pertaining to the Turco-Persian negotiations," *Schofield I*, 306–44.

[34] PRO.FO 78/2711, Minutes of the 7th Conference of Erzurum, 1843. The Ottoman commission also presented copies of Reisü'l-küttab Sarı Abdullah Efendi's *Düsturu'l-İnşa* (1643); see Aykun, "Erzurum," 117–18.

of historiography from Mirza Taqi, who alleged that such chronicles were written to curry favors and hence were inherently unreliable.[35] The Iranians, in turn, attributed their loss of the original treaty to the upheavals of the mid-eighteenth century and presented Sultan Murad's letter confirming the treaty.[36] Despite questioning the reliability of historical texts, however, Mirza Taqi built his own argument on extracts from Katib Chelebi's *Cihannümâ*,[37] the Ottoman geographical work *Mukhtasar'ul mübin*,[38] and Muhammad Yusuf Vallah (Valih) Isfahani's pre-Safavid chronicle *Khuld-i Barin*. Not surprisingly, Enveri Efendi imitated his counterpart by rejecting history books as valid proof. Criticizing Chelebi's prose in *Cihannümâ* as messy and imprecise, he also argued that as a book of geography, it was not a rigorous historical source.[39] Mirza Taqi, however, insisted on presenting it, along with accompanying maps, to highlight its claim that the Ottoman districts of Ahiska, Kars, Van, Shahrizor, Baghdad, and Basra belonged to Iran. He stressed that because Chelebi's account was published in Turkish and bore the stamp of the sultan's censor, it should be accepted as convincing evidence.

Faced with divergent versions of the original treaty (including yet another one procured by Canning from the library of the Vienna Museum) and various historical accounts (including the famous Kurdish history *Sharafnama*), the conference became a critical historical documents and chronicles reading session. The commissioners compared accounts whose language was vague enough and different enough to justify their time-consuming labors. Yet some arguments were advanced for bargaining purposes and therefore judged by the British representatives as unworthy of serious consideration. This was certainly the case with Iranian claims to Suleimanieh, or Baban province. As the previous chapter showed, ownership of this region was a long-standing point of contention between Istanbul and Tehran, and the debates over it exemplified the process by which ambiguous suzerainty would come to be replaced by territorial sovereignty. Maintaining that they had appointed

---

[35] Aykun, "Erzurum," 118. Mirza Taqi also refused *Gülşen-i Maarif* because it contained only the reply to Shah Safi and not the original *ahidname* he sent to Istanbul.

[36] Mirza Ja'far Khan, *Risalah-i Tahqiqat-i Sarhadiyyah*, ed. Muhammad Mushiri (Tehran: Bunyad-i Farhang-i Iran, 1348/1969) 64.

[37] Aykun, "Erzurum," 148.

[38] Enveri Efendi maintained that if Iran based its claims on *Mukhtasar*, it should recognize that this text shows the district of Ushnu, under Iranian authority at the time, as Ottoman and so return it. Adamiyat, *Amir Kabir*, 92.

[39] BOA.I.MSM 40/1081, 05 Ra 1260/March 25, 1844.

the Baban governors from the time of Karim Khan Zand to that of 'Abbas Mirza, the Iranians insisted that the province was historically theirs and should be returned to them. However, following the shah's instructions, Mirza Taqi offered a compromise: Iran would renounce its right to Suleimanieh in exchange for the right to jointly appoint the Baban governor and an annual payment of thirty thousand tomans for the use of Baban summer grounds on the Iranian side. In response, Enveri Efendi declared that all of the Baban governors had the title of pasha, not khan, and were appointed by Istanbul. He also reminded the mediating commissioners of Iranian complaints to Istanbul regarding pashas supposedly appointed by them. Mirza Taqi continued to insist that Suleimanieh (and, as a result, Kurdistan) was historically and actually Iranian.[40] Echoing the Persian irredentism still prevalent in certain nationalist circles, he further argued that Memalik-i 'Ajam, with Iraq-i 'Arab at its heart, extended from Amu Darya to Shatt al-Arab, and that the Ottomans had exploited periods of instability to occupy Iranian lands.[41] In addition to his somewhat extravagant arguments regarding Suleimanieh, Mirza Taqi asserted Iranian rights to the Ottoman-held districts of Hakkari, Mahmudi, Bayezid, Kazlıgöl, and Khanaqin, as well as Muhammarah, Shatt al-Arab, and all of Khuzistan.[42] To counterbalance such demands, Enveri Efendi claimed the Iranian-held districts and castles of Heftedar, Dairna, Chahrik, Somai, Akhurek, Serdesht, Baitush, Maku, and Bradost, together with 322 villages. Despite this proliferation, all discussions soon came to be dominated by Muhammarah/Shatt al-Arab, Zohab, and Posht-e Kuh, with the Kotur and Chahrik regions described in Chapter 1 a distant second.

In Zohab, the Iranian town of Kerrind and Ottoman town of Khanaqin, located on opposite sides of the region, were the most important points of entry from Iran to the Ottoman Empire. Almost all Iranian pilgrims to Hijaz and the holy Shi'i shrines of Iraq, most caravans carrying the corpses of the Iranian Shi'i faithful to be buried in the precincts of those shrines, and much

---

[40] PRO.FO 78/2711, Minutes of the 4th, 5th, 6th, and 10th Conferences. Also, Canning to Lord Aberdeen, Istanbul, August 31, 1844, *Schofield I*, 378.

[41] Aykun, "Erzurum," 105–12.

[42] Afshar, *Amir Kabir*, 92. Ridiculing Iranian claims to Baghdad, Van, and Shahrizor (BOA. HR.SYS 719/1, 68), Enveri Efendi underscored that Kars and Bayezid, occupied by Russia during the 1828–29 war, were returned to the sultan, not the shah. Aykun, "Erzurum," 105–12. For Iranian counterclaims, see "Hajji Mirza Aqasi to Mirza Taqi," January 26, 1844, in Salehi, *Erzetelrum*, 66–68. For Iranian claims to Hakkari and Mahmudi, see Mirza Ja'far Khan, *Tahqiqat*, 177.

FIGURE 2. The town of Qasr-i Shirin.
Reproduced from G. E. Hubbard, *From the Gulf to Ararat* (Edinburgh and London: William Blackwood and Sons, 1916), 160.

interstate trade passed through these towns.[43] More strategically important, from a military point of view, was the Pass of Zagros, Taq-i Girra, or Kerrind, as it was variously called, known as the door leading to the heart of Persia.[44] Meanwhile, the town of Muhammarah offered little to the Ottomans in terms of territory or revenue, but its ownership ensured complete control over the navigation of the Shatt al-Arab River and likely would enable interference with that of the River Karun and the ability to place restrictions on commerce in adjacent Iranian provinces.[45] The situations in Zohab and Muhammarah were helpfully summarized by Canning: "The

---

[43] This information is based on Mehmed Hurşîd, *Seyâhatnâme-i Hudud* (Transcription Alaatttin Eser (Istanbul: Simurg, 1997), hereafter Hurşîd, *Seyâhatnâme*; and on statistics from the Ottoman Empire's sanitary administration. *Administration Sanitaire de L'Empire Ottoman: Bilans et Statistiques* 1.1 (Mars 1872–29 Février 1884) and 2.1 (Mars 1899–29 Février 1904), (Constantinople: Typographie et Lithographie Centrales).

[44] Y. I. Tchirikof [Russian Survey Commissioner, 1848–52], *Traveling Diary of Yegor Ivanovich Tchirkovff*, 16. Hereafter Tchirikof, *Diary*. British Library, IOR-L/P/S 11/29 and also PRO.FO 881/10116.

[45] "Detailed Statement by Sir S. Canning," *Schofield* I, 338.

interests involved in the territorial claims apart from those of domain and tribute, were with respect to Muhammarah: freedom of navigation and right of toll, with respect to Zohab, the possession of the pass of Kirrind and of the capital of the district [Kirrind]."[46]

When considering these matters, the mediating powers concluded that free access to the Karun River from the Persian Gulf was essential to Iran, and the possession of the Pass of Kerrind was crucial as a defensive position to the Ottoman Empire. They thus suggested giving uninterrupted navigation of the Karun to Iran and that of the Euphrates to the Ottoman Empire, whose only sacrifice would be the insignificant town of Muhammarah.[47] British diplomats opined that the possession of the western side of the Pass of Kerrind, which depended on the occupation of Zohab, would confer no additional political advantage on Iran, other than that of carrying out hostile operations in the plains of the Ottoman Empire.[48] Hence, they suggested the western side of the pass be accorded to Istanbul and the eastern to Iran.

GEOPOLITICS AND BOUNDARY MAKING: THE CASE OF ZOHAB/QASR-I SHIRIN

Composed of districts, farmlands, rich pastures, and barren lands, the *mamlakat* of Zohab was bounded in the north by the Shemiran plains and in the south by the town of Mendeli and was drained by the Sirwan (Diyala), Kuretu, and Holwan (Elvend) Rivers.[49] It lay to the west, or on the Ottoman side, of the great chain of mountains that formed the boundary between Iran and the Ottoman Empire at their northeastern point of contact. However, the mountains suddenly ceased to form a natural boundary near Zohab, making its physical division problematic.[50]

At the time of the 1639 Treaty – which never mentions Zohab by name, but rather refers to it as where the districts of Darneh and Dartang divide at Sermil – the region was under the authority of the Shi'i Kalhor Kurds. When Murad IV (r.1623–40) defeated the Iranians in 1639, he made

---

[46] Ibid.
[47] Ibid.
[48] Ibid.
[49] Kaiyan Homi Kaikobad, *The Shatt-al-Arab Boundary Question: A Legal Reappraisal* (Oxford, UK: Oxford University Press, 1988), 41. For a detailed geography of Zohab district, see ibid., 41–51; and Mirza Ja'far, *Tahqiqat*, 104–15.
[50] "Detailed Report by Sir S. Canning..." *Schofield I*, 321.

Zohab a *pashalık* and awarded it to the Sunni Kurdish family of Bajlan (Bajilan/Bajalan), in recognition of services rendered in the capture of Baghdad. In 1700, with the help of the government of Kermanshah, a group of Kalhor (who, according to Rawlinson, had renamed themselves Guran) drove the Bajlan out of Darneh. Confined to the plains, the Bajlan founded the town of Zohab. To further weaken them, Nadir Shah removed most of tribespeople to Khorremabad. Still, some remained, professed allegiance to the sultan, retained the title Derneh Begi, and

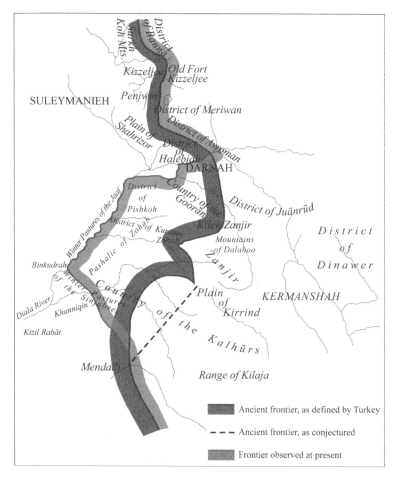

M A P 4. Ancient and Modern Frontiers of Suleymanieh
PRO.FO 881/2600, Sketch map to illustrate the ancient and modern frontiers of Zohab and Suleymanieh.

engaged in constant hostilities with the Guran.[51] Just before the 1821–22 war, Muhammad ʿAli Mirza occupied the land and, according to the *Gazetteer of Iran*, ruined it.[52] Even though the treaty of 1823 stipulated that Iran would return all occupied territory, Zohab was never restored to the Ottoman Empire and tribal, sectarian, and imperial rivalries continued to make it a contentious frontier zone.

Nevertheless, if one believes the British traveler James Silk Buckhingham, in 1830, the town of Zohab, home to a Sunni population of approximately one thousand households, was the seat of the Kurdish Pasha of Bajlan, Fettah Pasha, and a tributary of Baghdad. Still, Buckhingham notes, "properly speaking" it defied all masters and belonged to neither Persia nor Turkey.[53] Silk also observes that the pasha's lands came to an end after passing through the small village of Serpol, also known as Serpolc Zohab, ascending the Zagros Mountains, and crossing the narrow pass known as Tak-i Girra. Only here, he argued, would the traveler enter Iran. Even though the inhabitants of each side of the Zagros were Kurds, those on the west were "subject to the Pasha of Zohaub, who is tributary to Baghdad; and those on the east to the Shah Zadé of Kermanshah himself, without the intervention of a Pasha of their own."[54] In 1850, a local elder maintained that "in the course of thirty years he had seen Zohab plundered twenty-two times, by Mehmet Ali Mirza, by the Vali of Senne, by the Turks, by Djaffs, by Kelhurr, &c."[55] It was within this complex historical context that the parties at Erzurum attempted Zohab's division.[56] At the time, it was under Iranian authority and the governor of Kermanshah was renting the pastures of Sahra-i Zohab, or the Plain of Zohab, to the Kurdish Guran tribe, which spent its summers in the Delehu Mountains.[57] Locals reported that the

---

[51] Dervish Pasha claims the Bajlans left Zohab because of Karim Khan Zand's campaigns. *Tahdid-i Hudud-u İraniye* (Istanbul: Matbaa-i Amire, 1326 (1910), 29. Also, Memoranda by Major Rawlinson on 1639 Treaty, *Schofield I*, 362–70.

[52] Memoranda by Major Rawlinson on 1639 Treaty, *Schofield* I, 368; Ludwig Adamec, *Historical Gazetteer of Iran*, vol. 1 (Graz: Akademische Druck-u. Verlagsanstalt, 1976–89), 712–13.

[53] J. Silk Buckingham, *Travels in Assyria, Media, and Persia*, vol. 1 (London: Colburn & Bentley, 1830), 46–49.

[54] Ibid., 62. In other accounts, Sermil (the frontier pillar) is noted as the former boundary mark. For example, see Tchirikof, *Diary*, 341.

[55] Tchirikof, *Diary*, 68.

[56] For some time, Mirza Taqi refused to discuss Zohab because it was not included in his instructions. IMoFA claimed this was because it was not a disputed district for Iran. "IMoFA to Mirza Taqi" December 17, 1843, Salehi, *Erzetelrum*, 53–5.

[57] Tchirikof, *Diary*, 19, 57; and James Felix Jones, *Memoirs of Baghdad, Kurdistan and Turkish Arabia* (Selections from the Records of the Bombay Government, No. XLIII, New

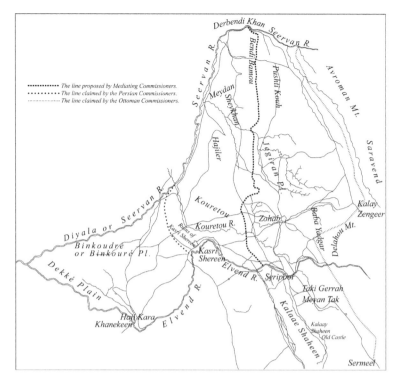

MAP 5. The Province of Zohab
Adapated from PRO.FO 881/2585/002, Sketch Map of the Province of Zohab.

Ottomans had previously sold Dartang to the Gurans, and the Kale-i Shahi, or King's Fort (sometimes called the Shahin or Hawk's Fort) to the Kalhor.[58]

Operating under the assumption that the status quo would be preserved, the Erzurum congress had decided that lands under the authority of one party (*uti possidetis*) should remain so until a final solution was found, which left Zohab with Iran. To find a permanent solution, the congress asked the parties to provide proof of ownership to the districts they claimed. From August to November 1843, the Ottoman commissioner supplied documents to prove Istanbul's territorial right to Zohab and Muhamamarah. These included "letters Patent issued by Sultan

Series, Bombay: 1857; reprint, Buckinghamshire, UK: Archive Editions, 1998), 164. For Guran, see Vladimir Minorksy, "The Tribes of Western Iran," *The Journal of Royal Anthropological Institute of Great Britain and Ireland* 75.1/2 (1945): 73–80; also "The Guran," in *Bulletin of the School of Oriental and African Studies* 11.1 (1943): 73–103.
[58] Tchirikof, *Diary*, 53.

Ahmed III granting tithings of Dairna, Dairtenk, and Shaikhan in Zohab, 1710"; a document "confirming grant of tithings" to the Bajlan and another addressed to a Kurdish chieftain named Suleiman; and extracts from the geographical memoir of John Macdonald Kinneir, which identified the pass of Kerrind as the boundary and Zohab as an Ottoman territory.[59] Enveri Efendi further argued that Muhammad 'Ali Mirza, the governor of Kermanshah, in contravention of existing treaties, occupied Zohab after Fath 'Ali Shah had returned it to the Ottomans. However, as Mirza Taqi rightfully pointed out, the provided documents corresponded to a temporary possession during an unstable period in Iranian history. Thus, the mediators did not accept them as proof of the Porte's claims; they did, however, ask the Iranian plenipotentiary to deliver similar ancient proofs. He declined, instead stressing his sovereign's right of possession based on the fact that from the most remote period Zohab had belonged to Iran. Hiding behind the ambiguity of the 1823 treaty, which stipulated the return of occupied territories without specifying names, he concluded that that document would have provided for Zohab's surrender had the district really belonged to the Ottoman Empire.[60] Thus, both plenipotentiaries adamantly argued that Zohab was an inalienable part of their respective sovereign's domain.[61]

Consequently, the commission revisited the existing copies of the original treaty. Yet, as Schofield maintains, "as the allocation of territory was concerned, the 1639 instrument could do no more than identify a wide strip of land in which the authority of both Sultan and Shah was weak and disputed."[62] Additionally, some of the smaller settlements mentioned in the old document were not inhabited at the time of the conferences, whereas others had names that existed on both sides of the frontier or might refer to distinct places. Among the areas described, Baghdad, Jessana (Jassan), Badra, and Mendeljeen (Mendeli) were Ottoman possessions at the time of the conferences, whereas Darneh and Dartang, which made up most of Zohab, were Iran's. Further complicating matters was the emergence of new settlements, such as Shelir and Nakhvan in Zohab, the

---

[59] For the text of Sultan Ahmed III's letter patents, see PRO.FO 78/2711; also *Schofield I*, 111–14. John MacDonald Kinneir, *A Geographical Memoir of Persian Empire* (London: John Murray, 1813), 140–41, 302. The Ottoman commission carefully reproduced these quotes and their translations for the conference. BOA.I.MSM 40/1094, 7.

[60] BOA.HR.SYS 719/1, 68. Also Harari, *Turco-Persian*, 72; Curzon and Williams to Sheil, Erzurum, August 13, 1843, *Schofield, I*, 115.

[61] For Enveri's arguments, see BOA.I.MSM 40/1081, 10; and Aykun, "Erzurum," 143–50.

[62] Introduction, *Schofield I*, xvi.

dispersal of tribes such as the Bajlan, and the disappearance of some branches of the Jaff specified in the treaty.[63]

Examining available versions of the 1639 document, the conferees at Erzurum, like the survey commissioners that followed them, tried to locate the places it listed to fix the boundary according to the foundational text. However, the disparity between the *hudud-u kadime*, or old border, and the *hudud-u haliye*, or present one, proved difficult to reconcile. This difficulty was further compounded by Tehran's and Istanbul's clashing ambitions and the borderlanders' sectarian affiliations. Two centuries of intermittent conflict and competition, modifications to the balance of power, migrations, conversions, environmental changes, diseases, and other factors had indelibly altered the world of the borderland and its imaginable or imagined limits.

When textual evidence fell short, the congress frequently turned to the geography itself, that is, to the idea of natural frontiers based on geopolitical and strategic concerns related to offensive and defensive strategies, such as mountain passes that would permit or halt trade and military expeditions. Rawlinson, for example, suggested that were Zohab to remain in Iran's possession, the most natural frontier line would be the course of the Holwan and Diyala Rivers to their point of confluence. However, he worried that "this further concession ... would involve a serious forfeiture of the Ottoman rights, as the lands enclosed between the two streams are exceedingly productive, and are thickly studded with villages dependent upon Khanikin."[64] Sharing Rawlinson's concerns regarding the Porte's right to the land, Canning suggested that the natural features of the country might allow the eastern part of the district, Dairna/Derna, to go to Iran, and the western slope of the Pass of Kerrind and all the low country to the west of the mountains could be ceded to the Ottomans.[65] Supporting Canning's argument, Layard wrote the following:

By this division – of frequent occurrence in territorial demarcation – the pass would be divided between the two Powers, and whilst the means of unexpected aggression are taken from one party, the means of just defense are conferred upon both. This would appear the most reasonable and equitable mode of determining a frontier,

---

[63] PRO.FO 78/2712, Foreign Office Memorandum, May 12, 1845; and Mirza Ja'far, *Tahqiqat*, 126. As Iraj Afshar maintains, the district was actually divided between both states. The confusion arose because both parties claimed its entirety. Adamiyat, *Amir Kabir*, 88.

[64] "Memorandum by Major Rawlinson on Perso-Turkish Frontier as Defined in the Treaty of 1639, between Sultan Murad IV and Shah Sefi," in *Schofield I*, 367.

[65] Sheil to Lord Aberdeen, July 12, 1844, *Schofield I*, 358.

when a mountain chain, with an important pass forming a great military road between the two countries, is claimed by two Powers.[66]

The Russian survey commissioner of 1848–52, Colonel Tchirikof, concurred with his British counterparts: "It is there that all means of defense must be concentrated in the event of an attack from the direction of Baghdad."[67] Such agreement among the mediating parties was perhaps to be expected because, as Sahlins perceptively notes, when military strategists and diplomats look at mountains, they see passages, not barriers, for mountains are not effective barriers unless the passes are held.[68]

In addition to local geography, conferees also consulted local populations in their search for convincing proof of ownership. Thus, when his documentary evidence was challenged, Enveri Efendi called in Osman Pasha (Bajlan), a previous *mutasarrif* of Zohab, to provide *viva voce* evidence.[69] Questioned in the presence of the other commissioners, Osman declared that he had become pasha in 1812, but that the province had been granted to his ancestor Abdal Bey after the 1638 Ottoman occupation of Baghdad and had remained in his family's possession ever since. Maintaining that Nadir Shah and Karim Khan Zand had pillaged the province, he described how Moḥammad ʿAli Mirza Dawlatshah took possession of it and how, between 1811 and 1823, it had changed hands several times, with members of his family instated and reinstated as rulers.[70] When Mirza Taqi suggested that the region's inhabitants belonged to a Shiʿi sect, the Ahl-i Haq, and were thus Iranian, Osman vigorously objected: "I never commanded under the Persians; they hate me because my name is Osman. Zohab contains 300 villages and 6,000 families, all of them Sunnis; the boundaries were settled by Sultan Murad."[71] Despite Osman's knowledge of the area, the portion of testimony emphasizing the sectarian divide was received with caution because it came from a "refugee" who had been appointed to a one-year term as governor and who,

---

[66] "Memorandum by Mr. Layard respecting the Mode of Settlement of the Turco-Persian Frontier Question proposed by Sir Stratford Canning, with special reference to Colonel Sheil's observations thereon" (August 1844), *Schofield I*, 379–82.

[67] Tchirikov, *Diary*, 16.

[68] Peter Sahlins, *Boundaries: The Making of France and Spain in the Pyrenees* (Berkeley: University of California Press, 1989), 42.

[69] Curzon, *Armenia*, 80; BOA Cevdet HR 5609, 8 C 1260/June 25, 1844.

[70] See "Zehav Sancağı Esbak Mutasarrıfı Saadetlü Osman Paşanın Takriridir," BOA.HR. SYS 719/1, 50; and Aykun, "Erzurum," 150–52. See also Enveri Efendi's minutes for the 14th conference, January 23, 1844; BOA.I.MSM 40/1081, 10.

[71] PRO.FO 78/2711, Curzon and Williams to Canning, Enclosure No.4, Erzurum, August 11, 1843.

under Ottoman protection, was seeking to reestablish himself. Still, Iranian Prime Minister Mirza Aqasi chastised Mirza Taqi for approving the pasha's appearance before the commission.

Although, as this case shows, the ethnic identities and especially religious affiliations of the borderland communities were considered, they were not emphasized in the meetings. The tendency was to leave Shiʻi tribes with Iran and Sunni tribes with the Ottoman Empire wherever possible. Hence, it was not Lek or Kalhor's Kurdishness, but their Shiʻi affiliation that mattered. In his sketch of the Zohab region and its inhabitants, which he based on local accounts, Williams noted that parts of each tribe had been previously subject to each empire, with the Kalhors moving from the Somar, Ghilan, and Mendeli regions to Zohab at the time of Nadir Shah, and the Leks leaving for the Iranian side when troops were sent to make them pay taxes. Yet, at the time of the conferences, only a few Kalhor were under Ottoman sovereignty. Meanwhile, upward of three thousand Lek families resided in villages around Kirkuk, an Ottoman province, and some Lek subdivisions were found in Zohab and great numbers in Iran. Most striking, and a testimony to how borders form identities, was Williams's observation that the "part of each tribe that remains in Turkey speaks Turkish Kurdish [sic], dresses like them, and are Sunnis, and those in Persia quite the contrary."[72] Information gathered from local sources in the following decade by the Ottoman survey commissioner Dervish Pasha corroborates these reflections.[73]

Further underscoring the preeminent importance of religious identity is Rawlinson's "Observations on the proposed transfer of Zohab [to the Ottoman Empire]." In this document, the British diplomat best acquainted with the region openly supports the Porte's rights to it but concludes that because of the religious affiliation of the majority of its inhabitants, it should be left to Iran. Whereas the once-dominant Sunni Bajlan were now sparsely scattered over the area, every year at the approach of winter some six or seven thousand Kalhor and Lek families would descend from the Iranian mountains and assert their control. These nomads, Rawlinson thought, would not respect agricultural settlers sent by Istanbul the way they respected cultivation by Iranian subjects. The only way to establish Ottoman control would be to summarily abrogate the Kalhors' and Leks'

---

[72] PRO.FO 78/2711, Williams to Sheil, October 25, 1843. In 1844, James Felix Jones gave the number of Kalhor as 7,000 families. See his *Memoirs of Baghdad*, 194; Mary Leona Sheil estimates 11,500 families in 1849. See her *Glimpses of Life and Manners in Persia* (London: John Murray, 1856), 401.

[73] Dervish, *Tahdid*, 35–36.

right of pasturage and establish an Ottoman force in the region. As this would be difficult and costly, he suggested the Ottomans abandon their rights to Zohab in exchange for the tranquility of their border and good neighborly relations.[74] The Porte did not accept Rawlinson's advice, however, and the question of Zohab continued to haunt negotiations for a long time.

SHATT AL-ARAB, MUHAMMARAH, AND THE KAʿB TRIBE

Even Zohab, however, was not Erzurum's most contentious issue. That dubious honor belongs to Shatt al-Arab, a conflict-prone region that has been the subject of many studies.[75] Under debate at the conference table was the right to control the waterway known as Shatt al-Arab, as well as ownership of the city of Muhammarah and the Island of Khizr. Today, Muhammarah is the sizeable Iranian city of Khorramshahr, and the Island of Khizr (Abadan) and anchorage of Muhammarah firmly belong to Iran. Still, after seventeen treaties, the Shatt al-Arab question remains relatively unresolved. In the last quarter of the twentieth century, it figured significantly in two international crises, both informed by larger unresolved issues of the Ottoman-Iranian border. The first was when Saddam Hussein accepted the conditions regarding the Shatt al-Arab laid out by the shah of Iran in the Algiers Treaty of 1975, in return for the shah halting his cross-border support of the Kurdish rebellion in the northern part of the Ottoman-Iranian frontier. The second occurred when the Shatt al-Arab became an apparent cause of the Iran-Iraq War of 1980–88, which left hundreds of thousands of people dead and destroyed many of the border towns, including Abadan and Khorramshahr. Shortly after abrogating (and publicly tearing apart) the Algiers Treaty, and before launching a full-scale invasion of Iran, Saddam Hussein vowed, "This Shatt shall again be, as it has been throughout history, Iraqi and Arab in name and reality."[76] His absolute claim to this territory stands irreconcilably alongside those made by Iran and the Ottoman Empire. The following discussion challenges all of these nationalist narratives by providing an account of

---

[74] "Observations by Major Rawlinson on the proposed transfer of Zohab" (possibly November 1844), in *Schofield*, I, 411–14.

[75] Among many studies on the Shatt, see Richard N. Schofield's works, especially *Evolution of the Shatt al-'Arab Boundary Dispute* (Cambridgeshire, UK: Middle East & North African Studies Press, 1986). For legal aspects, see Kaikobad, *The Shatt-al-Arab Boundary Question*.

[76] Swearingen, "Geopolitical Origins of Iran-Iraq War," 408.

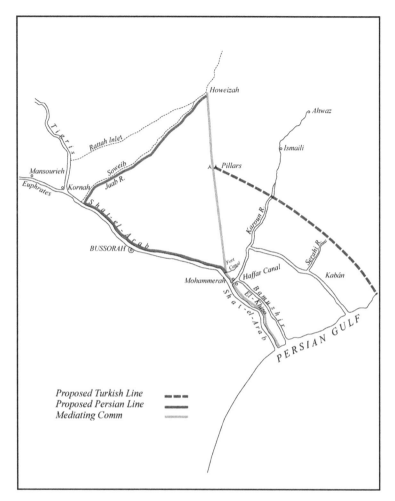

MAP 6. Shatt al-Arab/Muhammarah Region Map
Based on Differing Claims
Adapted from PRO.FO 881/2585, Map of Muhammarah and district prepared
in 1850.

earlier negotiations regarding the Shatt and tracing historical changes in
the human and physical geography of the region, which reveal how the
identities of this land and its people were not fixed but rather evolved in a
dialectical fashion.

The division of the Shatt was difficult because previous treaties made no
specific mention of any frontier point south of Mandali, Badra, Jassan, and

Zarbatya, and the 1639 treaty contained only a general allusion to Basra and its dependencies as the southern limit of the Ottoman Empire.[77] Defending their right to the Shatt, Muhammarah, and the Island of Khizr, the Iranians declared that if the region had belonged to the Ottomans, Murad IV would have claimed it in his letter confirming the 1639 treaty. Ipso facto, Istanbul did not own land east of the Shatt.[78] Istanbul, naturally, begged to differ.

A waterway stretching 120 kilometers, Shatt al-Arab literally means "the shore of the Arabs" and is formed by the waters of the Tigris and Euphrates after they meet at al-Qurnah. At its southern extremity, the Shatt incorporates the waters of the Karun, the longest river in Iran, which made it difficult to define it as an exclusively Ottoman body of water. Along the Shatt's course – which runs from the K/Gurmet Ali confluence to the mouth of the estuary at Fao on the Persian Gulf and discharges into the gulf's lakes and wetlands – are located the important ports of Basra and Muhammarah.[79] Geographical changes further complicated the division of the Shatt and its delta. These included the redirection of some rivers, notably the Karun, whose waters join those of the Tigris and Euphrates below Muhammarah through the Haffar Canal. However, the Karun also flows to the gulf through another branch called the Bamishere (or Bahmanshir). In the triangle formed by the Haffar and Bamishere Canals and the Shatt was the Island of Khizr, today Abadan, an important Iranian port city established in the early twentieth century. Layard summarized the history and debates surrounding the Shatt al-Arab as follows:

A canal had been cut to unite this river and the Shat al-Arab, known as Hafar … and upon its banks Mohammarah had been built by the Sheykh of the Ca'ab Arabs. In the course of time the waters of the Karun had enlarged the canal, and through it the main body of the river was directed into the Shat al-Arab; consequently Persia now claimed the left bank of Shat al-Arab below the Hafar, with the town and district of Mohammarah as Persian territory. The original mouth of Karun the Bahmeh-shire was still open and navigable at least to vessels of moderate draught. The Porte contended that as the Tigris and Euphrates were Turkish rivers, running through the dominions of the Sultan from its source, it was unjust, and against universally recognized principles to give Persia control of its outlet into the sea, merely because a Persian stream had changed its course and had invaded a territory

---

[77] *Schofield I*, Introduction, xvi.
[78] Mirza Ja'far, *Tahqiqat*, 64.
[79] S. H. Amin, "The Iran-Iraq Conflict: Legal Implications," *The International Law Quarterly* 31 (Jan. 1982): 169.

which did not belong to the Shah. The command of the trade and navigation of a great river, which had flowed more than one thousand miles through Turkish territory, would thus be transferred to a power which might, if hostile to Turkey, close the river at its mouth.[80]

The Porte also claimed that Iran could, without much trouble, make the Bamishere navigable to vessels of any size and consequently would not need the Shatt al-Arab and added that Iran's frontier had never reached the Euphrates, whereas the entire delta between the mouth of that river and the Bamishere originally belonged to the Ottoman Empire.[81]

Disagreements over the Shatt were not limited to its physical geography. Questions surrounding the migration, survival, religious affiliation, and national belonging of its inhabitants, the Ka'b (also Chaub, Caab, Chaab) tribes exemplify how such factors shape an international boundary and how making frontiers is a process rather than a rupture in time and space. Composed of about nine thousand households in the 1850s, the Ka'b occupied the southern area of the Shatt al-Arab; the Island of Khizr; and the lands between Behbehan, Shuster, and Hawiza (also Hoveyze, Hawizah), with some households also living on the Basra side of the river.[82] Because of their religious affiliation and historical settlement patterns, the majority of the Ka'b preferred Iranian sovereignty. It is not an exaggeration to claim that these two factors secured for Iran the strategically and economically crucial cities of Khorramshahr and Abadan as well as navigational rights over the Shatt. Despite claims by the likes of Saddam, it was in fact the alliance of the region's Arab inhabitants with Iran that secured Abadan and Khorramshahr for the latter.

The Ka'b, however, were migrants to the region. An offshoot of the Banu Khafaja of Arabia (Najd), they arrived between the fifteenth and early seventeenth centuries and had occupied nearly all the deltaic land at the head of the Persian Gulf by the late eighteenth century. In time, they Ka'bisized[83] and "Arabicized all inhabitants of the wetlands and marshes –

[80] Layard, Austen Henry, *Early Adventures in Persian, Susiana, and Babylonia, Including a Residence Among the Bakhityari and Other Wild Tribes Before the Discovery of Nineveh* (London: John Murray, 1887), 434–36.

[81] Ibid.

[82] Mirza Ja'far, *Tahqiqat*, 58.

[83] Mirza Ja'far maintained that some individuals registered as Ka'b were from the Bavi Arab tribe. *Tahqiqat*, 59. Dervish Pasha claimed that because of their fights with Iranian Arab tribes, Iranians destroyed the Ka'b's Sabilah dam and redirected the Karun to its present course through the Haffar Canal. The dam's destruction forced a Ka'b relocation to Fallahiyeh, which was in *memalik-i 'Ajam*. Dervish, *Tahdid*, 7. Layard suggested that

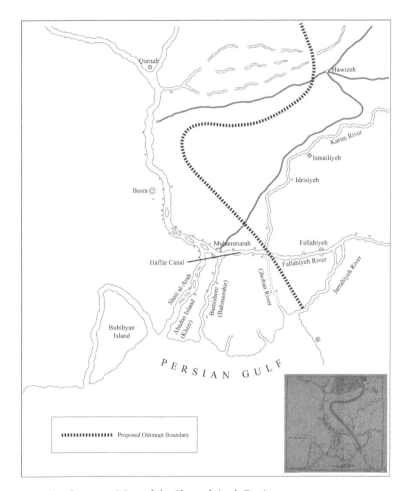

MAP 7. An Ottoman Map of the Shatt al-Arab Region
BOA-IMSM 40/1094, Map of the Shatt al-Arab region showing the proposed Ottoman boundary.

a triangular area between the southern suburbs of Ahwaz and the rivers Zohreh and the Shatt al-Arab."[84] In 1810, after camping on the banks of the Haffar and Karun for six months, Kinneir wrote that "The island, or delta, between the *Shat-ul-Arab* and the Bamishere (the ancient Mesene), was

the Ka'b were originally from Wasi, but the Sheikh of Ka'b told him they emigrated there from Kuwait and the Arabian coast of the Persian Gulf.
[84] John R. Perry, "The Banu Ka'b: An Amphibious Brigand State in Khuzistan," *Le Monde Iranien et L'Islam: Sociétés et Cultures* (Geneve: Libraire Droz, 1971), 135.

formerly included in the *Pashalick* of *Bagdad*" until it was conquered by the Ka'b leader Sheikh Solyman.[85] By the eighteenth century, the area was known as Arabistan and the Ka'b had constructed one of the gulf's largest seagoing fleets. Different accounts indicate that during this period of transition, the Ka'b recognized Ottoman sovereignty, and that it was only after their post-1720 expansion into Khuzistan that the question of their allegiance came to the fore. This was when Nadir Shah (1732–47) "dispatched Muhammad Husayn Qajar to besiege Quban and the Ka'b sued for peace thereby accepting Iranian suzerainty for the first time."[86] The Ka'b reached the zenith of their power under Sheikh Salman, who by the early 1760s controlled most of southeast Khuzistan. With a navy of some eighty boats, they controlled all traffic between Basra and the mouth of the Shatt,[87] conducting their "piratical fleet into the Gulph."[88] Thanks to a favorable location and the activities of this fleet, the economy on both sides of the Shatt flourished, and Ka'b rulers were able to incorporate the Persian lands along the Karun as well as the nominally Ottoman districts of Muhammarah, Haffar, and Tamar, while retaining a degree of autonomy from both the Ottomans and the Iranians.[89] After many failed attempts by Iranian, Ottoman, and East India Company authorities to stop the Ka'b threat to trade routes, the Ottoman military joined forces with the British East India Company to defeat the energetic Salman in 1765, at which time Salman moved his seat of government to Fallahiyeh, in the Persian province of Fars.[90] This move might have been facilitated by the Ka'b conversion to Shi'ism, which would play a crucial role in their preference for Iran.[91] That conversion coincided with the rise of the *mamluks* in Baghdad, whose neglect of southern Iraq and the concurrent weakening of the Ottoman fleet in the Persian Gulf also strengthened Iran's hold. It was only after driving

---

[85] Kinneir, *Geographical*, 294.

[86] Ibid., and Mirza Ja'far, *Tahqiqat*, 58–59.

[87] Perry, "Banu Ka'b", 134; and Mehrdad R. Izady, "The Gulf's Ethnic Diversity: An Evolutionary History," in Lawrence G. Potter and Gary G. Sick, eds., *Security in the Persian Gulf* (New York: Palgrave, 2002), 63.

[88] Kinneir, *Geographical*, 293.

[89] Schofield, *Evolution of the Shatt*, 23; Mustafa Al-Najjar and Safwat Najdat Fathi, "Arab Sovereignty over the Shatt al-Arab during the Ka'bide Period," in M. S. el–Azhary, ed., *The Iran-Iraq War: An Historical, Economic and Political Analysis* (London: Croom Helm, 1984), 20–37.

[90] Schofield, *Evolution of the Shatt*, 23; and Al-Najjar and Safwat, "Arab Sovereignty," 20–37.

[91] According to Yitzak Nakash, the tribes of the southern marshes converted to Shi'ism in the fifteenth and sixteenth centuries, but most large confederations converted in the nineteenth century. The Ka'b, Nakash suggests, converted in the late eighteenth century. Nakash, "The Conversion of Iraq's Tribes to Shi'ism," *International Journal of Middle East Studies* 26.3 (Aug. 1994): 443–63. See also Mirza Ja'far, *Tahqiqat*, 59.

out the *mamluks* that Istanbul again turned its attention to the gulf. According to the Ka'b leader Sheikh Hajji Jaber, Muhammarah – which was built in the second half of the eighteenth century by the Ka'b, with the help of Turks and Persians fleeing the persecution of frontier authorities – became an important place (and a true frontier town) in the 1820s.[92] Consequently, Baghdad authorities began demanding taxes. When Muhammarah did not comply, Baghdad's governor, 'Ali Rıza Pasha, attacked it in 1839 in the name of the sultan, who, constrained in the west, desired to reestablish control of the increasingly vital Persian Gulf.

Their economic vitality also piqued British interest in the Shatt and the Persian Gulf, which was further intensified by a perceived Russian threat toward India and the resulting desire to demarcate the unstable frontier.[93] Starting with Colonel Chesney's expeditions (1835–37) to prove the navigability of the Tigris and Euphrates, which concluded that Muhammarah should be the center of communications between India and Europe, the East India Company tried to establish a foothold in the region. As Gamazof notes, the scramble over Muhammarah was understandable, for it had many desirable features. These included its anchorage in the deep and broad Haffar Canal; its good weather, safe harbor, and sweet water; the possibility of constructing stores and a wharf, or even a complete port; its strategic command of the Karun and the Shatt and the great rivers forming it; and its proximity to the trade of Baghdad, Basra, and the many local tribes that carried on commerce independently.[94]

Pressured by imperial actors, on the one hand, and struggling to hold on to their relative autonomy, on the other, the Ka'b responded to the question of which empire possessed their land by recognizing dual sovereignties. As the land occupied by Muhammarah originally belonged to an Ottoman subject, they paid a sum in kind to the governor of Basra until 1844, thus recognizing Ottoman territorial rights. At the same time, they paid tribute to Iran for the large swaths of indisputably Iranian lands they inhabited. Yet, according to Rawlinson:

[T]he distinction between the liability for the payment of rent as tenants of the soil, and of a fixed tribute as subjects became gradually lost sight of, and the Chaab,

---

[92] In 1851, the Russian topographer Gamazof wrote: "The inhabitants [of Muhammarah], about 2,000 in number, were rascals of many different races, Arabs, Turks, Persians, Guebers (Parsees), Indians, Sabæns, Negro slaves from Abyssinia, Barbary, Nubia, and coasts of the Persian Gulf. These slaves form more than half of the whole population." Gamazof in Tchirikof, *Diary*, 173.

[93] Adamiyat, *Amir Kabir*, 85–86.

[94] Gamazof in Tchirikof, *Diary*, 177.

residing the most part in the Persian territory, governed by a chief whose capital of Fellahieh was within the well established frontier of the province of Fars, and subject almost yearly to demands for revenue from the Persian crown, came to be regarded as Turkish colonists who emigrated to the Persian territory, and by a continued residence of many years had naturalized themselves as Persian subjects.[95]

According to local lore, when they first began to settle the lands beyond Muhammarah, the Ka'b offered annual gifts to the chiefs of the Iranian Afshar tribe; later, they instead gave gifts to the *wali* of Hawiza. After establishing themselves and increasing their power, they bypassed the weakened *wali* in favor of the Iranian governors of Fars and Shiraz.[96] This, however, was only one side of the coin, for they also paid tribute (*kalemiye* or *miri kalemiye*) to the Ottoman governors of Basra.[97]

Despite such payments, whose purpose was to evade state intervention and occasional military campaigns such as that of 1837, the remoteness to Anatolia and Syria and the inaccessibility of the eastern Tigris-Euphrates marshlands made the subjugation of Ka'b lands by Ottoman authorities nearly impossible. The same conditions also protected them from intrusive Iranian interference, while acceptance of the suzerainty of Iran's rulers further ensured independence from Ottoman interference. Yet acceptance of suzerainty did not necessarily mean recognition of sovereignty, and the multiple claims of suzerainty over them, which continued through the second half of the nineteenth century, gave them even more room to maneuver. With the process of demarcation, however, the end of this period was approaching.

When the commissioners began discussing Muhammarah, Mirza Taqi declared that the town had historically been part of Khuzistan and demanded £1 million in compensation for 'Ali Rıza Pasha's 1837 attack. He argued that the governor had killed many, carried away significant wealth, and sold women and children in Baghdad's slave markets.[98] Thus, while the Ottomans focused on the question of who rightfully possessed Muhammarah and its environs, the Iranians not only claimed such possession outright, but also forcefully raised the issue of compensation for the town's destruction. Faced with such conflicting approaches, the mediating

[95] "Memorandum by Major Rawlinson, British Consul, Baghdad on the Subject of Muhammara and the Chaab tribe", January 6, 1844, *Schofield, I*, 281–303. Dervish Pasha claims that the *pishkesh* (gifts) the Ka'b gave the Iranians became regular over time, giving the impression they were Iranian subjects. Dervish, *Tahdid*, 8–9.

[96] Henry A. Layard, "A Description of the Province of Khuzistan," *JRGS* 16 (1846), 41–43.

[97] Kaikobad, *The Shatt-al-Arab Boundary Question*, 10.

[98] Enveri Efendi rejected those claims. Enveri Efendi's minutes of the seventh conference, 7 December 1843, BOA.I.MSM 40/1081, 5; and Aykun, "Erzurum," 120.

commissioners concluded that the Ka'b's professed religious affiliation could not be taken as conclusive proof in favor of Iran, and the negotiating parties were asked to provide documentary and *viva voce* evidence. The Ottomans submitted old deeds, court rolls, and treaties dated between 1627 and 1768, all of which indicated the Karun as the boundary. However, as they were dated no later than 1768, they were considered inconclusive. As it had done in the case of Zohab, the Iranian side declined to present documentation and instead based its claims on its current occupation of the country (*uti possidetis*)and local allegiance.[99] Responding to Iranian complaints regarding Ali Rıza's attack on Muhammarah, Enveri Efendi claimed that the Ka'b had originally been an Ottoman tribe and noted that Iran had disputed no previous punitive campaigns against them. Moreover, he argued that there was little difference between the seasonal migrations of some Ka'b branches into Iranian lands and the similar movements of other indisputably Ottoman tribes, and he even suggested that Iran forced some Ka'b to remain in its territory. Finally, he noted that 'Ali Rıza warned Iranians about his attack out of respect and not in recognition of their sovereignty. In any case, the pasha's supposed punishment of the Ka'b living in Iranian Fallahiyeh could not be considered a transgression because they were originally Ottoman subjects and therefore still under Ottoman sovereignty. And besides, he concluded, as the pasha campaigned "in parts of the eyelet of Basra" that likely belonged to the sultan, his actions were an internal matter, thus negating Iranian claims to compensation.[100]

Such Ottoman arguments were supplemented by information provided to the British commission by its representatives, who were well acquainted with the region. This included material from Colonel Chesney's exploration; General Monteith's rough notes on the frontier;[101] notes from Taylor, the late British consul of Baghdad, who regarded Muhammarah as Ottoman; and observations from A. Malcolm, the chief Armenian merchant of Bushrie, who shared Taylor's view. In light of these opinions, the British commissioner concluded that "the balance of probabilities is immeasurably in favor of Turkey."But to preserve the peace, he suggested that the Porte model its actions after those of London during its boundary dispute with

[99] PRO.FO 78/2711; also *I*, 363.
[100] "Enveri Efendi's Minutes of the Seventh Conference, 7 December 1843 and Eighth Conference of 12 December 1843," in BOA.I.MSM 40/1081, 5.
[101] Colonel (later General) Monteith of the Madras Engineers (1809–47) served in Persia between 1810 and 1829. His journal of northern Iran was published as "Journal of a Tour Through Azerbaijan and the Shores of the Caspian," in *JRGS* 3 (1933): 1–58; it does not provide a map of the Persian Gulf.

America and either compromise or give up part of its territory. Layard, who claimed that Iranians had only occupied Muhammarah in 1840s, also favored the Ottoman claims, basing his opinion on his extensive travels in Luristan and Khuzistan and his study of documents furnished to Canning by the Iranian government.[102]

Such clear British support for Ottoman claims put the Great Powers at loggerheads. The British government suggested the new frontier line be drawn through the desert to the west of Hawizah at some distance from the Shatt al-Arab, across the Hafar, and midway down the delta to the sea. This would leave the Ottomans in the possession of the banks of the Euphrates along its entire course. The Russian government, which supported Iranian claims, responded by increasing Iranian demands and insisting on the ceding of territory on the Shatt's east bank, which had not been previously claimed, almost to the junction of the Euphrates and Tigris at Kornah. This would have given Tehran rights to the chief line connecting Asia Minor to the gulf.[103] Despite Canning's opposition, Lord Aberdeen and consequently London deferred to the Russian view. The Porte was forced to yield. The underlying motivation for the British decision was that the Karun, Tigris, and Euphrates were thought to become "great military and trading highways" in the future, and London preferred to cede their mouth to the weaker power, Iran.[104]

Russians were not alone in their support of Iran. On the question of Muhammarah, Colonel Sheil, unlike his peers, produced strong evidence in Iran's favor.[105] A closer look at this evidence elucidates the terms and conditions by which the boundaries were delimited. According to Sheil, one factor in favor of Iran was that the British government of India recognized the Sheikh of Muhammarah as independent or subject to the Sheikh of the Ka'b. As the Sheikh of Fallahiyeh, whose authority was accepted by the Sheikh of Muhammarah, recognized the shah as sovereign, Muhammarah also belonged to Iran. Moreover, Sheil claimed that since the time of Karim Khan Zand (1752), the Iranian flag had flown at Muhammarah and its vessels were under Iranian dominion.[106] As a final

---

[102] Layard, "Description," 1–105; Layard, *Early*, 434–36.
[103] Layard, *Early*, 438.
[104] Ibid.
[105] Sheil to the British Commissioner at the Conference of Erzurum, Tehran, September 27, 1843, *Schofield*, I, 124.
[106] A. B. Kemball added that this might be a consequence of their *creed*, not an acknowledgment of subjection to Iran. Kemball to HM's Minister at Tehran, August 27, 1843, *Schofield*, I, 124.

proof, Sheil noted that in 1837, while the shah was at Herat, Ottoman troops destroyed Muhammarah: if it had been regarded as an Ottoman dominion, he concluded, the sultan would not have sanctioned its destruction. Referring to maps and Kinneir's book, which showed Muhammarah as Iranian, Sheil also pointed to the rivers, physical entities that have always helped draw natural boundaries:[107] as the Karun was undoubtedly under Iranian authority, he suggested that its tributaries around the Shatt should be so too. Muhammarah's location on the eastern, or Iranian, side of the river, left no doubt for Sheil regarding the town's ownership. As for the written proof produced by the Ottomans, Sheil, like Mirza Taqi, stressed the slippery truth value of historical documents. As the indisputably Iranian city of Tabriz had been under Ottoman rule for eighteen years at the beginning of the seventeenth century, he argued, the Ottomans could have produced ample documents showing it to be an Ottoman possession as well.[108]

Faced with so many conflicting arguments, the commissioners again turned to the local population, procuring oral testimony from the chiefs of tribes who might possess documents that would help settle the problem and who, moreover, would be acquainted with the country's geography and culture. The Ottomans, for example, presented Sheikh Thamir (al Ghazban, of Al-Bu Nasir), a former chief, or *sheikh al-mashaikh*, of the Ka'b who had been deposed by the Iranians and had resided in Basra since his expulsion.[109] Mirza Taqi objected to his testimony – on which Ottomans now based their claims to Muhammarah, Ghoban, and the environ – on the basis that Iran did not recognize him. He relented, however, when the mediating delegates approved Thamir as an informed local who could provide useful information regarding topographical points of reference.[110] Although he steadfastly

---

[107] Whereas the mediating commissioners concluded that Kinneir's map showed the Shatt al-Arab as the boundary, Enveri Efendi opined that Kinneir clearly showed Muhammarah as Ottoman. Aykun, "Erzurum," 195. Noting that the southwestern boundaries of Kuzistan were the Tigris and Shat al-Arab, Kinnier maintained that the Pashalik of Baghdad "extends in a N. W. direction, from the mouth of the Shat-ul-Arab to the rocks of Merdin." *Geographical*, 85, 237.

[108] Sheil to the British Commissioner at the Conference of Erzurum, Tehran, September 27, 1843 and Kemball to HM's Minister at Tehran, August 27, 1843, *Schofield*, I, 124.

[109] The British vessel *Nicotris* brought the sheikh from Basra to Baghdad for his journey to Erzurum. Jones, *Memoirs of Baghdad*, 136, 145.

[110] Mirza Taqi was reprimanded for allowing subjects such as Thamir, Hussein Beg of Zilan, and the people of Hakkari to present petitions. Hajji Mirza Aqasi warned him if he accepted such documents or testimonies again, he would be considered a traitor [khaine dowlete Shahenshah]. For the letters of IMoFA and Hajji, see Salehi, *Erzetelrum*, 62–68.

maintained that his ancestors had been in possession of Ghoban [Dura] for generations, Thamir's testimony reveals how ambivalent some border-landers felt about their allegiance. For example, he described the tribute, a fixed sum, paid by his tribe without respect to the districts it occupied but stated that because both the Ottomans and Iranians claimed the disputed lands, "last year's tribute is in the hands of a banker, but we do not know who to pay it to, as Persia and Turkey both claim the land."[111]

In response to Mirza Taqi's questioning, Thamir stated that the land of Muhammarah had been in the possession of the Ottoman Empire from ancient times (*minel kadim*). Despite its location at the boundary (*sinor*) of Ghoban, it was dependent on Basra *vilayat* and its inhabitants were primarily Ka'b with some *fellah*. He admitted that at the incitement of Karim Khan Zand, a branch of the tribe under Sheikh Suleiman had migrated to the Iranian town of Fallahiyeh but insisted that they too were the sultan's subjects. Thamir also declared that Basra's notables, through imperial *berat*s, owned some of the *muqataa*s (taxfarms) in and around Muhammarah, whereas others were royal lands that passed into Ka'b hands in 1822. He also stated that Baghdad's pasha carried out his punitive expedition because parts of the tribe refused to pay tribute and that Iranians were not present at the time of the attack. Not wholly convinced, the bureaucrats asked him for papers to substantiate his claims. But he declared he had none, adding, "We do not understand such things." This lack of documentation no doubt reflected the lack of government control of the region, as well as the fact that – as a sheikh of the Banu Lam explained to survey commissioners a few years later – the great families of the region considered reading and writing a shameful activity.[112]

Shaped by signs of ambiguity of allegiance and a fragility born of a lifetime of living on contested grounds, the sheikh's testimony confirmed that the Ka'b center of gravity was the larger town of Felahiyeh, which was indisputably Iranian, rather than Muhammarah, which consisted of a few hundred houses.[113] Thamir, like Osman Pasha of Zohab, had been deposed and his family ruined by Iranian machinations. For this reason, the commission found both men's knowledge of topographical points useful but viewed their oral testimonies with some skepticism. Additionally, while Thamir

---

[111] For the text of Thamir's testimony, see BOA.HR.SYS 719/1 p.48; and *Schofield, I*, 108, 119.
[112] Hurşîd, *Seyâhatnâme*, 65.
[113] BOA.HR.SYS, 719/1, 48; and Aykun, "Erzurum," 129–30. Enveri Efendi's minutes of the 8th conference (December 12, 1843) indicate that he had coached Thamir's answers. See BOA.I.MSM 40/1081, 5.

supported the Ottomans, his successors backed Iran. As the inhabitants of the city were inclined toward their co-sectarians, the Ottoman plenipotentiary's argument that the land of Muhammarah was a dependency of Basra and the Sheikh of Ka'b's inclination toward Iran and proximity of those lands to Iran will not cause those places to belong either to the sheykh or Iran proved to be less than convincing.[114]

IMPERIAL DECISION MAKING

While the delegates were engulfed in minutiae, their capitals were becoming impatient with the inconclusive and costly meetings. When Tsar Nicholas I visited England in September 1844, his foreign minister, Nesselrode, proposed a project of compromise, a conclusive settlement of the whole frontier. It appears that his proposal was in favor of Iran. Alerted, Canning argued that the plan was not consistent with the objective of mediation. Agreeing that the principle of *uti possidetis* might be applied to Muhammarah, he added, "the Persians are not in possession of the left bank of the Shatt al-Arab higher than Mohammarah, nor can they navigate any part of that river without being liable to the duties levied on shipping and merchandise by the Ottoman authorities."[115] Thus, if the proposal were accepted, Istanbul would lose a portion of this revenue, along with a fertile, well-populated, and well-cultivated district. It might, in addition, suffer the withdrawal of the region's inhabitants, who belonged to subject tribes. Similarly, he opposed Nesselrode's suggestion that Zohab should also be left to Iran, reasoning that historical and documentary evidence in favor of Istanbul abounded and that Iran had violently appropriated the land in dispute.[116] The Russian representatives in Erzurum rejected Canning's arguments, and Canning accused them of being blinded by their zeal for Iran.[117]

Russia's pro-Iranian intervention infuriated other Britons such as Layard and Williams and no doubt Istanbul.[118] The latter was of the opinion that ceding these two provinces, which had been seized by Iran, would be so degrading that the Ottoman Empire would be forced to enter into hostilities with its neighbor to regain them. Stressing that the

---

[114] For details of the discussions on the topic, see Aykut, "Erzurum," 120–35.

[115] Canning to Lord Aberdeen, 1 and 2 November 1844, in *Schofield I*, 388, and 391.

[116] Ibid.

[117] Canning to Aberdeen, November 2, 16, and 22, 1844, *Schofield, I*, 391, 401, 403.

[118] For Layard's response see "Observations sur le Mémorandum de Sir Stratford Canning, concernant les bases d'une solution arbitrale du Litige Turco-Persan, Le 1er Septembre, 1844," *Schofield I*, 391–99. For Istanbul's perception, BBA.A.DVN 8/16, 260.

Ottomans had presented more evidence than their rivals, Williams suggested the division of Zohab between the two parties.[119] Russia's backing of Iranian claims and London's tacit approval upset even the pro-Iranian Sheil. Criticizing Nesselrode's proposal that Iran renounce its claims to Suleimanieh, and the Porte its to Zohab, he maintained that the former were groundless, whereas the latter were supported with *viva voce* evidence. Despite these objections, however, pragmatic considerations compelled him to support Nesselrode's suggestion that Zohab be left to Iran. These included its occupation by the Iranian Guran tribe and the real necessity for Iran to retain its plain as a winter pasture ground for its tribes.[120] With all of these considerations in play, the commissioners decided that the Shatt boundary should run along the low-water mark of the left, east, or Iranian bank of the river.[121] Although they conceded the contested lands to Iran, they granted the Ottoman Empire right of control over the whole Shatt al-Arab. Even though in the concluding treaty and subsequent negotiations, Iran secured the eastern bank, free right of passage on the waterway, the Island of Khizr, and Muhammarah, this latter decision remained a constant source of complaint, with Tehran insisting that the boundary should run down the center of the river.

It is probable that Ottoman evidence and the opinions of the British diplomats were so easily dismissed because London's first priority was to maintain good relations with Russia. Russia's support of Iran helped Tehran secure its most valuable frontier possessions – namely, the eastern bank of the Shatt and the Island of Khizr – by lending weight to its arguments regarding the historical and actual allegiance of the Ka'b tribe, as evidenced by its Shi'ism, use of the Iranian flag, payment of tribute to Iranian authorities, and strong presence in Fellahiyeh. Thus, the balance of power between Russia, England, and the Ottoman Empire, combined with Ka'b religious and political loyalties, played a conclusive role in the temporary resolution of a very contentious issue.

PASTURE POLITICS: FRONTIERS AND TRIBES

The problems of the frontier were not always territorial in nature. Although the division of geo-strategically important places such as Zohab and the Shatt al-Arab dominated the conferences, the most

---

[119] Williams to Canning, Erzurum, December 4, 1844, *Schofield I*, 415–16. [Emphasis added.]
[120] Sheil to Aberdeen, Tehran, 29 December, 1844, *Schofield I*, 417–20.
[121] Eliyahu Lauterpacht, "River Boundaries: Legal Aspects of the Shatt al-Arab Frontier," *The International and Comparative Law Quarterly* 9.2 (Apr. 1960): 209.

recurrent theme in Ottoman-Iranian relations was the cross-border movement of mostly Kurdish tribes, many of which had pastures on both sides of the divide. Under the watch of regional rulers such as the Babans, after paying their pasturage dues, these tribes were accustomed to making their seasonal migrations. However, the parallel processes of boundary making and the destruction of the Kurdish dynasts fundamentally changed this dynamic, forcing them to choose the territorial base of their belonging, loyalties, and allegiances.

At the conferences, the Ottomans asked for an agreement on the allocation and governing of border tribes and for the surrender of certain tribes that had migrated to the Iranian side. In contrast, the Iranians asked about tax arrears for pasturage fees and the restoration rather than surrender of various historically Iranian Kurdish tribes, such as the Haydaran, Jalali, Sipki, Zilan, Jamaledin, Takori, Shemski, and Shekefti, which had crisscrossed the frontier before settling within Ottoman dominions.[122] The Ottomans responded that most of those tribes were originally part of the Milan of Diyarbakir that, because of wars with Russia and Iran, had resided temporarily in Iran but were now returning.[123] Complicating these issues, especially on the northern Kurdish frontier, was the question of religious identity. The Kurdish tribes of the north were Sunnis living under the Shi'i shah. Given the sensitive nature of the issue, the negotiating commissioners refrained from claiming these groups on religious grounds, relying instead on arguments about historical precedence and long-term allegiances.[124] However, the role played by sectarian affiliation in a tribe's selection of citizenship was not lost on the interested parties. When the conferees discussed the case of the Zilan tribe, for example, the pro-Iranian Sheil warned Canning in Istanbul and his counterparts in London that they had moved to the Ottoman side not for pasture and climate but because they were Sunni.[125]

The Zilan lived at the intersection of Russia, the Ottoman Empire, and Iran. Their migrations through these frontier regions vividly illustrate the transition from indefinite frontier to the new realities of a bordered life. Traditionally, they roamed among the three sovereignties almost at will

---

[122] "IMoFA to Mirza Taqi," Salehi, *Erzetelrum*, 61–62.

[123] Enveri Efendi's minutes of the 14th and 15th conferences, BOA.I.MSM 40/1081, 14 and 15.

[124] Mirza Taqi argued that the Jamaladdin branch of the Zilan were Iranian and famous for their courage in the shah's campaigns around Yazd, Kerman, and Khorassan. Enveri Efendi's minutes of the 15th conference, BOA.I.MSM 40/1081, 15.

[125] PRO.FO 78/2709, Williams to Canning, March 23, 1850.

and with apparently no state intervention. The testimony of their chief, Hussein Agha, shows how such pastoral nomadic communities coped with environmental changes, population pressure, and a seminomadic lifestyle dependent on available and adequate pasturelands. According to Hussein, the Zilan and its subsidiary, the Jamaladdin, were originally inhabitants of Diyarbekir and were *tebaa-i sahih*, or true subjects of the sultan. As their numbers increased along with the difficulty of procuring subsistence, they were obliged to turn their tents in the direction of Bayezid and Kars, which lay hundreds of miles away in present-day northeastern Turkey. There, they settled in lands straddling Russian, Ottoman, and Iranian territories. When "a great number of Kurdish and Parthian tribes were gathered" under Hussein's authority, they were forced to pick up their tents once more: "in the hope of procuring the comfort, well-being and the subsistence of the whole, it was deemed advisable to pass into the neighborhood of Revan [Yerevan, in present-day Armenia, then under Iranian rule] being a spacious country, and one where the rigors of the winter season are not so much felt."[126] Leaving a part of the tribe in Kars and Bayezid, they wandered in Revan until it was occupied by Russia. "[N]ot deeming [this occupation] to their advantage," they returned to Ottoman territory, to the zone between Mush and Bayezid. When the Russians invaded that area as well, destroying the land's prosperity, they picked up once more. This time, they looked toward Iran, attracted by the perceived lack of a firm frontier in that direction: "the fact of there being no ceremony between the two high and mighty states of Turkey and Persia tempted us to go as sojourners and strangers, and establish our tents in the direction of Khoi [Persia]." Yet, after only eight years in Khoi, and thanks to the efforts of Kamili Pasha, the governor of Erzurum, they returned to Kars. In an effort to stop them, Tehran imprisoned one of Hussein's wives along his son Qasim Agha. Ignoring these tactics of intimidation, Hussein completed the move.[127] These final events coincided with the Erzurum conferences. After listening to Hussein's testimony, Mirza Taqi insisted that the Zilan were the shah's subjects and that Qasim, along with other chiefs of his tribe, had given Iran an official petition to this effect. Hussein protested, claiming that his son and wife were still being held hostage in Khoi.[128]

---

[126] PRO.FO 78/2711, Testimony of Hussein Bey of the Tribes of Zeelan Dwelling in Kars, January 13, 1843.

[127] Ibid. For similar information see Hurşîd, *Seyâhatnâme*, 264–65; and Dervish, *Tahdid*, 162–64.

[128] PRO.FO 78/2711 Testimony of Hussein Bey, and "IMoFA to Mirza Taqi," in Salehi, *Erzetelrum*, 61.

Although the conferees were unable to resolve the Zilan case, it appears that soon thereafter Hussein died and Tehran called Qasim back, treating him well and urging him to return with the rest of his tribe. To please Iran, he convinced about one hundred households to return to Khoi, after which his family members were released. But such coercive measures did not prevent the Zilan from returning to Ottoman lands. Thus, in 1850, the Iranian plenipotentiary sent a note to a mediating commissioner claiming, "Kasim Aga of Zilan, with 300 families of an Iranian tribe has escaped from Makho to Bayazid where, instead of being turned back, they have been received by the governor as guests."[129] When the survey commission passed through the northernmost part of the frontier in 1851, an estimated 1,000 Zilan households lived in Kars and Kağızman on the Ottoman side, whereas 1,650 families were Russian subjects who spent winters in Revan and summers in Sinek, Balık Gölü, and Pirlu around Bayazid on the Ottoman side. Only about 100 families remained in Maku as Iranian subjects.[130]

The tangled history of the Zilan is not unique. Indeed, after many similar cases were presented, each negotiating commissioner blamed the other for inciting cross-border migrations and demanded the return of "fugitive" tribes as required by existing treaties. The story of the Zilan (which will continue in the following chapters) and other similar stories not recounted in these pages demonstrate how settlement and migration throughout the borderlands tended to be gradual and influenced by various factors, including the availability of adequate pastures, drought and famine, epidemics and population pressure, religious discrimination or affiliation, disagreements with local authorities, internal divisions among tribal confederations, vendettas, resistance to conscription, and displacement resulting from interstate wars. Recognizing this complexity and despairing of any imminent solution, Enveri Efendi pushed for the formation of a separate commission to definitively decide the subjecthood of tribes.[131] The delegates, however, resolved that such a project would be impossible. The better solution would be to demarcate the boundaries to force the tribes to choose one side or the other. And so it was. Notwithstanding the efforts of both states, it was only finalization of the

---

[129] The same information is in Hurşîd, *Seyâhatnâme*, 265. In March 1849, the Vali of Erzurum was ordered to settle the Zilan tribe, "a part of which is in Iran." See BOA. BEO.A.MKT 167/7, 1265.2.6/March 18, 1849. They were settled in Kars. See BOA. BEO.A.MKT 168, 63, 1265.2.16/ March 28, 1849.

[130] Dervish, *Tahdid*, 159.

[131] BOA.IMM, 40/1082, also in Aykun"Erzurum," 167–68.

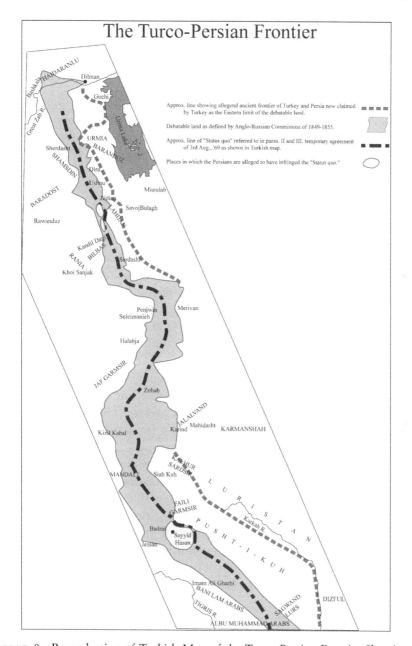

MAP 8. Reproduction of Turkish Map of the Turco Persian Frontier Showing Different Claims
Adapted from PRO.MFQ 1/1344.

boundary and the routinization of modern state practices that brought tribal cross-border movements to an end.

OTHER ISSUES AT THE CONFERENCE

Tribes were not the only fugitives whose fate occupied the commissioners. For Tehran, an equally important matter was the surrender of members of the Qajar family who had escaped to the Ottoman Empire and lived near the border, in places including Baghdad. As their proximity to Iran might facilitate a challenge to the legitimacy of Qajar rule, Tehran was especially sensitive about the topic. When requesting their return, the Iranian delegate always made reference to the 1590 treaty and subsequent ones, in which each side pledged not to harbor rebels and refugees.[132] Istanbul responded that because they belonged to a ruling dynasty, returning the princes would be undignified and contrary to international law and human rights (*hukuk-u düveliye ve insaniye iktizasınca*).[133] It is interesting that this diplomatic back-and-forth had the unintended consequence of introducing the notion of political refugees to Ottoman-Iranian relations, for Istanbul argued that the princes were not fugitives but refugees. Iran responded that the 1590 treaty called for the return of refugees who could effectively cause mischief, not ordinary refugees who wielded little or no power.[134]

The problem of the princes, however, paled in comparison to the constant stream of Iranian pilgrims whose presence, augmented by traveling merchants and Iranians living in Ottoman domains, made policies regarding border crossing and control a grave concern. A snapshot of the voluminous Ottoman documentation on the topic shows that Iranians were especially concerned about the unfair treatment of pilgrims as well as legal problems related to Iranian merchants and the estates of deceased Iranians and the imposition of *jizya* (Islamic poll tax imposed on non-Muslim male adults) on Iranian *dhimmi*s (non-Muslims).[135] Hence, during the conferences, Istanbul intermittently ordered frontier governors in Erzurum, Van, and Baghdad to redress the complaints of Iranian citizens. However, this was to be done according to the necessities of the

---

[132] Ernest Tucker, "The Peace Negotiations of 1736: A Conceptual Turning Point in Ottoman-Iranian Relations," *The Turkish Studies Association Bulletin* 20,1 (1996): 19.

[133] Aykun, "Erzurum," 196.

[134] Mirza Taqi insisted that the princes were *firaris* who should be returned. See Enveri Efendi's summary of the January 16, 1844 meeting, in BOA.I.MSM 40/1081, 4.

[135] BOA.IMM 40/1082–10.

modern state – Iranians, like all other foreigners, were asked to observe the rules of *murur tezkeresi*, the travel papers that were precursors of the passport.[136]

Inextricable from pilgrimage was what I have elsewhere referred to as Iranian charitable involvement in the affairs of Ottoman Iraq.[137] Whether as an expression of piety or a way of legitimizing their rule in the eyes of the Shi'i faithful, Iranian dynasties from the Safavids onward appealed to Istanbul for permission to maintain and furnish (*tefriş*) the shrines of Shi'i imams and erect Shi'i mosques in Ottoman territory. Likewise, Iran chafed against the Ottoman prohibition on Sunni-Shi'i intermarriage, which lasted as long as the Ottoman Empire.[138] The mediating parties stood aloof from religious questions. Still, they understood that Iranian insistence on "building mosques and contracting marriages according to Persian tenets in Turkey would be to admit what the Mohammedans of this empire hold to be highly illegal, irreligious and immoral," as Canning expressed it.[139] In response to Mirza Taqi's insistence that the marriage prohibition was a later tradition or *bid'at* that should be eliminated, Enveri Efendi argued that many Iranians who married Sunnis left their wives and children, making it only logical that the ban continued.[140] Similarly, when Mirza Taqi broached the building of Shi'i mosques in Baghdad – where, he pointed out, there were already Christian churches and Jewish synagogues – Enveri Efendi became infuriated: "Consider that I did not officially hear what you said, nor is there a possibility of me hearing it! Regard this as something you did not utter and I did not hear."[141] No doubt this reaction was related to ongoing Shi'i proselytizing, which had resulted in the conversion of many tribes of the southern borderland. At a time when the centralizing empire struggled to extend its control, such challenges to its legitimacy were inflammatory.[142]

---

[136] For this order, see BOA.A.MKT 21/97, 1260/1844. For the *murur tezkeresi* see Musa Çadırcı, *Tanzimat Döneminde Anadolu Kentlerinin Sosyal ve Ekonomik Yapıları* (Ankara: Türk Tarih Kurumu Basımevi, 1991), 46.

[137] Sabri Ateş, "Bones of Contention: Corpse Traffic and Ottoman-Iranian Rivalry in Nineteenth Century Iraq," *CSSAME* 30, 3 (2010): 512–32.

[138] See Karen M. Kern, "The Prohibition of Sunni-Shi'i Marriages in the Ottoman Empire: A Study of Ideologies" (Ph. D. diss., Columbia University, 1999).

[139] Canning to Aberdeen, Constantinople, November, 15, 1845, *Schofield I*, 507–15.

[140] Aykun, "Erzurum," 191.

[141] BOA.IMM 40/1082–10, Aykun, "Erzurum," 185.

[142] For the later phase of Shi'i-Sunni competition, see Selim Deringil, "The Struggle Against Shi'ism in Hamidian Iraq: A Study in Counter Propaganda," *Die Welt des Islams* XXX (1990), 45–62.

Notwithstanding sectarian differences, Iran continually asked that disputes between Iranian Muslims and other Muslims be referred to religious courts and not tribunals of commerce, which were bound by conventional law. Furthermore, it requested the renunciation of all distinctions between Sunnis and Shi'is in weighing the validity of evidence given before sharia courts. Tehran also insisted on the rights of consular and diplomatic agents to protect its subjects, Christian or Muslim. Such protection was necessary because Iranian Armenians were sometimes imprisoned and asked to pay *jizya*. There were, moreover, complaints that some Iranians were forced to serve in the Ottoman army or navy or were jailed without the presence of Iranian representatives. Another well-documented sore point was the confiscation of the property of deceased and murdered Iranians. Mirza Taqi brought to the conference the brother of a deceased Iranian whose property was not given to his children, as well as an Iranian who was robbed and, despite the sultan's order to the contrary, had received no justice.[143]

Although orders and treaties, when respected, might minimize complaints of merchants and travelers, they were helpless where highway robbery (*kat' al-tarik*), the twin brother of commerce, was concerned. Because the robbed party would record his loss with and request compensation from local authorities, this is a well-documented aspect of border crossing. Hence, Mirza Taqi gave specific examples of groups of Iranian pilgrims being robbed as they traveled between Mecca and Medina and reiterated his demand for official protection, arguing that such acts were a crime against religion and their punishment sanctioned by the Qur'an. They were, moreover, a major impediment to trade. After the conclusion of negotiations, it became obvious that these issues were related, not only to the process of boundary making but also to the rise in state capacity at the peripheries. For example, when the culprits belonged to large Arab tribes and their activities were sanctioned or directly carried out by the chiefs, their punishment required major operations that were often beyond the power of local authorities.[144]

Iranians thus desired the secularization and modernization of the Ottoman border regime as regarded pilgrims, visitors, marriages, and corpse caravans bringing Shi'i dead to be buried in the precincts of holy shrines of Iraq. They did not, however, want to include tariffs and customs in this new international regime. As we have seen, Tehran strongly resisted

---

[143] Aykun, "Erzurum," 181–83, 186.
[144] For one such operation by Bagdhad's governor against an Arab tribe that robbed Daghestani and Iranian pilgrims, see Aykun, "Erzurum," 192; and BOA.IMM 40/1082–2.

inclusion in the free-trade Balta Limanı system that incorporated the Ottoman Empire into the emerging global economic system, preferring the status quo of the 1823 treaty, which had established the flat rate of 4 percent *ad valorem*. The Ottoman delegate repeatedly argued that changing conditions warranted Iran's inclusion in the new system and warned that further resistance would result in Iranian merchants being barred from the internal trade of the Ottoman Empire.[145] His warning was unnecessary, however, because the conferees were preparing the text of a new treaty to further standardize Ottoman-Iranian relations and their frontier regimes. Iranians would no longer benefit, or suffer, from being the members of an ambiguous *umma* but would be treated as citizens of a separate nation with attendant rights and responsibilities.

THE ERZURUM TREATY OF 1847

After two years, so many points of difference remained that it seemed the conferences would be fruitless. To break the deadlock, the influential ambassadors of England and Russia submitted a joint plan of compromise composed of nine articles regarding indemnities, territory, political refugees, religious freedom, travel, security, and normalization of commercial relations. Essentially a draft of the final treaty, it proposed the following:

- The mutual relinquishment of pecuniary claims.
- Iran's relinquishment of its claim to the town and province of Suleimanieh and agreement either to cede the plain of Zohab or to offer adequate compensation. The Porte's relinquishment, in turn, of the eastern, mountainous part of Zohab, the island on which Muhammarah was located, and the section of the left side of the Shatt al-Arab where Iranians were known to be residing, plus free navigation of the river from its mouth to the point of contact of the respective territorial limits.
- Both parties' relinquishment of all other territorial claims and agreement to appoint a delimitation/survey commission.
- Both parties' agreement to refer claims for indemnity to a special commission.
- The Porte's designation of a town far from the border for the residence of the Qajar princes, who would be forbidden from leaving this town or entering into clandestine relations with Iran.

---

[145] For the Ottoman account of tariff and customs issues, see Aykun, "Erzurum," 168–82, 196.

- Iran's willingness to enter into a new commercial treaty with the Porte (not necessarily the Balta Limanı Treaty).
- In conformity with previous treaties, the Porte's ensuring a safe and duty-free passage for Iranian pilgrims. Also, the granting of all privileges and rights extended to Ottoman consular agents in Iran to consular agents nominated by the shah. Also, the Porte's agreement to settle amicably and reciprocally questions of a religious nature brought to the Erzurum conferences by Iran.
- The introduction, by both states, of measures to prevent acts of brigandage by nomadic frontier tribes by establishing military posts and taking responsibility for the incursion of tribes into one another's territory; and a mutual agreement that tribes with an ambiguous dependency would permanently select their territory of residence, whereas those whose dependency was uncontested would return to their home state.
- All clauses from the 1823 Treaty of Erzurum not expressly modified should be included verbatim in the new treaty.[146]

The Ottoman Council of Ministers was conciliatory toward most of the articles and formed a commission to further examine the proposal. Still, it rejected outright all concessions of a religious nature, including the appointment of Iranian consuls to Mecca, Medina, Najaf, and Karbala. It did, however, allow for such appointments to commercial centers.[147] Not surprisingly, the territorial questions, especially regarding Zohab and Muhammarah, also remained contentious. After internal debate, Istanbul concluded that Muhammarah should be given to Iran in exchange for all of Zohab. This position, and Istanbul's refusal to offer concessions, angered Canning, who suggested that Russia and Britain recall their commissioners. However, lacking official authorization to do so, Titow, the Russian charge d'affaires, refused to comply, thereby saving the negotiations.[148] In a meeting with Canning and Titow, high-ranking Ottoman officials – including Ali Efendi, the acting MoFA (Minister of Foreign Affairs); Rıfat Pasha, the president of the Council of Ministers; and Fethi Ahmed Pasha, the sultan's brother-in-law – reiterated their offer.[149] The mediators again rejected it and accused the Porte of exaggerating

---

[146] PRO.FO 78/2712, Joint Memorandum of Canning and M. de Titow to the Porte and Court of Persia, Istanbul, March 24, 1845, *Schofield I*, 436–37; and Harari, *Turco-Persian*, 76–77. I relied heavily on Harari's translation of this note from French.

[147] Canning to Aberdeen, Constantinople, May 19, 1845, *Schofield I*, 447–50.

[148] PRO.FO 78/2713, Canning to Aberdeen, September 29, 1845; Canning to Aberdeen, September 17, 1845, *Schofield I*, 487–95.

[149] Canning to Aberdeen, Constantinople, October 16, 1845, *Schofield I*, 496–506.

Muhammarah's importance out of fear that its future development as a hub of trade might weaken Basra.[150]

Similar meetings were held in Tehran, which increasingly relied on the mediating powers to provide a counterbalance. The shah even stated that "he felt himself unable to resist the united will of two governments like England and Russia, and that he must forcibly yield to their opinion."[151] Such amicable words did not signify passive acceptance, however. In meetings with the mediating ambassadors, Hajji Mirza Aqasi squarely rejected the Ottoman proposal regarding Muhammarah, noting that Iran had already agreed to relinquish its claim to part of Zohab. He also maintained that Tehran was not asking for the free public display of Shi'i ceremonies or separate places of worship, but rather for recognition of the validity of Iranian evidence in courts of law, permission for Shi'i-Sunni intermarriages, security for Iranian pilgrims, the right of appeal to a Shi'i qadi when two Iranian subjects had differences, and the same privileges and honors for Iranian consuls as were conferred on European agents of similar rank.[152]

Although unhappy with the negotiating parties' intransigence, the Russian and British ambassadors pressed on, meeting with the highest echelons of power in Tehran and Istanbul (although, unlike the shah, the sultan did not meet with them personally). After a February 1846 meeting with Titow and Reşit Pasha (the MoFA), Canning informed London and Sheil in Tehran that obstacles to solving the Muhammarah-Zohab problem and various religious issues had been removed. A protocol had been signed and Istanbul had, albeit reluctantly, agreed to Iran's permanent possession of Muhammarah. Moreover, an acceptable solution to the problems of intermarriage and Shi'i testimony in Ottoman courts had been worked out: "The only point, upon which it has not been found possible to shake the objections of the Porte, is the proposed impunity of any Persian, who being in Turkey might through ignorance break out into public demonstration of faith offensive to those of Soonite creed."[153] The Porte also promised protection from unprovoked injury and insult to every Iranian in the sultan's domains, as long as Iran reciprocated. Canning urged Sheil to press the Iranian government for the immediate execution

---

[150] Canning to Aberdeen, Constantinople, November 15, 1845, *Schofield I*, 507–15.
[151] PRO.FO 78/2713, Sheil to Aberdeen, Tehran, June 3, 1845.
[152] Sheil to Aberdeen, Tehran, December 16, 1845, *Schofield I*, 518–29.
[153] "Protocole d'une Conference tenue a Pera de Constantinople," February 26, 1846, in BOA.HR.SYS 719/1, pp. 98–102, 107; and also in Canning to Sheil, Constantinople, February 12, 1846, *Schofield I*, 537–47.

of the protocol.[154] However, the painfully protracted negotiations, for whose conclusion Canning prematurely congratulated Sheil, did not so easily come to an end.

For example, Hajji Mirza Aqasi sent all parties a draft of articles emphasizing Iranian views, an uncharacteristic act of assertion that Sheil attributed to Russian machinations.[155] In it, he argued that Iran should be awarded the town and port of Muhammarah and the island and anchorage of Khizr, as well as much of the eastern bank (occupied by an Iranian tribe), and it should enjoy rights of navigation from the Shatt's mouth to the point of contact of the two parties. As for Suleimanieh and Zohab, the Porte should be given Suleimanieh and the plain of Zohab, and Iran should keep Zohab's eastern portion including the pass of Kerrind. Suggesting that a commissioner and engineers be appointed immediately to determine the frontier, Aqasi requested that pecuniary claims be abandoned and arrears in pasturage fees collected by authorities of both states, that the Iranian princes be settled in Bursa, that tariffs be organized in accordance with the 1823 treaty, and that the security and free passage of Iranian pilgrims be guaranteed. Additionally, Aqasi again demanded that Istanbul grant consuls appointed by the shah (except to Mecca and Medina) the privileges enjoyed by consuls from other friendly states. The last article concerned the need to establish military posts to prevent tribes from crossing the border to pillage. Echoing the joint plan of compromise, it suggested that uncontested tribes be restored to their home country, whereas contested ones be allowed to choose their place of abode.[156]

The long negotiations thus became a game of one-upmanship between Tehran and Istanbul. In the summer of 1846, however, a violent attack on the Erzurum quarters of the Iranian plenipotentiary incited an international crisis that halted negotiations for months. Curzon attributed the attack to religious animosity from a "fanatical mob of Soonis" and Turkish disdain for "Mirza Tekee's" stately manners, which provoked "various accusations against him and some members of his household."[157] Ottoman records, however, show that a member of the Iranian delegation

[154] Ibid.
[155] Canning to Aberdeen, April 30, 1846; and Sheil to Aberdeen, June 1, 1846, *Schofield I*, 565–73.
[156] "Draft of Articles of Agreement Signed by Hajji Mirza Aqasi," April 6, 1846, *Schofield I*, 557–64.
[157] Curzon, *Armenia*, 57.

sodomized a young boy on July 18. In response, a mob gathered at Mirza Taqi's residence to demand that the culprit be handed over. A confrontation followed in which a servant and Mirza Taqi's secretary, Mirza Hasan Monshi, were killed. Mirza Taqi was saved by Ottoman officers and moved to a more protected residence.[158] The insulted plenipotentiary refused to participate in the conferences until his demands for an apology, compensation, and an official investigation were met.[159] Istanbul complied and replaced the governor and dismissed the town's qadi. Although a special tribunal concluded that the events had indeed been set off by the sexual assault of a boy, it nevertheless ordered the arrest of the provocateurs, who were sentenced to various punishments.[160]

Mere weeks after Mirza Taqi, under orders from the shah, returned to the negotiating table, yet another crisis erupted after the Porte discovered that Muhammarah was not situated on an island, but on the mainland. This rather belated finding resulted not only in renewed objections to Iran's possession of the town, but also in a refusal to cede even the left bank of the Shatt. Exasperated, the British and Russian representatives jointly threatened to abandon the negotiations and suspend all discussions with the Porte pertaining to the border.[161] In response, the Porte requested assurances on three points: (1) that the anchorage of Muhammarah be more accurately defined so that Istanbul, in ceding the town with its port and anchorage, would not inadvertently sacrifice additional territories or resources; (2) that when most of a tribe resided in Iranian lands, Iran would not have the right to claim the territory where the balance of the tribe resided; and (3) that clarifications on the matter of compensations be made. The mediating powers offered assurances on the first two points. Regarding the third, they reiterated that in conformity with the treaty, all governmental claims would be canceled and individual claims referred to a commission.[162] Of the three points, the first – that is, the Porte's insistence

---

[158] For the Ottoman version of events, see Aykun, "Erzurum," 208–17. For an Iranian account based on British documents, see Afshar, *Amir Kabir*, 104–17.

[159] Sheil to Hajji Mirza Aghassee, 5th Shavval 1262, September 27, 1846, *Schofield I*, 590–91.

[160] For many British reports on the issue, PRO.FO 78/2715. For Mirliva Arif Pasha's Report (Layiha), BOA.I.MSM 82/2344. As the treasury was in dire straits, the highest officials active in Ottoman-Iranian peace negotiations were made to pay the compensation. Aykun, "Erzurum," 214–17; Curzon, *Armenia*, 32.

[161] Wellesly to Lord Palmerston, Buyukdere, November 3, 1846, *Schofield I*, 595–97.

[162] Mirza Ja'far, *Tahqiqat*, 43; Harari, *Turco-Persian*, 82–83; and PRO.FO 78/2716, Joint Memo of mediators to the Porte and Persia, February 15, 1847. Also see Wellesly to Palmerston, Constantinople, February 3, 1847, *Schofield I*, 643.

on having full control of the Shatt and giving Iran no lands or ports beyond the city of Muhammarah – would, not surprisingly, contaminate negotiations for the longest time.

It was now that Britain's queen, either uninformed or hoping to increase pressure on Istanbul, "trusting to the assurances conveyed to her by her Majesty's representatives [in Istanbul and Tehran], declared to her parliament, and through that parliament to Europe [that] Turco-Persian differences were settled."[163] Soon afterward, the shah accepted a draft of the treaty drawn up by the mediating commissioners. The Porte then withdrew its objections to ceding the Island of Khizr, with the stipulation that no fortifications be erected on it.[164] Yet the deadlock continued, reportedly because the sultan was unhappy, despite his ministers' acquiescence.[165] Infuriated, in February 1847, Tehran threatened to break off negotiations, even as the mediating governments continued to pressure the Porte while warning Tehran to stay put.[166] The Porte stood its ground, reiterating its three points and informing London and St. Petersburg of an additional claim to the islands on the Shatt. It also insisted that Iran not claim lands situated on the Shatt's right bank, even if tribes recognizing Iranian suzerainty lived there. Finally, it notified the mediators that unless the assurances they had provided were officially accepted by Iran, the treaty must be considered null and void.

If the mediating parties could not come up with a formula that would satisfy Istanbul, the negotiations would fail. Determined to avoid such an outcome, they continued to give Istanbul assurances but kept the Iranians ignorant of them, hoping Tehran would thus endorse the assurances. Placated, in early April 1847, the Porte ordered Enveri Efendi to sign, without alteration, the nine articles first suggested by Titow and Canning on March 25, 1845, but only on the condition that "if the Persian Government

---

[163] Memorandum on proposed territorial arrangement for Muhammarah, Enclosure, Wellesley to Palmerston, Buyukdere, November 3, 1846, *Schofield I*, 604–5.

[164] Wellesley to Palmerston, Constantinople, December 19, 1846; and to Ottoman minister of foreign affairs, December 13, *Schofield I*, 628.

[165] For Canning's and Russian Ambassador Oustinoff's warning to Istanbul about the Island of Khizr, BOA.I.MSM 40/1094, 1 and 12. For British chargé d'affaires Wellesly's and Oustinoff's letters to the Porte, BOA.HR.SYS, 736/13. Wellesley to Palmerston, Constantinople, February 3, 1847, *Schofield I*, 643. Mirza Ja'far claims the Porte became alarmed because Hajji Mirza Aqasi ordered the building of a fort and caravanserai at Muhammarah, appointed a governor to Arabistan, and ordered the appointment of an Amir al-Hajj, *Tahqiqat*, 40.

[166] PRO.FO 78/2716, Sheil to Palmerston, Tehran, February 24, 1847.

should refuse to abide by the declaration made by us, the Porte will not ratify the treaty."[167]

In the meantime, Ottoman armies continued the pacification and reconquest of Kurdistan. Pointing to this activity, Wellesly, the British representative in Istanbul, drew attention to "the immense advantage the Porte would derive by having the question settled before it managed in hostilities with Bedr Khan Bey, and other Kurdish tribes." As the previous chapter showed, his prediction that "as the frontier tribes were already in arms, bloodshed was likely to ensue unless a speedy termination was put to the present uncertain state of the things" proved to be correct.[168] It was under these circumstances that the negotiating commissioners, while still waiting for the finalization of discussions in Tehran and Istanbul, signed the Erzurum Treaty on May 31, 1847. Happy the conferences were finally over, Williams and Mirza Taqi departed on June 2, and on June 26, Sheil informed London of the shah's ratification of the treaty.[169] Unhappy with the loss of lands it considered to be the sultan's, the Ottoman *Meclis-i Has-ı Vükela* (cabinet) discussed the possibility of rejecting it but finally agreed to ratification.[170] This, however, was not the end of the drama.

In late October, Tehran's messenger Mirza Jawad departed for Istanbul with the ratified copies of the treaty. He arrived toward the end of January 1848. It was at this point that the mediating ambassadors devised a diplomatic maneuver that poisoned the fruit of the long labors of the Erzurum Congress. The Porte insisted that it would not ratify the treaty before obtaining an Iranian declaration confirming the three previously mentioned points. Titow and the new British ambassador, Lord Cowley, not wanting to raise Tehran's suspicions, attempted to convince its envoy to Paris, Mirza Mohammed 'Ali Khan, who was in Istanbul, to agree to the declaration the Porte had requested. When he refused, the mediators declared they would not accept his refusal and issued a communication to the effect that unless he complied, he should consider all relationships between Iran and Russia and England to be terminated.

Probably unwilling to accept the responsibility for the threatened break, Mirza Muhammad Ali Khan agreed to sign the required declaration

---

[167] Wellesley to Palmerston, Constantinople, April 2, 1847, *Schofield I*, 661.
[168] Ibid.
[169] PRO.FO 78/216, Protocol of Special Conference held for exchange of signatures, May 31, 1847, also Williams to Lord Cowley, Erzurum, May 31, 1847, *Schofield, 1*, 673–74. PRO.FO 78/2716, Sheil to Cowley, Camp near Tehran, June 26, 1847, and BOA.A.DVN. MHM 3-A/91, 1263.4.25/July 7, 1847.
[170] Aykun, "Erzurum," 240–41.

alternately called *Explanatory Note* or *Clarifications* (*Izahatname*) in exchange for an official statement signed by Lord Cowley and M. de Titow saying unless he had done so, the mediators would have broken relations. The European representatives agreed to issue the statement and the respective declarations were finally exchanged.[171]

Still not content, the Porte asked the mediators to prepare a final *Explanatory Note* that more formally presented the assurances they had previously given. The mediators complied and on March 21, 1848, the final ratifications were exchanged.[172] Consequently, the same Great Powers that advocated Iran's right to Muhammarah and the Island of Khizr ceded its control of the Shatt al-Arab River without even informing Tehran of the fact. Once again, the balance of power between the Ottoman Empire, Russia, and England defined the future of the most contentious zone of the frontier.

Expectedly, the *Explanatory Note* would become a major impediment to all future negotiations. As Arnold Kemball would later maintain, it negatively influenced the treaty's terms and restricted the labors of the newly appointed survey commission to the mere acquisition of topographical and statistical information.[173] Iran's subsequent efforts concentrated on reversing the terms of the note by claiming that the Iranian ambassador to Paris had not been authorized to sign it and that his government did not recognize it. The Ottoman representatives, in turn, repeatedly urged that the note be treated as the basis of the delimitation of the frontier's southern extremity.[174] The legacy of the *Explanatory Note* also marred relations between Iran and the post-Ottoman state of Iraq. When the latter was created and made independent in 1932, Iran rejected its sovereignty over the Shatt's navigation by again claiming that the Erzurum Treaty of 1847, and the note, had been forced on it by Britain and Russia: Tehran argued that such a treaty is a relic of the colonial era and therefore could no longer be accepted by a free and independent Iran. Iraq, in turn, noted that Baghdad had accepted the terms of the treaty even though the Ottoman Empire had agreed to cede Arab territory on the left bank of the Shatt to

---

[171] Harari, *Turco-Persian*, 85; and PRO.FO 78/2717, Cowley to Palmerston, February 2, 1848. Mirza Ja'far claims that in the name of a sultanic gift, Mirza Muhammed 'Ali was given a bribe of four thousand tumans; see *Tahqiqat*, 40.

[172] PRO.FO 78/2717, Cowley to Palmerston, March 21, 1848.

[173] PRO.FO 881/2586 General Sir A. B. Kemball, "Memorandum on the present state of the Turco-Persian Boundary Question, and the conditions on which the solution would seem to depend," April 2, 1875, *Schofield I*, 63–71.

[174] Tchirikof, *Diary*, 11.

Iran. Moreover, it argued that Iran's ratification of the treaty implied its acceptance of its terms.[175]

Despite the *Explanatory Note*, the Erzurum Treaty allowed Iran to make significant gains. Its refusal to be included within the regime of the Balta Limanı Treaty paid off, because the new treaty preserved the tax rate set in 1823. Whereas the import rate for France and Great Britain was 12 percent, and the tax rate for Ottoman citizens was 12 percent, the subjects of the shah enjoyed a 4 percent rate reaffirmed in an order issued on January 4, 1859, which added an additional 2 percent *ad valorem* to be collected at the time of sale of goods. Another groundbreaking clause of the treaty was its seventh article, which stipulated that the shah would be allowed to have consuls in all major Ottoman cities.

Ernest Tucker correctly suggests that the 1746 Treaty of Kurdan was a turning point in Ottoman-Iranian relations, but I agree with Bruce Masters that it was the Erzurum Treaties and the negotiations leading to it that prompted both parties to embrace a Western view of nationality by compelling the Ottomans to recognize Iranians as constituting a "nation" along the model they had established for European communities in their empire.[176] After the conclusion of the treaty, Iran was no longer an ambiguous part of *dar al-Islam* but rather a distinct state. Likewise, Iranians were no longer subjects of the shah and part of the *umma*. They had become citizens of Iran with the same rights as other foreigners. The legal and theoretical basis for this new classification was forged at Erzurum under the mediating eyes of the imperialist powers. Now, it was time to end ambiguity in the borderlands by demarcating the limits of both states.

Parallel with the process of demarcation, many new institutions of the modern state took shape. Alongside age-old institutions, such as border patrols and customhouses, came quarantine stations, passports, and identification cards. It was also at this time that Istanbul asked the provinces, in accordance with the treaty, to send officials to the tribes to inquire about their choice of citizenship.[177] As the *tanzimat* state expanded, Ottoman frontier authorities increased their surveillance at the eastern borders while Istanbul warned them to prevent cross-border

---

[175] Tareq Y. Ismael, *Iraq and Iran: Roots of Conflict* (Syracuse, NY: Syracuse University Press, 1982), 24.

[176] Bruce Masters, "The Treaties of Erzurum (1823 and 1848) and the Changing Status of Iranians in the Ottoman Empire," *Iranian Studies* 24.1/4 (1991): 3, 9.

[177] See Ahmed Izzet's memo, BOA.BEO.A.MKT 100/15, 1263.11.19/January 31, 1848.

movements or attacks.[178] With the signing of the treaty, the borderland came into legal existence and moved toward the second stage of its transformation, to be accomplished by the cartographic, trigonometrical, and astronomical measurements of the survey that would allow the next wave of commissioners to cartographically construct the geographic limits of territorial sovereignty of the two states.

[178] See, for example, Şukka to the Vali of Erzurum, BOA.A.MKT 236/16, 1265.12.21/ March 5, 1850.

3

The Long Journey of the First Survey Commission

Following four years of negotiations, the Erzurum Congress's mediating and negotiating parties and their respective capitals decided that Iran and the Ottoman Empire should formally and finally settle their borders. It was a pressing project, for they believed that the ongoing disputes threatened the precarious peace, not only of the two states, but also of the two world powers.[1] The Erzurum Treaty of 1847 was hailed as a diplomatic triumph by Russia and England, the so-called mediating powers, and as a prelude to a growing Anglo-Russian entente in the East. Ironically, only six years before the Crimean War would pit the Ottoman Empire, England, and France against Russia, the joyous Russian chancellor, Count Nesselrode, hoped that "the good understanding which has lately existed between England and Russia on Eastern affairs, may be permanent, and that their policy in the East may be such, as to enable them to act in concert and in mutual confidence in any question which may arise in that quarter of the world."[2] Such desire for cooperation did not extend to the governments of Iran and the Ottoman Empire. Still, in accordance with the treaty, they approved the appointment of a joint survey commission to trace the line that would separate the dominions of the shah and the sultan.[3] Each country was asked to appoint a commissioner, and commission members were instructed to survey the borderland and determine the boundary line.

[1] James Felix Jones, *Memoirs of Baghdad, Kurdistan and Turkish Arabia, 1857* (Reprint, Buckinghamshire, UK: Archive Editions, 1998), Introduction.
[2] PRO.FO 78/2717, British Embassy to Palmerston, St. Petersburg, April 13, 1948.
[3] Wellesley to Lord Palmerston, Constantinople, April 2, 1847, and Canning's Report to Earl of Aberdeen, April 27, 1844, *Schofield* I, 325, 661.

The ink of the treaty was scarcely dry when the Delimitation Commission hit the road.

Consisting of four commissioners and their technical, diplomatic, and scientific staff, the commission worked from January 1849 to September 1852, nearly completing the survey of all border regions and generating sufficient information to make the boundary clear and unmistakable, at least on an abstract map. Constructing such a map, however, proved to be daunting because of the variegated geography of deserts, rivers, and high mountains. Inhabited by a multiplicity of communities that lived without regard to Ottoman or Iranian claims of proprietorship, the ownership of many parts of this geography was highly debated.

This chapter examines how the decisions of the Erzurum Congress were put into practice and once more highlights the cases of Zohab, Muhammarah, and the borderland tribes. Tracing the process by which "territoriality unfolded in actuality," it aims to show how the boundary line emerged as "the negotiated result of a variety of territorialization strategies" employed by local and imperial actors.[4] Tracing the surveyors' steps, it argues that the very act of surveying accelerated the transformation of the borderlands into bordered lands, or *sarhadd* into *sınır*. The survey helped crystallize allegiances and identities and forced once-autonomous peoples to abandon itinerant lifestyles and become citizens of Iran or the Ottoman Empire, entrenched behind a cartographically determined line. The borderlanders were doubtless aware of the survey party, which resembled a large military expedition. Although the many military expeditions in their lands had been devastating, they had always been temporary. The survey, however, heralded permanent change. Indeed, the commissioners' interactions with the peoples they encountered were explicitly designed to transmit the message of this change, to warn them that the era of "state evasion" was over. From this time forward, they would be incorporated into the fiscally legible economy of a central state. The labors of the surveyors thus made notions of boundary and sovereignty more coterminous by cartographically defining the limits of each state's authority. In this way, they marked the transition from a political sphere organized by suzerainty, or allegiance of semiautonomous local rulers to one or another center, to a territorial sovereignty marked by discernible limits. The surveyors thus strove to concretize the bounds of Iranian and Ottoman authority, while defusing tensions over disputes regarding pastures, plains, valleys, fields, villages, rivers, and – equally importantly – peoples. A later British memo summarized the

---

[4] Paolo Novak, "The Flexible Territoriality of Borders," *Geopolitics* 16.4 (2011): 751.

survey's objective as "to determine and establish the boundary between the Ottoman Empire and Persia so as to prevent the conflicts and disputes which had arisen from generations of contested jurisdictions and to confirm a permanent peace in that region for the benefit of humanity and commerce."[5]

Tasked with bringing administrative order, progress, and civilization to the imperial peripheries, the diplomats, engineers, botanists, geologists, archeologists, meteorologists, cartographers, and military personnel of the tsar and her majesty, in the company of the servants of the shah and the sultan, located, classified (in very similar terms), and mapped the physical and human geography of the region. As they proceeded, they marked the locations of mountain passes, water resources, forts, villages, and towns; noted possible outlets to be used in military campaigns; and kept careful records of roads, irrigation schemes, gorges, peaks, ridges, defiles, bridges, valleys, plains, deserts, marshes, and the like. In addition to their geodetic and topographical work, they collected and cataloged geological, botanical, and zoological specimens.[6] They also inevitably interacted with different ethnic, linguistic, and religious groups. Even as they alerted these groups to the coming of the border, they also collected ethnographic and socioeconomic data about them, information from which this study makes ample use.

Data gathering and reconnaissance sometimes preceded the survey party. Even before the commissioners were appointed, Captain Felix Jones, a commander in the Indian navy and surveyor of Mesopotamia, and Major Rawlinson, the British consul at Baghdad and a famed archeologist, carried out a preliminary survey between Baghdad and the Luristan Mountains to assess the feasibility of the larger project. In addition to reports on archeological sites, they produced accounts of subjects as varied as tribes, public buildings in Baghdad, goods (from broccoli to gazelles) sold in bazaars, prices and currencies, administrative structures, water resources, land tenure, the situation of women, types of houses and accommodation, cuisine, zoology, and botany. As part of his duties, Jones also carried out astronomical and traverse operations. To determine the routes to be followed by the commission, he mapped the distances between stops and the longitude and latitude of various points and provided

[5] PRO.FO 78/2726, Memo on Turco-Persian Boundary Question (1865).
[6] For the extensive notes of William Kenneth Loftus, the British team's geologist, including diagrams of the region's mountains and rock types, see "On the GEOLOGY of portions of the TURKO-PERSIAN FRONTIER and of the DISTRICTS ADJOINING" in *The Quarterly Journal of the Geological Society of London* 11 (1855): 247–344.

synoptical tables of daily distances between destinations.[7] If the survey extended the reach of Ottoman and Iranian hegemony to some of the most intractable parts of their respective domains, it did so only with the help – and, when necessary, the clout – of the tsar's and queen's cadres. In this sense, it also established the geographical gaze of the empires in the borderland.[8] The travelers, officials, officers, and surveyors who followed, literally, in the footsteps of Jones and Rawlinson, would multiply this gaze.

Even if in the short run it left no visible mark on the landscape, the work of the first survey commission deserves attention for a variety of reasons. First, through its analysis, we can demonstrate the role and contribution of the Ottoman and Iranian bureaucracies and the borderland societies in shaping the boundary. Second, the survey confirmed Britain and Russia as the new brokers in Ottoman-Iranian relations, while introducing the borderlanders to the notion of boundary, direct imperialist intervention, and expanding state authority in their habitat. Third, to paraphrase James Scott's observations in a different context, the very act of surveying the landscape and its inhabitants was an effective strategy to bring less-governed or virtually autonomous peoples and spaces to a heel.[9] Developments in military, transportation, and (soon thereafter) communication technologies would further facilitate this smoothing of the rough edges of the land and its inhabitants to fit them, by force if necessary, into the newly constructed geo-bodies.

THE COMMISSIONERS AND THEIR DUTIES

One of the authors of the Erzurum Treaty, British commissioner Lieutenant-Colonel W. F. Williams, volunteered to lead the survey's British team.[10] Initially rejected, he was later appointed as the British plenipotentiary.[11] As

---

[7] James Felix Jones, "Narrative of a Journey to the Frontier of Turkey and Persia, through Part of Kurdistan," in *Memoirs of Baghdad*, 135–213. Like the British, the Russians collected data. For example, the orientalist N. V. Khanykof visited the surveyors' camp in Lahijan. Y. I. Tchirikof, *Traveling Diary of Yegor Ivanovich Tchirikof*, 125, in British Library, IOR, L/P/S 11/29 and also PRO.FO 881/10116.

[8] Mathew H. Edney, *Mapping an Empire: The Geographical Construction of British India, 1765–1843* (Chicago: University of Chicago Press, 1997).

[9] James C. Scott, *The Art of Not Being Governed: An Anarchist History of Upland Southeast Asia* (New Haven, CT, and London: Yale University Press, 2009), 3–4.

[10] PRO.FO 78/2705, First correspondence started on June 16, 1848.

[11] PRO.FO 78/2717, 24 June 1848, and FO to Admiralty, June 16, 1848, *Schofield 2*, 19–22. In June 1848, Williams returned to the frontier accompanied by Lieutenant Glascott of the Royal Navy, who served as the British commission's surveyor and astronomer. Glascott had employed methods of geodetic triangulation and measuring by means of signals in Venezuela, Brazil, and British Guiana in 1841–43. Tchirikof, *Diary*, 34.

Colonel Dainesi, the Russian commissioner at Erzurum, had become a general and was assigned elsewhere, Colonel Yegor Ivanovitch Tchirikof was appointed to represent the tsar at the end of September 1848.[12] Also in September, Tehran appointed its previous ambassador to Istanbul, Mirza [Sayyid] Ja'far [Hoseyni] Khan (Mohandis Bashi, Mushir al-Dawleh), who was educated at Woolwich Military Academy.[13] The high-ranking bureaucrat Mehmet Emin Dervish Pasha (also known as Kimyager, or the Chemist), who was educated in Istanbul and Paris, was appointed Ottoman plenipotentiary, in part because it was thought that his knowledge of French (and some English) would enable him to communicate directly with the mediating commissioners.[14]

Soon after their appointments, with instructions in hand, the commissioners advanced to Baghdad, the settled-on meeting point. Stratford Canning's letter of instruction to Williams answers the question of why the Great Powers undertook the survey operation. Benevolently, Canning urged the commissioners to guard the interests of the inhabitants of the vast lands through which the boundary was intended to run. In addition to drawing the line between the states, they were to

Lay the foundation of much social improvement to be gradually developed among the wild inhabitants of those countries, at the same time they will contribute powerfully to the maintenance of peace between respective governments. Nor is it too much to hope that by bringing the local features and natural productions of a region hitherto little or at all frequented by intelligent travelers to the notice of the civilized world, your commission may assist in extending the sphere of useful knowledge, and eventually in opening new channels of commercial intercourse.[15]

[12] PRO.FO 78/2717, Bloomsely to Palmerston, St. Petersburg, September 26, 1848. Tchirikof's name is spelled differently by each source. I prefer the most common form. Among his staff, we could identify his secretary, 'M. A. Gamazof; Staff-Captain, Proskuriakoff; and topographer, Ogranovitch.

[13] For his life, see Mirza Ja'far, *Risalah-i Tahqiqat-i Sarhadiyyah*, ed. Muhammad Mushiri (Tehran: Bunyad-i Farhang-i Iran, 1348/1969), Introduction.

[14] For a short biography and a list of his later positions, see Mehmed Süreyya, *Sicilli Osmanî* 2 (Istanbul: Tarih Vakfı Yurt Yayınları, 1996) and Mehmed Es'ad, *Mir'at-ı Mekteb-i Harbiye* (Istanbul: Şirket-i Mürettibiye Matbaası, 1310/1895), 142–43. Dervish Pasha's staff included his secretary, Hurşîd Efendi, later pasha; chief engineer, Kaimmakam Tahir Pasha, later Es'ad Efendi; second engineer, Kolağası Yunus Efendi; cartographic engineer, Mustafa Efendi of Soma; doctor, Konstantin; and pharmacist, Nove. See Ibrahim Aykun, "Erzurum Konferansı (1843–1847) ve Osmanlı-Iran Hudut Antlaşması" (Ph.D. diss., Erzurum Atatürk Üniversitesi, 1995), 245. Also PRO.FO 78/2717, Canning to Palmerston, Theracia, September 25, 1848.

[15] For Canning's Letters of Instruction, see PRO.FO 78/2705, December 9, 1848, and 78/2717, December 16, 1848.

Moreover, as agents of this civilizing mission, the commission members were "to endeavor to obtain information as to the state of commerce and capability of extension."[16] Warned that he and his men were mediating commissioners whose job was to act as auxiliaries to the negotiating commissioners, Williams was advised to maintain close ties with his Russian counterpart to implement the survey according to scientific principles. Even though it did not lie within the strict definition of his duties, he was instructed to pay attention to "the fourth and eighth articles of the treaty, relating to dues for pasturage, to the establishment of military stations and to the settlement of the tribes hitherto fluctuating in their allegiance."[17] Canning later forwarded an additional letter, along with a detailed memorandum written by Henry A. Layard, the future British ambassador to Istanbul, who was at the time a traveler and archeologist of biblical and mythological sites. In the latter, Layard emphasized that the surveyors also gather commercial, ethnographical, linguistic, zoological, and botanical data.[18]

Copies of Williams's instructions were forwarded to M. de Titow, the Russian representative in Istanbul, who confirmed that he was issuing the same instructions to his plenipotentiary, Tchirikof. In addition, "Chirikof was told that the delimitation was based on Article III of the Treaty of Erzurum, that the Russian cabinet urged the commission to indicate on maps, and on the frontier itself, the path of the boundary wherever accepted by the principals."[19] On the contested portions of the boundary, Russia advocated that the lines claimed by Iran and the Ottoman Empire be traced on a map, and that the mediators then trace their own recommendations on the same map in accordance with the Treaty of Erzurum. Having thus put down in different colors three possible lines, the delegates should proceed, avoiding delays by leaving the final negotiations to be settled in Constantinople.

The Great Powers were not alone in their desire "to integrate and monetize the people, lands, and resources of the periphery."[20] As agents

---

[16] Ibid., December 16, 1858.

[17] Ibid.

[18] PRO.FO 78/2707, Additional Instructions Given to Turco-Persian Frontier Commission (no date). Also PRO.FO 78/2717 Canning to Williams – Letter of Instructions, December 16, 1848.

[19] Maurice Harari, *"The Ottoman-Iranian Boundary Question: A Case Study in the Politics of Boundary Making in the Near and Middle East"* (Ph.D. diss., Columbia University, 1953), 94. For Tchirikof's instructions, see Titow to Tchirikof, *Schofield* III, 115–17.

[20] Scott, *The Art of Not Being Governed,* 4.

of the states claiming those spaces, the Iranian and Ottoman plenipotentiaries must have received similar instructions. Although we were unable to
locate such documents, their accounts, which detail the population, agricultural production, and fiscal capacity of the borderland communities,
suggest that they, too, were ordered to collect information about the
regions' inhabitants and write detailed reports on local administration as
well as agricultural and industrial production.[21] Not limiting itself to
decidedly Ottoman lands, the Ottoman commission's general report was
meant to be a statistical collection and (as its author, Hurşîd Efendi, states)
to provide more accurate knowledge about the borderlanders, whose real
character and lives had been surrounded by a cloud of mystery and
exaggerated hearsay.[22] Indeed, the effendi completed a very detailed
account of the frontier districts and the groups inhabiting them. Despite
his intention to transcend stereotypes, however, his account differs little
from the reports produced by London's representatives. He classified the
inhabitants using categories analogous to contemporary European notions
of so-called oriental races and detailed the manners and customs of countries and groups that any imperial servant from the self-styled civilized core
might encounter. His superior, Dervish Pasha, also penned a long *layiha*,
or pamphlet, describing the frontier delimitation.[23] The pasha's stated goal
was to analyze the *hudud-u kadime*, or ancient frontier, and the situation
of its *ashair*, or tribes. Like Hurşîd Efendi, he provided valuable information about local histories and some of the *ashair* and *tavaif*, or clans, while
also achieving the overtly political goal of claiming most of the disputed
and some undisputedly Iranian districts for the Ottoman Empire.

---

[21] Following Dervish Pasha's appointment, the governors of Mosul, Baghdad, Kurdistan, and
Erzurum were informed that besides carrying out the delimitation, he would also report on
the region's general conditions and should be assisted accordingly. See BOA.A.MKT 169/92,
1265.2.26/08 May 1849; A.MKT 175/69, 1265.3.25/06 June 1849; A.MKT 211/5,
1265.8.13/25 October 1849.

[22] Mehmed Hurşîd Effendi (later a pasha, minister, and governor) published his *Seyâhatnâme-i
Hudud* in 1860. He also published a *lâyiha* (pamphlet), *Tahdid-i hudud-u Iraniyye me'mur-
iyetiyle fi 28 sefer sene 65 ve fi 11 Kanun-u Sani sene 64 tarihinde taraf-ı devlet-i âliyeden i'zam
buyurulmuş olan müteveffa Derviş Paşa ile birlikde bulunan Ankara valisi esbak Hurşîd Paşa
tarafından keleme alınmış olan lâyihadır* (Dersaadet: Mahmud Bey Matbaası 1300 (1883)).
Gamazof, secretary to the Russian commissioner and later Directeur de l'institut des Langues
Orientales du Ministère des Affaires Étrangères, translated *Seyâhatnâme* into Russian in
1863. For the pasha's life, see *Evkaf-ı Hümayun Nezaretinin Tärihçe-i Teşkilatı ve Nuzzar
Teracim-i Ahvali* (Darülhilâfetil'Aliye: Evkaf-i Islamiye Matbaası, 1335/1919): 142–44.

[23] *Devlet-i Aliye ile Iran Devleti Beyninde Olan Hudud-un Layihasıdır* (Istanbul: Matbaa-i
Amire, 1870), in BOA.A.DVN.NHM 32/9. The *layiha* was also published as Derviş Paşa,
Tahdid-i Hudud-u İraniye (Istanbul: Matbaa-i Amire, 21.Ş.1267/1870). [Hereafter,
Dervish, *Tahdid*.]

The account of the Iranian commissioner, Mirza Ja'far Khan, makes plain that his goals were similar to those of the Ottoman officials. His detailed defense of Iranian claims is mainly concerned with the topography of rivers, mountains, hills, valleys, and settlements. Understandably devoting many pages to show why, in geographical and historical terms, the disputed districts belonged to Iran, he also provided productive ethnographic and historical data on borderland communities.[24] In accordance with his instructions, Tchirikof also penned a detailed account of the survey that includes invaluable geographic, ethnographic, and historical information.[25] Williams, too, was to have written an account; regrettably, before he could do so, his personal notes "had the misfortune to be dropped overboard near Gravesend and found a sepulchre in the mud of the Thames."[26] Despite this loss, the surviving accounts and the instructions to the mediating commissioners, augmented by official correspondence and the nearly unmanageable notes of auxiliary personnel and travelers, make this survey one of the best-documented imperial expansion and enclosure projects in this part of the world. Providing a wealth of data on the local peoples and illuminating the objectives of the commission's various parties, they articulate the goal of transforming the borderland into a fully governed, fiscally fertile zone. They also show how this goal combined the mediating parties' political and commercial concerns with the negotiating parties' surveillance and control-oriented goals.

CREATING FACTS ON THE GROUND, OR DERVISH PASHA'S LONG DETOUR AT KOTUR

The British commission, and possibly the Russian one, departed Constantinople around Christmas 1848, traveling via the port of Samsun on the Black Sea coast. After an arduous journey, they arrived at Baghdad

---

[24] See Mirza, *Tahqiqat*.

[25] Tchirikof's incremental notes were edited and expanded by his secretary, Gamazof, who added his own account to the final product, published in St. Petersburg in 1875 as No. 9 of the publications of the Caucasian Section of the Imperial Russian Geographical Society. Here I used the abridged translation prepared by G. F. Fairholme for the Foreign Office in 1912. Unfortunately, Fairholme excludes most of the information useful for social history. See British Library, IOR.L/P/S 11/29 and also PRO.FO 881/10116, *Traveling Diary of Yegor Ivanovich Tchirikof*, hereafter Tchirikof, *Diary*. An abridged translation also appeared in Persian: *Siyahatnameh-e Mosyo Chirkiof*, tr. Akbar Masihi (Tehran: Moassesee Entesharate Amir Kabir, 1379/2001).

[26] G. E. Hubbard, *From the Gulf to Ararat: An Expedition through Mesopotamia and Kurdistan* (Edinburgh: William Blackwood and Sons, 1917), 10.

expecting to find the Ottoman and Iranian plenipotentiaries. Neither was there. The Iranian delegate, who was already late, further postponed his departure after Istanbul dispatched Dervish Pasha to Van, ostensibly for the adjustment of some local questions to prevent a later disruption of the delimitation. This adjustment, which would give rise to the so-called Kotur dispute, interrupted the work of delimitation before it began and created lasting problems for the frontier negotiations. It is important to study the case of Kotur, not only because it would be a hotly debated issue even at the Congress of Berlin in 1878, but also because it provides a good example of changing population dynamics at the borderland and evolving Iranian and Ottoman conceptualizations of *hudud*.

Taking advantage of the instability caused by Muhammad Shah's death, Istanbul instructed Dervish to go to the district of Kotur, a source of much tension in the 1820s, accompanied by troops provided by the *serasker* of the eastern regions, Gözlüklü Mehmet Reşid Pasha, to offer Iranian troops stationed there an opportunity to withdraw. Iran claimed Kotur's thirty-nine villages as part of Khoi. Istanbul, however, asserted that it was part of the Mahmudi *kaza* of Van province, and that the Iranians had taken control of it after the Mahmudi dynasts were eliminated. The pasha was provided with documents to prove that Kotur was Ottoman, but he was also instructed to consult with knowledgeable locals to determine the *hudud-u kadime*, or old boundary, and build (*alamet-i serhaddiye*) boundary signs accordingly. The locations of those signs, with their names and drawings, were to be registered in the *sicil* (register) of the Van court and a map to be sent to Istanbul. This plan no doubt defied the status quo considered the basis for the new frontier commission's negotiations.

Offering Ottoman citizenship to the borderlanders and promulgating an expansionism that would be imitated by later generations of pashas, Dervish also used the occasion to rout Iranian authorities and establish an Ottoman garrison of regular troops. He then occupied Kotur's *nahiya* (township) and all its villages, as well as the district of Akhorek, with its twenty-one villages.[27] He laid the foundation for two fortified barracks to

---

[27] Muhammad Amin Riyahi, *Tarikh-e Khoi* (Tehran: Tarhe Nu, 1378), 325. Mirza Ja'far claims that Dervish Pasha additionally occupied Hevder/Hoder[?], Derik, Chahrik, Shapiran, and some villages of Maku. See Mirza Ja'far, *Tahqiqat*, 168–69, 184. Dervish, *Tahdid-i Hudud-u İraniye*, 84, and an 1852 British "General Report on Border Region" PRO.FO 78/2706 maintain that those districts originally belonged to the Hakkari but were occupied by Abbas Mirza.

house three hundred soldiers, a third for artillery and the commander, a hospital for fifteen men, and other fortifications. Further east, at the village of Esteran (Astaran), he placed another three hundred men, under the newly appointed *kaimmakam* of Kotur and an officer.

According to the pasha, after thorough research, he discovered the old boundary at a place called Damğacıtaşı, ninety minutes on horseback from Esteran, where he erected inscribed pillars to mark the spot and separate Ottoman from Iranian villages. He also stationed forty soldiers to protect it and put signs on top of mountains such as Pirzade to further assert Ottoman ownership.[28] When the other commissioners asked him to relinquish possession of the district and its dependencies, demolish the guardhouse, dismantle newly established passport controls, and proceed to Baghdad, Dervish refused. He maintained that the district belonged to the Ottoman Empire, its inhabitants were Ottomans, the guardhouse was erected on Ottoman soil, and the "viseing [issuing of visas] of traveler's passports is simply a consequence of the system of police and general administration observed anywhere."[29] However, he noted that if the inhabitants were to claim Iranian citizenship, he would withdraw.[30]

The Kotur dispute illustrates how military-strategic considerations influenced the decision making of the statesmen of the time. With sixty homesteads, the village of Kotur was insignificant. However, the defile leading from it ran in the direction of the town of Khoi and beyond and constituted a difficult passage for troops, whereby a small force could stop a large one. By establishing the post at the end of the defile, in the village of Esteran, three hours from Khoi, Dervish Pasha gained possession of one of the chief passes leading toward Tabriz and Urumieh. As Tchirikof described it, the defile was a scaling-ladder thrown across Persian lands;

---

[28] Hurşid claims that the name Damğacıtaşı comes from Damgacıtaşı, where previously the *damga rusumu* (stamp tax) was paid. Mehmed Hurşîd, *Seyâhatnâme-i Hudud*, transcription Alaatttin Eser (Istanbul: Simurg, 1997), 240, and Mirza Ja'far, *Tahqiqat*, 177–78. Dervish maintains that he was told to uncover the ancient (kadim) *hudud* of the *nahiya* of Kotur, and that the people referred to Damğacıtaşı as the beginning of the boundary. Dervish, *Tahdid*, 83, 138. For Dervish's other activities, see Tchirikof, *Diary*, 142–43. For a British account, see PRO.FO 881/2586, General Sir A. B. Kembal, "Memorandum on the present state of the Turco-Persian Boundary Question, and the conditions on which the solution would seem to depend," April 2, 1875, *Schofield* III, 63–71.

[29] PRO.FO 78/2718, Prince Governor of Azerbaijan to Amiri Nizam and Amiri Nizam to Colonel Farrand, April 29, 1849. Farrand to Canning, Tehran, April 30, 1849, Farrand to Palmerston, Goolaheck, May 23, 1849. Also PRO.FO 78/2709, Dervish Pasha to Mirza Jafar Khan, September 12, 1849.

[30] Aykun, "Erzurum," 247.

its whole length was lined, on both sides, by Iranian territories.[31] Although such strategic considerations played a pivotal role in Dervish's occupation of Kotur, the claims and counterclaims that followed also show that the elimination of the Kurdish dynasts had resulted in a proprietary and administrative vacuum that various parties were rushing to fill. Claiming that his actions were guided by a *ferman-i 'ali*, or royal decree, Dervish argued that he had in fact liberated (*istihlas*) a region that belonged to the Mahmudi dynasty for two centuries, from 1630 to 1830.[32]

Winning Kotur, however, did not satiate the pasha's appetite for the socio-geographic engineering of the borderland. He now set his sights on almost the entire Sunni Kurdish borderland. Beginning with the districts neighboring Kotur, he tried to lure Iran's Sunni Kurdish subjects to the Ottoman side. No doubt such actions stirred not-so-dormant sectarian sensitivities. Moved by the prospect of relief from Shi'i rule, Sunni Iranian subjects began applying for Ottoman citizenship and protection in a process that would end only after the First World War.[33] As we will see in the following chapters, Dervish Pasha's agenda defined Ottoman policy in the borderland for six decades, until the end of its 1905 to 1912 occupation of northwestern Iran.

FINALLY AT WORK: SURVEYORS ON THE GO

Furious over Dervish Pasha's activities, Tehran refused to allow its plenipotentiary to join his colleagues. The impasse lasted for about eight months and was broken only when the mediators guaranteed that the Kotur *fait accompli* would not prejudice their final decision on that district. Reserving its rights to the embattled district, Tehran dispatched its commissioner. The delegates assembled in Baghdad in the summer of 1849, but they were

---

[31] Tchirikof, *Diary*, 29–30. [Gamazof] Tchirikof, *Diary*, 172. Gamazof lists districts and villages occupied by Dervish. This list would prove crucial when Russia made Kotur's return an article of the 1878 Paris Peace Treaty.

[32] According to Dervish, a member of the Mahmudi family, Musa Bey, held the districts in *yurtluk-ocaklık* status but as a result of his recklessness, some Iranians murdered him and took possession. Dervish, *Tahdid*, 123–24. There are other indications that Mahmud acknowledged Iranian authority and was even given the title of *khan*. Sinan Hakan, *Osmanlı Arşiv Belgelerinde Kürtler ve Kürt Direnişleri* (Istanbul: Doz Yayınları, 2011), 50. In addition to the *nahiyas* of Abghai, Aland, Satmanis, Akhorek, Sharafkhana, and Sarai, all of which gradually passed into Iranian hands, the pasha provides the names of other villages sold by lesser *agha*s to Iranian subjects from Khoi. Ibid., 127.

[33] The people of Yezdigani near Kotur made one such appeal, complaining of Iranian oppression and applying for Ottoman citizenship. BOA.A.MKT 215/96, 1265.9.6/ August 21, 1849.

unable to begin work immediately because of a fever epidemic in the region between Suleimanieh and Baghdad, spread by the flooding of the Tigris.

When they finally commenced, they spent months on particulars such as arranging security and planning where to start and how to move forward. They also gathered information on the most disputed locales, including Muhammarah/Shatt al-Arab, where they agreed to begin their mission. When they at last set off, the vessel that carried them along the Tigris was the East India Company's armed steamer, the *Nitocris*, which bore both British and Russian flags. Arab vessels were hired for transport, and mules, horses, and servants were to proceed by land, guarded by troops commissioned by the Ottoman government.[34] The Iranian commission traveled on the *Nitocris*, but Dervish Pasha "went on a gunboat expressly built for him at Baghdad and armed with eight guns. His troops later embarked on two Turkish war-ships stationed in the Shatt al-Arab."[35] When the parties reached Muhammarah, the sheikhs of Ka'b, complying with instructions issued by Mirza Ja'far, accorded them "a most polite and honorable reception."[36] It was early January 1850, exactly a year after the British surveyors departed from Istanbul.

Providing an idea of the size of the retinues and the kind of auxiliary personnel that accompanied the commissions, the "Muster Roll of the Servants and Camp Followers" of the British team for 1851 lists one steward, six servants, three cavaliers, seven horse keepers, twelve muleteers, five tent pitchers, one cook and assistant, one washer man, four baggage men, four porters, four instrument carriers, and one water carrier. Along with a handful of auxiliaries, the total number of men came to fifty-six. Later with the addition of a *mirahor* (stable master), another attendant, and five muleteers, as well as staff turnover, the number rose to sixty-two. Additionally, the British team had saddle horses for its members and their servants as well as sixty-nine mules and packhorses for the conveyance of tents, baggage, litters for the sick, supplies, and when necessary forage.[37] One may assume that the

---

[34] William Kenneth Loftus, F.G.S., *Travels and Researches in Chaldea and Susnia; with an Account of Excavations at Warka, the "Erech" of the Nimrod, Shush, "Sushan the Palace" of Eshter, in 1849–1952* (New York: Robert Carter and Brothers, 1857), 72.

[35] Tchirikof, *Diary*, 9–10.

[36] Ibid. and Mirza Ja'far, *Tahqiqat*, 49.

[37] "Muster Roll of the servants and camp followers of the Turco-Persian Boundary Commission" in PRO.FO 78/2704, Sura, February 8, 1851. Tchirikof supplied a similar list, which is unfortunately excluded from the English and Persian translations I have employed. For the personnel and expenses of the British commissions, see PRO.FO 78/2708. This dossier, like many others, contains ample documents related to expenditures. The list supplied is as follows:

Russian, Ottoman, and Iranian commissions were not smaller than the British, as they also wanted to project the grandeur of their empires and enumerate and classify the human and physical geography of the region.

Traveling with such large parties, the commissioners were aware of the potential for causing disturbance among the borderlanders. Long traditions of imperial rule had taught them that the locals would resent their presence and identify their activities with surveillance, conscription, and new taxes. To avoid "provoking among the frontier tribes any suspicion that coercive measures against them were intended, it was decided to restrict the escort to the number necessary for the security of the mixed commission."[38] In spite of such precautions, however, the operation indeed had the aura of a military campaign.[39] Its spectacle sent a strong signal to the borderlanders that the time of evading state control was coming to end. Yet, this did not deter some from resisting. More than once, the large caravan was harassed and daring thieves occasionally curtailed it.

On January 17, 1850, the conferences began. The first eight extended over three weeks and allowed the negotiating commissioners to bring forward their proposals. The mediating commissioners then presented their ideas for the settlement of the questions in dispute. They soon discovered, however, that inscribing the terms of the Erzurum Treaty onto the variegated geography of the borderland would be a process fraught with difficulties.

LOCATING THE BOUNDARY OF MUHAMMARAH AND SHATT AL-ARAB

As the previous chapter detailed, proprietary and navigational rights over the Shatt al-Arab River and ownership of the small town of Muhammarah and the Island of Khizr constituted the most contentious issues of the frontier. In

Annual Expenses
1843 176,940 piasters, 22 paras
1844 99,662 piasters, 39 paras
1845 97,895 piasters, 2 paras
1846 109,118 piasters, 25 paras
1847 47,047 piastess, 10 paras
1849 516,878 piasters, 30 paras
1850 611,530 piasters, 30 paras
1851 561,189 piasters
1852 601,801 piasters (in another account, 740,180)

[38] Tchirikof, *Diary*, 8–9.
[39] Ibid., 9. Also Mirza Ja'far, *Tahqiqat*, 49. It appears that the warships had the intended effect. The Arab tribesmen confessed they were more afraid of the ships than the Turkish troops that had previously plundered Muhammarah. Tchirikof, *Diary* 13–14.

this region, strategic, religious, economic, ethnic, and geographic boundaries merged like nowhere else. Additionally, the Shatt seemed to defy any fixed category of river boundary delimitation – including "joint sovereignty," "bank as boundary line," "median line," "thalweg," and "arbitrary straight line" – because different criteria applied to its different parts.[40] Claiming that the Tigris and Euphrates were Ottoman rivers, Istanbul was reluctant to share jurisdiction of the Shatt and questioned why it should allow Tehran to control its outlet to the sea merely because an Iranian stream – that is, the Karun River – had changed its course. The Ottoman claim had some validity, as British reports from before the formation of the commission, based on historical as well as contemporary information, argue that Ottoman sovereignty on the Shatt was the more tenable option. As an indication of this, Iranian vessels entering the Shatt had to pay dues to Ottoman authorities before the 1847 treaty.[41]

Istanbul, as we have seen, signed the Erzurum Treaty only after the Iranian ambassador to Paris was made to sign an extra document, the *izahatnama*, or *Explanatory Note*. The Ottomans considered the *izahatnama*, which gave them control of the Shatt, to be as binding as the treaty itself and insisted that Iran accept it as a prerequisite to negotiations. That document did grant specific sections of Muhammarah to Iran, including its *lengergah* or anchorage (i.e., the broad and deep arm of the Karun River), the Haffar Canal where the Karun enters the Shatt al-Arab, and the Island of Khizr (present-day Abadan). However, it also specified that the Sublime Porte did not cede any other parts "there may be in this region."[42] Using this clause to justify his actions, Dervish Pasha advanced his territorial claims deep into Khuzistan. If the map his engineers drew had been accepted, it would have left Muhammarah and the Island of Khizr as Iranian enclaves within the sultan's domains.[43] Not surprisingly, the

---

[40] For these terms, see Richard N. Schofield, *Evolution of the Shatt al-'Arab Boundary Dispute* (Wisbech, Cambridgeshire, UK: Middle East & North African Studies Press, 1986), 13. In river boundaries, *Thalweg* signifies a stream's line of maximum depth.

[41] Kaiyan Homi Kaikobad, *The Shat-al-Arab Boundary Question: A Legal Reappraisal* (Oxford, UK: Clarendon Press, 1988) 15.

[42] This dispute continued long into the twentieth century and Iran continuously denounced the *Explanatory Note*. See Schofield, *Evolution of the Shatt*, 45–46.

[43] According to this map, (See Map 7) the border would have started at the mouth of the Jarrahiyah River, with a line cutting through Ghoban, passing from the point where the Karun River meets the Haffar Canal. From there, it would have passed through the environs of Hoveyze (Hawiza), leaving the Hor Marsh on the Ottoman side. BOA.HR.SYS 96/19. Defining the *eyalet* of Basra, Hurşîd mentions Ghoban sanjak, the Island of Khizr, and Muhammarah as parts of the province, maintaining they were given to Iran. The word

Iranian plenipotentiary denounced Dervish's claims, arguing that the ambassador to Paris had been sent to Istanbul to ratify the treaty as it stood and was not authorized to modify its clauses or append explanatory notes.[44] Insisting that the *izahatnama* was not binding, he suggested a different demarcation, closer to the present-day one, through the middle of the Shatt. Such a line would grant the islands on the river to Iran and give both parties joint use of and sovereignty over the waterways. The Muhammarah dispute, which the mediators thought they had resolved in Istanbul, once again clogged negotiations from beginning to end.

Once again, the negotiating parties were asked to provide documentary and *viva voce* evidence to authenticate their claims to all districts over which they asserted ownership. Following the pattern set at Erzurum, the Ottomans submitted various documents and brought locals to testify, whereas the Iranians clung to actual possession as proof of historical ownership. In addition to what the Ottoman commission had previously provided at Erzurum, Dervish Pasha submitted deeds of conveyance and sale (*timar beratı, hujjet,* and *buyuruldu*) and old decrees partly provided by the Basra government. Dating mostly to the seventeenth century, these documents reiterated Istanbul's claims to Haffar, Ghoban, and the Island of Khizr.[45] However, as happened at the previous conferences, the mediating commissioners considered them inconclusive because they dated to the times of the Ottoman occupation. Similarly ineffective was the Ottoman reliance on the celebrated Arabic dictionary *Al-Qamus* and (yet again) the *Geographical Memoirs* of John M. Kinneir. Likewise, the testimony of thirty-five residents of Kuwait, affirming Muhammarah as Ottoman and Fallahiyeh (the main town of the Ka'b tribe) as Iranian, did not pass muster.[46]

Lacking documents but secure in Iran's current occupation and the allegiance of the local population, Mirza Ja'far emphasized that the status quo required the parties to accept the situation on the ground, except in the cases of the Shatt and Zohab.[47] Any claim to the Island of Khizr or beyond should be seen as a reneging on the treaty. He also noted that the absence of any reference to them in the 1639 treaty was proof that the lands south of Badra-Jassan – those claimed by Dervish Pasha – were Iranian. Moreover,

"given" disturbed Iranian authorities, who claimed those regions as part of historical Iran. See Hurşid, *Seyâhatnâme*, 3; Dervish, *Tahdid*, 3; Mirza Ja'far, *Tahqiqat*, 60–1, 63.

[44] PRO.FO 78/2719, Journal des conferences pour la delimitation de la frontiere Turco-Persane, Premiere Conference, Mohammera, 16/ Janvier 28, 1850. Harari, *Turco-Persian*, 104.

[45] For these documents see Dervish, *Tahdid*, 5–9.

[46] Aykun, "Erzurum," 250.

[47] PRO.FO 78/2711, Williams to Canning, July 10, 1844, *Schofield I*, 373.

Mirza Ja'far noted that the same treaty urged Iran not to meddle in the affairs of Basra and Baghdad but made no mention of Khuzistan. The original treaty's silence on the matter was proof that the lands belonged to Iran.[48] Similarly, he observed that despite its emphasis on tribes, the 1823 treaty did not ask that the Ka'b be returned to the Ottomans. Recalling the 1837 Ottoman attack on Muhammarah, Mirza Taqi argued that 'Ali Rıza Pasha would not have pillaged that town if the Ottomans had truly considered it theirs. If Istanbul believed Muhammarah to be its own, why did its envoy Sarim Efendi agree to pay compensation for it? And why did the people of Muhammarah remain loyal to Iran, refusing Ottoman approaches and monetary incentives even when Tehran increased their annual taxes tenfold?[49]

In addition to advocating these arguments, Tehran ordered Mirza Ja'far to make a display of Iranian sovereignty. To comply, he hoisted the Iranian flag on the walls of Muhammarah; appointed several Iranians to public office; and made Sheikh Hajji Jaber, the Ka'b chief, governor with the title of *khan*. In response, Dervish Pasha blockaded the town from the Haffar Canal with two warships. Meanwhile, ships of the British Persian Gulf flotilla were also anchored in the waters of Muhammarah.[50] To relieve the escalating situation, the mediators – who had in the meantime realized that the *Explanatory Note* had been drawn up without knowledge of local conditions – proposed that several alternative lines for the Shatt al-Arab delimitation be submitted to the negotiating parties' respective courts and, pending their decision, the commission should continue northward.[51]

As Williams wrote to Canning, the meditating commissioners had to "combat the Turkish pretensions to the east of Muhammarah and the Island of Khizr [while abstaining] from admitting Persian claims to the Islands in the Shatt al-Arab."[52] They (in essence Williams) proposed that the boundary should run southward from Hawizeh, pass through the towers named by Dervish to the junction of the Jiyedeh (Abu Jeddeh/ Jazih) River south of the Shatt al-Arab, and from there along the east bank of the Shatt to the Persian Gulf. Distancing the Porte from territories east of the Shatt, and Tehran from the islands in the Shatt, the proposal allowed Iran navigation of the Karun and free entrance to and security in

---

[48] Mirza Ja'far, *Tahqiqat*, 93–94.
[49] Ibid., 64–65.
[50] Tchirikof, *Diary*, 13.
[51] "Memorandum Respecting Turco-Persian Boundary Delimitation" [by Arnold Kemball], March 1875, *Schofield III*, 87–163, hereafter Kemball Report.
[52] Williams to Canning, Muhammarah, February 4, 1850, *Schofield II*, 111–12.

the port of Muhammarah, while also connecting Muhammarah with Iran. The proposal also granted Istanbul all the navigable parts of the Shatt, ensuring its navigation "by the destruction of the fort built by Sheikh Jabir (Kal'a Filiyah), during the conferences of Erzeroum."[53] Because Basra previously received customs taxes from ships passing up through the Shatt, Istanbul was concerned it would lose its commercial significance if Muhammarah, where large ships could dock at high tide, emerged as the *entrepôt* of the Gulf for European and Indian goods, as well as Ottoman and Iranian merchandise destined for export.[54] The mediating proposal aimed to safeguard navigation up to Basra, thereby guaranteeing the future security and prosperity of both Basra and Muhammarah. The Porte predictably rejected the Williams line, even as Tehran consented to it and surrendered its claim to territories lying four miles further upstream on the condition that the Ka'b living north of the line be transferred to Iran.[55] Tehran's claims to the Ka'b, as we have seen, were not baseless. During this period, they remained steadfast in their allegiance to Iran. Aware of Dervish's plans to enter Goban, they had taken up arms and sent their livestock and property away in preparation for his possible advance.[56]

Although such provocative posturing and diplomatic bickering hindered the work of the commission, the unbearable heat, high humidity, and simoom of the gulf also impeded their efforts.[57] As a result, toward the end of May 1850, in the company and at the suggestion of Ja'far Khan, the mediating commissioners temporarily adjourned to the cooler mountains of Luristan, where members of the British commission carried out excavations at the ancient city of Susa, thus fulfilling another part of their mission.[58] In the meantime, the Russian commission and a few members of the British one went to Khorramabad, Borujerd, Gulpayagan, Isfahan, Hamadan, Kermanshah, and Dezful, finally returning from Susa to Muhammarah. Dervish, to the great anger of Mirza Ja'far, carried out his own surveys along the frontier, interviewing and trying to lure local communities to the Ottoman side, while keeping two warships and troops in Muhammarah. To prevent an Ottoman *fait accompli* that might create grounds for *uti possidetis*, Mirza Ja'far sent most of his troops to

---

[53] Ibid.
[54] Dervish, *Tahdid*, 11. Dervish also wanted to retain Muhammarah so that Istanbul would benefit from Iranian trade.
[55] Schofield, Introduction, *Schofield II*, xiii.
[56] Williams to Canning, Muhammarah, February 4, 1850.
[57] Loftus, *Travels*, 280.
[58] Tchirikof, *Diary*, 14.

Muhammarah and Fallahiyah to strengthen the forces of the Ka'b's *sheikh al-mashaikh*, leaving only a detachment of soldiers and thirty cavalry to protect the mediating commissioners.[59]

Their sojourns completed, the commissioners reconvened and the negotiators picked up where they left off. Mirza Ja'far protested the Ottoman military guards stationed in locations where Dervish thought the boundary should pass and objected to the pasha's attempts to entice the Ka'b and other tribes away from the shah.[60] To counterbalance Ottoman claims to lands east of the Shatt, he also reiterated Tehran's old argument that because the Iranians were not interfering in Suleimanieh, which they had once claimed, the Ottomans should not meddle in Muhammarah. Finally, he again stressed the importance of the nationality of the region's tribes, contending that the Ka'b were Iranian because they were Shi'i.

Desiring to avoid the diplomatic perils that came with the conflation of nationality and religious identity, the mediators underscored that the real objective of the treaty was to make Muhammarah a viable commercial center and ensure the passage of ships navigating from the interior through the Karun River. At the same time, the mediators believed that allotting any location east of Muhammarah to the Porte would be like creating a colony or an island in the midst of Iranian territory. Hence, they continued to insist on the Williams line, which ensured Ottoman rights to the navigation of the Shatt toward Basra and left to Iran the lands up to six miles north of Muhammarah.[61] Dervish Pasha, unsurprisingly, continued his vigorous protest. Insisting that his rivals had no sovereignty on the Shatt, he demanded assurance that Iran would not erect fortifications along its banks or have right of possession to its bed. Allowing the Persian merchant navy freedom of navigation on the Shatt al-Arab to the mouth of the Karun, he declared, should in no way impair the rights of the Porte to the full possession of the riverbed.[62]

Deadlocked once again, the commission sent all four governments a map with three separate lines, as proposed by Dervish Pasha, Mirza Ja'far, and the mediating commissioners (i.e., the Williams line). While waiting for their governments to respond, the mediators decided to continue northward. Dervish Pasha, however, refused to leave Muhammarah until his engineers

[59] See the detailed Kemball Report, *Schofield III*, 87–163.

[60] Harari, *Turco-Persian*, 111, PRO.FO 78/2720, Sheil to Palmerston, Tehran, January 25, 1851.

[61] PRO.FO 78/2719, Première Conference, Muhammarah, 16–18 Janvier; Deuxième Conference, Muhammarah 19–29 Janvier, 1850; Harari, *Turco-Persian*, 105.

[62] Harari, *Turco-Persian*, 106, and PRO.FO 78/2719, Deuxième Conference, Muhammarah, 19/29 Janvier 1850.

had finished collecting the information he needed to draw a map of the Island of Khizr and its environment. He also insisted that no Iranian troops or employees be left behind and no taxes or customs be collected in the area; otherwise, he would consider it necessary to leave behind an equal number of troops and employees. In protest, the Iranian plenipotentiary decided to remain at Muhammarah until he received instructions from his government.[63] As the commissioners' work stalled once more, Ottoman tribes manifested their resistance to the delimitation efforts. The sheikh of the large Muntafiq confederation, theoretically an Ottoman subject, for example, did not allow Dervish and his entourage to enter the town of Suk al-Sheikh (Suku's-Shuyuh), an act that Istanbul described as "unbefitting."[64]

In response to Mirza Ja'far's refusal to proceed northward, the British Foreign Office directed Sir Justin Sheil to warn Tehran that if it left the settling of the dispute to force of arms with the Ottoman Empire, it would be the losing party.[65] At the same time, to alleviate Iran's fears, Sheil endeavored to obtain assurances from Palmerston and Canning that if the commission moved northward before settling the question of Muhammarah, the mediating powers would not then grant the Ottoman Empire a portion of Zohab province, the other hotly disputed area. Such assurances did not satisfy the Iranians, who expressed an utter lack of confidence in the Porte's intentions. An official joint note from the Russian and British ambassadors asking the Porte to accept the Williams line was likewise of no avail.[66] With no resolution in sight, the mediating governments finally agreed to proceed along the remaining parts of the frontier.

A breakthrough seemed to arrive in early 1851, with the news that that Iran's prime minister had promised to accept the Williams line, provided

---

[63] Harari, *Turco-Persian*, 108; PRO.FO 78/2719, Troisième Conference, Muhammarah, 23 Janvier-4 Fevrier and Quatrième Conference, Muhammarah, 2–14 Fevrier, 1850.

[64] BOA.A.MKT.UM 33/19, 17 C. 1266 /April 30, 1850. Two years later, the Muntafiq were still defying Ottoman authority, whereas the two other large Arab tribal confederations, the Shammar and the Banu Lam, were ready to fight against them on behalf of the government. Similarly, the inhabitants of Karbala and Najaf had rebelled against the governor. Karbala was easily quelled, but "the Turkish governor has been compelled to quit the town with the garrison," wrote Williams, who also opined, "The Turks hold Iraq very much on the same tenure as the British held Cabul and Kandahar. There is the same numerical disproportion between the rulers and the ruled. The same bitter animosity of race. Baghdad is not less distant from Kharpoot the nearest valid military support than the Kabul from Sutlej, and the marches of Chaleda are not less difficult for troops, than were the passes of the Afghan Mountains." See PRO.FO 78/2723. Williams to Canning, May 23, 1852.

[65] PRO.FO 78/2719, Foreign Office to Sheil, September 11, 1850.

[66] PRO.FO 78/2719, Joint Official Note from Canning and Titow to Ali Pasha, September 20, 1850.

that the status quo was restored, which in essence meant the acceptance, by the Ottomans, of the principle of *uti possidetis*.[67] But the interpretation of the status quo itself was another source of contention. Thus, when the commissioners reconvened at Muhammarah in mid-February, Dervish Pasha's new instructions were irreconcilable with the Iranian demand, and the commissioners, stymied once more, dispersed at the beginning of April.[68] Two years had passed since they had set off for the frontier, yet only three weeks had been spent in the real work of delimitation.[69]

Exploiting the stalemate, the negotiating parties amped up their efforts to win over the borderlanders. Dervish Pasha, for example, instructed Ka'b chiefs including Sheikh Hajji Jabir and Sheikh Faris [Khan] to refuse to pay revenue to the shah, resist Iranian authorities, and apply for assistance when necessary to the governor of Basra. Sheikh Faris, in response, insisted that although his people had once been Ottoman subjects, he and all the Ka'b tribes and clans were loyal subjects of Iran and had been since the time of Karim Khan Zand.[70] Undeterred, Dervish offered a ten-year period of no taxation as well as future tax breaks. Despite their clear declaration of loyalty and identity, the pasha's offer provided the Ka'b with an opportunity to demand the same from Mirza Ja'far. Allegiance, no doubt, must have tangible benefits, and material interests figured prominently in identity formation. However, the Iranian commissioner claimed that he was able to convince them to reject the Ottoman offer while still raising their yearly tax (although given the delicacy of the times, the raise was minimal). Mirza Ja'far continued to rely on Ka'b allegiance to claim Iranian rights over the lands they inhabited,[71] whereas the pasha kept asserting that Muhammarah was Ottoman land and should be returned.[72]

[67] Harari, *Turco-Persian*, 112; Sheil to Palmerston, Tehran, January 29, 1851.

[68] Dervish left for Baghdad in April 1851. With the goal of organizing Ka'b affairs, Mirza Ja'far went to Falahiyah, later advancing to Brujerd, while the Europeans journeyed to Kerrind for its climate and because the negotiations were to be held there if reopened. After five months, they, along with the Iranian commissioner who had since joined them, went to Sinne, the seat of the Vali of Ardalan, to escape a cholera epidemic that had reached Baghdad from Basra and Muhammarah.

[69] Kemball Report, *Schofield, III*, 132.

[70] For Dervish's letter to Sheikh Faris (April 13, 1851) and the sheikh's answer (June 19, 1851), see Mirza, *Tahqiqat*, 69–71, and *Guzidah-i Asnad* I, 433–36; see also PRO.FO 2720 Sheil to Palmerston, Tehran, 7 May 1851.

[71] Mirza Ja'far, *Tahqiqat*, 60, 63.

[72] PRO.FO 78/2704, Mirza Ja'far to Dervish 11 Jemazeel Evvel 1267/March 14, 1851; and Dervish to Mirza Ja'far, March 16, 1851. Dervish to the Mediating Commissioners, March 17, 1851; and Mirza Ja'far to the Mediating Commissioners, March 16, 1851.

Recognizing that the religious underpinnings of Ka'b allegiance to Iran were a mighty obstacle, Dervish Pasha set about trying to convince the Sunni borderlanders of Iran to switch their loyalty to the caliph sultan.[73] Iranians noted that, however, he was not the only Ottoman official given to intrigues, procrastinations and inciting the tribes. Tehran complained that by going to Hakkari with his troops, Mehmed Reshid Pasha had violated the frontier and sent spies to Iran to incite Iranian subjects to rebel.[74] Dervish similarly claimed to have received intelligence that the Iranian commissioner was holding secret meetings with the Ottoman Jaf tribe.[75] All the while, Iranian authorities flew their flag and maintained their garrison, while Ottoman warships remained anchored across from Muhammarah and Dervish continued communicating with the Ka'b chiefs.[76]

Alarmed by Ottoman propaganda and the resultant agitation and fearful that the Ottomans might succeed in persuading some borderlanders to switch their allegiances, Nasir al-Din Shah ordered between thirty thousand and forty thousand troops to gather in Sultaniya, near Zanjan, for a military review, which was intended to be a show of force.[77] News soon spread that considerable levies of troops in Azerbaijan and elsewhere were on the move and that the adjutant general of the Iranian army was inspecting and organizing troops on the Kurdish frontier. As tensions increased, three Ottoman men-of-war anchored opposite Muhammarah. In the meantime, increased conflict among the tribes rendered the implementation of the Erzurum Treaty ever more difficult. The open revolt against Istanbul on the part of some of the powerful tribes of the Baghdad and Mosul regions worsened the situation. Fearing the worst, the British and Russian representatives in Tehran formally expressed their disapproval.[78] This prompted the shah to cancel his plan to go to the border, easing tensions.[79]

---

[73] For letters about Dervish's conduct, see PRO.FO 78/2709, Williams to Canning, Baghdad, August 14, 1849; and Canning to Williams, February 20, 1850, and July 30, 1851.

[74] PRO.FO 78/2705, Mirza Ja'far to Canning [n.d.].

[75] Dervish, *Tahdid*, 62.

[76] PRO.FO 78/2707, Sheil to Canning, Isfahan, August 16, 1851.

[77] Amanat argues that this demonstration was closely linked to Ottoman mistreatment of Iraq's Shi'ites and the shah's desire to be the "Sultan of the Shi'ite nation," as well as the fact that Istanbul permitted his exiled brother, Abbas Mirza, to receive British protection. See Abbas Amanat, *Pivot of the Universe: Nasir Al-Din Shah Qajar and the Iranian Monarchy, 1831–1896* (Berkeley: University of California Press, 1997) 233.

[78] Harari, *Turco-Persian*, 113; PRO, FO 78/2720, Canning to Palmerston, May 28, 1851.

[79] PRO.FO 78/2720, Sheil to Palmerston, March 25, 1851.

Apprehensive and tired of paying for an inconclusive operation, the cabinets of London and St. Petersburg endeavored to effect an agreement that would allow the delimitation work to proceed. Feeling the pressure, the Porte made concessions, including the withdrawal of its warships, and in August 1851, Dervish Pasha was instructed to join his colleagues, but on conditions unacceptable to Persia. Once again, before they started, negotiations reached a standstill. The mediating governments concluded that only joint action of a more conclusive character could restart the proceedings.

Canning and Titow thus drew up a memorandum, which was submitted to London and St. Petersburg[80] and supplemented by a proposal from London to St. Petersburg, calling for their diplomatic agents in Istanbul to work with the commissioners to trace the frontier line on a map in conformity with the Erzurum Treaty.[81] Representing a transition, or potential transition, from the Great Powers serving as mediators to full-fledged arbitrators, the proposal then recommended that London and St. Petersburg should mark the boundary on the ground, prepare maps on the basis of this demarcation, and present Tehran and Istanbul with the results. To force the rival states to agree, the British suggested that if one of them subsequently violated the frontier, the two mediators should promise the aggrieved party their full aid and support. The Russian chancellor, Count Nesselrode, clarified that such an intervention would be moral support and not military in nature.[82]

As London grew even more impatient, Canning reminded Palmerston of the commission's central goal of delimitation: "it must not be forgotten that the interests of humanity, of commerce and of civilization are involved, together with important political questions, in the just and complete execution of the Treaty." Even though drawing a map was costly, he emphasized "it should be remembered that for geographical purposes alone, to say nothing of commercial interests, precise knowledge of the position, character, and direction of the heights and water-courses of those unexplored regions would be indisputably desirable."[83]

While such exchanges were taking place, the commissioners spent most of the spring and summer of 1851 in Sinne, until they were informed that

---

[80] PRO.FO 78/2732, Canning to Palmerston, September 17, 1851; Harari, *Turco-Persian*, 98; PRO.FO 78/2732, Palmerston to G. H. Seymour, October 11, 1851.

[81] Palmerston to Seymour, PRO.FO, October, 11, 1851; in Kemball Report, *Schofield III*, 143–44.

[82] PRO.FO 881/2585, Seymour to Palmerston, St. Petersburg, October 29, 1851, *Schofield III*, 144.

[83] Canning to Palmerston, Therapia, September 17, 1851, *Schofield, III*, 137–39.

St. Petersburg and London had agreed that the delimitation should recommence as quickly as possible.[84] In the company of Mirza Ja'far, the mediators departed on November 7 to conduct surveys and enquiries in the Zohab-Qasr-i Shirin, Mendeli, and Khanaqin areas, which comprised the central zone of the frontier.[85] Dervish Pasha joined them two weeks later. At their first meeting, on November 22, the negotiating commissioners provisionally accepted the status quo at Muhammarah, as defined by the Williams line, and agreed to set aside previous recriminations and renounce any change in the allegiance of the disputed territories' inhabitants. Despite its reluctant acceptance, the Williams line of February 4, 1850, remained the generally accepted interpretation of the territorial provisions of both the 1847 treaty and the annexed "clarifications."[86]

LOCATING THE BOUNDARY OF ZOHAB-QASR-I SHIRIN

As the previous chapter related, Zohab, like Muhammarah, was a region of overlapping boundaries. The commission spent two months trying to untangle its complicated geographical, social, and political topographies, reaching as far as the town of Mendeli. But rather than clarifying the situation, their work revealed that the realities traced on paper were different from those inscribed on the ground. It would not be easy to reconcile text and terrain. Because of the absence of any continuous physical feature, the Treaty of Erzurum had stipulated that the western, or flat lands, would go to the Ottoman Empire, whereas Iran would receive the eastern, or hilly lands. The survey, however, showed that despite the existence of eastern and western directions, there was nothing like a natural line dividing flat and hilly lands because the whole province was a mixture of those features and would not admit the proposed partition.[87] The problem was that in the district of Zohab, the great chain of mountains that formed the boundary between Persia and the Ottoman Empire from the northeastern point of contact changed its topography. Rather than containing a relatively continuous north-to-south ridge, Zohab was crossed by numerous chains of parallel mountains of secondary height that enclosed a number of interior plains and plateaus. These plains and plateaus constituted the focal point of the mediation because tribes loyal to each party used them.[88]

---

[84] Tchirikof, *Diary*, 18.
[85] Ibid., 17–19.
[86] Schofield, Introduction, *Schofield II*, xiii.
[87] Tchirikof, *Diary*, 18–19.
[88] Harari, *Turco-Persian*, 119–20.

On the Ottoman or western side, Sunni Kurds populated a district that also contained the summer pastures of the ʿAli Ilahi Kurds of Sinjabi and Shabankara, who professed allegiance to Iran.[89] The Iranian-dominated south was inhabited by the Guran confederation and included the pasture-lands of two groups of Kalhor Kurds, the Mansuri and the Shahbazi, both of which had ʿAli-Ilahis and Twelver Shiʿi branches and were confessedly Iranian.[90] Further complicating the matter was the frequent presence of the large Ottoman Sunni Kurdish tribal confederation of the Jaf and some Sinne tribes who paid *ser alef*, or pasturage dues, to the *wali* of Sinne.[91] Despite recurrent disagreements, land use was regulated, and Iranian and Ottoman tribes paid pasturage fees to pertinent parties.[92] For example, the Kalhors, Sanjabis, and Shabankara used winter pastures in Khanaqin, Qizil Rabat, Sherban, and Mendeli and paid *ser alef* to Ottoman authorities, whereas the Jaf paid *sar alef* to the *hakim* of Zohab.[93] Because of the porous nature of the frontiers and pressure applied by administrators, many groups changed their permanent habitations even as they continued to seasonally migrate. According to Mirza Jaʿfar, many tribespeople from the Iranian side left and settled in Baghdad or its dependencies; at the same time, numerous inhabitants of Badrai, Jassan, Khanaqin, and Mendeli had originally dwelled in the lands of the tribes of Kermanshah.[94] Even though the province had changed hands numerous times, it was accepted that Muhammad ʿAli Mirza had occupied it during the 1821–22 war. The consequent treaty obligated Tehran to restore all occupied lands but did not name specific regions. As a result, Zohab was never restored. Nor did the 1847 treaty mention restoration; rather, it divided the province between the two parties.

Zohab provides us with various examples that defined a boundary. As noted in the previous chapter, it was a region where strategic

---

[89] For a history of the Sanjabis, see ʿAli Akbar Khan Sanjabi, sardar-i muqtadir, *Il-i Sanjabi va mujahidat-i milli-i Iran: khatirat-i Ali Akbar Khan Sanjabi, sardar-i muqtadir* (Tehran: Shirazah, 2002).

[90] Tchirikof, *Diary*, 67.

[91] Mirza Jaʿfar, *Tahqiqat*, 127

[92] According to the traditional arrangement, if an Ottoman tribe entered a pasture considered Iranian, it would pay taxes to the Ottoman authorities, who would deliver a prearranged sum to the Iranian authorities. A reciprocal policy was practiced by Iranian tribes pasturing in an Ottoman *yaylak* (summer pasture).

[93] Dervish claims that before Dawlatshah's occupation of Zohab, they paid one sheep per hundred (which was accepted as a *sürü*-flock) and a certain amount of money for each family. Dervish, *Tahdid*, 37–38.

[94] Mirza Jaʿfar, *Tahqiqat*, 106–13; Tchirikof, *Diary*, 67.

considerations and the religious affiliations of the province's inhabitants were of primary importance. The politics of pasture – that is, of migration patterns and the location of summer and winter camps – was a secondary, but still significant, consideration. After their survey, the mediators concluded that Iran should be granted the paths leading to Zohab's heartland as well as the winter pastures for its tribes. As the main road from Kermanshah to Baghdad went through Zohab, it was additionally decided that Iran would have Sar-i Pol as a point of assembly for its pilgrims before they entered Ottoman territory. The mediators also claimed that their proposed line interposed geographic barriers between enemy nomadic tribes.[95] Consequently, they suggested an uninterrupted connection between Ottoman possessions on the Sirvan (the upper waters of the Diyala River) as far as the Bamu range and along the lower part of the Elvend River, which would separate Iranian nomadic tribes from the Ottoman frontier town of Khanaqin by an undulating strip extending from Qasr-i Shirin to Sar-i Pol and Bamu.

Not surprisingly, this proposal was strategically and economically unacceptable to Dervish Pasha, because it left the passes and valleys of Taq-i Girra and Qal'a Zenjir, which led to Mendeli, in Iran's hands, a situation that would allow Tehran to direct its forces toward Baghdad without difficulty. If, on the contrary, these areas were left under Ottoman control, the passage of pilgrims, armies, and tribes could be controlled and the establishment of quarantine and customhouses facilitated. As Iranian tribes would continue to cross the frontier for winter pastures, the pasha argued, leaving the passes in Ottoman hands would allow them to collect *kışlak rüsümatı*, or winter pasture dues, and restrain the tribes. Dervish concluded that the towns of Qasr-i Shirin, Kuretu, and Maydan should be made Ottoman. In response, Mirza Ja'far argued for pushing the Iranian frontier further west.[96] Once more the conferences succumbed to conflict. Rejecting the Zohab plan as pro-Iranian, the Porte prohibited Dervish from taking part in further discussions.[97] Disturbances along the frontier and in the Shatt region (allegedly fomented by the pasha himself) caused further delays, which the Porte blamed on the Iranians, whom they accused of violating Ottoman territory.[98] As a result, in Zohab, as in Muhammarah, the making of the boundary was left to the future.

[95] Mirza Ja'far, *Tahqiqat*, 119; Tchirikof, *Diary*, 19.
[96] Dervish, *Tahdid*, 41–47; Hurşîd, *Seyâhatnâme*, 15.
[97] Tchirikof, *Diary*, 20; Kemball Report, *Schofield III*, 148.
[98] Kemball Report, *Schofield III*, 147.

COMMISSIONERS AND BORDERLANDERS: INSCRIBING
SUBJECTHOOD ON THE PEOPLE OF THE FRONTIER

After Dervish Pasha's withdrawal, the remaining parties decided to survey a portion of the frontier still unknown to them (although twice traveled by Dervish): the dry country between Mendeli and Hawiza. Provided with sixteen days of supplies and shadowed by stealth robbers, they departed Zohab on January 31, 1852, and reached Hawiza in nineteen days.[99] From south of Zohab to the environs of Basra, they discovered few permanently inhabited places. In fact, of the settlements referred to in the 1639 Treaty, only Mendeli was a fairly important town, whereas Zorbatya, Badrai (Badrah), and Jassan were villages. Between these places and Muhammarah, they encountered only desert dotted with marshes. These barren regions still had to be surveyed and delimited, however, a task made more difficult by an almost total lack of natural boundaries. The exceptions

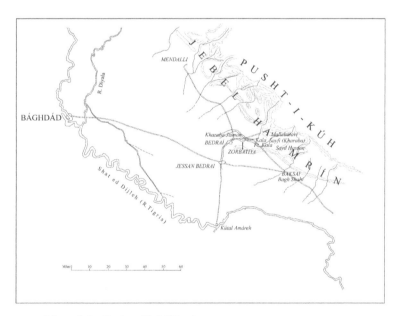

MAP 9. Map of the Posht-e Kuh District
Adapted from PRO.MFQ 1/573 Posht-e Kuh District.

[99] Tchirikof, *Diary*, 21. For a history of Hawiza (also Hawizeh, Huwayza, Huwaizah, Hoveyzeh), see Mirza Ja'far, *Tahqiqat*, 88–90; Tchirikof, *Diary*, 21, 36; and Ludwig W. Adamec *Historical Gazetteer of Iran*, 2 vols. (Graz: Akademische Drucku. Verlagsanstalt, 1976), .2.308.

were the Tigris River in the west, on whose banks dwelled the Ottoman Banu Lam Arabs, and the Luristan Mountains in the east, whose interiors were inhabited by the Failis of the Posht-e Kuh, Iranian subjects. Smaller Arab tribes lived on the Hawiza side, and the strip of land where the desert and mountains met was a liminal space where all these peoples met for fighting or fraternization. The desert area between Hawiza and Muhammarah was inaccessible because of a total absence of water.[100]

Once their work was completed, the commissioners returned via a circuitous route through the ancient ruins of Susa, Dezful, and Posht-e Kuh to avoid the dangers of spring flooding. Leaving Hawiza on March 3, 1852, they arrived at Mendeli on April 4, 1852, where Dervish Pasha awaited them.[101] Their subsequent activities in Mendeli and the Posht-e Kuh region offer a clear example of how the new international order, with its insistence on clear-cut boundaries, was inscribed on the region and its inhabitants, not only by the hand of modernizing regional states but also by European powers.

The legacy of the partition of this stretch of the frontier would be both immediate and long lasting. In the short run, despite its failure to finalize the demarcation of Muhammarah and Zohab, the commission paved the way for the future by sending a clear message that local populations must choose sides and identities. Aware of the extensive crossing and mixing characteristic of said populations, and of the somewhat autonomous political structures they enjoyed, the surveyors strove to make the sparse populations they encountered understand that the new frontier would become an increasingly tight filter. Moreover, their mere presence offered a clear sign that the borderland was no longer a space of ambivalence, but rather one of well-defined allegiances, which would be called "citizen-ships." Launching the process by which fluid and inclusive borderlands became exclusive bordered lands, they signaled encroaching limits on the movement of itinerant populations by extending the authority of the central state over those territories that had, up to this point, allowed tribes to maneuver and preserve some element of autonomy. Nearly a century and a half later, such limits were firmly entrenched within state ideologies when Saddam Hussein ethnically cleansed "Arab Iraq" by expelling the Failis on the Iraqi side of the boundary for the alleged offense of being Iranian. History, however, shows that Faili migration to what would become the nation-state of Iraq long predated the formation of that state.

---

[100] Tchirikof, *Diary*, 20–21.
[101] Ibid., 23.

Moreover, at the time of the making of the boundary, it was not easy to define the autonomous Failis as Iranian subjects. It was the very act of boundary and state making that further integrated them into the geo-body of Iran and imposed imperial, and later national, identities on them and groups like them, allowing them to become inadvertent victims of nationalist regimes such as the Ba'athist Iraq.

THE CASE OF THE FAILIS OF POSHT-E KUH

Posht-e Kuh was part of Luristan, which at the time was divided into two provinces, Luri-Buzurg, or Greater Luristan, and Luri-Kuchak, or Lesser Luristan. The former was composed of the mountainous country of Bakhtiyaris stretching westward from the frontiers of Fars to the Dezful River. The latter, a frontier district to the west of the river, was inhabited by Faili Kurds[102] and divided into the Pish-e Kuh and Posht-e Kuh, or the country before and behind the mountains. The mountains, in this case, were the great Zagros chain, whose most notable peak was Kabir Kuh. Pish-e Kuh lay north and northeast of Kabir Kuh, whereas Posht-e Kuh faced its south and southwestern sides on the Mesopotamian slope of the western wall of the Zagros.[103] Small intra-mountain plains or valleys dominated the Posht-e Kuh landscape. Larger plains used in the seasonal migrations of local tribes extended toward the Khuzestan Province in the south and the Pish-e Kuh in the east.[104] Because of its frontier location and inaccessible geography, the *walis*, or hereditary governors, of the region were for a long time only nominally dependent on Iran. However, as a result of internal strife, the family that had ruled the Luri-Kuchak since at least the time of Shah Abbas lost control of Pish-e Kuh to the government of Kermanshah during the time of Mohammad-'Ali Mirza Dawlatshah (1789–1821).[105] However, they remained as *walis* of Posht-e Kuh through

---

[102] Of the Failis, Hurşid wrote: Aşâyir-ı merkûmenin kâffesi Ekrâd olarak hemân cümlesi Fârisi dahi bilirler ve Farîsice ve kendi lisanlari olan Güranca okur-yazarları ve münşi ve şâirleri vardir. Hurşid, *Seyâhatnâme*, 69. *Sharfnama* classifies the Lurs as Kurds.

[103] H. C. Rawlinson, "Notes on a March from Zohab ... in the Year 1836," *JRGS* 9 (1839), 49. Also Vladimir Minorsky, "The Tribes of Western Iran," *The Journal of the Royal Anthropological Institute of Great Britain and Ireland* 75.1/2 (1945), 77.

[104] See EIr, Pošt-e Kūh.

[105] Tchirikof, *Diary*, 86. According to Rawlinson, in 1836, the tribes of Luri-Kuchak and their dependencies numbered 56,000 families, 12,000 of which inhabited Posht-e Kuh. After the death of Hussein Khan (Hasan Khan's father), the inhabitants of Posht-e Kuh lost their attachment to the Faili chiefs. See "Notes on a March from Zohab," 52, 104–9 for their organization and relations with Tehran.

the 1850s, where they ruled over Failis who, although settled in villages, seasonally migrated to the other side of the mountain to summer pastures that ranged as far as Khorramabad in the west. At the time of the survey, three sons of Hasan Khan, the last great ruler of Posht-e Kuh, ruled over three zones of Posht-e Kuh.[106] Khan's sons were 'Ali Khan, Ahmed Khan, and Haidar Khan.[107] Although their power was much diminished since their family's defeat at the hands of Dawlatshah, the brothers maintained a semblance of military strength and independent rule, symbolized by their *naqqarakhana* (drum and trumpet house), *eshiq aghasi* (chief of the guards and official doorkeeper), *tufengchi* (musketeer), and *farrash-bashi* (head chamberlain).[108] In the mid-1840s, they could jointly furnish about four thousand armed men and two thousand horsemen.[109]

Facing Posht-e Kuh on the Ottoman side were three settlements identified in the 1639 Treaty as frontier towns: Cessan (Jassan), Badra (Badrah, Badrai, Bedre), and Zorbatya (Zurbatiyah, Zurbatiya, Zorbatieh). According to Hurşîd Pasha, in 1851, the first of these was a village with about three hundred households, mostly composed of people who moved in from elsewhere. The second, with six hundred households, was a small town. The third, farther east and closer to the mountains, was a well-cultivated district inhabited by many Faili who had bought land there. Hurşîd explains the heightened presence of Failis in both Zorbatya and Badra by claiming that before the rule of Davud Pasha Mamluk, Baghdad's governors had oppressed the region's original inhabitants, forcing them to sell their lands to the Failis.[110] What complicated the issue was

---

[106] Dervish Pasha defines the Failis [Fîlî] as the leading tribe of the Luri Kuchak Kurds, whose center is Khorramabad. However, because of the problems between Hasan Khan's father and "Iranlular," toward the last quarter of the eighteenth century, some Failis were forced to move to Posht-e Kuh, which they and the Lek used as *garmsir* or winter grounds. As a result of political pressure and forces sent against him, Hasan's father moved to Posht-e Kuh, which was subject to Baghdad. Even though Hasan ruled in Khorramabad for some years, he too fell out with Tehran and moved to Posht-e Kuh, where his people became agriculturalists and in time mixed with (*bir nev'i birleşmiş olduklar*) the Qara Ulus tribe of Mendeli. Dervish, *Tahdid*, 21–22.

[107] For a history of Luristan during the Qajar period, see Muhammad Riza Valizadah Mu'jizi, *Tarikh-i Luristan: Ruzgar-i Qajar, az Ta'sis ta Kudita-yi 1299* (Tehran: Hurufiyah, 1380 [2001]).

[108] Mirza Ja'far, *Tahqiqat*, 100.

[109] Henry Layard "A Desciption of the Province of Khuzistan," *Journal of Royal Geographical Society of London* 16 (1846), 5.

[110] Hurşîd also claims that most of the Cessan, Badra, and Zorbatya were Shafi'is, and some were Shi'is, and their language was Turkish, but because of mixing they also spoke Persian, Kurdish, and Arabic. Even though he thinks it exaggerated, he gives the number of Faili as twelve thousand families in 1850. *Seyâhatnâme*, 69.

that towns such as Mendeli were dependent for water on rivers originating in Posht-e Kuh, making interdependence between desert and mountain a fact of life, and people moved and settled without regard for imperial pretentions to frontiers.[111] The trans-frontier crossings and settlement patterns of the area helped create the situational nature of the local borderlanders' identity. As Andrés Résendez notes in a different context, "what started out as opportunistic or optimizing choices over time acquired a life of their own, and perhaps in this way even seeped into the deeper psyche of the frontier," defining citizenship choices.[112] The Faili were not the only ones to change places and allegiances. Just as they had moved from Iran to the Ottoman Empire, so too about twelve thousand Ottoman Banu Lam households relocated to Iran.

Trying to explain this migration, Dervish identified oppression of the Banu Lam by Baghdad governors, as well as internal squabbles among their chiefs.[113] Turning to territorial claims, he argued that Ottoman lands extended to the village of Dehloran and even up to the heights of Kabir Kuh, thus effectively asserting ownership of the lands of Posht-e Kuh. Despite such extravagant claims, he rather surprisingly asked the mediating commissioners to persuade the brothers, 'Ali, Ahmed, and Haidar, to submit to the shah's government. The letter Williams sent to the three Faili *khan*s again demonstrates how the survey inscribed imperial order and notions of geographical space onto the borderland for the expressed purpose of ending state evasion and autonomy. Its clear delineation of the various boundaries that coexisted in the borderland makes its text worth examining at length:

Sent by the English government to investigate and decide upon all matters relating to the final frontier between Turkey and Persia, I have had the pleasure of meeting and conversing with all the governors of the provinces which lie near the line, namely the Sheikhs of Chaabs, the Vali of Hawiza, the governor of Shuster and Dizfool, the Chiefs of Kalhoors and Goouran and the Vali of Senne. You and your brothers the joint Valis of Poosht-i Kooh have to my great regret, abstained from visiting me and entering into friendly intercourse so necessary to the prosecution of our investigation.

---

[111] For the payment of *gheymete ab* (water money) to the Eyvan (Kalhor) Khans by the people of Mendeli, see Mirza Ja'far, *Tahqiqat*, 105. For Dervish's claims that Eyvan belonged to the Ottoman Empire, see Dervish, *Tahdid*, 32–34.

[112] Andrés Résendez, *Changing National Identities at the Frontiers: Texas and New Mexico, 1800–1850* (Cambridge, UK: Cambridge University Press, 2004), 3. For his notion of "situational," see his Introduction.

[113] Dervish, *Tahdid*, 18–20.

Your own reflections will doubtless lead you to conclude that such a state of things is very much against your future interests, and also convince you that the time is come when the frontier line will be distinctly drawn between Persia and Turkey, and it is necessary for me to hint to you, that all those chiefs who do not obey, but fly to either side of the frontier (whether it be from Persia into Turkey or from Turkey into Persia) will by the stipulation of the new treaty of Erzeroom, be sent back to their lawful sovereign . . .

I shall most probably pass through your country in the course of a month's time from this date, and I shall give you due notice of any approach and I conjure you to come and meet me, that I may converse with you, for your good, and that of your family. It will be the last opportunity presented to you to make your peace with the Shah and thus reestablishing your family under . . . the government of His Majesty. I hope you will favor me with an answer to this letter in order that I may send a copy of it to the English Ambassadors at Constantinople and Tehran.[114]

As the letter indicates, and Tchirikof's and Mirza Ja'far's accounts confirm, most of the lords of the marches had already met the commissioners and shown themselves to be more compliant than the Failis. Mirza Ja'far maintains that the chiefs of Bakhtiari, Dezful, Hawiza, and many others who were in revolt for years, escaping to foreign countries when pressed, took advantage of the survey's passage through the region to declare their allegiance officially. Raheem Khan of Segvend went even further. As Williams later related to Sheil, this chief demonstrated a keen understanding of the new order and power relations when, while safeguarding the commissioners' passage through his tribe's lands, he "especially begged me to inform you of his friendly deportment towards me, and I promised him to do so."[115] Like the commissioners, the Faili chiefs wanted to make their authority known and respected. Perhaps, like Raheem, they sensed the end of an era, but they chose to resist rather than accept what was forced on them.

At first, 'Ali sent a messenger to plead ill health. Ultimately, however, he came within a *farsang* (six miles) of the camp, accompanied by two hundred horsemen, to propose that the Iranian and the two mediating commissioners come to meet him, each with two attendants. The commissioners refused, thinking this to be beneath the dignity of their governments and unlikely to produce beneficial effects on a man so distrustful of their "real intentions, which centered on getting the necessary information respecting his portion of the frontier, and in offering him advice." Apprised of their refusal, 'Ali – who, Rawlinson noted, possessed "a regal dignity,

---

[114] PRO.FO 78/2722, Williams to Sheil, Near Mendeli, April 12, 1852.
[115] Ibid. See also, Mirza Ja'far, *Tahqiqat*, 101.

and in his black tent affects all the etiquette of a Fet-h-ʿAli Shah" – returned to his remote mountains.[116]

The next district the commissioners passed through belonged to Haidar Khan, the most powerful of the brothers, who had twelve sons and seventy wives. Having sent his tents and families away with the pretext of changing places, Haidar went to the camps to welcome the commissioners. Accompanied by at least two thousand armed followers, he was so suspicious that his armed guards waited beside him during his meeting at Mirza Jaʿfar's tent, and he declined to eat or drink anything for fear of being poisoned.[117] After the meeting, however, like Raheem Khan of Segvend, Haidar asked Williams, via an agent, to send a letter on his behalf to Sheil. Williams's answer was a stark reminder of changing power relations. He informed the agent that such a document was unnecessary; he would report his visit to Sheil and attest to the *khan*'s loyal behavior. The third brother, Ahmed Khan, answered the letters he received but did not appear at the camp, although he had previously sent his secretary and fifty armed men to join the commissioners while they traveled through the Zorbatya-Posht-e Kuh region.[118]

If one is to believe Dervish Pasha's account, the Faili chiefs were uncertain about where the future frontier would be. Aware that their autonomy was coming to an end, they hedged their bets. Possibly after the pasha asked the mediating commissioners to ask the Faili Khans to submit to the shah's government, Haidar sent the pasha a trusted person to confirm his loyalty and declare that since the time of Büyük Süleyman Pasha (r. 1780–1802), the governor of Baghdad, his ancestors had submitted to Baghdad. Moreover, his family and tribe had lands in Badrai, Jassan, and Zorbatya, and others had settled in Baghdad. Consequently, he asked to be accepted as an Ottoman subject.[119] Although the pasha's account suggests that Haidar approached him of his own volition, Williams's correspondence

---

[116] PRO.FO 78/2722, Williams to Sheil, Near Mendeli, April 12, 1852. Layard "A Description," 5.

[117] He had grounds to be suspicious: "attempts of this kind had already once been made on him and his brother Ali Khan by the Persians. The two brothers were seized at an audience with the Iranians, and afterwards escaped from prison at Tehran." Tchirikof, *Diary*, 24, 100; and Mirza Jaʿfar, *Tahqiqat*, 100–1.

[118] Mirza Jaʿfar, *Tahqiqat*, 101–3; Tchirikof, *Diary*, 83, 85.

[119] Dervish argues that the Failis could be considered a tribe with disputed subjecthood (*munaziʿi fih*). However, he only claimed the land of Posht-e Kuh, not the Failis, because doing the latter would have given Iran grounds to dispute the subjecthood of the Banu Lam living in Iran. Unable to produce documents to corroborate his claims, he based his argument on natural features and local accounts. Dervish, *Tahdid*, 24.

describes another possibility. When advising the chiefs he met as to their future line of conduct, he was informed that members of the Ottoman commission had already passed through Faili country under the pretext of taking testimonies regarding the old frontier. Dervish's real objective, Williams guessed, was to undermine the fealty of the chiefs to Iran. It seems that this strategy worked. Haidar's agent warned Williams (and through him the Iranian government) that if the *khan*s were pressed by the Iranian government, "they would be obliged to run away to Baghdad, where many of their tribe already lived."[120] In response, the British and Russian commissioners warned the Faili Khans to maintain their current allegiance to Iran and be aware of foreign agents trying to deceive them. They also warned the three brothers to stop attacking local villages by invoking the Erzurum Treaty, which required the mutual surrender of fugitives. If they continued their raids, the new frontiers would render escape impossible and punishment certain.[121] The commissioners' combined efforts appear to have had their intended effect. The brothers eventually yielded to the new international order. When the survey party again passed through their lands, all three brothers met with and provided them escort.[122]

USING THE STATE TO ADVANCE LOCAL CLAIMS: THE CASE OF BANU LAM

The autonomy of the frontier peoples thus waned as state capacity, symbolized by the tightening of the frontier filter, waxed; the survey's message that the time of state evasion and autonomous rule was coming to an end was being received. According to British documents, this message was vigorously communicated throughout the countryside. When the commission was not in active session, its members traveled the land encouraging representatives of Tehran and Istanbul posted at the frontiers to be vigilant in maintaining tranquility and communicating their message of inevitable centralization to tribal chiefs.[123] Although the commissioners tried to inscribe boundaries on the borderland and identities on its peoples, the peoples themselves sought the backing of one state or the other to justify

[120] PRO.FO 78/2722, Williams to Sheil, Near Mendeli, April 12, 1852.
[121] Ibid.; Tchirikof, *Diary*, 24; and Dervish, *Tahdid*, 22.
[122] PRO.FO 78/2710 Williams to Canning, Hawiza, February 29, 1852; Enclosure: circular letter to the three joint Valies of Poosht-i Kooh, Ahmed Khan, Hyder Khan and Alli Khan, Baksai, February 15, 1852.
[123] PRO.FO 78/2710 Williams to Canning, Persian Koordistan, Bana, March 10, 1852.

their right of possession to the lands, pastures, and water resources they claimed as communities or as towns and villages. Casting doubts on the reality of a frontier purported to have been in existence for more than two hundred years, their testimonials and petitions show how they tried to use the survey as an opportunity to make such claims. The *mazbata*, or letter, of the Banu Lam of Badra to Dervish Pasha, for example, declares the following:

> We, who belong to the Beni Lam ashair, do not have the knowledge of the actual boundaries of Iran and the Ottoman Empire. We know, though, that from the ancient times [kadim zamandan beru] onward the river Dowirij is the boundary [hadd-i fasıl] between the Beni Lam and the 'Ajam ... The 'Ajam have no districts on the right side of the river, which is our country [diyar] ... [The land] from the source of the river to Mendeli and beyond is divided between the Faili ashiret and us, with the mountains being the boundary.[124]

In their attempt to persuade Dervish of their assertions to lands and resources they did not necessarily control, the petitioners also claimed the district of Baghsai (Baksai, Beksaye), which would be the subject of intense debate in later decades, as well as Dehloran and Bayat (Beyad), located farther from the present frontier.[125] At the time the Banu Lam wrote this petition, the Failis controlled the latter two locations, whereas Baghsai and Zorbatya had mixed populations of Failis and Arabs. However, the petitioners claimed this was not the case, and that they had been collecting taxes from all of these districts on behalf of the Baghdad treasury. Denying Faili – and, accordingly, Iranian – claims, they argued that to keep the peace, they annually sent the gift of a horse to the Faili chiefs. However, after Hasan Khan's death, his three sons took control of Bayat and Dehloran and began collecting half of Baghsai's *khum* (one-fifth income tax) and *baş parası* (tax paid for the flocks) from the Faili tribes around Zorbatya.[126]

Listening to these and similar claims, the commissioners concluded that the boundary line in this area should run along the heights known to geographers as Jabal Hamrin and the Duwarij (Dovaridj, Diuveridj) River and proceed down the course of that river to the Ghor-Azem swamps, which join the Tigris. Essentially reiterating the 1639 treaty,

---

[124] Dervish, *Tahdid*, 26–27. Dervish added that none of the tribes knew of the *hudud-u kadime*, or old boundary.

[125] About thirty families of Failis and Arabs cultivated the village of Baghsai in 1851 and paid a tax of a fifth of the grain, which was divided between Ali Khan Faili and Meskut, the Sheikh of the Banu Lam. Tchirikof, *Diary*, 86, 88.

[126] Dervish, *Tahdid*, 26–27.

they decided that "the country at present occupied by the Banu Lam Arabs, by the villages of Bedrai, Djessan and Zorbatiye, and by the town of Mendeli (Mendeljin) would remain Ottoman and Posht-e Kuh and the dominions of Hawiza Persian."[127] (See Map 9) This arrangement left Zorbatya on the Ottoman side and rejected the Banu Lam's tenuous assertions to Bayat and Dehloran. As such, not only did the Baghsai problem remain unresolved, but many members of Arab tribes were left on the Iranian side and many Failis on the Ottoman side. As we have seen, in the late twentieth century, this situation would provide ammunition for Ba'athist ethnic-cleansing policies. Although the land between Mendeli and Zohab remained to be delimited after a map was prepared, it was suggested that a line drawn through the desert divide the territories south of Zohab up to Muhammarah. These latter places were, in any case, of secondary political importance because, as Tchirikof argued, they bene-fited from natural boundaries: "Turkey is protected by the stream of Tigris, Persia by the mountains of Luristan. In between lies the great desert; consequently, attention ought to be entirely concentrated on the water-ways of the Shatt al-Arab and the Karun."[128]

SUNNIS FOR THE CALIPH: CLAIMING THE LANDS IN THE NAME OF DEFUNCT KURDISH DYNASTS

At this point, the commissioners left the Banu Lam Arabs and advanced to Kurdish occupied lands. Unlike in Zohab, where they struggled to find a balance between strategic space and religious affiliations, sectarian bounda-ries were not easily detectable in this part of the frontier, because inhabitants on both sides were Sunni. There were, however, other discernible boundaries in the region, namely the historical limits of Suleimanieh, the seat of the Baban family, and Sinne, the seat of the Ardalan family. North of Suleimanieh was the Ottoman district of Koi Sanjak (Köysancak), the frontier district of which was Pishder. Opposite Suleimanieh was the Iranian province of Sinne (Senna, Sanandaj), with its districts of Merivan, Avroman (Hawraman), Baneh, Saqez, and Sardasht. The border districts of the eastern part of Suleimanieh

[127] This decision accepted the 1639 Treaty as the point of departure, as Mirza Ja'far desired. *Tahqiqat*, 93–95. See also Tchirikof, *Diary*, 22. Of Badrai, Layard wrote, "we crossed the Turkish frontier and reached Badrai without further incident . . . The Turkish Governor received us with much civility." Henry A. Layard, *Early Adventures in Persia, Susiana, and Babylonia, Including a Residence Among the Bakhtiyari and Other Wild Tribes Before the Discovery of Nineveh* (London: John Murray, 1887), 337.

[128] Tchirikof, *Diary*, 22.

were Gulambar and Kizildja, with their chief places being Panjwin and Qala-Chuvalan. Divided for centuries between the Ardalan and Baban principal-ities, the southern portion of this frontier presented, in principle, few grounds for dispute, with the exception of some villages. At the time the surveyors arrived, however, the power of the Babans and Ardalans had diminished, but Iran and the Ottoman Empire had yet to solidify their control in the region. Here, then, the act of boundary making was also the act of filling the power vacuum created by the destruction of the autonomous wardens of the marches and the surveyors strove to integrate the indirectly controlled terri-tories into the new geo-bodies they were creating.

The Ottomans, for example, declared ownership of the whole strip of territory situated to the east of the high peaks of Surkev, Belu, and Qandilan – "the wildest of all frontier mountains," according to Tchirikof – up to but not (yet) including Baneh. The mediating commis-sioners rejected these claims on the grounds that although the districts did belong to the Sunni Babans, Ottoman interests were not driven by religious but by economic and strategic considerations.[129] Namely, they were inter-ested in gaining two difficult-to-follow caravan routes that passed through the mountains from Suleimanieh into Iran: the first, to Tabriz, went through Baneh, Saqez, and Meragha; the other, to Urumieh, went through Sardasht, Soujbulak, and Salduz. While laying claim to the aforemen-tioned districts in official meetings, Dervish Pasha continued to make unofficial forays into nearby towns, where he attempted to coax Kurdish subjects of the shah to the subjecthood of the Sunni sultan. While the commissioners were in the Merivan region, for example, the pasha argued, in his official capacity, that Sunnis who tended to rebel against rather than submit to Iran populated the villages of Merivan and Avroman. At the same time, he unofficially tried to convince a certain Sheikh ʿAli to provide a *şehadetname*, or testimonal, indicating that his people were Ottoman subjects forcefully conquered at the time of Nadir Shah. Initially, Sheikh ʿAli was fearful of Iranian reprisals; later, however, thanks to the efforts of Suleimanieh's *kaimmakam*, the *şehadetname* was procured.[130] Dervish also frequently appeared in mosques to emphasize the Sunni-Shiʿi divide and stress the role of the sultan as the Sunni caliph. Aware of the ambiguity of the ancient frontier, he employed such strategies in the hope of pushing the new frontier westward. The mediating commissioners repeatedly warned him against a course of action that undermined their fundamental

---

[129] Ibid., 26.
[130] Dervish, *Tahdid*, 50.

task[131] and complained, in official correspondence, that he was visiting the Sunni Kurdish towns of Baneh, Sardasht, Lahijan, and Ushnu "for the purpose of seducing Iranian subjects from their allegiance to the shah [and that] his conduct . . ., to a great extent, retarded the progress of the commission."[132]

Iran, of course, did not idly sit by as its rival tried to snatch territories it considered its own. Indeed, while the commissioners were surveying the Kurdish districts, reports reached London of Iranian attempts to provoke frontier tribes against the Ottomans, and when Mirza Ja'far and the mediating commissioners reunited with Dervish at the beginning of May 1852, the latter accused his rival of inciting the population of Suleimanieh.[133] Mirza Ja'far likewise complained that the Ottomans were trying to lure away even the inhabitants of regions they did not officially claim. One such example was Baneh. In his account of the survey, Mirza Ja'far included a letter written by thirty-four notables of this district, including *ulama, a'yan, ashraf*, and *mearif*, who – no doubt aided by Iranian authorities – maintained that Baneh was part of Kurdistan, which in turn was Iranian. They had served under previous shahs and participated in Nadir Shah's campaigns under the *wali* of Kurdistan. These petitioners noted that prior to the arrival of the Ottoman survey team, they had never heard that Baneh belonged to the Ottoman Empire or that it was forcefully taken by Iran. They claimed that the Ottomans offered them a ten-year tax exemption, which they rejected and reported to Iranian authorities.[134] Indeed, even Dervish's research showed that Baneh was Iranian, although the Babans had occasionally held it. However, the pasha decided that because it was located at a sensitive part of the *hudud*, it would be beneficial to claim. Additionally, he asserted that its Sunni population was inclined toward the Ottoman Empire.[135] In spite of his subsequent formal claim to the region, however, the mediating commissioners held firm in their conviction that Baneh had never belonged to the Babans or the Ottomans.[136]

---

[131] PRO.FO 78/2723, Joint Official Note, Tchirikof and Williams to Dervish Pasha, June 28, 1852.

[132] Kemball Report, *Schofield III*, 149.

[133] PRO.FO 78/2721, Canning to Palmerstone, Therassia, June 25, 1851. Dervish also speaks of the intelligence he received about Iranian authorities secretly meeting with Jaf leaders. Dervish, *Tahdid*, 62.

[134] Mirza Ja'far, *Tahqiqat*, 136–37.

[135] Dervish, *Tahdid*, 63–64.

[136] Tchirikof, *Diary*, 26.

Another district the pasha thought prudent to claim was Sardasht, which had 8 *nahiyah*s, 130 villages, 2,800 Shafi'i Muslim Kurdish families, and 25 Jewish families. Claiming that the Iranians had taken it from the Babans in 1811, the pasha wanted it returned to the Ottoman Empire. Dervish based his information about this region on a petition, forwarded from Istanbul, from the people of Sardasht, who claimed to be tired of Iranian oppression and desirous of being included within Ottoman domains.[137] Mirza Ja'far likewise produced a letter in which seventeen dignitaries from the town of Sardasht reported that after the other commissioners departed, Dervish stayed under the guise of carrying out research. He then assembled the dignitaries at the mosque to ask them to "give a sealed paper stating that Sardasht and its dependencies belong to the Turkish Government." In the letter, the dignitaries claim to have refused and emphasized their loyalty.[138]

The Pasha claimed Mergever and Tergever based on similarly sketchy evidence. He argued that previous sultans had granted not only these places to the local dynasty, but also Berdesor, Bradost (Baradust), and Somai (also Somay or Sumay). According to his argument, these districts' proximity to Urumieh facilitated a gradual alignment with the 'Ajams, and it was not until the time of Fath 'Ali Shah that they came completely under Iranian jurisdiction.[139] The pasha also presented a translation of the *şehadetname* of the *ehli vukuf*, or knowledgeable people, of Imadiye, who testified that Berdesor, Tergever, and Mergever *nahiya*s had historically [az kadim] been part of the Imadiyah sanjak, and that the rulers of Berdesor had come from the Imadiyah family, another local Kurdish dynasty subject to Istanbul. According to this testimonial, the Iranians had established themselves there only gradually and only at the turn of the nineteenth century, when internal discord weakened the rule of the descendants of Ismail Pasha of Imadiyah.[140] Such petitions and counter petitions show that although it inscribed imperial identities on them, the survey also uncovered considerable ambiguity of belonging and allegiance among borderland communities religiously tied to the Ottomans but historically connected to Iran. Nor were the peoples of frontier towns such as Sardasht and Bane unique.

[137] [Iranlunun zulm ve teaddilerine tabaver olamadıklarına mebni yine tabiiyet-i saltanat-ı seniyyeye dehalet ve iltica eyledikleri...] BOA.I.HR 4165, 2 C 1268 / 23 March 1852. See also Dervish, *Tahdid*, 64, 68.

[138] Mirza Ja'far, *Tahqiqat*, 150.

[139] Dervish, *Tahdid*, 97–102.

[140] Ibid., 102–3.

TO WHICH PASTURE THE NOMADS BELONG, AND TO WHICH COUNTRY THE PASTURE?

Even though the Erzurum conferees had concluded optimistically that the division of the borderland tribes would automatically follow the final demarcation, the survey commission soon realized that the two processes were inseparable. Transhumant populations combining permanent settlements with mobile camps straddled both sides of the divide. Such populations, more reliant on ecological patterns than political ones, demanded mobility for the optimal utilization and conservation of resources and the preservation of their social organization and sustainable pastoralism.[141] More specifically, they required seasonal utilization of pastures and hence seasonal, or at times permanent, migration. It is true that borderland communities competed for access to land and other resources, but under the management of frontier principalities such as the Baban and Ardalan, they managed to live in uneasy coexistence. As we have seen, local power brokers had to be defeated to extend state capacity and incorporate borderland populations into the bordered empire. The latter efforts, moreover, could not tolerate the fluidity of movement and identity that accompanied the borderlanders' mobility. To decrease their mobility and, with it, the porosity of the frontier filter, the states needed to increase their surveillance capacity, turning the peoples of the margins into fiscally accountable units. This was only possible with the demarcation of the boundary.

The Jaf were a large seminomadic tribe that seasonally migrated between the lands of both states and, therefore, posed a direct challenge to this intertwined process. The largest group of the Jaf, called the Muradi, had a population of up to six thousand tents and recognized Ottoman sovereignty. They wintered in Shahrizor and the northern parts of Zohab and spent the most of the summer months in the mountains of the Iranian district of Merivan.[142] Yet, not all of their migrations were seasonal. When the commission passed through their region, a small group of Muradi, consisting of four hundred tents, had already crossed the mountains to Jawanrud, in Sinne on the Iranian side. Responding to the commission's

---

[141] Mahmud Mamdani, *Citizen and Subject: Contemporary Africa and the Legacy of Late Colonialism* (Princeton, NJ: Princeton University Press, 1996), 166.

[142] Jaf chiefs in the 1920s told Cecil J. Edmonds that they originally moved from Jawanrud to Ban-i Khêlan, in Baban territory, in the 1770s. See chap. XI of *Kurds, Turks and Arabs* (London: Oxford University Press, 1957).

inquiries, they reported that they were waiting to be joined by the others. It is likely, however, that competition for resources eventually compelled parts of this subgroup, now known as the Jaf Jawanrudi, to break away definitively and move to Kermanshah. To illustrate the fluid, syncretistic nature of the borderland communities, they ultimately joined the ʿAli Ilahi Guran confederation, despite the fact that the two groups belonged to different religious sects.[143]

Jaf crossings into Iran for pastures, and their harassment of local villages on arrival, had long occupied the negotiating and mediating parties. For example, a few months earlier, on their return trip from Hawiza to Mendeli, the mediating commissioners had visited two prominent Jaf chiefs to ask them to cease attacks on area villages. Deflecting blame, the chiefs replied that lesser chiefs whom they did not control were responsible, whereas they observed the law. Such apparent compliance, however, did not signal an easy surrender of traditional rights and pastures, but rather suggested they would not cause outright trouble. Indeed, the commissioners were unable to solve the Jaf problem and concluded to leave the division of Sinne-Suleimanieh as it was. The long-term difficulty of solving this problem is suggested by the fact that in the 1920s, Cecil J. Edmonds noted that shepherd sections of the Jaf and other Iraqi tribes spent their summers "in the Persian highlands between Senna and Saqqiz."[144]

From Jaf country, the commissioners advanced into territories occupied by the Bilbas (Belbas), another tribal confederation whose allegiance and belonging did nothing to clarify the task of delimitation.[145] Various branches of the Bilbas nomadized in Pishder and Dasht-e Vezneh, as well as in eastern sections of the well-watered Lahijan district. Their geographic location in the high Qandil Mountains, between the domains of the two states, allowed them to retain a degree of independence; yet, their seasonal migrations allowed both states to claim them and the lands they inhabited. Thus, although they had formerly recognized only their own authority, Mirza Jaʿfar opined that the need for pasture would triumph over other forms of identity and, following the delimitation, the Bilbas would choose

---

[143] Edmonds, *Kurds, Turks*, 141. Volumes 2/1 and 2/2 of Mohammad Ali Soltani's multivolume *Jughrafiai Tarikhi va Tarikhe Mofassale Kermanshahan* (Historical Geography and Comprehensive History of Kermanshahan), subtitled *Ilat va Tavaif-e Kermanshahan*, give a detailed history of the region's tribes, including the Jaf, especially the Jaf Muradi who migrated to Iran.

[144] Edmonds, *Kurds, Turks*, 143.

[145] For Bilbas in the 1850s, see Dervish, *Tahdid*, 79–80; Hurşîd, *Seyâhatnâme*, 210–14; and Mirza Jaʿfar, *Tahqiqat*, 147.

Iranian citizenship because they spent seven months in Iran and only five in the Ottoman Empire.[146] Meanwhile, in addition to Lahijan and Vezneh, Dervish, like Enveri Efendi before him, claimed Ushnu, Mergever, Dasht, Tergever, Bradost, and Somai, on the Iranian side of the Qandil mountains facing Rawanduz and Amadia.[147] Contending that all of these lands originally belonged to defunct Kurdish dynasts, the pasha bolstered his argument by pointing to the existence of *ashair* and *tavaif*, including the Surchi (Bavomer), who spent summers in Ushnu pastures and winters in Rawanduz ones, and the three-thousand-household Ottoman Herki, which straddled both sides of the frontier and had bought extensive lands in the Urumieh region. Such cases further aggravated the complicated process of separating lands,[148] and the survey commissioners once again deferred any conclusion regarding the citizenship of the peoples and the territoriality of their lands.

Relieved by its indecision, the survey party determined that to continue its investigations while avoiding the cholera epidemic raging at Urumieh, Salduz, and Savojbulagh, it would advance to Kotur, which, like Qandil, featured high mountains on the Ottoman side and high valleys and plateaus on the Iranian one.[149] However, because, as we saw toward the beginning of this chapter, Dervish had already occupied Kotur, secured certain districts in Bradost and Salmas, and signaled the Ottoman intention to expand the occupation, the commissioners again found themselves at an impasse.[150] Still, to collect the data necessary for the completion of a map, they advanced closer to the northernmost frontier. Here, in the districts of Bradost, Chahrik, Somai, Derik, Hoder, and Salmas, Ottoman and Iranian attempts to win over or coerce frontier tribes, mostly the pro-Iranian Shi'i Turkic Karapapak and the Sunni Kurdish Shekak, were again on full display.

---

[146] Mirza Ja'far, *Tahqiqat*, 147–48, maintains that the Mangur spent summers and winters in Naleyn-i Mengur, whereas Dervish and Hurşîd claim they spent summers in Naleyn-i Mengur and Savojbulagh in Iran, and winters in Pishder and Koi Sanjak on the Ottoman side. The Ottomans referred to Nadir Shah's anti-Mangur campaigns, mentioned in *Tarikh-e Jahangoshay-e Naderi*, and other Iranian campaigns against the Bilbas as proof that they acknowledged Ottoman authority. Mirza Ja'far, however, describes a carrot-and-stick policy in which the *aş'ar* (tax/tithe) of Mangur-occupied villages was left to the chiefs so they would be inclined toward Iran. See Dervish, *Tahdid*, 71–73; Hurşîd, *Seyâhatnâme*, 213.

[147] Mirza Ja'far, *Tahqiqat*, 164.

[148] Tchirikof, *Diary*, 28; Mirza Ja'far, *Tahqiqat*, 150, 160.

[149] Tchirikof, *Diary*, 28.

[150] See also Mirza Ja'far, *Tahqiqat*, 160.

LIMITS OF SECTARIANISM: OTTOMAN EFFORTS TO LURE THE SUNNIS

Because they were Sunnis, the Ottoman authorities tried to secure the loyalty of the Shekak, whereas the Iranians did their best to coerce them into submission. Russian commission members noted that between seven hundred and eight hundred Shekak families with allegiance to Iran had settled in Hakkari, on the Ottoman side, motivated by persecution by Urumieh authorities as well as certain advantages provided by the Ottomans. Then, in 1840, under Omar Agha, more than one thousand Shekak tents joined by two hundred non-Shekak ones moved to Albak, also in Hakkari.[151] Claiming that the Shekak were originally from Diyarbakir, Dervish attributed the move to Iranian arrogance and aggression (*ruunet ve khushunet*) because they were Shafiʿi Sunnis. He might have had a point. It seems that Tehran had long harbored suspicions against them. Indeed, in 1849, Tehran accused their grand chief, Ali Agha, of being pro-Ottoman and imprisoned him while launching a campaign against his people. This move effectively prevented the Shekak from further defecting to the Ottoman side and weakened Dervish's claims to the lands they occupied.[152]

The pasha nevertheless forged ahead, contending that the districts in question had previously belonged to Hakkari.[153] Some of them, he maintained, passed into Iranian control as a result of Afshar stratagems and proximity to Urumieh. Others changed hands because of disagreements among members of the ruling Hakkari dynasty. Most had been decisively occupied only in the war of 1821–22. Underscoring his determination to return the lands to Ottoman sovereignty, Dervish also emphasized that with the exception of some Armenians (whom he confuses with Nestorians) and small numbers of Jews, their population was made up of Sunni Shafiʿi Kurds.[154] Although unpersuasive to the mediating commissioners, the argument that these lands were Ottoman because they had been ruled by now-defunct Kurdish dynasts and were currently inhabited by Sunnis would become a mantra repeated not only by the Ottoman commissioners who followed Dervish, but also, as we shall see in the

---

[151] For the Shekak, see Gamazof/Tchirikof, *Diary* 28–29, 136, 167; Mirza Jaʿfar, *Tahqiqat*, 161; Hurşîd, *Seyâhatnâme*, 247–48.

[152] Dervish, *Tahdid*, 103–15.

[153] Ibid., 116.

[154] Ibid., 106–18.

final chapters of this study, by the Ottoman troops that occupied many of Iran's Sunni Kurdish regions from 1905 to 1912.

Beyond claiming these districts in oral arguments and on paper, Dervish made a final effort to convince local Sunnis to declare themselves loyal to the Sunni caliph by visiting the mosques of towns and villages where he invited the inhabitants to acknowledge Ottoman suzerainty and citizenship (*bay'at va tabi'iyyet*).[155] The mediating commissioners informed their ambassadors of his activities and also met with regional chiefs, advising them to remain tranquil until the boundary was finalized. It was during this period that Williams, after praising the chiefs of Merivan, Baneh, and Sardasht for being "most attentive to the safety of our camps," reflected on the corrosive and even dangerous effects of an undefined boundary: "The ordinary and very slender bonds of society were daily weakened by the uncertainty which hangs over the solution of this disputed frontier."[156]

But before this task could be completed, the negotiating commissioners continued collecting local testimonies in support of their claims. Of the many testimonials Dervish Pasha included in his account, one is worth highlighting because it shows how the boundary was shaped by local conditions and agency that did not always follow ethnic and sectarian lines. It came from the people of Ushnaviyah (Ushnu), a town composed of 600 Muslim, 20 Jewish, and 6 Armenian families, which had 39 villages that annually paid 4,500 tuman to Tehran.[157] Sent to him by Mufti Abdulkadir on August 2, 1852, it declared that Dervish Pasha, the *muhaddid* of the *hudud*, or delimiter of the boundary, had come to the *kaza* of Ushnaviyah and inquired about the *vilayat*. The greybeards and notables of the district of Ushnaviyah and Lahijan testified that it had been part of the Ottoman Harir sanjak under the Babans. However, in the struggle between the Turkish Shi'i Afshars and the Kurdish Dunbulis of Khoi for domination of Urumieh, the Sunni Kurdish *khan*s of Ushnaviyah and Karani Agha of the Piran branch of the Bilbas that lived in the area allied themselves with the Afshars and established marriage connections with them, only to be undermined because of those connections. The *pishkesh* or gifts they sent to Urumieh gradually

---

[155] Mirza Ja'far writes that in the northern part of the frontier, Dervish claimed the districts of Baitush, Sardasht, Savojbulagh, Baneh, Mergever, Tergever, Ushnu, Somai, Bradost, Chahrik, Kal'a Khud, Derik, Salmas, the Kotur valley, Lahijan, Vezne, Akhorek, Abghai, and Maku, which the Ottomans also claimed at Erzurum. See *Tahqiqat*, 74; for Friday prayers, 149. For inviting the populace to Ottoman citizenship ["da'vat va istimalet"] in the Shapiran district, see 167.

[156] PRO.FO 78/2723 Williams to Sheil, Serdesht, Persian Kurdistan, June 9 and 23, 1852.

[157] Tchirikof, *Diary*, 129–30.

turned into taxes, and alliance into recognition of Iranian suzerainty. According to their petition, Ushnaviyah had been an Iranian province paying taxes and maliyat (*maliyat va kharaj*) to the 'Ajam for between forty and fifty years.[158] Recognizing Iranian sovereignty did not mean that Ushnaviyah was under direct Iranian control. Tchirikof maintains that following Muhammad Shah's death, the Khan of Ushnaviyah, with two thousand men, sustained a siege of the town, which lasted for two months, by six thousand Persians from Tabriz and Urumieh. Even though Tchirikof does not provide any other detail, this could be seen as an indication that direct Qajar authority was established only around 1850. When the commissioners were there, the governor of Mergever and Tergever was Shahzade Melik Mansur Mirza, who visited them. Previously, these two districts, along with Dasht and Salduz, were part of Ushnaviyah and under the authority of the Khan of Ushnaviyah.[159]

Like his rival the pasha, Mirza Ja'far also collected petitions and testimonials. One came from the notables of Baradost and Somai and declared that after the commissioners left, Dervish sent agents to inform them that their districts were now Ottoman and the Iranians had no right to interfere in them. In spite of promised rewards for declaring Ottoman *teba'iyyet*, fifteen signatories claimed they informed the pasha's agents that the districts were Iranian, as their forefathers had told them. They, the notables, wrote, who know the reality, could withstand such falsehood, "but what do the simple folk [*avam ol nas*] know about such claims [naql]?" Echoing Williams, they observed, "As a result of such activities, these frontiers [*in hadd*] are very much confused and disturbed."[160]

In his account, Mirza Ja'far describes another letter, sent to him by thirty-seven notables, including *ulama*, *kedkhoda*, and priests of Chahrik, that describes how the Ottomans sent *mudir*s and other notables from Bashqala and Albak to Chahrik, Derik, and elsewhere to stir up the people with gifts and promises of a ten-year tax exemption in exchange for testimony that the district was Ottoman and that they desired Ottoman

---

[158] To prove the letter's veracity, Dervish refers to the *Tarikh al-Akrad* (Sharafnama) and claims that the letter shows that Ushnaviya and Lahijan had been Ottoman lands forty years before the 1639 Treaty. He attributes some forged stamps on the letter to local residents' fears of the 'Ajam and adds that, in any case, they learned such trickery from the 'Ajam. Dervish, *Tahdid*, 84–90. For Afshar-Kurdish relations, see Nobuaki Kondo, "Qizilbash Afterwards: The Afshars in Urmiya from the Seventeenth to the Nineteenth Century," *Iranian Studies* 32/4 (1999): 537–56.

[159] Tchirikof, *Diary*, 130.

[160] Mirza Ja'far, *Tahqiqat*, 165.

citizenship. In certain villages, people were urged to go to Dervish to claim they were Ottoman subjects who had been forced to declare allegiance to Iran. The *hakim* of Chahrik, Teymur Khan, vouched for the contents of this letter and declared that by provoking local clergymen to lead ordinary people to Dervish, these Ottoman agents were corrupting the Armenian and Kurdish *reaya*, who, in turn, created such disorder at the *sarhadd* that no *divani* (or fixed) taxes could be collected. To bolster Teymur's claims, Mirza Ja'far's account includes a petition by the Sunni Shafi'i khalifah of Salmas, which similarly describes the *reaya* of Chahrik as devoted followers of Dervish who had been stirred up into a state of revolt.[161] Similarly, the hereditary governor of Somai complained about Dervish's efforts to lure him with flattery, gifts, and promises.[162] In the end, Dervish Pasha's propaganda did not produce any beneficial results. This was first and foremost because the survey operated according to the principle of *uti possidetis* and the preservation of the status quo, but also because for many borderlanders historical affiliation with Iran superseded their sectarian affiliation with the Ottoman Empire. Despite these obstacles, however, Dervish's strategies would remain central to Ottoman claims for decades to come.

THE END OF THE SURVEY

While the negotiators gathered their final petitions, the mediators collected local histories and data for their map-making project, which they presented at the joint meetings. Because the survey's goal was not to make final decisions regarding ownership of all frontier regions, but rather to gather information, they were able to complete their operations despite the many setbacks they faced along the way. Hence, from Ushnaviyah, they moved to the frontier's northernmost section, arriving at the village of Bazargan on August 29, 1852, where 'Ali Khan Makoi hosted them for eight days. Here, as to be expected, Dervish attempted to woo the inhabitants of towns and villages on the banks of the Araxes River. In his absence, the other commissioners celebrated the end of their labor with a "splendid banquet" that Ali Khan and Mirza Ja'far gave in honor of the Europeans.[163] Mirza Ja'far, however, was utterly disappointed with the survey's inconclusive termination. In a letter addressed to the banquet's

---

[161] Ibid., 171.
[162] Tchirikof, *Diary*, 166.
[163] Mirza Ja'far, *Tahqiqat*, 185; Tchirikof, *Diary*, 31.

honorees, dated September 10, 1852, he listed his grievances. The *Explanatory Note*, he complained, had caused great delay in the execution of the terms of the Erzurum Treaty, and the mediators' awarding of a great portion of the mountainous territory of Zohab to the Ottoman Empire, at variance with the treaty, would endanger the peace and tranquility of that region's tribes. He protested the Ottoman occupation of "Kalai Berderesh and its dependencies, Penhan Nesheen, belonging to Yahya Khan, some of the grounds of Shepiran, &c., but more especially with respect to the villages and grounds of Khotour, Satmanis, Sherefkhaneh, Akhoorek, Yarim Kaya, and Dambat of Makoo." Because the mediating commissioners had "reiterated a promise to annihilate those encroachments and irregularities," he demanded that they take such measures for the restitution of the seized territories and also fugitives and runaway Iranian tribes. Bitterly protesting Dervish's conduct, he also asked them to reverse their decisions about Zohab and Muhammarah. The mediating commissioners responded, tersely, that his points had been repeatedly discussed and they had been mindful of their duty.[164]

Despite such last minute recriminations, the survey team considered its task completed by September 14, 1852.[165] Nonetheless, Williams asked London for permission to return to Constantinople to complete his notes and prepare his report in conjunction with the Russian mediator and technicians. Mirza Ja'far went to Tehran and the Ottomans to Istanbul: "The Russian commission, which had to complete its surveys round the little Ararat, went north-east, proceeded round Ararat, and reached the Russian frontier on the 6th September 1852. Traveling by way of Erivan, Kağızman, Erzurum, and Trebizond it returned to Constantinople on the 21st October 1852 – almost four years after it had left this place."[166] Through their joint labors, the commissioners collected enough technical information to complete a map of the whole boundary. The work of transforming their voluminous data on geography, commerce, ethnography, and history into a definitive map began in Istanbul but later was transferred to London and St. Petersburg. All told, it took more than two decades to complete. It appears that throughout this long process, neither Tehran nor Istanbul was consulted. Map making, a modern and technical

---

[164] The Persian text of the letters is in Mirza Ja'far, *Tahqiqat*, 190–93; here, I relied on the English translations in *Schofield II*, 287–89.

[165] PRO.FO 78/2723, Williams to H. A. Addington, Near Mount Ararat, September 14, 1852.

[166] Tchirikof, *Diary*, 31.

feat, was seen as a task that could be undertaken only by the European powers. Indeed, because of this belief, many British accounts of the survey do not even mention the names or deeds of the members of the Ottoman and Iranian technical teams, who were seen as amateurs at best. It is now to the aftermath of the survey that we turn our attention.

4

The Borderland between the Crimean War
and the Berlin Congress

After finishing their pioneering survey of the Ottoman-Iranian borderlands, the British, Russian, and Ottoman commissioners returned to
Istanbul to translate their findings into the first modern and complete
map of the frontier. The map, Britain and Russia hoped, would facilitate
their trade and telegraphic communications, reaffirm their central roles in
the politics of the Ottoman Empire and Iran, and define the limits of the
negotiating states' legal authority. This, in turn, would allow the mediating
states to define their de facto spheres of influence, which would become
official five decades later. Intended to be completed in six months, the work
of the cartographers and engineers was interrupted by the Crimean War
(1853–56). Although the Russo-British teams returned to their labors after
the war's end, it took them an additional twelve years to produce the final
map, the *Carte Identique*, which was presented in May 1869.[1] Although
not accepted as authoritative for many years, this document represented
the first time the Ottoman-Iranian boundary had been definitively traced
on paper. As such, its completion marked an important turning point.

After this, negotiations gained pace and, as we will see, a series of new
commissions was formed. However, none of these resulted in definitive
progress, and all diplomatic work again ground to a halt during the Russo-
Ottoman War of 1877–78, which caused catastrophic changes in the
borderland and beyond. Two years after the end of this war, from 1880
to 1881, a combined force of Ottoman and Iranian Sunni Kurds inhabiting
the northern zone of the borderland rose in revolt against the process of

---

[1] PRO.FO 78/2728, Galscott to Clarendon, Petersburg, May 20, 1869. The correspondence
describing their travails could be the topic of a separate book and is not detailed here.

boundary formation, as well as against Qajar attempts to make Shi'ism supreme in Kurdistan. The rebels' desire to unite Kurds across the boundary line posed the most direct challenge yet to that line, but their ultimate failure further integrated their peoples into the realms of their respective sovereigns. These developments mark the general outlines of the history of the borderland region between the first survey commission, which ended in 1852, and the Ottoman occupation of northwestern Iran, which began in 1905. Shifting between the global, regional, and local, the following pages analyze this long period, during which cross-border movements – including trade, migration, pilgrimage, and struggles for scarce resources – continued unabated and document how the events just sketched augmented sectarianism as a form of identity and belonging, thus preparing the way for the many tragedies that followed.

THE CRIMEAN WAR AND THE NORTHERN BORDERLAND

As the survey commission completed its arduous task, the Porte increasingly became the focus of Great Power rivalry. The Hungarian refugee crisis of 1848–49, incited by Polish-Hungarian revolutionaries fleeing to the Ottoman Empire, served as a harbinger of what was to come. When Austria and Russia demanded extradition, Istanbul, supported by London and Paris, refused. The issue was quickly and peacefully resolved. In its aftermath, however, relations between Russia and other European powers deteriorated as a result of competition between Catholic France and Orthodox Russia regarding which church should control Christian Holy Places in Palestine. Istanbul was drawn into this struggle when France demanded that it turn these places over to the Latin Church. In response, Russia asked Istanbul to recognize it as the protector of the Orthodox Church and the Orthodox subjects of the sultan, who represented a significant chunk of his subjects.[2] Seeking to protect its sovereign rights, Istanbul was caught between the ambitions of Napoleon III and Tsar Nikolai I. Nikolai's blatant disregard of those rights and French and British support of them further raised tensions. The Crimean War thus began on October 4, 1853, when the Porte declared war on Russia and was soon joined by French and British forces.[3] The war's fronts extended from

---

[2] Candan Badem, "The Ottomans and the Crimean War 1853–1856" (Ph.D. diss., Sabancı University, 2007), 61–63. (Hereafter Badem, "Crimean War.") For an Ottoman account of the war, see Ahmet Cevdet Pasha, *Tezâkir*, 1–12, hz. Cavid Baysun (Ankara: TTK, 1991).
[3] Eric J. Zürcher, *Turkey: A Modern History* (London: I. B. Tauris, 1997), 55–56.

the Baltic Sea to the Ottoman-Iranian border. In the latter region, some familiar names were involved, including the British representative to the Erzurum Conferences and survey commissioner, William Fenwick Williams, and Erzurum's British consul and a key initiator of the frontier negotiations, James Brant.[4]

After nearly two years of bloodshed, the Treaty of Paris was signed on March 30, 1856. A defeated Russia conceded to the demands of France, Britain, and Austria, and the Ottoman Empire was admitted into the Concert of Europe. The treaty guaranteed the independence and integrity of the empire by all major European powers, demilitarized the Black Sea (on the Ottoman side), and ended Russian influence in Moldavia and Wallachia. Britain, Austria, and France signed a convention declaring that they would consider any violation of these terms as *casus belli*.[5] In the meantime, the contemporaneous Anglo-Iranian conflict, incited when Iran attempted to invade Herat during the war, ended with the Peace Treaty of March 4, 1857.

The repercussions of the Crimean War were not limited to interstate relations. Many borderlanders participated in the struggle as *başıbozuks*, or irregulars, though they proved to be mostly ineffective against the regular Russian army.[6] At the same time, Istanbul used the war as an opportunity to increase state capacity at the borderland. As the first chapter showed, following the repression of the Kurdish dynasts, Istanbul began including Kurdish provinces within *daire-i tanzimat*, or the bounds of reform, registering nomadic males for tax and conscription purposes and introducing new taxes such the 1852 *iane-i umumiye*, or temporary tax, along with new administrative divisions. The Crimean War allowed Istanbul to further spread its administrative net. During the Crimean War, it introduced additional *avarız* taxes, including *iane-i cihadiye* or *iane-i harbiye* (contributions or subsidies to war). In spite of local

---

[4] Lieutenant Colonel Williams was appointed commissioner to the Anatolian army on August 2, 1854. In December, he was promoted to the rank of brigadier general in the British army and *Ferik* (lieutenant-general) in the Anatolian army, where he soon assumed the role of de facto commander-in-chief. Although he surrendered to the Russians in September 1855 because of a lack of provisions, Williams distinguished himself as defender of Kars and received the honorific title, Sir W. F. Williams of Kars. The sultan awarded him the rank of vizier and granted him a first-grade Mejidi medal. Cevdet, *Tezâkir*, 60; Badem, "Crimean War," 196–1–97; James J. Reid, *Crisis of the Ottoman Empire: Prelude to Collapse 1839–1878* (Stuttgart: Steiner, 2000), chap. 5; and BOA.A.DVN 110/64, 04/Ca/1272–13 January 1856. Williams's correspondence regarding the Crimean War was published in his William Fenwick Williams, *The Siege of Kars, 1855: Defense and Capitulation* (London: Stationery Office, 2000).

[5] Zürcher, *Turkey*, 56.

[6] Badem, "Crimean War," 3, 189–90.

authorities' petitions testifying to the destitution of their communities, the Porte insisted on the collection of these taxes, even as it distributed gifts to sheikhs in frontier districts such as Hakkari to encourage them to keep their populations under control.[7] Despite these latter efforts, and no doubt in response to the state's wartime push into its peripheries, a revolt broke out in the interior borderland. Centered in Bohtan (Cizre or Jazira ibn Omar), it was known by the name of its leader Ézdin Şêr (Yezdan Şer), a cousin of Bedirkhan.[8] Possibly beginning in November 1854, Ézdin Şêr and his men captured Bitlis and subordinated Musul, Siirt, and Van. In addition to Kurds, many Arabs, Nestorians, and Greeks participated in the revolt, and reports reached Istanbul that it was "far bigger than [the uprising] of Bedirhan, with an unheard of union and alliance among the Kurds from the time of the conquest of Kurdistan by the Ottomans and with unequalled violent battles,"[9] during which the Ottoman army destroyed villages from Mosul to Cizre.[10] The rebellion and its possible impact on the war front and the Iranian frontier worried British, French, and Ottoman authorities, leading Williams to intervene by sending messengers to Ézdin Şêr to offer him a guarantee of life and property. The maneuver was successful.[11] The failure of this last great effort by the members of the old Kurdish nobility to revive their family rule and repel centralization resulted in further pacification and facilitated the delimitation of the boundary and extension of state capacity.

THE CRIMEAN WAR AND OTTOMAN-IRANIAN RELATIONS

The allied worries about the Iranian frontier were not baseless. Shortly before the war and while the survey commission was still at work, on June 15, 1851, Istanbul appointed the able diplomat Ahmed Vefik Efendi (who later became the *sadrazam* of the empire) as ambassador to Tehran, where he served until September 12, 1854. It was thought that his knowledge of Persian language, politics, and geography would allow him to continue

---

[7] Ibid., 318.
[8] For more information on Ézdin Şêr, see Badem, "Crimean War"; and "Kırım Savaşı Sırasında İsyanlar ve Asayiş Sorunları (1353–1856)" in *Savaştan Barışa 150. Yıldönümünde Kırım Savaşı ve Paris Antlaşması (1853–1856)* (Istanbul: Ist. Ün. Ed. Fak. Araştırma Merkezi, 2007): 285–327.
[9] Badem, "Crimean War," 323–24.
[10] Reid, *Crisis*, 301–2; and Atwell Lake, *Narrative of the Defence of Kars: Historical and Military* (London: Richard Bentely, 1857), 37–39.
[11] Badem, "Crimean War," 324.

Dervish Pasha's *hudud* work.[12] As *tahdid-i hudud*, or frontier delimitation, was the most troublesome issue between the parties, he received the necessary information about Ottoman claims regarding the making of the boundary.[13] Before he even began his work, however, efforts to form alliances intensified with the approaching Crimean War. Suspicious that Russia might instigate Iran to occupy the disputed districts, Istanbul reinforced its army at Baghdad. In response, Tehran bolstered its troops, and both sides sent soldiers to the frontier.[14] To the dismay of Ahmed Vefik, the Russian representative in Tehran, Prince Dimitri Dolgorukov (Dolgorouki), manipulated existing rifts between Tehran and Istanbul by advising Iran to take precautionary steps against a possible amassing of Ottoman troops in Erzurum.[15]

Shortly before the war, Russian efforts to cajole or threaten Iran into an alliance escalated. The shah also faced pressure from his own people. The Iranian plenipotentiary to the survey commission, Mirza Ja'far Khan, hastened to the shah's camp near Tehran to convince him of the "opportunity which the threatened hostilities offered for regaining at least the districts of Kotoor and Tanbat, so arrogantly seized by Turkey."[16] For Tehran, which wanted Istanbul to accept some of its long-standing demands and redress its grievances regarding Karbala and the treatment of Shi'is in Iraq, the timing was ideal. Hence, the shah decided to review his troops near the border at Sultaniya, close to Zanjan; still, when pressed, he insisted his goal was to rein in unruly frontier tribes, prevent Ottoman Kurds from crossing into Iran, and limit the adverse effects of war.[17]

[12] Ibnülemin Mahmud Kemal İnal, *Osmanlı Devrinde Son Sadrazamlar*, V. cüz (Istanbul: Maarif Matbaası, 1944), 651–54; Mustafa Aydın, "Kırım Harbi Esnasında Osmanlı-İran-Rus İlişkileri (1853–55)," in *Savaştan Barışa 150. Yıldönümünde Kırım Savaşı ve Paris Antlaşması*, 131–50.

[13] For the instructions he received, his voyage to Tehran, and the diplomatic crisis that ensued when he raised the Ottoman flag at Tehran, see Mohammad Reza Nasiri, *Nāṣīreddin Şah Zamanında Osmanlı-İran Münasebetleri (1848–1896)* (Tokyo: Institute for the Study of Languages and Cultures of Asia and Africa, 1991), 61–63.

[14] PRO.FO 78/2723, Rawlinson to Principal Secretary of State, Baghdad, January 24, 1853; and PRO.FO 78/2724, Rawlinson to Clarendon, Baghdad, April 13, 1853.

[15] Abbas Amanat, *Pivot of the Universe: Nasir Al-Din Shah Qajar and the Iranian Monarchy, 1831–1896* (Berkeley: University of California Press, 1997), 235.

[16] PRO.FO 78/2724, Thomson to Clarendon, July 8, 1853.

[17] Amanat, *Pivot*, 233. For details of this period, I benefited from *Pivot*, chap. 6; see also Caner İ. Türk, "1853–1856 Kırım Harbi Sırasında Osmanlı-İran İlişkileri, Osmanlı Devletine Karşı Russian-İran Gizli Antlaşması." (M.A. thesis, Atatürk Universitesi, 2000), 24, and Mustafa Aydın, "Kırım Harbi Esnasında Osmanlı-İran-Rus İlişkileri (1853–55)," in *Savaştan Barışa 150. Yıldönümünde Kırım Savaşı ve Paris Antlaşması* 135.

Regardless of Nasir al-Din's true objectives, his preparations displeased the British, who distrusted assurances that his troops would not move a step beyond Sultaniya.[18] In a note to his own prime minister, the shah conveyed his belief that the Ottomans were behind continuing British pressure and expressed irritation at being prevented from moving inside his own domain. Recalling the Karbala incidents that had briefly put a stop to previous boundary negotiations, he articulated his enduring anger at Ottoman authorities:

Ten years ago they repeatedly killed and plundered and gradually laid down a precedent [literally an "innovation"]. In whatever way they could they have offended and degraded *shari'at*. But on the last day we will be responsible. No doubt we will pay for it. Certainly God disapproves that thirty thousand Shi'ite human beings can be violated so much in that province [i.e., Baghdad]. What is the purpose of this life? To hell with [political] expediency [*bar padar-i mulahiza la'nat*]. I am not the sultan of the Shi'ite nation! I am not! That is all.[19]

Despite his outrage, the self-appointed "sultan of the Shi'ites" remained constrained by circumstances as well as stronger opponents. British pressure, along with an outbreak of cholera in Tehran, economic limitations, and logistical problems, effectively halted his show of force. One day after his arrival at Sultaniya, he canceled the review of troops and returned to his camp outside Tehran.[20] No doubt the shah's displeasure with the Ottomans and his anti-British sentiments prompted his aborted display of force. Yet, continued Russian instigations and his own dreams of grandeur also played a role.

Keenly aware of Ottoman-Iranian tensions, Dolgorukov believed that Tehran would ally itself with Moscow if Russia could force Istanbul to pay indemnities for the Karbala incident of 1843 and acquire Kotur for Iran. Shortly after the Ottoman declaration of war, in early November 1853, in a private audience with the shah, Dolgurukov and the tsar's special envoy Bebitove forcefully requested that "a strong military demonstration" be made against Turkey in Azerbaijan and Kermanshah.[21] Ottoman sources suggest that possible Iranian advances into Erzurum-Bayezid and Baghdad, Karbala, and areas around Najaf were also discussed. Both Ottoman and Russian sources assert that in clandestine one-on-one meetings, Dolgorukov offered the shah a secret program. In exchange for Iran's contribution of sixty

[18] PRO.FO 78/2724, Thomson to Clarendon, July 8, 1853.
[19] Nasir al-Din to Nuri, quoted in Amanat, *Pivot*, 234.
[20] For Thomson's pressuring of Iranian authorities on the subject of the military review, PRO.FO 78/2724, Thomson to Clarendon, July 8, 1853.
[21] Amanat, *Pivot*, 249; and Aydın, "Kırım Harbi," 136.

thousand soldiers, acceptance of the authority of Russian officers, and permission for Russian troops to withdraw to Iran in case of defeat, Russia promised, among other things, to cancel the debts agreed to by the Turkmanchay Treaty, allow Iran to keep any lands it occupied during the war, and pay for Iranian troops if the war became protracted.[22] As further incentive, Russia offered the long coveted Herat as well as other regions of Afghanistan and Central Asia, pending Russian victory, while threatening Tehran with occupation of its Caspian provinces if it refused to cooperate. The shah did not forget to ask, as well, for the return of Kotur.[23] As rumors of this alliance spread, Ottoman frontier authorities monitored Iranian military activities and prepared for a confrontation. Because Ottoman Kurds were serving as *bashibozuks* (irregulars) and Iranian Kurds were sympathetic to the Ottomans, Iran took necessary measures to thwart its Kurds from joining the Ottoman forces.[24] As we will see, this was not the last time Iran prevented its Kurds from joining their co-sectarians against Russia.

Enticed by Russia's promises and his own dreams of becoming the sultan of the Shi'is or, at least, of convincing the Ottomans to follow a more tolerable policy toward their Shi'i subjects, the young shah once again "ordered an assembly of troops to be sent to the Turkish frontiers under the Kurdish officer 'Aziz Khan Mukri, now the commander of the army (*sardar-i kull*), and Muhammad Khan Qajar, the chief of the royal bodyguard."[25] When asked, Tehran insisted the troops were sent only for the tranquility of the frontier. Rumors of a possible Iranian march on Baghdad circulated at the war front,[26] however, even as it was also speculated that Tehran would declare for the allied powers.[27] Others noted that Nasir al-Din "made overtures to Great Britain and France, and was advised by those Powers, which had now joined in the Russo-Turkish war, to remain neutral."[28]

---

[22] 'Ali Asghar Shamim, *Iran dar dawrah-i Qajar: Qarn-i sizdahum va nimah-i avval-i Qarn-i chahardahum* (Tehran: Entesharate Zariab, 1387/2008), 221–22. İ. Caner Türk, "1853–1856 Kırım Harbi Sırasında Osmanlı-İran İlişkileri, Osmanlı Devletine Karşı Rus-İran Gizli Antlaşması" (M.A. thesis, Atatürk Universitesi, 2000), 17.

[23] Türk, "1853–56 Kırım Harbi," 23; Amanat, *Pivot*, 249.

[24] Türk, "1853–56 Kırım Harbi," 20.

[25] Amanat, *Pivot*, 250; and Reid, *Crisis*, 249–50.

[26] Adolphus Slade and M. S. Anderson, *Turkey and the Crimean War: A Narrative of Historical Events* (London: Smith, Elder, 1867), 227.

[27] Laurence Oliphant, F. Straker, and M. S. Anderson, *The Trans-Caucasian Campaign of the Turkish Army under Omer Pasha: A Personal Narrative* (London: W. Blackwood, 1856), 227–28.

[28] Percy M. Sykes, *A History of Persia* (London: Macmillan and Co.1915), vol. 2, 450; Aydın, "Kırım Harbi," 134.

While rumors flew, Iranian Prime Minister Mirza Aqa Khan Nuri, who advocated for cooperation with the allies to regain the Caucasian provinces lost to Russia,[29] informed British chargé d'affaires Taylor Thompson that the shah would not exploit the plight of his Muslim neighbor but rather would "abstain so long as the war continued ... from bringing forward the claims of Persia against Turkey with regard to Kerbela, Mohammera, Kotoor and the other grievances."[30] Notwithstanding the prime minister's words, the shah's change of heart arose, not from sympathy for his coreligionists, but as a response to continuing pressure from Britain as well as France.[31] This pressure, along with Nuri's more sober calculations, the antiwar gatherings of *ulama* and merchants in front of the palace, and the fact that Britain had already declared in favor of Iran on the Kotur issue, convinced the shah to refuse even a defense treaty with Russia, declare his neutrality, and exchange notes of friendship with Istanbul.[32]

Buffeted between the Great Powers, as Abbas Amanat observes, "Perhaps at no time in the diplomatic history of Qajar Iran other than the turbulent period between 1852 and 1857 did the two European powers use their capitulatory rights so unreservedly to try to force the host government to submit to their vengeful and often opposing views."[33] Possibly wanting to show that he could negotiate directly with his Sunni half brothers, in late 1853, the shah lifted the three-year-old ban on visitations to Karbala as a goodwill gesture. He then sent the Iranian chargé d'affaires at Istanbul, Hajji Mirza Ahmad Khan, to the Porte with a list of Iranian demands: the return of Kotur, favored nation status, the right for Iranians to be tried in their own courts, and the easing of restrictions on corpse traffic from Iran to the holy Shi'i cities. He also requested that Iranians already in the holy cities be allowed to repair their (unlawfully acquired) properties and that the shah's mother be authorized to build a series of mosques in Iraq. Maintaining its rights to Kotur, Istanbul was nevertheless conciliatory. It canceled taxes on pilgrims and corpses (*bac* or *nakil vergisi*) and eased restrictions on existing Iranian properties. But the Ottoman

---

[29] Shamim, *Iran dar dawrah-i saltanat-i Qajar*, 222–23.

[30] PRO.FO 78/2724, Thomson to Clarendon, January 23, 1854; Türk, "1853–56 Kırım Harbi," 39.

[31] 'Ali Asghar Shamim argues that Nasir al-Din was unhappy with British and French support of the Ottomans and hence became sympathetic to Russian offers. *Iran dar dawrah-i saltanat-i Qajar* 221.

[32] Aydın, "Kırım Harbi," 137–42.

[33] Amanat, *Pivot*, 236–37, 250.

Advisory Council (Meclis-i Meşveret) also suggested that Iranians no longer be allowed to buy property in the Ottoman Empire and sent additional forces to Van and Bayezid.[34]

Russia nevertheless continued to pressure Iran, replacing Dulgorukov with Nikolai Anichkov, who gradually recognized that Iran would not participate in the war and shifted his efforts toward a policy of neutralization. His efforts paid off when, following Ottoman defeats in August and September of 1854, a secret treaty was exchanged under the shah's personal auspices, in which Iran agreed "to halt the movement of arms, namely British consignments via Azerbaijan, to the Ottoman side, prevent the transport of food and provisions to the Ottoman Empire,"[35] and prevent Kurdish incursions into Russian frontiers. In return, it would be relieved from paying 473,000 tumans, the last of the 1828 war indemnity.[36] Although it failed to arrange an alliance, Russia thus prevented its neighbor from cooperating with its enemies. Moreover, after signing the treaty, Iran ceased pressing the Kotur issue until the return of general peace, even as Istanbul, ignoring London's pleas, continued its occupation there. The British ascribed this intransigence to Sultan Abdulmecid I (r. 1839–61), who was said to adhere to the policy of retaining Kotur more obstinately than his ministers.[37]

Even as he cooperated with Russia, however, the shah continued his efforts to improve relations with Istanbul, whose borderland authorities became more tolerant toward Iranian pilgrims and the Shi'is of Iraq. Rashid Pasha, the governor-general of Iraq and commander of the Iraq-Hijaz army, for example, assured authorities in Tehran of the safety and provisioning of the great caravan route to the holy cities of Karbala and Najaf, and the better treatment of Iranian merchants at Ottoman ports. In addition, he temporarily suspended the *iane-i sultani* tax on Iranians in Najaf and Karbala and abolished various taxes on ferries, canals, caravansaries, and the like. Still, he claimed that other irritants, such as fees on the washing and internment of the dead or monopolies on *kefens* (shrouds), rosaries, and cakes of Karbala earth (all items used by Shi'is for prayer), could not be abolished without direct orders from Istanbul. Moreover, the Ottoman government remained vigilant in its enforcement of another institution of the modern border, the quarantine. Despite complaints about ongoing

---

[34] Aydın, "Kırım Harbi," 138; and Türk, "1853–56 Kırım Harbi," 26.
[35] Amanat, *Pivot*, 254, 248.
[36] Türk, "1853–56 Kırım Harbi," 43–44; Aydın, "Kırım Harbi," 146–48.
[37] Kemball Report, *Schofield III*, 150.

oppression suffered by Iranians in quarantine stations and official calls for their abolition, Rashid received orders to double the required time spent in quarantine at the frontier from five to ten days.[38]

Soon after the Treaty of Paris was signed on March 30, 1856, and despite his state's declared neutrality, the Iranian ambassador Farrukh Khan Ghaffari traveled to Istanbul on his way to Paris to discuss French support for Iran's planned campaign at Herat.[39] His efforts to win Ottoman support for this campaign, and to convince them to prevent the British navy from using the Shatt al-Arab, failed. London's friendship was no doubt more valuable than any benefit that could come from supporting Nasir al-Din Shah's "youthful ambitions," a term coined by Abbas Amanat. Although the shah initially succeeded in capturing Herat, by December 1856, British forces had occupied the southern port of Bushehr, from which they advanced farther into Iran. Anglo-Persian hostilities ended with the Paris Peace Treaty signed on April 5, 1857, and the Herat debacle not only dimmed Tehran's hopes of expanding its eastern frontiers but also subjected it to Britain's whims for the period to come.[40]

For a few years, the Crimean War and ensuing British-Iranian hostilities overshadowed the ongoing problems faced by borderland communities. Tehran, rocked by internal problems, also faced external political, territorial, and economic pressures from both England and Russia. Istanbul, meanwhile, faced huge debts and renewed Great Power pressure. Despite these latter challenges, however, in 1856, the Porte declared the Imperial Rescript (*Hatt-ı Hümayun*) that opened *tanzimat*'s second phase and a new era in the reorganization of the Ottoman state and society. As a result of factors such as the Russo-Iranian threat, the slow rise of Armenian nationalism, and the power vacuum created by the campaign against the Kurdish dynasts, the borderland thus became a main focus of the *tanzimat* state's drive to increase its capacity and territorial sovereignty. This drive was facilitated by one enduring legacy of the Crimean War, the introduction of the telegraph lines that would soon extend into Iran.[41] After the

---

[38] PRO.FO 78/2724, Rawlinson, British Residency, Baghdad to London, April 15, 1854; Türk, "1853–56 Kırım Harbi," 38–40.

[39] Nasiri, *Nāsıreddin*, 85.

[40] For the Herat campaign and Anglo-Iranian relations in this period see Amanat, *Pivot*, chap. 7.

[41] Yakup Bektaş, "The Sultan's Messenger: Cultural Constructions of Ottoman Telegraphy, 1847–1880," *Technology and Culture* 41 (2000), 684; H. C. Rawlinson *Notes on the Direct Overland Telegraph From Constantinople to Kurrachi* (London: John Murray, 1861).

installation of the first lines that linked the Crimean fronts to Istanbul,[42] and then Istanbul to the European system (1856), a separate Ottoman-Iranian Telegraph Treaty was signed in 1857.[43] The telegraph was introduced to Iran in 1858 and spread thereafter, opening up the country to additional economic concessions.[44]

These developments were further spurred by the Indian Mutiny of 1857, which increased London's need for an overland electric telegraph line to India that would traverse the length of Iran and Ottoman dominions in Asia. The Anglo-Iranian telegraph convention of February 6, 1863, called for the construction of a line from Baghdad to the Persian Gulf through Iranian territory. The Anglo-Ottoman telegraph convention, meanwhile, was signed on October 20, 1863.[45] Promising to bring the British Empire into daily contact with its Asian colonies, while also providing direct communication between Tehran and Istanbul, the line created a new urgency for the demarcation of the boundary, because the dispute in Zohab about the seventeen miles of territory between Qasr-i Shirin and Khanaqin was delaying its completion. Istanbul's reluctance to allow the extension of an overland route from Baghdad through Iran to India further exacerbated the problem, generating a flurry of diplomatic activity. Only the signing of the Russo-Iranian telegraphic convention of August 1864, which resulted in the prospect of an alternative line advancing from Russia via Tiflis, Tehran, and Bushehr, forced Istanbul to consent to the neutralization of the disputed territory.[46] Tribal revolts, such as that of the Muntafiq confederation of lower Iraq (1863–65), halted the construction of the line in the peripheries for some time, but in the end modernity and the tools that it put into the service of

[42] Ahmet Cevdet Paşa, *Tezakir*, vol. 1 (Ankara: Turk Tarih Kurumu Basımevi, 1953), 56.

[43] For the signing of the Ottoman-Iranian telegraph treaty, see BOA.A.DVN.NMH, 8/6, 1271.N.10/ May 27, 1855–1273.Ş.25/April 20, 1857.

[44] Nikki R. Keddie, *Roots of Revolution: An Interpretive History of Modern Iran* (New Haven, CT: Yale University Press, 1981), 58.

[45] Soli Shahvar, "Iron Poles, Wooden Poles: The Electric Telegraph and the Ottoman-Iranian Boundary Conflict, 1863–1865," *British Journal of Middle Eastern Studies*, 34.1 (2007): 23, 27.

[46] After lengthy discussions, it became obvious that whoever built poles in disputed territories could later claim proprietorship. Thus, after much debate, it was decided to set up alternating rows of iron and wooden poles, as the Ottomans were using the former and the Persians the latter. See ibid.; G. E. Hubbard, *From the Gulf to Ararat* (Edinburgh and London: William Blackwood and Sons, 1916), 12; Maurice Harari, "The Ottoman-Iranian Boundary Question: A Case Study in the Politics of Boundary Making in the Near and Middle East" (Ph.D. diss., Columbia University, 1953), 138.

the state won the day.[47] The line, to be patrolled mutually, was built at the joint expense of Tehran and Istanbul, and in early January 1865, London was finally connected directly to India.[48] During the next two decades, the construction of new lines extended to all corners of both states, and telegraph technology became an important tool of empire that symbolized the sultan's and the shah's authority and geographic reach. By facilitating the rapid deployment of troops and sharpening the gaze of the states at the *sarhaddat*, the telegraph significantly decreased the porosity of the frontier as a filter.

THE LOCALS AND THE LOCALITIES: HOW TO CONTROL, WHOM TO STOP

Greater Ottoman surveillance at the frontiers raised familiar Iranian complaints about the treatment of Shi'is. Defeated in Afghanistan, the sultan of the Shi'is increasingly took refuge in religious piety and, following the example of many predecessors, became involved in charitable work in Ottoman Iraq. In addition to petitioning for protection and free access for pilgrims and corpse caravans, his dignitaries requested permission to erect Shi'i mosques and madrassas in Ottoman territory and appealed for the maintenance and furnishing (*tefriş*) of the shrines of the imams, especially those of 'Ali and Hussein. In 1857, the shah sent money to the highest Shi'i religious authority of the time, Abd al-Hussein Tehrani, to furnish, maintain, and enlarge the shrines in Iraq. Such charitable intervention was a threat to the sultan's authority and put Istanbul on alert. Thus, when the shah bought buildings around Hussein's shrine with the intention of enlarging it, Istanbul ordered the governor of Baghdad to intervene. It was only further Iranian lobbying and French intervention that allowed its construction to be completed. Still, Istanbul remained wary of the Shi'ization of southern Iraq and restricted work on other shrines to necessary repairs.

Iran's potential for interference in Iraq and other Ottoman territories was exacerbated by the fact that its subjects lived and traded all over the Ottoman Empire, where they had long enjoyed special advantages. For example, they were allowed to buy real estate and avoid paying many

---

[47] Soli Shahvar, "Tribes and Telegraph Lines of Lower Iraq: The Muntafiq and the Baghdad-Basrah Telegraph Line of 1863–1865," *Middle Eastern Studies*, 39.1, 94.

[48] Bektaş, "The Sultan's Messenger"; Amanat, *Pivot*, 404–5.

taxes, privileges not extended to other foreigners. As we have seen, the Erzurum treaties stipulated that such privileges be proscribed, and that Iranians be treated like citizens of any other nation. The Porte embraced this reform, not only because it would help prevent Iranian involvement in Iraq, but also because it fell in line with *tanzimat* principles, which aimed at creating a bounded, unified citizenry irrespective of religious affiliation. The vaguely bounded space of the *umma*, which Iranians had metaphorically and physically occupied, needed to be delimited so that the citizen could be defined. Thus, to comply with the Erzurum treaties, expand *tanizmat* reforms, and protect Iraq from the shah's influence, Iranians, some of whom had resided in Ottoman lands for generations, were asked to make a choice: become Ottoman citizens or sell their real estate and stay as guests. It was only after serious diplomatic wrangling that Istanbul agreed to allow them to keep land they already owned. Further investments, however, were prohibited and existing real estate became taxable.[49]

While Sultan Abdulaziz (r. 1861–76) promoted administrative reform and centralization with the help of the *tanzimat* pashas, Tehran's energies were absorbed by the disastrous Marv campaign against the Türkmens and a massive famine that resulted in bread riots.[50] At the same time, disputed frontier districts such as Kotur and Muhammarah continued to trouble internal and external relations of both parties. As the power struggles over real estate and citizenship revealed, clashes during the period of Abdulaziz's reign were as much about the inhabitants of the land as they were about the land itself. In the borderlands, with the vanquishing of local dynasties such as the Baban and Ardalan and further territorialization of sovereignty, seminomadic groups that had been unable to adjust to the new realities of a tightening frontier filter now became the principal focus of dispute.

Despite sharing common linguistic, ethnic, and religious identities, which were deepened by social and economic relations that extended across both sides of the line, such groups were obliged to adopt the citizenship, and later the nationality, of one state or another. Yet, abstract imperial loyalties could not easily displace long-standing notions of place, and for a long time, the borderlanders clung to the localities that had shaped their collective identities since time immemorial.[51] The

---

[49] Nasiri, *Nāsīreddin*, 91–107.
[50] For a detailed account, see Amanat, *Pivot*, 378.
[51] Peter Sahlins, *Boundaries: The Making of France and Spain in the Pyrenees* (Berkeley: University of California Press, 1989), 33.

boundary line itself – invisible but, thanks to the work of previous commissions, ever more tangible – was the first new reality they had to confront because of their seasonal reliance on pasturelands on both sides. Their attempts to assert traditional rights to these lands increasingly brought them into confrontation with the state authorities that were aggressively guarding their limits.

These populations were, moreover, deprived not only of pasturelands but also of the fluidity of itinerancy, which had long allowed them to flee overtaxation, conscription, and other types of limitation or oppression. As the border filter closed and the passport became the magic key to open it, nomads – who traveled without documents and in groups for which no modern border filter would open – faced a stark choice: to settle, permanently, on one side of the divide or the other. In response, communities reacted with distinct positions and expressions of identity.[52]

The case of Mangur tribe of the northernmost zone, mentioned at the end of the previous chapter, exemplifies how the local sense of space clashed with the process of boundary making. A branch of the Bilbas tribe mentioned in the 1639 treaty, they spent most of the year in the Lahijan district, in pasturelands claimed by both Iran and the Ottoman Empire. After the demise of Rawanduz, the emirate of Soran, under whose authority they had been, the Mangur disregarded the newly negotiated boundaries and moved freely between pastures, as they had traditionally done. On the one hand, their autonomous movement was facilitated by the absence of the Kurdish emirates that had previously regulated pasture usage. On the other, the same power vacuum also increased tensions with neighboring tribes that were loyal to Iran, including the Mamesh, another branch of the Bilbas, and the Shi'i Turkish Karapapak tribe. It seems that the competition for resources with these and other tribes might have prompted the Mangur to favor Ottoman sovereignty even as they continued their seasonal migrations.

In any case, their activities drew the attention, and the ire, of Iranian and Ottoman officials, both of whom claimed authority over them and their habitat. To further its territorial claims, Tehran built forts at Lahijan, Merivan, and Hawraman – all points along the tribe's migration routes – to block their movement through its guarded domains. Ottoman authorities, in turn, backed the Mangur with claims that the forts were illegitimate because they were built in districts marked as disputed in the status quo.

<hr />

[52] T. M. Wilson and Donnan Hastings, *Border Identities: Nation and State at International Frontiers* (Cambridge, UK: Cambridge University Press, 1998), 10.

The mediating governments were informed accordingly, but this did not hinder the Iranian authorities.[53] In 1864, the governor of Iranian Savojbulagh mounted several cannons on the walls of the Lahijan fort and garrisoned it with three hundred soldiers.[54] Comparing these actions to those of Ottoman authorities in places such as Bayazid and Van, Iran argued that they were solely "for the management of the interior and to improve the condition of some of their own subjects, at their own request."[55]

In 1866, while in Iranian lands, the Mangur were involved in a quarrel with the Karapapak, who bested them with the help of Iranian authorities. After they retreated to the Ottoman side, Namık Pasha, the governor of Baghdad, demanded indemnities from Iran and was refused. The Mangur – possibly with the pasha's encouragement – then embraced the first opportunity to forcefully recover their losses.[56] One British observer described the resulting dilemma as follows:

The merits of the present discussion are not easily determined. They are as usual complicated by the divided nationality of the tribe in question, who enjoying the rights of pasturage on both sides of the border, alternately claim the protection or repudiate the authority of either government, as the interests of the day may prompt them.[57]

Iranian attempts to compel the Mangur to recognize the limits of the guarded domains failed. They had the numbers to resist and so continued to tread their long-traveled paths. In 1867, while in Lahijan, they again came into conflict with Iranian authorities and, again, returned to Ottoman territory. Led by their chief Hamza Agha on their trek back, they raided local villages, prompting Iran to dispatch about five hundred horsemen. Under cover of night, Hamza and his men attacked these horsemen, killing about one hundred at a place called Bairam Shah and taking horses and flocks of sheep. They then stealthily entered a fort garrisoned by additional Iranian troops, where they killed about fifteen more men and took everything they could find. After retreating to the Qandil mountains, Hamza went to Takiyeddin Pasha, the governor of Kirkuk, and related the whole affair, for which he reportedly received praise.[58] Tehran, unsurprisingly, reacted

---

[53] See, among many examples, PRO.FO 78/2726, Turkish Mission to Mirza Said Khan, August 31, 1865.

[54] PRO.FO 78/2727 Mr. Rassam's Report, Mossul, July 13, 1867.

[55] PRO.FO 78/2726, Mirza Said Khan to Ottoman Consul at Tabriz, September 15, 1865.

[56] Ibid.

[57] PRO.FO 78/2727. H. P. T. Darron to Lord Stanley, Constantinople, August 5, 1867. See also British Consulate General, Baghdad, June 27, 1867.

[58] PRO.FO 78/2727, Mr. Rassam's report, Mosul July 13, 1867.

less positively. In June 1867, it sent ten thousand troops from Tabriz to near the frontier. Further, it demanded that Namık Pasha remove Takiyeddin Pasha and Ömer Pasha, the governors of Kirkuk and Suleimanieh, and extradite Hamza and his men. Three additional divisions of troops were then sent to Rayat, Serdesht, and the pass of Suleimanieh, and Tehran threatened to loose Iranian tribes along the whole line of the frontier to ravage Ottoman territory. In response, Ottoman authorities gathered men from all the Kurdish tribes belonging to Kirkuk, Suleimanieh, and Rawanduz and ordered commanders in Mosul to send troops and ammunition to Rawanduz.[59] Namık sent twelve hundred carabineers to reinforce Takieddin in Kirkuk, among other measures. News of the conflict soon reached British representatives in Mosul and Baghdad, and it was their diplomatic interference that prevented a war.

This turbulent episode seems to have eroded the resistance of the Mangurs. Although they continued their cross-border migrations for some time, they finally put an end to their divided nationality. As Mirza Ja'far predicted, pasture trumped politics. Under Hamza's leadership, they chose allegiance with Iran, the location of most of the lands that made their subsistence possible.[60] This choice, however, did not put an end to their tribulations. They were now forced to alter their traditional cycle of migration and compete with rival tribes for limited resources, while being pressured by Iran to pay new taxes. Their unease with the limitations imposed by demarcation, coupled with ever-harsher Iranian policies, would soon put them at the forefront of a rebellion against Tehran's hegemony and against the very fact of increasingly tangible boundaries.

Far from unique, the trajectory of the Mangur is representative of many other tribal groups whose migratory patterns, ambivalent state allegiances, and local concepts of belonging ran up against an increasingly surveilled, less porous frontier. The Mangurs' sense of place and identity, incongruent with a citizenry defined by boundaries, made them unable or unwilling to adapt to the new realities pushed on them by the states. As is so often the case with peoples of the margins, increasingly frequent references to them in state registers and diplomatic correspondence signaled state encroachment on their land and in their lives. As state capacity increased, so did state unease with seasonal border crossings and tribal unease with the

---

[59] Ibid.

[60] Hurşîd Pasha adds that the Mangurs' acquisition of fields around Savojbulagh coupled with Iranian pressure, gradually made them lean toward Iran. Mehmed Hurşîd Paşa, *Seyâhatnâme-i Hudud*, transcription Alaatin Eser (Istanbul: Simurg, 1997), 213.

decreasing porosity of the frontier filter. Mutual apprehension thus became magnified through many similar cases, and the negotiating and mediating parties began to consider the formation of a new commission to finalize the demarcation of the frontier.

FORMING A NEW COMMISSION, TEACHING THE BORDERLANDERS A LESSON

At the same time that the 1869 *Carte Identique* was finally being completed, Tehran and Istanbul began building additional military stations along the frontier to stop border crossings and justify claims to disputed lands in future negotiations. In addition to those previously mentioned, Tehran built fortifications in the highly debated plain of Zohab, and Istanbul strengthened its installations in Kotur.[61] The resultant threat to the status quo again drew British and Russian representatives into the situation. Hoping to use this involvement to his advantage, the shah informed Charles Alison, the British envoy extraordinary and minister plenipotentiary from April 1860 to April 1872, that "Turkey should abstain from taking any independent action in regard to the frontier, and that nothing should be done by either party without the full cognizance and approval of England and Russia."[62] In response, the Ottoman grand vizier assured the British ambassador that Istanbul had no such intentions to strike out on its own. Even as it looked at Ottomans and Iranians with suspicion, London also suspected that Russian representatives were instrumental in promoting ill will between the negotiating governments and provoking the movement of Iranian troops toward the frontier.[63] While London worried about a possible military confrontation, Tehran requested the appointment of a special commission to inspect all frontier districts, including Kotur, and to destroy all buildings erected on disputed territory since the conclusion of the Erzurum Treaty.[64]

Although Tehran's request was not immediately granted, subsequent correspondence and negotiations resulted in a convention whose purpose was to resolve problems that had emerged along the frontier. At the convention's conclusion, on August 3, 1869, Tehran and Istanbul reaffirmed

---

[61] Nasiri, *Nāsīreddin*, 38–40.
[62] For the British intervention and Iran and Istanbul's assurances, see PRO.FO 78/2728, Alison to Clarendon, February 6, 8, and 9, 1869.
[63] PRO.FO 78/2728, Foreign Office to Alison, March 4, 1869.
[64] Harari, *Turco-Persian*, 13.

their pledge to maintain the status quo pending final agreement.[65] The pledge, however, had little positive effect. Exploiting ambiguity regarding whether disputed lands could be cultivated, occupied, or pastured by nomads, each side raised or destroyed structures on said lands in an attempt to appropriate the larger share of the total territory.[66] Moreover, they strategically encouraged itinerant populations to claim their traditional rights, further exacerbating tensions.

When Tehran complained that the prominent Ottoman reformer and governor of Baghdad Midhat Pasha had violated the status quo reiterated by the 1869 convention, the mediating powers decided that additional complaints would be referred to a new boundary commission. In September 1870, however, before the commission was scheduled to begin its work in Baghdad, Nasir al-Din Shah decided to visit the holy Shi'i sites in Iraq. Despite the trip's sensitive political nature and the huge financial burden it would impose on Istanbul, the sultan granted him permission.[67] The shah and his large retinue were well received and, in a reciprocal gesture of Shi'i-Sunni reconciliation, he bequeathed one hundred thousand Iranian tumans for the beautification of the tomb of Abu Hanifa, the founder of the Hanafi school of law.[68] This success led to renewed attempts by the negotiating states to circumvent Great Power mediation. For example, during his visit the shah suggested that both parties should keep what they now held: Kotur for the Ottomans and Zohab for Iran. His proposal produced no practical result,[69] but Midhat did sign an agreement with the Iranian ambassador Hussein Khan to regulate corpse traffic between Iran and Ottoman Iraq. Emerging global awareness about cholera, and suspicions that corpses and pilgrims might be agents of its spread, facilitated this agreement. An international demand that the Ottomans increase surveillance at the frontiers thus played a

[65] Ali Pasha and Mirza Muhsin Khan signed the convention. For the Ottoman version, see BOA.A.DVN.NMH 19/3, April 30, 1869/January 14, 1871. PRO.FO 78/2732, Foreign Office Memorandum, February 8, 1869, and PRO.FO 78/2728, Elliot to Clarendon, Constantinople, August 6, 1869.

[66] Kemball's Report, *Schofield III*, 157.

[67] Midhat Paşa. *Midhat Paşa Hayat-ı Siyasiyesi, Hidematı, Menfa Hayatı: Tabsıra-i İbret*, ed. Ali Haydar Midhat (Istanbul: Hilal Matbaası, 1320/1903), 4, 97–98; and Ali Haydar Midhat, *The Life of Midhat Pasha* (London: John Murray, 1903), 96.

[68] Nasiri, *Nāṣīreddin*, 155.

[69] PRO.FO 78/2729, Elliot to Clarendon, Constantinople, May 30, 1870, PRO.FO 78/2729, Baron Ernest Philip Brunnow (Russian ambassador to Britain) to Lord Granville, November 5 (17), 1870, and Mirza Saed Khan to Charles Alison, September 20, 1870.

significant role in accelerating the need for a less porous frontier filter.[70] Another agreement promised to limit the cross-border movement of tribes and fugitives. Soon afterward, however, claiming lack of Iranian cooperation in the surveillance of the frontier, Midhat unilaterally established frontier posts, or *karakol*s, in Baghdad province composed of local people, a technique he had previously used in Tuna *vilayet*.[71]

The shah's visit thus had limited positive effects. On July 24, 1871, another temporary document exchanged between the Ottoman Empire and Iran reconfirmed the status quo. It reiterated noninterference in disputed lands until a commission decided their fate, clarified that present ownership or pretense to such was not a justification of that right, and declared that future disputes should be settled without the mediators' involvement unless absolutely necessary.[72] Nevertheless, both sides continued to claim proprietorship by sending troops or loyal tribes to build barracks or small buildings in unpopulated or deserted regions that were used as pasture grounds in other seasons. As such actions constrained the movements of pastoralists, IMoFA Mirza Sa'id Khan blamed Ottoman petty officials for the tribes' unsettled state, warning that Iran could not be held responsible for what might happen and expressing the hope that Britain, "who has so fully exerted itself in establishing peace and tranquility in the East, will never permit that the welfare of these countries should be thus exposed to dangerous disorders and confusion through the unwise proceedings of these insubordinate Turkish officials."[73]

Consequently London – this time acting independently of Russia – once more urged Tehran and Istanbul to choose representatives for the new commission. They complied, appointing Ottoman Commissioner Miralay Abdurrahman Bey and Iranian Commissioner Mirza Mohib 'Ali Khan Nizam al-Mulk, a general in the Iranian army and consul general in Tiflis.[74]

---

[70] For the role of corpse traffic and emergence of cholera in the making of the boundary, see Sabri Ateş, "Bones of Contention: Corpse Traffic and Ottoman-Iranian Rivalry in Nineteenth Century Iraq," *Comparative Studies of South Asia, Africa and the Middle East* 30.3 (2010): 512–33; and Naseri *Nāsireddin*, 156.

[71] Midhat Pasha, *Hayat-ı Siyasiyesi*, 53. According to the policy, every local male older than fifteen was to be stationed at a karakol for four separate weeks annually, serving once a decade so as not to affect agricultural activities.

[72] Translation in PRO.FO 78/2729, July 2–4, 1871.

[73] Ibid.

[74] PRO.FO 78/2729, Thomson to Granville, Tehran, October 14, 1872. 'Ali Asghar Shamim maintains that the Iranian representatives were Haj Mirza Mohsen Khan Mushir al Dawla and Mirza 'Ali Khan Nizam al-Mulk. See *Iran dar Dovre-e Saltanat-e Qajar*, 224. Mirza Mohib 'Ali Khan wrote a treatise on the Bagsa/Malhatavi/Sayfi dispute, entitled *Ahdnameh-e Dawlatayn-e Iran va Usmani* (Ketabkhane-e Majlis-e Shora-e Eslami, No. F1919).

They also agreed to pay the expenses of the British "referee," Colonel J. Herbert, consul general of Baghdad, who then informed Mirza 'Abbas Khan, the Iranian special commissioner at Baghdad, of the following conditions:

1) Both sides should forget past offenses and accept the demarcation of the survey commission.
2) Each side should prohibit subject tribes from passing into the territory of the other and refuse protection to any group who defied this order.
3) Tribes should be punished without inquiry should they, after crossing the frontier, be accused of any act of aggression by the government into whose territory they had passed.
4) Each side should commit itself to preventing, to the extent possible, the passing of the tribes of the neighboring state into its own territory under a penalty to be decided by mutual consent.[75]

In spite of such counsel, Herbert's mediation produced no tangible results. The sole exception, a significant incident in which he intervened, exemplifies how and by what means his advice would be put into practice and how violence was used to inscribe the notion of the boundary and territorial sovereignty on the borderland and its peoples through the intervention of central states and imperialist powers.

According to available accounts, the episode in question began when a group of Iranian Kurds, under the order of Iranian authorities, demolished a guardhouse built by Ottoman authorities at Laveran, on the frontier of Shahrizor and Jawanrud, located halfway between Kermanshah and Halabja. To determine ownership of the land, Herbert proceeded to the town of Alusreha. There, he questioned the locals after being received by Mahmud Pasha, the chief of the large Jaf confederation and governor of the district, as well as *miralay* Abdurrahman Beg and *kaimmakam* Shaban Beg. The joint testimony of Mahmud and the influential Sheykh 'Ali Effendi indicates that the district belonged to the Ottoman Empire and had previously been under the control of the house of Baban. After the Baban's demise, they maintained, they had taken control and collected its revenue. Despite this testimony, Iran's vociferous claims to the same tract of land complicated the commission's decision-making process. Herbert concluded that the land was indeed Ottoman but also agreed that when

[75] PRO.FO 78/2729, Herbert to British Envoy Extraordinary and Minister Plenipotentiary at the Court of Persia, Baghdad, August 16, 1872. Also *Schofield II*, 700–702.

Ottoman tribes were not there, Iranians had used it. As this lent some credence to Iranian claims, his subsequent suggestion that the guardhouse be repaired and the culprits punished infuriated Iranian authorities. They agreed, however, to punish the culprits, who, according to Herbert, had been instigated by 'Ali Akbar Khan Sharaf ol-Molk, the governor of Jawanrud, and Shahzade Farhad Mirza, the governor of Iranian Kurdistan. A certificate signed by two Ottoman observers, Mahmud Agha and Mahmud Sadık Bey, confirms that the "delinquents" were severely penalized: four *beg*s (chiefs) received one thousand lashes each and two to three months of confinement in chains, whereas the ordinary *rayah*s of the Kokooe tribe each received one thousand lashes. The hand of the man who had first fired on the guardhouse was cut off, and the nose of the man who ordered its total destruction was pierced, a string inserted therein, and he was led thus through the markets and streets. Both men also spent three months in chains. Accompanying the Ottoman observers' certificate was a declaration from the *qadi*, deputy *qadi*, and *ulama* of Jawanrud certifying that the punishments were carried out. Protesting such brutality, Tehran complained that Herbert had exceeded his powers, but only the governor of Jawanrud was reprimanded for having exceeded the bounds of legitimate punishment.[76] Irrespective of such diplomatic wrangling, the borderlanders received a brutal message about the changing nature of frontiers.

Like the Iranians, Russian authorities were unhappy with the Herbert mission. After twenty years of close cooperation, the British representative had become the sole arbitrator in Iranian-Ottoman frontier negotiations. Russia's exclusion, they argued, was a result of Iranian attempts to shut them out while seeking the greater involvement of England.[77] To avoid further irritating Russia, it was decided to form yet another commission, this time with Russian participation.

BRINGING THE STATE INTO LOCAL DISPUTES

Before the new commission was able to begin its work, however, one of the longest-lasting disputes of the border – which would again beleaguer the commission in 1888 – resurfaced: namely, the division of the lands of the Faili

---

[76] PRO.FO 78/2730, Colonel Herbert's Report of December 11, 1872, Certificate of Mahmood Agha, Mahmood Sadeq Bey and of Turkish Consul of Iranian Koordistan, Khaled Beg, Sent to Hubert at February 13, 1873, Declaration of Kadi, Deputy Kadi and Ulema of Jawanrud (in Arabic) and Mirza Saed Khan's letter to Thomson, February 11, 1873.

[77] PRO.FO 78/2729, Brunnow to Granville, London, December 7, 1872 (enclosing dispatch, Gorchakow to Brunnow, November 28, 1872); Harari, *Turco-Persian*, 142.

Kurds and the Banu Lam Arabs. As we have seen, initially the dispute in the Posht-e Kuh area was about the division of the whole region. Thirty years later, it had been reduced to a smaller area. Known as the Bagsai dispute of Posht-e Kuh or, as Midhat Pasha and other Ottoman authorities called it, "the dispute over the lands of Seyyid Hassan," this new phase dragged on, stimulating voluminous correspondence among all parties.[78] The main point of contention were the well-watered, rich lands of the town of Baghsai (Baksaye in Ottoman documents), which lay seventy miles northeast of Mandali and fifteen miles east of Badra. Also implicated were three villages: Saifi, Ghorabieh, and Malhatari (Malhatavi in Iranian documents). These were located northwest of Baghsai in the frontier's central zone and occupied by a mixed population of Faili Kurds and Arabs.[79] The Ottomans contended that all of these localities were not part of Posht-e Kuh, but of another territory unknown to the Persians, called Seyyid Hasan, where the tomb of the saint of that name was located.[80] Tehran argued that the Ottomans used this name to cast doubt on Iran's proprietorship, and that Seyyid Hassan was actually the name of a votary chapel situated between Malkhatavi and Saifi, on lands that the Erzurum Treaty, the status quo, and the *Carte Identique* accepted as Iranian. British reports indicate that Sayyid Hassan was the name of the district that encompassed Malhatavi and Saifi, and that those areas frequently changed hands.[81]

This long-lasting dispute illuminates the process by which the border was transformed into a boundary, and also the ways in which pasture informed the politics of the frontier. It also demonstrates how some borderlanders sought state support when trying to appropriate shared resources. Protecting the pasture rights of the Shi'i Arab Banu Lam thus motivated Ottoman authorities, whereas advancing the rights of the Shi'i Faili tribes motivated Iranian ones.[82] On numerous occasions, Ottoman

[78] For some Ottoman documents on the topic, see files in BOA.HR.SYS 682/1 and 703/1.

[79] For Iranian views on the dispute, see Mirza Mohib 'Ali Khan *Ahdnameh-e Dawlatayn-e Iran va Usmani.* transliteration Nasrollah Salehi. Tehran: 1302/1885. [Ketabkhane-e Majlis-e Shora-e Eslami: No. F1919].

[80] Harari, *Turco-Persian*, 163. PRO.FO 78/4696, Thomson to Elliot, Tehran, July 7, 1873, and January 5 and 30, 1874, in Harari, *Turco-Persian*, 165. See also PRO.FO 78/4696 and Hertslet Memo, *Schofield III*, 472

[81] Mirza Mohib, *Ahdnameh*, 1; "Memorandum by Sir E. Hertslet on the Boundary Dispute between Turkey and Persia in the Posht-i Kuh district", March 17, 1884, *Schofield III*, 472.

[82] Mirza Mohib 'Ali maintains that the Banu Lam were divided into two parts: one Iranian, to the east of the Tigris, the other Ottoman, to the west; and that the names of some subgroups, such as the *qabila* of Abdalshah and Abdalkhan and the *taifa* of Al-e Alikhan, clearly indicate their Iranian connection; hence, the lands they occupy should be Iranian. See *Ahdnameh*, 2–3.

officials protested the cultivation by Iranian peasants of these resource-rich districts, which were much in demand by large flock-owning tribes.[83] Even as Iranians continued to use them, Midhat and others claimed Ghorabieh and Bagsai as integral parts of Ottoman territory.[84]

In his treatises on the issue, Mirza Mohib 'Ali Khan, like other Iranian representatives before him, used the writings of the Ottoman surveyors Dervish and Hurşîd Pashas to prove his case. He emphasized that their accounts describe the hospitality of 'Ali Khan Faili's son, an Iranian subject, who, when they passed through the area in question, accompanied them up to the boundary and hosted them in Baghsai. This, along with the fact that Hurşîd did not even bother to record the details of the district, proved that the lands belonged to Iran. Because the dispute was also about the allegiance of two tribal confederations struggling over rich but limited resources, Mohib 'Ali Khan went on to criticize Dervish's use of petitions from the Banu Lam to justify certain Ottoman claims. No doubt, he wrote, groups such as the Banu Lam would advance any claims that might help their own cause. Yet, their utilization of the lands and payment of taxes proved neither ownership nor Ottoman proprietorship because their *teba'iyyet* (citizenship) was as yet unresolved. Additionally, he asserted that because they were nomads who made seasonal use of pasturelands, they could not be the inhabitants of the region, as the Ottomans argued. Finally, turning to local records, Mohib 'Ali Khan demonstrated that the Posht-e Kuh governors had appointed various officers to Bagsai, further proof of Iran's sovereignty.[85]

Such claims solved neither the problem of the occupied districts nor the identity and citizenship issues of their tribes and in 1873, tensions again came to a head when Tehran claimed that "about 10,000 families of Turkish nomad tribes had crossed the frontier and encamped in the summer pastures of Oroomiah, and that when the Iranian frontier officials demanded their return, they replied that they had not received any prohibition from their own government."[86] The governor of Khoi, Shuja ud-Dawlah, decried the

---

[83] For instance, in 1866, Istanbul learned that the Vali of Luristan, Hassan Quli Khan, invaded Seyyid Hassan and attacked parts of the Banu Lam. See BOA.HR.SYS 723/31 and 41, June 8, 1866.

[84] Harari, *Turco-Persian*, 163. For example, in a letter written to OMoFA Rashid Pasha on June 26, 1873, Istanbul described the Iranian occupation of Bagsai and Seyyid Hassan. In his subsequent appeal to British authorities, Rashid declares the districts "terrains appartenant de temps immémorial a l'Empire Ottoman." See BOA.HR.SYS 683/15, p. 29.

[85] Mirza Mohib, *Ahdnameh*, 3–4.

[86] PRO.FO 78/2730, Mirza Saed Khan to Turkish Minister (attached is the letter of the Governor of Khoi, Shuja ol Dowleh), Tehran, June 16, 1873; Thomson to Granville, Golahak, June 19, 1873, in *Schofield II*, 739–41.

unjustness of a situation in which Ottoman tribes freely crossed the border, whereas Iranian ones such as the Jalali, in desperate need of summer pastures, were prohibited by Iranian frontier governors from doing the same. As hostilities rose in response to the subsequent occupation of Bagsai by Ottoman troops, Hussein Qoli Khan, the governor of Posht-e Kuh, gathered five thousand men from local tribes. As he readied them for a cross-border confrontation, one of his *ghulam*s (servants) passed over the boundary, sacked an Ottoman post, and plundered the Kara Ulus tribe near Bagsai-Seyyid Hassan.[87]

Ottoman authorities quickly retaliated. Midhat informed Hussein Qoli, and through him the area's Iranian inhabitants, that he intended to dispatch troops. The Iranians, in turn, informed the British representative that if Ottoman troops entered the disputed lands, Hussein Qoli would repel force with force.[88] When the Ottomans advanced, however, Iran took no such action. Instead, Mirza Sa'id asked Thomson, the British minister in Tehran, to convince them to withdraw and agree to the formation of a commission for the immediate demarcation of this tract of land.[89] In the meantime, Iran sent officers to control Hussein Qoli. After more telegrams and British (and Russian) interventions, Tehran and Istanbul ordered their commanders to withdraw. The problem of the nomads' need for pastures, however, remained unresolved, and troop deployments to Bagsai-Seyyid Hassan and other areas continued for many years.

NEW ACTORS AND NOTIONS: MIGRATION AS ASYLUM

The Erzurum Congress concluded that the cross-border migration of nomadic tribes could be checked only after the finalization of the boundary. This did not mean, however, that tribes were immune to new rules and regulations. The case of the Jaf is illustrative. The 1639 treaty divided the Jaf between the two states, but they continued, at times defying orders to the contrary, to use pastures on both sides of the dividing line. As one of the largest tribal confederations moving across the border, their migrations were a constant source of tension. Wintering in Shahrizor, they spent summers in pastures northwest of Panjwin, in Shelir Plain, between the mountains of Merivan, Saqqez, Bane, and Khorkhore.

---

[87] Ibid.
[88] Thomson to Granville, Tehran, February 15, 1884, *Schofield III*, 455.
[89] Thomson to Granville, February 16, 1884, *Schofield III*, 459–60; and Hertslet memo, *Schofield III*, 474.

Because there was no physical barrier between Merivan and the summer pastures, between 1865 and 1866 the shah ordered forts built at Merivan to prevent Jaf incursions and to control migration.[90] However, in 1874, Mahmud Pasha Jaf moved to the Iranian part of the frontier at Zohab with a portion of his tribe. The Porte demanded that he be returned or sent to Iran's interior. What is distinct about this case was not the cross-border migrations of all or part of a tribe – this was a *sine qua non* of life in the borderland – but rather the invocation of a new term to describe such migrations: the Jaf would soon become political refugees. The concept of the "political refugee" was itself not new to the region; it had been employed to describe the Qajar princes and the Hungarian revolutionaries in 1848. Never before, however, had it been applied to tribal migration. From this point forward, tribes that fled across the border would increasingly be treated, not as fugitives, but as political refugees.

When the Jaf moved to the Iranian side, Istanbul asked for their removal from the border area because it feared the remaining members of the tribe would follow, leaving large tracts of unprotected, uncultivated, and untaxed land. Iran responded that it had given Mahmud Pasha the status of political refugee. The Ottoman minister at Tehran conveyed his surprise to the IMoFA, declaring that the Jaf chief was not accused of a political offense, but rather of urging his people to cross the border. Such (apparently) nonpolitical behavior should exclude him from the class of political refugees. However, betraying his doubt that the Iranian government would agree to return the tribe to Ottoman lands, he temporarily took a conciliatory attitude by suggesting that "his and his tribe's removal from the frontier would gratify a friendly, neighboring and co-religionist power."[91] Consequently, Tehran ceased defining Mahmud and the Jaf as political refugees. Instead, they were Iranian subjects "who owing to some reason or other, fled to Turkish territory and have now without inducement returned of their own accord to their real homes with Mahmud Bey . . . Secondly they have broken off all connection with Turkish territory and have given up the lands they possessed, and now they intend to reside perpetually and not temporarily in Persia."[92]

---

[90] The forts were built at Shahabad and Farhadabad in Toraq Tappeh, and Lashkarabad in the Mirabad hills. Nasrollah [Khan] Muhandis, *Tahdid-e Hudud-e Merivan* (1878), transliterated by Reza Naqdi, 8–11; Sheikh Muhammad Mardukh Kordestani, *Tarikh-e Mardukh* (Tehran: Kharang, 1379–2000), 292.

[91] PRO.FO 78/2731, Thomson to Derby, May 21, 1874 and Turkish Minister at Tehran to Persian Minister of FA, March 25, 1874.

[92] PRO.FO 78/2731, IMoFA to the Turkish Minister at Tehran, March 30, 1874.

This change of strategy was ineffective, however, and Istanbul – as 'Abbas Mirza had done fifty years earlier in the Haydaran-Sipki case – reverted to threats of force: if Iran did not return or remove from the frontier any Ottoman tribe that had crossed the border, Istanbul would make them return by forcible measures. Intimidated, Tehran again appealed to Britain and Russia.[93] Initially refusing to intervene, Russian and British representatives eventually helped the rival states reach an agreement by which the Iranian government would remove Mahmud and the Jafs "to some other locality in the interior at such a distance as will prevent political intrigue being carried on by them within Turkish territory." It was also agreed "as regards the removal of Ottoman refugees in Persia and of Persian refugees in Turkey to a suitable distance in the interior of the respective states, there shall be complete reciprocity dating from the time of the arrival of the Jaf in Persian territory."[94]

Thus, directly or indirectly, the Jaf migration became a turning point in the history of tribal migration. Previously, borderlanders had been defined as itinerants moving between pastures, in search of better pastures or seeking to escape the reach of too-eager *tanzimat* pashas or their Iranian counterparts. Now they were refugees in need of protection. This new categorization may have offered some security, but it also complicated their migrations and ultimately accelerated the process by which they adopted Iranian or Ottoman citizenship. The frontier filter was becoming ever less permeable, and itinerant populations had to adapt to the limits of sovereign authority and its bounded territoriality.[95] No longer relatively unregulated and inhabited by diverse, autonomous, and mobile peoples, their traditional lands were increasingly politicized – and therefore contested, co-opted, and dominated – by the central states. Therefore, their movements had to be regulated or, better yet, altogether stopped.

THE COMMISSION OF 1874

The intensification of disputes such as those surrounding the Bagsai-Seyyid Hassan region or the Jaf tribe led to renewed calls to convene the elusive frontier commission. This time around, Russian and British authorities, once more coordinating their efforts, wanted to have it both ways: without

---

[93] PRO.FO 78/2731, Thomson to Derby, May 21, 1874.
[94] Ibid.
[95] In January 1877, Mahmud and his followers returned to Ottoman territory "at the urgent instance of the Ottoman local authorities." PRO.FO 78/2732, Thomson to Derby, Tehran January 18, 1877.

taking part in daily negotiations, they hoped to have their interests assured. Indeed, the Russian chancellor, Prince Gortchakow, suggested to the British ambassador, Lord Augustus Loftus, that

> The Turkish and Persian Governments should appoint Commissaries to decide upon and delineate the frontier as agreed upon in the Anglo-Russian Map submitted to them, and that if any differences of opinion should arise between the Turkish and Persian Commissaries they should be recorded, as a whole and not singly, in a Memoir drawn up by the respective litigants, and should then be referred for final decision to the English and Russian Governments.[96]

Tehran appointed Mirza Mohib 'Ali Khan as its commissioner; Istanbul chose the indomitable Dervish Pasha. However, at their initial meeting, Iran proposed the 1847 Erzurum Treaty as the point of departure, whereas the Ottomans – acting as if decades of negotiating, surveying, and diplomacy had never transpired – insisted on the 1639 treaty. The resulting deadlock led to the inclusion of the Russian and British mediators in the conferences, despite their desire to avoid such active participation as well as the Porte's aversion to their presence.[97]

When the fully authorized commission finally came together in June 1875, the mediators proposed that each party trace on the *Carte Identique* the boundary line according to its interpretation based on the official treaties.[98] When it was furthermore suggested that they begin by finding points of agreement, Dervish claimed that not a single such point existed. Refusing to be bound by either the 1847 treaty or the *Carte Identique*, he accused his surveyor colleagues from 1848 to 1852 of favoring Iran.[99] He then proposed to replace the Erzurum Treaty with information gathered from previous conventions, local traditions, and topographical features.[100] He also suggested substituting or supplementing the *Carte Identique* with a map made

---

[96] Granville to Thornton, April 19, 1884, *Schofield III*, 474–75.

[97] PRO.FO 78/2731, Persian Minister of FA to Turkish Minister in Tehran, May 7, 1874.

[98] The commission's first sittings were attended by the British Embassy dragoman, Robert Easolani; the Russian Embassy attaché, Colonel Zeharny; Dervish Pasha; Muhammad 'Ali Khan, who later became the Iranian minister in London and IMoFA; and Mirza Mohib 'Ali Khan. Afterward, Arnold Kemball, the former consul at Baghdad, was appointed as British commissioner, and Colonel Zelofinof [Zelenoy], the military attaché to the Russian Embassy, was selected as Russian commissioner. The commission held its first meeting on December 3, 1874. See Elliot to Derby, January 31, 1875; Elliot to Safvet Pasha, Constantinople, January 15, 1875, *Schofield III*, 59–61; Harari, *Turco-Persian*, 148.

[99] Harari, *Turco*-Persian, 150–54; PRO.FO 78/2732, Elliot to Derby, Therapia, July 1, 1875; Kemball to Elliot Therapia, July 22, Protocol of Sittings of the Turco-Persian Boundary Commission, Constantinople, May–June 1875.

[100] PRO.FO 78/2732 Elliot to Derby, Therapia, July 5, 1875.

by Ottoman engineers. Both suggestions were rejected, the latter because the mediators believed it would result in at least the partial invalidation of the *Carte Identique*, the only available basis for comparing rival territorial claims.[101] Even when the pasha finally agreed to use the 1847 treaty as the starting point, he claimed that his instructions did not allow him to trace a frontier line on a map drawn by the mediators. Consequently, he proposed that the discussion be concluded and that each party prepare a signed protocol stating his views and those of his counterpart. The commission approved this proposal, and the protocol was sent to the four participating governments on June 22, 1875.[102]

Two months later, the Porte recognized the authority of the *Carte Identique*, instructed Dervish to be more cooperative, and even expressed willingness to drop its claim to Muhammarah, provided the Iranians drop theirs to Kotur, which had by then been under Ottoman rule for a quarter of a century.[103] The British ambassador to Istanbul, Henry Elliot, convinced that the Porte would not withdraw from Kotur, suggested to London that the principle of *uti possidetis* be invoked so that negotiations could proceed.[104] Still, Grand Vizier Esad Pasha, in conformity with the wishes of the British representatives, remained open to new suggestions on Kotur's borders. For this reason, the British recommended that Dervish be sidelined and settlement of the question be pursued with Esad.[105] Before any real progress could be made, however, the threat of war between Russia and the Ottoman Empire again brought negotiations to a standstill. In January 1877, after nearly twenty months of inconclusive deliberations, the Russian commissioner was called to St. Petersburg and the commission disintegrated.[106]

THE RUSSO-OTTOMAN WAR OF 1877–1878 AND THE TRANSFORMATION OF BORDERLAND IDENTITIES

In the following months, reports of cross-border incursions continued to reach all four capitals, and frontier authorities on both sides began mobilizing troops.[107] But such struggles took a backseat to the Russo-Ottoman

---

[101] Harari, *Turco-Persian*, 152.
[102] Ibid., 153–54.
[103] PRO.FO 78/2732, Elliot to Derby, Therapia, August 29, 1875.
[104] PRO.FO 78/2732, Elliot to the Derby, Therapia, July 22, 1875.
[105] Harari, *Turco-Persian*, 156.
[106] PRO.FO 78/2732, Kemball to Elliot, Constantinople, January 14, 1877; and BOA.HR. SYS 685/4, 19.
[107] PRO.FO 78/2732, Thomson to Derby, March 16, and June 7, 1877.

War of 1877–78. Although the details of this conflict have been well studied, analysis of its repercussions has been largely limited to its impact on the Balkans and the Ottoman Empire's other European provinces, as well as the Armeno-Muslim struggles that erupted in its wake. In actuality, however, the communities of the Kurdish Ottoman-Iranian borderland, which actively participated in the war, were hardly immune to the catastrophic transformations it engendered. Most importantly for this context, the war strengthened sectarian sensibilities, heightening antagonisms between Christians and Muslims as well as Shi'is and Sunnis and fundamentally shifting the project of Ottoman citizenship from an ecumenical to a more explicitly Muslim venture.

The conflict began during a time of economic crisis in the Ottoman Empire, which was exacerbated by the Anatolian drought and famine of 1873–74 that killed thousands and depleted tax revenues.[108] Unable to secure loans from the European banks it had relied on since the Crimean War or to raise taxes in Anatolia, Istanbul pressured other regions for revenues. The first mass response was a revolt, in 1875, in Bosnia Herzegovina that the Porte, now officially bankrupt, was unable to suppress. By July 1876, the sultan's Bulgarian, Serbian, and Montenegrian "subjects" had also declared war. Further complicating the situation was a palace *coup d'état* on May 30, 1876, that deposed Sultan Abdulaziz and enthroned Crown Prince Murad as Sultan Murad V. Considered mentally unfit, Murad was pushed aside on September 1, 1876, and replaced by his brother Abdulhamid. Now faced with superior Ottoman powers, Serbia sued for an armistice. The suppression of the Bulgarian rebellion, however, resulted in the death of thousands of Muslims and Christians. Yet, it was the slaughter of between twelve thousand and fifteen thousand Bulgarian Christians, highly publicized in Europe and especially England as the Bulgarian Massacres, that cost Istanbul European goodwill. Ottoman politicians quickly announced plans to guarantee the rights of Christians throughout the empire, including Armenians in the Irano-Ottoman frontier region. Russia nevertheless

---

[108] My information about the Russo-Ottoman War depends mainly on Zurcher, *Turkey*; Reid, *The Crisis*, chap. 6; Mahmud Celaleddin Paşa, *Mir'ati Hakikat*, 3 vol., ed. Ismet Miroglu (Istanbul: Bereket Yayınevi, 1983); Charles Williams, *The Armenian Campaign: A Diary of the Campaign of 1877, in Armenia and Koordistan* (London: C. Kegan Paul & Co., 1878); and Charles S. Ryan, *Under the Red Crescent: Adventures of an English Surgeon With the Turkish Army at Plevna and Erzeroum, 1877–1878* (London: John Murray, 1897), 323.

declared war on April 24, 1877, after its demands for further reforms and Bulgarian autonomy were not met.[109]

As the fighting began, Muslims from the Caucasus and the Balkans, under attack, fled or were forced to move to Muslim-dominated regions of the Ottoman Empire, particularly the Anatolian peninsula. Under similar circumstances, Armenians and Pontic Greek Christians went to Russia. A proclamation by the tsar extending protection to all Christians and enjoining them to fight against the Ottoman Empire with the Russian army worsened the situation. Offering the same protections to Muslims under Russian sovereignty, the Ottomans likewise armed their constituencies on both sides of the border.[110] The conflict thus became a war of hearts and minds or, better put, a sectarian clash. Activating age-old religious, ethnic, and economic antagonisms, it transformed civilians into willing or unwilling participants, witnesses, victims, and villains of its many tragedies.

Although it suffered heavy casualties on the Balkan front, the Ottoman army fared well on the eastern front, which extended from Batum in the north to Bayezid in the east and Erzurum in the west. Even when a column of Russian cavalry captured Kars, Ardahan, and Artvin, a vigorous Ottoman response held the forward line. In many areas, the struggle turned into jihad against the Russian advance. In this context, a son of the legendary Sheikh Shamil led a revolt in Abkhazia from May to June 1877. Russia responded with a scorched-earth policy that increased the conflict's sectarian overtones.[111] In spite or because of such violence, Abkhazians and Circassians formed the nucleus of the Ottoman Caucasian Army. As a result, when the Ottomans lost, many of them were forced to migrate from Russia to the Kurdish- and Armenian-populated parts of the borderland, a move that further emphasized already activated sectarian boundaries. Nor was it only Circassian and Abkhazian Muslim subjects of Russia who fought on the side of the sultan, so too did those Zilan Kurds who had remained in Russia since migrating in the first part of the nineteenth century (see Chapter 2). Indeed, the Kurdish irregulars and Circassians who dominated the Ottoman cavalry in the region bested the Russians in several early battles in Bayezid.[112] Ayub Agha, son

---

[109] Zurcher, *Turkey*, 77. Kemal Karpat calls the 1877–78 war and the Berlin Treaty "the most important historical, cultural, and psychological watershed in the history of the Ottoman Empire." Karpat, *The Politicization of Islam* (Oxford, UK, and New York: Oxford University Press, 2001), 153.

[110] Reid, *Crisis*, 343.

[111] Ibid.

[112] Ibid., 349.

of Jafar Agha and chief of the Zilans, who "held the rank of honorary colonel in the Russian army, and was decorated by the Emperor Alexander on his visit to Alexandropol," was sentenced to death by Russia after being found guilty of participating in one such attack.[113]

Despite the relative success of Ottoman forces in the east, the war ended with Russia's victory and the signing of the Treaty of San Stefano (Yesilköy) on March 3, 1878. The treaty acknowledged the independence of Bulgaria, Montenegro, Serbia, and Romania and resulted in the Ottoman loss of Batum and the frontier districts of Kars, Ardahan, Aleshkerd, and Bayezid. Yet the war's repercussions throughout the empire, and especially along the northern Ottoman-Iranian frontier, extended far beyond territorial loss. Facilitated by the spread of firearms throughout the region on a previously unknown scale – auxiliary forces were given Henry Martini and Winchester rifles – sectarian animosities galvanized during the war intensified in the period that followed. The ensuing Christian-Muslim or Armeno-Muslim hostilities are well documented; however, corresponding Shi'i-Sunni antagonisms have not been studied.

Such absence does not accurately reflect the role played by Shi'i-Sunni sectarianism during and after the war, not only in Ottoman Kurdistan but also in Iranian Kurdistan, even though Iran was technically a neutral party to the conflict. Indeed, reports by William George Abbot, the British general consul of Tabriz, indicate that during the war, Kurdistan remained unsettled on both sides of the border.[114] As the conflict became a defense of Muslim lands against an arrogant Christian power, Ottoman Kurds participated on a mass scale as auxiliaries, or *muavene askeri*, under the leadership of *tariqa* (religious order) leaders and tribal confederation chiefs. Likewise, despite Iran's official neutrality, many Iranian Sunni Kurds responded to Ottoman authorities mobilizing troops and spreading the word of jihad. Here, as in the case of the Caucasians and Zilans, supranational religious identity, the Sunni caliph's authority, and cross-border *tariqa* networks trumped state allegiances.[115] No doubt as a result of Russian pressure, in May 1877, the new governor of Savojbulagh, Mohammad Hussein Khan, led an expedition to the border. He described his objective as follows: "To frighten the shah's subjects of the Sunni persuasion in Persian Koordistan, and prevent them

---

[113] Charles Boswell Norman, *Armenia, and the Campaign of 1877* (London and New York: Cassell, 1878), 250.

[114] PRO.FO 60/401 Abbot to Thomson, Tabreez, May 29–30, 1877.

[115] For the role of religious brotherhoods in Kurdistan, see Martin van Bruinessen, *Agha Shaikh and State: The Social and Political Structures of Kurdistan* (London: Zed Books, 1992), chap. 4.

from going to the assistance of their co-religionists the Turks. His highness the Prince Governor of Azerbaijan has issued orders that Persian subjects in Koordistan embracing the Turkish cause are to be punished with death and their houses burned."[116] Preventing Iranian Sunnis from participating in the jihad was a decision that would haunt the northern borderland in the years that followed.

This was largely the result of the increasing authority of religious figures, a development that illustrates the multifaceted transformations taking place in the borderlands. Religious leaders and *tariqa* networks connecting both sides of the frontier had, of course, long influenced the borderlanders' daily lives. However, as Chapter 1 discussed, in the 1840s, they began to assume roles previously played by hereditary dynasts. As van Bruinessen suggests, sociopolitical changes in Kurdistan "suddenly propelled the shaikhs into the role of political leaders."[117] Their rise, then, was fomented by the central governments, which rigorously co-opted religious networks to fill the power vacuum left by the dynasts. The ability of the networks' leaders to rally significant numbers of auxiliaries from across Kurdistan, which "proved to be an exception in *tanzimat* reformers' attempts to enforce the laws of conscription,"[118] made them valuable as brokers between state and society. Unlike the *khan*s and *beg*s, who recruited personal retinues in times of war and were spatially constrained, the most powerful sheikhs were able to influence large numbers of people spread over considerable distances. That is to say, rather than the vertical structures utilized by a *mir, beg*, or *khan*, they mobilized through horizontal organizations that provided access not only to the people of a certain locality, tribe, or tribal confederation, but also to much wider social networks. Such reach was immediately useful to central states struggling to control far-flung populations. However, the cross-border character of the *tariqa* was diametrically opposed to the limitation of movement imposed by the boundary line and could easily be turned against the states.

This double-edged dynamic is dramatized through the story of Sheikh Ubeidullah of Hakkari, who led troops in defense of the sultan during the Russo-Ottoman War before turning against both states to lead a revolt shortly thereafter. Abbot summarized Ubeidullah's participation in the war as follows: "The notorious Sheykh Obeidollah of Gewar has been preaching 'Djehad' in Koordistan and the Persian and Turkish Koords

[116] PRO.FO 60/401 Abbot to Thomson, May 30, 1877.
[117] van Bruinessen, *Agha*, 229.
[118] Reid, *Crisis* 159.

have alike obeyed his summons. Sheykh was accompanied by as many as thirty thousand men; three thousand of them being Persian Koords, and the Koords of Senneh and Saqqez are poised to follow."[119]

Abbot also underscored the religious motivation of the sheikh and his followers, observing that on learning about the expedition by Savojbulagh's governor, the "Koords of Persian territory [had determined] to fight at all risks on behalf of the Turks, if the Persian government meddled with their religious affairs and refused their petition of joining the war."[120] In his correspondence with Sultan Abdulhamid, Ubeidullah himself claimed to head a force of thirty thousand. Although Ubeidullah's numbers echo those of Abbot, Ahmed Mukhtar Pasha, the Ottoman commander of the Caucasian and Eastern front, declared that the sheikh, in addition to regular troops, had "raised 50,000–60,000 irregular soldiers, both infantry and cavalry from his districts of Van province."[121] Not all contemporary accounts were so admiring. The British minister at Tehran, Taylor Thomson, thought Abbot's numbers greatly exaggerated: "It is understood here that about 500 Sonnee Persian Koords have been induced to follow that religious Sonnee fanatic."[122] The Iranian bureaucrat Eskander Qurians and the Ottoman pasha Mahmud Celaleddin likewise denigrated the military performance of Ubeidullah's untrained tribal militia against the Russians in Bayezid.[123] Regardless of their numbers or level of prowess, the eager participation of jihadists from both sides of the frontier revealed the activation of once-dormant sectarian boundaries, which would reshape borderland politics in radical ways. In addition to the call to jihad, rising Armenian nationalism and seeming Russian support for it and increasing missionary activities in the region might have alarmed the Kurds. Indeed, in a letter he later wrote to Sultan Abdulhamid II, Ubeidullah warned that the Muslims would not allow the formation of an Armenian state and cautioned that *tanzimat* reforms had resulted in the diminishment of the sultan's authority.[124]

[119] PRO.FO 60/401 Abbot to Thomson, Tabreez, May 30, 1877.
[120] Ibid.
[121] Ahmed Muhtar Paşa, *Anadolu'da Rus Muharebesi, I*, ed. Enver Yaşarbaş (Istanbul: Petek Yayınları, 1985), 23–27, 44–45; Valentine Baker, *War in Bulgaria: A Narrative of Personal Experiences I* (London: Low, Marston, Searle, & Rivington, 1879), 351–60; and Reid, *Crisis*, 358.
[122] PRO.FO 78/2731, Thomson to Derby, Tehran, June 8, 1877.
[123] Eskender Qurians, *Qiyame Shaikh Ubeidullah dar Ahd-i Shah Nasir al-Din*, ed. Abdullah Mardugh (Tehran: Donyaye Danesh, 1356), 24; and Mahmud Celaleddin Paşa, *Mir'at-ı Hakikat*, 331.
[124] BOA.Y.PRK.KOM 3/66, August 21, 1882.

Motivated by such religious and political concerns, in the last months of 1880, under the leadership of Ubeidullah, thousands of Iranian and Ottoman Kurds marched on Iran and briefly conquered several cities in the area between Urumieh and Sovojbulagh (present-day Mahabad).[125] Among the most immediate reasons for their revolt were the public display, by Iranian authorities, of Shiʿi symbols and the forceful introduction of Shiʿi practices in Sunni settings. These intrusions, combined with the after-shocks of war and increasing missionary presence in the northern border zone, strengthened sectarianism as the new language and venue of mobilization and identity formation.[126] Moreover, as representatives of the royal family replaced the remaining vestiges of hereditary local dynasties, Iranian Sunni Kurds, lacking any polity member strong enough to mediate on their behalf, increasingly turned to the sheikh, an Ottoman citizen with family and lands on both sides. Moved by the petitions he received from them, Ubeidullah initiated direct communication with the sultan, secretly informing him via letters and telegrams of Iranian oppression and plans for establishing an independent Armenia. Always addressing him as caliph, and thus emphasizing the role of religion, the sheikh requested that the sultan intervene on behalf of their fellow Sunnis in Iran. He was disappointed when his appeals were ignored. Continuously pressured by Iranian Sunni Kurds of all classes to do something on their behalf, he was also troubled by the disorganization of the lands where his kinsmen lived: as he told the British consul of Tabriz, he hoped to reorganize the region and unite it as an autonomous entity under the caliph. To this end, Ubeidullah finally took matters into his own hands. In his resolve to resort to the force of arms, he was not alone.

At the end of August 1880, two columns of his followers advanced into Iranian territory. At the head of one column was the sheikh himself. At the head of the other was Hamza Agha Mangur, who, as we saw earlier, had been forced to submit to Iran but then became subject to various forms of oppression by local administrators. It appears that Ubeidullah's force was composed of no less than fifteen thousand poorly armed infantry and cavalry, some of whom carried the Winchester and Henry Martini rifles they received during the war. Initially, Hamza, aided by Ubeidullah's

---

[125] The following account is based on Sabri Ateş, "Empires at the Margin: Towards a History of the Ottoman-Iranian Borderland and the Borderland Peoples" (Ph.D. diss., New York University, 2006), chaps. 5–6.

[126] For the rise of sectarianism in another Ottoman setting, see Usama Makdisi, *The Culture of Sectarianism: Community, History, and Violence in Nineteenth-Century Ottoman Lebanon* (Berkley: University of California Press, 2000).

son Abdulkadir, triumphed in Sunni towns, where they insisted that the
Friday *khutba* be read in the name of the Caliph of Islam, the Ottoman
Sultan Abdulhamid, thus emphasizing their religio-political aspirations.
Militarily, however, the revolt was a disappointment. The sheikh failed to
conquer his main target, the Iranian provincial center of Urumieh, and his
forces faced stiff resistance in Shi'i towns and among some Kurdish tribes
loyal to Iran. Unable to further their advance, they withdrew after one
month.

The escalation of assaults and retaliations during and after this revolt
further polarized Shi'i-Sunni relations. Even those Kurds who were hedg-
ing their bets, or whose loyalties and identities were still ill defined, were
obliged to take a stand for or against the Iranian state or the sheikh.
Meanwhile, after the sheikh's withdrawal, the region's Sunni inhabitants
were left to the mercy of a galvanized Iranian army and its Shi'i tribal
supporters, whose brutality resulted in the destruction and depopulation
of villages and towns and the deaths of thousands. Many Sunnis fled to
inaccessible mountain regions. According to some accounts, up to one
hundred thousand families crossed the frontier into Ottoman lands,
whereas some who remained in Iran were forced to accept Shi'ism. Made
to choose political allegiances, the borderlanders confronted a crucible of
identity, which their communities handled with diverse strategies and
tools.

Only intense Ottoman persuasion and the arrival of Ottoman, Iranian,
and Russian troops to the frontier prevented the sheikh and his followers
from mobilizing for a second revolt. As fears of another assault grew,
Russian representatives who had promised to aid the Iranian military
began to threaten armed intervention within Ottoman borders. Given the
presence of Christian communities in the region and the risk that Russia
would make good on its threats, the British and French ambassadors also
put pressure on Istanbul to expel the sheikh from the region. The possibility of European and more importantly Russian involvement, the emer-
gent Armenian question, and the prospects for the sheikh's success, all
brought the Ottomans and Iranians into cooperation. Together, their
armies swiftly sealed the border to prevent Ottoman Kurds from joining
the rebels and sent emissaries to urge the sheikh's withdrawal.

Seven months after the end of the revolt, under international pressure,
the sheikh left for Istanbul, whereas the Iranian army's punitive expeditions and summary executions continued. The day after his arrival,
Ubeidullah received an audience with the sultan and a large house within
the palace compound. Yet, barely a year later, in August 1882, he escaped

house arrest and fled to his village. However, he succeeded neither in organizing another rebellion nor in negotiating permission to remain in his home region. Exiled to Mecca, he died in 1883. Despite its religious overtones, by connecting groups from both sides of the frontier, Ubeidullah's revolt was in a way an attempt to deactivate the boundary and generate an alternative understanding of space that would encompass the Kurdish ethnic group. Because of the difficulty of choosing, if not a national identity then a state with which to identify and subject themselves to, borderland communities struggled with enormous ambiguities. The revolt tapped into these ambiguities; its failure, in turn, demonstrated that identities such as Ottoman or Iranian, reinforced by the making of the boundary, clashed definitively and absolutely with the alternative collective identities promoted by ideologues such as Ubeidullah. The failure of the revolt thus became a testimony to the reality of the boundary and the identities that were formed by it.

THE END OF THE WAR: KOTUR AND MINOR MOVING INTO MAJOR

Perhaps expectedly, the repression of Ubeidullah's rebellion did nothing to settle matters in the frontier. Similarly, new diplomatic interventions by Europe after the signing of the Treaty of San Stefano failed to bring peace. These interventions were linked to European unhappiness with the treaty, which it feared would lead to Russian dominance in the Balkans and Anatolia. Such fears led Britain and Austria to convene an international Berlin Congress to rewrite the treaty and find an acceptable solution to the "Eastern Crisis." The congress succeeded in establishing the Commission de Délimitation des Frontières, or the Russo-Ottoman Frontier Commission, to delimit Ottoman boundaries with Serbia, Romania, Montenegro, Bulgaria, and Russia. It also produced the Treaty of Berlin, which mitigated some of the terms agreed on in San Stefano. For example, it reduced the territorial gains of Romania, Serbia, and Montenegro and created an autonomous Bulgaria that was much smaller than originally envisaged. Russia, however, held on to its acquisitions on the eastern front, whereas Austria annexed Bosnia-Herzegovina (though it technically remained part of the Ottoman Empire) and Britain occupied Cyprus. The Ottomans had no choice but to acquiesce.[127] Most important for our purposes is that Russia introduced

[127] This paragraph is adapted from Henry F. Munro, *The Berlin Congress* (Washington, DC: U.S. Government Printing Office, 1918); and Zurcher, *Turkey*, 79.

aspects of the ongoing Irano-Ottoman dispute into the congress's debates. In appreciation of Iran's strong support during the war, it had already made the return of Kotur part of the San Stefano Treaty. With Russian support, the Iranian representative Mirza Malkum Khan won an audience in Berlin with the congress's president to argue in favor of keeping this provision.[128] During the subsequent negotiations, the Russian representative, Count Shuvalov, further underscored Russia's promise to return Bayezid and Alashkerd in exchange for the restitution of Kotur to Persia. Protocol 16 of the Berlin Congress affirmed Russia's wish,[129] and Shulavov warned the Ottomans that his government would accept nothing less than the complete restitution of Kotur. Still, before making any final decisions, the congress awaited a response from the Porte.[130]

The restitution of Kotur proved to be easier said than done. As Sir Edward Hertslet reminded his audience in a memorandum on the town and district of Kotur, except for a limited area near Muhammarah the previous commissions had fixed no definite line in the region, neither did the *Carte Identique* contain any precise demarcation. Instead, it presented a tract of land within which (never appointed) special commissioners would lay down the line.[131] Given this stubborn ambiguity, a few months later yet another commission (the Kotur Commission) was formed. This time, it was decided that the British and Russian commissioners would mark the definitive line on the map, and the Iranian and Ottoman commissioners would mark it on the ground. In October 1878, possibly as a way of showing its displeasure, the Porte reappointed the doyen of boundary negotiations Dervish Pasha and his secretary Hurşîd Efendi (by then a high-ranking pasha) as its representatives. The British representative was Major General Sir Edward Hamley, and Russia appointed Zelenoy (Zelofinof), now a major general, who had also served on the unproductive 1874 commission.[132] Mohib 'Ali Khan, the Iranian representative, had likewise served on the failed previous commission and was well acquainted with the border issue. As negotiations were set to

[128] See the San Stefano Treaty protocols, *Schofield III*, 280–81; and Ali Fuat Türkgledi, *Mesâil-i Mühimme-I Siyâsiyye* (Ankara: TTK, 1957), 52, 82–86.

[129] Congress of Berlin Protocol No. 16, *Schofield III*, 280–81. According to this delimitation, the lowlands were to go to Istanbul.

[130] Congress of Berlin Protocol No. 15, *Schofield III*, 281.

[131] PRO.FO 78/4173, Memorandum by Hertslet on Kotur, London, October 23, 1873 in Harari, *Turco-Persian*, 160; and *Schofield III*, 271–73.

[132] BOA.HR.SYS 684/5, pp. 39 and 115. Also Mehmed Süreyya, *Sicil-i Osmanî* (Istanbul: Tarih Vakfı Yurt Yay, 1996).

begin, Iran warned the other parties that this commission's work in Kotur should not become confused with that of the separate Russo-Ottoman Frontier Commission. Moreover, Iran declared that its delegates would meet with the other delegates only after Kotur was surrendered.[133] To make matters worse, in December 1878, before the commission even convened, Istanbul received reports that Tehran was amassing troops in Khoi to occupy Kotur. Warning its own frontier authorities to prepare,[134] the Porte then disingenuously claimed to be unacquainted with the particulars of the frontier line in Kotur and requested to be enlightened so that the restoration could be successfully completed. At the Foreign Office's behest (and contradicting the ambiguities emphasized in Hertslet's earlier report), General Kemball responded that the 1874 commission had already testified that Kotur belonged to Persia and had clearly laid down on its working maps the line of the common frontier.[135]

Despite Kemball's chastisement, London confirmed its role as champion of Ottoman interests when it advised its representative on the Russo-Ottoman Frontier Commission, Major F. C. H. Clarke, to prevent the Russians from pushing too hard in Iran's favor. Authorizing him to participate in the demarcation of Kotur as well, it warned that "the frontier to be settled is one which Great Britain has undertaken, under certain conditions, and in certain contingencies to assist in defending."[136] London insisted it had no desire to push the terms of the treaty in the Ottoman Empire's favor, but instead was "naturally interested in seeing that none of the advantages secured to the sultan by the work of the Congress should be impaired or lost in the settlement of the details." Still, it urged Clarke to advise the Ottoman commissioners without provoking Russian protests.[137] British Foreign Secretary Marquis of Salisbury further reminded Clarke of "the expediency of assigning to the Turkish dominion in Asia generally as good a strategic frontier as possible."[138]

With this dizzying array of complex diplomatic, political, and historical factors in play, on January 25, 1879, the Ottomans officially ceded to Iran

---

[133] Layard to Marquis of Salisbury, Therapia, October 17, 1878, *Schofield III*, 282.

[134] BOA.HR.SYS, 684/4, p. 11.

[135] Marquis of Salisbury to Kemball, October 28, 1878; and Kemball to Lord Trentden, October 30, 1878, *Schofield III*, 284, 287.

[136] Marquis of Salisbury to Clarke, FO, March 27, 1879, *Schofield III*, 302.

[137] Ibid.

[138] Marquis of Salisbury to Clarke, FO, April 14, 1879, *Schofield III*, 308. In meetings regarding the Russo-Ottoman frontier in Asiatic Turkey, Russia threatened military action whereas the British commissioner supported the Ottoman point of view. At the end of 1879, the Asiatic Boundary Commission disbanded with no conclusive solution.

the town of Kotur, along with sixteen villages housing a total of 610 households, plus military barracks and a quarantine house, while holding on to fourteen villages that Iran continued to claim.[139] Coincidentally, the formal retrocession of the district occupied by Dervish three decades previously took place just twenty days after the pasha's death. It was more than a year later, in April 1880, that Hamley arrived in Istanbul to begin finalizing the division. In June, he was still waiting for Zelonoy. Because of Zelonoy's refusal to travel from the frontier to Istanbul – and because Istanbul could not come up with immediate funds to send its new representative, Miralay Cevad Bey, to Kotur – Hamley asked London to urge Petersburg to authorize General Stebnitzky, the Russian commissioner to the Russo-Ottoman Frontier Commission, who was still in Istanbul, to join him in drawing the boundaries.[140] Under these circumstances, Stebnitzky, Hamley, and Cevad held their first meeting on June 7, 1880, without Iranian participation and with the Ottoman and Russian delegates proposing their respective lines and the British commissioner mediating.[141] It was still necessary to survey and finalize the boundary on the ground. Thus, Hamley (and Cevad) arrived in Erzurum on July 4, and Hamley joined Zelenoy at Sarıkamış shortly thereafter. Hamley and Zelenoy signed the Sary Kamish (Sarıkamış) Protocol on July 27, 1880, to which they appended a copy of the *Carte Identique* with the new boundary marked in green:

The two generals recommended further that the boundary thus described on the map should be fixed on the spot by a Turco-Persian Commission, assisted by British and Russian officers, and that the functions of that commission be rigidly limited to the execution of the boundary tracing on the spot and not be allowed to involve a discussion of the rights and recriminations of the two Muslim governments over that portion of their common boundary.[142]

The topographical corps immediately set to work. Zelenoy's experiences and notes taken during his previous work with Kemball proved useful, and the commission was still at the frontier on August 14, 1880, when its

---

[139] BOA.HR.SYS 654/4, 19 and 67. For a list of the villages, see Nasiri, *Nāṣireddin*, 51; Sepehsalar to Thomson, February 24, 1879; Abbot to Marquis of Salisbury, February 27, 1879, *Schofield III*, 304–5.
[140] Hamley to Granville, Constantinople, May 18, 1880, *Schofield III*, 394.
[141] This commission consisted of the following: for Britain, Major General Sir E. B. Hambley, Engineer Captain Wolski, and Engineer Lieutenant Leverson; for Russia, General d'etat Major Stebnitsky and Advisor to the Court Emelianoff; and for the Ottoman Empire, Miralay Cevad Bey and Major Ishak Bey. In Sarıkamış and Kotur, Vice-Consul at Erzurum William Everett represented Britain and Zelenoy and Colonel Koulberg, Russia.
[142] Harari, *Turco-Persian*, 162. For the Protocol of Sarikamis, see *Schofield III*, 411–12.

members concluded that the map they had drawn should be accepted as authoritative, and that a mixed commission should finalize the delimitation.[143] Iran was expected to accept the territory as defined provided that Istanbul was amendable.[144]

However, because the Sheikh Ubeidullah rebellion of 1880–81 had severely disrupted the northern frontier zone, it was only in late November 1882 that the Porte informed the British, Russian, and Iranian representatives in Istanbul of the imperial sanction for the appointment of officers for the delimitation. London in turn advised the Porte that the commissioners would proceed as soon as it accepted Hamley and Zelenoy's line.[145] It did so in May 1883 and shortly thereafter appointed Miralay Cevad, Binbaşı Ibrahim, and Kolağası (Colonel d'état Major) Şakir to join Colonels Everett and Kulberg, the topographers who were serving, respectively, as the British and Russian commissioners.[146] However, just a few months later, the Porte backtracked, informing the British representatives that it feared losing more territory than expected. Meanwhile, because of winter conditions or as a stalling tactic, the Ottoman commission members left Kotur in December, promising to return the following spring. The mediating governments then communicated the Sarıkamış Protocol and the appended map to the Persian government, which swiftly supplied a commissioner to assist Colonels Everett and Kulberg in the on-the-ground demarcation. This marked Iran's first direct involvement in the delimitation of Kotur since the Berlin Congress. The Porte, meanwhile, once more voiced its substantial reservations and referred the matter to the grand vizier and the Council of Ministers,[147] which resulted in the repudiation of the Hamley-Zelenoy line in February 1884, once again dashing hopes of a resolution. It seemed that the Porte, shaken by the debilitating defeat of 1878 and the 1882 British occupation of Egypt, was averse to any British or Russian impositions, although Britain attributed the decision to the rise of German influence in

---

[143] This section and parts of the following are derived from sections of HR.SYS 685/4 and "Further Correspondence respecting the Demarcation of the frontier of Turkey in Asia including the Anglo-Russian delimitation at Khotour, 1880–1883," *Schofield III*, 393–451.

[144] Hamley to Julian Paunceforte, FO, December 30, 1880, *Schofield III*, 412–14.

[145] Hugh Wyndham to Granville, Constantinople, May 3, 1883, *Schofield III*, 429.

[146] BOA.HR.SYS 685/4, 70. Wyndham to Granville, May 6, 1883, *Schofield III*, 431–36. A note attached to this letter indicates that Majors Abdurrahman, Ibrahim, and Danyal and Adjutant Major Şerafeddin Efendi were also attached to the commission.

[147] Wyndham to Granville, Therapia, September 9, 1883; and Lord Duffrein to Granville, Constantinople November 20, 1883, *Schofield III*, 446–47, 448–49.

Istanbul.[148] In July, the British representative in Istanbul was still waiting in vain for the sultan's sanction of the arrangement on Kotur.[149]

With the Kotur dispute still unresolved, the question of the Bagsai-Seyyid Hassan region once again came to the forefront. The Convention of 1869 had stipulated that pending any final judgment, the status quo should be maintained. This meant no new buildings should be erected and all lands should remain intact, with neither side having the right to claim or institute any right of possession by cultivation. In the interim, the Ottoman government on numerous occasions had protested the cultivation by Iran of the disputed lands. In 1882, for example, "the Governor of Baghdad sent infantry and cavalry with the dual mission of protecting plantations owned by Ottoman subjects and of destroying Persian crops. Persia protested and demanded compensation but with no results."[150] A British memo on the question suggested that the mediating powers should settle the dispute, which the two Mohammedan powers "have shown themselves totally unable to arrange amicably between themselves," not only to facilitate the peaceful enjoyment of the productive districts in question, but also to prevent an inevitable conflict.[151] In April 1884, Earl Granville requested that Sir Edward Thornton, then British ambassador to Russia, consult with the Russian government for a joint representation to Istanbul and Tehran to demand the immediate withdrawal of troops and the submission of rival claims to the mediating powers.[152] This happened two months later, when the Russian and British representatives in Istanbul issued a joint memorandum urging withdrawal and requesting that the Porte agree on a boundary line to be traced on a map of that territory. The mediators asked for a "clear and lucid exposé" of the Porte's claims, to be compared with a similar memorandum from Persia so that they could make a final decision.[153] Although Persia embraced their further proposal that the negotiating parties appoint representatives to proceed immediately to Bagsai-Sayyid Hasan, the Porte claimed that more urgent matters were at hand.[154]

[148] *Schofield III*, xviii.
[149] Harari, *Turco-Persian*, 168; PRO.FO 78/4174, Dufferin to Granville, Therapia, July 15, 1884.
[150] Harari, *Turco-Persian*, 165.
[151] Further Memorandum on the Boundary Dispute by Hertslet, *Schofield III*, 473.
[152] Granville to Thornton, London, April 19, 1884, in Harari, *Turco-Persian*, 165.
[153] PRO.FO 78/4174, Joint Note from Thomson and Melikow to Ottoman and Persian Governments, Tehran, July 14, 1884, in Harari, *Turco-Persian*, 166.
[154] Harari, *Turco-Persian*, 167.

The unsettled state of the frontier and the threat that the Bagsai question could lead to serious conflict persisted, even though from 1886 to 1888 official diplomatic communications were greatly diminished. The exception was a rash of correspondence regarding the Porte's intention to construct a fort at the Fao peninsula, on the west bank of the Shatt al-Arab, which the British Foreign and India Offices deemed hazardous to their strategic and economic interests at the head of the Persian Gulf. This risk to British trade brought Tehran and London closer when the latter concluded that as it could not demand the destruction of the fortifications, it could at least lend stronger support to Iran. Around this time, Iran was increasingly alienated from Russia. The shah was of the opinion that to extort concessions from Iran, Russia was inviting Istanbul to create difficulties either on the disputed frontier or among tribes with undecided allegiance. London's representative in Tehran, Henry Drummond-Wolf, therefore argued that "either from the dictatorial tone of Russia or from some other reason the Shah seems to wish to place his main reliance on Her Majesty's Government [and] this is a disposition I think would be well to encourage."[155] Given this realignment, and perhaps as a result of the growing rift between Russia and Iran, or tensions caused by the Anglo-Russian rivalry in Central Asia and the Middle East, or a concomitant reluctance on the part of the mediators to cooperate, both the Kotur and the Bagsai-Sayyid Hassan questions remained unresolved until the last frontier commission of 1914.[156] In the meantime, some local communities attempted to exploit these interstate rivalries to their own advantage. One such example is a *note verbale* provided by the Porte to the British representative in 1899. Providing a plethora of documents to prove that the disputed lands were Ottoman, the note's signatories included tribal chiefs; notables; and officials of Zorbatia, Badra, and Kut al-Amarra.[157]

In this manner, small-scale clashes continued, along with fruitless diplomatic exchanges at the local, national, and international levels. Still, despite persistent complaints about frontier crossings for seasonal pasturing, state correspondence declined between 1890 and 1903. This did not mean the frontier region was stabilized. Rather, the grazing grounds of the borderlanders that busied the parties in the 1890s were momentarily of less interest to the players of the Great Game, whose eyes were increasingly

---

[155] Drummond-Wolf to Salisbury, Tehran, October 2, 1888, *Schofield III*, 527–30.
[156] Harari, *Turco-Persian*, 170.
[157] Sir A. White to Marquis of Salisbury, August 28, 1889; and Ottoman Note Verballe, *Schofield III*, 604–42.

focused on a new actor in the region. Although also concerned by the Russian advance into Central Asia, Britain was more and more uneasy about German efforts to develop relations with the sultan and the shah, build the Baghdad-Basra railway, and gain a foothold in the Persian Gulf. Abetted by the Russian defeat in the 1904–5 Russo-Japanese War, this uneasiness prepared the way for the signing of the 1907 Russo-British convention, which effectively divided Iran into a Russian zone of influence in the north and a British zone in the south, with a natural zone in between. Less than a decade into the twentieth century, Iran was thus officially divided even as it was suffering from the turmoil inflicted by the constitutional revolution that began in 1905. Russia, too, remained weakened after its defeat by Japan. Exploiting these circumstances, the Ottoman Empire launched what would become its last expansionist effort. Its attempt to conquer the northwestern Sunni Kurdish parts of the shah's domains was in direct contravention to the fifty-years-in-the-making frontier negotiations and, indeed, to all of the treaties that had thus far helped transform the Ottoman-Iranian frontier into a boundary.

5

Sunnis for the Sultan: The Ottoman Occupation of Northwestern Iran, 1905–1912

From 1905 to 1911, Ottoman troops and their Kurdish allies made a final effort to turn parts of northwestern Iran into the northeastern Ottoman Empire and to integrate the Sunni Kurdish subjects of the shah's "guarded domains" into the caliph-sultan's "well-protected realm." Allied against them were the Iranian state, such as it existed at the time; its Iranian Kurdish and Turkish allies; and the Russian and British governments. This final Ottoman expansionist or integrationist campaign, depending on one's point of view, had the potential to undo almost seventy years of intermittent boundary making and topple the shaky balance of power established by the Concert of Zagros. What follows is the tangled story of this curiously unstudied episode.[1]

A combination of historical circumstances and the consequent development of an ideology set this story in motion. As we saw in Chapter 1, the process of boundary making ran parallel to the process of reform, during which the Ottoman Empire modernized many age-old notions, passed new laws concerning citizenship, and developed Ottomanism as the formula for turning subjects into citizens. These measures, however, did not solve the monumental problems of the empire. Ottoman intellectuals and reformist bureaucrats responded to the crisis of nineteenth century by calling for a constitutional monarchy, which was declared in 1876 and was followed by the opening of the Ottoman parliament. It took the newly enthroned Sultan

---

[1] The first publication addressing aspects of this episode is by Ghilan, "Les Kurdes Persans et L'Invasion Ottomane," in *Revue du Monde Musulman*, 2nd Année, Mai, No. 5 (1908): 1–22, and No. 10 (1908): 193–210. Another short article is Sinan Kuneralp, "Ottoman Drang Nach Osten: The Turco-Persian Border Problem in Azerbaican, 1905–1912," in *Studies in Ottoman Diplomatic History IV* (Istanbul: Isis Press, 1990), 71–76.

Abdulhamid II less than a year to permanently suspend the constitution and disband the parliament, shattering the dreams of the intelligentsia. On the heels of this blow came the Russo-Ottoman War of 1877–78, which led to the loss of many European lands and Christian subjects, effectively making the empire more Asiatic in territory and Muslim in population. Under heavy pressure from imperialist powers and the competing ideologies of liberalism, nationalism, and constitutionalism, Abdulhamid II increasingly wrapped himself in the caliphial mantle, becoming a champion of (Sunni) pan-Islamism. His religious appeals reverberated in the borderland. As the previous chapter demonstrated, Tehran's suppression of Sunni Kurdish participation in the war with Russia, coupled with its aggressive push for Shi'i dominance in its periphery, only increased sectarian sensibilities, making some Kurds of eastern Kurdistan receptive to integration with the caliph's domains.[2] The Kurdish parts of Iran, however, were not the only targets of this last effort at Ottoman expansionism. Istanbul revived its claims to Al-Hassa in eastern Arabia, Kuwait, Qatar, and Yemen as well.

Apart from rising inter-Muslim sectarianism, the borderland was affected by increasingly militant cross-border Armenian activities, apparent Euro-Russian support of Armenian demands, and escalating confrontations between Muslims and Armenians that threatened Christian-Muslim coexistence in the region.[3] To secure the support of its Sunni brethren, the Porte developed a strategy to better incorporate the Kurdish tribes of the borderland and beyond into its military hierarchy. In doing so, it hoped to counter the Russian threat in Caucasus and Eastern Anatolia as well as the cross-border incursions of Iranian tribes and Armenian guerillas, and to prevent another Sheikh Ubeidullah from raising the banner of revolt and uniting the Kurds. Hence, the Hamidieh Light Cavalry Corps, named after the sultan and blamed for many of the atrocities of the period, was established and the chiefs of various tribes endowed with new status. These steps expanded the process of the re-clanization of the Kurds described in Chapter 1, or what Janet Klein called the strengthening the tribal system, further atomizing

---

[2] The Iranian ambassador to Istanbul, Irfa'a al-Dowleh, cites Ottoman bitterness dating from this period as one reason for the occupation. See his report of September 18, 1907, in *Gozidah-i Asnad*, vol. 6, Document No: 1019.

[3] This chapter does not address the Armenian side of the story because an established literature already exists. For Armeno-Kurdish relations, the Ottoman-Russian competition over Caucasus and Eastern Anatolia, and the tragedies that followed, I refer the reader to Janet Klein, *The Margins of Empire: Kurdish Militias in the Ottoman Tribal Zone* (Stanford, CA: Stanford University Press, 2011) and Michael A. Reynolds, *Shattering Empires: The Clash and Collapse of the Ottoman and Russian Empires 1908–1918* (Cambridge, UK, and New York: Cambridge University Press, 2011).

the borderland's social organization and buttressing its social boundaries.[4] They also furthered the process of erasing the non-Muslim populations from a region they had inhabited for millennia. Thus, the authority of Abdulhamid II, called Bavé Kurdan (the Father of Kurds), and the Ottoman administration of the northern borderland seemed solidified. It was under such circumstances that Istanbul undertook the occupation of Sunni Kurdish Iran.

Also facilitating this venture were events rocking the international arena. As emphasized previously, the balance of power among the Ottoman Empire, England, and Russia, rather than between Tehran and Istanbul, was crucial in finalizing the boundary as we know it today. Hence, when the Russo-Japanese War, the Russian revolution of 1905, the Moroccan Crisis, and the Boer War shook this balance, Istanbul exploited the moment. Beginning in late 1905, in defiance of previous frontier commissions and treaties and the apparent Russo-British control of Iran, Ottoman troops, in cooperation with some Sunni Kurdish tribes, gradually occupied the mostly Sunni Kurdish districts of northwestern Iran.

However acclaimed by the tribal nobility of the periphery, the absolutist sultan's position was far from secure at the center, and a constitutional monarchy was again declared in 1908. The following year, the Committee of Union and Progress forced Abdulhamid II to abdicate. Similarly, amid imperialist rivalries and as a result of the work of Iranian reformers and revolutionaries, Iran also witnessed a constitutional revolution from 1905 to 1911.[5] In 1907, in the midst of this latter struggle, Britain and Russia signed a treaty that officially divided Iran into spheres of influence, while vowing to respect its "integrity and independence."[6] Complicating the geostrategy of the region was the aggressive emergence of Germany and a concession granted to a German company to extend the Ottoman railway line from the central Anatolian town of Konya to Basra. This concession unnerved Russia and Britain, which were now securely in control of Iran. Whatever the case, Qajar Iran, in the throes of a constitutional revolution and civil war and caught between British, Russian, and Ottoman maneuvers, remained

---

[4] Klein, *The Margins of Empire*, chap. 2.

[5] For a comparative history of these constitutional revolutions, see Nader Sohrabi, *Revolution and Constitutionalism in the Ottoman Empire and Iran* (New York: Cambridge University Press, 2011). For the Iranian constitutional revolution, see Janet Afary, *The Iranian Constitutional Revolution 1906–1911* (New York: Columbia University press, 1996); for Azerbaijan, see James D. Clark, *Provincial Concerns* (Costa Meza: Mazda Publishers Inc., 2006).

[6] Firoozeh Kashani-Sabet, *Frontier Fictions* (Princeton: Princeton University Press, 1999), 123.

paralyzed. As the following pages will show, the Ottoman occupation and Sunni irredentism made Iran ever more dependent on the two Great Powers already "strangling Persia."[7]

At the same time, perversely, this strangling was the guarantor of Iran's independence as it faced the aggression of its Ottoman rivals. Two previous generations of Ottomans – the survey commissioner Dervish Pasha in the early 1850s and Sheikh Ubeidullah of Hakkari in 1880–81 – had attempted to take advantage of a weak Qajar state and incorporate Iran's Sunni Kurdish regions into the Ottoman Empire. The occupation of 1905–12 built on this legacy and ambitiously extended it. Curiously, even though it began under the reign of the pan-Islamist Abdulhamid II, the Committee of Union and Progress (CUP) unhesitatingly supported the occupation, despite CUP's reformist agenda and vocal support for its fellow constitutionalists in Iran. The histories of the Ottoman and Iranian constitutionalist movements, as well as British and Russian interventions in Iran during the same period, have been well studied. Less studied are these Ottoman efforts, not simply to carve out an alternative sphere of influence, but to transform that sphere into Ottoman lands *par excellence*. Although inflaming sectarian affiliations between Shi'i and Sunni Muslims, said efforts reinforced the impact on borderland communities of the state-initiated processes of boundary making and modernizing reform by forcing them to choose sides as well as the strategies and tools with which they would respond to their new reality.

JUSTIFYING THE INTEGRATION

Istanbul justified the integration of the occupied territories through various mechanisms. First, it claimed to be assisting a weakened Tehran in securing the borderland during the constitutional turmoil. The specifics of this claim shifted, however, with historical circumstances: during Abdulhamid's reign, Istanbul maintained it was helping the shah; during the CUP's rule, it professed to be aiding its revolutionary comrades. As its initial activities began before the start of the national movement in Iran, these assertions were dubious at best. Many British and Russian diplomats rightfully believed the occupation to be strategically directed against

---

[7] See Morgan Shuster, *The Strangling of Persia; A Story of the European Diplomacy and Oriental Intrigue That Resulted in the Denationalization of Twelve Million Mohammedans, a Personal Narrative* (New York: The Century Co., 1912).

Russia, not Iran, because some of the seized districts offered excellent passage to troops in northwestern Iran in case of a Russo-Ottoman confrontation. As Michael Reynolds demonstrates, the Russo-Ottoman rivalry over the Caucasus and Eastern Anatolia played a primary role in shaping the fate of the borderland and its peoples.[8] By increasing sectarian tensions as well as nationalist aspirations, this rivalry tore the region apart. As Richard Schofield argues, its actions also placed the Porte in a position to bargain with Russia for the simultaneous withdrawal of their respective troops from the area.[9]

Second, Istanbul turned to historical justifications, asserting that the districts in question had been reclaimed, not occupied, because they had been taken by Iran in the war of 1821–22 or integrated through various 'Ajam stratagems after the demise of Kurdish rule. For example, an Ottoman frontier commissioner of the period, the governor of Van, Tahir Pasha, argued in a pamphlet about the delimitation process that the Ottoman centralization efforts of the *nizam-i cedid* (new order) and *tanzimat* (reformation) eras had alienated the Kurds, who responded by declaring allegiance to Iran during the time of the first survey commission. Tahir additionally asserted that Iranian representatives manipulated the Porte's responses to Kurdish chiefs and sheiks by urging it to punish, and thus further alienate, them.[10] Tahir also extended his criticism to his Ottoman predecessors: he disparaged Istanbul for failing to provide documentation proving its ownership and complained that previous commissioners, including the indomitable Dervish, did not pay due attention to the rights of empire and thus fell prey to Iranian trickery. Because Ottomans generally saw deceit as an integral part of Iranian politicking, the pasha further asserted that the copies of the 1639 treaty held in London and St. Petersburg libraries had been corrupted by Iranians.[11] Basing his own claims on Dervish's map, an early seventeenth-century manual of Ottoman imperial provinces compiled by Ayni 'Ali Efendi, and another manual prepared for the frontier commissioners and based on the oldest available registers (*defter*), he concluded by proclaiming Ottoman rights

---

[8] Reynolds, *Shattering*, chap. 2.

[9] *Schofield IV*, Introduction, xxv.

[10] Tahir Pasha, *İki sene evvel hudud-u İraniye tahkikine me'mur olan hey'et-i resmiyye Erzurum valisi devletlü Tahir Paşa hazretlerinin hudud-u mezkureye dair ba'zı malumatı havi olarak Bab-ı 'Ali'ye takdim eyledikleri varakanın sūretidir* (Erzurum Matbaası, 1329), 7.

[11] For a warning to Dervish and the frontier province governors to be wary of Iranian deceit (*hile*), see BOA.A.MKT.MHM, 10/25, 26/s/1265.

to Ushnu, Mergever, Tergever, Bradost, Somai, Anzel, Maku, Baneh, and Savojbulagh, among others.[12]

Behcet Bey, another commissioner, illustrates a third line of argument with his blunt description of the issue as one of identity and belonging: Shi'is belong to Iran whereas Sunnis are Ottoman. He remarked that the 1746 Treaty of Kurdan accepted all villages inhabited by Kurds as belonging to the Ottoman Empire and that subsequent treaties reaffirmed this. Likewise, the two hundred thousand Kurdish-speaking households that made up the *nevahi-i cedide*, or new provinces, as the occupied districts were now called, were Sunnis, whereas those of the other side were Shi'is. Basing his assertions on books of history, including the Kurdish history *Sharafnama*, Behcet remarked that until the 1850s, Kurdish dynasts subject to the Ottoman Empire had ruled most of the occupied districts. Therefore, if asked, the inhabitants say they are Hakkarian (*Biz Irani değil Hakkariyiz derler*).[13]

Finally and related, the Ottomans defended their occupation by pointing to official appeals made by oppressed Sunni borderlanders.[14] Such appeals were facilitated by the Ottoman state's appropriation of a customary tribal institution of violence control called *dehalet* (Tr.) or *dekhalet* (Pr.), which was traditionally invoked by a party escaping from enemies or desiring to prevent further violence by taking refuge in a neutral "tent." As reinterpreted by Istanbul, *dekhalet* or *dekhaletname* was a declaration made by individuals or a community to the effect that being dissatisfied with their present condition, they requested Istanbul to accept them as subjects and protect them. In most of the newly occupied places, *dekhalet* preceded the Ottoman advance, justifying the expansion by allowing troops to appear in the role of "protectors of a population crying for assistance."[15]

---

[12] Ayni Ali Efendi counts Ekrad beni Kotur as part of Van; Mergeve, Oshnu, Mavran [Merivan?] as part of the Shahrizor *eyelet*; and Bayat, Kerend, Ghilan, Darna as parts of the Baghdad *eyelet*. See *Kavanin-i Âli Osman der Hulasa-i Mezamin-i Defter-i Divan*, ed. Tayyib Gökbilgin (Istanbul: Enderun Kitabevi, 1979), 33–37. For the manual, Erkan-ı Harbiye Kaimmakamı Cevdet, *Iran Hududunun Tahdidine Medar Olan Defatir-i Hakani Kaydından Istinsah Edilmişdir, Hudud Komisyonuna Mahsusdur* (Istanbul: Süleymaniye Matbaa-i Askeriye, 1327/1912 [BOA Library 3250].

[13] BOA.HR.SYS 720/13, Cipher from the Iranian Hudud Commissioner Behcet Bey, May 27, 1911.

[14] O'Conor to Wratislaw, Constantinople, October 12, 1907, *Schofield IV*, 217.

[15] Joint Report by Messrs. Shipley and Minorsky, British and Russian Delegates, on the State of Affairs on the Turco-Persian Frontier, June 8–September 16, 1911, *Schofield IV*, 555; hereafter Joint Report by Shipley and Minorsky. For the origins of *dakhala* (Ar) or entering protection, see Sulayman N. Khalaf, "Settlement of Violence in Bedouin Society," *Ethnology* 29.3 (July 1990): 225–42.

Petitions for Ottoman nationality or protection, and accompanying complaints about Shi'i oppression, were hardly new. During the first survey operation, the Crimean War, and afterward, the people of towns such as Ushnu and Sardasht emphasized their Sunni identity and asked for *iltica*, or refuge, and *dekhalet*. The novelty of these *dekhalet* lay in their active solicitation by Ottoman authorities, who even penned them, if one believes Russo-British sources. Throughout the occupation, many individuals, tribes, villages, and even entire small towns applied or occasionally were forced to apply for protection, after which they became Ottoman citizens, sometimes after buying Ottoman passports. In due course, Ottoman authorities began calling the occupied districts *vilayet-i şarkiyye* or *nevahi-i cedide*, that is, the eastern provinces or new districts. Categorized as extensions of existing eastern provinces, *kaimmakam*s and *mudir*s were appointed to administer their affairs. Most often using the *dekhaletname*s as their signposts, Ottoman forces and their Iranian Sunni Kurdish allies occupied some thirty-one districts, including Lahijan, Salmas, Chahrik, Somai, Bradost, Tergever, Mergever, Dasht, Baranduz, Deshtbil, Ushnu, Salduz, Sardasht, Alan, and Baneh, along with various villages in Saqqiz, Khoi, and Savojbulagh, in an area that spanned about 300 kilometers from north to south with a breadth varying from 20 to 80 kilometers.[16] The rivalry between chiefs of the Bilbas tribes in the Pesveh (Passova)-Vezneh (Vaznah)-Lahijan (Lajan) districts provided the initial pretext for the occupation.[17]

THE CASE OF THE BILBAS AND THE BEGINNING OF THE OTTOMAN OCCUPATION

Throughout the history of the frontier's transformation, commissioners had tried to solve the problem of the citizenship of the Sunni Bilbas (or Belbas) tribes and determine ownership of their lands. In the 1840s, the Piran, Mangur, Mamesh, and Gowrik (Gawrg) branches of the Bilbas confederation occupied districts in Vezneh-Lahijan identified as disputed by the *Carte Identique*. The Piran, Mangur, and Mamesh seasonally migrated across the frontier and on reaching Lahijan (Lajan), "which is Persian territory [paid] the revenues of their lands to the Mukri, proprietors of Soujboulagh," who

---

[16] This occupation surpassed even Dervish's claims, which included Baneh, Sardasht, Lahijan, and their dependencies but excluded Merivan, Saqez, and Savojbulagh. Dervish Pasha, *Tahdid-i Hudud-u İraniye* (Istanbul: Matbaa-i Amire, 1326 (1910), 52.

[17] Ghilan, "Les Kurdes Persans," II, 204.

were Iranian subjects.[18] In 1852, the Iranian survey commissioner Mirza
Ja'far counted more than two thousand households from the Mangur,
Mamesh, Zudi, Khadkar, and Senn (or Sin) branches of the Bilbas and
maintained that they all migrated to both sides. As we have seen, however,
he predicted that pasture would trump politics and that they and the rest
of the Bilbas would eventually choose Iranian citizenship because of
the Lahijan plain's ecological resources. Complicating the division of the
Vezneh-Lahijan area was the large non-Bilbas Ako tribe. Its two thousand
households summered on the Iranian side and wintered north of Ottoman
Beitush but did not serve Iran (*khedmeti be Iran nami koned*). According to
Mirza Ja'far, they were rivals of the mostly Iranian Bilbas.[19] Mirza Ja'far's

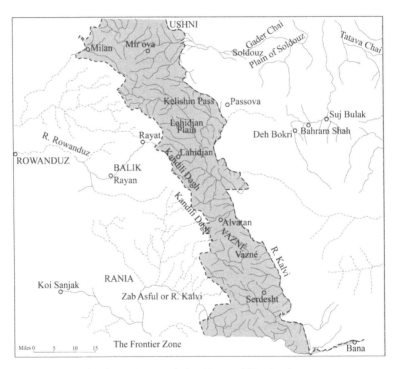

MAP 10. Map of Lahijan Area and the Disputed Territories
Adapted from PRO.MFQ 1/63, Map of the Part of the Turco-Persian Frontier
reduced from *Carte Identique*.

---

[18] Rawlinson to Canning, July 18, 1844. Quoted in Alwyn Parker Memo, December 6, 1906,
Schofield IV, 108.
[19] Mirza Ja'far Khan, *Risalah-i Tahqiqat-i Sarhadiyyah*, ed. Muhammad Mushiri (Tehran:
Bunyad-i Farhang-i Iran, 1348/1969), 147–48; "Memorandum by Lieutenant-Colonel

counterpart, Dervish Pasha, claimed that Lahijan was originally Ottoman. Given as *yurtluk-ocaklık* to the Mir Basakan, a *firka* (section) of the extensive Mukri *taifa*, it was seized by the Ottoman Bilbas of Koi Sanjak, who gradually submitted to Iran.[20] Given such claims, starting in the 1870s, Ottoman and Iranian troop movements in Lahijan-Vezneh preoccupied diplomats in all four capitals. This dispute and its trajectory exemplify how itinerant populations dealt with the extension of a state power that abandoned old notions of suzerainty and increasingly demanded that its citizens acknowledge its territorialized sovereignty.

In the 1880s, the dispute intensified until, in 1888, Istanbul complained that the Iranian Mangur tribe had occupied Vezneh, which it alleged was Ottoman territory.[21] Diplomatic correspondence gathered pace in July 1889, when the Porte threatened to expel the token Iranian force stationed at Lahijan if the Mangur did not evacuate in three weeks.[22] It did not follow through on its threat but did continue to assert ownership of the territory.[23] In the early 1890s, Tehran and Istanbul signed a protocol pledging "to evacuate Vezneh [within] one month." Both parties agreed to leave the place unoccupied pending the decision of a joint commission that would include representatives from all four powers.[24] This assuaged the issue for a time, but the commission had apparently still not met and the problem had returned full force. In a detailed memorandum, a well-informed British representative, Lieutenant-Colonel Francis R. Maunsell, noted the following:

The Kurdish tribal confederation of Bilbas occupies all these frontier districts on both sides of the line. They are mostly nomad, and call themselves subject to one or the other Government as suits them best, evading consequences of their misdeeds by crossing to the other side of the frontier and generally living in a state of semi-independence. The Persian government (previous to the present dispute) left them alone as long as they paid tribute and their Chiefs or "Aghas" ruled as they liked.[25]

Maunsell respecting the Turco-Persian Frontier near Lahjan and Wazna, December 20, 1906," in *Schofield IV*, 113–14.

[20] Dervish, *Tahdidi*, 64, 68.

[21] Correspondence between British representatives from 1889 to 1894 includes some four hundred dispatches and telegrams dealing principally with Vezneh and Lahijan. Alwyn Parker Memo, December 6, 1906, *Schofield IV*, 103.

[22] A. White, British Ambassador to Istanbul to Marquis of Salisbury, Constantinople, July 17, 1889, *Schofield III*, 591–95.

[23] White to Marquis of Salisbury, January 16, 1890, *Schofield III*, 646–68.

[24] For the text of the undated protocol, see *Schofield III*, 650–53.

[25] Maunsell Memorandum, December 20, 1906, *Schofield IV*, 113–14.

Similarly, the British vice-consul of Diyarbekir, Avalon Shipley, noted that although the Turks claimed that the mixed commission had adjudicated Lahijan to them thirty years previously, they had never exercised authority over the local tribes. As they were Sunni, if forced to choose, the Mamesh, Mangur, and Piran would opt for the Ottomans, "but hitherto they have refused to acknowledge either definitely, claiming Persian nationality when the Turks, and Ottoman when the Persians, claimed the payment of taxes."[26] Maunsell also noted that in 1906, most of the Bilbas seasonally migrated between Lahijan, Vezneh, and Savojbulagh on the Iranian side and the Rania and Pishder plains on the Ottoman side. The significant exception was the tribe's principal branch, the Gowrik, a sedentary group of six thousand households that lived under direct Iranian rule. Despite their independent attitude, the three thousand Mamesh households likewise recognized Iranian suzerainty. The three thousand Mangur households persisted in their independence and their transborder migrations, whereas the two thousand Piran households, which at one time lived on the Rania Plain, changed nationality and moved to Iran, "a thing fairly easy to accomplish," Maunsell remarked.[27]

No doubt the inaccessibility of the mountainous region facilitated the Bilbas' autonomy. As this brief sketch shows, however, they were not completely independent of the central governments. Moreover, like similar groups, they were most vulnerable to state control when different branches of their confederation competed, especially for resources and chiefdoms. After the demise of the Kurdish dynasts, such situations would arise when some branches approached central state representatives to gain legitimacy and even support – a move that in turn increased the legitimacy of the state itself. It was one such struggle that gave the Ottomans an excuse for occupation.

An influential wing of the Ottoman establishment, labeled "the war party" by British diplomats, was looking for just such an excuse. Troubled by Armenian guerilla incursions from Iran, this group was especially concerned about a possible Russian advance and argued for occupying parts of northwestern Iran to create a bulwark. Its fears regarding Russia were stoked by Moscow's plan to extend its railway to Julfa, the existence of its road to Tabriz, the appointment of a Russian vice-consul to Urumieh, and the conversion of Iranian Assyrians to the Russian church. As Van's British vice-consul Bertram Dickson observed, "If a railway were required

[26] Shipley to O'Conor, Mosul, April 9, 1906, *Schofield IV*, 39–40.
[27] Maunsell Memorandum, 113.

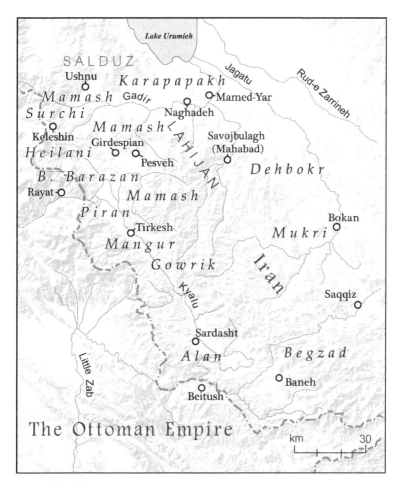

MAP 11. The Bilbas Country
Based on Alexander Iyas's expeditions of December 1912 and August 1913, reproduced by "Boundary Cartography" from John Tchalenko, *Images from the Endgame* with permission from John Tchalenko and Saqi Books.

to be constructed from Russia to Baghdad or the Persian Gulf," the easiest route was the Lahijan-Vezneh pass, and if a railway or cart road were to be constructed from Beyazid to Baghdad, it would have to follow through the same pass. This, he suggested, was the main strategic reason for the occupation.[28]

---

[28] See his report on Vezneh-Lahijan. Vice-Consul Dickson to O'Conor, Van, December 14, 1907, *Schofield IV*, 262.

The pretense for occupation arose as a result of leadership struggles among the region's Bilbas chiefs and were exacerbated by Iranian efforts to transform the Bilbas into Iranian citizens. In 1905, Prince Imam Quli, the governor of Savojbulagh, demanded five hundred tumans from the independent Mangur chief Baiz Agha, as part of a plan to replace him with his rival, the more pliant Bapir Agha. Unable to pay, Baiz fled to the Ottoman side and Bapir assumed power.[29] Even as Baiz plotted to reclaim his chieftaincy, a similar struggle was unfolding among the Mamesh, whose leader, Mamesh Muhammed Agha, was being challenged by his nephew Hamza. Seizing on the opportunity presented by this discord, Izzet Bey of Kerkuk, a *kaimmakam* and a leader of the expansionist war party, offered to help both Baiz and Hamza. In late August 1905, under the guise of sending an approved commission to inquire into the matter of tribal leadership, Izzet Bey placed two Ottoman staff officers, fifty cavalry, and two hundred men under their joint command and ordered them to attack their rivals. After forcing Mamesh Muhammad, his ally Bapir, and the new governor of Savojbulagh Shuja ud-Dawlah to flee, Hamza became Mamesh chief and Baiz, Mangur chief. It was reported that Baiz, who would later be made an Ottoman pasha, was given a salary and appointed

FIGURE 3. Baiz and Hamza Aghas.
Finnish Museum of Photography, Alexander Iyas Collection 114, Bayiz Agha (Pasha) Mangur (seated left) and Hamzeh (Seman) Agha Mamesh (seated right).

[29] John Tchalenko, *Images from an Endgame: Persia through a Russian Lens 1901–1914* (London: Saqi, 2006), 134; Ghilan, "Les Kurdes Persans," II, 203.

kaimmakam of Vezneh. For his part, Izzet Bey secured the loyalty of both chiefs' kinsmen and the right to claim the lands in which they resided. If one is to believe Vice-Consul Shipley's report, most of the tribes in question declared their loyalty to the Ottoman government and some even moved to the Ottoman side.[30]

Soon, Ottoman troops began gathering in Suleimanieh, from which point they entered Iran. Thus, with minimal effort, the war party claimed a part of Iran for the sultan, whereas Tehran, under Muzaffar al-Din Shah, was undergoing the first phase of the constitutional revolution and was therefore in no position to resist. Sir Nicholas R. O'Conor, the British representative in Istanbul, summarized the "the critical situation in Lahidjan" as follows:

An ordinary tribal quarrel, followed by the intervention of the neighbouring Turkish authorities at the instance of the weaker side, has been allowed to develop through the intrigues and ambitions of Izzet Bey of Kerkuk, supported by other persons of influence in high quarters, into an armed invasion of places lying beyond the neutral frontier zone, culminating in the occupation in force of Passova, and the concentration of a large number of Turkish troops on the Persian frontier.[31]

The first reports of Ottoman troop movements into Vezneh-Lahijan hit the diplomatic cables in October 1905, followed by news of regular troops and Hamidieh Cavalry moving into Lahijan. In the midst of the early tumult of the Iranian constitutional revolution, Tehran contacted British and Russian representatives in Istanbul, urging them to support the Persian ambassador in his protest of the aggression.[32] However, diplomatic inter-ventions did not stop the advance of the Kurdo-Ottoman troops into Bilbas territory. Afraid that their own plans for Iran might be endangered, London and St. Petersburg pressed Istanbul to accept the formation of yet another commission. Acceding, Istanbul nevertheless refused to withdraw, stating that Vezneh, Lahijan, and Pasveh formed part of its dominions and that troops were "dispatched there on our part whenever incursions have taken place from the other side."[33] Tehran also agreed to the commission, but insisted that as long as "the invaders" remained, any joint inquiry would be ineffective.[34]

[30] Shipley to O'Conor, Mosul, April 9, 1906, *Schofield IV*, 39–40; Ghilan, "Les Kurdes Persans," II, 205.

[31] O'Conor to Grey, May 2, 1906, *Schofield* IV, 38.

[32] Persian Embassy to OMoF, December 13, 1905, *Schofield IV*, 14.

[33] OMoF to Persian Ambassador, Constantinople, December 13, 1905, *Schofield IV*, 15.

[34] Moshir-ed-Dowleh to Persian Minister, January 31, 1906, communicated to London on February 1, *Schofield IV*, 16.

During subsequent diplomatic exchanges, Istanbul insisted that the disputed districts' inhabitants were Ottoman, that is, Sunni, and hence Ottoman citizens. Tehran, in turn, claimed that the Erzurum Treaty had decided that they were under Iranian occupation (*uti possidetis*) and that the status quo should be preserved. Careful not to offend the sultan, Tehran blamed the war party for the encroachment, which it called "entirely at variance with the unity which should prevail in the world of Islam."[35] It was because of its desire "to protect the honor of Islam" that it did not allow the inhabitants of places such as Urumieh to retaliate against nearby Ottoman troops. Still, Tehran noted that by asking their inhabitants to become Ottoman, Ottoman authorities simply provided further proof that the districts were Iranian.[36]

The honor of Islam was all but an empty cliché. As one British representative noted, the untrained and poorly equipped Iranian infantry was no match for the Ottoman troops.[37] Consequently, Tehran sought British help with the "withdrawal of the Turkish encroachers from Persian territory," after which they would have no objection to mixed inquiry or a commission.[38] When the British ambassador to Istanbul declared that England would remain neutral, Muzaffar al-Din was furious. Given that "England had so long been the friend of Persia," the shah told the British chargé d'affaires, Evelyn Grant Duff, that its support should not be withheld precisely at the time of need:

The friendship of Great Britain was more valued by Persia than that of Turkey, so HM's government must also set the friendship of Persia above that of Turkey, for Persia's policy was a constant one, whereas that of Turkey was ever changing. Moreover many of the inhabitants of India were Sunnis, and therefore co-religionists of the Turks, and Turkey might therefore some day create difficulties in India.[39]

Unconvinced, Duff responded that the shah's requests would be conditional on his government's settlement of some of "our long outstanding cases in token of their good-will, and on assuming a more conciliatory

[35] Note Communicated by Persian Government to Ottoman Government, December 8 (21), 1905; and Grey to Grant Duff, January 5, 1906, *Schofield IV*, 12.
[36] Extracts of Correspondence Passed between Persian Government and Ottoman Embassy at Tehran, *Schofield IV*, 17.
[37] Lieutenant Colonel J. A. Douglas, military attaché of the British Embassy in Constantinople, was in the region to report the number of troops on the frontier. See his reports to Duff January 31, and O'Conor March 5, 1906, *Schofield IV*, 19.
[38] Mushir-ed-Dowleh to Duff, December 26, 1905, *Schofield IV*, 18.
[39] Duff to Grey, Tehran, March 23, 1906, *Schofield IV*, 22.

attitude generally."[40] The shah's conversation with the Russian representative was more productive, and St. Petersburg urged London to adopt a more energetic attitude toward the Porte. Viewing cooperation as the best way to maintain its troops' position, in March 1906, Istanbul agreed to send commissioners to Lahijan. Similarly unenthusiastic, the Iranians agreed to do the same.[41]

Despite pressure from the mediating governments and vigorous internal debates, it was increasingly obvious that the pro-expansionist faction of the government was pushing forward with plans to annex Iranian Kurdistan, a possibility that excited the local population.[42] Iran was in such a precarious situation that IMoFA Mushir al-Dawlah asked Duff what military measures it should take. When the latter declined to offer advice, the former "begged that I would refer this question" to Edward Grey, the British foreign minister, and "asked also how far Great Britain and Russia considered it their duty to intervene in disputes on the Perso-Turkish frontier."[43] Kept abreast of Ottoman troop movements and weapons sent to the region, Grey responded that it was futile "for them [Tehran] to attempt to do anything themselves," while advising his diplomats such as Cecil Spring-Rice, plenipotentiary at Tehran, to press Istanbul to accept the "arbitration of Russia and Britain."[44] Aware of Iran's diminished military capacity, the Porte declined to withdraw its forces prior to the convening of the frontier commission. Tehran, following Russian and British advice, refrained from military action. Meanwhile, according to Shipley, the two leading spirits "of the party of aggression," Abdullah and Izzet Pashas, advocated for the immediate dispatch of all troops to the frontier.[45]

British diplomats clarified to the Porte that London would tolerate neither the disorder that would result from inciting the Kurds nor any disorder in the Persian Gulf and Southern Persia. Moreover, they indicated agreement with the shah's warnings about (Sunni) pan-Islamism, noting their concern that the occupation had "elements of complications possibly

[40] Ibid.
[41] See Irfa'a Dowleh's Report from Istanbul, September 18, 1907, in *Gozidah-'i Asnad*, vol. 6, Document No: 1019.
[42] According to O'Conor the war party was headed by Abdullah Pasha and Izzet Pasha of Kerkuk, whose brother Mustafa Pasha, the Vali of Mosul, was in the opposing camp along with Mushir Zeki Pasha. O'Conor to Grey, Constantinople, April 10, 1906, *Schofield IV*, 29–30.
[43] Duff to Grey, Tehran, April 22, 1906, *Schofield IV*, 31.
[44] Grey to Spring-Rice, FO, April 24, 1906, *Schofield IV*, 34.
[45] Shipley to O'Conor, Mosul April 7, 1906, *Schofield IV*, 30.

threatening the existence of Persia, which at present is wholly unable to offer any effectual armed resistance, and from another point of view, it opens a prospective of a Pan-Islamic propagandism which neither ourselves nor Russia could regard without serious concern."[46] The Russians, not ready to take military action suggested that the Porte should be pressed to accept joint arbitration. This was Tehran's position as well.[47]

Frequent meetings and correspondences continued through April 1906, and on May 7, Tehran finally reported that it would send its commissioners to join the Ottoman ones already at the frontier.[48] Meanwhile, eight thousand soldiers under Izzet's command and headquartered at the fortified village of Pesveh were occupying Lahijan, which had been proclaimed a sanjak of Suleimanieh for which a *kaimmakam* had been appointed.[49] By the end of April, Ottoman forces had taken complete possession of the districts of Dasht and Mergever, and armed soldiers prohibited Urumieh's governor from levying taxes along the frontier as they worked to win over the region's Christian inhabitants.[50]

If one is to believe the British representative at Istanbul, the war party headed by Abdullah Pasha and his chauvinistic supporters was dictating misleading reports issued by the Ottoman frontier commission, which in turn kept the other commissioners from concluding that Pesveh was Persian territory. Further, the commission was trying to convince the sultan that a withdrawal would upset local tribes and Hamidieh officers, and his prestige would suffer so seriously that he might be obliged to employ force to prevent a revolution of his own Kurdish subjects. Grand Vizier Avlonyalı Ferid Pasha, according to O'Conor, stood alone in attempting to persuade the sultan against the occupation. Whereas the expansionists presaged a possible Kurdish backlash, the British Embassy warned the Porte that uncontrollable disturbances stimulated by the occupation might spread to Baghdad and even Basra, possibly fomenting conditions for revolution in Asia Minor, where affairs in the Caucasus were

---

[46] O'Connor to Grey, Constantinople, April 10 and 27, 1906, *Schofield IV*, 32, 36.

[47] This would remain Iranian policy for a long time. For an example in later years, see Prince Irfa'a al-Dowleh to IMFA, October 25, 1907, in *Guzidah-'i Asnad*, vol. 6, Document No: 1019.

[48] The Iranian members of the commission were Mirza Mahmoud Khan, Ehtesham ol-Saltana, Iran's ambassador to Germany, commissioner; Nezam-ol-Molk, first deputy; M. de Bruk, chief engineer; Sadegh Khan, interpreter; and a secretary, a doctor, and other auxiliaries. PMoFA to Persian Ambassador at Constantinople, *Schofield IV*, 43. The Ottoman commissioner was Vecid Pasha; his deputy was Major Said Bey.

[49] Douglas to Duff, Tehran, April 24, 1906, *Schofield IV*, 41.

[50] Duff to Grey, Tehran, May 21, 1906, *Schofield IV*, 44.

already having an effect. O'Conor advised the grand vizier that such a development, especially in the Persian Gulf, was deeply worrisome to Britain and Russia.[51] There was reason to be concerned. Colonel Conyers Surtees, military attaché to the British Embassy in Istanbul, reported that between Mosul and the frontier, twenty thousand troops and forty-three thousand tribesmen from the Khosnao, Bilbas, Sheikh Bileni, Hemevend, and Jaf tribes were ready to swoop into the province of Azerbaijan, and military posts had been established at various places.[52] In his detailed report, Surtees remarked that only a fraction of Ottoman troops had been mobilized, whereas the "Persian army is practically a *quantité negliable*. Hence it appears that Turkey is in a position to impose her will upon Persia, unless other Powers should decide to intervene."[53] Britain and Iran again pressured Istanbul, and this time the sultan responded by sending the high-ranking Zeki Pasha to Pesveh to work with the Iranian commissioners to prevent a conflict that could include Russia. Still, the sultan's grand vizier opined that "the only course left open to Persia was to appeal to the arbitration of Great Britain and Russia," which is precisely what the Iranian ambassador, Mirza Riza Khan, did.[54]

In July, Tehran's commissioners finally arrived at the frontier and the joint Ottoman-Iranian frontier commission met on the twenty-seventh of that month, but the Ottoman commissioner left for Suleimanieh on August 18 with no tangible results. Ottoman authorities continued collecting taxes in certain districts and thousands of Ottoman troops remained in Pesveh. The Porte additionally began endowing tribal chiefs in the occupied zone with military ranks. Not to be outdone, the Iranian commissioner attempted to recruit some Kurdish tribes that had previously moved from the Iranian to the Ottoman side.

Soon Ottoman troops went to Anzel and, in the company of Ismail Agha Shekak, collected taxes in Chahrik. Meanwhile, Izzet Pasha, along with Herki Karim Khan, occupied villages around Baranduzchai, and additional soldiers went to Kohnashahr in the environs of Khoi. The government of Iranian Kurdistan informed Tehran that Ottoman soldiers were also collecting money from the villages of Baneh.[55] In October, news of an Ottoman advance toward Savojbulagh and tax-collecting activities within two miles of Urumieh confirmed Istanbul's assertion of claims over

---

[51] O'Conor to Grey, Therapia, June 26, 1906, *Schofield IV*, 47.

[52] H. Conyers Surtees to O'Conor, Constantinople, June 22, 1906, *Schofield IV*, 48.

[53] Conyers Surtees to O'Conor, Constantinople, July 2, 1906, *Schofield IV*, 49–51.

[54] O'Conor to Grey, Therapia, July 13, 1906, *Schofield IV*, 52.

[55] BOA.HR.SYS 742/20, IMFA to the Ottoman Embassy, August 24, 1906.

lands up to Urumieh Lake. Following the issue with interest but "leaving the Ottoman Government in doubt as to what it would do," London again warned the Porte that it would consider serious steps if its interests were threatened.[56]

Such warnings seemed to have a positive effect when, in February 1907, a new joint Iranian-Ottoman commission tasked with settling the dispute and delimiting the whole boundary met at Mosul.[57] Once more, however, its efforts were futile. Such repeated ineffectiveness frustrated London and St. Petersburg, which were suspicious that Istanbul's new friend Germany might try to solve the frontier question in Turkey's favor and subsequently demand a recompense, "which could take the shape of a coaling station or island on the Persian Gulf."[58] Consequently, in June, they again argued that disturbances in Iran might "eventually rebound upon Turkey herself," perhaps in the form of a Shi'i revolution in Baghdad.[59] The making of the boundary thus became part of the larger struggle over the region, even as the Ottoman expansionist party increased its efforts to procure *dekhalet* petitions.

A KURDISH TRIBE, AN AMERICAN MISSIONARY, AND THE *DEKHALET* PETITIONS

The spark that ignited these efforts and allowed further Ottoman expansion was the March 1904 killing of an American missionary, Rev. Benjamin W. Labaree, (also known as Dr. Labarre), who was active in Urumieh and Hakkari. The murder was committed by members of the Sunni Kurdish Begzadeh tribe of Dasht, at the instigation of a certain Sayyid Gaffar, who – along with the chief *mujtahid* of Urmieh, Mirza Hasan Khan – strongly objected to the missionaries on religious grounds.[60] The culprits were arrested but escaped from prison in when they were returned to Urumieh. Approximately two years later, in July 1906, the Begzadeh petitioned Tahir Pasha, then the *vali* of Van, to be commissioned as members of the Hamidieh and protected from the Iranian government

[56] Alwyn Parker Memo, December 6, 1906, *Schofield IV*, 106.
[57] O'Conor to Grey, Constantinople, February 18, 1907, *Schofield IV*, 115.
[58] O'Conor to Grey, Constantinople, April 17, 1907, *Schofield IV*, 115.
[59] O'Conor to Grey, Constantinople, June 13, 1907; and Grey to O'Conor, FO, June 18, 1907, *Schofield IV*, 116.
[60] Albert Charles Wratislaw, *A Consul in the East* (Edinburgh: W. Blackwood, 1924), 191–93; and Ghilan, "Les Kurdes Persans," I, 18–20, II, 209.

officials, Shiʻis, and Christian Assyrians who were oppressing them.[61] Agreeing with Dervish Pasha's reading of the Turkish claim that Sunni Muslims were naturally subjects of the sultan and that Mergever, Tergever, Baradost, Berdesor, and Somai were Ottoman, Tahir accepted their petition in October, even though Istanbul had warned him that the status quo should be preserved. By November, the *zabtieh*s (gendarmerie) and a detachment of infantry had temporarily occupied Mergever, furthering Ottoman claims already made to Vezneh-Lahijan.[62]

Around this time, Azerbaijan was the hotbed of the Iranian constitutional revolution and *anjuman*s, or city councils, ruled some of the towns there. According to British sources, because the Urumieh *anjuman* wanted to assert its authority and possibly gain the support of foreign powers, in June 1907, it authorized Mejd-es-Saltanah, the city's strongman, to carry out punitive expeditions against the Begzadeh, forcing them to pay the indemnity demanded by the American government. Mejd-es-Saltanah sent a detachment of five hundred men to occupy Jerma, in the hills above the Begzadeh stronghold of Berdesor. However, the Begzadeh attacked the detachment *en route*, killing two hundred. Rather than reporting the details of this encounter, pro-expansion Ottoman officers informed Istanbul that the Iranians had attacked Ottoman troops in Mergever. Meanwhile, Mejd-es-Saltanah and fifteen hundred additional troops – later reinforced by Assyrians and some Kurds from Tergever – arrived in Mergever.[63]

On June 26, Majd es-Saltanah's men attacked and set ablaze several Begzadeh villages. Kurds from the Ottoman side and the Ottoman authorities assured the Begzadeh that help was at hand and soon a large Ottoman force, buttressed by many Hamidieh Kurds, arrived at the scene. Through a messenger, Mejd-es-Saltanah expressed his surprise at finding Ottoman troops on Iranian soil, especially because he was carrying out an officially sanctioned punitive expedition. The Ottoman commanders responded that his forces were not sent by Tehran but by the revolutionary Urmi *anjuman* and were thus illegitimate. They further declared that the districts of Mergever, Tergever, Bradost, and Somai were Ottoman. In the ensuing confrontation, the Ottomans bombarded the Iranian camp, which quickly withdrew, leaving behind equipment and 150 dead. The retreating Ottoman troops, along with their Shekak and Herki auxiliaries, pillaged the large

---

[61] Report by Vice-Consul Dickson on His Recent Journey through Turco-Persian Territory, December 14, 1907, *Schofield IV*, 263–69.
[62] Ibid.
[63] Ibid.; Ghilan, "Les Kurdes Persans," II, 210.

village of Mawana, prompting thousands of frightened Christians and Shi'is to flee with their livestock and take refuge in Urumieh.[64] Tehran asked for prompt reparations and urged that measures be taken to prevent the recurrence of such events.[65]

In the wake of this conflict, grossly exaggerated reports of Ottoman deeds were reported throughout Europe, including stories of plundering, killing, and the kidnapping of Shi'i and Christian women. French, Russian, English, and American ambassadors – all of whom had missionaries in the region – strongly supported Tehran's demands.[66] The presence of Christian borderlanders and missionaries was thus a benefit for Tehran, which supplied constant updates to European and American representatives and portrayed the Ottomans as defenders of Labarre's killers and aggressors against local Christians. Tehran also appealed to the newly established international body, the Hague Conference, whose first convention in July 1899 had called for the settlement of international disputes through mediation.[67] Even as it attempted to further internationalize the frontier question, Tehran tried to win Istanbul's sympathies. Recalling the friendship "which has always existed between the two Mussulman Powers," the shah declared that the Ottoman incursions had caused him "profound astonishment and grief." Such an attack by a friendly neighboring state "would not be deemed justifiable even if made against Bedouins, much less when made against Persians without any previous signs of hostility being shown."[68]

None of this did anything to hinder Istanbul. After taking control of Mergever, Tergever, and Berdesor in early August 1907, Ottoman troops and their Kurdish allies occupied the districts of Chahrik, Dasht, and Bradost.[69] It was rumored that Saqqez, Urumieh, Salmas, Khoi, and

---

[64] BOA.HR.SYS 742/42, Tehran Embassy report to OMFA, August 17, 1907. See also E. G. Browne, *The Persian Revolution* (Washington DC: Mage Publishers, 2006), 149; "Report by Rev O. H. Parry (English Mission head of Archbishop's Assyrian Mission) respecting the Frontier Dispute between Turkey and Persia, English Mission, Urmi, August 27, 1907," *Schofield IV*, 148–51; Spring-Rice to Grey, Gulahek, August 15, 1907, *Schofield IV*, 157.

[65] *Takrir* sent to Turkish Ministry of Foreign Affairs by Persian Ambassador at Constantinople, July 26, 1907, *Schofield IV*, 155–56.

[66] Spring-Rice to Grey, Gulahek, August 7 and 15, 1907, *Schofield IV*, 119, 157. Grey to O'Conor, FO, August 8, 1907, *Schofield IV*, 119.

[67] Spring-Rice to Grey, Gulahek, August 6, 1907, *Schofield IV*, 123; and "Memorandum of information received during the month of September 1907, relating to affairs in Persia, and of the course of the Anglo-Russian negotiations from April to the end of September 1907," *Schofield IV*, 206.

[68] Persian Minister of Foreign Affairs to Persian Ambassador in Constantinople, August 7, 1907, *Schofield IV*, 156.

[69] IMFA to Persian Embassy in Constantinople, July 24, 1907, *Schofield IV*, 155.

Savojbulagh would follow. Ottoman commanders ordered Iranian troops in Savojbulagh to disperse. A British dispatch from the time noted that the whole frontier region, including many Christian villages, "appears to be in the hands of the Kurds, who rely on a large body of Turkish regulars for support."[70] Although it was not under immediate threat, Urumieh, where hundreds of Christians had taken refuge at the Russian Consulate, was also gripped by anxiety.[71] Further complications included cross-border Armenian activities, rumors that Russia's First and Second Caucasian Rifle Brigades were preparing to enter Iran, and news that Christians were being allowed to return to their villages provided they accepted Ottoman sovereignty.[72]

The Kurdo-Ottoman advance also reactivated Shi'i-Sunni sectarianism. Reports of desecrations of Shi'i places of worship as well as killings and decapitations of civilians fermented unrest in Azerbaijan and beyond. Dismissing such reports, Istanbul blamed Tehran for providing newspapers with "false and biased information" and retorted that "3,000 Persians in cooperation with a large number of Armenians" had raided and burned Sunni villages in Takovar and Baradostun and forced peaceful populations to take refuge in the mountains.[73] Under such attacks, the Sunni Kurdish population increased its appeals for Ottoman protection, while ethnically Turkish Shi'i tribes such as the Karapapak, who resisted Ottoman advances, wired the Iranian National Assembly to settle this unsatisfactory state of affairs.[74] Agitation in Tehran reached such levels that the Ottoman ambassador worried that the populace might attack the embassy.[75] As news of the Anglo-Russian Convention's division of Iran into spheres of influence began to circulate around this time, British interests and citizens were also under threat.[76]

This delicate situation forced London and St. Petersburg to intensify efforts to find a peaceful resolution, while also pressuring Istanbul to resolve ongoing disagreements between its pro- and anti-expansionist parties. To this end, O'Conor reminded the Porte of the "considerable political effervescence and

[70] Spring-Rice to Grey, Gulahek, August 15, 1907, *Schofield IV*, 157.
[71] For photos of the refugees, see Ghilan, "Les Kurdes Persans."
[72] "Memorandum of information received during the month of September 1907, relating to Affairs in Persia," *Schofield IV*, 207.
[73] Nicholson to Grey, St. Petersburg, September 1, 1907, *Schofield IV*, 160.
[74] Ala-es-Saltanah to Spring-Rice, September 7, 1907, *Schofield IV*, 178.
[75] HR.SYS 742/49, Ottoman Embassy of Tehran to OMFA, September 9, 1907.
[76] Spring-Rice to Grey, Gulahek, September 30, 1907, *Schofield IV*, 163–64. For the convention's background, see Firuz Kazemzadeh, *Russia and Britain in Persia, 1864–1914* (New Haven, CT: Yale University Press, 1968), chap. 7.

discontent" in its eastern provinces of Bitlis, Van, and Erzurum, and the danger "of a combination between Revolutionary party and the Kurds owing to the exactions and maladministration of the country."[77] O'Conor was referring to the sometimes violent resistance that had sprung up in various cities, including some along the frontier, against two types of poll taxes. The Armenian Dashnaktsutiun Revolutionary Party and the League of Private Initiative and Decentralization were responsible for turning this regional disturbance into a full-fledged constitutional movement,[78] and British representatives suspected that the sultan might have been influenced by such events when ordering the invasion of Iranian territory. Places such as Bitlis had witnessed unrest that resembled events taking place in Azerbaijan: telegraph offices had been seized and Fedavi or revolutionary devotees used.[79] Possibly responding to such fears, the sultan suggested that a new commission be sent to the frontier.

In Tehran, meanwhile, complicity between the shah and the sultan was rumored. It was generally believed that the shah, averse to the constitution and assembly, wished the disorder to continue because it discredited the assembly and, he hoped, would hasten and justify intervention. The Iranian historian A. A. Shamim argues that there was indeed a secret agreement between Muhammad 'Ali Shah and Sultan Abdulhamid, because Tehran took no steps to force the withdrawal of Ottoman troops. Similarly, M. Amin Riyahi argues that the shah's policy was to incite tribes to raid and loot in order to make the townspeople enemies of the constitutionalists. One such example was the powerful *sarhaddar* of Maku, Sardar Makoi, who, with the help of Kurds (some Ottoman) and Russians, wreaked havoc in the region.[80]

Because a sizeable number of Russian troops were stationed in Iranian Azerbaijan, London also feared complications between Istanbul and St. Petersburg.[81] However, encouraged by the Russo-Japanese War, Istanbul was confident in its ability to subdue Russia, especially as England

---

[77] O'Conor to Grey, Therapia, August 28, 1907, *Schofield IV*, 152–53.

[78] For this revolt, see Şükrü Hanioğlu, *Preparation for a Revolution* (New York: Oxford University Press, 2001), chap. 5.

[79] Spring-Rice to Grey, Gulahek, September 30, 1907, *Schofield IV*, 176–78.

[80] 'Ali Asghar Shamim, *Iran dar dawrah-'i saltanat-i Qajar, qarn-i sizdahum va nimah-i avval qarn-i chahardahum* Tehran: Entesharate Zariab, 1387/2008, 517–18 and Muhammad Amin Riyahi, *Tariki-i Khoi: sayr-i tahavvulat-i ijtima'i va farhangi-i shahr'ha-yi Iran dar tayy-i qurun*. [Tehran]: Intisharat-i Tarah-i Naw, 1999), 413.

[81] "Memorandum of information received during the month of September 1907, relating to affairs in Persia, and of the course of the Anglo Russian negotiations from April to the end of September 1907," *Schofield IV*, 211.

was occupied with its own difficulties in India and Egypt. The constitutional turmoil in Iran likewise heartened Istanbul. *The Times* reported that "the Sultan thinks it is time to crush Persia before the liberal movement comes to fruit or the Perso-Russian railway is built."[82]

Instead of waiting for that to happen, the Russo-British Entente again stepped up efforts to put an end to the occupation, which revealed as impotent Anglo-Russian promises of protecting Iran's integrity. The alarmed British representative to Tehran, Cecil Spring-Rice, wrote that given his rumored complicity with the sultan, the shah's life and throne would be in danger if the aggression continued. This in turn could draw the Christian powers deeper into the conflict and the ever-more-disgruntled public eye. If Russia and Britain could induce the sultan to withdraw, the dangerous agitation aroused by their division of Iran into spheres of power might be assuaged.[83]

This view was shared in St. Petersburg. Even though the Anglo-Russian Convention guaranteed the inviolability of Persian territory, the conservative Russian newspaper *Novoye Vremya* claimed that many viewed it as the first step toward Persia's partitioning, and that the lack of action against the Ottomans strengthened this theory. The suspicion that Istanbul was carving out a sphere of influence that encroached on Russia's unnerved St. Petersburg, as did the notion that Berlin was actuating the Porte's polices and so undermining Russian and British influence in Tehran. *Noveye Vremya* maintained that in order to consolidate its influence in Asia Minor and the Persian Gulf, Berlin had thrust the Baghdad Railway into the body of Western Asia

like a steel feeler. [Hence] the vital interests of Russia and Persia demand the adjustment of the Perso-Turkish conflict by peaceful means. [Persia,] ruined and disorganized by a regime long since not in accordance with the requirements of modern state life, with an empty treasury, without proper administrative and judicial organization, without any appreciable European education of the public class, without an army or military leaders, cannot hope to offer the requisite resistance to foreign invasion.[84]

The crux of the rivalry between European powers, according to a like-minded London *Times* correspondent in Iran, was the competition between the Baghdad Railway and the Russo-Persian line, which Russia planned to run from Julfa to Tabriz and then directly to Bushrie in the

[82] Extract from *The Times*, September 24, 1907, *Schofield IV*, 174–76.
[83] Spring-Rice to Grey, Gulahek, September 19, 23, 1907, *Schofield IV*, 173.
[84] Extract from *Novoye Vremya*, November 27 (December 10), 1907, *Schofield IV*, 240.

Persian Gulf. The parties were competing not only to build railroads but also to dominate the region economically, politically, and strategically. Berlin's donation to Tehran of a moderate banking concession and its appointment of a military attaché there only increased Russo-British trepidation.[85] The British foreign minister wanted the frontier settled before the Baghdad Railway reached the gulf. Hence, continuing to urge the Porte's withdrawal, London and Petersburg expressed their desire to participate in the delimitation by signaling that they would appoint commissioners.[86]

In the meantime, public opinion in Iran was increasingly anti-Ottoman. Fervor rose in the streets, along with a newfound patriotism. As Firoozeh Kashani-Sabet argues, in the midst of revolutionary change, the frontiers and their protection, concepts of citizenship, Iranian singularity (*mamlikat-i Iran*), and patriotic defense of the homeland penetrated intellectual and daily discourse.[87] At the same time, the intellectual milieu of the constitutional revolution, aided by the Ottoman occupation, began to alienate non-Shiʻi elements of society. As Kasahani-Sabet notes:

> Iranians increasingly had to adopt "Persian" and "Shiʻi" characteristics to become involved in constitutional politics. The supplementary laws, for instance, had declared Twelver Shiʻism the official religion of Iran. Whereas before, diversity was an attribute of Iranian unity, now ethnic difference threatened cultural homogeneity, which would be achieved through propagation of the Persian language and Twelver Shiʻism. In an attempt to stimulate national unity, constitutional institutions imposed a cultural order that privileged the Persian and Shiʻi heritage of some Iranians over the legacy of the others.[88]

No doubt these trends further estranged those Kurds already distraught by Tehran's Shiʻi push into Kurdistan. Their alienation helps us better understand both the anti-constitutionalism and the pro-Ottomanism increasingly prevalent in Iranian Kurdistan.

Since December 1906, Ottoman aggression had become a fairly regular topic in the Iranian parliament, and thus in the public discourse. The parliament's newspaper, for example, noted that the dispute centered on

---

[85] Extract from *Times*, 24 September 1907, "The Turco-Persian Frontier Question," *Schofield IV*, 174–76.

[86] Grey to O'Conor, September 14, 1907; O'Conor to Grey, September 15, 1907, *Schofield IV*, 170–71.

[87] Kashani-Sabet, *Frontier Fictions*, 107–8. Kashani-Sabet's account provides a thorough analysis of the Iranian press of the time, which I relied on here.

[88] Ibid., 111.

the Ottoman breach of an 1869 agreement to preserve the status quo and on Ottoman claims to the Urumiyeh-Savojbulagh region. Newspapers and satirical journals reminded their readers of Ottoman disregard of Iran's rights and territorial integrity. Some articles insightfully suggested that the Ottomans tried to avenge their European "injuries" in Iran. The occupation also brought back memories of the Safavid-Ottoman wars and reignited long-held animosities. At a time when the two European powers were dividing Iran into spheres of influence, another beleaguered Islamic state's territorial encroachment was all the more difficult to accept. It was even rumored that Russia and England were prepared to concede a sphere of influence to Turkey.[89] The situation was of concern, not only to politicians but to ordinary people as well. The people of Kermanshah, for example, asked the British consul there why Britain allowed the occupation, reminding him that according to the Anglo-Russian Convention, it was his duty to protect Iranian frontiers.[90] The so-called crisis of Urumiyah also troubled the wider Shi'i community, as it threatened the honor of Islam (*namus-i Islam*) – presumably Shi'i Islam. Tehran's dependency on Russia and Britain, its inability to protect its *sarhaddat*, and the Kurdo-Ottoman advance all brought to the fore the government's ineffectiveness and lack of military power. These, in turn, made the state's modernization and the frontier's finalization top priorities.[91]

Iranian resentment peaked toward the end of 1907, when the president of the Iranian parliament sought the British representative's personal opinion as to the advisability of armed resistance on the frontier. The representative responded that it would be disastrous, yet public opinion was highly agitated in Tabriz and Isfahan, where the "[Aghas] organized a monster demonstration to protest against the Turkish advance, and to call on the Government to take active steps against the Turkish encroachments."[92] Soon the Iranian parliament passed a national law declaring that "the boundaries of Iran and its provinces (*vilayat*), its states (*iyalat*), and its districts (*bulukat*) are immutable except on the basis of law."[93] Despite such largely rhetorical moves, however, Tehran, realizing that the

[89] Marling to Grey, October 10, 1907, *Schofield IV*, 220; Browne, *Persian Revolution*, 131.

[90] Haworth to Marling, Kashr-i Shirin, February 27, 1908, *Schofield IV*, 293.

[91] This paragraph is adapted from Kashani-Sabet, *Frontier Fictions*, chap. 4, esp. 114, 120, 128–29. Kashani-Sabet's chap. 4 "Political Parables: Iran's Frontier Crucible, 1906–1914" provides an in-depth account of Iranian responses to the Ottoman occupation as well as the larger developments surrounding Iran.

[92] Marling to Grey, October 7, 10, 1907, *Schofield IV*, 213, 220.

[93] Kashani-Sabet, *Frontier Fictions*, 115.

Ottoman end goal was to carry out a plan of annexation, faced a dilemma. Sending troops would give its rivals another excuse for invasion. Inaction would allow them to affirm the occupation as necessary for the tranquility of the region. Conscious of Iran's paralysis, the Ottomans and the Kurds who acted as their vanguard advanced farther into Azerbaijan, underscoring the occupation's sectarian nature.[94]

British representatives now also understood that the Porte's objective was annexation, not to build a strategic bulwark against Russia, as they had long surmised. As the signs of this plan multiplied, both London and St. Petersburg continued to worry that anti-Ottoman feeling in Iran would increase anti-British and anti-Russian sentiments, thus forcing them to confirm their intention of protecting Iran's territorial integrity. Because military intervention was not an option, finalizing the boundary emerged as the only way of preventing annexation.[95] Russia, in particular, pressed the Porte to agree to another frontier commission because of its fears that the occupation would lay the Caucasus open to a flank attack. Britain, feeling "bound to support Russia and Persia" after its 1907 agreement, concurred. It was thus decided that the British consul-general in Tabriz, Albert C. Wratislaw, and the Russian vice-consul in Urumieh, Baron Tcherkassov, would act as de facto members of the ineffective Ottoman-Iranian frontier commission.[96] Istanbul reappointed Tahir Pasha as its commissioner, even as its troops continued to push east and south. Tehran's representative, Muhtashamu as- Saltanah, arrived in Urumieh on December 22, 1907.[97]

Tired of commissions that led nowhere, some British diplomats believed that to reach a final solution on the frontier, "arbitration must be conceded to supersede mediation for the determination of final issues not otherwise reconcilable."[98] The growing push for arbitration, which had been on the table for a long time, coincided with the emergence of that crucial element of future Middle East politics: oil. Senior British diplomat Alwyn Parker argued that after sixty-four years of unsuccessful and costly efforts, and with the understanding that Great Britain and Russia expressly recognized the integrity of Persia, they had the right to energetically pursue

[94] Marling to Grey, Tehran, December 31, 1907, *Schofield IV*, 252.
[95] Memorandum Respecting the Turco-Persian Frontier Dispute, FO, October 14, 1907, *Schofield IV*, 215.
[96] Wratislaw, *A Consul*, 232.
[97] Browne, *Persian Revolution*, 156.
[98] Kemball to FO, September 14, 1907, *Schofield IV*, 164.

the finalization of the frontier. He added that the protection of "the D'Arcy petroleum wells at Mendali" at a time "when German enterprise is becoming more active every year" required Persia's suzerainty to be definitively recognized.[99] But London had to walk a thin line. While pressing for delimitation and keeping Russia in check and Iran under control, it also needed to avoid irritating Istanbul, because "British interests, and more especially, our chance of securing the Mesopotamian oil-fields for British concessionaires, will suffer seriously."[100] The combination of these factors made delimitation a necessity. This, however, required Ottoman consent.

RESPONSES TO THE OCCUPATION

In spite of a discourse of religious solidarity, not all Iranian Kurds welcomed the Ottoman occupation. Sheikh Mahmud Saddin, a landlord who was Sheikh Ubeidullah's cousin, claimed that "no one in those districts who was not an outlaw, wished the Turks to come, that they were Persians, and although the Persian might not be the best of Governments, they would rather have anything than the Turks."[101] According to Wratislaw, landowners, ecclesiastics, and officials in Urumieh opposed the Ottoman advance because it undermined their interests, whereas the town-dwelling lower classes remained indifferent and unaffected. Wratislaw went on to note that because of lower taxes and an improvement in security, the peasantry was well disposed toward the Ottomans. Indeed, the inhabitants of some villages in places such as Bradost had invited the occupation, and others had extended invitations yet to be answered. Wratislaw added, however, that Christian villages preferred Persian administration.[102]

As we saw in the previous chapter, sectarian tension was not a new phenomenon in the borderland. In the period following the Crimean War, various factors contributed to its rise. However, in the 1890s, it gained a new urgency as a result of various factors, including the rising role of Iranian *mujtahid*s in Iraq,[103] who were reportedly trying to lure the

---

[99] Further Memorandum on the Turco-Persian Boundary Questions (February to September 1907), *Schofield IV*, 166–69.
[100] O'Conor to Grey, Constantinople, September 15, 1907, *Schofield IV*, 164.
[101] Report by Vice-Consul Dickson on His Recent Journey through Turco-Persian Territory, December 14, 1907, *Schofield IV*, 265.
[102] Wratislaw to Marling, October 25, 1907, *Schofield IV*, 242–45.
[103] For Istanbul's inquiry regarding the number of *mujtahid*s in Baghdad, see BOA.YPRK. SRN 3/19, December 8, 1891.

sultan's Shi'i subjects to the shah;[104] Iranian attempts to introduce Shi'i symbols and ceremonies into Sunni Iran; and, as Kasravi notes, the ritual cursing by *la'natchi*s of "historical figures of the dawn of Islam."[105] Amir Nizam's appointment as *wali* of Kurdistan and his attempts to organize Shi'i ceremonies in places such as Saqqez and Baneh, in conjunction with the resurgence of *Omar Kushan* (the ritual destruction of the effigy of Omar, the second caliph) in Azerbaijan, resulted in sectarian clashes that further strained relations between government officers and the populace.[106] Consequently, various tribes expressed a desire to take refuge in the Ottoman Empire.[107] In November 1899, for example, the people of Savojbulagh appealed to their Ottoman consulate to ask the ambassador to Tehran to intervene to stop their oppression (*zulm va taaddi, harekat-ı gaddarane*). They also sent a deputation to Hakkari's *mutasarrıf* complaining of unbearable oppression by extremist Shi'i officials (*me'murin-i müteassıbe-i Şi'iye*).[108] They added that if the caliph would not accept them as citizens or take other action to protect their honor, they would initiate a revolt like that of Sheikh Ubeiduallh or take refuge in Russia. The petitioners then took refuge in the consulate, demanding and receiving the removal of the city's *hakim* or governor.[109]

Several years later, the occupation had further strengthened sectarian boundaries, exacerbating the uncertainty faced by borderlanders already living with the ongoing complexities created by indefinite national boundaries. Still, appeals like those made by the people of Savojbulagh were not limited to the disputed frontier region. In June 1902, the Sunni *ulama* and notables of Ardabil appealed to the Ottoman embassy in Tehran, complaining of attempts to forcefully convert Sunnis to Shi'ism.[110] Similarly, in 1908, the Taleshi Sunnis of Resht province (who first asked for asylum from Shi'i oppression in 1890)[111] sent a letter stamped by eighty-six individuals to the

---

[104] For ayatollahs' activities in Samarra, see BOA.YPRK.SRN 4/68, July 30, 1894. For a report explaining Ayatollah Mirza Hasan Shirazi's efforts to spread Shi'ism in Iraq, see BOA.Y. PRK 31/8, May 15, 1895. For later activities, see BOA.Y.A.HUS 453/4, July 26, 1903.

[105] Ahmad Kasravi, *History of the Iranian Constitutional Revolution* (Costa Meza: Mazda Publishers, 2006), 157–58.

[106] BOA.Y.PRK.EŞA 18/78, October 29, 1893.

[107] BOA.Y.A.HUS 390/48, August 18, 1896.

[108] BOA.Y.PRK.UM 48/25, October 8, 1899.

[109] BOA.Y.A.HUS 401/43–44–122, November 18, 1899.

[110] BOA.Y.A.HUS 430/62, July 15, 1902. The Ottoman prime ministry declared this counter to the principle of freedom of belief, and because Shi'is in Ottoman lands freely practiced their religion, it advised Tehran to extend the same right to Sunnis in Iran.

[111] BOA.Y.A.HUS 311/6, July 2, 1896.

Ottoman consulate at Tbilisi to petition for the protection of forty thousand members of their community against the humiliation they suffered at the hands of the Qajar government. The Porte responded that because they lived inside Iran, any attempt to protect them would be against international law. However, "if any of them seek refuge in our side, they would be treated as refugees and protected as such."[112]

Meanwhile, in November 1907, the situation in Savojbulagh reignited when the region's governor was forced to flee under threat by the Mangur chief Baiz Agha, now an Ottoman pasha. Afterward, some of the town's inhabitants, almost all Sunni Kurds, presented a *dekhalet* to the Ottoman commander at Pesveh, Mehmet Fazıl Pasha, for Ottoman nationality. Their request was forwarded to Istanbul.[113] Encouraged by such petitions, Tahir Pasha reiterated his claim that according to the 1639 treaty, "all the sanjaks of Kurdistan, including ... the inhabitants of the Kurdish villages scattered about the Urumia plain," had been under Ottoman possession until the beginning of the nineteenth century.[114]

FIGURE 4. Group of children at Savojbulagh, 1914.
Finnish Museum of Photography, Alexander Iyas Collection 173.

---

[112] BOA.HR.SYS 690/2, p. 3, November 1908.
[113] BOA HR SYS 742/84, Ottoman deputy consul of Soujboulagh's letter, February 23, 1908; Wratislaw to Marling, Urmi, December 28, 1907, *Schofield IV*, 271–72.
[114] O'Conor to Grey, Constantinople, January 1, 1908, *Schofield IV*, 251; O'Conor to Grey, February 1, 1908, *Schofield IV*, 260; O'Conor to Grey, February 3, 1908, *Schofield IV*, 261.

In early January 1908, while the Savojbulaghis were waiting for the sultan's reply, Prince Farmanfarma, the governor-general of Azerbaijan entered their district with between three thousand and five thousand soldiers and pillaged about twenty Sunni villages that had applied for Ottoman *teba'iyyet*, killing several individuals. Rebuffing the ensuing entreaties for help (*feryatnameler*), the local Ottoman commander claimed to lack sufficient troops and means of transportation. Baiz Agha, however, did not wait for troops or Kurds from the Ottoman side to come to the rescue. Writing to Savojbulagh's Sheikh-ul-Islam, he threatened to attack "if the citizens do not expel Farmanfarma from the city." At first, the governor general, with the help of pro-Iranian Kurds, attempted to stand his ground. Soon, however, facing attacks from the Mangurs and their Mamesh, Gowrik, and Dehbokri allies, and under pressure from Ferik Mehmet Fazıl Pasha, he left for Mianduab, accompanied by Iranian merchants and government officials. The Kurds, along with Ottoman officers, took his place. Two days later, Mehmed Fazıl arrived. Yet, under Iranian, British, and Russian pressure, Ottoman forces withdrew after only one month, on February 22, 1908.[115] It appears that during the brief occupation, Fazil Pasha lost the people's support by carrying out harsh policies, including pillaging the homes of officials and wealthy villagers. The town's newly approved Ottoman citizens told a different story, claiming the pasha ended the misdeeds of officials and *agha*s, who held a grudge against him as a result. After the withdrawal, the town again came under tentative Iranian control. The countryside, however, continued to identify with the Ottomans.[116]

Although Sunni Kurds were still utterly divided in their choices of belonging, the Shi'i Kurdish tribes of the frontier's middle zone – including the extensive Sanjabi, Zanganah, and Kalhor federations – unwaveringly supported Tehran. Even when most of the Sanjabis were wintering in their traditional Ottoman pastures, their chief, the Governor of Qasr-i Shirin, Samsam el-Mamalik, contemplated resisting the Turks if asked to do so by the shah.[117] Similarly, the wali of Posht-e Kuh was ready to defend the

[115] H. Diran Melik Vartanian (M.D. and British informer working with Persian army) to Vice-Consul Stevens, Mianduab, January 29, 1908, *Schofield IV*, 277–79. Also Browne, *Persian Revolution*, 198. Irfa'a al-Dowleh, the Iranian ambassador to Istanbul, claimed credit for Fazil Pasha's withdrawal. See Irfa' al-Dowleh to Iranian Ministry of Foreign Affairs, April 1907, *Gozidah-'i Asnad*, vol. 6, Document No: 1021, pp. 25–30.
[116] Savojbulagh's Ottoman shehbender reported on the general situation in the region; see BOA.HR.SYS 728/9, July 22, 1910.
[117] Wratislaw to Marling, Urmia, January 30, 1908, *Schofield IV*, 280. For Sanjabi's defense of the Iranian *sarhadd*, see 'Ali Akbar Khan Sardar Moqtadir Sanjabi, *Il-e Sanjabi va Mojahadate Melli-e Iran*, Karim Sanjabi, ed. (Tehran: Shiraze, 1380).

shah's domain at Badrai with several thousand *sowar*s, or horsemen. The Kalhor chief, Daoud Khan, boasted that he could take Khanikin in a day. The Zanganah chief, Zahir-ul-Mulk (also the governor of Kermanshah and a frontier commander) made similarly aggressive assertions; Captain Haworth, the British consul of Kermanshah, claimed to have had to convince him that Iran could not compete with the Ottoman Empire.[118]

Support for Tehran and Qajar rule was not as strong in the south. Aware of the Ottoman elimination of local dynasties and grandees, and fearing a similar fate, the Bakhtiyari Khans and the Sheikh of Muhammarah applied to the government of India for closer relations and guarantees of autonomy.[119] The chiefs of the Baktiyari tribe, which in the following year played a significant role in the Iranian constitutional revolution, spoke to British representatives of their utter dissatisfaction with Qajar rule. Aware of British relations with Kuwait and Muscat, the Bakhtiari and the Ka'b expressed interest in becoming quasi-independent British protectorates. In response, the British reassured them that they would take firm steps to prevent any serious disturbance of the status quo.[120] Criticized for taking no action against the Ottoman occupation, British Foreign Minister Grey informed his diplomats that England would defend Muhammarah if the need arose. However, because the currently occupied districts did not contain any British oil concessions and were in the Russian sphere of influence, London could not "take the initiative, as it would not be limited to the frontier and might give rise to trouble and excitement in Egypt and elsewhere." However, to offer Persia "protection against flagrant and unprovoked violations of her territory," he promised to support any initiative taken by Russia.[121]

At the same time that these exchanges were taking place, in May 1909, Percy Cox, the British representative for the south of Iran, visited the Sheikh of Muhammarah to negotiate on behalf of the Anglo-Persian Oil

[118] Haworth to Marling, Kashr-i Shirin, February 27, 1908, *Schofield IV*, 293.

[119] For Bakhtiari relations with the British, see Arash Khazeni, *Tribes and Empire* (Seattle: University of Washington Press, 2010), chap. 4. For Britain in South Persia, see Shahbaz Shahnavaz, *Britain and the Opening of South-West Persia 1880–1914* (London: Routledge-Curzon, 2005).

[120] Memorandum by P. Z. Cox, January 7, 1908, *Schofield IV*, 303–4; and Captain Lorimer to Cox, February 3, 1908, *Schofield IV*, 305–6. Marling to Grey, Tehran, April 23, 1908, *Schofield IV*, 310. For the Ka'b sheikh's relations with the British, see, among numerous, Cox to Marling, Bushrie, January 18, 1908, *Schofield IV*, 257; and from viceroy, July 10, 1908, *Schofield IV*, 326.

[121] Reports by Vice-Consul Dickson, Military Report, Van, March 15, 1908, *Schofield IV*, 310–16; Grey to O'Beirne (British ambassador to Russia), June 22, 1908, *Schofield IV*, 321.

Company. Fearing the inevitable domination that would come as a result, the sheikh asked for guarantees for his own and his heirs' hereditary and customary rights. These guarantees secured, he sold to the company "full way-leave for the pipe-line and sold the land they required, on the understanding that it would revert to him when the concession expired."[122] Such agreements with local rulers, however, did not mark the end of the frontier commissions.

COMMISSIONS AND CLAIMS: THE 1908 FRONTIER COMMISSION

Accompanied by the Russian and British representative, the Ottoman-Iranian commissioners reconvened in March 1908, and the Ottomans once more insisted that the 1639 rather than the 1847 treaty be the basis of negotiations, as the latter dealt only with Muhammarah, Zohab, and Kotur. The Iranians responded that this was because the Erzurum Conferences had settled all other frontier questions and highlighted only those places still in dispute.[123] Such wrangling had two root causes: the question of Kurdistan and the redefinition of the Ottoman citizenship project. The latter had been underway since the 1877–78 Russo-Ottoman War and had the Sunni Muslims at its core. Ottoman diplomats privileged the 1639 treaty because they believed it defined the frontier on the principle of distinction of religion. If it was insufficiently explicit regarding the northern portion of the frontier, that was because the region was so incontestably Ottoman that further explanation was unnecessary, beyond the statement that "the Shiis are not to interfere" and assurances by Iran that it would not interfere with the Kurds, "who are ours." Moreover, they claimed that Iran had reconfirmed its noninterference in the 1823 treaty. Using the *dekhalet* petitions as proof of the enduring ties that bound Iranian Kurds to their former sovereign, the Ottoman commissioner argued that although Iran may have seduced them in the early nineteenth century, "now the Kurds have returned to their ancient allegiance to the Sultan." As Iran had never profited from the Kurds, he requested, "in the name of Islam and humanity, that no obstacle will be placed in the way of a period of prosperity to assure peace and security along this part of the

---

[122] Arnold T. Wilson, *S. W. Persia: A Political Officer's Diary* (London: Oxford University Press, 1941), 93.

[123] Memorandum Communicated by Ottoman Government to Persian Ambassador at Constantinople, April 1908, *Schofield IV*, 307–8.

frontier."[124] In the same manner, Ottoman officials in occupied towns asked local Iranian authorities not to meddle in the "internal" affairs of the Empire, whereas Tahir Pasha requested that Tehran stay out of the affairs of "our Kurds." All of these authorities strove to make religious difference the principle by which territory would be divided. Accordingly, in July 1908, Sunni villages scattered about the plain of Urumieh were informed that they would pass under the benevolent sway of the sultan. The inhabitants of Anzel likewise were told they had been annexed to the Ottoman Empire; within weeks, the *kaimmakam* of Gever began collecting taxes from them.[125] By the end of the same month, Urumieh was cut off from the remainder of Azerbaijan on all sides except that of the lake.[126] Soon afterward, Kerim Agha, the Herki chief, was appointed *mudir* of Baranduz, and local peasants were ordered to cease paying taxes to the shah.[127]

In response, the Iranian commissioner Muhtasham-as-Saltanah again urged his rivals to cease provoking the Kurds and interfering in Iranian affairs, for Tehran believed that Ottoman authorities such as Ferik Fazil were inciting Kurdish attacks on villages on the banks of Urumieh to compel their alliance and aid.[128] The commissioner also challenged the historicity of Ottoman claims, arguing that the Kurds were of Iranian origin and spoke the ancient language of Persia. Both the 1823 and 1847 treaties explicitly affirmed that both states had dependent Kurdish tribes; thus, to challenge the historicity of his rival's claims, he argued that "the Ottoman Turks are parvenus in Asia compared to the Persians, and as such any claim they make to territory once belonging to the latter must be proved up to the hilt."[129] Additionally, he maintained, Ottoman support of Sunnis in one region alone did not make sense because Sunnis were scattered throughout Iran. The urgency of such debates and even of the Ottoman incursions into Urumieh was diminished by the fateful events of July 1908, when the Iranian constitutional revolution suffered a serious reversal just as monumental changes were brewing in Istanbul.

[124] Memorandum Handed on the 26 Kanun-i-Sani 1323, by Imperial Ottoman Commission of Inquiry to Imperial Persian Commission of Azerbaijan, *Schofield IV*, 289; Wratislaw to Marling, Urumia, July 12, 1908, *Schofield IV*, 336–38.
[125] Wratislaw to Marling, Urumia, July 12, 1908, *Schofield IV*, 336–38.
[126] Barclay to Grey, July 26, 1908, *Schofield IV*, 331.
[127] Wratislaw to Marling, Urumia, August 10, 1908, *Schofield IV*, 343.
[128] Note Communicated by Persian Ambassador to Ottoman Government, End of June 1908, *Schofield IV*, 323.
[129] Wratislaw to Marling, Urumia, July 12, 1908, *Schofield IV*, 336–38; Wratislaw to Marling, Urmia, August 10, 1908, *Schofield IV*, 343.

THE END OF ABDULHAMID II'S REIGN, THE CUP, AND THE BORDERLAND

The Iranian revolutionaries were dealt a crushing blow by the June 23, 1908, coup and the bombardment of the parliament, which ushered in a period known as Minor Despotism, lasting until July 16, 1909. With the fall of Tehran, Tabriz emerged as the new center of the revolutionary activity of the banned *anjuman*. To complicate matters, shortly after the bombardment, Britain struck oil at Masjid-i Sulayman, in an area of southern Iran that fell under the 1901 D'Arcy concession. While Russia continued its strong military presence in northern Iran, in Istanbul Abdulhamid II was forced to reopen the defunct parliament on July 23, 1908, reinstituting the constitution he had suspended more than thirty years previously. Now a constitutional monarchy, the Ottoman government introduced further reforms promising equality before the law without distinction of race or religion. Constitutionalists in Iran were encouraged by these events and expected that the Hamidian borderland policies would also be reversed.[130]

To be sure, at the beginning of their rule, the members of the CUP expressed sympathy for the Iranian revolutionaries and seemed eager to settle the frontier dispute. The Porte gave St. Petersburg and London formal assurances that the troops would be recalled and a frontier satisfactory to both parties delimitated. In fact, Ottoman troops did withdrew from some districts,[131] and the Young Turk Ottoman chargé d'affaires at St. Petersburg offered assurances that he welcomed the friendly mediation of Russia and Britain as essential for peace.[132]

In line with these gestures, and to everyone's surprise, at the end of August the expansionist Tahir Pasha was instructed to rejoin his post in Bitlis. This marked the end of the 1908 frontier commission. The other war party hard-liners, Izzet and Fehim Pashas, also left the frontier as the CUP's power extended. Soon thereafter, the Council of Ministers ordered most remaining troops to withdraw. As it turned out, however, that withdrawal was not comprehensive, and the expansionists began to organize their resistance. According to Wratislaw's reports, small numbers of troops remained to encourage the region's inhabitants to continue obeying the newly authorized Kurdish chiefs. Moreover, before leaving, Izzet Pasha

[130] Browne, *Persian Revolution*, 250.
[131] Nicholson to Grey, St. Petersburg, August 26, 1908; Marling to Grey, Gulahek, August 14, 1908, *Schofield IV*, 335–36.
[132] Nicholson to Grey, St. Petersburg, August 22, 1908, *Schofield IV*, 339.

had told the Herki and Begzadeh chiefs that without annexing additional Iranian territory, they "should repulse by force any attempt on the part of the Persians to regain what was already occupied."[133]

Nevertheless, for a short time it seemed that revolutionary solidarity was penetrating the frontier region. For example, bands of Hamidieh that crossed into Iran to help the Khan of Maku, a loyalist at the time, were taken into custody upon returning to the Ottoman side. It was even reported that the CUP sent a group of *silahşor*, or men at arms, to help the Iranian constitutionalists overthrow the shah. Headed by the CUP strongman Enver Pasha's uncle Halil, thirty members of the group crossed into Iran, where Halil met with the leaders of the Jalali, Haydaran, Takori, Milan, Shemski, and Hazeran tribes to convince them to join the pro-constitutionalist side.[134] To study the changing situation, a new Iranian-Ottoman commission, with Danyal Pasha as the Ottoman representative, was established in October 1908, with no results. Soon thereafter, reports emerged of new attempts to distribute Ottoman passports and intimidate borderlanders into soliciting Ottoman citizenship.[135]

Such reports were followed by drastic changes in the Ottoman Empire's western frontiers, which put an end to the already tenuous solidarity between constitutionalists on its eastern edges. Austria's occupation of Bosnia-Herzegovina in October 1908 was crucial to this shift. The opposition blamed this event on CUP ineptitude and on April 13, 1909, orchestrated a coup. Two weeks later, the CUP staged a countercoup, which allowed it to dethrone Abdulhamid II, punish the loyalists, and extend martial law. The struggle between the monarchists and the increasingly dictatorial and Turkish nationalist CUP was just getting started.[136] Meanwhile, Iranian freedom fighters from Tabriz, Ghilan, and Bakhtiyari-Isfahan had begun marching toward Tehran a few months earlier, in February 1909. Forcing the withdrawal of foreign troops – Ottoman, as well as Russian ones that arrived in Tabriz, Qazvin, and other frontier towns

[133] Wratislaw to Marling, Urmi, September 24, 1908, *Schofield IV*, 346.
[134] Halil [Kut] Paşa, *İttihat ve Terakki'den Cumhuriyet'e Bitmeyen Savaş* (Istanbul: Kamer, 1997), 59–73; and Şevket Süreyya Aydemir, *Makedonya'dan Ortaasya'ya Enver Paşa*, v. 2, 117–21.
[135] Note Communicated by Prince M. Riza Khan to Ottoman Government, November 10, 1908; Its Enclosure Telegram from Persian Ministry for FA to Prince M. Riza Khan, and Ala-us-Sultaneh to Barclay, November 4, 1908, *Schofield IV*, 348–49. Browne, *Persian Revolution*, 297.
[136] Aykut Kansu, *Politics in Post-Revolutionary Turkey 1908–1913* (Leiden: Brill, 2000), chap. 3.

in late 1908[137] – was high on their agenda. By mid-July, they had taken the capital under control. Delegates from the dissolved Majlis then gathered to form an assembly that deposed Muhammad 'Ali Shah on July 18, 1909, and named his twelve-year-old son, Ahmad Shah, the new king. The end of the Minor Despotism in Iran thus coincided with the end of the thirty-three-year absolute monarchy of Abdulhamid II.

With Iran ruled by an infant king and embroiled in revolutionary war, Istanbul, firmly under CUP control, definitively terminated its policy of revolutionary solidarity and took Abdulhamid's expansionism to a new level. In the summer of 1909, it increased its forces in Urumieh, occupying villages as far as Urumieh Lake.[138] Soon afterward, it took Savojbulagh and Salmas. In Savojbulagh, customhouses were established and the Ottoman consular agent invited applications for Ottoman nationality. Similarly, Ottoman passports were distributed and sold in Urumieh. Alarmed, a group of Urumians sent a delegation to Tabriz to complain about "the Kurdish raids and continual encroachments of the Turks." Some Urumians even discussed taking "a general bast [refuge] in the Russian Vice-Consulate" and asked the Russian Consul to send three hundred soldiers to aid them.[139]

Encouraged by such appeals and by continuing Russo-British influence, patriotic Iranian journals called on the people to protect Mother Iran's chastity from foreign violations. Such rhetoric reinforced the relationship between borders and nationalism.[140] Indeed, the Ottoman occupation was becoming a defining element of the Iranian nationalism of the period. Cognizant of this, London and St. Petersburg issued a joint memorandum to Istanbul, underscoring their guarantee of Iran's integrity and independence and accusing the Ottomans of provoking Kurdish attacks to force people to ask for protection and citizenship. They then demanded, once more, that the Porte refrain from interfering in Iranian affairs, cease forcing people to petition for citizenship, and withdraw its troops.[141] Assuming a conciliatory tone, the Ottoman grand vizier emphasized three reasons for not withdrawing: the absence of government authority in Iran, the lack of any guarantee that Russia would not occupy evacuated

---

[137] Browne gives their number at more than six thousand. See *Persian Revolution*, 297.
[138] Farajullah Hosseini, Istanbul, to IMFA, May 30, 1909, in *Gozidah-'i Asnad*, vol. 6, Document No: 1027, pp. 58–62.
[139] PRO.FO 371/710, Barclay to Grey, Gulahek, June 4, 11, 1909.
[140] Kashani-Sabet, *Frontier Fictions*, 135.
[141] BOA.HR.SYS 673/36, July 14, 1909.

territories, and the fear that withdrawal would leave the territory's Sunni inhabitants at the mercy of the Shi'is.[142]

The Russians opined that such foot dragging was motivated by plans to extend the occupation of Urumieh all the way to the lake. They were proven right when the Ottoman governor of the neighboring province of Van visited Urumieh to arrange the territory's administration from the *vilayat* of Van to "the new frontier," apparently Urumieh Lake.[143]

As more Ottoman troops were sent to the border, London once more suggested the appointment of a boundary commission.[144] Before any action could be taken, however, another political crisis erupted – namely, the revolt in northern Albania that began in the spring of 1910. Revolts in Macedonia and Yemen followed, and dissatisfaction with the CUP's centralist, nationalist policies rose among non-Turkish communities, including those of Arabs, Greeks, Kurds, and Bulgarians.[145] The year 1910 witnessed renewed crisis in Iran as well. The turning point came with a British ultimatum, backed by Russia and issued on October 14, 1910, that gave Iran three months to secure southern trade routes carrying British goods from tribal attacks. If Tehran did not comply, Britain would regulate the Bushrie-Isfahan road using a local police force placed under the authority of officers from India. Despite its claims to have only safety in mind, Britain's stance was seen as a first step toward direct occupation. As such, it caused great indignation and diverted attention from the Ottoman occupation, as Iranians in Istanbul organized a large protest meeting at the Odeon Theater in Pera. Their organization, *Anjuman-i Sa'adat*, sent a telegram to the kaiser, urging him to "resume his role as savior of a Moslem State."[146]

Soon after, at a Conference of Muslims in Istanbul, Iranian, Ottoman, and Caucasian intellectuals condemned the British ultimatum, spoke against Russia's continued occupation of Iran, and criticized the imperialist discourse of the civilizing mission. The speeches were published in various journals and subsequent protests were held in Tehran.[147] Such protests, however, did not stop the tsar and kaiser from meeting in

---

[142] Lowther to Grey, Constantinople, January 25, 1910, *Schofield IV*, 397.
[143] PRO.FO 371/710 Acting Consul-General Smart to Barclay, Tabriz, September 15, 1909.
[144] BOA.HR.SYS 683/8, December 9, 1909. Harding made this proposal to Tevfik Pasha.
[145] Kansu, *Politics*, 187; and Reynolds, *Shattering*, chaps. 2–3.
[146] John Gurney, "E. G. Browne and the Iranian Community in Istanbul," in Thierry Zarcone and Fariba Zarinebaf-Shahr, eds., *Les Iraniens D'Istanbul* (Istanbul-Teheran: IFEA/IFRI, 1993), 170.
[147] Afary, *The Iranian Constitutional Reform*, 305–8.

Potsdam to discuss Russo-German rapprochement and the German advance into the region. Germany agreed to recognize the Russian sphere of influence in return for economic concessions. In addition to the Baghdad railway concession, it was agreed that a new railroad from Khanaqin to Tehran would be jointly financed but would remain under Russian control.[148] At around the same time, Germany also asked Ottoman authorities to solve the frontier question, in order to put a stop to Russo-English actions in Iran.[149]

London protested the meeting at the Odeon Theater, which was well publicized in England, and questioned the image of the kaiser whom the protesters called "le Protecteur Providentiel du monde Musulman." Such demonstrations did indeed embolden Tehran, which sent a new governor to Fars and two thousand troops to the south to counter the British ultimatum and show its sovereignty.[150] Meanwhile, facing London's protests, Istanbul was forced to take a position. Confidential letters between the OMFA and the *sadrazam* show that the Porte was relying on Russian assurances that its forces in Iran would provide security and on the Russo-British guarantee of Iranian independence, and that it was considering a policy of noninterference in Iranian affairs. This did not mean that Istanbul was abandoning its interests entirely. To the contrary, it strengthened its troops in the region while lobbying on behalf of the Iranian constitution. *Sadrazam* ordered officers and administrators in the disputed territories under Ottoman control to prevent any causes of complaint while reinforcing consulate guards in Salmas (also known as Dilman), Urumieh, and Khoi.[151] Istanbul was now differentiating between Iran and the *nevahi-i şarkıyye*: supporting the constitution did not mean surrendering what it saw as historically Ottoman territories usurped by the Qajars.

As the British and Russians continued to dominate their affairs, Iranian nationalists were becoming impatient with the Ottoman occupation. The journal *Bargh* (Barq), for example, published an article "Nos amis à double face," complaining that the Ottomans shed crocodile tears for Iran while continuing to encroach on its territories. The article condemned stories from Young Turk publications such as *La Turquie*, which claimed that Iranians eagerly welcomed Ottoman troops as the best guarantee

---

[148] Ibid., 309.
[149] For a meeting between the Ottoman ambassador and the German deputy-minister of FA, see HR.SYS 728/13, October 7, 1910.
[150] Afary, *The Iranian Constitutional Reform*, 305.
[151] BOA.HR.SYS 683/16, Sadaret to OMFA [undated] and Imperial Ottoman Embassy, London to Rifat Pasha, OMoFA, October 28, 1910.

against Russia, for providing false justification for the occupation. Playing on the Persian word "Rum," used to refer to the Ottomans as the Greeks of Anatolia, it ended with a quote from Virgil, *"Timeo Danaos et donna farantes"* ("I fear Greeks even when they bring gifts"), before wryly concluding, "C'est malheureux, mais c'est vrai."[152]

Nationalist and anti-imperialist agitation was cresting in Tehran, where one after another, similarly passionate anti-imperialist declarations of independence were issued. For example, "Expose du Meeting de la nation Persane du 17 Novembre 1910," printed on a large sheet of paper in Persian and French, declared that Iran was upholding "les idées de liberté, de justice et l'égalité" even as Russia and England continually impeded the march toward progress and civilization. Upholding the notion of "La Perse aux Persans," the declaration urged Iranians, the parliament, and all freedom-loving peoples to rid Iran of foreign troops.[153]

French-educated intellectuals were not alone in demanding an end to the occupation. For example, the ranking pro-constitutionalist clerics of Najaf, the *mujtahid* Ayatollahs Muhammad Kazim Khurasani, Mirza Hussain Tihrani, and Sheikh 'Abdullah Mazandarani continued to send letters, telegrams, and manifestos from Iraq encouraging "the Persian people in their struggle for freedom, and to neutralize the influence of reactionary ecclesiastics" and the shah.[154] The Ottoman Embassy in Tehran kept Istanbul abreast of these activities, as well as of the "vain manifestations" that took place in December 1910 in Najaf, Qom, Isfahan, Qazvin, Shiraz, Astrabad, Rasht, Hamadan, and Ardabil. Focusing on Iran's occupation by Russia and England, these protests culminated in the transmission of signed telegrams to newspapers, foreign embassies (including Istanbul's), and members of the Iranian cabinet and parliament. Almost all identical, the telegrams were dated December 15, written by *mujtahid*s Mazandarani and Khurasani, and transmitted by Tehran's Sadr al-ulama, Muhammad Ja'far al-Husayni. Their authors underscored the centrality of an *ulama* that could not remain indifferent to Russo-British attacks on Iran's sovereignty in the age of freedom. Despite the Great Powers' duplicity, the telegrams concluded, as long as Iranians are led by

---

[152] BOA.HR.SYS 728/14, October 29, 1910.
[153] BOA.HR.SYS 673/48.
[154] Browne, *Persian Revolution*, 262. For Ayatollahs Khurasani and Mazendarani's declarations dated June 25, 1910, see BOA.HRS.SYS 673/13. For the "Extraordinary Statement of Iran's Independence" [Varagae Fowqal'ade-e Esteghlale Iran] declaring the unity of Iranian *sardars*, see HR.SYS 673/26. For the 1910 text of a "Suret-e Meramname" distributed at Resht against Russian encroachments, see HR.SYS 672/74.

*mujtahid*s like them, they will defend their *"watan"* and *"hakimiyet-i milliye."* The signatories then asked for freedom-loving peoples around the world to help them liberate their country.[155]

The *mujtahids'* letter never explicitly referred to the Ottomans. Curiously, however, the *Agence Télégraphique de St. Pétersburg* interpreted it as such when it reported that the clergy and notables of the *ulama*, in response to an invitation to unite with the Turks to expel European troops, had agreed that the best way for Turkey to show its sincerity was to withdraw from the occupied territories.[156] Similar reports appeared in *Novoye Vremya*, which alleged that Iranians, indifferent to their nation's fate, welcomed British and especially Russian troops. The European powers respected Iran's integrity, the paper argued, claiming that in areas under Russian control, "Persian courts, administration, and police operate and we do not present any danger to the Persian frontiers." In contrast, the Ottomans not only occupied its Muslim neighbor's lands, but also levied taxes, opened schools, obliged youngsters to learn Turkish, and replaced Tehran's officers with members of the CUP. Istanbul's true plan, backed by Germany, was to subjugate all of Iran. When the Ottoman Embassy denied *Novoye Vremya*'s charges, the *Agence Télégraphique* joined the fray, providing names of Iranian officers replaced by the CUP in Khoi, Urumieh, and Mawana, and evidence of the arrival in Van of a group of propagandists headed for Iran.[157] The CUP responded (not unlike the Russians) by arguing that its troops were protecting local inhabitants and would withdraw after Russia vacated Azerbaijan.

The Ottoman thesis had some adherents in Iran. Emphasizing the ties that bound them, an article in *Soruosh* emphasized unity among the citizens of the Muslim nations, declared the interdependence of their independence, and accused Russian agents of spreading rumors about Ottoman transgressions.[158] This view was shared by the Ottoman military attaché to St. Petersburg, who reported that *Novoye Vremya* had previously published nearly identical telegrams regarding joint Ottoman-Kurdish attacks on Shi'i villages in Urumieh and Salmas.[159]

---

[155] BOA.HR.SYS 673/54, December 15, 1910, Hasib Bey to OMFA; the file includes copies of telegrams from various cities and *mujtahid*s.

[156] BOA.HR.SYS 711/2, January 25, 1911.

[157] BOA.HR.SYS 711/2, p. 7 Extracts from *Novoye Vremya*, January 22, 1911; and *Agence Télégraphique*, Février 22, 1911, p. 9.

[158] BOA.HR.SYS 728/21, Tehran Embassy to Rifat Pasha, December 17, 1910.

[159] BOA.HR.SYS 673/47, November 28, 1910.

SUNNI APPEALS TO THE CUP AND THE IMPENDING
END OF THE ANNEXATION

No doubt there was some truth to the assertions of *Bargh* and the Russian papers. But they presented only one side of the story of suffering on the borderland. Weary of Iran's division between the two great powers, Shi'i pressure, and revolutionary turmoil, which they saw as a Shi'i affair dominated by the ayatollahs, some Sunnis placed their hope in the caliph. A letter written by Sheikh Hasan, the ex-Sheikh al-Islam of Iranian Kurdistan, to Talat Pasha of the CUP, minister of the interior at the time, offers a good example of this position. In its descriptions of its author's petitions to the Ottoman government in 1908, and now in 1910, the letter exemplifies how Kurdish perceptions of Ottomans were changing. In 1908, suspicious that the British and Russians would eventually partition Iran, Hasan noted that the geographically important "Kurdistan kıt'ası" lay in the allegedly neutral zone between Tehran, Kermanshah, and Urumieh. In their naïve hearts, the people of this region nurtured feelings of religious fraternity toward the Ottomans. Hasan argued that England clearly wanted to include Baghdad and Basra within its sphere of influence, while also coveting Kermanshah. Russia, meanwhile, desired to win over the north. But into which hands, he wondered, would Kurdistan fall, being attached to neither Russia's nor England's sphere of influence? And what would happen to its people, who were of *ahl al-Sunna wal-Jama'ah*, after the lamentable partition took place? "We, the people of Kurdistan, have discovered the colonialist plots for the division of our country," the sheikh declared. "Hence, the ulama, notables, and people of Sinne, the center of Kurdistan," had authorized him to petition Istanbul for their inclusion in the domains of the caliph. The sheikh noted that he had come to Istanbul in 1908, when *hürriyet* was declared, to meet with the *sadrazam*, Kamil Pasha, but that no action had resulted because Kamil's cabinet fell in February 1909. Now, in 1910, he understood that Istanbul was not prepared to fully incorporate Kurdistan. Nevertheless, he wanted to suggest steps it could take to increase its influence in Kurdistan and Iran. These included the development of good relations with Karbala's and Najaf's *mujtahid*s, the opening of schools (including one for at least one hundred pupils in Sinne), the appointment of efficient and informed representatives to Tehran and Kurdistan, increasing the number of consular guards, providing the Sinne consulate with a doctor to serve the local people, and ensuring that officials and troops in the *nevahi-i cedide* treat people with compassion. Finally, and most importantly, he argued that the frontier should not be delimited, because this would facilitate Russian and British plots to partition the region by allowing them to further incite, and so manipulate, the "puppet Iranian government."[160]

Anticipating the Ottomans' inability to integrate Iranian Kurdistan, Sheikh Hasan thus asked, more modestly, for the protection of Sunnis and an increased Ottoman presence. Some influential figures in the region, however, were still hopeful that the occupation would result in permanent annexation. In a private meeting with the Ottoman consul, Mushir-i Divan, one of the most important notables of Sinne, observed that the region had between four hundred thousand and five hundred thousand Sunni inhabitants with close geographic and sectarian ties to the Ottomans and argued that a majority of its *ulama*, *a'yan*, and *tujjar* wanted to be included in the Ottoman Empire (*devlet-i aliye-i Osmaniye-ye dehalet*) However, he warned that some were becoming pro-Russian.[161] Around the same time, the Ottoman consul of Urumieh informed Istanbul of poignant letters from the Sunni villages of Dilbende-i Ulya and Ghehchin (Keçin?) complaining about attacks on their properties and lives.[162] Most such requests came from Sunni villages, but not all of them. In an effort to lighten its tax burden, for example, the Shi'i village of Moghanjik near Dilman informed the local Ottoman commander of its long-standing desire to be under the rule of the sultan. It even hoisted the Ottoman flag and refused to pay Iranian tax collectors but was unable to sway Ottoman authorities because it lay outside the status quo line.[163]

With or without such appeals, throughout 1911, Ottoman troops gradually expanded their influence over Saqqez, Baneh, Savojbulagh, and Bukan. Tehran complained that several Ottoman soldiers were dispatched to each occupied village of Saqqez to prevent Iranian officials from carrying out necessary business, including tax collection.[164] Istanbul also appointed what it called frontier commissioners, who in reality were military administrators. Colonel Ali Riza Bey, for example, was assigned in this capacity to a district that extended from Khoi to Pesveh, and Miralay Refik Bey to one reaching southward from Pesveh.[165] Russia closely monitored these activities and,

---

[160] BOA.HR.SYS 728/30, ex-Sheikh al-Islam of Kurdistan Sheikh Hasan to Minister of Interior [Talat Bey] August 30, 1910.

[161] BOA.HR.SYS 673/62, December 22, 1910. For pro-Russian Kurds, see Reynolds, *Shattering*, chap. 2.

[162] BOA.HR.SYS 675/30, August 23, 1910.

[163] For correspondence regarding Moghanjik, see BOA.HR.SYS 673/104, February-April 1911.

[164] BOA.HR.SYS 711/2, p. 261, Iranian Chargé d'Affaires to OMFA, February 10, 1911.

[165] Lowther to Grey, Pera, March 1, 1911, *Schofield IV*, 460.

noting that the "commissioners" continued to collect *dekhalet* petitions, its ambassador in Tehran warned his Ottoman counterpart that such acts would provoke Russia's military circles.[166] Large troop movements were reported from Kirkuk and Suleimanieh, chaos reined in Iran, and it was feared that Istanbul would further its advance.

Instead, it strengthened its grip on already occupied districts, in part by adopting some of Sheikh Hasan's suggestions. In early spring 1911, the consul of Savojbulagh convinced the town's ulama to read the name of the sultan instead of the shah during Friday *khutba*. Then, with money collected from the notables, the Council of Islamic Education (*Encümen-i Maarif-i Islamiye*) began to build a school, with plans to recruit teachers from the Ottoman Empire. With an eye to strengthening Sunni education, the Ottoman Ministry of Education collected two hundred Qur'ans, an equal number of *Qisas al-Anbiya* (*Legends of the Pre-Islamic Prophets*) and *Mukhtasar Tarikh-i Islam* (*Short History of Islam*) and many maps.[167] Opening schools pointed to a shift in Ottoman policy. Acknowledging the difficulty of retaining the new provinces and facing increased criticism of its occupation, Istanbul, mimicking the Great Powers, was moving away from expansion and toward the establishment of a sphere of influence. Plans were developed to open schools in Tabriz, Hamadan, and Sinne, under the conviction that such institutions would ensure continued adherence to Sunni beliefs and provide political as well as religious benefits. In the absence of modern Muslim institutions, opening "une institution séculaire Ottoman Azerbaïdjan et l'éducation en Turquie d'un certain nombre de Jeunes Persans" was seen as a way of increasing Ottoman presence in Iran, like the European countries were doing in Istanbul.[168] Yet another unexpected turn of events shattered these policies.

THE "INDEPENDENT" 1911 COMMISSION

Just as Istanbul was exploiting a debilitated Tehran, so Italy took advantage of a paralyzed Istanbul and, in late September 1911, occupied Tripolitania, the last Ottoman province in Africa. Meanwhile, the CUP's

---

[166] BOA.HR.SYS 674/21, Soujboulagh to Tehran Embassy March 17, 1911, and Embassy to OMFA, 2/May 19, 1911.

[167] BOA.HR.SYS, 674/5, April 17, 1911; OMFA to Ministry of Education, and Ministry of Education to OMFA. HR.SYS 674/27, Saujboulagh Consulate to Tehran Embassy, April 2, 1911.

[168] BOA.HR.SYS 674/27, May 23, 1911; Tehran Embassy to Rıfat Pasha, OMFA to Ministry of Education, April 21 and 28, 1911.

secretive Central Executive Committee was still governing under emergency rules, the Albanian revolt continued, and Bulgarian revolutionary propaganda activities in Macedonia intensified, paving the way for the debilitating Balkan Wars.[169] At the same time, an increasingly vocal opposition charged the CUP with chauvinism toward ethnic and religious minorities and, under the auspices of the newly established Entente Libérale or Hürriyet ve İtilaf Fırkası, began advocating administrative decentralization. In October, embattled on all sides and amid the crisis with Italy, Istanbul declared that Turkey "had no ambitious designs against any country or any state."[170]

The only country that must have taken notice of this declaration was likewise besieged, still mired in the struggle between constitutionalists and anti-constitutionalists. Discontent with the constitutional regime was growing amid the havoc wreaked by various tribes, the introduction of new taxes on the lower classes, and the subsequent bread riots that took place in Tehran in the spring of 1911.[171] On May 11, the American financial adviser Morgan Shuster accepted the role of treasurer general of Iran and struggled with British, Russians, and anti-constitutionalists to secure Iran's financial and political independence.

In the midst of widespread anarchy and aware that a major confrontation with Italy would require vast resources, Istanbul recognized the difficulty it would face trying to control its new provinces while also keeping Russia in check. Thus, it asked Tehran for the appointment of a joint delimitation commission and signaled its willingness to accept the 1847 treaty as the starting point. To diminish Russo-British interference, it also suggested that any unresolved disagreement be submitted to the Hague Tribunal.[172] However, no commission was formed because Tehran required the withdrawal of the Ottoman troops as a prerequisite, which did not happen. Observing the utterly debilitated state of the negotiating parties, London and St. Petersburg took the initiative to appoint their own joint commission and authorized Hammond Smith Shipley, the consul general at Tabriz, and Vladimir Fedorovitch Minorsky, the second dragoman at the Russian legation in Istanbul and later celebrated scholar, to investigate the situation in the western frontier districts of Azerbaijan.

---

[169] For this period as it related to Russo-Ottoman relations, see Reynolds, *Shattering*, 32–40.

[170] Aykut Kansu, *Politics in Post-Revolutionary Turkey, 1908–1913* (Boston: Brill, 2000), 179.

[171] Afary, *Iranian Constitutional Revolution*, 315.

[172] Barclay to Grey, Tehran, April 22, 1911; and Grey to Buchanan, April 24, 1911; *Schofield IV*, 470–71.

As Istanbul did not reply to an invitation to appoint its own commissioner, Tehran also refrained.

Shipley and Minorsky were to examine how far the Ottoman occupation and administration extended, uncover ultimate Ottoman objectives, investigate local attitudes, and facilitate a possible arbitration. More particularly, they were to establish, as closely as possible, what had been the de facto frontiers in 1905. The commissioners were accompanied by consular guards and an Ottoman escort but were instructed to avoid military conflict, in case of Ottoman obstruction.[173] The Shipley-Minorsky commission, closely monitored by the Ottomans, traveled the region from June 8 to September 16, 1911, and submitted its findings as seven diaries and one joint report.[174] Meanwhile, negotiations to establish a quadripartite commission and a protocol to define the parameters of future frontier negotiations continued.

OTTOMAN POLICIES IN THE *NEVAHI-I ŞARKIYYE*

Concurrent with the commission, a reporter from *Novoye Vremya* named Terletzki toured the region. He noted that the root of the problem was located in the "zone," which ranged in width from 10 kilometers at its narrowest to 87 kilometers at its widest, that the first survey commission had defined in the *Carte Identique* as the yet-to-be-delimited borderland, a solution that had satisfied neither the Iranians nor the Ottomans (See Map 10). He noted that the Ottomans had established relative law and order in the occupied areas of the zone, which made the local population sympathetic to them.[175]

According to the Shipley-Minorksy reports, even though Ottoman consuls in places such as Savojbulagh and Khoi had become de facto administrators, the officers with whom they came into contact were almost without exception Kurds. In places such as Salduz, Sunnis, Jews, and even Armenians were pro-Ottoman, although, for reasons that will become clear, landlords often were not. Still, in many places, the commission encountered demonstrations, staged or genuine, in which Ottoman flags were flown and chants of "Long Live Sultan Mehmed V" filled the air.

[173] Barclay to Shipley, Tehran, May 12, 1911, *Schofield IV*, 485.
[174] For the diaries and related correspondence, along with the Joint Report by Shipley and Minorsky, see *Schofield IV*, 495–561.
[175] BOA.HR.SYS 711/2, p. 33, extract from *Novoie Vremya*, Juin 25–Julliete 8, 1911.

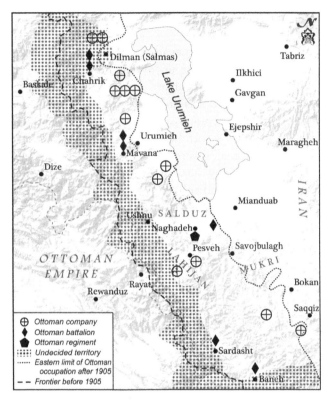

MAP 12. Map of Areas Occupied by the Ottoman Forces from 1905 to 1912 After Minorsky, 1911. Reproduced by "Boundary Cartography" from John Tchalenko, *Images from the Endgame* with permission from John Tchalenko and Saqi Books.

Ottoman reports confirm these observations when they describe more than five thousand armed and unarmed Sunni, Shiʿi, Armenian, Jewish, Nasrani, and Karapapak *millets* (peoples) of Salduz carrying star and crescent flags, chanting "Long Live the Ottoman Sultan and Down With the Iranian Tyranny" (*Yaşasın Padişahı Osmani Kahr Olsun Istibdadı Irani*), and pledging to sacrifice themselves for the sultan. They also submitted *mazbata*s, or prepepared petitions, to document their new allegiance. Such descriptions might indicate that the people of Salduz had resoundingly rejected Minorsky's alternative slogan, "Long Live all the Rulers," or *Umum Padişahlar Yaşasın*. The *Agence Télégraphique de St. Petersburg*, however, argued that the demonstrators had been obliged to sign the *mazbata*s and had subsequently sent a complaint to the governor of Urumieh regarding "les actes arbitraires des Turcs." Not surprisingly, Ottoman officials were deeply suspicious of Shipley and, especially, Minorsky. The Ottoman consul at Urumieh accused the latter of meeting with the Shekak leaders Ismail and Omar in order to incite them to violence and so justify Russian intervention. Ottoman reports also complained about Minorsky's undiplomatic behavior, including his destruction of a pro-Ottoman petition in front of a group of Jewish petitioners, who pieced together the shredded document to submit to the Ottoman Salduz civil administrator. The Russian commissioner's true goal, these and similar reports protested, was not to collect data but to sow confusion and provoke religious sentiments.[176]

Whatever Minorsky's intentions, it is indisputable that not everyone was content with Ottoman administration. Leaders of some branches of the ethnically Turkish Karapapak, for example, petitioned the commission:

We Karapapaks cannot renounce our love and sincere sentiments for Persia, our fatherland, we desire to live in our own country and with our own nation (Shi'is). To beg in our own country is better than to obtain honors in Turkey ... We have no strength left to endure Ottoman oppression ... If the Turks without any right, seize this land, help us to emigrate into Central Persia.[177]

These chiefs had a point. Minorsky-Shipley reported that in places inhabited by Shi'i peasantry, including Salduz, Baranduz, and Salmas, the agrarian policy of the CUP was directed at undermining the power and privileges enjoyed by landowners and encouraging *rayat* (peasants or subjects) emancipation. At times, even if left in possession of their villages, proprietors were ordered to reduce by half the taxes they collected.[178]

Such policies drew Tehran's attention. In his appeal to Istanbul to stop the practice of redistributing the khans' lands to the *rayat* in Salduz, the Iranian ambassador included a petition from twenty-seven notables complaining that the *mülkiye memuru* (administrator) in Salduz, Yusuf Ziya Bey, was distributing their hereditary lands and domestic animals to the *ahali* (common folk).[179] Another petition from nine individuals, including

---

[176] BOA.HR.SYS 711/1, various correspondence on pp. 1, 8, 18, and 35, July 4–10, 1911; HR.SYS, 711/1, p. 27, extracts from *Agence Télégraphique de St. Petersburg*, Juin 26, 1911.

[177] Shipley-Minorksy Diary No. 3, Urmia to Soujboulak, July 4–10, 1911, *Schofield IV*, 505.

[178] Joint Report by Shipley and Minorsky, *Schofield IV*, 554–55.

[179] BOA.HR.SYS 711/2, pp. 241, 244; Iranian ambassador to OMFA, October 9, 1911, and Iranian Khans to Iranian Embassy in Istanbul, Pesveh, August 29, 1911. Istanbul later ordered the commissioners not to distribute land. HR.SYS 711/2, p. 242.

one representing the Armenian community and another claiming to represent the people of Salduz, complained that the grievances of the poor and destitute of Salduz had only increased since the district had come under dispute. If the district was Ottoman, they argued, then Ottoman land law should prevail. If not, then their arbitrary oppression by Ottoman officials and Kurdish *agha*s should be stopped.[180]

Iranian authorities went so far as to claim that because the inhabitants of Salduz were Karapapaks who had emigrated from Russia, their grievances might bring about a Russian intervention. Ottoman authorities responded by pointing out that they had emigrated decades earlier and, more importantly, that the just administration of and consequent sympathy for Ottomanism (*Osmanlılık*) was the real source of Shi'i displeasure.[181] Unconvinced, Tehran also complained that Ottoman authorities were illegally interfering in the affairs and administration of Salmas, which "is part of Iranian domains and is temporarily occupied by the Ottoman troops."[182] Supporting such claims, Shipley and Minorsky noted that dispossessing traditional proprietors to bring about change in land tenure – especially when they were *agha*s of Iranian nationality or proclivities in Shi'i districts, and when those lands were transferred to Sunni Kurdish *agha*s – had the unfortunate effect of creating uncertainty and confusion.[183]

Indeed, no matter how carefully designed they might have been, such policies profoundly unsettled social relations in a region where landlords had long dominated. A Kurd summarized the situation best: "there are no more *agha*s left."[184] Despite the notables' complaints, however, villagers in many places indicated a preference for the new regime because of its milder treatment of the *rayat*. Such a preference might also have resulted from the fact that in some places, the peasantry and laboring classes stopped paying taxes altogether. For instance, in the village of Kahrize, located between Urmi and the lake and owned by a certain Nasr-ed-Dowleh, the villagers "themselves called in the Turks, refused to pay a penny to Nasser-ed-Dowleh alleging that the payments hitherto exacted by him had far exceeded the sum due to him from the small portion of the village really belonging to him, and that it was he therefore, who ought to

---

[180] BOA.HR.SYS 711/2, p. 267, to Iranian Embassy in Istanbul, December 14, 1911.
[181] BOA.HR.SYS 711/2, p. 264, Undersecretary of Ottoman Ministry of Interior to OMFA, January 30, 1912.
[182] BOA.HR.SYS 711/2, p. 269; Iranian Embassy to OMFA, May 15, 1912.
[183] Joint Report by Shipley and Minorsky, *Schofield IV*, 554–55.
[184] Ibid., 555.

make restitution to them." The residents of Kooloindji village, also owned by Nasser-ed-Dowleh, similarly stopped paying dues after a company of Ottoman soldiers arrived. In the nearby Protestant, Orthodox, and Catholic village of Gowlan, owned by Navid-ed-Dowleh, residents did not ask for *dekhalet* but nevertheless ceased paying dues, insisting: "As none were paid to the Nasr-ed-Dowleh [why] should we pay anything to Navid, who was no greater a personage than Nasr?"[185] Minorsky-Shipley suggested that many of *dekhalet* that were received were "written in good Ottoman Turkish, which is quite unknown by the Urmia population; others are drawn in stereotyped Persian form, where only the signatures vary." Whatever form they took, the report suggested, the *dekhalets* could be used to establish future rights over certain localities.[186]

A study of *dekhalets* shows that with the Iranian state incapacitated, the people of the region – landlords and peasants alike – were positioning themselves to benefit from the Ottoman expansion. For example, the inhabitants of the large Sunni village of Miava near the Urumieh shore, which lay entirely outside the zone of Ottoman influence, gave *dekhalet* and subsequently refused to acknowledge their landlords' authority. In response, the landlords leased their property to entrepreneurial Ottoman citizens while continuing to pay dues to Tehran.[187] Other landlords took a more preemptory tact: the proprietor of six villages in the Savojbulagh district, Samsam-es-Saltaneh, gave *dekhalet* himself, thus anticipating any action by his tenants.[188]

Despite their prevalence, there are some indications that Ottoman authorities did not force the population to give *dekhalets*. Rather, the occupation and the undefined character of the frontier created a conundrum. For example, the village of Toordjan in Bukan was owned by four brothers, three of whom remained Persian subjects, whereas one, Feth 'Ali Beg, gave *dekhalet*. Although his quarter share was now under Ottoman protection, the brothers still held the village in condominium. Nearby Karali similarly belonged to three brothers, only one of whom agreed to give *dekhalet*: "Thus while two-thirds of this village remain Persian the other third professes itself Turkish." Uncertainty became so acute that

---

[185] Shipley-Minorsky Diary No.7, Urmia to Tabreez through Anzal and Salmas, September 9–16, 1911, *Schofield IV*, 532–34, 535.
[186] Joint Report by Shipley and Minorsky, *Schofield IV*, 556.
[187] Shipley-Minrosky Diary No. 3, Urmia to Soujboulak, July 4–10, 1911, *Schofield IV*, 500.
[188] Shipley-Minrosky Diary No. 4, Soujboulak to Baneh, July 27 to August 2, 1911, *Schofield IV*, 508–11.

some Kurds, "being materially interested in the frontier question," consulted the Shipley-Minorsky commission for advice.[189]

No doubt sectarian affiliations played a significant part in identity and allegiance formation, but, as these examples demonstrate, material benefits were not to be ignored. Some *agha*s threw in their lot with the Ottomans, not only to benefit from conciliatory policies toward Kurdish chiefs, but also because of fears that Iranian constitutionalist *anjumans* would strip them of power and land. Rejecting one constitutional government, they took refuge in another. Even material benefits combined with shared religious affiliation did not convince some Sunni Kurds, who staunchly defended their Iranian connection. One such figure was Karani Agha of Mamesh, in Lahijan, the first district to be occupied. In a secret letter to Shipley-Minorsky, he maintained that the region was Iranian and its residents Iranian subjects who paid their taxes and held Iranian titles. Enumerating ongoing manifestations of Iranian authority, Karani attributed the silence of tribes in the region not to new allegiances but to Ottoman military superiority. People applied for *dekhalet* because they lacked the courage to refuse: "The Turkish authorities everywhere assemble the inhabitants by force, and, after threatening and warning them, obtain a paper saying that they gave up their nationality at their own pleasure and willingly accepted that of the Turks. The inhabitants and tribes accept Turkish nationality because they are helpless, and are afraid of losing their lives, property and honor."[190] As we have seen, however, such claims of force were simplifications at best.

At times, whole districts, such as Baneh, came under Ottoman authority because of interfamilial rivalries among notables. Mohammed (Mamed) Khan, who had been made governor of the town of Baneh by Tehran, secured his post by giving *dekhalet* when rivals challenged his authority.[191] The Ottomans, in turn, allowed him to appropriate villages belonging to other landlords and appointed him honorary *kaimmakam*. The actual governor of Baneh was a Kurd sympathetic to CUP policies: Suleyman Bey, a brother of the late Said Pasha, who had been minister for foreign

---

Ibid.
Shipley-Minorsky Diary No. 5, Baneh through Serdesht to Soujboulak, August 3–14, 1911, *Schofield IV*, 521; Diary No. 6, Soujboulak through Old Lahidjan, Ushnu, Dehtebil, Mergever, Desht, Tergever, and Inchkesu to Urmi, August 18–30, 1911, *Schofield IV*, 531.
Joint Report by Shipley and Minorsky, *Schofield IV*, 555; and G. E. Hubbard, *From the Gulf to Ararat: An Expedition through Mesopotamia and Kurdistan* (Edinburgh: William Blackwood and Sons, 1917), 206.

affairs and president of the Council of State. When meeting with Shipley
and Minorsky, he toed the party line, espousing plans for educating Kurds
in constitutional principles, insisting on the necessity of the occupation to
save the population from the landlords' tyranny, and alleging that the
Ottoman advance resulted from fears of Russian encroachment.[192]

Suleyman Bey was not the only pro-CUP activist in the new frontier.[193]
In Ushnu, where the commission was greeted with the usual shouts of
"Long Live the Sultan," revolutionary passion was in full swing. The
acting *kaimmakam* was a captain, or *yuzbashi*. The schoolmaster, who
wore a yellow badge with tricolor ribbons on his shoulder, explained to
them that his school depended on the Union and Progress Committee, and
that a new schoolhouse was being built thanks to funds procured from the
previous governor, who had now given *dekhalet*. That previous governor,
Suleiman Khan, did not meet (or was not allowed to meet) the delegates.
His cousins, Riza Khan and Mustafa Khan, however, did meet them after
returning from Mosul, where they had given *dekhalet* and returned with an
Ottoman detachment that proceeded to seize the Iranian customhouse:

Riza Khan, who as a reward for his services, had received permission to appropriate the Deshtbil district [which made him the master of twenty-two villages some
of which belonged to Agha Khan Mir Pendj], was loud in his praises of the Turks,
thanks to whom, he said, he had only now begun to understand what progress and
civilization meant, adding that he intended to make a trip to Europe.[194]

It is obvious that Riza Khan's appropriation of villages was not an anti-
landlord strategy. But it may have promoted the rights of the peasantry and
was therefore welcomed.

In spite of such enthusiasm, even some Ottoman officials disagreed
regarding their policies in the region. Sadi Bey, the Ottoman consul of
Urumieh, resigned, complaining that the military officers appointed to civil
positions were insufficiently qualified and created difficulties for the civil
administrators like him. Dubious of the military importance and commercial value of the occupied territories, he maintained that the occupation
should last only until the Persian government was able to provide security
in the region. In contrast, Kolagasi Remiz Bey, a military authority and
advocate of expansionism, maintained that Ottoman territory should

[192] Shipley-Minorsky Diary No. 4, *Schofield IV*, 511.
[193] For Ottoman patriotism among Kurdish intellectuals and the Young Kurds of the CUP,
see Djene Rhys Bajalan, "Kurds for the Empire 'The Young Kurds' 1898–1914" (MA
thesis, Istanbul Bilgi University, 2009).
[194] Shipley-Minorsky Diary No. 6, *Schofield IV*, 526.

extend to the shores of Urumieh Lake, adding that Turkey had historical rights to all of Azerbaijan up to Kaflan Kuh. Even the name "Urmia (Roomiye)" he argued, was proof of its having been in Turkey's possession. For Remiz Bey, the frontier "at present constituted, not a matter of any importance, as it would have to be rectified by inclusion of many places which had not yet come under Turkish sovereignty."[195]

Despite such extravagant claims, according to Shipley-Minorsky, except in the case of Salduz, the Ottoman administration was ad hoc. The Ottoman Code was not enforced in all occupied districts, neither had any laws applicable to it been promulgated. Civil cases were judged according to the shariah, and the commission members saw many mullahs, muftis, and kazis sent from Ottoman Kurdistan to arbitrate disputes between Kurds and, incidentally, aid in the propagation of Ottoman ideas. Indeed, the *Nuvvab Defteri*, or register of shariah judges, of the period shows the appointments of *naib*s to Salduz, Sardasht, and Baneh. Unlike most other judges, who were appointed from Istanbul after taking an exam, these were appointed by the *vilayet* of Mosul on the condition that they would take the necessary exam.[196] Locals were not appointed, most possibly because they were unacquainted with the Ottoman system. Ottoman officials also established customhouses in the eastern provinces and occasionally collected money and grain for the construction of schoolhouses and barracks, the Ottoman navy, and victims of a fire in Istanbul. There were also significant claims that they carried out a census, drafted locals for the army, and organized elections.[197]

Shipley and Minorsky concluded that it was impossible to find a geographically identifiable limit between occupied districts and those remaining under Qajar authority. Still, it was certain that Ottoman troops had taken control of all principal passes as well as wealthy districts that, if necessary, could ensure ample supplies for the maintenance of a large military force. Besides villages in Saqqiz, Khoi, and Savojbulagh, some thirty-one districts including Salmas, Chahrik, Somai, Bradost, Tergever, Dasht, Mergever, Baranduz, Dashtbil, Ushnu, Salduz, Lahijan, Sardasht, Alan, and Baneh were occupied at the time.[198] These districts, which Ottoman documents conspicuously refer to as *nevahi-i sharkiyye*, or

---

[195] Shipley-Minorsky Diary No.7, *Schofield IV*, 532.
[196] Nuvvab Defteri 1977, Müftülük archives, Istanbul. I thank Jun Akiba for providing relevant pages and aiding in their interpretation.
[197] Joint Report by Shipley and Minorsky; and Y. H. Bayur, *Türk Inkılap Tarihi* (Ankara: 1943), vol. II, pt. I, 171.
[198] Joint Report by Shipley and Minorsky.

mere extensions of the eastern provinces, were divided into two parts, each under the command of a colonel, styled as an Iranian Frontier First or Second Zone Commissioner (*Hudud-u Iraniye Birinci* or *İkinci Kısım Komiseri*).[199] In 1911, Behcet Bey was the *komiser* of the first zone, which extended from Chahrik to Ushnu, and Ahmed Refik Bey of the second, stretching from Salduz to Baneh. The first zone was divided into the *kaimmakamlıks* of Chehrik, Mavana, and Ushnu, which also included Shekeryazı, Hoder, Yumadi [Pomadi?], Enzel, Derik, Chubek, Bradost, Mergever, Shinova, and Tokzar [Togzar]. The second was partitioned into the *kaimmakamlıks* of Salduz, Sardasht, and Baneh and theoretically included the districts of Savojbulagh, Saqqez, and Sinne.[200] All *kaimmakam*s were officers who had held ranks before their appointment as civil officials. Because they had no staff of Ottoman clerks or properly qualified subordinates, their work was carried out with the assistance of local Kurds. Regarding their administration, the Russian consul of Saujbulagh, Alexander Iyas, later noted: "During their stay the Turks introduced a degree of order into the districts they occupied and, with the support of the troops they deployed in the contended zone, forced both settled and nomadic populations to buckle down."[201] Likewise, in his reports about the Shipley-Minorsky mission, Behjet Bey noted that the commissioners were impressed by the discipline of Ottoman troops and the loyalty displayed by chiefs and tribes for the caliphate and Ottoman justice. He also claimed they were dismayed by the tranquility reigning in the *nevahi-i şarkıyye*, because it invalidated their desire that the region and its peoples be returned to Iran.[202]

THE END OF THE OCCUPATION

Although those like Behcet Bey remained optimistic about the "new frontier," tensions between Istanbul and St. Petersburg mounted, not least because, by the end of 1911, Russia had completed the railway to Julfa and the road to Tabriz. At the same time, in an open letter to *The Times* dated November 11, 1911, Morgan Shuster accused Russia and England of obstructing his work in Iran through their persistent intrusion on its

---

[199] For example, see BOA.HR.SYS 711/1 and 2, 713/2, which includes hundreds of documents under the title, "Problems of the Eastern Districts."

[200] BOA.HR.SYS 720/13, May 27, 1911, Cipher from Kaimmakam Behcet Bey to OMI.

[201] Tchalenko, *End Game*, 112.

[202] BOA.HR.SYS 711/1 Hasib Bey to Grand Vezir Ibrahim Hakkı Pasha and Behjet Bey to General Staff, September 1, 1911.

independent and sovereign rights. This made him the target of British parliamentary discussions and Russian rancor. Days after the letter's publication, Russia demanded Shuster's dismissal. As thousands of Russian troops poured into its northern section, Iran agreed to seek Russia's consent when obtaining foreign advisors and to pay an indemnity for the maintenance of its forces in Ghilan but refused to dismiss Shuster. A serious boycott of Russian and British goods ensued. Eventually, the cabinet, more amendable to Russian demands, prevailed over the parliament, preventing a Russian occupation of the capital. The cabinet also succeeded in winning the support of the new regent, Nasir al-Mulk, who suspended the Majlis on December 24, 1911. At nearly the same time, the constitutionalist stronghold of Tabriz fell, effectively ending the constitutional revolution.[203]

Again demonstrating the nation's vulnerability, the Majlis sought Ottoman intervention to prevent Russia's attempts at partitioning Iran. Russia gave assurances to the Ottomans that it would not advance further if Iran dismissed Shuster. It must have been around this time that, as Shuster noted,

> A touch of grim humor was added to the situation by a declaration of the Turkish Minister of Foreign Affairs at Constantinople, in reply to a question in the Parliament. This Ottoman wag replied that Persia's independence could not be in danger, because the Anglo-Russian Agreement guaranteed it. At the time some 12,000 Russian troops were occupying the entire northern part of the Empire.[204]

In spite of its diplomatic maneuvers, Istanbul was aware that it could not hold on to the *nevahi-i şarkıye* and might not be able cope with the Russian troop concentration there. Having assumed governmental functions in Azerbaijan, Russian troop commanders and consuls were preparing to open a consulate in Savojbulagh, to be added to those in Tabriz, Urumieh, and Khoi. In a confidential letter, the Unionist minister of the interior, Celal Bey, warned that the Russians were waiting for an opportunity to intervene in the frontier. Because they, like the Ottomans, exploited Iranian insecurity and resultant tribal cross-border depredations

---

[203] Kashani-Sabet, *Frontier Fictions*, 141.

[204] Morgan Shuster, *The Strangling of Persia* (New York: Century Company, 1912), 183–84, 188; Afary, *The Iranian Constitutional Revolution*, 337–38. While Tabriz was under siege for months, the Ottoman consul kept Istanbul informed and reported on Russia's tacit support to the reactionaries, who were waiting for the town's surrender. BOA.HR.SYS 675/22, Deputy Consul of Tabriz to OMFA, October 15, 1911.

to legitimize their occupation, they believed that delimitation would allow them to construct military stations that could be used to end such depredations.

Moscow also increased its efforts to win over Nestorian communities, whom it urged to ask for Russian protection, just as the Ottomans had pressed Sunnis to ask for *dekhalet*.[205] Concerned that a Kurdish reaction could escalate the tension, Istanbul had to choose either facing the Russians or accepting the finalization of the frontier. As we will see in the coming chapter, new developments on its western frontiers forced it to opt for the latter. A gradual withdrawal followed and borderland communities such as the Bilbas branches, which had tried to exploit inter-imperial struggles to keep their autonomous status, were soon compelled to become citizens of a cartographically defined Iran.

For their part, England and Russia again pressured Istanbul and Tehran to form a frontier commission, in order to prevent what they called an Ottoman *fait accompli* and remain faithful to their declared guarantee of Iranian integrity. Perversely, the Russo-British colonial division of Iran into spheres of influence helped Iran preserve its integrity. The result was the signing of the Tehran Protocol of December 21, 1911, which established a new commission for the review and settlement of the entire boundary. A weakened Istanbul once again agreed to the 1847 Erzurum Treaty as the starting point of negotiations. In March 1912, the Ottoman-Iranian commission, made up of ranking bureaucrats, met in Istanbul.[206] This commission, along with the Russian expansion into Azerbaijan, marked the effective end of Ottoman efforts to turn northwestern Iran into the northeastern Ottoman Empire. It was also this commission that would, after long deliberations, finalize the Ottoman-Iranian frontier and make the borderlanders Iranian or Ottoman for good.

[205] BOA.HR.SYS 711/2, p. 37 OMW to OMFA, November 29, 1911, and p. 60; OMW to OMFA December 17, 1911.
[206] For names of the members of the commission, see BOA.HR.SYS 707/2 and 703/1, p. 61; and Lowther to Grey, Constantinople, April 23, 1912, *Schofield V*, 159.

6

Boundary at Last

The Tehran Protocol of December 21, 1911, established that the Ottoman and Iranian delegates, furnished with all necessary evidence in support of their claims, would base their work on the articles of the Erzurum Treaty. These guidelines technically invalidated most of the boundary work carried out between 1847, when the Erzurum Conferences concluded, and 1912, when the new protocol went into effect. It was also stipulated that as soon as the Joint Commission completed its work in Istanbul, a survey commission would mark the definitive line on the ground. The negotiating parties agreed to submit any points of divergence at the end of six months to the International Court of Arbitration at The Hague for final settlement. Istanbul, in particular, did so reluctantly. The worsening situation on its western frontiers coupled with the international realignments that preceded the Great War forced it not only to agree to delimit and demarcate its frontiers with Iran, but also to promise not to use its increasingly untenable military occupation as a legal argument to sway the demarcation.

Examining the end stage of the Ottoman occupation, this chapter traces the labors of the last frontier commission, which traveled the region from 1913 to 1914 and finally completed the process of boundary formation. The notion of a border had always existed in this region, but building on decades of negotiations, this commission's work finally turned that border into a boundary that significantly advanced the process of territoriality. Its survey, mapping, and especially placing of signs to mark the boundary on the ground firmly planted the symbols of territorial sovereignty into the soil of the borderland and the daily lives of the borderlanders. As had been true throughout the process of boundary formation, in this final stage, it was once again the balance of power among the Ottoman Empire, Russia, and England, rather than the imbalance between the Ottoman Empire and Iran, that allowed for this to happen.

On March 25, 1912, to enact the terms of the Tehran Protocol, the Joint Turco-Persian Commission held its first meeting in Istanbul.[1] Although officially not party to the commission, British and Russian representatives were also present and frequently consulted by the Iranian delegates. During these and subsequent negotiations, Iran's division into spheres of British and Russian influence at times proved valuable as it worked to reach a deal with its more powerful neighbor. Yet, more often than not, its dependence resulted in its total exclusion from negotiations. Three issues busied the delegates: the Ottoman insistence that the Iranian delegates accept the *Explanatory Note* attached to the Erzurum Treaty, vying claims to the province of Zohab, and questions regarding the limits of Suleimanieh.

As this book's second chapter recounted, the Erzurum Treaty and its much disputed addendum, the *Explanatory Note*, gave the waters of the Shatt al-Arab River to the Ottoman Empire but allowed Iran the town of Muhammarah and its anchorage on the Karun River. This time around, Britain was of the opinion that left to its own means, Iran would not be able to secure even that much.[2] Even so, arguments about the parties' respective claims to Zohab became bogged down once more in unwinnable arguments about the validity and authenticity of historical documents. Zohab's boundary and, more importantly, that of the Shatt al-Arab were therefore decided without Iranian input when a final agreement was reached in London.

The question of Suleimanieh, meanwhile, became the platform on which the Ottomans elaborated their claims to the occupied districts. The Iranians suggested a geographic frontier that would follow the region's natural features, such as crests, mountains peaks, and waterways. The Ottomans continued to insist that their rival had appropriated the lands of Kurdistan in defiance of previous treaties and countered with a line based on their reading

[1] The Ottoman commission included H. Adil Bey, *musteshar* of the Grand Vizirate (president); Danyal and Ali Rıza Pashas (both of whom left to participate in the Balkan Wars); Brigadier General Ali Nadir Pasha; and Aleko Effendi (secretary). They were later replaced by Sadreddin Bey, formerly chargé d'affaires at Tehran; Said Bey, under-secretary of state for FA; and Brigadier General Ziya Pasha. The Iranian commissioners were Ihtisham al-Saltanah Mirza Mahmud Khan, ambassador to Istanbul (president); Nazim-al-Mulk Jahangir Khan, deputy governor of Azerbaijan; and Ettela-al-Mulk Nasrollah Khan, head of Ottoman section, in IMFA. BOA.HR.SYS 707/2 and 703/1, p. 61; Lowther to Grey, Constantinople, April 23, 1912, *Schofield V*, 159.

[2] Percy Cox to the Secretary of the Government of India in the Foreign Department, Simla, August 25,1912, *Schofield V*, 441.

of the 1639 treaty, which would give them most of the occupied regions. According to various reports and diaries of Hammond Smith Shipley and Vladimir Fedorovitch Minorsky, members of the Anglo-Russian commission investigating the Ottoman occupation, that were extensively quoted in the previous chapter, the Ottomans presented documents dating back to the sixteenth century in order to argue that Suleimanieh's borders extended from the eastern shores of Lake Urmia to Mount Sahand, near Tabriz, and incorporated districts extending from Ushu, Lahijan, Baneh, Maragha, and Sqqez in the north, and Posht-e Kuh and Zohab in the south. A confidential report prepared by the Ottoman Frontier Commission for the Grand Vizier likewise stated that according to the Land Records Office (*Defterhane*), the frontier began at the Aras River, which left the greater part of Lake Urmi and places such as Avroman, Sinne, Afshar, and Merivan on the Ottoman side. This argument presupposed that the lands in question had been ruled by Kurdish dynasts recognizing Ottoman hegemony and that as the Ottoman government had terminated their rule, Istanbul retained the prerogative to govern the districts of the defunct dynasts. Iranian Kurdistan was thus defined as the natural extension of Sunni Ottoman Kurdistan unjustly appropriated by the Shi'is. The Porte's delegates also made reference to the 1823 treaty in which, they maintained, Persia accepted the empire's ancient limits and promised to return territories and fortresses that had passed into its hands during the 1821–22 war. Ottoman assertions were not limited to Kurdistan proper: the report also claimed the *liva* (sub-province) of Dartang and the *nahiyah* (district) of Luristan, both located on the Delahu-Posht-e Kuh chain of mountains, as well as Hawiza and the *liva* of Ghoban; the Ottomans did, however, acknowledge that various treaties had ceded Iran the Island of Abadan, the eastern part of Zohab *sanjak*, and the lands of Qoutra [Fotura?].[3] These were by far the grandest of all Ottoman claims made during the process of boundary making. The Iranian delegates, like their predecessors, responded by resorting to the principle of *uti possidetis*. Additionally, they argued that both parties had abandoned previous territorial claims when they agreed to the 1847 treaty. The Ottomans countered by pledging to take their case, if necessary, all the way to The Hague.

Neither the British nor the Russians were willing to let the issue go so far. They had invested almost seventy years of labor and money into finding a solution and did not want to risk a decision that would threaten their interests or international standing. As the Persians "were as helpless as children," and most of their remaining documentary evidence had been

---

[3] Report of the Ottoman Commission Addressed to the Grand Vizier, *Schofield V*, 228–31.

destroyed during the bombardment of the *Majlis*, the Russians and British demanded that if the matter did in fact reach The Hague, the Iranians had to "designate as one of their arbitrators either a Russian or a British jurist."[4] But they concluded that the best solution would be to convince Istanbul to agree to the formation of a commission that would empower its representatives as arbitrators rather than mediators, a proposal long in the making.[5]

In the midst of such political wrangling, the borderlanders, especially around the triangle of the Ottoman-Russian-Iranian frontiers, witnessed the waning of Ottoman authority and the daily increase of Russian troops. Aware of the storm in the Balkans and the near-absence of effective Iranian authority, groups such as the Nestorians, the Karapapaks, and the Kurdish tribes once more faced the vital question of whom to recognize as their sovereign authority. Louis Molyneux-Seel, the British vice-consul at Van, noted that these groups were becoming "uncertain where their best interests lie ... They were in doubt whether they are to remain Ottoman subjects or about to come under Russian control. Hence they remain in a state of unrest and the Turks are fully occupied in endeavouring to keep them under their influence."[6] As the Russians endeavored to do the same, both parties charged each other with inciting the region's tribes. Russian claims that its troop movements had nothing to do with Iran but rather with the Caucasus did not convince Turhan Pasha, the Ottoman ambassador to St. Petersburg, who urged the Porte to agree to the formation of the frontier commission with Iran in order to put a stop to such meddling.[7]

While the northernmost borderlanders were thus torn between empires, the Ottomans, as the previous chapter detailed, were forced to reexamine their expansionist policies as a result of developments at their western and southern frontiers. Indeed, their hand against Russia was significantly weakened by Italy's occupation of Tripolitania and the Balkan Wars of 1912–13. The latter, in particular, brought the expansionist project under ever-more-intense scrutiny. Even radical Unionists such as the ex-governor of Trabzon, Suleyman Nazif, publicly criticized "the policy of Turkey in regard to the Turco-Persian frontier question."[8]

---

[4] George W. Buchanan to Grey, St. Petersburg, March 17, 1912, *Schofield V*, 29.

[5] Memorandum on the Proposed Submission of the Turco-Persian Frontier Dispute to the Hague Tribunal, February 23, 1912, *Schofield V*, 9–15.

[6] Note Communicated to the Sublime Porte by Gerard Lowther Juin 1, 1912; and Note Communicated to Lowther by the Sublime Porte, June 12, 1912, *Schofield V*, 268; Vice-Consul Molyneux-Seel to Lowther, Van, March 25, 1912, *Schofield V*, 147.

[7] BOA.HR.SYS 711/2, 207, Turhan Pasha to OMoFA Asım Bey, Petersburg, May 25, 1912.

[8] Lowther to Grey, Constantinople, March 21, 1912, *Schofield V*, 38.

Nevertheless, in the spring of 1912, Ottoman forces occupied Merivan, where they appointed a *mudir*. At the same time, rumors reached London that the Ottoman cavalry was concentrating in Suleimanieh to move into Sinne.[9] Aware that Russia regarded the occupation as an effort to permanently control all the districts up to Lake Urumieh, Sadrazam Said Pasha urged officials not to transgress the status quo line, but to be ready to defend against any Russian troop movement while remaining mindful that a war was already in progress. He also asked the authorities of the *nevahi-i şarkıyye*, or new provinces, to refrain from carrying out a previously ordered census or organizing elections for the purpose of sending representatives to the Ottoman parliament.[10]

Under increasing pressure, but still unwilling to lose the occupied lands, Istanbul was at a crossroads. Its highest authorities discussed whether to unite the lands currently under the governance of two commissioners (*nevahi-i şarkiyye idaresinin tevhidi*) and whether civilian or military authorities should administer the region. The Ottoman Ministry of Foreign Affairs and some military authorities argued for strong civil service officers, whereas the Committee of Union and Progress (CUP) strongman, Talat Pasha, suggested a military-dominated system under the authority of an *umumi komiserlik*, or general commissioner directly responsible to the Ministry of War.[11] Because Russia was complaining about the Ottoman administrators in the region, Istanbul sent the deputy commander of the 11th Army, Mirliva Cabir Pasha, along with an inspector, Ali Seydi Bey, to investigate the situation on the ground and take measures to prevent Russian complaints about anti-Russian propaganda. After meeting with Ottoman and Russian authorities, they suggested replacing those administrators who had been targets of Russian complaints. To placate its rival, Istanbul agreed.[12]

Both sides wanted to avoid confrontation, which made delimitation a high priority for Istanbul and St. Petersburg, as well as for England, which wanted to protect its spheres of influence in southern Iran and Mesopotamia. Increasingly important as well was the D'Arcy Oil Concession of 1901, in which Iran had granted a British citizen that part of its territory bordering on Mesopotamia, from Khanaqin southward. As this oil-rich region fell on both sides of the status quo line, for the British "it mattered less where the line

[9] Lowther to Grey, Constantinople, April 18, 1912, *Schofield V*, 154.
[10] BOA.HR.SYS 711/2, pp. 91, 92, 93; Sadrazam to OMFA, March 18, 1912. See also BOA.A.MKT.MHM 740/23, 1330. R. 11/March 30, 1912.
[11] BOA.HR.SYS 711/2, p. 143, Dahiliye Nazırı vekili Tal'at to Sadaret, May 18, 1912.
[12] BOA.A.MKT.MHM 741/8 1330.C.2 / May 19, 1912, deciphered telegrams from Cabir Pasha and Ali Seydi Bey.

should lie than that it should be laid down definitely somewhere, for, until that had been done, no development was possible."[13] British anxiety was not baseless. Iraq's oilfields, railway placement and construction, and control of adjacent regions were becoming increasingly important to global strategic calculations; in addition, the Anglo-Persian Oil Syndicate; the German government; and smaller players such as Deutsche Bank, National Bank, Anatolian Railway Company, and Baghdad Railway Company were competing for mining and oil concessions in the region.

The Anglo-Persian Oil Syndicate already owned the Qasr-i Shirin Oilfields and, with the syndicate's interests in mind, Charles M. Marling, the British diplomat in Istanbul pushed for "the cession by Persia to Turkey of the Kasr-i Shirin districts" because Istanbul was "immeasurably more powerful" than Tehran and the Iranian inhabitants living along the possible pipeline route were considered "wild and lawless."[14] Fearing the legal ramifications of transferring a tract of land to a new owner and lobbied by the oil company to safeguard its investments, London urged that the original concessions be maintained if the land were indeed granted to the Ottomans. The oil company was of the opinion that "[t]he oilfields in Zohab will, when the Baghdad and other contemplated railways in Mesopotamia and Northern Persia are operating, be of considerable value, as oil will be the only cheap fuel available for these railways."[15] London was ultimately able to secure "its own interests and those of Mr. W. K. D'Arcy by obtaining a formal assurance that the D'Arcy Concession would be kept alive in any districts transferred *de jure* to Turkey from the *de facto* rule of Persia as a result of the arbitral labors of the British and Russian Commissioners."[16]

At the time of the commission, important wells had been sunk in Qasr-i Shirin, but their location was remote and their production limited. When another supply was tapped at Ahwaz, within reach of the Persian Gulf, a pipeline was laid down to Abadan, where a refinery was erected before the start of World War I. With Abadan's resultant emergence as an industrial hub, the dynamics of the region were transformed.[17] The British navy's conversion from coal to oil made control of the Persian Gulf and a

---

[13] Arnold T. Wilson, *S. W. Persia: A Political Officer's Diary* (London: Oxford University Press, 1941), 270–71.

[14] Marling to Grey, Constantinople, August 13, 1912, *Schofield V*, 323.

[15] C. Greenway, Managing Director, Anglo-Persian Oil Company to FO, September 3, 1912, *Schofield V*, 476.

[16] Wilson, *SW Persia*, 270–71.

[17] For a description of Abadan, see G. E. Hubbard, *From the Gulf to Ararat: An Expedition through Mesopotamia and Kurdistan* (Edinburgh: William Blackwood and Sons, 1917), 31.

definitive decision on its boundaries ever more vital to London's interests. Delimiting the Shatt was also necessary because the river had changed course since 1860, with the result that modern steamships could no longer lie, as before, in the mouth of the Karun opposite Muhammarah. Instead, they had to anchor in the mainstream, considered Ottoman waters.[18] This change effectively denied Iran its control of navigation. Accordingly, Britain wanted to dredge the bar of the Shatt to make it useful for average-sized oceangoing steamers while also promoting the speedy movement of commerce over it and other international waters. No progress could be made in these matters until a final settlement had been reached.[19]

For these reasons, Muhammarah and its anchorage, sovereignty over and navigation rights to the Shatt, and ownership of the islands in the Shatt once again took center stage. Although it continued to nurture its relationship with the Ka'b chief, Sheikh Khaz'al, London decided to negotiate directly with Istanbul to speed the process, a decision that again left Tehran out in the cold. The Russian minister of foreign affairs described the situation succinctly: "as [the Muhammarah] question has become object of direct negotiation between G. Britain and Turkey, Persia's attitude in regard to the question has no longer any importance."[20] Thanks also to the efforts of Tevfik Pasha, the Ottoman ambassador in London, London and Istanbul established the Shatt al-Arab Navigation Commission, which would lead to a convention. In the meantime, to avoid unpleasant surprises, the Ka'b chief implored the British to protect his interests, offering his full support in exchange. Despite sending him appeasing messages, however, London made certain that the sheikh would be treated as an Iranian subject rather than the semi-independent ruler he hoped to be.[21]

Meanwhile, London continued to cooperate with Moscow to preserve mutual spheres of influence in Iran and advise Tehran, in the hopes of avoiding a trip to The Hague. Well aware that in comparison to Istanbul, Tehran "had been excessively remiss in the preservation and collection of papers establishing [its] ancient rights in the contested districts," British and Russian authorities agreed that some concessions might be made to Istanbul.[22] They tried also to reach an understanding with Iran regarding

[18] Wilson, *SW Persia*, 271
[19] Ibid., 272.
[20] Buchanan to Grey, St. Petersburg, July 14, 1912; and Enclosure No. 1 to Grey's Letter to Buchanan, FO, July 17, 1912, *Schofield V*, 275, 285.
[21] Lieutenant-Colonel Percy Cox to Grey, Bushrie, July 18, 1912; and Grey to Townley, FO, July 22, 1912, *Schofield V*, 290, 296.
[22] Hugh O'Beirne to Grey, St. Petersburg, June 30 to July 4–5, 1912, *Schofield V*, 257, 264.

Zohab and what it would give in return for the procurement of an advantageous frontier.[23] Istanbul, meanwhile, concluded that it would not be able to push past the Russo-British alliance farther eastward into Iran. Hence, its priority was to acquire a secure and strategic frontier. Finally, most everyone's interests converged to make delimitation a reality.

By August 1912, even as they continued to pressure Istanbul to withdraw to pre-1905 frontiers, London and St. Petersburg had persuaded the Iranian delegates at Istanbul to accept the 1852 *Explanatory Note* without conditions. Under growing pressure in the Balkans, the Porte too adopted a conciliatory attitude. Concurrently, Russia increased its troop numbers around Khoi and appropriated all transport in and around Khoi, Julfa, and Salmas, making continued Ottoman presence there even less tenable.[24] Istanbul's position was further weakened when Montenegro declared war on October 8, 1912, followed by Bulgaria, Serbia, and Greece a week later. The Balkan Wars had officially begun. Two days later, the British, French, Russian, German, and Austro-Hungarian ambassadors asked Istanbul to begin immediate discussions regarding reform proposals for the administration of Eastern Rumelia. Surprised by the swift advance of the nascent Balkan states, their troops already decimated by a cholera epidemic and weakened by political divisions, the Ottomans speedily lost ground. Lacking the ability to fight on both the Balkan and the Russian fronts, Istanbul capitulated. By the end of October, Russia informed England that the Porte would withdraw to the 1905 line as requested, provided that Iran officially promised to protect the life and property of the Sunni population. With St. Petersburg urging it to agree to the Ottoman request,[25] Tehran declared itself ready to retake control, "giving assurances that the populations of those districts will be treated in a spirit of justice and benevolence without distinction of religion or nationality."[26] As the withdrawal began, distraught Sunnis from inside and outside the *nevahi-i şarkıyye* made final pleas for protection. In one such case, when the *Sunni al-madhab* district of Saral (?) requested military aid, Prime Minister Kamil Pasha refused on the grounds that the arrival of troops would cause Russian complaints, but he added that anyone taking refuge on the Ottoman side would be accepted.[27] These words marked the end of the very last chapter of Ottoman

---

[23] Marling to Grey, Constantinople, August 8, 1912, *Schofield V*, 317.
[24] Townley to Grey, Tehran, October 23–26, 1912, *Schofield V*, 498, 500.
[25] Grey to Townley, FO, October 29, 1912, *Schofield V*, 502.
[26] Townley to Grey, Tehran, November 6–7, 1912, *Schofield V*, 504–6.
[27] BOA.HR.SYS, 690/2, pp. 10, 12, Prime Ministry to OMFA, OMFA to Prime Ministry, October 31, 1912.

expansionism, and the hopes of some Sunnis of the northernmost frontier to be included within the domains of the caliph. Apprehensive of the future, they were left to the mercy of their new masters.

CHANGING POWER DYNAMICS AND THE NORTHERN BORDERLAND COMMUNITIES

The Ottoman withdrawal came after a disastrous loss to the Bulgarians and Serbs in early November 1912, followed by the signing of an armistice on December 4. Soon after the withdrawal was complete, Russian troops moved into the evacuated districts. Several days later, Alexander Iyas, who spoke Kurdish, arrived in the recently evacuated town of Savojbulagh to begin serving as its first Russian consul. His arrival marked a new era, especially for the nomadic and seminomadic tribes of the northern borderland, which were struggling with complicated decisions about identities and subjecthood while trying to preserve traditional life cycles and habitats. Many of the previously Ottoman-occupied districts, including Salduz, Ushnu, Bukan, Lahijan-Pesveh, Mianduab, Baneh, and Sardasht, were put under Iyas's jurisdiction, whose post had been created at Vladimir Minorsky's suggestion before the withdrawal began. Minorsky argued that the absence of a Russian consul in the region had encouraged the Turkish occupation in the first place; thus, the appointment of one would dissuade them from returning.[28]

Iran, in the meantime, proclaimed a general amnesty and sent administrators to the region. Iyas noted that the swift Turkish withdrawal astonished the local population, which had been assured that the occupied territories would never again belong to Iran. Consequently, the chiefs of various tribes of Mukri Kurdistan "rushed to Soujbulak to profess their loyalty to the Shah's government at the first summon of the local quasi-authorities."[29] Nevertheless, all were aware that Russia was the new master. Indeed, Russia instructed its consuls to intensify its influence among the Kurds, drawing them away from the Ottomans. New alignments were about to take shape.

Minorsky remained cautious. The Ottomans, he noted, had established land reforms whose reversal would harm the local population and cause disorder. The Turks had many sympathizers, he warned, who could be

---

[28] John Tchalenko, *Images From an Endgame* (London: Saqi, 2006), 91.
[29] Iyas to the First Department of the Russian Ministry of FA, Secret, December 2, 1912, in Tchalenko, *Images*, 94.

used as an excuse to interfere once more. He thus urged the Russian consul to protect local peasants from renewed oppression by landowners and to warn recently installed Iranian administrators that

The departure of Turkish troops is a result of Russia's, not Persia's action. Responsibility for disturbances owing to the return to Persian rule will be attributed therefore to Russia. Russia cannot be seen to be less humane than the Turks, so Russia must take control of Persian actions ... On its own Persia cannot cope with the return of the border countries and it should agree that only Russia can keep the Turks from reoccupying. In case of difficulties, one should remind the Persians that they have recognized Russia's zone of influence.[30]

Neither Russian power nor Ottoman and Iranian weaknesses were lost on the borderland communities. Among the notables who appeared at the consulate to secure Iyas's patronage, in case they were harassed by the Iranian authorities, were leaders from the previously pro-Ottoman Bilbas subdivisions of the Mangur, the Mamesh, and parts of the Piran, as well as the Dehbokr, Gowrik, and Begzade, which had remained at least nominally under Iranian rule. Taken as a whole, their acknowledgment of Russian authority allowed Iyas to emerge as the de facto ruler of Mukri until the beginning of World War I. Privy to Russian efforts to win over the Kurds, Iyas argued that this population had "shown neither the remotest sign of tribal unity, nor even a shred of nascent national consciousness" and lacked any central lay or religious authority; he thought that their unification was "an issue for the very distant future; at the moment it would be all but impossible to resolve."[31] Still, he strove to make the Russians their indispensable leaders and patrons.

Iyas was correct in his assessment of the Kurds at the time. What he did not understand, however, was that it was the struggle over their lands and the very process of boundary making that had left them without any figure with "sufficient authority to act as a centre around which the leaders of other tribes might unify."[32] Nor did all Kurds rush to the Russian consul. Although many hedged their bets by visiting him, Iyas received news that the local population in Savojbulagh was agitating to send volunteers to help Istanbul in the Balkan Wars. These "Turcophiles," as he called them, had organized under the authority of Qazi Ali, a member of the large Quzat family and were issuing "prayers for the victory of the Turkish arms every Friday in the town's main mosque; in addition, [Qazi Ali] has energetically

---

[30] Quoted in Tchalenko, *Images*, 92
[31] Iyas to the First Department of the Russian Ministry of FA, Tchalenko, *Images*, 96.
[32] Ibid.

set about organizing collections for the Turks in their struggle against the cursed 'infidels.'" As proof of local enthusiasm, Iyas noted that, upon being approached by the qazi,

Hajji Ilhan Dehbokr, Gholabi Agha, Pirut Agha and other Dehbokr elders immediately donated 600 tomans to the Turks without so much as a thought; the Begzad landowners have donated 400 tomans; the Sunni merchants of Soujbulak jointly collected 1,500 tomans in the course of a single Friday. Altogether about 3,000 tomans have been donated by sundry persons in Soujbulak within a comparatively short time.[33]

Concerned that the ongoing failures of the Iranian administration coupled with tribal unrest could encourage Istanbul to return, Iyas requested additional troops and undertook a number of pacification missions. The first was in Lahijan, to stop a feud between the rival chiefs of the Mangur and Mamesh, which had arisen "partly as a result of Turkish, Persian, and now Russian interferences."[34]

As the previous chapter recounted, during the Ottoman occupation, Baiz Agha – who had replaced his cousin, Bapir, as the Mangur leader – forced the governor of Savojbulagh, Shuja ud-Dawlah, to leave town. After the Ottoman departure, the inept Shuja ud-Dawlah was named as the assistant governor general of Azerbaijan, whereupon he moved to restore Bapir to power. He also encouraged the Dehbokr, Begzad, Gowrik, Piran, Karapapak and Mamesh tribes to unite under Bapir and against his rival. Hard-pressed, Baiz appealed to the Russian consul for protection and even Russian citizenship. Iyas promised him protection on the condition that "he submit wholly to the authority of both the Shah's government and the local administration, that he return the villages seized by his tribe to their rightful owners and that he put a stop to the Mangur's robbing and pillaging."[35] Despite opposition from tribal elders and his family, Baiz agreed. Iyas then granted full support to this previously pro-Ottoman chief who had been given the rank of pasha. This intervention was significant because it targeted precisely the intra-tribe rivalry that had given the Ottomans their initial excuse to begin their occupation. It was now Russia's turn to display its imperial power to these recalcitrant tribes and turn them into Iranian citizens, while warning them to refrain from "causing complications on the border and thereby providing the Turks with a pretext for redeploying

---

[33] Ibid., 122
[34] Ibid., 97–99.
[35] Ibid., 133.

their soldiers."[36] Nevertheless, insecurity in the northern borderland was acute, and rumors of an Ottoman return abounded.

Like the *ashiret* (tribal) Kurds, the Karapapak Turcomans of Salduz and the region's Nestorian and Armenian Christians displayed an acute understanding of changing power relations. The latter groups, which would suffer most in the ensuing turmoil, also exhibited the greatest signs of divided loyalties and insecurity. Faced with increasing Russian military might and British power, as well as the unrelenting activities of American, French, Russian, and Vatican missionaries, the borderland's Christian communities weighed their options carefully. When Iyas returned from his pacification mission in the Mangur-Mamesh region, the inhabitants of an Armenian village, led by a priest in full regalia, lined up to greet him, singing psalms and slaughtering a ram. Enok Charbashian, a businessman from Van who had served as Naghadeh's police chief during the Ottoman occupation, had organized the ceremony. Visiting the consul that evening, Charbashian enthusiastically praised "the magnanimity accorded by Great Russia to the downtrodden Armenian people." It was this same Charbashian, however, who in 1911 "had attempted to hand over to Minorsky and Shipley a petition expressing the satisfaction of the local Christian population with the Turkish administration."[37]

Similarly, Nestorians, Armenians, Catholics, and Presbyterians, some wearing Ottoman fezzes, greeted Iyas enthusiastically in the large village of Mamed-Yar, the administrative center of Salduz. The Shi'i Karapapak Khans who now controlled the village complained about abuses suffered at the hands of both Turks and Christians during its occupation.[38] Iyas met with the Christians at the home of Absalom [Avessalom], a local priest who was receiving 150 tumans annually from the American mission in Urumieh. Also in attendance was a Catholic priest representing fourteen souls and an Assyrian with good Russian pretending to be Orthodox. Iyas attributed this multiplicity of affiliations to the fact that for strategic reasons, most Assyrian families had members belonging to various faiths and were willing to convert for personal gain. Confusion was not limited to religious affiliations. After being teased about his Turkish fez, Absalom donned his Persian hat to bid Iyas farewell and settle into his new identity.[39]

[36] Iyas's Secret Report on the December 1912 Expedition to Lahijan and Salduz, in Tchalenko, *Images*, 100–106.
[37] Tchalenko, *Images*, 107–8.
[38] Ibid., 110.
[39] Ibid., 110–12.

Not only the communities of the *nevahi-i şarkıyye* were changing hats. By the beginning of 1913, Istanbul had decisively lost Albania, Thrace, and Macedonia, which had been core areas of the empire for almost five hundred years. In a situation recalling the aftermath of the 1878 Russo-Ottoman War, massive numbers of refugees deluged Asia Minor and Istanbul. As the remnants of its empire convulsed under the CUP's chauvinistic rule, Istanbul faced ever-increasing pressure to finalize its boundaries with Iran, not only because of Russian interests in the north, but also because of British apprehensions concerning Zohab's still undefined status and the resultant lack of security on the vital commercial route between Baghdad and Kermanshah.[40] Russia made it known that any resumption of Ottoman expansion would force it to move toward Asia Minor. Alternatively, the settlement of the frontier would resolve tensions between St. Petersburg and Istanbul.[41]

EXCLUSION OF IRAN FROM NEGOTIATIONS

Preventing a Russian incursion into Asia Minor was high on Istanbul's list of priorities. In early 1913, Ibrahim Hakkı Pasha, ex–grand vizier and special representative of Istanbul, was in England looking for financial support and trying to negotiate the issue of the frontier directly with London and indirectly with Russia. London made clear that any economic assistance would be contingent on the finalization of the boundaries in Zohab and Muhammarah.[42] Hakkı insisted that Zohab's boundaries be defined according to religious affiliation. If Istanbul accepted Russia's wishes in the north and British wishes in the south, he reasoned, it should receive compensation in the middle, namely Zohab. The pasha furthermore claimed that parts of Zohab had only been incorporated by Iran during the Greek War. "This," he argued, "was a very unfair state of affairs, especially as a large portion of the population in the northern part of the province was Sunni."[43] After seventy years of negotiating on its own terms, Istanbul was now asking for a favor. Its position was so weak that Grey suggested "some slight cessions of territory to Turkey on some portions of the frontier will very probably be necessary in order that the

---

[40] McDovall to Townley, Kermanshah, December 5, 1912, *Schofield V*, 516.

[41] Grey to Buchanan, January 27, 1913; and Buchanan to Grey, St. Petersburg, January 28, 1913, *Schofield V*, 519–20.

[42] Burcu Kurt, "*Ortadoğuda Bir Istikrarsızlık Unsuru: Şattü'l-Arap Sorunu* (MA thesis, Marmara University, 2006), 79–85.

[43] Minute by Parker, March 4, 1913, *Schofield V*, 532.

settlement should appear in the light of a compromise and not of a Turkish surrender."[44]

Having failed to integrate the Sunnis of the shah more broadly into the domains of the Sunni caliph, Istanbul now advocated the principle of "Sunni for Turkey and Shia for Persia" in Zohab only.[45] After much back-and-forth, Hakkı agreed to cede Qasr-i Shirin and Zohab to Iran in exchange for the Chia-Sourkh petroleum fields. Not coincidentally, Qasr-i Shirin was also the planned terminus of the future Russian railway; hence, the limits of Russia's sphere of influence delimited the shah's domains. Istanbul, meanwhile, was forced to rely on Russia and England to induce Iran to leave the Sunni-occupied territories to the sultan. They consented on the condition that religious affiliation would not be adapted as a general principle of delimitation but rather limited to Zohab.[46] As the resultant agreement left the Sinjabi winter quarters in the Ottoman Empire and its summer ones in Iran, Hakkı requested that any final decision not impede the tribe's rights to their pasturelands. Following this breakthrough, Russia accepted Istanbul's proposed boundary line from Ararat to Baneh (with the exception of modifications pertaining to specific villages). This long-in-the-making line, ironically, followed the guidelines set out by the Erzurum Treaty many decades before.

The definitive demarcation, however, would be left to the survey commission. Before that could happen, the Porte authorized Hakkı to reach a final agreement with England. On July 29, 1913, he and Grey signed the Anglo-Turkish Agreement, which included, among other items, one convention to establish a commission to improve navigation on the Shat-al-Arab and another that included a secret declaration providing for the settlement of both nations' respective interests in the Persian Gulf region. Also included was the pasha's suggestion for "a declaration, with the necessary maps, indicating the line of the Turco-Persian frontier from the region of Hawizeh to the sea," and the foreign office's recommendation that the remaining part of the frontier also be settled. Other issues addressed pertained to trade and customs, railway transport and river navigation, the borrowing power of Egypt, and the autonomy of Kuwait. Moreover, Istanbul explicitly recognized the independence of Bahrain and

---

[44] Grey to Lowther, FO, March 6, 1913, *Schofield V*, 533.
[45] Lowther to Grey, Constantinople, March 20 and 25, 1913, *Schofield V*, 542, 545.
[46] Lowther to Grey, Constantinople, April 5, 1913, *Schofield V*, 553; Prince Said Halim to Russian Ambassador, Sublime Porte, March 31, 1913, *Schofield V*, 554.

Qatar, and with it the changing power dynamics in the gulf.[47] On July 3, 1913 *The Times* reported from Constantinople that "an agreement has been fully concluded on the question of the delimitation of the Turco-Persian frontier, and it has been decided to appoint a Commission composed of delegates of Turkey, Persia, G. Britain, and Russia for the purpose of demarcating the boundary."[48]

Following this agreement, communications between St. Petersburg, London, Istanbul, and occasionally Tehran gained momentum as preparations for the logistical and technical aspects of the commission began. This time around, London and St. Petersburg wanted to ensure that their representatives had the power of arbitration and that the final protocol would be absolutely binding.[49] Regional representatives and technical teams provided the British and Russian ambassadors in Istanbul with memos, notes, and detailed district maps, which they, in turn, used to try to persuade Istanbul to accept a definitive line on the map before the commission's work commenced. As Iran was practically excluded from negotiations, the British representative in Tehran, Walter Townley, warned Grey, "It was by no means unlikely that the Persian Government may resent not having been consulted about the last details of Turco-Persian frontier, and we may experience some difficulty in securing their concurrence." Although anxious to avoid future Turkish aggression, the Persians were "apt to be obstinate when they think that their national *amour-propre* has been wounded," he noted.[50]

Despite such concerns, Tehran continued to be inconsequential. Russo-British cooperation was peaking, and protecting each other's interests in their respective spheres of influence, they occasionally referred to the frontier's "Russian" or "British" portions. According to Marling, even if Tehran criticized decisions regarding the zone that stretched from Ararat to Zohab, an area in which Britain took no special interest, "Russia and the Russian Legation at Tehran will no doubt be in a position to explain and defend against Persian criticism of the various arrangements."[51] Marling moreover expressed surprise that Tehran was dissatisfied at all, as the Ottoman occupation had been settled in a way it could never have achieved without Russo-British intervention. For this reason, and to protect the interests of the

---

[47] FO Draft Memorandum for Hakki Pasha, June 1, 1913, *Schofield V*, 593–96; and Wilson, *SW Persia*, 272.

[48] The short report is attached to Grey to Buchanan, FO, July 3, 1913, *Schofield V*, 613.

[49] Buchanan to Grey, St. Petersburg, August 24, 1913, *Schofield V*, 714.

[50] Townley to Grey, Tehran, August 8, 1913, *Schofield V*, 701.

[51] Marling to Grey, Constantinople, August 21, 1913, *Schofield V*, 705.

Anglo-Persian Oil Company, Tehran should acquiesce to the suggested line in Zohab.[52] Knowing the importance the British placed on oil, Istanbul soon alleviated London's concerns regarding the Anglo-Persian Oil Company. In early November 1913, the company's managing director informed London's Foreign Office that the Turkish government was pre-pared to recognize his company's rights in any district transferred from Persia to Turkey north of the Elvend River, which contained valuable oil-fields. He suggested the same policy be followed in territories south of Mendeli to Hawizeh.[53]

Just previously, in October, the Russian and British Embassies in Istanbul had submitted a *Draft Protocol Respecting the Turco-Persian Frontier* to Tehran and Istanbul. British and Russian representatives in Tehran met with Iranian Prime Minister Ala-es-Saltanah to persuade him that the protocol satisfactorily settled an old and thorny question. Although he acknowledged that Iran alone would not have been able to make such an agreement, and that his country would acquire significant land in some parts of the frontier, Ala-es-Saltanah complained that in other parts Iran would lose large tracts of territory that had been in its possession for centuries. London and St. Petersburg urged their representatives to dispel Tehran's objections.[54]

Despite some continued wrangling, Ottoman and Iranian powerlessness meant that, after decades, the frontier negotiations were drawing to a close. At the beginning of November, commissioners representing each of the four powers presented their governments with a new draft protocol. The debates this time around focused on only minor details, such as rules of procedure or limited pasturage or water rights in places such as the Ganguir River in Somar, which was used by both the Kalhur tribe and the inhabitants of Mendeli. In the latter case, the commissioners agreed that as with the Sanjabis, existing rights should be maintained regardless of a tribe's citizen-ship. Likewise, they concluded that the Sheikh of Muhammarah "shall continue to enjoy in conformity with the Ottoman laws his rights of own-ership in Ottoman territory."[55] After such particulars had been decided, the

[52] Ibid.
[53] Marling to Grey, Constantinople, September 24, 1913, *Schofield V*, 726. Greenway, Managing Director Anglo-Persian Oil Company, to FO, London, November 12, 1913, *Schofield V*, 766.
[54] Townley to Grey, Tehran October 27–28, 1913, *Schofield V*, 747.
[55] For the Shatt's boundaries in the 1913 Protocol, see Richard N. Schofield, *Evolution of the Shatt al-'Arab Boundary Dispute* (Wisbech, Cambridgeshire, UK: Middle East & North African Studies Press, 1986), 48–52.

Constantinople Protocol was signed on November 17, 1913, and the final commission was ready to hit the road.[56]

THE FINAL COMMISSION, 1913–1914[57]

The search for commission members had commenced several months earlier. The Russian and British ambassadors believed that their commissioners should be familiar with the tribal conditions along the frontier and the Turkish and Persian languages and cultures, so as to be able to keep the peace between the Iranian and Ottoman commissioners. Thus, Albert Charles Wratislaw, the British consul-general at Crete, previously of Tabriz, was appointed as the principal British commissioner.[58] Captain Arnold T. Wilson, who would become the British civil commissioner for Iraq at the time of its making, was appointed assistant commissioner with power to act in the event that Wratislaw became unable to fulfill his duties.[59] Lieutenant-Colonel Ryder, who had previous experience in boundary commissions in India and China, was made deputy-commissioner and head of the survey; he worked with another survey officer from India, Major Cowie.[60] G. E. Hubbard, who knew French, Turkish, and Arabic, was named secretary.[61] All told, the British commission totaled 150 men, the majority from India.[62]

---

[56] For the Ottoman version see BOA.HR.SYS 701-1, Constantinople, Imprimerie "Osmanie," 1914; and Protocol Relatif a la Délimitation turco-persane, signé à Constantinople, also in *Schofield V*, 757; for English, *Schofield V*, 427.

[57] The following account is based on an *Abstract English Translation of the Proceedings of the Turco-Persian Frontier Commission, 1913–14*, British Library, L/P&S/10/932. [Hereafter L/P&S/10/932 *Abstract English Translation*]; the original is *Recueil des Procès-Verbaux des Séances de la commission de Delimitation de la Frontière Turco-Persane 1913–1914*, British Library, L/P&S/10/522 [Hereafter L/P&S/10/522], also *Schofield VI*, 55–253.

[58] Wratislaw wrote *A Consul in the East* (Edinburgh: W. Blackwood, 1924), about his years as a consul. For his appointment, see Marling to Grey, Constantinople, July 21, 1913; and Grey to Buchanan, FO, July 25, 1913, *Schofield V*, 637, 639. Wilson replaced him when he fell ill toward the commission's end.

[59] Maurice Harari, "The Turco-Persian Boundary Question: A Case Study in the Politics of Boundary Making in the Near and Middle East" (Ph.D. dissertation, Columbia University, 1953), 184. Wilson wrote about the commission in *SW Persia*.

[60] C. H. D. Ryder later became deputy-director of surveys of Baghdad and surveyor-general of India. On the Ottoman-Iranian frontier, he wrote "The Demarcation of the Turco-Persian Boundary in 1913–14," *Geographical Journal* 66.3 (1925): 225–39.

[61] Hubbard, *From the Gulf*.

[62] Lists of all four parties' members are available at BOA.HR.SYS. 703/1 p. 52, Tahran Sefaretinden Hariciye Nezaretine, 15 Kanun-u Evvel 914, and also in L/P&S/10/522. Ryder provides a slightly different list in Final Report on the Turco-Persian Frontier Commission, April 1, 1915, in L/P&S/10/522. Hubbard also provides a list.

Mr G. E. Hubbard.   Lieut.-Col. Ryder, R.E.,   Capt. A. T. Wilson,
D.S.O., C.I.E.   C.M.G.

Capt. A. H. Brooke.   Major H. M. Cowie,   Mr A. C. Wratislaw,   Capt. H. W. Pierpoint,
R.E.   C.B., C.M.G.   I.M.S.
(*British Commissioner*).

The British Commission.

FIGURE 5. British commission members 1913–14.
Reproduced from G. E. Hubbard, *From the Gulf to Ararat* (Edinburgh and London: William Blackwood and Sons, 1916), 16.

FIGURE 6. British commission members 1913–14.
Chris Seaton/A. C. Wratislaw Archives, with permission from Chris Seaton.

Russia's choice of commissioner was obvious: Vladimir Fedorovich Minorsky, who would become a well-known scholar of Iran and historian of the peoples and geography of the northern borderland. He had served as a diplomat in Tabriz and Tehran and traveled the northern borderland extensively. As the previous chapter noted, in 1911, he had carried out a joint survey of regions under Ottoman occupation with Colonel Shipley. Indeed, his interest in the borderlanders was such that Wilson described him as "Minorsky, who talks Kurdish indefatigably and is more interested in them, I believe, than in the frontier."[63] A graduate of Moscow University's Faculty of Law and the Lazarev Institute of Oriental Languages, where he studied Turkish, Arabic, and Persian, Minorsky was secretary of the Russian Embassy in Istanbul at the time of his appointment.[64] Deputy Commissioner M. D. Belaiew (deputy consul at Bushehr), a naturalist, officers of the General Staff, a guard of Cossacks, a doctor, topographical corps, auxiliary camp staff, and his wife accompanied him.[65]

Istanbul appointed Binbaşı (Major) Ali Sami Bey, who had been a commissioner in the frontier region since 1905. Yüzbaşı (Captain)

FIGURE 7. Russian Commissioner Vladimir Minorksy with Russian officers and Iranian Commissioner members.
Finnish Museum of Photography, Alexander Iyas Collection 192.

[63] Wilson, *SW Persia*, 282.
[64] For Minorsky's career see D. M. Lang, "Obituary, Vladimir Fedorovich Minorsky," *Bulletin of SOAS* 29.3 (1966): 649–99.
[65] Aide-memoire communicated to Buchanan, St. Petersburg, Juliet 13 (26), 1913, *Schofield V*, 644.

FIGURE 8. Vladimir Minorksy, Iranian Commissioner Ittila al-Mulk, and members of their retinue.
Finnish Museum of Photography, Alexander Iyas Collection 195.

FIGURE 9. Vladimir Minorsky and Mrs. Minorsky with a group of Cossacks.
Finnish Museum of Photography, Alexander Iyas Collection 233.

Abdulhamid Bey and Basri Bey of the Foreign Ministry were made his deputy commissioners, and like the other parties, he was assigned auxiliary personnel. The Iranian commissioner was Ittila al-Mulk. His deputy was Mansour es-Saltaneh and his military advisor was Salar Mozaffar, who had been trained at French Ecole Polytechnique and the Berlin Military

Academy. A surveyor, a technical team headed by Abdul Rezak Khan, two topographers, Mohsen Khan and Asghar Khan an escort of forty Cossacks, a doctor, a secretary, and other camp followers joined him. His appointment, however, was delayed because of lack of funds. Tehran ultimately borrowed the money for its commission's expenses and for boundary signs from London and St. Petersburg and acquired its equipment from India.[66]

The survey commission began at Muhammarah. The British arrived in mid-December, and as a reminder of the increasingly surveilled state of the frontier, they were put in quarantine for several hours before being allowed to debark. The Russians, who traveled via ship from Istanbul, arrived next. The Ottoman and Iranian commissioners, traveling overland, reached Muhammarah a month later.[67] Because Russo-British cooperation was so intense, the arbitrating commissioners agreed, with little fanfare, that the British team would focus on the south and the Russians on the north. As happened in 1848–52, smaller surveys were carried out in advance of the commission's arrival. Russian Consul Iyas, for example,

Our Turkish and Persian Colleagues.
Etela-ul-Mulk (*Persian Commissioner*).
Major Aziz Samih Bey (*Ottoman Commissioner*).

FIGURE 10. Ottoman and Iranian commission members.
Reproduced from G. E. Hubbard, *From the Gulf to Ararat* (Edinburgh and London: William Blackwood and Sons, 1916), 18.

[66] Grey to Townley, FO, November 13 and 16, 1913, *Schofield V*, 768, 770.
[67] Hubbard, *From the Gulf*, 32.

FIGURE 11. Iranian commission members, 1913–14.
A. C. Wratislaw Collection with permission from Chris Seaton.

undertook a one-month journey through Savojbulagh to "map the mountain passes connecting the two countries, investigate the conditions the commissions would be encountering and gather information about where the various Kurdish tribes placed the natural frontier between the two countries."[68] Along the way, he was hosted and guided by tribal leaders who informed him about the mountains that had long served as the ad hoc border.[69] Also like 1848–52, the military, diplomatic, technical, and logistical components of the large survey caravan brought together global,

---

[68] Iyas, "Journey to Western Kurdistan 2 August–2 September 1913," in Tchalenko, *Images*, 150–60.

[69] For the logistics and a colorful composition of the entire caravan, see "Notes by Wilson for Information and Guidance of Survey Party Which Is to Be Sent to Mohammarah to Join the Turco-Persian frontier Commission," August 16, 1913, *Schofield V*, 687–99; Wilson, *SW Persia*, 279–90; Hubbard, *From the Gulf*, 15.

regional, and local actors. Advancing through difficult terrains and accompanied by hundreds of pack mules and horses, the miles-long cavalcade no doubt appeared to the local populations as an intimidating military expedition. In many ways, however, it was a curious procession. Representing Britons, Russians, Indians of various regions, Persians, Turks, Kurds, Lurs, Arabs, Armenians, Nestorians, and others, its members displayed a wide variety of costumes and customs.

Policies and procedures for the commission were quickly established. French would be the official language of the proceedings and the 1869 *Carte Identique* would serve as the topographical basis for the delimitation. The negotiating parties would share the financial burden of the boundary pillars, whose construction would be supervised by a subcommission of at least two delegates or other personnel. Upon completion of its labors, the commission would submit a detailed description of the frontier based on the verbatim proceedings as well as copies of the map approved by the four delegations to each of the participating governments and to their ambassadors in Tehran and Istanbul.[70]

To put into action the November 17, 1913, protocol, the commission initiated a series of meetings beginning on January 21, 1914 and ending on October 26 of the same year. The first was held in a fine house belonging to the Sheikh of Muhammarah, whereas subsequent ones took place on ships, in the houses of other local notables, or in tents in the desert or mountains.[71] Moving from south to north, in just ten months the commission demarcated 1,180 miles and erected 227 boundary pillars, most of which would be destroyed by the local inhabitants immediately after their construction. Contemporary technologies of triangulation, topography, astronomy, and telegraph were used to pinpoint the latitude, longitude, and azimuth of each point, and technical and all other aspects of the demarcation process were recorded in miniscule detail.[72]

Such technologies not only bolstered the survey's scientific credentials; they also proved to be crucial to its progress. Before its members departed Istanbul, their ambassadors had sketched on the *Carte Identique* the main outlines of about three-quarters of the frontier and charged the commissioners to fill in the details. As work progressed, however, it became obvious that the *Carte* was not sufficiently accurate. For example, a group of previously nonexistent islands on the Shatt al-Arab had to be

[70] Harari, *Turco-Persian*, 181.
[71] L/P&S/10/932, *Abstract English Translation*, 9.
[72] BOA.HR.SYS 703/1 and L/P&S/10/522.

added to it. Indeed, with the exception of areas comprising a single topo-graphical feature that itself formed the frontier (for which an accurate map was not even necessary), the *Carte* proved worthless. Thus, the commis-sion employed triangulation through the whole length of the boundary in order to create a new and accurate map.

Technology, however, was not an all-encompassing solution. Environmental changes and the instability and unpredictability of the natu-ral environment proved to be the biggest obstacles. The Shatt-al-Umma (or Armah) River, which ran for about twenty-seven miles between the Duvarij River and Umm Chir, provides a good example. The ancient channel of the Duvarij, this Shatt was boldly marked on the *Carte* as the status quo frontier, a classification confirmed by local testimony. Yet, at the time of the com-mission, portions of its main bed had disintegrated, splitting it into two or more courses, which in some cases were little more than ditches. This situation made it practically impossible to locate the status quo. Moreover, as Wratislaw remarked, such terrain complicated the building of permanent markers: "The mounds of earth erected to mark the frontier line as laid down in these doubtful sections were liable to be carried away by floods, any dispute will have to be decided by the map."[73]

Notwithstanding such difficulties, the British were tasked with complet-ing a technical survey up to latitude 36° near Lahijan, whereas the Russians did most of the work from there northward. Having less technical expertise, the negotiating parties accepted their findings, "a fact in great part due to the confidence inspired by our Indian surveyors, all Muhammedans," Ryder surmised.[74] Hubbard described their task as follows:

A section of frontier would be described in the Protocol as following the crest of a certain mountain, for instance, and passing thence to a neighbouring peak, leaving such and such a village to Turkey or Persia as the case might be. The line being thus broadly indicated, the engineers went ahead, surveyed a strip of country eight or ten miles wide, and had a detailed map waiting for the Commissioners by the time they arrived. The latter then, after examining the map and the ground, met in solemn conclave and debated the precise line of the frontier, which when agreed upon was described in writing, marked on the map with red ink, and on the ground with a line of boundary pillars. Along the undelimited part the matter was, of course, less simple. The only basis for the Commissioners' guidance was the status quo frontier of 1848 – a very illusive ghost, as one may well imagine. The rival claims in this region were often as much as twenty miles apart, and a compromise was next door

[73] L/P&S/10/522 Notes by Wratislaw on the Demarcation of Turco-Persian Frontier from Mohammarah to Vazneh, Enclosure No. 1 of Wratislaw to Grey, London, December 21, 1914.

[74] Ryder, The Demarcation of the Turco-Persian Boundary, 236–37.

to impossible, so that in the end almost the whole of this section was settled by Russo-British arbitration.[75]

Indeed, it was due to Russia's and England's newly acquired powers of arbitration that the parties were efficient enough to become the last boundary commission. The November protocol had established that in the event of any difference of opinion, the negotiators would have forty-eight hours to submit their arguments in writing to the Russian and British delegates. The latter would then consult in private and issue a binding joint decision. As the commission progressed, all delimitations would be considered as absolutely fixed.[76] Such binding decisions could be challenging to reach because of the sorts of ambiguities described by Hubbard, as well as the difficulty of obtaining reliable information from local inhabitants. As Wratislaw noted, despite many treaties and the work of various commissioners, there were still "immense tracts of debatable territory over which neither Power in the distant past had ever established permanent sovereignty; the inhabitants thereof were more or less independent and were quite ready to change their allegiance from one side to the other when circumstances rendered it desirable to do so."[77] Still, such ambiguities offered few lasting impediments. Hence, a few miles upstream from Muhammarah, in the village of Diaiji, Boundary Pillar No. 1 was erected in the last week of January 1914.[78] Before its construction began, a sheep was sacrificed and each of the four commissioners laid a brick at its foot before a group of local masons completed the edifice. The celebrations continued with an elaborate feast organized by Sheikh Khaz'al, who was secure in the knowledge that the Ottoman threat had been vanquished.[79]

Despite such celebrations, Iranian claims to the waters of Shatt al-Arab proved to be a sticking point. As the new frontier line followed the Persian coast instead of passing down the middle of the river, Tehran again pushed for its traditional rights of navigation. In response, Grey pointed to the Anglo-Turkish Convention of July 29, 1913, which declared that such navigation was open to all nations; therefore, he maintained, Persia "should pay dues for the services rendered, [because such dues] would be levied impartially on all shipping of all countries, and ... are indispensable

[75] Hubbard, *From the Gulf*, 21–22.
[76] Harari, *Turco-Persian*, 178.
[77] Wratislaw discussing Ryder's paper, *Geographical Journal* 66.3 (September 1925), 239–40.
[78] Ryder, The Demarcation of the Turco-Persian Boundary, 229.
[79] Hubbard, *From the Gulf*, 59.

The Sheikh's Feast.

FIGURE 12. Sheikh Khaz'al's feast for commission members, January 1914. Reproduced from G. E. Hubbard, *From the Gulf to Ararat* (Edinburgh and London: William Blackwood and Sons, 1916), 48.

if the river is to be adapted to the developments of modern shipping."[80] Once more excluded from the delimitation of its own frontier, Iran was forced to comply to the dictates of London and Istanbul, which stipulated that "the modern port and anchorage of Muhammarah, above and below the junction of the river Karun with the Shat-al-Arab" were to remain within Persian jurisdiction, but "the Ottoman right of usage of this part of the river shall not, however, be affected thereby, nor shall Persian jurisdiction extend to the parts outside the anchorage."[81] This unceremonious severing of Iran from the Shatt al-Arab would leave a scar that would occasionally reopen.

After the Shat-al-Arab, the commission moved into the harsh desert where environment played a defining role in its decision making. As Ryder noted, the scarcity and poor quality of water made even the fieriest disputant become meek as a lamb, bleating out, "[p]ut the boundary where you like, only let us get away."[82] Given such conditions and because it was impossible to erect boundary marks in the desert with sand the only

[80] Townley to Grey, Tehran, November 16, 1913, *The Times*, November 17, 1913, attached to Grey to Townley, November 18, 1913, *Schofield V*, 770–72.
[81] See Harari, *Turco-Persian*, Appendix F.
[82] Ryder, The Demarcation of the Turco-Persian Boundary, 232.

material available, it was agreed that here the map was sufficient to guide the frontier. The same principle was upheld for the marshes and extensive swamps between parallel 31 and Umm Chir, as this region was bereft of landmarks or any clear-cut passageway that coincided even approximately with the frontier line laid down by the protocol. In any case, as Wratislaw noted in his final report, the difficult nature of the district and its paucity of inhabitants rendered any disputes unlikely unless at some future time the marshes should be drained.[83]

From these bleak regions, the commissioners advanced northward into Posht-e Kuh, where the ownership of many districts was highly disputed. Yet, instead of becoming mired in minutiae, this commission summarily put into practice the principle that the hill country of Posht-e Kuh belonged to Iran (i.e., the *wali* of Posht-e Kuh) and its plains to the Ottoman Empire. Thus, the district of Bagsai, which lay entirely inside the plain, was given to the latter. The land of Seyyid Hassan, situated in a gap between the two ranges of hills in such a way that it appeared to belong to the hills rather than the plain, was awarded to Iran, along with Seifi and Malhatavi. The commissioners did not ignore private property rights for the benefit of state territorial sovereignty. In this spirit, because members of the Faili tribe, who were subjects of the *wali* of Posht-e Kuh, had long cultivated fields in the region, they were granted rights to considerable properties in Bagsai (Bakche-Chai) and Zorbatia that were to be given to the Ottomans.[84] Although solving a stubborn issue, this decision created one of the lasting legacies of the forceful division of borderland communities by the international boundary: the Failis, divided between Iran and the Ottoman Empire, would be expelled from Iraq almost seventy years later by Saddam Hussein, who accused them of being Iranian.

As in Baghsai, in Qasr-i Shirin and Zohab, the commissioners upheld the principle of private property rights. Hence, they agreed that the Sanjabis should retain full grazing rights on their traditional pastures between Mendeli and Qasr-i Shirin, which were to be transferred to the Ottomans. Similarly the rights of Ottoman tribes coming to Dalamper Mountains near Urumieh were protected.[85] These decisions set a precedent that allowed most tribes to retain their traditional pasturage rights no matter on which side of the boundary their citizenship came to lie.

---

[83] Ibid.
[84] L/P&S/10/522, Notes by Wratislaw..., December 21, 1914.
[85] Ibid.; Declaration, signed by Minorsky and Wilson, Balkha, May 13, 1914, in L/P&S/10/ 932, *Abstract English Translation*, 38–39.

Whereas the example of the Sanjabis involved communal pasturage usage, other cases highlighted individual property rights. Because it was agreed that the demarcation should not impair such rights, Wratislaw observed, "it is evident that the frontier will not prejudice the possession of fields of one party or the other which may happen to be situated on the other side of the frontier."[86] The Iranian and Ottoman commissioners not only defended the rights of their own subjects, but also accepted the corresponding rights of their counterpart's subjects as well. For example, when the Yarim Kaya swamps were left to Tehran and the neighboring Bulak Bashi district to Istanbul, the Iranian commissioner asked his colleague to allow the inhabitants of Yarim Kaya to pasture their herds in Boulak-Bashi. In return, he promised to guarantee the rights of Ottoman subjects to cut reeds in the marshes.[87]

While respecting cross-boundary private and communal property rights, the commissioners were bent on finalizing debates about borderlanders' citizenship. One place that the ambiguous subjecthood of the inhabitants played a significant role was the district of Vezneh, where, as the previous chapter recounted, questions of ownership as well as Ottoman and Iranian

FIGURE 13. Last frontier commission camp.
Finnish Museum of Photography, 135.

[86] L/P&S/10/932, An Arbitral Decision with Reference to the Village of Tchamperaw, Signed by Wratislaw and Minorsky on June 14, 1914, *Abstract English Translation*, 50.

[87] L/P&S/10/932, 46th Sitting, Tavile, June 1, 1914; 72nd Sitting, Sero, August 24, 1914; 84th Sitting, Bazargan, October 20, 1914; 86th Sitting, Boulak Bashi, October 23, 1914, *Abstract English Translation*, 42, 65, 74, 76 respectively.

meddling in the affairs of the Bilbas tribes had first triggered the occupation of the parts of northwestern Iran. When both mediating commissioners once more claimed the Bilbas as subjects, Minorsky noted that the first Russian surveyor, Tchirikof, described them as *les Bilbas Turcs* and reported that they spent summers in Vezneh and winters on the Ottoman side. Nevertheless, Minorsky remarked, at present all of these tribes (Mangur, Mamesh, Piran) were settled in Iran and could therefore no longer be said to inhabit both countries. Thus, he concluded,

The subjection of these nomads is no longer affected by the consideration of their sojourn in the territories of the two powers. At present their subjection is a purely personal matter, and depends on their choice, within the limits laid down by the treaties for the preservation or the alteration of their nationality. In so far as they claim always to have been Turkish subjects, they can not be prevented except by what is laid down by the treaties.[88]

Even though the Iranian commissioner Ittila al-Mulk stated that they had no power to decide the nationality of the Bilbas, with Minorksy's help, the Bilbas tribes, whose chiefs had already submitted to Iran, were declared Iranian citizens because their main residences were located there.

This did not mean that the Bilbas preferred to be the subjects of one power or the other. Not long after the commission left, they pulled down the pillars erected by the Russian commission's triangulation party.[89] The commission was aware of such resistance. From Vezneh to its northernmost point at Ararat, the frontier followed, with few exceptions, a well-marked watershed that formed a natural boundary. Yet even such a clear-cut natural division was not sufficient, as Colonel Ryder observed: "It never has and never will however be a true frontier as the Kurds from either side come up into the hills for the summer and by mutual arrangement amongst each other."[90] Years later, Ryder, with some sympathy for the Kurdish borderlanders, noted that

The fixing of a frontier was however repugnant to the finer feelings of the Kurds, and from "evidence received" we were left in no doubt that most of our pillars survived their erection a bare twenty-four hours. It is so easy to lay down a frontier in the chancelleries of Europe and to agree that if Turkey makes a concession in the south, Persia shall respond in the north; but this is no consolation to the inhabitants

[88] L/P&S/10/932, 65th Sitting, Khane, July 25, 1914, *Abstract English Translation*, 56–57.

[89] L/P&S/10/522, Report on the Proceedings of the Turco-Persian Frontier Commission from July 16 until Its Termination on October 26, 1914, by A. Wilson, C.M.G., Political Department, Government of India. [Hereafter Wilson Report.]

[90] L/P&S/10/522, Turco-Persian Frontier Commission, Report by Colonel Ryder April 1, 1915.

concerned: they will not stand it at any price, when they live in inaccessible country remote from central governments. Full consideration must always be given to local opinions.[91]

It was, of course, not delicate sentiments but rather the forceful division of their habitat and customary lands that made the Kurds resist the imposition of limits. Consequently, they were represented by observers less sympathetic than Ryder as wild, uncivilized hordes resisting the civilizing mission of empires.

Moving northward from Vezneh, the commissioners reached the town of Ushnu on July 26, where they were hosted by the Russian detachment stationed there. On August 3, just as their work was coming to an end, they received news of the outbreak of war in Europe. Unlike previous commissions that disbanded when given similar news, this one accelerated its efforts. While the commissioners finished demarcating the watershed, a subcommission left for Kotur. It was fated to represent yet another failed attempt to mark that forty-mile stretch of frontier. This time, however, the locals rather than the negotiating governments were the obstacle. Even though the British surveyors had prepared a detailed map of the region, the Ottoman commissioner objected to making any definite decision. His hesitation, Wilson recorded, was due, at least in part, to the resistance of a local tribe:

The inhabitants (Shemski tribesmen) of the six villages destined to be transferred to Persia, alarmed at the prospect of being handed over to the tender mercies of the local Persian chiefs, of the rival Avdoi clan, their hereditary foes, had been protesting by telegram to Van and Istanbul. Emphasis was added to their representations by the fact that in the course of general mobilization the villages in question had furnished a number of men for the army, and these men were actually under training in the disputed villages, which were all occupied by detachments of Turkish troops.[92]

Another complicating factor was the emergence of new villages. Between Kotur and Maku, for example, in the Egri Chai valley, various villages had appeared since the last frontier commission, making delimitation here almost impossible. As a result of such complications, this section of the boundary was decided two decades later, following a Kurdish revolt in the Ararat region.[93]

[91] Ryder, The Demarcation of the Turco-Persian Boundary, 236–37.
[92] L/P&S/10/522, Wilson Report.
[93] G. R. C. [Gerald R. Crone?], "The Turkish-Iranian Boundary," *The Geographical Journal* 91.1 (Jan. 1938): 57–59.

The Shemskis were but one example of how the borderland peoples continued to negotiate their identities, which were formed, not through simple directives, but rather through exchanges between periphery and center.[94] It was due to such exchanges that the commission, when faced with the problem of pastures and tribes, so often decided to respect existing pasturage rights.

Unable to solve the enduring case of Kotur, the now-dwindling commission proceeded to the final sections of the border. In spite of snowstorms and other obstacles, the commissioners signed the last protocols and maps not far from Bayezid, at the foot of Mount Ararat, on October 27, 1914, and a final meeting was held the following day. Hubbard summarized the scene as follows:

> In the autumn of 1914, a few weeks after the outbreak of the War, a small party consisting of Englishmen, Russians, Turks, and Persians arrived on a snow-clad spur of Mount Ararat, constructed an unobtrusive stone pillar beneath the shadow of the great 17,000-foot peak, and swiftly dispersed, each to his own country. Such (thanks to the Hun) were the inglorious circumstances which attended the culminating act of seventy odd years of diplomatic *pourparlers*, special commissions, and international conferences between the four Powers concerned.[95]

Minorsky and his deputy were the first to cross the frontier into Iran, leaving Ryder and Wilson to follow. Under dark of night, Wilson escaped to Maku two hours before Istanbul declared war on Russia on October 29.[96] Thus, the long transformation of the Ottoman-Iranian borderland into a boundary came to an end. Two hundred twenty-three boundary pillars marked the labors of this final commission, and the limits of the domains of the shah and the sultan. Of these, 10 were natural objects, rocks, and shrines; 18 were made of large mounds of earth; 79 were piles of stones without cement or mortar; and 116 were piles of stones set in cement or mortar.[97] It appears that most were erected in the northern parts of the frontier, a testimony to the nature, both contentious and fluid, of the physical and social geography of the region. Istanbul complained that they were not sufficiently strong. Wilson similarly noted that most were mere piles of stones carelessly erected, adding that the earthen ones were the most

---

[94] Peter Sahlins, *Boundaries: The Making of France and Spain in the Pyrenees* (Berkeley: University of California Press, 1989), 267–76 and Andrés Résendez,*Changing National Identities at the Frontiers, Texas and New Mexico, 1800–1850* (Cambridge, UK: Cambridge University Press, 2005), 268.

[95] Hubbard, *From the Gulf*, 1.

[96] Wilson, *SW Persia*, 299–301.

[97] L/P&S/10/522, Wilson Report.

satisfactory, as they were difficult to destroy. In fact, the only safe pillars were those that shared space with *nazargah*s, heaps of stones marking sacred spots identified with local saints.

Yet there was a good reason for the poor construction of the pillars: the commission knew that no matter what, they would likely be destroyed. As Hubbard noted, "No token of government is popular with the Kurds, and we should have known . . . that our carefully built monuments were lucky if they stood for a day once the back of authority had been turned."[98] Another member observed,

The Commission was not encouraged to spend much money or time on the erection of frontier pillars by the fact that, Arabs and Lurs took pleasure in destroying them almost as soon as erected, and even boasted in advance of their intention of doing so as soon as the Commission left . . . It is very doubtful whether one pillar in twenty is still standing.[99]

Seen as imprudent investments, the commission spent a trifling 300*l* to build the pillars, the same amount the British commissioners alone spent on presentation articles for the chiefs of large tribes they hoped would protect the boundary.[100] It would, however, take time for the boundary to become a real force in the everyday lives of ordinary borderlanders. Thus, when the commissioners inquired of shepherds in the south, "Whose country are you feeding your goats in?" the answer was not the shah's or the sultan's but "Allah's."[101] Yet cartography, trigonometry, and other map-making technologies allowed the commissioners to be less attentive to wanton acts of destruction or alternative ideas of space. Once agreed upon by them, the precise limits of the states, etched in black and white, were beyond the reach of the shepherds and other native inhabitants.

---

[98] Hubbard, *From the Gulf*, 23.
[99] Ibid., 78.
[100] L/P&S/10/522, Wilson Report.
[101] Hubbard, *From the Gulf*, 78.

Conclusion

In a famous 1907 lecture, Lord George Curzon observed that the demarcated frontier is an essentially modern conception and expectedly ascribed the precision necessary for its successful implementation to the European mind. In Asia, he noted,

There has always been a strong instinctive aversion to the acceptance of fixed boundaries, arising partly from the nomadic habits of the people, partly from the dislike of precise arrangements that is typical of the Oriental mind, but more still from the idea that in the vicissitudes of fortune more is to be expected from an unsettled than from a settled frontier. An eloquent commentary on these propensities is furnished by the present position of the Turco-Persian Frontier, which was provided for by the mediation of Great Britain and Russia in the Treaty of Erzerum exactly sixty years ago, and was even defined, after local surveys, by Commissioners of the two Powers as existing somewhere in a belt of land from 20 to 40 miles in width stretching from Mount Ararat to the Persian Gulf. There, unmaterialized and unknown, it has lurked ever since, both Persia and still more Turkey finding in these unsettled conditions an opportunity for improving their position at the expense of their rival that was too good to be surrendered or curtailed. In Asiatic countries it would be true to say that demarcation has never taken place except under European pressure and by the intervention of European agents.

Despite his undisguised bigotry and factual errors, Curzon correctly observes the adversarial relation between the socio-ecological organization of the frontier society and the notion of fixed boundaries. Moreover, as he claims, the Iranians and the Ottomans repeatedly exploited the unsettled frontier to improve their position at the expense of their rival. What he fails to note is that they did so mostly to the detriment of the frontier communities. Indeed, even as Curzon was delivering his lecture, Ottoman troops were busy trying to turn northwestern Iran into the northeastern Ottoman Empire, creating a conundrum of identity for the borderlanders. It was only Russo-British pressure, compounded by the Italian occupation of Libya and the tragedy of the Balkan Wars, that forced Istanbul to cease its efforts and accept the final demarcation of the frontier.

As this book has shown, the long road toward that demarcation began with the emergence of the Safavids and the Ottoman Empire's eastward expansion and ended days before World War I. All along the way, contradictory forces swirled around the peoples of the frontier, impinging on their loyalties and collective sense of self.[1] A cursory look at transborder movement and migration shows that as the border slowly took form, borderland communities struggled with enormous ambiguities as they were made to choose, if not a nationality, then a state subjecthood. As Andres Resendez has argued in a different context, at key moments they faced stark and very public choices and were forced to act as Iranians or Ottomans, however uncertain they privately felt about these categories.[2] By analyzing their various and varying identity choices, this book has shown that these communities were not and are not monolithic, neither can their identity choices be understood in terms of a single factor. For example, even although sectarian affiliations played a significant role in their lives, for the branches of the seminomadic Bilbas tribe, geography, natural resources, and intra-tribal rivalries were often more influential factors in shaping their choices. In contrast, Iran secured rights to Muhammarah and the strategic Abadan Peninsula, and to Zohab and Qasr-i Shirin, precisely because of the Shi'i affiliation of the Arab Ka'bs and the Sinjabi and Kalhor Kurds, respectively. Meanwhile, the Kurdish Dehbokri tribe remained loyal to Iran despite its Sunni affiliation, because of its historical ties to Iran and the influence of local rivalries. As Peter Sahlins has argued, identities – be they ethnic, national, or otherwise – are not simply imposed from the center on the peripheries. Rather, the process could best be described as a two-way exchange.[3] Indeed, as Andrés Résendez notes in some instances, frontier peoples struggling with questions of identity "found it convenient to uphold and maintain" boundaries in order to further their interests.[4] As the examples of the Mamesh, Sinjabi, Banu Lam, or Ka'b show, they at times appropriated and brought the state

---

[1] Andrés Reséndez, *Changing National Identities at the Frontiers: Texas and New Mexico, 1800–1850* (Cambridge, UK: Cambridge University Press, 2005), Introduction.

[2] Ibid., 2.

[3] Peter Sahlins, *Boundaries: The Making of France and Spain in the Pyrenees.* Berkeley: University of California Press, 1989, 267–76.

[4] Reséndez, *Changing National Identities*, 269.

to the frontier to further their local interests. Some of them, such as the Banu Lam in the Zorbatiyah area, actively petitioned the Ottoman commissioner to secure state support in exchange for their loyalty, in the process becoming Ottoman and binding their part of the borderland firmly to the imperial center.

It was not only the borderlanders who redefined their identity in a dynamic or situational way. The states, too, responded quickly to changing times and geopolitical realities. The transformation of the Ottoman Empire throughout the tumultuous "long nineteenth century" is a case in point. When the reform and centralization projects and the policy of Ottomanism failed to hold the empire together, and especially in the wake of the disastrous Russo-Ottoman War of 1877–78, Istanbul redefined itself as a (Sunni) Muslim state and developed policies accordingly. One such policy was the Ottoman occupation of Sunni northwestern Iran. I argued that this project, later formulated as "Sunnis for the sultan and Sh'is for the shah," began with the aggressive claims and actions of the first Ottoman survey commissioner Dervish Pasha, continued with the Sheikh Ubeidullah rebellion, and reached its logical conclusion with the 1905–12 occupation.

The Ottomans failed to integrate western Iran into their domains. However, helped by Russia and Britain, both they and their rival Iranians expanded state power in the peripheries through the boundary-making process and its twin, the centralization and modernization project. The resultant rise in the capacity of states required replacing the autonomous lords of the marches and their indirect rule with state appointees and direct rule, a strategy that fundamentally changed the socio-organizational life of the borderland communities by establishing the center's authority at the peripheries. The Kurdish communities of the borderland embodied this change. In the tradition of scholars such as Martin van Bruinessen and Janet Klein, this book challenges nationalist interpretations of these communities' history by analyzing how their sociopolitical structures were shaped by the interconnected dynamics of state centralization, imperialist intervention, and boundary making. Employing van Bruinessen's ideas to analyze what might be called "reverse evolution" of nineteenth-century Kurdish sociopolitical organization, I shed light on the failure of Kurdish nationalism to build a nation-state. Specifically, I argued that developments surrounding the making of the Ottoman-Iranian boundary – including the state-imposed destruction of local dynasties and the founding of the Hamidiye corps, among others – fundamentally atomized Kurdish society. This proved costly. Although many constituencies in the Middle East successfully organized central leadership during World War I, the Kurds, divided by boundaries and conflict among various petty chiefs, failed to do so. As a result, they had no one to broker for them with the imperialist powers that were once more dividing the region according to their interests. By destroying the foundation of Kurdish political organizations, the making of the Ottoman-Iranian boundary coupled with the imperialist remaking of the Middle East sealed the fate of this ethnic group.

Although unique in many ways, the Kurdish story told in this book is inseparable from the long, complicated history of the Iranian-Ottoman border. It is an iteration of the larger narrative of how the spatial strategy of territorialization unfolded in actuality, or on the ground, transforming the relationship between center and periphery from one of suzerainty to one of sovereignty. Underscoring the ongoing nature of this process, I conceive of borders not as zones but as filters whose porosity varies in time and space and changes, not only when state-centered order inscribes itself onto the borderlands, but also when local populations transgress and challenge that order. Hence, the movement toward territoriality that this study highlights is neither static nor unilaterally imposed.[5] Understanding this allows us to challenge the sacralization and mythologization of boundaries by nationalist regimes and their ideological apparatuses, including those supported by historians or the borderlanders themselves. For example, the myth of Qasr-i Shirin, analyzed in the first pages of this study, suggests that the Iranian-Ottoman frontier was firmly established in 1639; it is one of the oldest boundaries of the world, and even before the nineteenth century, it was well defined. However, the history of this polyglot borderland defies such a simplistic description. As we have seen, even in the nineteenth century, it resembled many things, but a pacified and settled frontier it was not. In times of war and peace, it witnessed a relatively free flow of goods and ideas, as well as of diseases, refugees, nomadic and seminomadic tribes, fugitives, and pilgrims. And throughout it all, Iran and, especially, the Ottoman Empire tried to redefine the boundary line, pushing it out at the expense of their rival.

Such unmaking or remaking of a supposedly settled boundary recalls Curzon's notion that "more is to be expected from an unsettled than from a settled frontier." But the process of boundary making also had its advantages, not only for the Great Powers of Europe, but also for Iran and the Ottoman Empire. For example, it allowed them, to greater or lesser degrees,

---

[5] Paolo Novak, "The Flexible Territoriality of Borders," *Geopolitics* 16.4 (2011): 747.

to tighten the border filter by controlling crossings at the border and criminalizing its transgression, thus increasing their surveillance capacity at their peripheries. This had the effect of weakening the cross-border networks that had once weaved the borderland together. Pastoral nomads who crisscrossed the borderland and tribes with branches straddling both sides of the line were forced to adapt their migratory patterns and social organization to the boundary's new contours. Indeed, these contours increasingly turned long-standing cross-border kin and social relations into "problems."[6] Such problems were magnified when the formalized boundaries were sacralized by the nation-states that inherited the imperial limits. It was at this point that the borderlanders became minorities distinct from "the nation," and their resistance to the impositions of newly minted nation-states became demonized as endangering the unity and indivisibility of the nation, so cogently symbolized by the boundary line.

Undoubtedly the boundary-making process inscribed the central states' regulatory regimes onto the borderland, defined the legal limits of state and human action, and reshaped patterns of life and identity. The boundary line that was, over the course of decades, inscribed on the region's physical and mental maps turned the borderlanders into Ottomans or Iranians, and over time it became a dividing wall. Yet it was not capable of transforming the essential cultural identity of the borderland peoples. As Rachel St. John argues about the U.S.-Mexico border, state power is never absolute. Even though the national states that inherited imperial boundaries "became stronger and more entrenched on the border over time, they never achieved complete authority over it."[7] Nor could they fully or exclusively impose their sovereignties or their conceptions of space and identity on the borderland peoples. Alternative conceptions of space and identity always persisted, whether or not recognized. For example, the Herki tribe wintered around Ottoman Mosul and spent its summers in Iranian Mergever and Tergever until the finalization of the boundary. At present, its territories occupy the triangle at the Turkish, Iranian, and Iraqi frontiers (about twenty villages each in Turkey and Iran, and about thirty villages in Iraq). Although such fragmentation inevitably shifted the rhythms of their life cycles, it did not considerably alter their social organization or kinship ties, which continued to be cross-border. Hence, until the 1970s,

---

[6] Michiel Baud and Willem van Schendel, "Toward a Comparative History of Borderlands," *Journal of World History* 8.2 (1997): 224.

[7] Rachel St. John, *Line in the Sand: A History of the Western U.S.-Mexico Border* (Princeton, NJ: Princeton University Press, 2011), 7.

their grand-agha, Mala Seyide Herki, who lived in Iraq, directed the voting patterns of the Herki residing in Turkey.[8] This phenomenon fundamentally changed, however, with the introduction of the deadliest of frontier policies: the line that divides them is now a field of mines. Commissioners and pillars no more, men with prosthetic body parts tell the observer where the border lays.

---

[8] See Kardeş Türküler, CD, *Traditional Music of Hakkari* (Istanbul: Kalan, 2005).

Select Bibliography

Archives

Başbakanlık Osmanlı Arşivi, Istanbul
British National Archives (Formerly PRO)
British Library, India Office Records
Ketabkhane-e Majlis-e Shoraye Eslami, Tehran

Official Publications and Collections of Documents

Administration Sanitaire de L'Empire Ottoman: Bilans et Statistiques. 2 vols. 1872–84, 1899–1904. (BOA Library, old registration number 2741) Constantinople: Typographie et Lithographie Centrales and Typo-Lithographie du Journal La Turque.

Cevdet, Erkan-ı Harbiye Kaimmakamı. *Iran Hududunun Tahdidine Medar Olan Defatir-i Hakani Kaydından Istinsah Edilmişdir, Hudud Komisyonuna Mahsusdur*. Istanbul: Süleymaniye Matbaa-i Askeriye, 1327. [BOA Library 3250]

Commission Mixte Chargée La Révision Tarif des Droits Sanitaires dans L'Empire Ottoman. Constantinople: Typographie et Lithographie Centrales, 1882. [BOA Library No. 5296]

Daftar-i Mutala'at-i Siyasi va Bayn al-Milali (Iran). *Guzidah-'i asnad-i siyasi-i Iran va Usmani: dawrah-'i Qajariyah*. 7 vols. Tehran: Daftar-i Mutala'at-i Siyasi va Bayn al-Milali, 1990.

Evkaf-ı Hümayun Nezaretinin Tarihçe-i Teşkilatı ve Nuzzar Teracim-i Ahvali. Darülhilâfetil'Aliye [Istanbul]: Evkaf-i İslamiye Matbaası, 1335 (1919).

Maunsell Lt. F. R. *Reconnaissances in Mesopotamia, Kurdistan, North-West Persia, and Luristan from April to October 1888. Vo. I: Narrative Report, Description of Larger Towns and Routes Leading from Them*. Simla: Printed at the government Central Printing Office, 1890. [BL-IOR, L/PS/201/44]

Salehi, Nasrollah. *Asnadi az In 'ikad-e 'Ahdnameh-e Dovvome Erzetelroum*. Tehran: Daftar-i Mutala'at-i Siyasi va Bayn al-Milali, 1377 (1999).

Schofield, Richard, ed. *The Iran-Iraq Border: 1840–1958*. 11 vols. Buckinghamshire, UK: Archive Editions, 1989.

Primary Sources and Chronicles

Adamec, Ludwig W. *Historical Gazetteer of Iran*, 2 vols. Graz: Akademische Drucku. Verlagsanstalt, 1976.

Ahmed Cevdet Paşa. *Târih-i Cevdet*. Dersaadet [Istanbul]: Matbaa-i Osmaniye, 1309 (1893) vols. 1–12.

Ahmed Cevdet Paşa. *Tezâkir*, ed. Cavid Baysun. Ankara: TTK, 1991.

Ahmed Muhtar Paşa. *Anadolu'da Rus Muharebesi I*, ed. Enver Yasarbaş. Istanbul: Petek Yayınları, 1985.

Ali Fuat Türkgledi. *Mesâil-i Mühimme-i Siyâsiyye*, ed. Bekir Sıtkı Baykal. Ankara: TTK, 1957.

Ayni Ali Efendi. *Kavanin-i Âli Osman der Hulāsa-i Mezāmīn-i Defter-i Divān*, ed. Tayyib Gökbilgin. Istanbul: Enderun Kitabevi, 1979.

'Azîz Efendi, and Rhoads Murphey. *Kanûn-nâme-i Sultânî Li 'Azîz Efendi: Aziz Efendi's Book of Sultanic Laws and Regulations: An Agenda for Reform by a Seventeenth-Century Ottoman Statesman*. Sources of Oriental Languages and Literatures, 9. Cambridge, MA: Printed at Harvard University Office of the University Publisher, 1985.

Dervish Pasa. *Tahdid-i Hudud-u İraniye*. Istanbul: Matbaa-i Amire, 1326 (1910).

Esat Efendi, Bâhir Efendi. *Vak'a-nüvîs Es'ad Efendi Tarihi: 1237–1241/1821–1826*, ed. Ziya Yılmazer. İstanbul: Osmanlı Araştırmaları Vakfı, 2000.

Eskandar Beg Monshi. *History of Shah 'Abbas the Great (Tārīḵ-e 'Ālāmāra-ye 'Abbāsī)*, trans. Roger M. Savory. Boulder, CO: Westview Press, 1978.

Feridun Bey, et al., eds. *Mecmua-yi Münşeat-i Feridun Bey or Münşe'at-i Selatin.* 2 vols. Istanbul: Darüttıbattil'âmire, 1265–1274 (1848–1857).

Hasan Fasa'i. *History of Persia under Qajar Rule*, trans. H. Busse. New York: Columbia University Press, 1972.

Hubbard, G. E. *From the Gulf to Ararat: An Expedition through Mesopotamia and Kurdistan*. Edinburgh: William Blackwood and Sons, 1917.

Koca Ragıp Mehmed Pasha. *Tahkik ve Tevfik: Osmanlı-Iran Münasebetlerinde Mezhep Tartışmaları*, ed. A. Zeki Izgözer. Istanbul: Kitabevi, 2003.

Kurdistani, 'Ali Akbar Vaqaya' Nigar. *Ḥadiqah-'i Naṣiriyah dar jughrafiya va tarikh-i Kurdistan.* ed. Muhammad Ra'uf Tavakkuli. Tehran: Tavakkoli, 1985.

Mahmud Celaleddin Paşa. *Mir'ati Hakikat*, Vols. 1–3, ed. İsmet Miroğlu. Istanbul: Bereket Yayınevi, 1983.

Mehmed Hurşîd Paşa. *Seyâhatnâme-i Hudud*, transcription Alaatin Eser. Istanbul: Simurg, 1997.

Mehmed Süreyya. *Sicil-i Osmanî*. Istanbul: Tarih Vakfı Yurt Yay, 1996.

Mirza Ja'far Khan, and Muḥammad Mushiri. *Risalah-i tahqiqat-i sarhaddiyah.* Tehran: Intisharat-i Bunyad-i Farhang-i Iran, 1969.

Mirza Mohib Ali Khan Nizam al-Mulk. *Ahdnameh-e Dawlatayn-e Iran va Usmani.* transliteration Nasrollah Salehi. Tehran: 1302/1885. [Ketabkhane-e Majlis-e Shora-e Eslami: No. F1919]

Mustafa Selaniki. *Tarih-i Selânikî*, ed. Mehmet İpşirli, 2 vols. Ankara: TTK Yayınevi, 1999.

Naima, Mustafa. *Târih-i Na'îmâ (Ravzatü'l-Hüseyn fî hulâsati ahbâri'l-hâfikayn)*, ed. Mehmet İpşirli. 2 vols. Ankara: Türk Tarih Kurumu, 2007.

Nasrollah Khan Mohandis. *Tahdid-e Hudud-e Merivan*, transliteration Reza Naqdi, 1878. [Ketabkhane-e Astan-e Qods, 5442]

Naṣūhü's-Silāḥī Maṭrāḳçī. *Beyān-ı Menāzil-i Sefer-i 'Iraḳeyn*, ed. H. G. Yurdaydın. Ankara: TTK Yayınevi, 1976.

Sanandaji, Shukullah, and Hishmatallah Ṭabibi. *Tuhfa-i Nasiri dar tarikh wa jugrafiya-i Kurdistan*. Tehran: Mu'assasa-i Intisharat-i Amir Kabir, 1987.

Şânî-zâde Mehmed 'Atâ'ullah Efendi, *Şânî-zâde Târîhi: 1223–1237/1808–1821*. ed. Ziya Yılmazer. İstanbul: Çamlıca, 2008.

Selâniki Mustafa Efendi, *Tarih-i Selâniki*, ed. Mehmet İpşirli. Ankara: Türk Tarih Kurumu Basımevi, 1999.

Şem'dânî-zâde Fındıklılı Süleyman Efendi. *Şem'dânî-zâde Fındıklılı Süleyman Efendi târihi: Mür'i't-tevârih*, ed. M. Münir Aktepe. İstanbul: İstanbul Üniversitesi Edebiyat Fakültesi, 1976–81.

Sıdkî Paşa. *Gazavât-ı Sultân Murâd-ı Râbi': IV. Murâd'ın Revan seferi*, ed. Mehmet Arslan. İstanbul: Kitabevi, 2006.

Tahir Paşa. *İki sene evvel hudd -u İraniye tahkikine me'mur olan hey'et-i resmiyye Erzurum valisi devletlü Tahir Paşa hazretlerinin hudud-u mezkureye dair ba'zı malumatı havi olarak Bab-ı 'Ali'ye takdim eyledikleri varakanın suretidir*. Erzurum Matbaası, 1329.

Türkgeldi, Ali Fuat. *Mesâil-i Mühimme-i Siyasiye*, ed. Bekir Sıtkı Baykal. 3 vols. Ankara: TTK, 1960.

Zeyrek, Yunus. *Tarih-i Osman Paşa: Özdemiroğlu Osman Paşa'nın Kafkasya Fetihleri (H. 986–988 M. 1578–1580) Ve Tebriz'in Fethi (H. 993 M. 1585)*. Ankara: Kültür Bakanlığı Yayınları, 2001.

Secondary Sources

Abou-el-Haj, Rifaat A. "The Formal Closure of the Ottoman Frontier in Europe: 1699–1703." *Journal of the American Oriental Society* 89, 3 (1969): 467–75.

Adamiyat, Faridun. *Amir Kabir va Iran*. Tehran: Intisharati Kharezmi, 2006.

Adelman, Jeremy, and Stephen Aron. "From Borderlands to Borders: Empires, Nation-States and the Peoples in between in North American History." *The American Historical Review* 104, 3 (1999): 814–41.

Afary, Janet. *The Iranian Constitutional Revolution 1906–1911*. New York: Columbia University Press, 1996.

Agoston, Gabor. "A Flexible Empire: Authority and Its Limits on the Ottoman Frontiers." In Kemal H. Karpat and Robert W. Zens, eds., *Ottoman Borderlands: Issues, Personalities and Political Changes*. Madison: University of Wisconsin Press, 2003: 15–31.

al-Najjar, Mustafa, and Najdat Fathi Safwat. "Arab Sovereignty over the Shatt al-Arab during the Ka'bide Period." In M.S. el-Azhary, ed., *The Iran-Iraq war: An Historical, Economic and Political Analysis*. London: Croom Helm, 1984, 20–37.

Amanat, Abbas. *Pivot of the Universe: Nasir Al-Din Shah Qajar and the Iranian Monarchy, 1831–1896*. Berkeley: University of California Press, 1997.

"Dawlatšāh, Moḥammad-ʿAlī Mīr-za," in *Encyclopedia Iranica*, http://www.iranicaonline.org/articles/dawlatsah-mohammad-ali-mirza

Amin, S. H. "The Iran-Iraq Conflict: Legal Implications." *The International Law Quarterly* 31, 1 (1982): 167–88.

Anderson, James, and Liam O'Dowd. "Borders, Border Regions and Territoriality: Contradictory Meanings, Changing Significance." *Regional Studies* 33, 7 (1999): 593–604.

Anderson, Malcolm. *Frontiers: Territory and State Formation in the Modern World*. Cambridge, UK: Polity Press, 1996.

Arfa, Hasan. *The Kurds: An Historical and Political Study*. London: Oxford University Press, 1966.

Ateş, Sabri. "Bones of Contention: Corpse Traffic and Ottoman-Iranian Rivalry in Nineteenth Century Iraq." *CSSAME* 30, 3 (2010): 512–32.

"Empires at the Margin: Towards a History of the Ottoman-Iranian Borderland and the borderlan people". Ph. D. dissertation, New York University, 2006.

Aydemir, Şevket Süreyya. *Makedonya'dan Ortaasya'ya Enver Paşa 2, 1908–1914*. Istanbul: Remzi Kitabevi, 1971.

Aydın, Mustafa. "Kırım Harbi Esnasında Osmanlı-İran-Rus İlişkileri (1853–55)." In *Savaştan Barışa 150. Yıldönümünde Kırım Savaşı ve Paris Antlaşması (1853–1856)*. Istanbul: Ist. Ün. Ed. Fak. Araştırma Merkezi, 2007, 131–50.

Aykun, İbrahim. "Erzurum Konferansı (1843–1847) ve Osmanlı-Iran Hudut Antlaşması." Ph.D. dissertation, Erzurum Atatürk Üniversitesi, 1995.

Bacqué-Grammont, Jean-Louis. "The Eastern Policy of Suleymân the Magnificient." In Halil İnalcik and Cemal Kafadar, eds., *Süleymân the Second [i.e., the First] and His Time*. Istanbul: Isis Press, 1993, 219–28.

Badem, Candan. "Kırım Savaşı Sırasında İsyanlar ve Asayiş Sorunları (1353–1856)." In *Savaştan Barışa 150. Yıldönümünde Kırım Savaşı ve Paris Antlaşması (1853–1856)*. Istanbul: Ist. Ün. Ed. Fak. Araştırma Merkezi, 2007, 285–327.

"The Ottomans and the Crimean War (1853–1856)." Ph.D. dissertation, Sabancı University, 2007.

Bailey, Frank E. "The Economics of British Foreign Policy, 1825–50." *The Journal of Modern History* 12, 4 (1940): 449–44.

Bajalan, Djene Rhys. "Kurds for the Empire 'The Young Kurds' 1898–1914." MA thesis, Istanbul Bilgi University, 2009.

Baker, Valentine. *War in Bulgaria: A Narrative of a Personal Experiences I*. London: Low, Marston, Searle, & Rivington, 1879.

Bassin, Mark. *Imperial Visions: Nationalist Imagination and Geographical Expansion in the Russian Far East, 1840–1865*. Cambridge, UK: Cambridge University Press, 1999.

Baud, Michiel, and Willem van Schendel. "Toward a Comparative History of Borderlands." *Journal of World History*, 8, 2 (1997): 211–42.

Bauer, Ralph W. *Boundaries and Frontiers in Medieval Muslim Geography*. Philadelphia: American Philosophical Society, 1995.

Bektaş, Yakup. "The Sultan's Messenger: Cultural Constructions of Ottoman Telegraphy, 1847–1880." *Technology and Culture* 41 (2000): 669–95.

Brower, Daniel, and Edward J. Lazzerini, eds. *Russia's Orient: Imperial Borderlands and Peoples, 1700–1917*. Bloomington: University of Indiana Press, 1997.

Buckingham, James Silk. *Travels in Assyria, Media, and Persia*. London: Colburn & Bentley, 1830.

Çadırcı, Musa. *Tanzimat Döneminde Anadolu Kentlerinin Sosyal ve Ekonomik Yapıları.* Ankara: Türk Tarih Kurumu Basımevi, 1991.

"Osmanlı İmpartorluğunda Askere Almada Kura Usulüne Geçilmesi – 1846 Tarihli Akerlik Kanunu." *Askeri Tarih Bülteni* 18 (1985): 59–75.

Cole, Juan R., and Moojen Moomen. "Mafia, Mob and Shiism in Iraq: The Rebellion of Ottoman Karbala 1824–1843." *Past and Present* 112 (1986): 112–43.

Crone, G. R. "The Turco-Iranian Boundary." *The Geographical Journal* 91, 1 (1938): 57–59.

Curzon, Robert. *Armenia: A Year at Erzeroom, and on the Frontiers of Russia, Turkey, and Persia.* London: Cambridge Scholars Press, 2002.

Darling, Linda T. "Contested Territory: Ottoman Holy War in Comparative Context." *Studia Islamica* 91 (2000): 133–63.

Deringil, Selim. "The Struggle Against Shiism in Hamidian Iraq: A Study in Ottoman Counter-Propaganda." *Die Welt des Islams* 30 (1990): 45–62.

Dessouki, Ali E. Hillal, ed. *The Iran-Iraq War, Issues of Conflict and Prospects for Settlement.* Princeton, NJ: Center of International Studies, 1981.

Edmonds, C. J. "The Iraqi-Persian Frontier: 1639–1938." *Asian Affairs* 62 (1975): 147–54.

el-Azhary, M. S. ed., *The Iran-Iraq War: An Historical, Economic and Political Analysis.* London: Croom Helm, 1984.

Faroqhi, Suraiya. *The Cambridge History of Turkey,* Vol. 3: *Later Ottoman Empire, 1603–1839.* Cambridge, UK: Cambridge University Press, 2008.

Febvre, Lucien. "Frontière: The Word and the Concept." In P. Burke, ed., *A New Kind of History from the Writings of Lucien Febvre.* New York: Harper Torchbooks, 1973: 208–18.

Findley, Carter V. "Sir James W. Redhouse (1811–1892): The Making of a Perfect Orientalist?" *Journal of the American Oriental Society* 99, 4 (1979): 573–600.

Fraser, J. Baillie. *Travels in Koordistan, Mesopotamia, &c. Including an Account of Parts of Those Countries Hitherto Unvisited by Europeans. With Sketches of the Character and Manners of the Koordish and Arab Tribes.* London: Richard Bentley, 1840.

Ghilan. "Les Kurdes Persans et L'Invasion Ottomane." In *Revue du Monde Musulman,* 2/5 Mai 1908: 1–22; 2/10, Octobre 1908: 193–210.

Gökhan, Çetinsaya, "Challenges of a Frontier Region: The Case of Ottoman Iraq in the Nineteenth Century." In A. C. S. Peacock, ed., *The Frontiers of the Ottoman World.* Oxford and London: Oxford University Press, 2009, 271–87.

Gurney, John. "E. G. Browne and the Iranian Community in Istanbul." In Thierry Zarcone and Fariba Zarinebaf-Shahr, eds., *Les Iraniens D'Istanbul.* Istanbul-Teheran: IFEA/IFRI, 1993, 149–75.

Halil [Kut] Paşa. *İttihat ve Terakki'den Cumhuriyet'e Bitmeyen Savaş.* Istanbul: Kamer, 1997.

Hämäläinen, Pekka, and Samuel Truett. "On Borderlands." *The Journal of American History* 98, 2 (2011): 338–61.

Harari, Maurice. "The Turco-Persian Boundary Question: A Case Study in the Politics of Boundary Making in the Near and Middle East." Ph.D. dissertation, Columbia University, 1953.

Herkless, J. L. "Stratford, the Cabinet and the Outbreak of the Crimean War." *The Historical Journal* 3 (1975): 497–523.

Heywod, Colin. "The Frontier in Ottoman History: Old Ideas and New Myths." In Daniel Power and Naomi Standen, eds., *Frontiers in Question: Eurasian Borderlands, 700–1700*. New York: St. Martin's Press, 1999, 228–50.

Hobsbawm, Eric. *Nations and Nationalism since 1870: Program, Myth and Reality*. Cambridge, UK: Cambridge University Press, 1990.

Hopkins, B. D. "The Bounds of Identity: The Goldsmid Mission and the Delineation of the Perso-Afghan Border in the Nineteenth Century." *Journal of Global History* 2 (2007): 233–54.

İnal, Ibnülemin Mahmud Kemal. *Osmanlı Devrinde Son Sadrazamlar. v. cüz.* Istanbul: Maarif Matbaası, 1944.

İnalcık, Halil. "Autonomous Enclaves in Islamic States." In *History and Historiography of Post-Mongol Central Asia and the Middle East: Studies in Honor of John E. Woods*. Weisbaden: Harrasowitz, 2006, 112–34.

"Islam in the Ottoman Empire." In *Essays in Ottoman History*. Istanbul: Eren Kitabevi, 1998, 229–45.

"Ottoman Methods of Conquest." *Studia Islamica* 3 (1954): 103–29.

İnalcık, Halil, and Donald Quataert, eds. *An Economic and Social History of the Ottoman Empire, 1300–1914*. Cambridge, UK: Cambridge University Press, 1994.

Ismael, Tareq Y. *Iraq and Iran: Roots of Conflict*. Syracuse, NY: Syracuse University Press, 1982.

Issawi, Charles. "The Tabriz-Trabzon Trade, 1830–1900: Rise and Decline of a Route." *International Journal of Middle East Studies* 1, 1 (1970): 18–27.

Izady, Mehrdad R. "The Gulf's Ethnic Diversity: An Evolutionary History." In Lawrence G. Potter and Gary G. Sick, eds., *Security in the Persian Gulf*. New York: Palgrave, 2002, 63.

Jones, James Felix. *Memoirs of Baghdad, Kurdistan and Turkish Arabia, 1857*. Reprint, Buckinghamshire, UK: Archive Editions, 1998.

Kafadar, Cemal. *Between Two Worlds: The Construction of the Ottoman State*. Berkeley: University of California Press, 1995.

Kaikobad, Kaiyan Homi. *The Shat-al-Arab Boundary Question: A Legal Reappraisal*. Oxford, UK: Clarendon Press, 1988.

Kalantari, Yahya. "Feth Ali Şah Zamanında Osmanlı-İran İlişkileri." Ph.D. dissertation, Istanbul Üniversitesi, 1976.

Kansu, Aykut. *The Revolution of 1908 in Turkey*. Leiden: Brill, 1997.

Politics in Post-Revolutionary Turkey, 1908–1913. Boston: Brill, 2000.

Kern, Karen M. "The Prohibition of Sunni-Shi'i Marriages in the Ottoman Empire: A Study of Ideologies." Ph.D. dissertation, Columbia University, 1999.

Karpat, Kemal. *The Politicization of Islam: Reconstructing Identity, State, Faith, and Community in Late Ottoman State*. Oxford, UK, and New York: Oxford University Press, 2001.

Kashani-Sabet, F. *Frontier Fictions: Shaping the Iranian Nation 1804–1946*. Princeton, NJ: Princeton University Press, 1999.

"Picturing the Homeland: Geography and National Identity in Late Nineteenth – and Early Twentieth Century Iran." *Journal of Historical Geography* 24, 4 (1998): 413–30.

"Fragile Frontiers: The Diminishing Domains of Qajar Iran." *International Journal of Middle Eastern Studies* 29 (1997): 205–34.

Kazemzadeh, Firuz. *Russia and Britain in Persia: A Study in Imperialism, 1864–1914*. New Haven, CT: Yale University Press, 1968.

Keddie, Nikki R. *Roots of Revolution: An Interpretive History of Modern Iran*. New Haven, CT: Yale University Press, 1981.

Khalaf, Sulayman N. "Settlement of Violence in Bedouin Society." *Ethnology*, 29, 3 (1990): 225–42.

Khodarkowsky, Michael. *Russia's Steppe Frontier: The Making of a Colonial Empire 1500–1800*. Bloomington: Indiana University Press, 2002.

Kinneir, John Macdonald. *Journey through Asia Minor, Armenia, and Koordistan, in the Years 1813 and 1814, with Remarks on the Marches of Alexander, and Retreat of the Ten Thousand*. London: John Murray, 1818.

A Geographical Memoir of Persian Empire. London: John Murray, 1813.

Kılıç, Orhan. "Van Eyalet'ine Bağlı Sancaklar ve Idari Statüleri (1558–1740)." *Osmanlı Araştırmaları* 21 (2001): 189–210.

"Yurtluk-Ocaklık ve Hükümet Sancakları Üzerine Bazı Tespitler." OTAM, 10 (1999): 119–37.

Kılıç, Remzi. *XVI-XVII Yüzyıllarda Osmanlı-İran Siyasi Antlaşmaları*. Istanbul: Tez Yayınları, 2001.

Klein, Janet. *The Margins of Empire: Kurdish Militias in the Ottoman Tribal Zone* Stanford, CA: Stanford University Press, 2011.

"Power in the Periphery: The Hamidiye Light Cavalry and the Struggle over Ottoman Kurdistan, 1890–1914." Ph.D. dissertation, Princeton University, 2002.

Kondo, Nobuaki. "Qizilbash Afterwards: The Afshars in Urmiya from the Seventeenth to the Nineteenth Century." *Iranian Studies* 32, 4 (1999): 537–56.

Kuehn, Thomas. *Empire, Islam, and Politics of Difference: Ottoman Rule in Yemen, 1849–1919*. Leiden: Brill, 2011.

Kütükoğlu, Bekir. *Osmanlı-İran Siyasi Münasebetleri 1578–1612*. Istanbul: Istanbul Fetih Cemiyeti, 1993.

Osmanlı-İran Siyasi Münasebetleri. Istanbul: Istanbul Fetih Cemiyeti. 1963.

Lang, D. M. "Obituary, Vladimir Fedorovivh Minorsky." *Bulletin of SOAS* 29, 3 (1966): 649–99.

Lamar, Howard, and Leonard Thompson. "Comparative Frontier History." In H. Lamar and L. Thompson, eds., *The Frontier in History: North America and Southern Africa Compared*. New Haven, CT: Yale University Press, 1981, 3–13.

Lane-Poole, Stanley. *The Life of the Right Honourable Stratford* Canning, vol. II. London: Longmans, Green, and Co., 1888.

Lattimore, Owen. *Studies in Frontier History; Collected Papers, 1928–1958*. London: Oxford University Press, 1962.

Lauterpacht, Elihu. "River Boundaries: Legal Aspects of the Shatt al-Arab Frontier." *The International and Comparative Law Quarterly* 9, 2 (1960): 208–36.

Layard, Henry Austen. *Early Adventures in Persia, Susnia and Baylonia*, vol. 2. London: Longmans, Green & Co., 1887.

Early Adventures in Persia, Susiana, and Babylonia, Including a Residence Among the Bakhtiyari and Other Wild Tribes Before the Discovery of Nineveh. London: John Murray, 1887.

Discoveries in the Ruins of Nineveh and Babylon; with Travels in Armenia, Kurdistan and the Desert: Being the Result of a Second Expedition Undertaken for the Trustees of the British Library. London: John Murray, 1853.

"A Desciption of the Province of Khuzistan." *Journal of Royal Geographical Society of London* 16 (1846): 1–105

Leslie, Shane. *Mark Sykes: His Life and Letters.* London: Cassel and Company Ltd., 1923.

Loftus, William Kenneth. "On the Determination of the River 'Eulœus' of the Greek Historians." *JRGS of London,* 27 (1857): 120–133.

Travels and Researches in Chaldea and Susnia; with an Account of Excavations at Warka, the "Erech" of the Nimrod, Shush, "Sushan the Palace" of Eshter, in 1849–1952. New York: Robert Carter and Brothers, 1857.

"On the Geology of portions of the Turko-Persian Frontier and of the Districts Adjoining." *The Quarterly Journal of the Geological Society of London* 11 (1855): 247–344.

Longrigg, Stephen Helmsley. *Four Centuries of Modern Iraq.* Oxford, UK: Oxford University Press, 1925.

Maier, Charles S. "Transformations of Territoriality 1600–2000." In Oliver Janz, Sebastian Conrad, and Gunilla Budde, eds., *Transnationale Geschichte: Themen, Tendenzen Und Theorien.* Gottingen: Vandenhoeck & Ruprecht, 2006: 32–55.

Makdisi, Usama. *The Culture of Sectarianism: Community, History, and Violence in Nineteenth-Century Ottoman Lebanon.* Berkley: University of California, 2000.

Mamdani, Mahmud. *Citizen and Subject: Contemporary Africa and the Legacy of Late Colonialism.* Princeton, NJ: Princeton University Press, 1966.

Mardukh Kordestani, Muhammad. *Tarikh-e Mardukh.* Tehran: Kharang, 1379 (2000).

Masters, Bruce. "The Treaties of Erzurum (1823 and 1848) and the Changing Status of Iranians in the Ottoman Empire." *Iranian Studies* 24, 1–4 (1991): 1–15.

Matthee, Rudi. "Between Arabs, Turks and Iranians: The Town of Basra, 1600–1700." *Bulletin of SOAS* 69, 1 (2006): 53–78.

"The Safavid-Ottoman Frontier: Iraq-i 'Arab as Seen by the Safavids." *International Journal of Turkish Studies* 9/1–2 (2003): 157–73.

Mc Lachlan, Keith. "Borders of the Ottoman Empire." In E. Yarshater, ed., *Encyclopedia Iranica.* London: Routledge, 1989.

McAdam, Doug, Sidney G. Tarrow, and Charles Tilly. *Dynamics of Contention.* Cambridge, UK: Cambridge University Press, 2001.

McChesney, Robert D. "Barrier of Heterodoxy"?: Rethinking the Ties Between Iran and Central Asia in the 17th Century." *Pembroke Papers* 4 (1996): 231–67.

McDowall, David. *A Modern History of the Kurds.* New York: I. B. Tauris, 1977.

McLachlan, Keith, ed. *The Boundaries of Modern Iran.* New York: St. Martin's Press, 1994.

Midhat Paşa. *Midhat Paşa Hayat-ı Siyasiyesi, Hidematı, Menfa Hayatı: Tabsıra-i Ibret,* ed., Ali Haydar Midhat. Istanbul: Hilal Matbaası, 1320/1903.

Midhat, Ali Haydar. *The Life of Midhat Pasha.* London: John Murray, 1903.

Minorsky, Vladimir, V. V. Bartol'd, and Clifford Edmund Bosworth. *Hudūd Al-'Ālam; "The Regions of the World"; A Persian Geography, 372 A.H.–982 A.D.* London: Luzac, 1970.

"The Tribes of Western Iran." *The Journal of the Royal Anthropological Institute of Great Britain and Ireland* 75, 1/2 (1945): 73–80.

Tadhkirat Al-Mulūk, A Manual of Ṣafavid Administration. London: Luzac & Co, 1943, reprinted 1980.

Munro, Henry F. *The Berlin Congress.* Washington DC: Government Printing Office 1918.

Murdoch, Jonathan, and Neil Ward, "Governmentality and Territoriality." *Political Geography* 16, 4 (1997): 307–24.

Murphey, Rhoads. "The Resumption of Ottoman-Safavid Border Conflict, 1603–1638: Effects of Border Destabilization on the Evolution of State-Tribe Relations." *Orientwissenschaftliche Hefte*, Mitteilungen des SFB "Differenz und Integration" 5: Militär und Integration, Halle (2003): 151–70.

"Süleyman's Eastern Policy." In Halik İnalcik and C. Kafadar, eds., *Süleyman the Second [i.e., the First] and His Time.* Istanbul: Isis Press, 1993, 259–79.

Münir Aktepe. *1720–1740 Osmanlı-Iran Münâsebetleri ve Kemânî Mustafa Ağa'nın Revân Fetih-Nâmesi.* Istanbul: Ist. Ed Fak. Yay, 1970.

Nakash, Yitzak. "The Conversion of Iraq's Tribes to Shi'ism." *International Journal of Middle East Studies* 26, 3 (1994): 443–63.

The Shi'is of Iraq. Princeton, NJ: Princeton University Press, 1994.

Nasiri, Mohammad Reza. *Nāsīreddin Ṣah Zamanında Osmanlı-İran Münasebetleri (1848–1896).* Tokyo: Institute fort the Study of Languages and Cultures of Asia and Africa, 1991

Norman, Charles Boswell. *Armenia, and the Campaign of 1877.* London: Cassell, Petter & Galpin, 1878.

O'Shea, Maria T. "The Demarcation of the Turco/Persian Border." In Keith McLachlan, ed., *The Boundaries of Modern Iran.* New York: St. Martin's Press, 1994, 47–57.

Oliphant, Laurence, Frederic Straker, and M. S. Anderson. *The Trans-Caucasian Campaign of the Turkish Army under Omer Pasha: A Personal Narrative.* Edinburgh and London: W. Blackwood, 1856.

Orhan Şaik Gökyay. *Katip Çelebi: Yaşamı, Kisiliği ve Yapıtlarından Seçmeler.* Ankara: Türkiye İş Bankası Kültür Yayınları, 1982.

Öz, Mehmet. "Ottoman Provincial Administration in Eastern and Southeastern Anatolia: The Case of Bidlis in Sixteenth Century." In Kemal H. Karpat and Robert W. Zens, eds., *Ottoman Borderlands: Issues, Personalities and Political Changes.* Madison: University of Wisconsin Press, 2003, 145–57.

Peacock, A. C. S., *The Frontiers of the Ottoman World.* Oxford, UK: Oxford University Press, 2009.

Perry, John R. "The Banu Ka'b: An Amphibious Brigand State in Khuzistan." *Le Monde Iranien et L'Islam: Sociétés et Cultures.* Geneve: Library Geneve, 1971.

Posch, Walter. "What Is a Frontier? Mapping Kurdistan between Ottomans and Safavids." In Éva M. Jeremiás, ed., *Irano-Turkic Cultural Contacts in the 11th–17th Centuries.* Philiscsaba: Avicenna Institute of Middle Eastern Studies, 2003, 203–15.

Potter, Lawrance G. "The Evolution of the Iran-Iraq Border." In Reeva Specter Simon and Eleanor H. Tejirian, eds., *The Creation of Iraq 1914–1921*. New York: Columbia University Press, 2004.

Prescot, J. R. V. *The Geography of Frontiers and Boundaries*. Chicago: Aldine Publishing Company, 1965.

Ra'iss Tousi, Reza. "The Persian Army, 1880–1907." *Middle Eastern Studies* 24, 2 (1988): 206–29

Rabino di Borgomale, H.L. *Great Britain and Iran: Diplomatic and Consular Officers; or Material for a List of British Diplomatic and Consular Officers Who Have Served in Iran and of Iranian Diplomatic and Consular Officers Who Have Served in Great Britain and in the British Empire*, 1946, n.p.

Rawlinson, H. Creswicke. *Notes on the Direct Overland Telegraph from Constantinople to Kurrachi*. London: John Murray, W. Cloves and Sons, 1861.

"Notes on a March from Zohab, at the Foot of Zagros, along the Mountains to Khuzistan (Susnia), and from Thence through the Province of Luristan to Kirmanshah, in the Year 1836." *JRGS* 9 (1839): 22–116.

Reid, James J. *Crisis of the Ottoman Empire: Prelude to Collapse 1839–1878*. Stuttgart: Steiner, 2000.

Reinkowski Maurus. "Double Struggle, No Income: Ottoman Borderlands in Northern Albania." *International Journal of Turkish Studies* 9 (2003): 239–53.

Résendez, Andrés. *Changing National Identities at the Frontiers, Texas and New Mexico, 1800–1850*. Cambridge, UK: Cambridge University Press, 2005.

Reynolds, Michael A. *Shattering Empires: The Clash and Collapse of the Ottoman and Russian Empires 1908–1918*. Cambridge, UK, and New York: Cambridge University Press, 2011.

Rich, C. James. *Narrative of a Residence in Koordistan and on the Site of Ancient Nineveh with Journal of a Voyage Down the Tigris to Baghdad and an Account of a Visit to Shirauz and Persepolis*, vol. 1. London: James Duncan, 1836.

Riyahi, Muhammad Amin. *Tarikh-i Khoi: sayr-i tahavvulat-i ijtima'i va farhangi-i shahr'ha-yi Iran dar tayy-i qurun*. [Tehran]: Intisharat-i Tarah-i Naw, 1999.

Rogan, Eugene L. *Frontiers of State in the Late Ottoman Empire: Transjordan, 1850–1921*. Cambridge, UK: Cambridge University Press, 1999.

"Aşiret Mektebi: Abdulhamid II's School for Tribes (1892–1907)." *IJMES* 28, 1 (1996): 83–107.

Ryan, S. Charles. *Under the Red Crescent: Adventures of an English Surgeon with the Turkish Army at Plevna and Erzeroum, 1877–1878*. London: John Murray, 1897.

Ryder, Colonel C. H. D. "The Demarcation of the Turco-Persian Boundary in 1913–14." *Geographical Journal* 66, 3 (1925): 225–39.

Sack, Robert. *Human Territoriality: Its Theory and History*. New York: Cambridge University Press, 1986.

Sahlins, Peter. *Boundaries: The Making of France and Spain in the Pyrenees*. Berkeley: University of California Press, 1989.

Salzmann, Ariel. *Tocqueville in the Ottoman Empire: Rival Paths to the Modern State* (Leiden: E. J. Brill, 2004).

Sanjabi, 'Ali Akbar Khan, and Karim Sanjabi. *Il-i Sanjabi va mujahidat-i milli-i Iran: khatirat-i 'Ali Akbar Khan Sanjabi, sardar-i muqtadir*. Tihran: Shirazah, 2001.

Schofield, Richard N., and K. McLachlan. *A Bibliography of the Iran-Iraq Borderland*. London: Menas Press Ltd, 1987.

Schofield, Richard N. *Evolution of the Shatt al-'Arab Boundary Dispute*. Wisbech, Cambridgeshire, UK: Middle East & North African Studies Press, 1986.

Schroeder, Paul W. "The 19th Century International System: Changes in the Structure." *World Politics* 39, 1 (1986): 1–26.

Scott, James C. *The Art of Not Being Governed: An Anarchist History of Upland Southeast Asia*. New Haven, CT: Yale University Press, 2009.

Shahvar, Soli. "Iron Poles, Wooden Poles: The Electric Telegraph and the Ottoman-Iranian Boundary Conflict, 1863–1865." *British Journal of Middle Eastern Studies* 34, 1 (2007): 23–42.

"Tribes and Telegraph Lines of Lower Iraq: The Muntafiq and the Baghdad-Basrah Telegraph Line of 1863–1865." *Middle Eastern Studies* 39, 1 (2007): 89–116.

Shamim, 'Ali Asghar. *Iran dar dawrah-'i saltanat-i Qajar, qarn-i sizdahum va nimah-i avval qarn-i chahardahum*. Tehran: Entesharate Zariab, 1387/2008.

Shuster, Morgan. *The Strangling of Persia*. New York: Century Company, 1912.

Sinclair, Tom. "The Ottoman Arrangements for the Tribal Principalities of the Lake Van Region of the Sixteenth Century." In Kemal H. Karpat and Robert W. Zens, eds., *Ottoman Borderlands: Issues, Personalities and Political Changes*. Madison: University of Wisconsin Press, 2003, 119–45.

Slade, Adolphus, and M. S. Anderson. *Turkey and the Crimean War: A Narrative of Historical Events*. London: Smith, Elder, 1867.

Smith, A. D. "War and Ethnicity: The Role of Warfare in the Formation, Self-Images and Cohesion of Ethnic Communities." In John Hutchinson and A.D. Smith, eds., *Nationalism: Critical Concepts in Political Science*, vol. 5. London: Routledge, 2002.

Sohrabi, Nader. *Revolution and Constitutionalism in the Ottoman Empire and Iran*. New York: Cambridge University Press, 2011.

Soltani, Mohammad Ali. *Coghrafiai Tarikhi va Tarikhe Mofassale Kermanshahan*, vol. 2/1, 2/2, *Ilat va Tavaif-e Kermanshahan*. Tehran: Soltani, 1372.

Stein, Mark L. *Guarding the Frontier Ottoman Border Forts and Garrisons in Europe*. London: Tauris Academic Studies, 2007.

Stoye, John. *Marsigli's Europe, 1680–1730: The Life and Times of Luigi Ferdinando Marsigli, Soldier and Virtuoso*. New Haven, CT: Yale University Press, 1994.

St. John, Rachel. *Line in the Sand: A History of U.S.-Mexico Border*. Princeton, NJ: Princeton University Press, 2011.

Swearingen, Will D. "Geopolitical Origins of Iran-Iraq War." *Geographical Review* 78, 4 (1988): 405–16.

Sykes, Mark. "Journeys in North Mesopotamia." *The Geographical Journal* 30, 3 (1907): 237–54 and 4 (1907): 384–98.

Sykes, P. M. *A History of Persia*, vol. 2. London: Macmillan and Co., 1915.

Tahir-Kheli, Shirin, and Shaheen Ayubi, eds. *The Iran-Iraq War: New Weapons, Old Conflicts*. New York: Praeger, 1983.

Tansel, F. A. "Ahmed Vefik Paşa'nın Şahsiyeti'nin Teşekkülü, Hususi Hayatı ve Muhtelif Karakterleri." *Belleten* 113 (1965): 121–75.

Tchalenko, John. *Images from an Endgame: Persia through a Russian Lens 1901–1914*. London: Saqi, 2006.

Tekindağ, M. Şahabettin. "Yeni Kaynak ve Vesikaların Işığı Altında Yavuz Sultan Selim'in İran Seferi." *İst. Ün. Ed. Fak. Tarih Dergisi* 17 (1967): 49–78.

Tezcan, Baki. "The Development of the Use of 'Kurdistan' as a Geographical Description and the Incorporation of This Region into the Ottoman Empire in the 16th Century." *The Great Ottoman-Turkish Civilization* 3, Ankara: Yeni Türkiye Yayınları, 2000, 540–53.

Toynbee, A. J. "The Controversy over the Frontier between Iran (Persia) on the One Side and Turkey (Iraq) on the Other." *Survey of International Affairs*. Oxford, UK: Oxford University Press, 1937.

Tucker, Ernest. *Nadir Shah's Quest for Legitimacy in Post-Safavid Iran*. Gainesville: University Press of Florida, 2006.

"The Peace Negotiations of 1736: A Conceptual Turning Point in Ottoman-Iranian Relations." *The Turkish Studies Association Bulletin* 20, 1 (1996): 16–37.

Türk, İ. Caner. "1853–1856 Kırım Harbi Sırasında Osmanlı-İran İlişkileri, Osmanlı Devletine Karşı Rus-İran Gizli Antlaşması." M.A. thesis, Atatürk Universitesi, 2000.

Unat, Faik Reşit. *Osmanlı Sefirleri ve Sefaretnameleri*, Ankara: Türk Tarih Kurumu, 1968.

Uzun, Ahmet. *Tanzimat ve Sosyal Direnişler: Niş Isyni Üzerine Ayrıntılı Bir İnceleme*. Istabul: Eren, 2002.

Valizadah Mu'jizi, Husayn, and Muḥammad Valizadah Mu'jizi. *Tarikh-i Luristan: ruzigar-i Qajar, az ta'sis ta kudita-yi 1299*. Tehran: Ḥurufiyah, 2001.

van Bruinessen, Martin. "Kurds, States and Tribes." In Faleh A. Jabar and Hosham Dawod, eds., *Tribes and Power: Nationalism and Ethnicity in the Middle East*. London: Saqi, 2003, 165–83.

Mullas, Sufis and Heretics: The Role of Religion in Kurdish Society. Istanbul: The Isis Press, 2000.

Agha Shaikh and State: The Social and Political Structures of Kurdistan. London: Zed Books, 1992.

Von Moltke, Helmut. *Essays, Speeches, and Memoirs, vol. 1*. New York: Harper & Brothers, 1893.

Williams, Charles. *The Armenian Campaign: A Diary of the Campaign of 1877, in Armenia and Koordistan*. London: C. Kegan Paul & Co., 1878.

Williams, William Fenwick. *The Siege of Kars, 1855: Defense and Capitulation*. London: Stationery Office, 2000.

Williamson, Graham. "The Turco-Persian War 1821–1823: Winning the War but Losing the Peace." In Roxane Farmanfarmaian, ed., *War and Peace in Qajar Persia*. London: Routledge, 2008, 88–109.

Wilson, Arnold T. *S. W. Persia: A Political Officer's Diary*. London: Oxford University Press, 1941.

Wilson, T. M., and Donnan Hastings. *Border Identities: Nation and State at International Frontiers*. Cambridge, UK: Cambridge University Press, 1998.

Winichakul, Tongchai. *Siam Mapped: A History of the Geo-body of a Nation*. Honolulu: University of Hawaii Press, 1994.

Wratislaw, Albert Charles. *A Consul in the East*. Edinburgh: W. Blackwood, 1924.

Yalçin-Heckman, Lale. *Tribe and Kinship among the Kurds*. New York: Peter Lang, 1991.

Zarcone, Thierry, and Fariba Zarinebaf-Shahr, eds. *Les Iraniens D'Istanbul*. Istanbul-Teheran: IFEA/IFRI, 1993.

Zarinebaf-Shahr, Fariba. "The Iranian Merchant Community in the Ottoman Empire and the Constitutional Revolution" In Thierry Zarcone and F. Zarinebaf-Shahr, eds., *Les Iraniens D'Istanbul*. Istanbul-Teheran: IFEA/IFRI, 1993, 203–12.

Zürcher, Eric J. *Turkey: A Modern History*. London: I. B. Tauris, 1997.

Index

Lightning Source UK Ltd.
Milton Keynes UK
UKOW06f1904180616

276557UK00008B/217/P

Whitehall Paper 94

The Future of NATO Airpower
How are Future Capability Plans Within the Alliance Diverging and
How can Interoperability be Maintained?

Justin Bronk

www.rusi.org

Royal United Services Institute for Defence and Security Studies

The Future of NATO Airpower
First published 2019

Whitehall Papers series

Series Editor: Professor Malcolm Chalmers
Editor: Emma De Angelis

RUSI is a Registered Charity (No. 210639)
ISBN [978-0-367-46823-1]

Published on behalf of the Royal United Services Institute for Defence and Security Studies
by
Routledge Journals, an imprint of Taylor & Francis, 4 Park Square, Milton Park, Abingdon OX14 4RN

Cover Image: US Air Force fourth and fifth-generation aircraft fly in an echelon formation with a Royal Air Force Typhoon and a French Rafale in support of exercise Point Blank 19-2, over the North Sea, 27 June 2019. *Courtesy of US Air Force/Tech Sgt. Matthew Plew*

SUBSCRIPTIONS
Please send subscription order to:

USA/Canada: Taylor & Francis Inc., Journals Department, 325 Chestnut Street, 8th Floor, Philadelphia, PA 19106 USA

UK/Rest of World: Routledge Journals, T&F Customer Services, T&F Informa UK Ltd, Sheepen Place, Colchester, Essex, C03 0LP UK

Contents

About the Author

Justin Bronk is the Research Fellow for Airpower and Military Technology in the Military Sciences team at RUSI. He is also Editor of the *RUSI Defence Systems* online journal. Justin has written on airpower issues for the *RUSI Journal*, *RUSI Defence Systems*, *RUSI Newsbrief*, the *Journal of Strategic Studies* and the RAF's *Air Power Journal*, as well as contributing regularly to the international media.

Justin is a part-time doctoral candidate at the Defence Studies Department of King's College London and holds an MSc in the History of International Relations from the London School of Economics and Political Science, and a BA (Hons) in History from York University.

Acknowledgements

I would like to thank the many officers in the Royal Air Force, United States Air Force, Armée de l'Air and Luftwaffe who have been so generous with their time, experiences and patience with my many questions over the last five years. I would also like to thank my colleagues in the Military Sciences team at RUSI, especially Peter Roberts, for supporting this project, and Jack Watling and Sidharth Kaushal, for always being willing to talk through and lend their expertise on thorny topics, often at considerable length. Finally, I would like to thank my partner Melanie Thienard for her love and encouragement.

INTRODUCTION

This Whitehall Paper argues that there is an increasing divergence between the pace and trajectory of airpower capability development in the US and the rest of the NATO Alliance. While the US has held an overwhelming capability lead for decades, the emerging focus on countering Chinese capabilities at scale in the Pacific theatre, coupled with a continuing resource imbalance, is further eroding the ability of other NATO air forces to keep pace.

Specifically, this study argues that there are major changes on the horizon in terms of the way that the US wages war from the air and as a joint force. These are likely to make it significantly more technically difficult and politically complex for other NATO air forces to 'plug into' US-led coalitions as they have done for decades. From the way that sensor data, weapon allocation and targeting are cued within the kill chain, to a step change in how enablers like AWACS aircraft are provided, to the scale of cross-domain integration, the US is aiming to revolutionise the way it fights. In some cases, other NATO members may not wish to go down the same developmental pathways, even if they are able to do so. This might be because combat aircraft, concepts of operations (CONOPS) or weapons systems developed by the US with a Chinese threat in the Pacific in mind might be judged unsuitable for European needs. However, there are potentially more disruptive ethical and legal issues to do with fighting as part of a future US-led coalition as the latter pursues extensive automation to improve its lethality in a major war. For an alliance whose airpower edge is highly dependent on US enablers, command and control (C2) infrastructure and in some cases equipment, this has major implications. NATO is first and foremost a political organisation rather than a military one. However, this should not obscure the fact that it is a political organisation with a central purpose – mutual defence and deterrence against state opponents – which requires strong, interoperable military capabilities in addition to political will and unity.

Airpower has been key to NATO's deterrence posture ever since the organisation was founded. Since the Alliance has generally been unwilling (and unable) to match potential state opponents like Russia or previously the Soviet Union in terms of the ability to rapidly mass armour and artillery firepower on land, its members have placed heavy reliance on being able to deliver firepower against critical targets from the air in the event of a major conflict.[1] The air domain is also one where the core NATO member states have traditionally maintained close tactical cooperation and interoperability, with a variety of US- and European-made platforms designed according to similar mission requirements and with crews and supporting structures trained regularly in multilateral exercise environments. The Soviet Union was a useful unifying influence for NATO air forces, as it meant that the pacing threat systems were clear, and the likely potential operational environment and geography were established. Since the mission sets – such as offensive counter-air (OCA), defensive counter-air (DCA), suppression of enemy air defences (SEAD), strike, interdiction and anti-shipping strike – were relatively straightforward conceptually, the fact that different states approached each tactical problem slightly differently was seldom an issue.

The centrality of the nuclear mission to NATO's defence plans also meant that resilient and regularly exercised Alliance-wide C2 arrangements were essential for all major air forces, given the potentially catastrophic results of any failure in that regard. Compatible communications and tactics, techniques and procedures (TTPs) were usually the main interoperability obstacles, and ones which were relatively easy to overcome. However, over time the decisive attributes of combat aircraft have shifted away from airframe performance characteristics towards sensors, smart munitions and networked situational awareness. Greater software complexity and dependence has increased the interoperability obstacles that must be overcome at both a platform and national force level. However, it has also led to a situation where the gap in whole-force combat capability between those at the cutting edge of airpower technology and those struggling to catch up is much greater than the individual system differences would suggest.

The modern air environment is particularly unforgiving for forces operating second-tier equipment. The speed of engagements is faster than ever, with extremely capable missiles fielded by the US, European powers, Russia, China and Israel for both air-to-air and surface-to-air use. The fighter that detects another first and gets the first shot away has a huge advantage, since even if the other aircraft detects the incoming threat and manages to defeat the missile, it is forced to 'go defensive' and sacrifice energy and situational awareness, giving the offensive pilot

---

[1] For a breakdown of the usable force ratios in Eastern Europe in terms of tanks, artillery and infantry fighting vehicles, see Scott Boston et al., *Assessing the Conventional Force Imbalance in Europe* (RAND Corporation, 2018).

plenty of opportunity to fire again or escape as needed. Furthermore, individual platforms' differences are greatly magnified by modern networking capabilities using directional jam-resistant datalinks which enable the various sensors throughout a force to maximise any competitive advantages across a whole strike package

By contrast, there were tactics and scenarios which enabled Soviet-made MiG-17s and MiG-21s over Vietnam to remain somewhat competitive against the US's more technologically advanced F-4 Phantom IIs. Already by the 1980s and early 1990s, the Israeli air force over Syria and US Air Force over Iraq and the Balkans were brutally demonstrating the overwhelming dominance of superior technology with extremely lopsided kill ratios. Comparable airframe performance of MiG-29 and Mirage-series fighters was simply not competitive with the F-15 and F-16 series' advanced sensors, missiles and ability to receive and utilise data from off-board sensors such as Airborne Warning and Control System (AWACS) aircraft.

Since the 1990s, the introduction of fighter platforms with extremely low radar signatures and excellent situational awareness which can be gathered and shared without alerting hostile forces has enabled the US to achieve an even greater leap in airpower capabilities, not only compared to rival powers but also to other NATO member states. However, the F-22 and F-35 have themselves in turn stimulated a vigorous response from Russia and China, with both investing heavily in modern, mobile, long-range air defence systems and a myriad of radar techniques to try to unmask US stealth aircraft. These long-range surface-to-air missile (SAM) systems, ever-improving sensor technologies and long-range anti-enabler missile systems are much cheaper for rival powers like China and Russia to produce than for the US to counter. China has also begun fielding its own low-observable fighter, the Chengdu J-20 *Mighty Dragon*.

Seeking to stay ahead of this rapid Chinese and Russian threat system growth and to address the problems posed by distances in the Pacific theatre, the US is now looking for the next leap beyond what stealthy tactical fighters like the F-22 and F-35 alone can provide. Meanwhile, other NATO member states are still in the early stages of trying to catch up with US capabilities and find answers to the evolving Russian threat systems developed to counter them. Many are purchasing limited numbers of F-35s, while France and Germany have started their own new fighter development programme and the UK and Italy are hoping to do both.[2] In

---

[2] See Global Participation page, 'F-35 Lightning II', Lockheed Martin, <https://www.f35.com/global>, accessed 22 October 2019. See also Craig Hoyle, 'Airbus, Dassault warn over FCAS funding need', Flight Global <https://www.flightglobal.com/news/articles/airbus-dassault-warn-over-fcas-funding-need-461365/>, accessed 22

basic terms, European NATO members are trying to play catch-up over the next decade and a half in tactical fighter terms, but the US Air Force (and US Navy and Marine Corps) are already aggressively pursuing the next capability leap. This threatens to widen the already significant capability gap between the US and other NATO members in the air domain, and to reduce interoperability.

The more visible combat aircraft programmes tell only part of this story, with developments in US intelligence, surveillance, target acquisition, and reconnaissance (ISTAR) systems and C2 architectures likely to have at least as great an impact on how the US Air Force, Navy and Marine Corps fight future wars. European air forces have traditionally lagged even further behind the US in ISTAR and other enabling capabilities such as air-to-air refuelling (AAR) tankers than they have in combat aircraft. While some states like the UK and France operate a range of enabling capabilities, they still rely to a significant extent on the US in coalition operations. Smaller states are extremely reliant on US Air Force support to make their limited numbers of fast jets effective on overseas combat operations or against peer opponents. In the past, this has been largely an issue of duplication of effort, rather than a serious barrier to interoperability. Put simply, the US has plenty of tactical fighters and its air operations are typically capped by the availability of tankers and other enablers. When Allied air forces join coalitions, they often bring more tactical fighters but seldom more than one or two enabling assets, increasing theoretical firepower but actually acting as a further pressure on the enabler bottleneck.

It is natural for smaller countries with limited funds to prioritise fast jets over less politically evocative tankers and ISTAR aircraft. However, there are a variety of factors, including longer-ranged threat systems and a strategic rebalancing towards the Pacific theatre where operational distances are greater than in Europe, that are putting pressure on the traditional US Air Force enabler fleets. Large sensor or AAR platforms derived from wide-bodied airliners are increasingly vulnerable and having to operate at ever-greater distances from contested airspace, rendering them less effective. As part of its response, the US is pursuing a more network-centric ISTAR and C2 concept with an emphasis on smaller distributed platforms with sensors cross-referenced and cross-cued automatically.[3] The US Air Force's main effort in this area is centred

---

October 2019; 'Future Combat Air System', BAE Systems, <https://www.baesystems.com/en/future-combat-air-system-fcas>, accessed 22 October 2019.
[3] Multiple author interviews with US Air Force senior officers, London and Washington, DC, 2017–19.

around the Advanced Battle Management System (ABMS) and is part of a broader Pentagon project called Multi-Domain Operations (MDO).[4]

If the US successfully changes the way in which its combat airpower depends on large, airliner-derived ISTAR and tanker enablers, it will have the unintended side effect of forcing other NATO air forces to seriously examine how they intend to 'plug into' any future US-led coalition. In broader C2 architecture terms, ABMS and MDO also have significant implications for national sovereignty and tolerance for automation as part of lethal combat operations in US-led coalitions. The speed of automated sensor-shooter cueing processes are likely to outstrip the ability of NATO member states to meaningfully scrutinise and approve strikes involving their assets through traditional means such as national red card holders in a combined air operations centre (CAOC).

With this in mind, Chapter I explores some of the contextual factors driving modernisation across NATO, including the impact of years of counterinsurgency on force structures and training, and gives an overview of particularly significant capabilities being fielded and developed by the two major peer-threat actors: Russia and China. Chapter II examines the US response to these challenges and why it represents a significant departure from its Europe-focused strategies of the Cold War. Chapter III examines the current state of the 'mid-tier' NATO air forces such as the UK's Royal Air Force and France's Armée de l'Air and shows how these states are trying to catch up with current US warfighting capabilities, while also pursuing subtly different future plans. Chapter IV looks at some of the capability plans of smaller member states such as Belgium, the Netherlands and Poland, and the problems facing them in the form of increasing technological barriers to entry and a renewed focus on high-intensity warfighting as a planning assumption. Finally, the paper argues that while there are significant challenges implied by NATO Allies' increasingly different modernisation trajectories and future force ambitions, there are also potential opportunities to enhance NATO airpower in the coming decades if policies are pursued that take into account the trends outlined in this Whitehall Paper.

---

[4] For detailed information on MDO and its broader implications see Jack Watling and Daniel Roper, 'European Allies in US Multi-Domain Operations', *RUSI Occasional Papers* (September 2019).

I. THE CONTEXT: HOME-GROWN PROBLEMS AND ADVERSARY INNOVATIONS

Aside from the US, NATO's air forces have suffered a considerable decline in their ability to conduct sustained combat operations against a near-peer or peer state opponent since the end of the Cold War.[1] Badly delayed modernisation plans, inadequate weapons stockpiles, inflexible C2 arrangements, reduced fleet sizes, and pilots highly experienced in dropping munitions on insurgent groups but lacking the intense training required for proficient operations in highly contested airspace are problems that affect all Alliance members. NATO efforts to reverse these trends, such as the so-called 'Four Thirties' force generation and readiness plans, still sit largely in the realm of political statements of intent rather than concrete programmes to generate increased military power.[2] Increased readiness levels, while necessary, are also not a solution in and of themselves to the gulf in combat capability and enablers between the US and other member states. While Russia has also seen a significant decline from over 2,650 to around 1,250 modern combat aircraft compared to the Soviet Union, its greater reliance on a mixture of heavy ground forces and modern ground-based air defence systems in large numbers renders it less dependent on large-scale airpower than NATO.[3]

Almost three decades of discretionary, limited wars against sub-peer threat states and long counterinsurgency campaigns since 1991 have served to demonstrate many of the inherent strengths of airpower,

---

[1] For an overview of these trends see Frank Gorenc, 'Transatlantic Air Power and What to Do Now', Atlantic Council, Issue Brief, April 2019.

[2] NATO Press Conference, 'NATO Secretary General Jens Stoltenberg Following the Meeting of the North Atlantic Council at the Level of Heads of State and Government (NATO Summit Brussels)', 11 July 2018, <https://www.nato.int/cps/en/natohq/opinions_156733.htm>, accessed 10 October 2019.

[3] Boston et al., *Assessing the Conventional Force Imbalance in Europe*, pp. 4, 8.

including responsiveness, precision and often decisive battlefield effects. However, they have also demonstrated that despite all these advantages, airpower usually struggles to deliver campaign-level or long-term strategic victories by itself in complex discretionary conflicts. This is a major challenge for political and high-level military thinkers in terms of the place which airpower should occupy within global power-projection efforts and counterinsurgency and stabilisation operations. However, it is not the challenge with which this Whitehall Paper is primarily concerned. This study looks at efforts by NATO air forces to retain and in some cases regain the capability to deter and, if necessary, successfully fight a high-intensity conflict with another state. Despite years of counterinsurgency operations and the difficulties just listed, this shift need not require dramatic changes for many air forces in terms of primary combat aircraft types.

With the exception of the remotely piloted aerial systems (RPAS) such as the MQ-1 Predator and MQ-9 Reaper, which have become synonymous with counterinsurgency and counterterrorist operations, the platforms used to fight these discretionary conflicts were largely developed or at least conceived during the late Cold War. The Eurofighter Typhoon and F-22 Raptor – conceived at the end of the 1980s to overmatch the next generation of Soviet-built combat aircraft in a high-intensity conflict – have instead been employed for dropping precision-guided munitions on terrorist targets in the Middle East. However, this has not blunted their theoretical potency in a high-intensity conflict. In terms of weapons, even the RAF's signature low-collateral damage Brimstone missile, celebrated for its pinpoint accuracy against Muammar Qadhafi's rusting armour in Libya and Daesh's (also known as the Islamic State of Iraq and Syria, ISIS) technicals in Iraq and Syria, was originally conceived as a fire-and-forget salvo missile to be ripple-fired at massed Eastern Bloc tanks before being adapted.[4]

This is the result of a longstanding assumption among airpower planners that if an air force is equipped and trained to fight a high-intensity conflict under the least likely, but most serious, threat scenarios, then it will be capable of performing well (if not necessarily efficiently) in low-intensity, discretionary operations. Since the potential requirement to conduct air operations as part of stabilisation operations and/or in support of counterinsurgency efforts seems unlikely to fade despite a return to planning for high-intensity scenarios, this is an

---

4 See Development section of 'Brimstone', ThinkDefence.co.uk, <https://www.thinkdefence.co.uk/uk-complex-weapons/brimstone/>, accessed 8 May 2019.

assumption which NATO air forces have little choice but to fall back on as they once again confront peer threats.

Advances in precision-guided munitions and targeting pod technology have made fast jets designed for peer conflict highly capable in the close air support (CAS) role in support of friendly troops in permissive airspace. However, the training and organisational structures required to excel in this sort of environment often differ greatly from those demanded by high-intensity scenarios against a peer or even near-peer state opponent. The majority of NATO aircrew today have spent most of their operational careers conducting CAS missions in largely permissive airspace over the Middle East and North Africa. Due to smaller operational fleets since the Cold War and the relentless demands for airpower as a force multiplier in long counterinsurgency operations, the operational tempo for these tasks has been extremely high, resulting in pilot retention issues, airframe fatigue overuse and perhaps most significantly of all, high-intensity mission set skills fade.[5]

Fast jet aircrew require a great deal of practice to become and then remain proficient in many complex but often critical mission sets. This is in addition to basic currency requirements to remain certified for operational flying under various conditions including night operations, bad weather and in some cases from aircraft carrier decks. Thanks to budgetary pressures, and with airframe fatigue and maintenance cycle disruptions well in excess of long-term planning assumptions, aircrew flight hours currently sit well below what they were during the Cold War in most NATO air forces.[6] Readiness for high-intensity mission sets is far lower still, with fewer than 50% of even US Air Force squadrons classed as ready for full-spectrum missions as of late 2016.[7] Synthetic training is an increasingly valuable and important part of efforts to solve this problem. Modern, sophisticated simulators are not only a way to substitute for lost live flying training hours, they also allow aircrew to practice complex and dangerous scenarios which are hard to reproduce safely in live sorties. However, for many skills and currencies there is no adequate substitute for live flying.

---

[5] See Stephen Losey, 'Fewer Planes are Ready to Fly: Air Force Mission-Capable Rates Decline Amid Pilot Crisis', *Air Force Times*, 5 March 2018.

[6] John Venable, 'U.S. Air Force: An Assessment of U.S. Military Power', Heritage Foundation, 4 October 2018, <https://www.heritage.org/military-strength/assessment-us-military-power/us-air-force>, accessed 9 October 2019.

[7] David Goldfein, 'Testimony to US Armed Services Committee at Nomination Hearing', 16 June 2016, <https://www.armed-services.senate.gov/hearings/16-06-16-nomination_-goldfein>, accessed 18 June 2019.

With only a limited number of available live flying hours and many of those taken up with basic flight currency maintenance, as well as training for and conducting counterinsurgency operations, the all-important practice sorties for each squadron's primary mission(s) in a high-intensity conflict scenario are not being conducted with sufficient regularity to maintain, let alone grow, skills.[8] What this means is that while the platforms and even weapons systems have not lost theoretical relevance for high-intensity warfighting during years of counterinsurgency operations, the effects on training hours and pilot experience levels have damaged NATO air forces' ability to fight against a peer or near-peer opponent. This has prompted urgent efforts on the part of the US Air Force to refocus and improve training towards high-intensity warfighting, especially under the auspices of the famous *Red Flag* series of exercises – the most recent of which have included enemy stealth fighters, long-range SAM threats, cyber threats and heavy electronic warfare elements.[9]

Air Threat Landscape from Russia and China

With a return of great power competition in the Pacific – this time against a modern China with rapidly expanding military capabilities and political ambition to replace the US as the dominant regional power within the next decade and a half – high-intensity conflict is once more on the US Air Force and US Navy planning agenda. Equally, Russia's aggression in Ukraine and tensions over competing military and political activities in the Baltic region, Syria and the Eastern Mediterranean and Black Sea have forced a reluctant NATO to start increasing defence spending after years of decline and, at least internally, confront the spectre of a military confrontation with Moscow.

While on the surface Russia and China possess many comparable systems, especially in the airpower domain (as shown in Table 1), they pose very different military challenges. Both are nuclear powers, although Russia is much more willing to use its enormous nuclear arsenal for direct threats and strongman tactics than China with its more limited deterrent. However, since conventional deterrence is still a major factor in US relations with China, as well as NATO's complex relationship with Russia in Europe, the conventional airpower picture will be the focus in this paper. The relationship between nuclear and conventional deterrence in the modern world is the subject of many other studies.

---

[8] Author interviews with US Air Force pilots with experience of flying F-15C, F-15E, F-16CJ and F-22, Washington, DC, February 2019; London, March 2019.
[9] Robert Novotny, 'Close Air Support on the 21st Century Battlefield', speech given at Close Air Support Conference, London, 29 May 2019.

Table 1: Russia and China's Combat Aircraft.

	Russian Federation	**People's Republic of China**
Combat aircraft (fourth generation)	approximately 1,250	approximately 1,500
Combat aircraft (fifth generation)	15 (limited combat capability)	approximately 30–40
Heavy bomber aircraft	139	193
Aerial refuelling tankers	15	18
Intelligence, surveillance and reconnaissance aircraft	18	29

Sources: Author analysis based on: International Institute for Strategic Studies (IISS), *The Military Balance 2019* (London: Routledge, 2019); Andreas Rupprecht, *Modern Chinese Warplanes: Chinese Air Force – Combat Aircraft and Units* (Houston, TX: Harpia Publishing, 2018), pp. 45–46; Scott Boston et al., *Assessing the Conventional Force Imbalance in Europe* (Washington, DC: RAND Corporation, 2018).

Combat Aircraft

In conventional combat airpower terms, both Russia and China rely for the bulk of their fighter strength on a mix of Sukhoi Su-27/30/35 Flanker family derivatives, alongside bombers, interceptors and multilayered integrated air defence systems. Therefore, the capabilities of the Flankers are important to examine up front.

The Flanker family remains a pacing threat for many air forces in NATO, since it remains the most potent non-Western fighter in large-scale service. The various versions of the Flanker possess decent range on internal fuel, high speed and reasonable high-altitude performance, along with startling within-visual range manoeuvrability and heavy missile loadout options. The more modern derivatives such as the Chinese J-11B and Russian Su-35S Flanker-E variant operated by Russia's Aerospace Forces (VKS) and the Chinese People's Liberation Army Air Force (PLAAF) offer improvements in cockpit interface, datalink and radar performance. The Russian approach with the Su-35S's Irbis-E passive electronically scanned array radar was to prioritise acquisition range and 'burn through' performance in heavy jamming environments.[10] China's J-11B employs a more traditional pulse Doppler radar but its J-11D prototype and J-16 multirole variant equip the Flanker with Chinese-developed active electronically scanned array (AESA) radars to give much better multirole, track while scan (TWS) and electronic counter-countermeasures (ECCM)

---

[10] Carlo Kopp, 'Flanker Radars in Beyond Visual Range Air Combat', Air Power Australia, <https://www.ausairpower.net/APA-Flanker-Radars.html>, last updated April 2012, accessed 22 October 2019. See also Andreas Rupprecht, *Modern Chinese Warplanes: Chinese Air Force – Combat Aircraft and Units* (Houston, TX: Harpia Publishing, 2018), pp. 38–39.

capabilities.[11] For now, the PLAAF seems content to purchase small numbers of the Su-35S to evaluate the type's attributes against its own J-11B/D and J-16 domestic variants in terms of Flankers. However, China is rapidly expanding its airpower capability ambitions beyond what the Flanker airframe can deliver.[12]

The biggest drawback of the Flanker airframe is its enormous radar cross-section (RCS) which means it shows up on hostile radars from great distances. It is also large and has a distinctive shape which makes it easier for infrared and electro-optical passive search and track systems to pick it up at range when compared to smaller fighters. While the Su-35S does offer impressive radar performance in terms of range and jamming resistance, it does not possess the ability to actively scan for targets without giving away its location to any hostile asset with a modern radar warning receiver (called low probability of intercept/low probability of detect, or LPI/LPD). The Chinese AESA radar on the J-16 might remedy the latter deficiency to a degree, but there is little that can be done about the huge signature of the basic airframe configuration.[13] This means no Flanker derivative is ever likely to be able to compete with fifth-generation stealth fighters such as the F-35, which will have an overwhelming situational awareness advantage over it in almost any situation.

As a result, China has been actively developing the J-10 series of lightweight multirole fighters as a cheaper and lower signature multirole fighter to lessen dependence on the Flanker series. The latest model J-10C has an AESA radar, as well as the option for thrust vectoring, multi-band satellite communication (satcom) and datalink connectivity, and a truly modern glass cockpit.[14] It should be considered a worthy rival to the latest Lockheed Martin F-16 and Saab Gripen variants and may well see significant export sales to non-Western-aligned states in coming years. Meanwhile, China has also been developing a very long-range air-to-air missile – codenamed PL-XX by Western observers – to make the most of the Flanker's strengths in the support and anti-enabler role.[15]

To enable the PLAAF to compete directly against the US Air Force (as well as the Japan Air Self-Defense Force and Republic of Korea Air Force,

---

[11] Rupprecht, *Modern Chinese Warplanes*, pp. 38–40, 58.
[12] *Ibid.*, pp. 39, 44–45.
[13] For more detail on this, see Justin Bronk, 'Next Generation Combat Aircraft: Threat Outlook and Potential Solutions', *RUSI Occasional Papers* (November 2018), pp. 6–7.
[14] Rupprecht, *Modern Chinese Warplanes*, pp. 34–35.
[15] *Ibid.*, p. 112. See also Jeffrey Lin and P W Singer, 'China is Testing a New Long-Range, Air-to-Air Missile that Could Thwart U.S. Plans for Air Warfare', Popular Science, 22 November 2016.

both of which possess modern and well-trained fighter fleets), China has developed the J-20 Mighty Dragon heavy stealth fighter. It is a compromise between the specific range requirements of the Pacific theatre and radar signature reduction features. The airframe is large, employing forward-mounted canards to maintain agility and vertical stabiliser surfaces both above and below the rear of the aircraft. The canards and under-fuselage strakes are a design concession since they will increase the RCS of the aircraft. However, by carrying weapons internally, the J-20 has already achieved an 80–90% reduction in RCS compared to traditional fighters that carry munitions on underwing hardpoints, since those hardpoints and external weapons typically constitute around this level of a non-stealth fighter's RCS in combat configuration.[16] This relatively low radar signature will mean Western radars will detect the J-20 at significantly shorter ranges than other Chinese combat aircraft. If managed carefully, this lower signature may enable the J-20 to effectively blend into the background radar clutter and 'noise' created by large numbers of aircraft and missiles within the heavy jamming environment of any future state-on-state clash.

Alongside the J-20, China is also pursuing active unmanned combat aerial vehicle (UCAV) programmes, including but almost certainly not limited to the GJ-11 Sharp Sword, Dark Sword and the newly unveiled CH-7.[17] Given the requirement to operate in high-intensity conflict scenarios which would involve heavy jamming, including denial of satellite communications, by both sides, it must be assumed that China's UCAV designs (as elsewhere) are intended to be capable of high levels of in-flight automation to avoid dependence on real-time datalinks for remote control: in other words, lethal autonomous weapons systems.

The GJ-11 Sharp Sword has been flying, most likely in technology demonstrator form, since 2013 and is one of a series of low-observable tail-less flying wing type UCAVs designed for strike and survivable intelligence, surveillance and reconnaissance (ISR) missions.[18] In October 2019, a new version of the GJ-11 was paraded through Tiananmen Square

---

[16] Author discussions with Lockheed Martin operational analysis specialists, Fort Worth, TX, 19 February 2019.

[17] On CH-7, see Liu Zhen, 'China's Latest Stealth Drones Go on Display at Airshow China 2018', *South China Morning Post*, 7 November 2018, <https://www.scmp.com/news/china/military/article/2172176/chinas-latest-stealth-drone-goes-display-airshow-china-2018>, accessed 17 March 2019. For an example of the initial examination being carried out around the leaked Dark Sword, see David Axe, 'China Apparently is Developing a Stealth Fighter Drone', War is Boring, 8 June 2018, <https://warisboring.com/china-apparently-is-developing-a-stealth-fighter-drone/>, accessed 17 March 2019.

[18] Rupprecht, *Modern Chinese Warplanes*, p. 105.

featuring a noticeably more stealthy, redesigned jet exhaust fairing than previous flying prototypes, showing that iterative development continues at pace.[19]

The Dark Sword is a long-running PLAAF concept for a supersonic UCAV capable of fighter-like agility for so-called 'loyal wingman'-type operations,[20] a full-sized mock-up of which was leaked in a photograph release in 2018.[21] It suggests that China is at least exploring the concept of UCAVs for air superiority tasks.

CH-7 is a separate, large cranked-kite type stealth UCAV design apparently optimised for long-range strike missions which was unveiled at the 2018 Zhuhai Airshow as a possible export product.[22] The WZ-8, an entirely new supersonic rocket-propelled ISR drone designed for release from bombers in flight, was also revealed in October.[23] There are undoubtedly further technology demonstrator and conceptual studies for possible future UCAVs being explored in China, and if the technology is adopted en masse it could further complicate the ability of the US to sustainably project airpower within range of Chinese bases.

UCAVs offer huge benefits in terms of available combat mass for a given fleet size due to the fact they do not require aircrew. Without the need to train a large aircrew cadre and have multiple squadrons for each one at readiness to allow a training/deployment/rest cycle as piloted combat aircraft fleets must, in theory almost every UCAV in an inventory can be part of the front line. Despite having made significant progress in the past decade in increasing the realism and rigour of aircrew training, the PLAAF still lags well behind the US and most NATO air forces in this

---

[19] Joseph Trevithick, 'China Showcases Stealthier Sharp Sword Unmanned Combat Air Vehicle Configuration', The Warzone, 1 October 2019.

[20] 'Loyal wingman' is a concept frequently used in discussing UCAV possibilities. It envisages UCAVs operating very closely alongside conventional piloted combat aircraft rather than as separate elements within a strike package. In this concept, the UCAVs would act as wingmen for fast jets, contributing missiles, electronic warfare support and, if necessary, taking risks to prevent the piloted aircraft from having to do so. However, that sort of concept of operations relies on the UCAV airframes having performance similar to fast jets to enable them to fly mission profiles alongside them, and effectively tethers them to constant datalink connectivity and human control, removing many potential UCAV advantages such as endurance, machine reaction times and lower detectability.

[21] Tyler Rogoway, 'Image of China's Stealthy "Dark Sword" Fighter-Like Combat Drone Emerges', The Warzone, 5 June 2018. See also Rupprecht, *Modern Chinese Warplanes*, p. 105.

[22] On CH-7, see Zhen, 'China's Latest Stealth Drones Go on Display at Airshow China 2018'.

[23] Tyler Rogoway, 'China's High-Speed Drone is Rocket-Powered and All about Doing What Satellites Can't', The Warzone, 1 October 2019.

regard.[24] By contrast, China is at the forefront of cutting-edge research into military usage of artificial intelligence, machine learning and lethal autonomous weapons systems, alongside the US. As a recent Center for New American Security (CNAS) report assessed, 'Chinese officials generally expect drones and military robotics to feature ever more extensive AI and autonomous capabilities in the future. Chinese weapons manufacturers already are selling armed drones with significant amounts of combat autonomy'.[25] There are questions around the current level of technological maturity of these weapons but the direction of travel is clear, and China has shown an impressive ability to rapidly mature advanced weapons once past the initial production stage.[26] In the combat air domain, UCAVs with high levels of in-flight autonomy offer the PLAAF more than simply a way to increase combat mass. Since UCAVs are not dependent on the skills of a cadre of human pilots and are also an emerging class of aircraft which no country has yet put into series production, they represent a disruptive capability development pathway where China is already closer to parity with Western-style air forces. Many of the latter are also still hesitant to openly pursue UCAVs for political reasons.

By contrast, while Russia has proven highly adept at getting the last word in performance out of its Cold War airframe designs such as the Flanker fighter series, Tu-22M3 and Tu-160M bomber fleets and Mig-31 interceptors, it has so far failed to demonstrate a credible capability to produce either true fifth-generation fighters or UCAVs.

The Su-57, formerly known as PAK FA and T-50 during its prototype development stages, is the closest Russia has come to the US F-22 and Chinese J-20A stealth fighters. However, the programme has been beset with technical difficulties, most notably affecting the intended engines which are still not ready, issues with the airframe including metal patching to cover wing cracks, and difficulties integrating the complex multi-band radar arrays given the limitations of Russian military electronics manufacturing. The airframe is also inherently less stealthy than the F-22 or F-35 due to its greater emphasis on supermanoeuvrability over

---

[24] Author interview with Ken Allen, China Aerospace Studies Institute, Washington, DC, 22 February 2019.

[25] Gregory C Allen, 'Understanding China's AI Strategy', Center for a New American Security, 9 February 2019, <https://www.cnas.org/publications/reports/understanding-chinas-ai-strategy>, accessed on 13 May 2019.

[26] For example, the rapid maturation of the indigenous J-10 from the 'A' standard through much more advanced, multirole 'B' and new even more capable 'C' blocks in the five years since 2014. See Rupprecht, *Modern Chinese Warplanes*, pp. 32–35.

signature reduction, and intake and engine configuration stemming from its Flanker-family development heritage.[27]

Production of combat-capable Su-57 aircraft was initially limited to a single squadron of 12 aircraft, which is far short of a sustainable fleet size for regular combat operations.[28] This did not bode well for the future of the type, despite the official explanation citing the performance of the Su-35S meaning there was no need for the Su-57 in large numbers. Ongoing technical difficulties with both quality control for the stealth features and inability to make the complex radar arrays work properly, along with scarce funding, were likely behind Deputy Defence Minister Yury Borisov's statement in July 2018 that the Su-57 would not enter series production for the foreseeable future.[29] As a result it came as a surprise when in May 2019 President Vladimir Putin announced plans to procure an additional 76 Su-57s by 2028, which would bring total numbers to around 100 by the end of that decade.[30] The extremely low contract price of $2.7 billion (or $35.5 million per aircraft, compared with $334 million per F-22 as part of a programme over twice the size) quoted, in addition to continued problems with the design and the withdrawal of India from the programme, cast doubts on the viability of this order. However, even if all of the announced aircraft are purchased and delivered by 2028 as claimed, the Su-57 will fall far short of replacing most of Russia's frontline tactical fighter inventory.[31]

The limited (at best) production prospects for the Su-57 mean that for European air forces concerned primarily with Russia, the threat of hostile stealth fighters in any significant numbers appears to be receding. As for UCAVs, it was only in January 2019 that the first images emerged of a credible Russian test programme. The Sukhoi S-70 Okhotnik-B appears to be a heavy strike and reconnaissance subsonic UCAV prototype.[32] However, the airframe has a standard AL-31F series fighter engine in a

---

[27] Author calculations based on analysis of Su-57 exterior airframe features, along with interior construction shots where available. See also Tyler Rogoway, 'No, The Su-57 Isn't "Junk": Six Features We Like on Russia's New Fighter', The Warzone, 30 April 2018.

[28] Franz-Stefan Gady, 'Russia's Defense Ministry to Ink Contract for 12 Su-57 Stealth Fighters Soon', The Diplomat, 22 August 2018.

[29] Franz-Stefan Gady, 'Russia Will Not Mass-Produce 5th Generation Stealth Fighter Jet', The Diplomat, 12 July 2018.

[30] Joseph Threvithick, 'Russia Now Claims it Will Buy 76 Su-57 Advanced Fighter Jets by 2028', The Warzone, 16 May 2019.

[31] TASS, 'Russian Defense Ministry to Get 76 Su-57 Fighter Jets', 27 June 2019.

[32] Miko Vranic and Nikolai Novichkov, 'Russia Unveils Okhotnik Heavy UAV', Jane's Defence Weekly, 28 January 2019.

simplistic mounting configuration which would significantly compromise its stealth properties from below, above and behind.

Russia is clearly interested in UCAV technology but heavy Russian reliance on imported Western electronics for high-end military systems and continuing Western sanctions blocking access to these components since the annexation of Crimea in 2014 are likely to significantly hinder these efforts.[33] In essence, Russian airpower is a concern for Western militaries due to both long-range strategic nuclear-capable bomber forces and the ability to operate large numbers of modern but non-stealthy fighters against NATO ground troops in a scenario where Western OCA and DCA sorties were not reliably available during the initial phases of a conflict due to extensive Russian ground-based air defences.[34] The prospect of being qualitatively matched or even outmatched by Russian combat aircraft is not a major concern for the leading NATO air arms, particularly as F-35 squadrons start to become operational.[35]

Ground-Based Integrated Air Defence Systems

However, the other major threat component for NATO air forces in high-intensity scenarios involving Russia or China is modern ground-based integrated air defence systems (IADS). Russia is the unquestioned leader here, but China has also developed a formidable IADS. The core of both are long- and very long-ranged SAM systems developed on the basis of the Soviet-era S-300 family. The most modern Russian variants are the S-400 and S-300V4, both of which fire a variety of missiles including the 400-km range 40N6 and 9M82MD respectively.[36] However, the limitations imposed by the radar horizon and the time of flight and kinematic energy

---

[33] For example, the upgraded modern avionics and cockpit electronics which differentiate the Su-35S from previous Su-27 Flanker variants are largely imported from Western companies such as Thales. For more detail on Russian military electronic components import dependence, see Igor Sutyagin and Justin Bronk, *Russia's New Ground Forces: Capabilities, Limitations and Implications for International Security*, RUSI Whitehall Paper 89 (London: Taylor & Francis, 2017), pp. 85–88.

[34] Since 2011 Russia has inducted almost 500 new fixed-wing combat aircraft – almost all Flanker derivatives, as well as undertaking large-scale modernisation and upgrades for its existing MiG-31, Su-25, Su-24, Tu-95, Tu-160 and Tu-22M fleets. See Piotr Butowski, *Flashpoint Russia: Russia's Air Power: Capabilities and Structure* (Austria: Harpia Publishing, 2019), p. 6.

[35] Author interviews with fast jet aircrew from the RAF, US Air Force, Armée de l'Air and Norwegian Air Force, London, Paris, Berlin, Munich, Washington, DC, 2015–19.

[36] For more information on the component parts of the S-400 system, see Army Technology, 'S-400 Triumph Air Defence Missile System', <https://www.army-technology.com/projects/s-400-triumph-air-defence-missile-system>, accessed 17

profile of these huge long-range missiles when engaging targets beyond 250km make them most useful against large surveillance aircraft and other enablers like tankers rather than against smaller, agile combat aircraft. Smaller, cheaper and more agile missiles are also loaded into the transporter erector launcher (TEL) canisters in each battery, allowing the S-300V4 and S-400 to engage a wider variety of targets within around 250 km. The systems have a modular architecture enabling multiple radar types to feed into their situational awareness picture. This also enables upgraded radar types to be rapidly integrated into existing batteries as they become available. The S-400 and S-300V4 are also capable of limited ballistic missile defence duties, are highly mobile with set-up, shoot and scoot times measured in minutes, and are protected in the field by Pantsir S-1/2 series point defence systems.

China has purchased several S-400 batteries for its own use, and they currently form the most capable part of the Chinese IADS.[37] China has also produced its own derivative of the S-300 family, the HQ-9 series. The HQ-9 uses very similar TELs and core concepts to Russian S-300 variants but pairs them with Chinese electronics, seeker heads and radar units, many of which are thought to be based on reverse-engineered components from a covertly acquired US MIM-104 Patriot PAC-2 SAM system.[38] It has also developed a specialised anti-radiation missile called the FT-2000 for use against aircraft which emit a great deal of electromagnetic energy such as AWACS, Joint STARS (Joint Surveillance Target Attack Radar System) and the US Navy's EA-18G Growler electronic warfare fighter aircraft.[39] The People's Liberation Army Navy (PLAN) also deploys a navalised variant called the HHQ-9 on its major surface combatants, enabling China to extend its SAM coverage significantly beyond the reach of land-based batteries.

So-called 'strategic SAMs' such as the S-400 and HQ-9 are usually deployed as part of the layered network of overlapping radars and medium- and short-ranged SAMs which make up a modern IADS. Taken together, these systems present a formidable but not insurmountable

---

May 2019. For the 9M82MD see *TASS*, 'Russia's New S-300V4 Air Defense System to Get Three Types of Hypersonic Missiles', 9 September 2016.

[37] Jeremy Chin, 'China Conducts BMD Test with S-400', CSIS Missile Defense Project, 29 December 2018, <https://missilethreat.csis.org/china-conducts-bmd-test-with-s-400/>, accessed 17 May 2019.

[38] Army Technology, 'HQ-9 Medium-to-Long Range Air Defense Missile System', 31 January 2019, <https://www.armyrecognition.com/china_chinese_army_missile_systems_vehicles/hq-9_ground-to-air_medium_range_air_defense_missile_technical_data_sheet_specifications_pictures.html>, accessed 17 May 2019.

[39] *Missile Defense Advocacy Alliance*, 'HQ-9', 20 June 2018, <http://missiledefenseadvocacy.org/missile-threat-and-proliferation/todays-missile-threat/china-anti-access-area-denial-coming-soon/hq-9/>, accessed 17 May 2019.

challenge for Western air forces. Degrading these defences requires large-scale SEAD and destruction of enemy air defences (DEAD) campaigns. These must employ a mix of cyber attacks, standoff and stand-in electronic warfare (jamming), large numbers of standoff weapons such as cruise missiles and, most of all, either fighters, bombers or UCAVs stealthy enough to penetrate deep inside the layered defences to pinpoint the most important radar and command units and either attack them directly or guide in the standoff munitions. Such operations would be costly in terms of munitions and likely combat losses, and require a great deal of military preparation, coordination and political risk tolerance on the part of an attacking force. They also force large enabler aircraft to operate beyond the missile engagement zones of the long-ranged strategic SAMs.

IADS are an inescapable part of the modern combat air environment, and a challenge to which NATO air forces must have answers. However, while Russia relies extremely heavily on its IADS to the extent that it is fair to characterise the combat aircraft of the VKS as playing a subordinate and supporting role to the ground-based sensor network and SAM systems, China poses a different and more flexible long-term threat. While China has a potent IADS of its own, the PLAAF and the air wing of the PLAN are being developed with a greater capacity for operations beyond its coverage.[40] China's IADS sits alongside the People's Liberation Army Rocket Force as more of a joint force enabler out to the first island chain rather than the main pillar of defence against Western airpower. It is against the PLAAF and PLAN that the latest wave of transformation and modernisation efforts for the US Air Force and US Navy is increasingly being tailored.

---

[40] Author interview with Japanese expert on Chinese security trends, National Institute for Defense Studies, Tokyo, 14 June 2019.

II. THE BIG PLAYER: THE UNITED STATES

When seeking to understand airpower within the NATO Alliance, the United States must be the starting point for any discussion. The US possesses a greater combat air capability than the rest of NATO put together. The US Air Force is by far the largest within the Alliance, and the US Navy operates what would be the second-largest air force. The discrepancy in capability between the US and other Allies is already far greater than mere platform numbers or budgetary comparisons would suggest. The critical enablers that allow a modern air campaign to be conducted – tankers, strategic and penetrating ISTAR assets, C2 and network infrastructure, munitions stocks and more – are overwhelmingly provided by the US. For example, in 2014, the proportion of AAR tankers provided by the US compared to the remainder of NATO was 9:1. While 17 of 28 (61%) of the NATO member states operated fast jets which draw on AAR, only nine (32%) had a national tanker capability.[1]

In this context, the fact that the US Air Force is aiming to increase from its current front line strength of 312 squadrons to 386 squadrons by 2030, in order to fulfil what it sees as the mission sets implied by the latest National Security Strategy, is a powerful reminder of the increasing quantitative gap between the US and other NATO air forces.[2] This significant expansion plan is underpinned by an attempt to change the narrative around how the US government perceives military spending in an era of great power competition. As the Chief of Staff of the US Air Force General David L

---

[1] Joint Air Power Competence Centre, 'Air-to-Air Refuelling Consolidation: An Update', March 2014, pp. 8–10. This ratio has not significantly improved in 2019, despite the long delays in the US KC-46 tanker replacement programme which has constrained USAF numbers.

[2] Heather Wilson, 'The Air Force We Need', speech given at the Air Force Association's Annual Air, Space and Cyber conference, 17 September 2018. For detailed numbers, see US Air Force, 'The Air Force We Need: 386 Operational Squadrons', 17 September 2019, <https://www.af.mil/News/Article-Display/Article/1635070/the-air-force-we-need-386-operational-squadrons/>, accessed 8 April 2019.

Table 2: US Air Force and US Navy Aircraft Fleets vs. Other NATO Member States

	United States Air Force and Navy	Other NATO Member States (Total)
Combat aircraft (fourth generation)	approximately 3,000 (approximately 1,400 combat-ready)	approximately 2,500 (fewer than 50% combat-ready)
Combat aircraft (fifth generation)	approximately 420 (F-22 x 187 – 121 combat-coded) (F-35 x 300, not fully operational)	approximately 50 (all F-35s, not fully operational)
Heavy bomber aircraft	157	0
Aerial refuelling tankers	530	61
Intelligence, surveillance and reconnaissance aircraft (including RPAS)	625	44

Source: Author analysis based on IISS, *The Military Balance 2019*; John Venable, 'US Air Force: An Assessment of US Military Power', Heritage Foundation, 4 October 2018; Boston et al., *Assessing the Conventional Force Imbalance in Europe*; author interviews with NATO and US Air Force commanders, London, 2019; Washington, DC, 2019; Berlin, 2019.

Goldfein put it at the Air Force Association's Air, Space and Cyber Conference in 2018, 'We usually have the dialogue about the Air Force we can afford. This is different. This is about the Air Force we need to present credible options to compete, deter, and if deterrence fails, win'.[3] A move to force structure planning that is led more by threat/mission requirements rather than budget limitations is completely at odds with how most NATO forces are organised and, perhaps more importantly, funded. There are certainly questions as to the long-term financial viability of the US Air Force's expansion plans as the funding boon from the era of President Donald Trump is not expected to last, but the contrast in terms of language and ambition with other NATO member air forces is nonetheless striking and instructive in terms of broad trends, as shown in Table 2.

Air-to-Air Refuelling Aircraft

When considering the combat air outlook for the US Air Force and other air arms, the AAR enabler picture must always be borne in mind because in most scenarios it is the availability and standoff distance of tanker orbits which constrain US strike options.[4] As General David Deptula said of AAR

---

[3] US Air Force, 'The Air Force We Need'.
[4] '[T]he number of refueling aircraft available in each theater is one of the biggest limiting factors to the scale and scope of aerial power projection'. David A Deptula and Douglas A Birkey, 'The Force We Need: Key Factors for Shaping the Air Force

capability, 'There is no alternative when it comes to this mission that underpins America's global reach'.[5] While AAR is important for enhancing the endurance of large enablers such as AWACS, the most pressing customer group for their fuel offload capacity is short-ranged tactical fighters. Tactical fighters impose a high degree of tanker dependence on air forces even in the context of a potential European conflict, where ranges are typically measured in hundreds of nautical miles between bases and potential combat zones.

However, the primary focus for the Pentagon as it looks to the next half century or so is not Europe or Russia, but rather a rising Chinese threat in the Pacific.[6] In the vast distances of the Pacific, the US has a serious tanker dependence and tanker vulnerability problem.

The Boeing KC-46A Pegasus next-generation tanker programme is still beset by troubles, with multiple outstanding design and quality control issues in addition to being chronically behind schedule and over budget. The state of the programme is casting doubt over the ability of the US Air Force to increase the size of its tanker fleet, let alone start to replace the ancient KC-135 Stratotankers which make up the bulk of its current 40 AAR squadrons.[7] The US Air Force claims it needs an additional 14 squadrons (roughly 210 tanker aircraft) and is also aiming to retire its fleet of 59 KC-10 Extender tankers as the KC-46 comes into service. Clearly, the existing order for 179 KC-46s by 2028 would not come close to providing for another 14 squadrons in addition to replacing the KC-10 fleet. The Pegasus acquisition programme in its current state 'will replace less than half of the current tanker fleet and will leave the Air Force with over 200 ageing KC-135s awaiting recapitalization'.[8] When one includes the Air National Guard and Air

for the Future', *Mitchell Institute Policy Papers* (Vol. 19, March 2019), p. 7, <http://docs.wixstatic.com/ugd/a2dd91_7f1dd52770df4faa993a3f90df9622b3.pdf>, accessed 16 April 2019.

[5] David Deptula, 'Pegasus Arrives: KC-46 Tanker Makes America More Effective in Era of Growing Threats', *Defense News,* 16 January 2019.

[6] Patrick Shanahan quoted in Ryan Browne, 'New Acting Secretary of Defense Tells Pentagon "to Remember China, China, China"', *CNN,* 2 January 2019. See also the strong focus on China in White House, 'National Security Strategy of the United States of America', December 2017, <https://www.whitehouse.gov/wp-content/uploads/2017/12/NSS-Final-12-18-2017-0905.pdf>, accessed 16 March 2019.

[7] For details on KC-46A programmes, see Joseph Trevithick, 'USAF Finally Accepts its First KC-46A Tanker, but the Design Still Needs Years Worth of Fixes', The Warzone, 10 January 2019.

[8] Arnold W Bunch, Jr, Jerry D Harris and Scott A Vander Hamm, 'Hearing on Air Force Bomber/Tanker/Airlift Acquisition Programs – Hasc Seapower and Projection Forces', hearing before the Committee on Armed Services, US House of Representatives, 25 May 2017, p. 10, <http://docs.house.gov/meetings/AS/AS28/

Force Reserve squadrons in this total, Air Mobility Command operates 396 KC-135s.[9] Since the youngest KC-135 in the fleet was delivered to the Air Force in 1965, making it 54 years old in 2019, the entire fleet is increasingly expensive to maintain and operate.[10]

However, perhaps the largest problem facing the US Air Force (as well as the US Navy and Marine Corps aviation elements) in terms of AAR enablers in high-intensity contingency planning is not scarcity or fleet age but rather the vulnerability of these assets in combat.

China is developing weapons systems specifically geared towards hunting large US tanker and AWACS aircraft, as a means to neutralise much of the US Air Force tactical fighter fleet in any armed clash. One notable example is the J-20A with its combination of low observability (LO), ability to carry up to four jettisonable external fuel tanks, large internal weapons bays and fuel capacity.[11] Another is the PL-XX missile seen in carriage testing on J-16 fighters in 2017 with what appears to be a dual-mode seeker and a range based on a loft-coast trajectory of around 400 km.[12] The Chinese concept is relatively simple: the US Air Force can be kept at bay if its tankers can be effectively targeted or forced to operate so far from the battlespace as to lose most of their efficiency in terms of boosting fighter reach. While the KC-46 will incorporate the latest self-defence capabilities – most likely in the form of modern active chaff and flare dispensers, as well as possibly towed decoys and even, in future, directed energy-based active defence systems – it is ultimately hard to ensure the safety of an airliner-derived large aircraft with huge RCS and very limited manoeuvrability. These aircraft are the most obvious weak link in the US Air Force's ability to generate sorties near the Chinese mainland in a conflict and China is well aware of this. Almost as high on the Chinese (and Russian) priority target list are ISR enablers which typically operate behind the main battlespace with the AAR tankers, using powerful sensor suites to provide the whole force with wide area situational awareness.[13]

20170525/106013/HHRG-115-AS28-Wstate-BunchA-20170525.pdf>, accessed 9 April 2019.

[9] US Air Force, 'KC-135 Stratotanker', Fact Sheets, 14 May 2018, <https://www.af.mil/About-Us/Fact-Sheets/Display/Article/1529736/kc-135-stratotanker/> accessed 9 April 2019.

[10] *Ibid.*

[11] Rupprecht, *Modern Chinese Warplanes*, pp. 40–44.

[12] *Ibid.*, p. 112; see also Lin and Singer, 'China is Testing a New Long-Range, Air-to-Air Missile'.

[13] Author interview with Chinese PLAAF expert, National Defense University, Washington, DC, 23 February 2019.

AWACS and Intelligence, Surveillance and Reconnaissance Aircraft

The US Air Force has traditionally relied on a series of large airliner-derived platforms for both airborne AWACS and standoff ISR. There are three main families of such 'big-wing ISR' aircraft: the E-3G Sentry AWACS fleet; the RC-135 Rivet Joint family of specialised signals intelligence and electronic intelligence types; and the E-8C Joint STARS ground radar surveillance and battle management fleet. In addition, the US operates a range of smaller piloted and unmanned ISR aircraft including the high-flying U-2S Dragon Lady spy plane and RQ-4 Global Hawk UAVs, and the stealthy and only semi-acknowledged RQ-170 Sentinel stealth UAV for penetrating ISR missions.[14]

As the first of the big-wing ISR classes approaches retirement, the US Air Force has moved to firmly kill off the expected effort to replace the E-8C with a similar type of aircraft.[15] Instead, the service intends to extend the E-8C fleet into the mid-2020s and upgrade at least seven E-3G Sentry AWACs aircraft in order to provide a bridge until a totally new ISR and C2 approach is mature enough to replace them.[16] The US Air Force is counting on a distributed network of sensors mounted on multiple piloted and unmanned platforms, as well as space-, ground- and maritime-based sensors linked together and processed by its nascent ABMS.[17]

The US Navy is already working on a similar concept called Naval Integrated Fire Control – Counter Air (NIFC-CA), which is intended to allow situational awareness sharing, sensor cross-referencing and enhanced cooperative engagement capability (CEC) across multiple different airborne and surface platforms.[18] In 2016, it conducted a live fire test in which the sensor picture from an F-35 was used to successfully cue in an SM-6 missile from an Aegis test platform beyond the range of the Aegis array's own radar picture.[19] The US Air Force has been experimenting with platform-to-platform CEC for more than a decade alongside the US Navy, to allow tactical sensor-shooter flexibility in

---

[14] Tyler Rogoway, 'Rare Video of an RQ-170 Sentinel Making a Low Approach at Dawn is Both Spooky and Glorious', The Warzone, 11 July 2016.

[15] Venable, 'U.S. Air Force'.

[16] Kris Osborn, 'The Air Force is Creating a System to Manage the Military's Forces in War', *The National Interest*, 1 March 2018.

[17] *Ibid.*

[18] For more discussion on NIFC-CA and some key assets such as the E-2D Hawkeye, see Justin Bronk, 'A Quiet Take Off – US Navy Deploys E-2Ds to Japan', *RUSI Commentary*, 24 January 2017.

[19] Naval Sea Systems Command, 'Navy Conducts First Live Fire NIFC-CA Test with F-35', F35.com, 13 September 2016, <https://www.f35.com/news/detail/navy-conducts-first-live-fire-nifc-ca-test-with-f-35>, accessed 10 April 2019.

specific scenarios.[20] However, what the ABMS architecture is trying to do is beyond the current scope of NIFC-CA or CEC. Rather than simply providing an architecture of datalinks to connect weapons, sensors and command centres – itself a complex undertaking – ABMS is an attempt to provide automated data fusion, analysis and optimal sensor-shooter combinations for the whole connected force.[21] In other words, in its advanced phases at least, it is planned as an information processing, translation and analysis architecture rather than just a networked approach to kinetic engagements and situational awareness. If the ABMS project is successful, it will significantly change the way in which platforms throughout the joint force integrate, and how targeting and C2 is conducted by US forces. ABMS also has implications for how the US Air Force and the other E-3 operators within NATO will eventually choose to replace their E-3 Sentry fleets in the AWACS role when the type reaches its end-of-service date, currently set for 2035.[22]

The E-3 Sentry has set the global standard for AWACS aircraft since its introduction in the early 1970s by the US Air Force and subsequent acquisition by the Royal Air Force, French Air Force, NATO AWACS Force, and Royal Saudi Air Force. The E-3 has proven to be a critical force multiplier in every conflict in which the US Air Force has taken part since the Gulf War in 1991, when it was instrumental in enabling coalition fighters to rapidly overmatch and destroy the Iraqi Air Force.

Fighter aircraft carry small radars primarily in the nose with limited scanning arcs depending on which direction the nose is pointing at any given time. Using these radars to actively scan for targets without a LPI/LPD capability also reveals an aircraft's location to any opponent equipped with a radar-warning receiver. In effect, a traditional fighter radar can be thought of like using a handheld flashlight to spot enemies in a dark warehouse: it illuminates whatever it is pointed at well but does not show the whole picture, while also giving away the user's own location. An AWACS, meanwhile, employs a large rotating radar array at high power levels and from high altitudes; to continue the analogy, it is like turning on a ceiling light. It provides a much more comprehensive view of the battlespace for friendly units than any fighter radar can offer alone and can also help provide positive identification of unknown contacts. The latter capability is particularly useful for fighters with older

---

[20] Author interview with senior US Air Force aircrew officer with extensive fast jet combat and testing experience, London, 29 May 2019.
[21] Author interviews with Northrop Grumman subject matter experts, London, 4 March 2019.
[22] Justin Bronk, 'The Future of Air C2 and AEW: E-3 Sentry, Threat Technologies and Future Replacement Options', *RUSI Occasional Papers* (June 2017), p. 6.

radars that lack advanced non-cooperative target recognition (NCTR) or similar capabilities to identify contacts which are not squawking a transponder identification or broadcasting 'Identification Friend or Foe' (IFF) at significant distances – critical for beyond-visual-range (BVR) engagements.

The E-3 also offers a comprehensive suite of Very High Frequency/ Ultra High Frequency (VHF/UHF) Secure Voice/Data Systems, Link 16, Link 11 and satcom channels to act as a core network node for the whole force. Finally, it also offers human capacity with a large mission system crew to act as battlespace managers to coordinate combat and logistical tasks, such as AAR tanker allocations within a given area of operations. The US Air Force's Sentry fleet is currently in the middle of a mid-life upgrade process to bring its fleet of 31 active duty aircraft to Block 40/45 E-3G standard through a thorough computer system and data-processing upgrade package.[23] However, as with the E-8C Joint STARS fleet, advances in long-range surface- and air-launched missiles and low-observable (stealth) fighter technology threaten the ability of the E-3 to fulfil its traditional AWACS function in a modern high-threat environment.[24]

Just as the Chinese J-20A low-observable fighter and very long-range PL-XX air-to-air missile threaten to hunt down US tanker orbits at significant combat ranges, they are also able to threaten AWACS, E-8 Joint STARS and other ISR platforms. In fact, the electronic emissions which radar-based surveillance assets generally must give off to do their jobs make them easier to find, track and engage than tankers. From the ground, Russia's S-400 and S-300V4 SAM systems with the 40N6 and 9M82MD 400 km-class missiles respectively threaten to keep large airliner-derived ISR platforms so far from the battlespace that their own sensor utility is largely negated, though they still fulfil a crucial airborne communications node and C2 capacity function.[25] China has also purchased the S-400 and, as noted earlier, has its own HQ-9/HHQ-9 series of long-range SAMs based on the S-300 family with new radar and seeker components.[26] Chinese SAMs are both land-based and deployed on PLAN surface combatants, as well as on

---

[23] Darren D Heusel, 'Upgraded E-3 Sentry Deploys to Combat Theater', US Air Force, 19 November 2015, <https://www.af.mil/News/Article-Display/Article/630606/upgraded-e-3-sentry-deploys-to-combat-theater/>, accessed 10 April 2019.

[24] For a detailed discussion of this, see Bronk, 'The Future of Air C2 and AEW'.

[25] For more information on the component parts of the S-400 system, see Army Technology, 'S-400 Triumph Air Defence Missile System', <https://www.army-technology.com/projects/s-400-triumph-air-defence-missile-system/>, accessed 9 October 2018. For an announcement on the S-300V4's new 9M82MD missile, see *TASS*, 'Russia's New S-300V4 Air Defense System to Get Three Types of Hypersonic Missiles', 9 September 2016, <http://tass.com/defense/898884>, accessed 11 April 2019.

artificial reefs such as Fiery Cross Reef, Subi Reef and Mischief Reef in the Spratly Islands to enable the projection of SAM engagement zones far beyond the Chinese mainland.[27] In a recent report for the Department of Defense, the Center for Strategic and Budgetary Assessments (CSBA) judged that in the future planning scenario of a conflict with China, contested airspace for non-stealthy, big-wing tankers and ISR aircraft could extend up to 1000 nm from Chinese territory.[28] If held this far from potential targets, the on-board sensor suite of ISR platforms would not be directly useful due to radar horizon and line of sight limitations.

What this means is that during any future conflict with Chinese forces in the Pacific theatre, US (and regional allies') combat aircraft will be forced to operate significantly further forward from their supporting enablers than previously. This means longer penetrations from AAR tanker support, less assistance with situational awareness and real-time targeting from big-wing ISR and more defensive patrol and escort responsibilities for the air superiority fighters having to protect the enablers themselves. For fighters, especially legacy fourth-generation fighters, it also means the prospect of significant attrition, especially from pop-up SAM threats based on Chinese PLAN vessels, reefs and atolls. The answer to at least some of these issues for many in the US Air Force is a combination of novel unmanned solutions, space-based ISR, and eventually the ABMS and large numbers of F-35s.

Combat Aircraft

The largest single component of US combat airpower for the foreseeable future will be the F-35 Lightning II. The programme of record includes 1,763 of the conventional take-off and landing (CTOL) F-35A variant for the US Air Force, and a mixture 693 F-35C catapult-assisted take-off but arrested recovery (CATOBAR) and F-35B short take-off, vertical landing (STOVL) variants for the US Navy and US Marine Corps.[29] With an

---

[26] For S-400 deliveries to China, see Franz-Stefan Gady, 'Report: China Completes User Trials of S-400 Air Defense System', *The Diplomat*, 17 January 2019.

[27] Paul McLeary, 'China Has Built "Great Wall of SAMs" in Pacific: U.S. Adm. Davidson', *Breaking Defense,* 17 November 2018. See also Amanda Macias, 'China Quietly Installed Missile Systems on Strategic Spratly Islands in Hotly Contested South China Sea', *CNBC,* 2 May 2018.

[28] Author interview with Mark Gunzinger, Washington, DC, 11 July 2019. See also Mark Gunzinger et al., 'An Air Force for an Era of Great Power Competition', Center for Strategic and Budgetary Assessments, 29 March 2019, pp. 113–15.

[29] Lockheed Martin, 'F-35 Lightning II Program Status and Fast Facts', 5 March 2019, <https://www.f35.com/assets/uploads/documents/F-35_Fast_Facts-_March_2019. pdf>, accessed 16 March 2019.

estimated acquisition cost of $406 billion, and a total through-life cost of an estimated $1.1 trillion, the F-35 programme dwarfs any other in history.[30] The aircraft is without doubt the most sophisticated fighter aircraft ever made, with situational awareness and advanced information sharing and electronic warfare/cyber capabilities which eclipse even those of the US Air Force's premier air dominance fighter, the F-22 Raptor.[31] It was designed specifically to counter modern IADS such as those being fielded today by Russia and China, as well as to be able to out-position and destroy or evade advanced hostile fighters through its combination of very low observability (stealth) and superior situational awareness. As part of this, the F-35 has a particularly impressive capability to precisely locate, classify and attack hostile SAM radars including strategic SAMs like the S-400 and HQ-9, all while providing the pilot with a dynamic display of the range at which the target is likely to detect them.[32]

Fighter Aircraft: Range Limitations in the Context of the Pacific

In this respect, the system which the US armed services are already receiving and will continue to procure in large numbers is a great success. Before its more advanced capabilities are unlocked in the upcoming Block 4 software versions and beyond, the F-35 is already proving formidable in the most challenging and realistic threat scenarios that the US Air Force can generate, even in the hands of very inexperienced pilots.[33] Nonetheless, there are currently no external fuel tanks available for the F-35, and they would in any case increase drag and severely compromise its stealth properties.[34] This limitation is partially compensated for by its impressive internal fuel capacity compared to legacy fighters, with a combat radius of

---

[30] US Government Accountability Office, 'F-35 Joint Strike Fighter: Development is Nearly Complete, but Deficiencies Found in Testing Need to be Resolved', Report to Congressional Committees, June 2018, pp. 6–8.

[31] For more information, see Justin Bronk, 'Maximum Value from the F-35: Harnessing Transformational Fifth-Generation Capabilities for the UK Military', *Whitehall Report*, 1-16 (February 2016).

[32] See John Venable, 'The F-35A Fighter is the Most Dominant and Lethal Multi-Role Weapons System in the World: Now is the Time to Ramp Up Production', Heritage Foundation Backgrounder, 14 May 2019.

[33] Many of the F-35's most advanced warfighting features are software dependent and will be introduced or matured in the upcoming Block 4 software standard. At the time of writing, F-35s around the world are flying on Block 3F software. For more details on *Red Flag* performance, see David Cenciotti, 'The First Reports of How the F-35 Strutted its Stuff in Dogfights Against Aggressors at Red Flag are Starting to Emerge', The Aviationist, 16 February 2019, <https://theaviationist.com/2019/02/16/the-first-reports-of-how-the-f-35-strutted-its-stuff-in-dogfights-against-aggressors-at-red-flag-are-starting-to-emerge/>, accessed 16 March 2019.

up to 600 nm for the F-35C variant, but it still leaves the F-35 heavily dependent on AAR tankers in many potential Pacific scenarios.[35] It is a dependency which China is well aware of, and it creates a significant limitation for US planners in that if China can push tanker orbits back beyond the combat radius of the F-35, then the F-35 cannot reach Chinese targets.

The CATOBAR and STOVL variants of the F-35 offer basing flexibility in that they can operate from the US Navy's nuclear-powered aircraft carrier fleet in the case of the F-35C and the US Marine Corps' smaller amphibious assault landing ships in the case of the F-35B. The latter can potentially also operate from rapidly deployed 'lily pad' bases on small islands if other assets such as landing ships and heavy rotary-winged assets can bring the required materials ashore. However, both of these options present their own difficulties and potential vulnerabilities. For lily pad bases, a key concern would be the ability to maintain supply lines by sea and air to bring in sufficient fuel, munitions and spare parts to generate useful sortie rates from such far forward and widely dispersed bases. For aircraft carriers and amphibious assault ships, potential threats from undersea, shore-based and air-launched weapons threaten to keep these floating operating bases sufficiently far from Chinese shores to make the F-35's unrefuelled combat radius a key limiting factor once more. China is fielding a number of systems aimed at keeping the US Navy's carrier battle groups at least 1,000 nm from the Chinese coastline, notably the DF-21D anti-ship ballistic missile, with its hypersonic glide vehicle warhead, and a large arsenal of conventional anti-ship missiles and submarines.[36]

Recent studies suggest initial fleet deployments in the early stages of a war could be up to 2,000 nm from the Chinese mainland and a need to maintain combat air patrols out to 1,000 nm from the carrier.[37] The power of the US Navy's carrier battle groups also means that they cannot be exposed to serious risk of loss since each one would be a huge hit to total US strike power. With only 'buddy-buddy' refuelling available to US

---

[34] Briefing given to author by Manager, Operations Analysis, Lockheed Martin Aeronautics division, Fort Worth, TX, 19 February 2019.

[35] Combat radius is a complex figure to measure because a great deal depends on the altitude profile flown in a given mission, the task required once 'at the target area', atmospheric conditions, payload, and other factors. For the internal fuel ranges of the CTOL, STOVL and CATOBAR F-35 variants, see Lockheed Martin, 'F-35 Lightning II Program Status and Fast Facts'.

[36] For DF-21D, see Tyler Rogoway, 'Is This China's DF-21D Air Launched Anti-Ship Ballistic Missile Toting Bomber?', The Warzone, 15 August 2017.

[37] For detailed information on the range implications of Chinese A2/AD threats for US carrier forces, see Bryan Clark et al., 'Restoring American Seapower: A New Fleet Architecture for the United States Navy', CSBA, 2017, pp. 92–95.

carrier-based fighters since the retirement of the S-3 Viking fleet in 2016, the ability of the US Navy to generate combat sorties if pushed back beyond around 400 nm from the battle space would drop dramatically.[38]

Part of the solution may be the upcoming MQ-25 tanker UAV, which offers a significantly lower signature compared to older, manned tanker solutions. It should therefore be able to operate closer to enemy territory and thus provide greater combat range for the strike assets through fuel offloads closer to target. However, with only four initial airframes on contract for initial deck operating capability by 2024, there will be a limited number of MQ-25s available to any given carrier air wing for the foreseeable future.[39] In addition, while the MQ-25 will offer a usable fuel offload capacity of at least 15,000 lbs at 500 nm from the carrier, which is valuable for extending the range of a small strike package, this is still less than 10% of the fuel provided by large airliner-derived solutions such as the KC-135 and KC-46A.[40] Therefore, the Chinese ability to push the carrier group further from any contested area will still have a significant effect on practical sortie rates even once the MQ-25A is in service, limiting the degree to which the F-35 and F/A-18E/F Super Hornet combined air wing alone can offer solutions to the range-centric challenges of the Pacific.

Operating Fourth- and Fifth-Generation Fighters Together
In terms of developmental pathways that the rest of NATO can follow, the F-35 remains a generally positive trend. The UK, Italy, the Netherlands, Norway, Belgium, Denmark, Poland and Turkey have already committed to buying the F-35, and other NATO member states are likely to follow over the coming decade.[41] The all-important software capabilities which sit at the heart of the F-35, and its ability to exchange information discreetly with other F-35s through the multifunction advanced datalink (MADL), are interoperable by design between different national

---

[38] Dario Leone, 'U.S. Navy Bids Farewell to the S-3 Viking', The Aviationist, 14 January 2016. Buddy–buddy refuelling is a technique whereby a non-dedicated aerial refuelling aircraft such as a fighter jet uses auxiliary fuel tanks and pods to refuel another aircraft of the same type in flight.

[39] Megan Eckstein and Sam LaGrone, 'Navy Picks Boeing to Build MQ-25A Stingray Carrier-Based Drone', *USNI News*, 30 August 2018.

[40] *Ibid*. For comparison, the KC-135 can offload 150,000 lbs of fuel at 1,300 nm; US Air Force, 'KC-135 Stratotanker'.

[41] At time of writing, Turkey's continued participation is in question due to President Recep Tayyip Erdogan's refusal to cancel the acquisition of S-400 air defence systems from Russia. See Jim Inhofe et al., 'A U.S. Fighter Jet or a Russian Missile System. Not Both.', *New York Times*, 9 April 2019.

operators.[42] In that sense, there is likely to be a significant measure of commonality within NATO fighter fleets going forwards, which should greatly enhance interoperability within the force when compared to the wide range of legacy fast jet fleets in service today.

It is important to remember, however, that even if the US Air Force manages to secure the funding it has requested from Congress to cover 72 new fighters a year for the foreseeable future to allow expansion above the rate of old airframe retirement, and even if all 72 were to be F-35As, then the US Air Force fighter fleet would still be composed of 50% legacy fourth-generation platforms like the F-15 and F-16 in 2030.[43] In fact, the latest US Air Force budget estimates plan instead on 48 F-35s per year from 2020, augmented with eight new F-15EX fighters in the 2020 financial year, rising to 18 per year from 2021–24.[44] Eventually, the US Air Force may purchase as many as 144 F-15EXs to replace ageing F-15Cs in the air superiority and air defence roles by the mid-late 2020s, which will further reduce the ratio of fifth-generation fighters in the force.[45]

How the US Air Force maintains the viability of the large number of fourth-generation tactical fighters remaining in its inventory out to well past 2030 will be critical, since they will still form a majority of available fighter numbers.

The F-35 force will be working alongside F-15s, F-16s, F/A-18E/Fs and EA-18Gs for decades and these legacy platforms will rely to an increasing degree on the ability of the F-35 to share its situational awareness in real time, without compromising its own survivability, in order to remain competitive in high-threat environments. This will require either upgrading the datalinks and software architecture of these legacy fighters to allow them to receive and decode MADL from F-35s, or continued reliance on relay and 'translation' nodes such as the business-jet derived E-11A and EQ-4B Net Hawk variant of the Global Hawk UAV, both of which loiter at high altitudes to facilitate interoperability but represent additional cost and mission complexity.[46] No other NATO member state has yet decided to invest in this relay and MADL translation function – which is currently provided by a system known as the Battlefield Airborne Communications Node (BACN) with a Freedom 550 module on the E-11A

---

[42] For more information, see Bronk, 'Maximum Value from the F-35'.

[43] John Venable, speech given at Combat Air Survivability Conference, RUSI, London, 20 March 2019.

[44] Department of Defense, 'Fiscal Year (FY) 2020 Budget Estimates: Air Force Justification Book Volume 1 of 2', March 2019, pp. 68–69.

[45] David Axe, 'Boeing's F-15EX: We Have the Air Force's Master Plan for This New Warplane', *National Interest*, 19 March 2019.

[46] For more information, see Bronk, 'Maximum Value from the F-35', p. 4.

and EQ-4B platforms – although the RAF has conducted numerous trials with its own F-35B and Typhoon fighters using US Air Force assets.[47]

Long-Range Strike Bomber Programme: The B-21
Alongside the F-35 Joint Strike Fighter programme, the B-21 Raider programme is a critical part of the US Air Force strategy for the coming decades. It is intended to replace the current fleet of 20 iconic B-2 Spirit stealth bombers, which have provided the US Air Force with the ability to strike targets almost anywhere on earth with conventional or nuclear weapons since the mid-1990s. The new B-21 will also replace the non-stealthy but supersonic-capable B-1B Lancer, which is no longer part of the US nuclear triad but still regularly flies conventional missions around the world.

In terms of design, the B-21 will almost certainly be similar to the B-2: a large tail-less flying wing design with advanced, very low observability properties across the electromagnetic spectrum to allow it to effectively evade radar and infrared detection systems.[48] While it is an extremely capable aircraft, only 21 B-2s were ever built and it is still the single most expensive combat aircraft ever made when measured by unit cost.[49] The approach being taken with the B-21 programme envisages at least 100 aircraft. It also aims to avoid the cost spiral which plagued and ultimately limited the B-2 by relying to a much greater extent on proven and mature technologies.[50] However, it is also intended to be a much more multirole aircraft than the B-2, with a modern AESA radar and LPI datalinks providing superb situational awareness, in addition to sophisticated jamming, electronic warfare and surveillance possibilities.[51] Such a radar, coupled with a minimal signature in all spectra, would also allow the B-21

---

[47] For example, see Northrop Grumman, 'Northrop Grumman and Royal Air Force Demonstrate Enhanced Airborne Communications Interoperability Between 5th and 4th Generation Fast-Jet Aircraft', 15 February 2017, <https://news.northropgrumman.com/news/releases/northrop-grumman-and-royal-air-force-demonstrate-enhanced-airborne-communications-interoperability-between-5th-and-4th-generation-fast-jet-aircraft>, accessed 15 April 2019.

[48] For examples of some of the concepts being employed, see Tyler Rogoway, 'The B-21's Three Decade Old Shape Hints at New High Altitude Capabilities', The Warzone, 6 October 2017.

[49] Counting development costs, each B-2 Spirit cost $2.1 billion. See Sebastien Roblin, 'B-2 Spirit Stealth Bomber: The Air Force's "Silver Bullet" Super Weapon', *National Interest,* 4 January 2019.

[50] Jeremiah Gertler, 'Air Force B-21 Raider Long-Range Strike Bomber', Congressional Research Service, 7-5700, 12 October 2018, p. 9.

[51] For examples of some of the concepts being employed, see Rogoway, 'The B-21's Three Decade Old Shape'.

to engage hostile aerial threats if long-ranged air-to-air missiles were carried as part of the huge internal payload, giving it some measure of self-escort capability in hostile territory.

Most importantly of all, however, the B-21 is being designed to perform combat operations over the vast distances of the Pacific theatre, if necessary, from the continental US. The B-2 has a combat range of around 6,000 nm with over 10,000 nm possible with a single aerial refuelling, which can take place while at a very long distance from potential threats.[52] It is fair to assume that the B-21's range will be in a similar ballpark and so it will be a large aircraft requiring long runways and specially designed base facilities. This makes it a fundamentally different proposition to operating tactical fighters, both in terms of cost and infrastructure requirements, making it unlikely that any European country will follow suit in developing similar aircraft. Indeed, no European NATO air arm has developed or fielded heavy bombers since the British V Bomber force, which was designed during the 1950s.

For the US, however, such large aircraft are an essential component of its Pacific strategy, since they go some way towards reducing the current Achilles' heel of US airpower in the region: significant dependence on tanker support for in-flight refuelling. Put simply, reducing reliance on multiple refuellings per sortie would greatly increase the potential combat power which the US could project into areas contested by modern Chinese (or Russian) threat systems. Therefore, if the B-21 successfully proves the concept of a long-range, very low observable (VLO) bomber and multirole aircraft, then there is every chance that the US Air Force will place a heavy reliance on the type, possibly to the detriment of tactical fighter programmes like the F-35. There are already multiple voices and studies within the US Air Force calling for a significant uplift on the initial fleet target size of 100, with numbers of between 145 and 200 bombers being suggested.[53] Another possibility might be the further development of the B-21 into an even more capable future variant of the basic design. The latter would almost certainly involve realigning many of the US Air Force's other capabilities to leverage the B-21's unique reach and flexibility to the maximum extent possible in a Pacific context.

In either case, there is very little chance that other NATO air forces will be able or inclined to follow suit given the constraints of European budgets, airspace and range requirements. The B-21 itself is planned as part of a system of systems, with a range of airborne, space-based, inter-agency and cyber tools envisaged as part of a future 'toolkit' to create desired

---

[52] Deptula and Birkey, 'The Force We Need', p. 7.
[53] *Ibid.*, p. 18.

effects on target.[54] This is not only a question of leveraging maximum operational utility from the aircraft, but also a way to reduce technological risk within the programme by accepting reliance on off-board sensors and enablers to overcome high-threat mission challenges rather than having to be self-supporting in all contexts.[55]

Achieving Next-Generation Air Dominance

Changing Procurement Processes

The B-21 and most of its enabling capabilities are being run through the US Air Force's Rapid Capabilities Office rather than the usual procurement mechanisms, with a more ambitious timeframe and smaller overheads. It also relies heavily on leveraging technologies already proven in prototype form.[56] Beyond the headline airframe development and procurement efforts under way in many countries, this new 'experimentation, prototyping, and agile acquisition strategy' is where the US is really pulling away from the other NATO member states.[57] From expendable swarming UAVs such as the Gremlin to 'loyal wingman'-type UCAVs like Boeing's Airpower Teaming System and the XQ-58A Valkyrie, to space-based kinetic effects, the US is actively exploring technologies that are well beyond the current scope or reach of European NATO member states.[58] What is more, the timeframe envisaged for the testing and deployment of these capabilities is extremely ambitious, and designed to get inside a rapid Chinese iterative development cycle.

As part of this, there is an ongoing effort to break the procurement and development paradigm of the past 30 years, which has seen a platform-centric approach and timescales for new capabilities measured in decades. As the Air Superiority 2030 Flight Plan strategy states upfront, 'The rapidly changing operational environment means the Air Force can

---

[54] Author interview with senior US Air Force officer, The Pentagon, Washington, DC, 21 February 2019.
[55] Gertler, 'Air Force B-21 Raider Long-Range Strike Bomber', pp. 2, 5.
[56] *Ibid.*, pp. 4–5.
[57] See Conclusion section of Enterprise Capability Collaboration Team, 'Air Superiority 2030 Flight Plan', US Air Force, 2016.
[58] For Gremlin, see Scott Wierzbanowski, 'Gremlins', Defense Advanced Research Projects Agency (DARPA), <https://www.darpa.mil/program/gremlins>, accessed 16 March 2019. For info on the Airpower Teaming System, see Nigel Pittaway, 'Boeing Unveils "Loyal Wingman" Drone', *Defense News,* 27 February 2019. For info on the XQ-58A, see Tyler Rogoway, 'Air Force's Secretive XQ-58A Valkyrie Experimental Combat Drone Emerges After First Flight', The Warzone, 6 March 2019.

no longer afford to develop weapon systems on the linear acquisition and development timelines using traditional approaches.[59]

Fortunately, by embracing modern computer modelling and additive manufacturing techniques, it is possible to explore and prove core technologies to a much more advanced level than in previous generations when using technology demonstrators and small-scale experimental programmes.[60] The upshot is that within the top secret 'black world' the US is likely to be testing, proving and evaluating radical new approaches to delivering airpower effects at a much faster pace and on a broader scale than was previously possible. If programmes can be de-risked and then committed to and developed quickly once their military value is understood, then the need to develop a capability to last decades would also be reduced, allowing for smaller procurement programmes, for less money and with a faster refresh rate.

There have already been various hints within congressional programme status reports suggesting that the B-21 itself might be the first visible example of this new approach in action – with the design and even initial flight test programme well ahead of expectations given that the contract award to Northrop Grumman was only announced in 2015.[61] A first flight target of December 2021 and initial operational capability (IOC) expected in around 2024–25 is significant for future Alliance dynamics, since the pace and level of ambition behind these efforts is not something which European NATO members are likely to be able to approach.[62]

Unmanned Combat Aerial Vehicles

In the case of UCAVs and other weapons systems incorporating a high degree of autonomy once in the air, there may also be capabilities which other NATO members are not politically willing to develop or field. However, their combat utility is unquestionable, and as the US finds itself increasingly challenged in terms of the quality as well as quantity of

[59] US Air Force, 'Air Superiority 2030 Flight Plan', May 2016, pp. 3–5.

[60] Author interview with senior US Air Force officer, Pentagon, Washington, DC, 21 February 2019.

[61] Secretary of the Air Force Public Affairs, 'Air Force Selects Locations for B-21 Aircraft', 2 May 2018, <https://www.af.mil/News/Article-Display/Article/1510408/air-force-selects-locations-for-b-21-aircraft/>, accessed 17 March 2019. See also Tyler Rogoway, 'Congressman Details Integration Issues with the B-21's Exotic Air Inlet Design', The Warzone, 8 March 2018; John A Tirpak, 'B-21 Update', *Air Force Magazine*, 3 March 2017.

[62] Joseph Trevithick, 'New B-21 Raider Stealth Bomber Scheduled to Make its First Flight in Late 2021', The Warzone, 24 July 2019.

fielded systems by the PLAAF,[63] it may be simply unrealistic to expect the US to hold back on deploying highly autonomous lethal capabilities.

The Department of Defense's Directive on Autonomy in Weapons Systems defines acceptable systems as '[a] weapon system that, once activated, can select and engage targets without further intervention by a human operator. This includes human-supervised autonomous weapon systems that are designed to allow human operators to override operation of the weapon system, but can select and engage targets without further human input after activation'.[64] The Directive sets out guidelines to ensure that such systems include safeguards so that they do not behave unexpectedly if confronted with unanticipated scenarios or hostile behaviour, and remain subject to human supervision and override authorisation. It also sets out responsibilities for commanders and test and evaluation officials.[65] What it implicitly makes clear, however, is that the Department of Defense has had a framework in place to handle the development and potential deployment of weapons systems incorporating a high degree of autonomy under certain operational scenarios since 2012.

The UCAV question is already feeding into the debates around the Next-Generation Air Dominance (NGAD) concepts that are supposed to provide the basis for the next generation of fighter for the US Air Force and US Navy. Some, such as CSBA and the Mitchell Institute for Aerospace Studies, continue to advocate for a medium-sized stealthy fighter/electronic attack aircraft, sometimes labelled Penetrating Counter-Air/Penetrating Electronic Attack (PCA/P-EA).[66] However, while major Original Equipment Manufacturers (OEMs) such as Northrop Grumman and Lockheed Martin have been circulating artworks with tail-less super-fighter concepts for years, a powerful body of opinion

---

[63] As described earlier, China itself is experimenting with UCAVs, with Dark Sword, Sharp Sword and the newly unveiled CH-7 likely representing only the publicly admitted tip of the iceberg. Russia, too, is experimenting with its Su-70 Okhotnik heavy UCAV as a complement to its largely unsuccessful Su-57 programme, which aimed to develop a rival stealth fighter to those being fielded by the US and developed by China. On CH-7, see Zhen, 'China's Latest Stealth Drones Go on Display at Airshow China 2018'. For an example of the initial examination being carried out around the leaked Dark Sword, see Axe, 'China Apparently is Developing a Stealth Fighter Drone'. See also Military Factory, 'Sukhoi Su-70 Okhotnik (Hunter)', edited 27 August 2019, <https://www.militaryfactory.com/aircraft/detail.asp?aircraft_id=2067>, accessed 3 April 2019.
[64] Department of Defense, 'Autonomy in Weapons Systems', Directive Number 3000.09, 21 November 2012, pp. 13–14.
[65] *Ibid.*, pp. 2–15.
[66] Author interviews with US Air Force and civilian SMEs, Washington, DC, 10–13 July 2019. See also Gunzinger et al., 'An Air Force for an Era of Great Power Competition', pp. 142–43.

within the Pentagon is now pushing for a much more diverse approach based on rapidly proving and developing systems to enable a mix of manned and unmanned capabilities very different from the single major fleet solutions of previous generations.[67] This is partly driven by recent estimates for the likely cost of fielding a fighter-style PCA/P-EA replacement for the F-15 and F-22 air superiority fleets within the 2030–40 timeframe. The Congressional Budget Office placed a price estimate of around $300 million in 2018 dollars per PCA assuming a programme of 414 aircraft.[68]

One of the reasons for the current shortfall in the US Air Force's estimates of its ability to establish air dominance in a future high-intensity conflict was the decision in 2009 by then Secretary of State for Defense Robert Gates to terminate F-22 Raptor production after only 187 airframes out of an original target of 750.[69] This was largely due to the very high acquisition and operating costs of the Raptor, as well as concerns about its relevance to future conflicts in an age of counterinsurgency. The B-2 Spirit bomber suffered a similar fate, with an anticipated 100–30 strong fleet reduced to 21.[70] Few expect the PCA/P-EA to avoid such a fate if numbers like $300 million per aircraft are involved, giving ammunition to those in the Pentagon and US Air Force looking to a different, modular 'system of systems' approach under the NGAD programme umbrella. A third approach has been proposed by Will Roper, the assistant secretary of the Air Force for acquisition, technology, and logistics. This involves designing a series of new aircraft for shorter service lives than usual and in much shorter, more limited production runs along the lines of the so-called 'Century Series' fighters produced during the 1950s.[71] The idea would be to draw on novel manufacturing and design approaches to break the cost- and time-growth paradigm outlined by defence economist Norman Augustine in favour of more competition and risk-taking at the design and industrial base level.[72] However, at this stage this remains a

---

[67] Author interviews with US Air Force and civilian SMEs, Washington, DC, 20–22 February 2019 and 10–13 July 2019. See also, for example, Steve Trimble, 'USAF Acquisition Head Urges Radical Shift for Next-Gen Fighter Program', *Aviation Week,* 5 March 2019.

[68] Valerie Insinna, 'Budget Watchdog Warns This Fighter Could Cost Three Times That of the F-35', *Defense News,* 14 December 2018.

[69] Tyler Rogoway, 'Now the Head of the USAF is Jumping on the F-22 Production Re-Start Bandwagon', The Warzone, 26 May 2016.

[70] Mark F Cancian, 'U.S. Military Forces in FY 2020: Air Force', Center for Strategic and International Studies, 21 October 2019.

[71] Sydney J Freedberg, Jr, 'A New Century Series? Will Roper Takes Air Force Back to the Future', *Breaking Defense,* 12 April 2019.

[72] Norman Augustine, *Augustine's Laws,* 6th edition (Virginia: American Institute of Aeronautics & Astronautics, 1997).

conceptual outlier without widespread buy-in from the Pentagon's acquisition community or the US Air Force, due to the complexity of integration and testing required to produce competitive fifth-generation, let alone next-generation, combat air systems.[73]

Diverging from NATO Allies

At this point, it is important to return to the US Air Force's ambitions for ABMS in the 2030–40 timeframe. As has already been discussed, the ABMS architecture is hugely ambitious in terms of data fusion, real-time coordination of assets across multiple domains, and high levels of automated analysis and decision-making capability. However, beyond this, ABMS is also intended to help the US Air Force and the joint force more broadly transition to a posture more suitable for conducting MDO against state opponents in large-scale conflict scenarios.[74]

MDO is central to the Department of Defense's plan for modernisation of the entire US Armed Forces. It involves land, maritime, air, cyber and space forces operating in a fully synchronised and integrated system down to the tactical level in real time with command held at theatre level or even higher, since the essential convergence of effects (including inter-agency effects) can only be adequately organised and synchronised at a field army or equivalent headquarters.[75] In this sense, ABMS is not a tactical battle management or C2 architecture; rather it is an architecture designed to coordinate a truly joint task force at theatre-wide scale during a major war.

MDO – and ABMS as a core overarching component of the MDO vision – also involves a great deal of automated machine-machine cueing, requiring the integration of data from multiple sensors. This will by necessity place humans *on* rather than *in* the decision-making loop, which may create concerns among Allies as well as in the US itself about the maintenance of meaningful human control over lethal force. This is because the scale of cross-cueing of sensors from multiple platforms in multiple domains will make it practically impossible for a 'shooter' to track in real time the process by which the target data was created. Indeed, the aim of ABMS and MDO more broadly is to create a system within which

---

[73] Author interviews with subject matter experts, Washington, DC, July 2019; Warsaw, September 2019; Berlin, October 2019.
[74] Osborn, 'The Air Force Is Creating a System to Manage the Military's Forces in War'.
[75] Goldfein, speech given at RAF Air and Space Power Conference, 18 July 2019. For more information, see Jack Watling, 'Allies in the Multi-Domain Task Force', *RUSI Defence Systems*, 5 April 2019.

an automated network of cross-domain sensors detects, classifies, corroborates and then provides weapons track information to the most efficiently placed and armed 'shooter' without needing human intervention or guidance.[76] As such, the first human 'yes/no' authorisation in this system, exercising real-time human control, might well be the pilot launching a weapon.[77]

It is important to note that at this stage, the command arrangements and even architectural specifics of how the ABMS will incorporate assets from the US Navy, Army and Marine Corps are still unclear. The discussion is also heavily siloed, with the Air Force focusing on ABMS, the Navy and Marine Corps on NIFC-CA, and the US Army on MDO with the assumption of an army-centric command structure.[78]

Nevertheless, the US Air Force's plan to eventually phase out the big-wing ISR roles of E-8C and E-3G, and instead rely on ABMS and distributed smaller platforms once the system starts to mature in the 2030s, is a mark of the seriousness of the intended pivot to planning for large-scale wars against state opponents rather than multiple low-intensity intervention or counterinsurgency operations.[79] However, it also threatens to leave smaller Allies unable to integrate their forces effectively since even if they managed to meet the technical standards required, the size of their military forces would preclude them from exercising, let alone operating, at corps scale or above.[80] Partner states are also likely to have political and possibly legal objections to the levels of automation in target detection, classification and weapons release recommendations implied by ABMS.

At present, the envisaged ABMS approach of marshalling multi-domain and inter-agency kinetic and non-kinetic effects as a key part of real-time combat operations through a single command and situational awareness architecture remains an ambition rather than a capability for the US. Importantly, however, it is not only a real ambition and a funded one at that, but also a core part of MDO and is far beyond any envisaged capability being considered by other NATO Allies. The fact that the B-21 is, as already discussed, being designed with an inherent reliance on off-board ISR and unspecified enablers, orchestrated in real

---

[76] Author interview with senior US Air Force aircrew officer with extensive fast jet combat and testing experience, London, 29 May 2019; Goldfein, speech given at RAF Air and Space Power Conference.

[77] Goldfein, speech given at RAF Air and Space Power Conference.

[78] Author interviews with OF5 grade US Army officers from US Army War College, London, 23 April 2019.

[79] For E-8 recapitalisation withdrawal and ABMS replacement capabilities, see Venable, 'U.S. Air Force'.

[80] Watling, 'Allies in the Multi-Domain Task Force'.

time, to accomplish its core mission set in high-threat environments is evidence of the faith that the Department of Defense is placing in the ABMS approach when planning future platform configurations.

Plans for future US airpower capabilities beyond the F-35 programme, including B-21 and the broad NGAD efforts, are not only being designed from the outset to integrate within the future ABMS architecture but are being designed in such a way that they rely on operating within such a networked joint force construct. This is a crucial point to understand in a broader NATO context, since the way in which the US Air Force equips, trains and organises to fight wars dictates to a great extent how the rest of the Alliance does the same. This is because other member states are reliant on being able to 'plug in' to the US airpower framework for most, or in some cases all, of their enablers and logistical support.

However, as the weapons systems which grew out of the Reagan-era spending boom in the 1980s begin to show their age, and the US looks to yet another new generation with a mix of F-35, B-21 and potentially UCAV-based capabilities, as well as other exotic effectors under the NGAD umbrella, European NATO members are still years away from catching up with current US theatre-entry standard capabilities. The F-22 Raptor, B-2 Spirit, AIM-120 advanced medium air-to-air missile (AMRAAM) series and a host of other important US Air Force systems which date from the late 1980s or early 1990s were, at least, designed with similar requirements to their European counterparts: high-end deterrence and overmatch capability against the fourth generation of Russian fighters and air defence systems. The capabilities and ABMS-centric tactics that the US Air Force and US Navy will develop over the coming decade or so to counter Chinese advances and the demands of the Pacific theatre are less likely to share similar requirements and so will have a profound effect on how the Alliance is able to apply airpower.

III. THE MEDIUM POWERS: EUROPE'S LEADING AIR FORCES

The 28 non-US NATO members collectively possess well over 1,000 fast jet aircraft and as such represent a potentially highly potent part of the Alliance's airpower. However, a significant number of smaller member states do not possess combat aircraft, while the majority operate comparatively small fleets of between 40 and 60 aircraft and few enablers. Most of the non-US airpower in the Alliance is fielded by a few large European states, including the UK, France, Italy, Germany and Spain.[1]

A Survey of European NATO Members' Air Forces

The two most potent air forces in Europe at the end of the 2010s are the UK's Royal Air Force (RAF) and the French Armée de l'Air. Both states also operate smaller naval air forces which are closely tied to their land-based counterparts – the Fleet Air Arm (FAA) and the Aéronavale, respectively. The UK and France have also been the two foremost expeditionary-minded military powers in Europe since the end of the Second World War and, as such, have traditionally been the most concerned with developing and maintaining the sort of high-end power projection capabilities fielded by the US.

Both the RAF and Armée de l'Air operate a core fast jet fleet composed of advanced fourth-generation multirole fighters. The Typhoon FGR4 and Rafale F3-R are both extremely capable air-to-air fighters against non-fifth-generation opponents and both can carry a wide range of direct attack munitions and the long-ranged standoff Storm Shadow/SCALP cruise missile. However, neither aircraft is designed to survive within the

---

[1] Turkey also fits within this category in terms of numbers of combat aircraft but the practical capabilities of the Turkish Air Force have been severely degraded by political purges of aircrew and commanders since the attempted coup in 2016. It is assessed as no longer capable of performing at the level required to be discussed in this category. For outline figures, see Michael Peck, 'How Turkey Destroyed its Own Air Force', *National Interest,* 16 March 2018.

missile engagement zones (MEZ) of the latest Russian or Chinese SAM systems. For the task of operating within areas covered by such systems, the UK has introduced the F-35B into both the RAF and the FAA as a joint carrier and land-based fleet. France, however, has traditionally relied on electronic warfare and stand off weapons for such tasks, and has not developed an equivalent capability to the F-35 yet. Despite the Rafale's highly regarded SPECTRA electronic warfare system, it would struggle to sustain operations against an opponent fielding S-300V4 or S-400 SAM systems without incurring serious losses unless operating as part of a coalition force in which others are able to conduct the crucial 'sensors forward in the MEZ' task.[2]

The other relatively large air forces in European NATO are the German Luftwaffe, the Italian Aeronautica Militare and the Spanish Ejército del Aire.

Germany

Germany operates a mixed fleet of ageing Tornado IDS strike bombers, Tornado ECR electronic warfare and SEAD aircraft and the multirole Eurofighter Typhoon. However, Germany's Eurofighter fleet lags significantly behind those of the UK and Italy in terms of strike capabilities, having maintained an almost exclusive air defence mission focus for much of the aircraft's life. Like France, Germany has chosen to forgo involvement in the F-35 programme and has, so far, not fielded any strike aircraft which can credibly penetrate heavily defended airspace.[3] Having explicitly chosen to reject the F-35 as a possible replacement for the Tornado fleet in the conventional strike, electronic warfare/SEAD and nuclear roles, the only remaining options for Germany are the US F/A-18E/F Super Hornet or an additional purchase of the latest Eurofighter standard.[4] The timescales involved in the development of European platforms to replace the Eurofighter (and Rafale) are such that Germany will have to replace its Tornados with one of these two existing aircraft despite the fact that neither is currently cleared for the B-61 tactical nuclear delivery role which the Luftwaffe's Tornados still technically fulfil.

German combat aircraft procurement decisions have historically been largely driven by industrial concerns rather than operational requirements

---

[2] Author's own analysis, informed by multiple discussions with Rafale aircrew in London and Paris, 2015–19.
[3] Sebastian Sprenger, 'Germany Officially Knocks F-35 Out of Competition to Replace Tornado', *Defense News*, 31 January 2019.
[4] Andrea Shalal, 'Germany Drops F-35 from Fighter Tender; Boeing F/A-18 and Eurofighter to Battle On', *Reuters*, 31 January 2019.

analysis, and the Eurofighter is in any case a platform with significantly superior kinematic performance, power and capability growth potential compared to the Super Hornet. As a result, Germany is most likely to purchase additional Eurofighters to fulfil its future strike needs.[5] However, this will not provide Germany with an ability to operate without accepting high risk levels within airspace threatened by Russian long-range air defences. That said, there are efforts underway to improve the Eurofighter Typhoon's end-game missile survival capabilities[6] and ability to contribute standoff munitions and jammers to a broader SEAD effort using the SPEAR 3 range of munitions being developed by the UK, alongside existing cruise missiles like Storm Shadow and Taurus.[7]

Italy

Italy operates a very similar mix of combat aircraft to the RAF: the Tornado IDS is still in service although drawing down and looking towards retirement in the early 2020s; the Eurofighter Typhoon provides the backbone; and the F-35A and F-35B are intended to provide the ability to operate in high-threat environments, with plans for 30 F-35Bs and 60 F-35As on record.[8] It is not surprising, therefore, that Italy has chosen to partner with the UK's Team Tempest efforts to develop future combat air systems.[9] However, plans for F-35 acquisition and Typhoon modernisation already stretch the Italian air force budget; as such, adequately funding future acquisition and development efforts whilst also maintaining the current force modernisation plan may be even harder than for the UK, France and Germany. Nonetheless, Italian industrial capabilities, especially in developing advanced radar technology, will be valuable for future combat air efforts as part of the Tempest programme.

Despite the active participation of Italian Tornados in Operation *Unified Protector*, which first degraded and subsequently helped to defeat Qadhafi's forces in Libya, munitions costs alone forced their relegation to tactical reconnaissance during early phases of the conflict against Daesh

---

[5] For more information on German Tornado-replacement issues, see Justin Bronk, 'Next Generation Combat Aircraft: Threat Outlook and Potential Solutions'.

[6] 'End-game' refers here to the defensive ability to successfully evade or otherwise defeat a hostile missile once it has been launched and acquired a lock on the aircraft.

[7] Briefing by Paul Smith, BAE Systems Air, RUSI Combat Air Survivability Conference, London, 20 March 2019.

[8] Gareth Jennings, 'Italian MoD Takes Delivery of First Non-US Built F-35B', *Jane's Defence Weekly*, 29 January 2018.

[9] Alistair Smout, 'Italy to Join Britain's Tempest Fighter Jet Project', *Reuters*, 11 September 2019.

in Iraq.[10] As part of cost-cutting measures, the small but combat-proven reconnaissance and ground attack AMX-1 Gibli fleet will also be phased out by 2021.[11] While the retirement of the AMX-1 will reduce Italian tactical reconnaissance and light attack capacity in permissive air environments, the type was not suitable for high-intensity scenarios in any case. Given Italy's strained budget, the urgent need to procure F-35s to replace the Tornado by the early 2020s, and the need to ensure its Eurofighter fleet stays operational and up to date with the latest multirole standards, the AMX-1 retirement choice was a logical one.

Spain

Spain operates a mix of F/A-18 Hornet and Eurofighter Typhoon, as well as a small number of AV-8B Harrier IIs for its aircraft carrier, the *Juan Carlos I*. However, it has suffered significant affordability issues for its current fleets, and while there has been an ambition for many years to replace both the AV-8Bs and potentially the F/A-18 fleets with F-35s, the cost implications have prevented a commitment to this course so far.[12] In fact, Spain has previously explored the sale of part of its Tranche 1 Eurofighter fleet to Colombia due to budgetary concerns, although these plans were not carried through in the end.[13] The Ejército del Aire also currently lacks any tanker capacity, although plans were announced in 2018 to replace the retired KC-707 with three A-330 MRTTs as already flown by the RAF and Armée de l'Air.[14]

The UK

In terms of the way in which European NATO air forces operate, the RAF is currently closest to the US Air Force, both in terms of its working relationship and operational practices.

---

[10] Author interview with Aeronautica Militare General Staff officer, Rome, 15 January 2015.

[11] For more information on the AMX-1, see MilitaryFactory.com, 'AMX International AMX', <https://www.militaryfactory.com/aircraft/detail.asp?aircraft_id=464>, accessed 3 May 2019.

[12] Miguel González, 'Spain's Air Force and Navy Have Sights Set on New American Fighter Aircraft', *El Pais*, 5 June 2017.

[13] Carlos Vanegas, 'Espana y Colombia negocian la adquisicion de Eurofighter del Ejercito del Aire espanol para la FAC [Spain and Colombia negotiate the acquisition of Eurofighter of the Spanish Air Force for the Colombian air force]', *Defensa.com*, 12 December 2017.

[14] Esteban Villarejo, 'Spanish Air Force: The Six Top Modernization Priorities of 2018', (translated by) *Defense-Aerospace.com*, 7 February 2018, <http://www.defense-aerospace.com/articles-view/release/3/190575/spanish-air-force-lists-top-modernization-priorities-of-2018.html>, accessed 3 May 2019.

The Typhoon FGR4 fleet provides a robust fourth-generation air superiority capability which has long operated and trained closely with the US F-22 and F-15C communities. With exceptional climb performance, high-altitude supercruise and energy retention capabilities, the Typhoon lends itself uniquely well to cooperation with the F-22 since almost any other fast jet struggles to keep pace with the Raptor at very high altitudes and speeds, which places certain limits on tactical options for combined formations. Successive *Red Flag* exercises and bilateral exercise programmes have given the RAF Typhoon community a significantly deeper operational understanding of the challenges and benefits of integrating fourth- and fifth-generation assets than other European air forces.[15] While other states including Italy, Germany and more recently France have also participated in these exercises alongside and sometimes against fifth-generation opponents, the UK is afforded a level of training exposure to the full US Air Force Fighter Integration 3-1 standard tactics which exceeds that of these partner countries.[16] In addition, the joint RAF/Royal Navy F-35 force declared IOC in January 2019 at RAF Marham, marking the UK's transition to an operational mixed fourth-/fifth-generation fast jet fleet, just as the US Air Force has operated since the F-22 came into service.[17] RAF aircrew on exchange tours have also flown many high-sensitivity US Air Force platforms including the F-22, F-117 Nighthawk, RC-135 series and even the B-2 Spirit.[18]

Long-term cooperative exchanges on sensitive technology areas have also enabled the UK to buy into other sensitive US Air Force programmes, including acquisition of three RC-135W Rivet Joint aircraft, known as Airseeker in RAF service. Within this programme, the RAF's aircraft are operated closely with the US Air Force RC-135 fleet, with US crews often crewing RAF aircraft and vice versa.[19] However, to get the best value out of the data which its Airseekers gather, the UK relies on feeding that data into the US Distributed Common Ground System (DCGS), and then receiving actionable intelligence product back as an

---

[15] For more detail, see Justin Bronk, 'Maximising European Combat Air Power: Unlocking the Eurofighter's Full Potential', *Whitehall Report*, 1-15 (April 2015), p. 12.

[16] Author interviews with *Red Flag*-experienced RAF Typhoon pilots at RAF Leuchars, December 2014.

[17] Gareth Jennings, 'UK Declares IOC Land for F-35 Force', *Jane's Defence Weekly*, 10 January 2019.

[18] Author interviews with former exchange pilots, London, Paris, 2016–19. See also Mikal Canfield, 'Royal Air Force Pilot Makes History in B-2 Spirit', US Air Force, 8 August 2006, <https://www.af.mil/News/Article-Display/Article/130151/royal-air-force-pilot-makes-history-in-b-2-spirit/>, accessed 30 April 2019.

[19] Author interview with RAF RC-135 pilot, RAF Coningsby, 12 October 2015.

output.[20] The DCGS is a global network construct through which intelligence data from multiple sources is passed to specialist intelligence units and agencies to enable the generation of intelligence products for use at both the strategic and tactical levels.[21] One way of looking at the RAF's participation in the Airseeker programme, therefore, is as a relatively cheap means of purchasing access to the DCGS intelligence product from the US RC-135W big-wing ISR ecosystem.

Similarly, the UK's early adoption of the US Air Force ISTAR workhorse, the MQ-9 Reaper RPAS, and co-location of the initial training and operational unit 39 Squadron at Creech Air Force Base with the bulk of the US Predator and Reaper force, allowed the RAF to take advantage of US expertise and global RPAS infrastructure.[22] Despite having moved the Reaper (soon to be MQ-9B Certifiable Predator B or 'Protector') force to RAF Waddington in the UK, the RAF still operates its RPAS fleet according to similar CONOPS in combination with heavy use of US Air Force communications networks and the DCGS network to allow optimal processing and exploitation of the surveillance that they provide.

This sort of operational integration has given the UK a detailed view into ISR-exploitation best practice as conducted by the US Air Force, and as such it is no surprise that the UK's ISTAR fleet as a whole largely mirrors that of the US Air Force. In place of Joint STARS, the RAF operates the Sentinel R1, which carries a similar high-resolution synthetic aperture radar for long-range slant-surveillance and ground moving target indicator (GMTI) tracking capabilities, but on a smaller and more efficient Global Express business jet.[23]

The system was designed from the outset to be compatible with Joint STARS and carries an even more modern and capable radar, albeit with a smaller mission crew.[24] Despite being slated for retirement following the withdrawal of combat troops from Afghanistan in 2014, the type has proven so valuable to commanders in a variety of theatres – most notably Syria and Iraq in the campaign against Daesh – that it has been repeatedly extended and its out-of-service date is now set for 2021 at the

---

[20] Author interview with RAF Intelligence Officer with experience of DCGS, London, January 2016.
[21] US Air Force, 'Air Force Distributed Common Ground System', 13 October 2015, <https://www.af.mil/About-Us/Fact-Sheets/Display/Article/104525/air-force-distributed-common-ground-system/>, accessed 30 April 2019.
[22] Royal Air Force, '39 SQUADRON', <https://www.raf.mod.uk/our-organisation/squadrons/39-squadron/>, accessed 30 April 2019.
[23] Royal Air Force, 'SENTINEL R1', <https://www.raf.mod.uk/aircraft/sentinel-r1/>, accessed 3 May 2019.
[24] Tyler Rogoway, 'USAF or NATO Should Snap Up the RAF's Retiring R1 Sentinel Radar Planes', The Warzone, 16 June 2017.

earliest.[25] There is every chance that the fleet may continue in service through the 2020s, given that the US Air Force has decided to tide over the Joint STARS fleet until ABMS is ready rather than replace it with a similar capability which the RAF might in theory have then procured in the 2020s.[26]

Another possibility might be an adaptation of the new P-8 Poseidon maritime patrol aircraft (MPA) to carry a similar large synthetic aperture radar pod to replace the Sentinel. The US Navy has been testing just such a pod, known as the Advanced Airborne Sensor (AAS), on its P-8s since at least 2015, with the aim of allowing the MPAs to scan vast areas of open ocean, but also giving them a potential secondary synthetic aperture radar (SAR) mapping and GMTI capability overland.[27] The RAF took delivery of the first two aircraft in its own nascent Poseidon fleet in 2019 and has previous experience with modifying MPAs to undertake overland ISR missions in the shape of the Nimrod R1, which was retired in 2011 following a deadly crash over Afghanistan and subsequent public airworthiness criticisms.[28] Given that the US Navy has mounted AAS on the P-8 to enhance the MPA's ability to act as a situational awareness force multiplier and network node for multiple vessels and air assets as part of its NIFC-CA concept, having a similar capability would be hugely attractive for the UK. It would enable the RAF to enhance joint force interoperability, especially with the US Navy and also between the RAF and Royal Navy during littoral operations. It would also provide a much-needed additional option for network resilience between RAF assets.

The E-3D Sentry AWACS fleet which has long provided the RAF's air battle management and surveillance (ABM&S) capability – just as the E-3G fleet still does for the US Air Force – has suffered significant obsolescence and reliability issues after cost-cutting measures led the RAF to forgo a midlife upgrade in 2009.[29] Extending the E-3D's life into the mid-2020s, let alone to the 2035 out-of-service date tentatively set for the E-3G replacement, was going to cost at least £2 billion.[30] As a result, the RAF

---

[25] Royal Air Force, 'SENTINEL R1'.

[26] On the Joint STARS replacement decision, see Venable, 'U.S. Air Force'.

[27] Department of Defense, 'P-8A Poseidon Multi-Mission Maritime Aircraft (P-8A)', Selected Acquisition Report (SAR), 2016, p. 7. See also Tyler Rogoway, 'Exclusive: P-8 Poseidon Flies with Shadowy Radar System Attached', Foxtrot Alpha, 14 April 2014, <https://foxtrotalpha.jalopnik.com/exclusive-p-8-poseidon-flies-with-shadowy-radar-system-1562912667>, accessed 3 May 2019.

[28] Ministry of Defence, 'Nimrod R1 Retires from Service', GOV.UK, 7 July 2011, <https://www.gov.uk/government/news/nimrod-r1-retires-from-service>, accessed 3 May 2019.

[29] For more information, see Bronk, 'The Future of Air C2 and AEW', p. 1.

[30] Howard Wheeldon, 'UK Defence (254) – RAF Waddington Prepares for Exciting Future', CMS Strategic, 6 June 2016, <http://www.cmsstrategic.com/news/3106/uk-defence-254-raf-waddington-prepares-for-exciting-future>, accessed 3 May 2019.

has decided not to wait to see how the US ABMS effort develops before deciding on an E-3 replacement, and has instead opted to purchase a new fleet of five Boeing E-7 Wedgetail aircraft.[31] The Wedgetail was developed for the Royal Australian Air Force and features a relatively modern AESA radar on a 737 airliner-derived airframe – itself similar to the P-8. The aircraft will offer several advantages over the E-3D as an ABM&S role, including a more capable and flexible radar, lower operating costs and the likelihood of significantly enhanced operational availability. However, the £1.51 billion deal locks the RAF into a 'traditional' AWACS solution to the airborne C2 and network relay problem, and one which will come into service just as the US Air Force starts its push to transition to a more distributed and modular ABMS approach. One of the objectives laid out in the official RAF Strategy in 2017 is to 'become an integrated air force that recognises information is its lifeblood', but its ISTAR enabler and C2 roadmap as currently laid out is markedly less ambitious than the US Air Force's ABMS architecture within MDO.[32]

France

France, by contrast, upgraded its E-3 fleet to the same E-3G Block 40/45 standard as the US Air Force during the early 2010s and intends to replace the type in the same timeframe as the US – that is, during the 2030s. While this technically leaves the Armée de l'Air with a less modern AWACS than the RAF will have in the E-7 Wedgetail, it gives France the ability to more closely coordinate its future air C2 and airborne networking plans with the US Air Force's decisions for after the E-3.

Aside from the E-3F/G fleet of AWACS aircraft, France also operates two C-160G Gabriel aircraft which are C-160 Transall twin-turboprop, medium-lift transport aircraft converted to the electronic warfare/ electronic intelligence role. They are ageing aircraft and will be replaced by 2025 by the Dassault Falcon Epicure – a business jet-derived, multi-mission ISR aircraft.[33] France's pre-eminent ISTAR fleet remains the 22-strong Aéronavale fleet of Breguet/Dassault Atlantic Nouvelle Generation or ATL2 MPAs. Developed from the Breguet 1150 Atlantic, the

---

[31] Royal Air Force, 'Wedgetail to be RAF's New Early Warning Radar Aircraft', *RAF News*, 22 March 2019, <https://www.raf.mod.uk/news/articles/wedgetail-to-be-rafs-new-early-warning-radar-aircraft/>, accessed 3 May 2019.

[32] Royal Air Force, 'Royal Air Force Strategy: Delivering a World Class Air Force', 2017, p. 23.

[33] Matteo Sanzani, 'France Selects the Replacement of the C-160G Gabriel', *Blog Before Flight*, 4 March 2018, <https://www.blogbeforeflight.net/2018/03/france-selects-replacement-c-160g-dassault-falcon-epicure.html>, accessed 3 May 2019.

ATL2 carries a ground- and maritime-focused AESA radar array, forward-looking infrared (FLIR) ball, weapons bay capable of delivering precision-guided munitions, Exocet anti-ship missiles and torpedoes, and assorted Electronic Intelligence (ELINT) and SIGINT sensors. ATL2s have been regularly deployed to the Middle East and North Africa to perform ISR and strike missions, in addition to the traditional SAR, anti-submarine warfare and deterrent submarine support tasks inherent in the naval MPA role.[34] The type offers excellent persistence on station and good range, as with most MPAs, but lacks the high-altitude performance and transit speed of turbofan-powered big-wing ISR aircraft such as the E-3 and RC-135 series. Just like the P-3 and P-8 MPAs, the ATL2 is also tied to the MPA mission set first, with overland and littoral ISTAR capabilities in support of land operations as a secondary task, which limits the potential availability for the latter within a given fleet. In common with most ISR platforms, the ATL2 is also unable to operate within range of modern air defence systems or in the presence of enemy air threats.

Although France is increasingly vying with the UK for 'preferred ally' status in Washington, it remains fundamentally less connected to the US than the UK in many of the more sensitive data- and technology-sharing fields.[35] France is still outside the Five Eyes community and has traditionally maintained a degree of independence from NATO structures for most of its critical military capabilities – most notably its nuclear deterrent force. Therefore, France is both less likely to accept reliance on US technology than the UK, but also correspondingly less tightly integrated at the technical level in research and development, testing and evaluation and operational spheres.[36] Independent development costs more than the UK's traditional strategy of attempting to develop niche areas of technical excellence, with resultant intellectual property and expertise that can be traded for access as a junior partner in cutting-edge US-led programmes. This is one of the reasons why, despite a comparable level of defence spending and larger fighter fleet, the Armée de l'Air lags somewhat behind the UK in terms of its ISTAR capabilities.

---

[34] For example, see Navy Recognition, 'First Air Strike with GBU-12 Against ISIL in Iraq for French Navy ATL2 Maritime Patrol Aircraft', 22 August 2015, <http://www.navyrecognition.com/index.php?option=com_content&view=article&id=3028>, accessed 3 May 2019.

[35] This has been a trend visible since at least 2015. For example, see Michael Shurkin and Peter A Wilson, 'France is Replacing the UK as America's Top Ally in Europe', *RAND Commentary*, 30 March 2015, <https://www.rand.org/blog/2015/03/france-is-replacing-the-uk-as-americas-top-ally-in.html>, accessed 6 May 2019.

[36] Confirmed in author discussions with French military officials, Paris, 9 April 2018 and 19 June 2019.

European NATO's Dependence on US ISTAR Capabilities

The other mid-tier European air forces do not operate large ISTAR fleets. Germany contributes aircrew and basing facilities to the common NATO E-3A AWACS force. Funded and crewed by multiple Alliance members, this NATO force is designed to alleviate some of the European dependence on US Air Force E-3 assets for coalition operations. However, it is not a solution to the broader European dependence on US enablers. The Multinational MRTT Fleet (MMF) initiative started in 2011 to establish a pool of shared European tankers has also failed to generate much actual capability so far.[37] Put simply, apart from the UK and France, which are capable of fielding sufficient tanker and ISTAR enablers to broadly support their own combat fleets, European NATO remains heavily dependent on US-provided enablers in any complex operational scenario. All European NATO member states, including the UK and France, lack the ability to conduct dynamic targeting beyond the range of standoff ISR sensors inside territory covered by modern IADS, except for a few F-35s currently at or nearing IOC.

This is a significant issue given that using standoff weapons such as air-launched cruise missiles is, in theory, the main European response to Russia's IADS during any conflict. Cruise missiles such as Storm Shadow that can be fired from outside the range of an S-400 are of limited use without the ability to know to a high degree of accuracy where that S-400 battery is – something that the on-board sensors of a Rafale or Typhoon are unlikely to be able to pinpoint under combat conditions at that range.[38] Furthermore, since the flight time of a subsonic cruise missile from 400 km is around half an hour, and given that most modern SAM systems are highly mobile, real-time target data is required to update the missile in flight as it makes it way to the target, as and when the target system relocates.[39] Russian propensity for using high-fidelity inflatable decoys, electronic warfare and active camouflage techniques to protect SAM batteries – not to mention European weather conditions – means

---

[37] So far, the MMF programme has only procured two A-330 MRTT aircraft, although the plan is for up to eight to be operational by 2024. Current programme members include the Netherlands, Luxembourg, Germany, Norway and Belgium; however, Luxembourg does not field an air force itself and as such has no receiver requirement. The first two MMF tankers will in practice merely replace Royal Netherlands Air Force KDC-10 tankers which are being retired. See David Pugliese and Aaron Mehta, 'NATO's Tanker, AWACS Programs See Membership Increase', *Defense News*, 14 February 2018; Andrew Chuter, 'Netherlands, Luxembourg Pitch in Two Airbus Tankers for NATO Fleet', *Defense News*, 28 July 2016.

[38] For more information, see Bronk, 'Maximum Value from the F-35', pp. 9–11.

[39] Author calculations. S-400 and other modern mobile SAM systems can set up and fire in minutes. They can be on the move after firing within at least five minutes.

that standoff ISTAR techniques such as orbital observation, while helpful, cannot be relied upon for this task.[40]

As larger numbers of F-35s begin to be fielded in Europe, the ability to penetrate at least some way inside Russia's IADS (or one fielded by a near-peer) should help somewhat with European SEAD/DEAD capabilities. However, if those European F-35s are to provide targeting data to larger numbers of Typhoons, Rafales and F-16s without compromising their own position by broadcasting on Link 16, then a translation and relay node is required.

As previously discussed, only the US Air Force currently fields a system capable of translating the F-35's MADL into Link 16 and relaying it to legacy assets in combat. If the major European air forces are to lessen their dependence on US enablers for the critical SEAD/DEAD mission in a Russia context, then they will need more than the F-35; they will also have to get serious about funding, procuring and then exercising with the requisite C2 and datalink translation/relay capabilities. How they do so within the context of the broader attempt to catch up with the US platform capabilities within perennially constrained defence budgets remains an unanswered question. Until one or more of the UK, France, Germany or Italy does so, however, Europe's major air forces will remain dangerously reliant on US dynamic targeting and C2 support if forced to confront a modern IADS, despite having standoff weapons and modern fast jets.

Catching Up with the US: Two European Visions

The current European fourth- and fifth-generation connectivity shortfall exists in a context where the equipment and techniques required to enable effective coordination between the F-35 and legacy jets in high-intensity scenarios are known and relatively simple to adopt. The UK has undertaken a series of successful trials known as Babel Fish in the US, using a US-provided BACN with a Freedom 550 radio module to relay F-35 MADL data to Typhoon via Link 16.[41] However, as noted earlier, even the UK still has no funded acquisition plans for BACN-style capability at a national level.[42] Once the US moves further towards a fully integrated, networked ABMS architecture with the B-21 and likely also with UCAV elements, space-based enablers, national cyber capabilities

---

[40] Sutyagin and Bronk, *Russia's New Ground Forces*, pp. 72–82.

[41] Northrop Grumman, 'Northrop Grumman and Royal Air Force Demonstrate Enhanced Airborne Communications Interoperability'.

[42] Author briefings on RAF future combat air strategy, RAF Marham, 10 January 2019.

and other exotic enablers, it will be much harder for even the larger European states to catch up than is currently the case.

In this context, there are two competing visions for the future of combat airpower in Europe. One, the Future Combat Air System/Système de combat aérien futur (FCAS/SCAF) programme, started as a bilateral project between France and Germany, which Spain later joined as a signed partner at the Paris Air Show in June 2019.[43] The two core industrial partners in this are Dassault Aviation in France and Airbus Defence and Space in Germany.

The second project is Team Tempest led by the UK's BAE Systems, with Rolls-Royce, joint Anglo-French weapons developer MBDA and Italian-headquartered firm Leonardo as core industry partners.[44] There were early influential calls in Italy to join Team Tempest due to the strong level of commonality in fleets between the Aeronautica Militare and the RAF with the Typhoon and F-35, and the fact that Leonardo's UK-based business unit was involved from the start.[45] In September 2019, the Italian government announced that it intended to join the UK as a Tempest partner.[46] Sweden has also signed a memorandum of understanding with the UK to enter into a joint combat air development and acquisition programme but has declined to become a member of the Team Tempest industrial partnership group.[47] Meanwhile the UK remains open to future participation by non-European partners in Team Tempest: for example, discussions are ongoing with the Japanese Air Self-Defense Force

---

[43] Sylvia Pfeifer and Tobias Buck, 'Spain Joins Franco-German Alliance to Develop Fighter Jet', *Financial Times*, 17 June 2019. See also David Donald, 'Spain Joins FCAS/SCAF Program', AIN Online, 14 February 2019, <https://www.ainonline.com/aviation-news/defense/2019-02-14/spain-joins-fcas-scaf-program>, accessed 3 April 2019.

[44] Defence Contracts Online, 'Government Holds Team Tempest Industry Day in Farnborough', 20 March 2019, <https://www.contracts.mod.uk/do-features-and-articles/government-holds-team-tempest-industry-day-in-farnborough/>, accessed 3 April 2019.

[45] For example, see Tony Osborne, 'Think Tank Urges Italy to Join UK Tempest Fighter Project', *Aviation Week*, 25 March 2019.

[46] Smout, 'Italy to Join Britain's Tempest Fighter Jet Project'.

[47] Author interviews with senior Saab and RAF officials and officers, Royal International Air Tattoo, Fairford, 21 July 2019. See also Royal Air Force, 'UK and Sweden Partner on Future Combat Air', *RAF News*, 19 July 2019, <https://www.raf.mod.uk/news/articles/uk-and-sweden-partner-on-future-combat-air/>, accessed 26 July 2019.

concerning the replacement of its F-15J fleet; there is even an expression of interest from Boeing in the US.[48]

Domestic Industrial Factors at Play

In effect, two blocs are already drawing up alliance structures for the next generation of combat aircraft in Europe based on industrial and political factors. The Franco–German FCAS/SCAF programme was an overtly political creation born out of the wishes of French President Emmanuel Macron and German Chancellor Angela Merkel in 2018.[49] Meanwhile, the UK–Italian Team Tempest initiative is at least as much about ensuring that BAE Systems, Leonardo and Rolls-Royce can stay in the combat aircraft business as a matter of national sovereign industrial capability management, as it is about any specific anticipated operational requirements.[50]

This is nothing new, in the sense that political and industrial considerations have been the dominant factor in the development and procurement of combat aircraft fleets for decades – an unavoidable result of the strategic importance, huge capital investment and long timescales inherent in such projects. However, there are likely to be significant cracks within the blocs as discussions move from who the main players in each respective project are going to be onto scoping out the level of capability ambition and mission sets that each project seeks to create. Put simply, the more ambitious the capability sought, the higher the cost and programme risk are likely to climb. Spain and Italy face more significant budgetary pressures than the UK and France, while Germany places a much lesser political importance on credible long-range strike and expeditionary capabilities than the latter two states. Nonetheless, all are keen to maximise the industrial workshare which they can secure for their respective domestic industries and are unlikely to be content with relegation to junior partner status. This will almost inevitably lead to pressure from the UK in Team Tempest and France within the FCAS/SCAF programme for a greater level of capability ambition than the other international partners are keen to pay for.

---

[48] Author interviews with Japanese Air Self-Defense Force officers, Tokyo, 11–14 June 2019. On Boeing's interest, see Andrea Shalal, 'Boeing Would be "Thrilled" with Role on New UK Fighter – Defence CEO', *Reuters*, 20 July 2018.

[49] Pierre Briançon and Joshua Posaner, 'Angela Merkel and Emmanuel Macron Rekindle German–French Romance', *Politico*, 13 July 2017.

[50] For the importance of Team Tempest announcement to BAE Systems' Warton capacity, see Sylvia Pfeifer, 'BAE Systems Eyes a Brighter Fighter Jet Future', *Financial Times*, 7 November 2018.

There has also been a notable cooling of relations between France and Germany in the defence cooperation realm since the German decision to block arms sales to Saudi Arabia on human rights grounds in response to the Kingdom's ongoing war in Yemen and the assassination of journalist Jamal Khashoggi.[51] In the immediate term, this threatens to undermine current efforts to secure a follow-on order for 48 advanced Typhoon variants to augment the 72 already operated by the Royal Saudi Air Force, since the German division of Airbus Defence and Space is one of the core manufacturing partners for the Eurofighter consortium. However, France has long relied on aggressive export strategies, supported strongly by the French government, to bring down unit costs and help fund capability upgrades for its combat aircraft programmes. The Mirage III, Mirage F1, Mirage 2000 and in recent years the Rafale have all benefited greatly from export successes in the Middle East, North Africa and further afield, often to governments whose human rights record is less than spotless.[52] If Germany is setting a political precedent that as a consortium member it will block sales of combat aircraft, associated weapons and support contracts on human rights grounds, this is extremely problematic for the future commercial viability of the FCAS/SCAF programme in French eyes.

Pursuing a 'System of Systems' Approach
Both the FCAS/SCAF and Tempest programmes are notable for their explicit goal of developing a 'system of systems', rather than just a replacement fighter aircraft for the Eurofighter Typhoon and Rafale.[53] This is primarily because both the UK–Italian and Franco–German-led programmes have identified that it is not feasible within the budgets and technology available for a traditional fighter to have the desired level of organic lethality and survivability against projected threats beyond 2030. The Armée de l'Air deputy chief of staff for procurement, Major General Frédéric Parisot, has stated, 'the survivability of SCAF cannot be based on the capabilities of one single platform, even if taken to the very highest level – our adversaries would soon develop a countermeasure. It must be a family of systems and

---

[51] Rick Noack, 'Germany Halted All Arms Exports to Saudi Arabia. It Worked Too Well, and Now Berlin is Looking for a Way Out', *Washington Post*, 27 March 2019.
[52] For example, see Tyler Rogoway, 'Rafale has Gone from Long-Time Export Flop to Huge Success in 45 Days', Foxtrot Alpha, 30 April 2015; John Irish and Sophie Louet, 'Despite Criticism at Home, French Arms Sales Double in the Middle East', *Reuters*, 3 July 2018.
[53] Author interview with Armée de l'Air officer, Future Capability Plans Department, Balard HQ, Paris, 9 April 2018; briefings provided to the author on RAF future combat air strategy, RAF Marham, 10 January 2019.

capabilities'.[54] Likewise, Air Commodore Dan Storr, head of the Combat Air Acquisition Programme at the Ministry of Defence, said that as part of the evidence case which the RAF is building to narrow down requirements for Tempest, it had concluded that '[Tempest] needs to be a system with unmanned multiplier components'. It also concluded that, as a whole, the system must: be able to place sensors in proximity to targets; offer standoff options; and 'be reusable, and, therefore, survivable' in high-threat areas.[55]

From a requirements perspective, then, both the British and Franco–German projects are taking a similar route to the US NGAD efforts in designing next-generation combat air systems from the outset to operate as part of a system of systems rather than trying to make individual platforms self-sufficient in terms of survivability and lethality. However, differences remain when the underlying assumptions driving each programme are examined.

The UK's Combat Air Acquisition Programme process is currently working to define requirements for the system of systems based on the likely effects required in terms of sensor picture and kinetics on defended targets in future. This concept phase is currently expected to last until late 2020; this will be followed by an assessment phase during which options for realising the concepts will be examined, before the Ministry of Defence makes its final selection in 2025.[56] As part of this action, an active process of engagement with a range of potential industrial and technology suppliers is being pursued, with an intention to integrate and test key technologies for Tempest on Typhoon as a first step in de-risking and defining future capabilities.[57] This approach not only reduces programme risk for Tempest but also offers the prospect of significant new capabilities for RAF and Italian Typhoons in the interim.

While part of the answer for the UK may well include a future piloted fighter-type aircraft, Tempest is currently pursuing a desired-effects and technology potential-led approach, despite the fighter-style mock-up revealed at Farnborough when Tempest was announced in July 2018.[58]

---

[54] Major General Frédéric Parisot, 'Future Rafale Survivability Evolution/SCAF Programme', speech given at the Combat Air Survivability Conference, RUSI, London, 20 March 2019.
[55] Dan Storr, briefing provided to the author at RAF Marham, 10 January 2019.
[56] Michael Christie, BAE Systems' Strategy Director, quoted in Tony Garner, 'Team Tempest Takes Shape', *Eurofighter World Magazine,* 2 July 2019.
[57] Simon Rochelle, 'Next Generation Threats, Opportunities For the RAF', speech given at the Combat Air Survivability Conference, RUSI, London, 20 March 2019; Storr, briefing at RAF Marham, 10 January 2019.
[58] Briefings provided to the author on RAF future combat air strategy, RAF Marham, 10 January 2019. See also Michael Christie quoted in Garner, 'Team Tempest Takes Shape'.

Storr's comments also make clear that UCAV capabilities will be a key part of the Tempest system of systems, alongside standoff weapons, stand-in jammers and most likely a piloted aircraft to replace Typhoon.[59]

One of the first solid concepts to emerge from this process is the Lightweight Affordable Novel Combat Aircraft (LANCA) demonstrator, known as Project Mosquito, which was unveiled officially in July 2019.[60] The project aims to develop technology demonstrators for a small air vehicle class sitting somewhere between a full-sized UCAV and a long-range smart weapon. The Ministry of Defence has defined LANCA as an 'additive capability' for manned fighters and elaborated that LANCA would carry sensors or payloads for ISR or stand-in jamming.[61] The Ministry of Defence and the RAF are clearly seeking to conceptually differentiate Team Tempest from being a traditional fighter programme to replace Typhoon, and in this at least they are thinking more like those in the Pentagon who no longer see NGAD as a PCA/P-EA style 'super F-22'. This incremental system-of-systems development pathway for core capability elements is seen as reducing risk and keeping open more options for partnering on both sides of the Atlantic and even further afield in the long term.[62] There is also still an open question about the affordability of a full-scale fighter replacement programme for Typhoon given the UK's F-35 purchase ambitions.[63]

By contrast, the model unveiled by Dassault Aviation at the Paris Air Show in June 2019 suggests that, at least as far as Dassault is concerned, FCAS/SCAF will involve a different conceptual approach: that while a system of systems is a natural part of combat aircraft design going forwards, the starting point for FCAS/SCAF is a new piloted fighter, with Dassault as the lead design authority.[64] That fighter is currently envisaged as a twin-engine supersonic, carrier-capable low-observable aircraft with thrust vectoring for enhanced agility and substantial internal fuel and weapons capacity resulting in a larger airframe than Rafale, at around 30–35 tonnes.[65]

As a fighter aircraft manufacturer, this Dassault view is unsurprising, and is not necessarily representative of the French Ministry of the Armies or

---

[59] Tim Martin, 'UK "Likely" to Add Remote Carrier to Tempest Programme', *Shepherd Media*, 27 June 2019.

[60] Royal Air Force, 'Defence Ministry Praises UK's "Cutting Edge Air Power"', *RAF News*, 19 July 2019.

[61] Craig Hoyle, 'RIAT: UK Takes Wraps Off Unmanned LANCA Concept', Flight Global, 21 July 2019.

[62] Discussions with experts at closed roundtable on Future UK Combat Air options, RUSI, London, 24 September 2019.

[63] For more details see Justin Bronk, 'Enter the Tempest', *RUSI Defence Systems,* 16 July 2018.

[64] Author interview with senior Dassault adviser, Paris Air Show, 19 June 2019.

[65] *Ibid.*

the French government. Officially, the Direction Générale de l'Armement (DGA) – the French government's defence procurement and technology agency responsible for the programme management, development and purchase of weapon systems – will decide on French requirements in coordination with the Armée de l'Air and Aéronavale. However, Dassault has a much closer link with the French state than equivalent industrial players elsewhere in European NATO and DGA specifications have traditionally been developed in close collaboration with Dassault as the sole manufacturer. As such, the Dassault vision outlined at the Paris Air Show can be taken as a strong indicator of French priorities in negotiations with Germany and Spain regarding FCAS/SCAF at this early stage.

A strong push by the design lead for FCAS/SCAF to have a fighter at its core would naturally leave Airbus Defense and Space in Germany as the leader on the other system aspects – presumably including advanced standoff munitions, unmanned wingmen-type UCAV elements and dispensable stores. However, Germany is extremely cautious about any development of lethal autonomy in future weapons systems, making an Airbus lead on developing a UCAV component for FCAS/SCAF a politically fraught prospect for the weapons system as a whole.[66] There is a strong argument for future collaboration between France and the UK on at least the unmanned weapons carriers/loyal wingmen/UCAV components of their respective combat air programmes. The UK fundamentally understands France's three core capability drivers for any eventual Rafale replacement: long-range power projection; carrier capability; and the nuclear delivery role. Germany shares neither of the first two and is instinctively hostile to the third. For the UK, collaboration with France, while it will be politically difficult so long as Brexit-related uncertainty and potential design-authority arguments persist, is attractive for the same reasons.

Whatever FCAS/SCAF and Tempest produce in the end, interoperability with the US will remain key. However, the smaller NATO air forces may be forced ultimately to choose between joining the European programmes as junior partners or continuing to buy from the US. Both courses of action present significant potential difficulties, as will be explored in the following chapter.

---

[66] German discussions on lethal autonomous weapons system (LAWS) and UCAV development are almost exclusively conducted in the arms control and international regulation space, with domestic participation in development programmes almost unthinkable under current political conditions. Author interviews with Bundeswehr capability development officers and civilian SMEs at Federal Foreign Office, Berlin, 15 March 2019; author interviews with Luftwaffe officers, Berlin, 14–15 November 2018.

IV. THE SMALLER NATO AIR FORCES: IN SEARCH OF A VIABLE NICHE

The majority of NATO member states operate small air forces, with limited fleets of older third- or fourth-generation fast jets, alongside rotary-winged assets for search and rescue as well as army-cooperation duties. A few countries such as Poland and Norway, as well as NATO partner states Sweden and Finland, do consider self-defence in a kinetic conflict against Russia as part of their core defence planning assumptions. However, for many smaller NATO states which operate fast jet fleets, it is not always clear what the national requirements for combat air capabilities are beyond quick reaction alert (QRA) scrambles within national airspace.[1] Nonetheless, many of these countries regularly join US-led air campaigns, including those against Daesh in Iraq and Syria, Qadhafi's forces in Libya and the Taliban in Afghanistan.[2] The Baltic states, Luxembourg, Iceland, Montenegro, Albania and Slovenia do not field combat aircraft at all, requiring other NATO members to conduct air policing on their behalf on a rotational basis.[3]

Combat Aircraft

During the early Cold War, most smaller countries in Europe still fielded combat aircraft, often as part of the Warsaw Pact or NATO depending on which side of the Iron Curtain they were on. However, as the technological barriers to entry, the acquisition costs and operating costs rose with each generation of jet fighters, it has become harder for small

---

[1] All NATO member states are required to field at least two fast jets ready for QRA at all times, although those without fast jets can request air policing support. For more information, see NATO, 'NATO Starts Montenegro Air Patrols', 31 May 2018, <https://www.nato.int/cps/en/natohq/news_154999.htm>, accessed 28 June 2019.
[2] For example, Operation Inherent Resolve, 'Coalition', <https://www.inherentresolve.mil/About-CJTF-OIR/Coalition/>, accessed 28 June 2019. See also Todd R Phinney, 'Reflections on Operation Unified Protector', *Joint Force Quarterly* (No. 73, April 2014).
[3] NATO, 'NATO Starts Montenegro Air Patrols'.

countries with limited defence budgets to field sufficient numbers of modern aircraft to maintain a viable fleet. As such, NATO's smaller air forces today tend to field lightweight multirole fighters which offer the most flexible and affordable type of fast jet but have traditionally been outclassed in high-intensity warfighting by twin-engine air superiority types.

Europe's F-16 States
Since the end of the Cold War, the signature fast jet flown by these smaller states has been the US F-16 Fighting Falcon, a single-engine lightweight multirole fighter which has been progressively modified and upgraded to carry modern radar, sensor pods and precision-guided munitions. Norway, the Netherlands, Denmark, Belgium, Portugal, Greece, Turkey and Poland all operate the type, and have deployed on combat operations with it alongside the US.[4] The F-16 is relatively cheap and simpler to operate than larger twin-engine fast jets. It is also reliable, easy to fly, and can employ a wide variety of modern weapons.

Even more crucially for smaller European F-16 operators, however, is the fact that it has been the US Air Force's most numerous fast jet since the 1990s and as such the US has continually invested in integrating new sensors, weapons options and multirole capabilities onto the aircraft. This has ensured that midlife upgrades to periodically keep small fighter fleets up to date with crucial innovations such as targeting pods, precision-guided munitions and Link 16 datalinks were affordable and generally readily available for these states. This has been most recently demonstrated by Greece, Bulgaria and Slovakia purchasing the latest F-16V (Block 70) standard, which gives them relatively affordable access to high-end US-developed technologies – most notably the APG-83 AESA radar and the latest datalink and pilot interface standards – and full compatibility with the latest US weapons.[5] As a way to visualise what this means, Slovakia will – on current trends – operate a fighter with a modern AESA radar before Germany despite spending only a small fraction of the latter's defence budget. Without this commonality with the US Air Force, the F-16 states would have had to pay a great deal more to maintain the interoperability and common capabilities needed to fulfil a useful role in coalition air operations. A similar advantage has long been enjoyed by

---

[4] Lockheed Martin, 'F-16V: The Most Advanced Multirole Fighter for Greece', 2016, <https://www.lockheedmartin.com/content/dam/lockheed-martin/aero/documents/F-16/F-16V-Geece-Exec-Sum.pdf>, accessed 18 June 2019.
[5] *Ibid.*; Aaron Mehta, 'Slovakia Selects F-16 Over Gripen for New Fighter', *Defense News*, 11 July 2018; Sebastian Sprenger, 'US State Department Approves $1.7B Sale of F-16 Jets to Bulgaria', *Defense News*, 4 June 2019.

Canada with its fleet of CF-18 Hornet fighters, since the F-18 was also operated for decades on a much larger scale as the core of the US Navy and US Marine Corps tactical aviation fleets.[6]

A desire to maintain this ability to affordably keep up with the latest US platform capabilities by leveraging the benefits of a shared aircraft type has led many of the European F-16 countries to select the F-35 as a replacement tactical fighter. Norway, the Netherlands, Denmark, Belgium and Poland have all now selected the F-35, although most have accepted a smaller fleet size to afford the jet since it costs significantly more to both procure and operate than the F-16.[7] For example, the Netherlands is planning to replace its 61 remaining F-16s with 46 F-35s while Denmark is planning to replace 44 F-16s with 27 F-35s.[8] Just as with the F-16, shared training, maintenance and logistics arrangements for European F-35 states should help to keep costs down and overcome some of the drawbacks inherent in operating small national fleets.

However, deployability will remain challenging: in any fast jet fleet, only a small proportion are available for combat duties at any given time due to maintenance, training and reserve requirements, while availability rates are always a challenge with such complex machines. For example, both Belgium and Denmark were forced to withdraw their contingents of six and four F-16s respectively from operations over Iraq in 2015 due to lack of aircraft availability within fleet-wide maintenance cycles.[9] The Netherlands' decision in October 2019 to increase its initial purchase of F-35s from 37 to 46 was explicitly to enable a deployable force of four aircraft in addition to national airspace defence commitments.[10] As such, these smaller European states operating the F-35 will possess a formidably

---

[6] The Royal Canadian Air Force originally purchased 138 CF-18A/B Hornets, but only 79 modernised aircraft remain in service. Todd Balfe, 'The Royal Canadian Air Force CAS Programme', speech given at Close Air Support Conference, London, 29 May 2019.

[7] Author interviews with European air force officers, London, Copenhagen, Brussels, Warsaw, 2017–19. See also Niall McCarthy, 'The Evolution of the F-35's Unit Cost', *Forbes*, 14 September 2018.

[8] For F-35 purchase numbers, see Lockheed Martin, 'Global Participation', f35.com, <https://www.f35.com/global>, accessed 18 June 2019; for F-16 fleet sizes, see IISS, *The Military Balance 2016* (London: Oxford University Press, 2016), pp. 90, 123.

[9] At the time, Belgium had 59 F-16s in service with six deployed on operations, while Denmark had 47 F-16s in service and deployed four for operations with three extra as deployed reserves in case of mechanical failures or other issues. See Beth Stevenson, 'Danes Withdraw F-16s from Iraq Deployment', Flight Global, 27 August 2015, <https://www.flightglobal.com/news/articles/danes-withdraw-f-16s-from-iraq-deployment-416107/>, accessed 26 July 2019.

[10] Sebastian Sprenger, 'The Netherlands to Buy Nine More F-35s for $1.1 Billion', *Defense News,* 9 October 2019.

capable front line machine, but within force structures only able to sustainably deploy a handful of aircraft.[11] Such small air forces also offer almost no inherent ability to absorb attrition while remaining combat effective. On the flip side, the F-35 is inherently less dependent on off-board enablers than legacy fighters due to better pilot situational awareness. At a software level, the F-35 is also interoperable by default with other states' F-35s, thereby allowing even small numbers to more effectively integrate into larger coalitions than with previous generations of aircraft.

Those states trying to follow the previous F-16 or F-18 approach of combat aircraft commonality with the US through purchasing the F-35 can only afford small fleets. The risk is that this will leave them only able to field tiny, politically significant but operationally irrelevant contributions to expeditionary coalitions. The number of sustainably deployable airframes is simply too low for each national contingent to make a meaningful contribution to a major campaign. Only if genuinely pooled and operated almost as a single fleet could Europe's smaller air forces' planned F-35 purchases make a significant difference to the Alliance's aerial warfighting capabilities. As already noted, the F-35's software and networking architecture makes interoperability of this sort theoretically easier than with previous generations of aircraft, especially since US-generated software upgrades should be universally rolled out across the Alliance's user community. However, these states are geographically dispersed, have different national defence priorities and political caveats on the use of armed force, making this degree of integration extremely challenging.

Europe's Gripen States
The only other European aircraft type of note for small air forces is the Swedish Gripen, which is operated not only by Sweden as an officially non-aligned NATO partner state, but also by Hungary and the Czech Republic.

The Gripen is a similar aircraft to the F-16 in that it is a single-engine, lightweight, multirole fighter. However, the similarities largely end there as the Gripen was designed from the outset to meet Sweden's unique territorial defence requirement set. As such, it has a greater focus on: electronic warfare capabilities tailored for operations against Russian radars than the F-16; ease of maintenance for conscript crews in harsh winter conditions; and operating from strips of highway to reduce reliance on vulnerable airfield runways. Capability ambition was carefully managed to keep costs as low as possible, while one of the key design features is excellent

---

[11] Confirmed in author interviews with Chiefs of Staff of three European air forces which have purchased F-35s, RAF Air and Space Power Conference, 17–18 July 2019.

reliability. These considerations together meant that Sweden could maintain a decent number of combat-worthy jets at any given time from a limited defence budget as a small, non-aligned country.[12]

This makes it a compelling prospect for those smaller NATO member states with small defence budgets but which still want to operate some level of fast jet capability. On the downside, the Gripen's light weight and small overall size mean that external stores such as large munitions, targeting pods and fuel tanks impose a greater performance penalty than on larger aircraft which harms its competitiveness for long-range strike missions. On the other hand, it has very advanced datalink capabilities, with Swedish Air Force aircraft having to 'downgrade' their datalink to standard NATO Link 16 functionality in order to integrate fully into coalition air operations over Libya in 2011.[13] These excellent datalinks make networked situational awareness easier, while the Gripen's modern radar options, long-range Meteor missile armament, electronic warfare suite and ability to generate high sortie rates at low cost even from highways and temporary airstrips make it a highly efficient and capable air defence asset. For countries whose defence requirements are limited to territorial defence of their own airspace and that of neighbouring countries, the Gripen offers a compelling package from an operational point of view.

Saab is also producing a new evolution of the Gripen C/D model, known as Gripen E/F or Gripen NG, for the Swedish Air Force and Brazilian Air Force (as its first export customer). Much like the relationship between the US Navy's F/A-18E/F Super Hornet and the legacy F/A-18C/D Hornet, the Gripen NG looks externally very similar to previous Gripen A–D variants, but is a slightly larger and almost completely new aircraft in terms of systems and components. Having decided that developing VLO fighters like the F-35 was not an affordable option, Sweden opted for a completely different approach with the Gripen NG, designing the whole aircraft around a powerful electronic warfare suite.[14] Rather than attempting to hide a fighter from hostile radars like a VLO design, the Gripen NG is built around blinding those radars with sophisticated electronic attack and self-defence capabilities optimised for defeating specific Russian threat radars which are particularly relevant to Sweden.

---

[12] Author interviews with Saab subject matter experts and former Gripen aircrew, London, October 2016.

[13] Author interviews with commanders and aircrew who participated directly in Operation *Unified Protector*, London, Copenhagen, Rome, Berlin, 2015–16.

[14] Author interviews with Saab subject matter experts and former Gripen aircrew, London, October 2016.

The benefits of this approach are that the airframe is much easier to maintain than a stealth aircraft and can be significantly smaller, since it does not have to carry weapons internally to maintain a minimal RCS. The reliance on electronic warfare also offers the potential to be highly responsive to threat evolution when compared with a VLO approach that is reliant on airframe shaping. This is because electronic warfare relies on countering hostile radar signals as they adapt, meaning that EW suites have to be regularly patched and updated – a process which is dependent on having excellent intelligence on enemy radar developments. The disadvantage, however, is that it cannot be known for sure whether an approach that relies on electronic warfare will work in live fire combat until it goes up against the threat system. In addition, any advantages will be temporary, given that the enemy will rapidly adapt its own radar and electronic warfare techniques in response.[15]

For Sweden, a history of heavy political emphasis on self-sufficiency in defence and of producing highly economical and successful fighter aircraft for the Swedish Air Force means that the Swedish fighter fleet will likely be comprised of Gripen E/F for the foreseeable future. Following Russian aggression in Ukraine and provocations in the Baltics, Sweden has ordered a total of 60 Gripen E/F airframes due for delivery between 2019 and the mid-2020s, and has also announced that it is likely to maintain up to 60 of the older C/D models well into the 2030s.[16]

It is notable, therefore, that despite the Gripen E/F's likely service live of 40+ years from the point of its delivery in the mid-2020s, the Swedish defence minister confirmed in May 2019 that Sweden and Saab were in talks exploring joining the UK-led Team Tempest programme.[17] Subsequently in July 2019, it was announced that Sweden had instead signed a memorandum of understanding for joint future combat aircraft development work with the UK government but that Saab would not be joining the Team Tempest group as an industrial partner in the foreseeable future.[18] This suggests that, despite its long history of strict neutrality, lack of interest in power projection and consequent internal defence focus, even Sweden sees difficulties in maintaining credible

---

[15] Author interview with F-22 pilots with recent deployment experience in Eastern Europe, London, 3 May 2016.

[16] Craig Hoyle, 'Gripen E Production Tweak Safeguards Swedish Fighter Fleet', *Flight Global*, 2 January 2019. See also Craig Hoyle, 'Sweden Weighs Extending Gripen C/D Operations by a Decade', *Flight Global*, 1 May 2019.

[17] Gareth Jennings, 'Sweden Confirms UK Tempest Talks, Ambivalent on Franco–German FCAS', *Jane's 360*, 21 May 2019.

[18] Author interviews with senior Saab and RAF officials and officers, Royal International Air Tattoo, Fairford, 21 July 2019. See also Royal Air Force, 'UK and Sweden Partner on Future Combat Air'.

warfighting capabilities in the combat air domain without cooperation with larger partners. There was significant cooperation between the UK and Sweden on the Gripen programme and both countries can offer value to the other for the future in both conceptual and technological terms. Since Tempest is aimed at developing a system of systems rather than simply a new fighter, one option might be for Sweden to partner with the UK and other potential Tempest programme members to develop UCAV, standoff and stand-in weapons and jammers, datalinks and other elements of the system while maintaining the Gripen E/F as the core fighter at the centre of that system. If a piloted fighter does emerge as part of Tempest for UK service in the 2040 timeframe, Sweden might eventually look to purchase a mature version of that platform to replace the remaining Gripen C/Ds and eventually the new Gripen E/Fs in following decades.[19]

For other small European air forces, a similar solution might be a long-term answer to the inability to purchase F-35s in sufficient numbers to generate sustainable combat power in a high-intensity scenario. They could try to buy into either the Franco–German–Spanish FCAS/SCAF programme or Team Tempest, or even purchase UCAVs and other system of system components from the US while keeping their existing fighters as the core of their combat air fleets. Whether membership of these programmes would be offered without a commitment to purchase the fighter component of any future system remains to be seen.

Enablers

None of these options for replacing combat aircraft in the future gets around the other major deficiency of the smaller European air forces – that of critical enablers and especially tankers, resilient bases, weapons stockpiles and spare parts available at short notice. These enablers are difficult for individual nations to justify spending scarce resources on when they are also struggling to afford sufficient fast jet capabilities to field operationally viable frontline fleets.

Even the UK and France are having to face the reality that credible and robust conventional warfighting capabilities against a peer opponent are once more called for but are increasingly unaffordable within politically feasible levels of overall defence spending. Smaller states within NATO face an even starker version of this dilemma. Those states that are seeking to replace their F-16s with F-35s (albeit in much smaller numbers, as discussed above) in order to sustain commonality, will nevertheless remain heavily dependent on the US for all enablers; from AAR to spare

---

[19] Author interview with Saab officials, Royal International Air Tattoo, Fairford, 21 July 2019.

parts, munitions resupply, ISTAR and operational C2 in a joint environment. With the US aiming to change its own operating paradigm by modernising and eventually completely overhauling the way it conducts complex joint operations (as explored in Chapter II), small European NATO states already struggling to afford membership of the F-35 club will also have to change the way they operate their air forces if they want to continue 'plugging in' to US architecture.

Equally, if smaller NATO member states attempt to purchase cheaper fast jet options such as the modernised F-16V or Gripen E/F, they will lose the direct benefit of ongoing US investment in improving its own premier fighter platforms, and be more dependent on ISTAR enablers due to being forced to stand off further from threats than an F-35. Even with cheaper fast jet fleets, national acquisition and operation of large airliner-derived enablers like AWACS and AAR aircraft will still remain unaffordable for most small states. The United States Government Accountability Office expects the US Air Force's future fleet of 179 KC-46A tankers to cost an average of $226 million each, whilst the RAF's purchase of five E-7 Wedgetail AWACS aircraft cost $1.98 billion.[20] For small nations, therefore, the looming choice on enablers is dependence on larger NATO partners or acquisition of enablers to contribute to the broader Alliance force at the expense of national fast jet capabilities. The latter course of action is one which Luxembourg has tried to take through its membership of the NATO MMF initiative despite lacking fast jets of its own. If more states chose to focus on enablers for the Alliance at the cost of national fast jet capabilities it would undoubtedly make European NATO airpower more potent, but for most governments foregoing fast jets for ISTAR aircraft and tankers would be a difficult political choice to sell to taxpayers.

The Challenges of Deterrence as a Smaller State

Two European states are already attempting to deploy a national deterrent capability against the Russian Federation on their own terms. Both Poland and Finland are concerned about the potential threat which Russia might pose to their territorial or political integrity in a much more immediate sense than other European countries and NATO members that are more

---

[20] Congressional Research Service, 'Air Force KC-46A Pegasus Tanker Aircraft Program', 17 October 2019, p. 7, <https://fas.org/sgp/crs/weapons/RL34398.pdf>, accessed 10 November 2019; Andrew Chuter, 'Britain to Buy Wedgetail Aircraft in Nearly $2 Billion Deal', *Defense News*, 22 March 2019, <https://www.defensenews.com/global/europe/2019/03/22/britain-to-buy-wedgetail-aircraft-in-nearly-2-billion-deal/>, accessed 10 November 2019.

geographically removed from Russia's borders. As a result, Poland and Finland have both sought to deploy some measure of independent, conventional standoff capability against Russia by acquiring the Joint Air-to-Surface Standoff Missile (JASSM) for use with their F-16s and F-18s, respectively.[21]

Finland maintains its limited JASSM numbers as one of the few potentially retaliatory/coercive elements in its national defence concept which, much like that in neighbouring Sweden, encompasses a range of defensive military and civil society resilience elements aimed at making it costly for any potential adversary to attempt to violate its territorial integrity as a non-aligned nation.[22]

For Poland, being part of NATO means that it is able to rely on Article 5-based collective defence in a way which Finland cannot.[23] However, it also has painful cultural memories of being conquered, along with extended and brutal occupation by both Nazi and Soviet forces. An understandable cultural fear of military threats from the east, coupled with the presence of the heavily armed Kaliningrad enclave to its northeast and Russian-controlled Belarus to its eastern flank, mean that Poland wants to do more than simply adopt a purely defensive military posture. It has undertaken the Polish Fang project to build a long-range conventional strike triad to enable the country to hold targets in both Kaliningrad and Russia at risk without having to rely on other NATO members' firepower in the first instance.[24] The programme aims to combine air-launched JASSMs with the M142 High Mobility Artillery Rocket System (HIMARS) long-range rocket artillery and even a submarine with cruise missiles, although constraints on funding and armed forces manpower may frustrate the full realisation of this ambition.[25] Like almost all other small European air forces, Poland currently lacks the ability to detect, track and guide such long-range weapons onto sensitive targets deep within the Russian IADS unless they are static and their locations known in advance – or unless real-time targeting data is provided by the US. However, with the F-35 now also on order, Poland might – in future – be able to leverage the aircraft's superb sensors and ability to operate much closer to Russian SAM systems and combat aircraft without being detected, in order

---

[21] Author interviews with Polish Ministry of Defence officials, Warsaw, 11 September 2018,
[22] Author interviews with Finnish Air Force officers, Helsinki, 29–30 October 2018.
[23] NATO, 'Collective Defence - Article 5', <https://www.nato.int/cps/en/natohq/topics_110496.htm>, accessed 12 November 2019.
[24] Author interviews with Polish Ministry of Defence officials and Polish Fang SMEs at Polish Institute of International Affairs, Warsaw, 11–12 September 2018.
[25] *Ibid.*

to locate and provide targets within Russian territory to its Polish Fang strike arsenal. Nonetheless, even this strong effort on the part of Poland illustrates the difficulties facing small European air forces.

Poland will face other challenges in using the JASSM missiles it has purchased (40 JASSM missiles with a range of around 400 km and up to 70 JASSM-ER variants with an extended range of up to 1,000 km, to be delivered from 2020).[26] The Polish Air Force will have to launch them using its limited numbers of F-16s, which are vulnerable to Kaliningrad-based S-400 long-range SAMs and operate from bases under threat of Russian missile and air strikes.[27] Even if provided with targeting data by a small Polish F-35 force, this number of missiles is simply too small to have anything more than a symbolic effect on Russia's ability to prosecute a conflict. To knock out a single airbase in Syria with no effective point defences in 2017, the US delivered 59 Tomahawk Land Attack Missiles (TLAMs); despite this, the base was being used to conduct fixed wing attack sorties again within hours.[28]

Poland's experience suggests that even when pursued as a core part of a national defence strategy, non-nuclear long-range precision strike capabilities are simply too expensive to be fielded in militarily significant numbers by small NATO member states. Their political deterrence value is more debatable but must be weighed against the opportunity cost in terms of simpler, reusable and more numerous defensive capabilities forgone in order to purchase expensive long-range missiles.

A focus on fitting into much larger Alliance-wide air operations has, therefore, been the traditional approach taken by most smaller NATO air forces. As those large air operations continue to get more technologically, operationally and conceptually complex, they will entail correspondingly higher barriers to entry and greater exercise and C2 requirements – as explored in previous chapters. Specialisation within a given future approach to airpower is likely to be essential. These smaller states will, hence, have to look closely at the different approaches being pursued by the three major next-generation combat air development blocs and decide which emerging 'ecosystem' of capability offers the elements best suited to obtaining maximum combat power and political leverage as NATO Alliance members with limited resources.

---

[26] US Defense Security Cooperation Agency, 'Poland – JASSM-ER with Support', News Release, 28 November 2016, <https://www.dsca.mil/major-arms-sales/poland-jassm-er-support>, accessed 12 July 2019.

[27] Author interviews with Polish Ministry of Defence officials and Polish Fang SMEs at Polish Institute of International Affairs, Warsaw, 11–12 September 2018.

[28] Josie Ensor, 'Syrian Warplanes Take Off Once Again from Air Base Bombed by US Tomahawks', *The Telegraph*, 8 April 2017.

CONCLUSION: CHALLENGES AND OPPORTUNITIES

In the airpower domain, NATO faces a looming challenge but one which is also a potential opportunity if understood and adequately planned for. Put simply, the US is gearing up to leave the rest of the Alliance behind in capability terms, as it has done in previous generational shifts, but this time with a different primary mission focus from other NATO member states. This is for two main reasons.

First, that there is a growing awareness in the US Air Force and in other branches of the US military that even with its unmatched defence budget, the country cannot afford to continue trying to maintain a dominant military position over China and Russia in their own immediate neighbourhoods by pursuing incremental upgrades to existing capabilities.[1] Long-range SAM systems, ever-improving radar and other sensor technologies and long-range anti-enabler missile systems are much cheaper for China in particular to produce than for the US to counter. Decades of airpower overmatch, which has become essential for the way NATO plans for operations, are being steadily eroded by rival powers and in terms of China, the picture will only get worse in the coming decades. China and Russia have studied the US dependence on tankers, big-wing ISR and tactical fighters in its conduct of warfare from the air and have found cost-effective ways to impose unacceptable risks to that family of capabilities.

The second, and linked, reason for the US shift in capability is the new focus on China rather than Russia as the US military's primary long-term peer threat. The demands of the Pacific theatre and the distances to which China as a potential air and maritime challenger can increasingly project (or create) contested and highly contested airspace call for new and different approaches to warfighting than has been the case in relation to Russia in

---

[1] For example, see Heather Williams, 'The Air Force We Need'.

Europe and the High North[2] – though Russia remains a threat which the Pentagon takes seriously in the short to medium term.

When the US started developing a suite of revolutionary capabilities based on ISR, real-time targeting of precision-guided munitions, and stealth fighters and bombers in the late Cold War and into the 1990s, it did so within the bounds of an established NATO conceptual framework for air operations. The B-2 was intended to fly from the continental US alongside the existing non-stealthly B-52 and B-1B bomber fleets. The F-22 (and now F-35A) was designed to operate from large permanent bases with a strong dependence on tankers, alongside legacy tactical fighters. The B-2 and F-22's ground breaking stealth and situational awareness capabilities gave the US Air Force more options and the ability to conduct strikes in a way not done previously, but they did not change the fundamentals of the NATO airpower machine. Likewise, the extraordinary US Air Force global ISR fleet of big- and smaller-wing aircraft and UAVs have all been designed to feed into the E-3 AWACS, Combined Air Operations Centre (CAOC) and tactical fighter-centric approach taken by NATO. Aside from the B-2, these capabilities were also ones which many NATO Allies aspired to develop or buy into themselves, since they were essentially a way to perform a common NATO mission-set more effectively.[3]

As the 1990s and 2000s progressed, NATO's medium powers and even many of the smaller powers were able to upgrade their tactical fighter fleets and C2 systems to be interoperable with US-led strike packages despite not being able to field many of the exquisite platforms like F-22, Joint STARS, RQ-170 and RC-135W. Since the high-end assets were designed to operate within and complement NATO's existing airpower ecosystem, it has not mattered too much whether and how quickly Allies have been able to close the gap with the US as it has advanced. Some of the medium states such as the UK and France were able to purchase and operate E-3 and in the UK's case RC-135W, while others like Germany and the Netherlands bought into pooling and sharing schemes like the NATO AWACS force.[4] The F-35 can be seen as a further example of this trend, with many European NATO states somewhat

---

[2] For more information on Russian military activities in the High North (Arctic), see Mathieu Boulègue, *Russia's Military Posture in the Arctic: Managing Hard Power in a 'Low Tension' Environment* (London: Chatham House, June 2019).

[3] The B-2 itself was truncated into a 20-strong fleet following the end of the Cold War and has since served as a unique and extremely potent but niche component of NATO's airpower arsenal.

[4] NATO, 'E-3A Component', <https://awacs.nato.int/page5835237.aspx>, accessed 23 July 2019.

belatedly taking delivery of a stealthy fifth-generation fighter with world-beating situational awareness much like the US Air Force's F-22 back in the late 1990s. Smaller air forces like the F-16 states have long been able to 'plug and play'. They have done so by: purchasing US tactical fighters or upgrading indigenous ones like Typhoon and Gripen to common datalink standards like Link 16; training for common operational procedures like AAR; and by delivering precision-guided munitions on target using data supplied by US or NATO partner states. While this does not overcome the serious dependence of other NATO states on US enabler assets and C2 support, and in fact increases the bottleneck for the US, these arrangements have long delivered political benefits by allowing smaller air forces to conduct complex combat operations alongside larger Alliance members.

The direction the US is pursuing today is likely to have a more disruptive effect. It is quietly attempting to change the whole way it fights in the air by developing not only new combat aircraft types, but also a family of systems to create effects on targets including UCAVs, space-based effectors, directed energy weapons and hypersonic missiles. Perhaps even more crucially, these new assets are being designed from the outset to be employed within a networked C2 architecture designed to leverage unprecedented levels of edge processing and automation.[5] In order to enable the Pentagon's MDO strategy, which involves simultaneously converging effects across all domains from national-level strategic assets down to the tactical level, ABMS is being developed to generate sensor-senor-weapon cueing automatically at the machine level.[6] This is a level of networked integration, automation and inter-platform dependency far beyond that being planned for by even the medium powers within NATO.

It is true that a system of systems approach is evident in the thinking driving both the UK-led Team Tempest and the Germany–France-led FCAS/SCAF. Nonetheless, this thinking is focused on eventually replacing Typhoon and Rafale with something capable of operating within heavily defended areas, rather than creating an entirely new airpower network and C2 architecture. Furthermore, for both European programmes it is envisaged that the core platform will enter into service only in the early 2040s. Put simply, in trying to leverage airpower against a rising China across the ranges inherent in the Pacific in a much shorter timescale, the US may well end up investing heavily in technologies, platforms and C2 architectures which other NATO member states are both unable to immediately attempt to follow but possibly also unwilling to adopt. It is not necessary in the European theatre to have long-range, multi-mission

---

[5] Author interview with senior US Air Force officer, The Pentagon, Washington, DC, 21 February 2019.
[6] Goldfein, speech given at the RAF Air and Space Power Conference 2019.

bomber-sized stealth aircraft, advanced UCAVs and potentially unmanned refuelling solutions to enable significantly greater range than piloted tactical fighters offer. Nonetheless, they are likely to prove an essential component of the US Pacific strategy by the late 2020s and certainly the 2030s.[7] Even the US cannot afford to have two separate force models for the Pacific and European theatres so platforms, enablers, CONOPS and C2 systems developed for the former will eventually shape those in the latter. The ability to leverage space, cyber and joint force-supporting effects which are held at the national level as part of tactical air operations in real time – necessary for long-term US military overmatch against China – will require exercising and operating forces at a theatre command level. This is a scale that will be impossible for smaller NATO members to exercise at, let alone operate at with any regularity. Furthermore, the level of automation and edge processing of data required to realise the ABMS vision for coordinating sensor and weapon effects at scale and at machine–machine speed will strain European NATO member states' political, ethical and legal tolerances around meaningful human control and supervision of decisions guiding the use of lethal force.

If the US is able to realise its MDO vision, which for the US Air Force is most closely tied to the more advanced stages of ABMS, then by the late 2020s and the 2030s other NATO member states will face a stark choice. If they want to be able to credibly join a US-led warfighting coalition in a warfighting scenario then they will have to operate within an ABMS C2 architecture. First, this will mean that all their platforms, sensors and weapons systems must be interoperable with the highly automated US system – not a conceptually new problem but a potentially more challenging programming and information security one compared to previous generations. Second, it will involve the US's NATO Allies accepting that their operators and sovereign platforms will be given sensor and weapon cues by a US C2 system which is not only highly automated, but also (due to its speed) almost impossible to scrutinise in real time. The current red card holder system used in coalition CAOCs to vet proposed strikes against national caveats and rules of engagement is time consuming and relies on human judgement.[8] It will simply not be compatible with the way that the US Air Force (and US Navy, Marine Corps and Army) is planning to operate against state opponents through

---

7 Author interview with Mark Gunzinger, Mitchell Institute for Aerospace Studies, CSBA and former US Air Force B-52 command pilot, Washington, DC, 11 July 2019.
8 Author interviews with senior US Air Force and RAF officers with command experience at the CAOC in Al-Udeid, London and Washington, DC, 2017–19. See also NATO, 'Allied Joint Doctrine for Air and Space Operations', Edition B Version 1, April 2016, p. 2-3, clause 2.2.1.: Authority and command relationships.

MDO. The speed of machine–machine sensor–shooter cueing, in addition to the threat level when operating in contested or highly contested airspace, will simply preclude reachback to national ground-based red card holders and legal teams. In other words, in high-intensity warfighting scenarios, non-US NATO air forces will eventually have to accept and operate within the automation and US mission command implied by ABMS and MDO or pursue an entirely different path without large-scale interoperability with US forces.

Part of the problem for the two most prominent medium powers in NATO, the UK and France, is that efforts to catch up with the US's current operating practices with regards to critical enablers – such as dynamic ISTAR, space-based observation and communication capabilities, stealth assets and network gateways – have so far been too slow. The limited size of the modern RAF and Armée de l'Air means that enabler acquisition and modernisation is being attempted at a scale which makes it extremely expensive in relation to the number of usable combat aircraft that are ultimately enabled. Meanwhile, the US is accelerating away again and in a new direction – already looking for the next leap in capability even as the first operational F-35 squadrons start hitting their strides. This presents a choice. The natural UK tendency will be to continue striving to operate like a small version of the US Air Force alongside the latter, with all the ABMS-compatibility implications in terms of automation, meaningful human control, information security and operational sovereignty. An alternative, and more instinctively appealing approach for France, would be to adjust plans in recognition of the fact that the next generation of European airpower may have to operate less like its US counterpart than today, but in a way that offers more capacity for independent action.

However, if the US push towards MDO, ABMS, and a family of exquisite platforms and weapons tailored for the vast Pacific theatre threatens to undermine long-term Alliance interoperability, it also offers an opportunity to reduce duplication and bottlenecking.

The current airpower dynamic in NATO, whereby many states provide fast jets to coalition operations but rely almost entirely on the US for enablers and munitions, is a weakness of the Alliance. While those fast jets may be credible in high-intensity warfighting as platforms, they are often operated by crews with far less training in complex contested operations than their US counterparts and they bring with them a host of national caveats which make them operationally cumbersome to use. There may be great political value to their inclusion within a NATO coalition but for important, urgent or dangerous missions, the US will generally much prefer to employ the huge numbers of fast jets it brings to the fight itself.

At the same time, those fast jets contributed to NATO operations by smaller states generally rely on the same US Air Force AAR tankers, ISR assets, C2 bandwidth and munitions stocks which in themselves represent the most significant bottlenecks for the US's own air operations tempo. Put simply, small national contingents of tactical fighters, however technically advanced, seldom add significantly to the total operational capacity of a US-led coalition to deliver fighting power unless they are also supported by non-US enablers. Moreover, they often consume a large part of the limited defence budgets of small NATO states, money that could be used for more national-critical capabilities. They also actively reduce operational fighting power by drawing on limited US enabler capacity at the expense of more capable and less politically restricted US combat aircraft. A timely recognition that the Pentagon's push towards MDO, and the demands of the Pacific theatre, will change the way that the US airpower machine works could act as a forcing function to develop a more balanced non-US suite of Alliance airpower capabilities.

The Team Tempest and FCAS/SCAF programmes will both be of much greater value to the Alliance as a whole if they included provision for European-developed network, logistics and C2 structures to enable their eventual deployment as part of a coherent force design. Despite the greater economies of scale enjoyed by the US and its traditional dominance as a provider of airpower enablers for NATO, the technical challenges and expense of developing sufficient European capacity in these areas by the late 2020s are hardly insurmountable. However, doing so would require governments throughout the Alliance to give greater prominence to network architectures, resilient operational C2 capacity, survivable ISTAR and munitions and spare parts stockpiling than they have in the decades since the Cold War. These elements are less exciting than the fast jets which typically dominate political discussions of air force issues but they are just as vital for combat effectiveness, especially when seeking to establish stable deterrence against an enduring military threat in the shape of Russia.

If smaller Alliance members were to decide that the cost of sustaining genuine interoperability between their ever-smaller fast jet fleets and that of the US Air Force, they could contribute a great deal more to total Alliance warfighting capabilities by specialising in enablers to replace some of the capacity the US has traditionally provided. Equally, they might decide to continue operating and procuring combat aircraft but accept they cannot or do not wish to fight like an ABMS-centric US Air Force. In that case, having a viable alternative European NATO airpower ecosystem developed through Tempest, FCAS/SCAF or a combination of the two could be doubly valuable in giving smaller NATO air forces a path to continued combat relevance within a force design which remains tailored to European geography and threats.

All this would require a large degree of coordination and technical cooperation between the British–Italian and Franco–German led programmes, even if they remain separate industrial efforts. However, this is clearly desirable in any case since the products of both will have to be interoperable in an operational context. The heavily interlinked nature of the European defence industry makes coordination likely in the long term anyway, Brexit-related uncertainty and disruption notwithstanding.

NATO's air forces will always wish to retain interoperability with the might of the US so long as the capability trade-offs involved do not distort their own forces to the degree that they lose relevance for their own national security outlook. A recognition that the US is moving towards a force design and China-focused CONOPS that may not be so appropriate for many smaller NATO members should prompt a mature debate about where non-US partners need to develop their own capacities, platforms and CONOPS. The goal should not be to replace US airpower capabilities, as these will almost certainly continue to represent the greatest military advantage which NATO can field against potential state opponents. Instead, it should be to improve the ability of the medium powers in NATO to field coherent air forces within a European security context, which are able to fight against state opponents in high-threat environments without being so dependent on US-supplied enablers. That way, the overall capability of the Alliance can be improved, and smaller air forces with limited budgets will have more options in charting a future course between the desire for political relevance within NATO, national defence requirements and rising requirements to 'plug and play' with the US Air Force.

The NATO Alliance is primarily a political rather than a military construct. As a vehicle for binding the interrelated security concerns of Europe and North America in a changing and multipolar world, it must remain the key organisation going forwards. However, the Alliance's ability to deter and, if necessary, fulfil its core function of mutual defence should deterrence fail ultimately rests on more than political will. It rests on having capable military forces able to deploy and fight as a coalition against the most powerful state-based threats in a decisive fashion. Since airpower is and will remain NATO's military tool of first resort due to its power, reach and responsiveness, it is critical that the Alliance does not lose coherence as a fighting force in the air domain as the US rebalances its forces for the challenge of China in the vast Asia-Pacific. European NATO members must decide which aspects of the emerging MDO-centric way of air warfare being developed by the US work for them and, by contrast, what they must be prepared to do for themselves in the coming decades.

ISLAM AND INTERNATIONAL RELATIONS

Islam and International Relations: Fractured Worlds reframes and radically disrupts perceived understanding of the nature and location of Islamic impulses in international relations. This collection of innovative essays written by Mustapha Kamal Pasha presents an alternative reading of contestation and entanglement between Islam and modernity.

Wide-ranging in scope, the volume illustrates the limits of Western political imagination, especially its liberal construction of presumed divergence between Islam and the West. Split into three parts, the essays cover Islamic exceptionalism, challenges and responses, and also look beyond Western international relations.

This volume will be of great interest to graduates and scholars of international relations, Islam, religion and politics, and political ideologies, globalization and democracy.

Mustapha Kamal Pasha is Chair in International Politics at Aberystwyth University, UK. He is the Editor of *Globalization, Difference and Human Security* (2013).